11492

Shakespeare in Africa (& Other Venues)

Shakespeare in Africa (& Other Venues): Import & the Appropriation of Culture

Lemuel A. Johnson

Africa World Press, Inc.

P.O. Box 1892
Trenton, NJ 08607

P.O. Box 48
Asmara, ERITREA

Africa World Press, Inc.

P.O. Box 1892
Trenton, NJ 08607

P.O. Box 48
Asmara, ERITREA

Copyright © Lemuel A. Johnson 1998

First Printing 1998

Cover design: Linda Nickens

Library of Congress Cataloging-in-Publication Data

Johnson, Lemuel A.
    Shakespeare in Africa (& other venues) : import and the appropriation of culture / Lemuel A. Johnson.
        p.   cm.
    Includes bibliographical references (p.   ) and index.
    ISBN 0-86543-536-7. -- ISBN 0-86543-537-5 (pbk. : alk. paper)
    1. Shakespeare, William, 1564-1616--Knowledge--Africa.
2. Shakespeare, William, 1564-1616--Knowledge--Foreign countries.
3. Shakespeare, William, 1564-1616. Othello. 4. Shakespeare,
William, 1654-1616.--Tempest. 5. English drama--Foreign influences.
6. Culture conflict in literature. 7. Caribbean Area--In
literature. 8. Exoticism in literature. 9. Culture in literature.
10. Africa--In literature. I. Title.
PR3069.A37J64 1996
822.3'3--dc20   96-43385
                                                                    CIP

Credits: Permission to reproduce Illustration 44 from *The Florentine Codex*, Book 12 (see page 268 of the present work) has been generously granted by the original publisher. The illustration originally appeared in: *A General History of the Things of New Spain. Florentine Codex.* Fray Bernardino de Sahagun. Trans. And ed. By Arthur J. O. Anderson and Charles E. Dribble. Salt Lake City and Santa Fe: The University of Utah Press and the School of American Research, 1955. Copyright the University of Utah Press. All rights reserved.

For T. I. & D. M. J.
—in Memoriam—

Contents

At that age I had a very faulty view of geography. . . . I discovered after a few days that I was heading due south, so instead of Alaska, I ended up in Africa. . . . [W]hen I walked into the jungle I was seventeen. When I walked out I was twenty-one. And, by God, I was rich!

Arthur Miller, *Death of a Salesman*

History adds that before or after dying [Shakespeare] found himself in the presence of God and told him: "I who have been so many men in vain want to be one and myself." The voice of the Lord answered from a whirlwind: "Neither am I anyone; I have dreamt the world as you dreamt your work, my Shakespeare, and among the forms in my dream are you, who like myself are many and no one."

Jorge Luis Borges, *Labyrinths*

"So descending into Hell was just a waste of time?" cried Esteban.

Alejo Carpentier, *Explosion in a Cathedral*

The Greeks first use the literal meaning for *basanos* of "touchstone," then metaphorize it to connote a test, then reconcretize, rematerialize it to mean once again a physical testing in torture. If a coin or bit of metal, applied to the touchstone, marks the stone in a distinctive way, how is this process figured in relation to the human body? The slave on the rack waits like the metal, pure or alloyed, to be tested. . . .This test assumes that the slave . . . will not spontaneously produce a pure statement. . . . The *basanos* assumes first that the slave always lies, then that the torture makes him or her always tell the truth, then that the truth produced through torture will always expose the truth or falsehood of the free man's evidence.

Page duBois, *Truth and Torture*

Acknowledgements

Segments of this work passed through several readers, and in a variety of versions. The results were sometimes unambiguous demands for discipline and genealogy of certain kinds. On other occasions, there was the razor's-edge stimulation of hard-to-read silences on what seemed to me to be pressing points; so, too, the productive comfort of great talk and open disagreement. I am grateful to my respondents and to other participants at the "Shakespeare and Cultural Traditions" seminar of the Fifth World Shakespeare Congress (Tokyo); and to Alden and Virginia Vaughan, of course, for extending the invitation to participate. Elsewhere, and some three years later, I was led to a certain sense of, well, extra delight about "How to Breathe Dead Hippo Meat and Live" by my fellow conferees at a Tel Aviv University conference on Africa. At one time or another Simon Gikandi, Jonathan Ngate, and Abiola Irele added to my sense of comfort and discomfort; as did the readiness of Eldred and Margery Jones to be appreciative in Tokyo. There were instances, too, of summary view and detail from Gary Taylor and Russell Fraser; William Ingram, Dan Fader, and Veronica Gregg; so, too, from Raymond Grew, Steven Mullaney, and Carol Neely. Throughout the several incarnations of the manuscript—and of its author—my publisher Kassahun Checole and his quite remarkable staff at Africa World Press-Lawrenceville were more than understanding (as epitomized, for me, in one editor's customary greeting: "Dr. Johnson—as you live and breathe!"). It would be impossible not to recognize the various ways in which the University of Michigan was quick to guarantee support, among them the uncomplaining competence of Sharon Gillespie; likewise thanks, too, to Brett Ashley and Sara Thomas for kind words in rough spots. Finally, and as has been her wont in quite a number of ways, my wife Marian read versions and sub/versions of page after page with unwavering pencil and astonishing patience.

There is Africa, no less than Shakespeare and the Americas, here; and in the final months of writing, I did so very much haunted by a sense of how Ama Ata Aidoo's "reflections from a black-eyed squint" once positioned Sissie in *Our Sister Killjoy*. For it is here that, answering, she "told her [alien] friend about her

> Mad country and her
> Madder continent."

For Aidoo, it all made for a mixture on the tongue that was "complete sweetness and smoky roughage"—and no doubt accounts for Sissie's "Oh, Africa. Crazy old continent." Sissie wondered, then, "whether she had spoken aloud to herself"; whether, as they flew over the continent but on the way down, "the occupant of the next seat probably thought she was crazy. Then she decided she didn't care anyway." Consider, otherwise, the nature of the call to attention that Austin Clarke's *Growing Up Stupid Under the Union Jack* once invited us to associate with being "*fool-fool*" so at "second-grade" Combermere School or else at "first-grade" Harrison College. And if not there, then among the "prefects" and round-mouthed English words of Tayeb Salih's Gordon College in *Season of Migration to the North*. For it was in such places that a surfeit of empire and colony once demanded of a set of schoolboys that they stand at attention, very much "like rulers. Not moving, even when the rain came down and changed [their] stiff khaki into plastic, and made the brass buttons dull and like lead, and the white-balanced belts turn into thick milky watercolours" (Clarke 1980:149). They did not move, not even when "flies were prevalent on . . . hot afternoons"; and certainly not when "proud" parents looked on as a certain model of an English

> Major, [but] without his pips and decorations, watched us, and said, "God save the Queen!"; and probably thought of his own days in Africa. We did not move. A fly would light on our bottom lip, and we could think and remember epidemics and plagues and typhoid fever. Still, we did not move. . . . We were at attention. The Governor was inspecting the ranks of his Guard of Honour. And he and we were English, overseas, colonial and dominion. How could we move? No one, in the long history of Guards of Honour and of Combermere, had ever, when the Governor was looking, moved a muscle because of a simple fly. (149-150)

Caught (up) in so fabulous a logic of unequal exchanges, some of us, Clarke remembers, "fell to the ground through sunstroke." There were those who fainted from "standing too long on empty bellies," while others "caught colds which turned into worse colds, doubled up with [a] triple-pneumonia [that] made us cough and spit blood." There were some who "broke wind just as the Governor passed," granted; however, "we did not move." But then, given the reach for import in what follows, it bears recalling the words with which, for his part, Amos Tutuola had brought *The Palm-Wine Drinkard and his Dead Palm-Wine Tapster in Dead's Town* (1953) to an end: "But when for three months the rain had been falling regularly, then there was no famine."

Introduction

I t is not quite categorical a thing that the engagement with Shakespeare here is "postcolonial studies" or "Renaissance revisionism" or some quick, recognizable "insurrection of subjugated knowledges." There is, moreover, the additional matter of terrain and type in "the still-vex'd Bermoothes" of the second chapter, where the focus is on the reach of the utopian bent in the lands of America. Here, the points of entry lie as much in Ariel's embrace of contraindication in *The Tempest*'s "Full fathom five thy father lies" as they do in that land's-end image, from Wallace Stevens, of a "virgin of boorish births" that was womb enough for "the dreadful sundry of this world." There is landfall, too, at the Citadelle La Ferrière of Alejo Carpentier's *The Kingdom of This World* (1949)—with its assurance that "Not for nothing had those towers risen [in Christophe's Haiti], on the mighty bellowing of bulls, their testicles toward the sun." Latitude and import also derive from the drama, the *auto sacramental*, that Sor Juana Inés de la Cruz makes of the conversion of Mesoamerica in *The Divine Narcissus* (1690); there is relevance, too, in the narratives of coercion—as in the *autos da fe*— that Fray Diego de Landa made of his campaigns of extirpation in the Yucatan. Given such a convergence of terrains and types, and this study's approach, it may prove helpful throughout to keep in mind the world-(un)making premise with which Jorge Luis Borges introduced the discovery of that third and brave new world of his, "Tlön, Uqbar, Orbis Tertius." "I owe the discovery of Tlön," Borges's protagonist explained, "to the conjunction of a mirror and an encyclopedia" (1964:4). But then, to also presume to anchor so much literary transport, and the utopian bent, besides, in "Africa" is to risk doing so in an exclamation point.

The reasons are no doubt various. For representations of "Africa proper" (Hegel) do tend to converge in certain ways, and thus to involve commerce in "difference" that has been peculiar enough to limn a Sir Thomas Browne in a Henry David Thoreau. In the early modern period that follows here, "Africa" also provides an anchor of sorts for degrees of dis/affiliation that involve Turk, Jew and Irish as well as Euro-America, Ethiope, and Amerindia. Its import thus converges in any number of generic and, what is more, heuristic, alignments. The signatures that matter are thus present in the invocations of "Africa" that we get in the Perry Miller of *Errand into the Wilderness* (with its "barbaric tropic" of a Congo) and in that *voyage au Congo* and *retour du Tchad* (1925-26) as a result of which André Gide found himself "under a sky with no promise in it, [and] in a landscape uninhabited by god, or dryad, or faun—an implacable landscape, with neither mystery in

1

it nor poetry" (1962:111). But then, an alchemy of sorts also leads to the Arthur Miller of *Death of a Salesman* (with its "Africa!" and jungle of diamonds). There is a recognizably hyperbolic experience of landscape in all this, of course; just as there had been in Pliny's *Natural History* and its early assurance of the permanently exotic: "*Ex Africa*," after all, "*semper aliquid novi.*" "I came here," Perry Miller explained in his twentieth-century context, "seeking 'adventure,' and jealous of older contemporaries." Miller thus surrendered, or better, resigned himself to a descent from pedigree; and he does so with some generic justification. He was, after all, positioned in quite the latter days of a genre of epiphany in which it had once "been given to Edward Gibbon to sit disconsolate amid the ruins of the Capitol at Rome, and to have thrust upon him the 'laborious work' of *The Decline and Fall* while listening to barefooted friars chanting responses in the former temple of Jupiter." For all that he was "equally disconsolate," it was in quite other times that Miller's *Errand into the Wilderness* sought to "bring into conjunction a minute event in the history of historiography with a great one." Confined to "the edge of a jungle of central Africa," Miller found himself poised on a *reductio ad absurdum*. For it was while "supervising, in that barbaric tropic, the unloading of drums of oil flowing from the inexhaustible wilderness of America" that the "mission of expounding what [he] took to be the innermost propulsion of the United States" had been "thrust upon" him.

The awkwardness is as inspired as it is predictable elsewhere. For where Africa does not display itself as a hyperbole in other-ness, its terrain and type remain recognizable in that "cosmography of [the] selfe" within which Sir Thomas Browne had hoped to resolve the matter with, famously, the view that "There is all Africa and her prodigies in us." For which reason, he that "studies [the selfe] wisely learnes in a compendium what others labour at in a divided piece and endlesse volume." This degree of access to Africa notwithstanding, evidence remains of its heuristic value as *the* site of an *otro incastrable*. With this phrase, in Italo Manzi's translation of the Daniel Sibony of *l'Autre incastrable* (1978), I borrow a thought ("El inconsciente es *un lugar*?"/Is the unconscious a *place*?) about recalcitrant difference and unstable constellations of experience. Consider, in this light, the fact that, for all that he is promiscuous in appetite, even the Jupiter of Rabelais's *Pantagruel* still found occasion to wonder about the limit(ation)s of terrain and type. If geographies of difference and ceremonies of conquest have been mapped into an acceptable new-world order, he wonders, "What devil is it, down there howling so horribly?" After all, "The question of Parma is solved. So are those of Mardeburg, of Mirandola, and of Africa—which is the mortals' name for the town on the Mediterranean Sea that we called Aphrodisium." Granted, "owing to some carelessness, Tripoli has changed its master"; but then, "Its hour had come anyhow" (*Pantagruel* 442).

For his part, the Thoreau of *Walden* (1854) found it easy enough to work his way to the conclusion that "The other side of the globe is but the home of our correspondent." The New Englander therefore oscillates between "home" and "difference" according to a formula that makes of him yet another "expert in home-cosmography" (218) who is grounded, as was Browne, in the explanatory category that "Africa" provided. "It is not worth the while to go round the world to count the cats in Zanzibar," Thoreau would write. Besides which, "What does Africa,—what does the West stand for?"—and in what shades of difference? "Is not our own interior white on the chart? black though it may prove, like the coast when discovered? Is it the source of the Nile, or the Niger, or the Mississippi, or a North-West passage?" From its black coast to the cats of its Zanzibar Africa was thus called upon to map a consciousness and to nuance a constellation of things within which "The light which puts out our eyes is darkness to us" (227). It was to arrive at just this Africa of insights that Thoreau had famously embarked upon an experiment in living which began when he borrowed an axe from a neighbor and set out for Walden Pond "near the end of March, 1845."

The date intrigues, and not quite so parenthetically, I might add—coming from Sierra Leone as I do. For 1845 and near the end of March (the twenty-fifth) marked the date on which the Church Missionary Society established the Grammar School for Boys in Freetown. This, the CMS had done with a curriculum that included lineal drawing, geography and Greek as well as English Grammar and Latin; so, too, a school motto, *dioko*, the greek word for "I pursue." Almost a century later, in 1926 and at the eastern end of the continent in Kenya, Alliance High School would be founded by a coalition of Missionary groups. "A programmed world modeled on the British public school, it [would] serve the cream of the cream." The Headmaster of the 1950s, Carey Francis, "a workaholic 'martinet' [maintained] Alliance as 'an abode of peace in a turbulent country' convulsed by the anti-colonial struggle. . . . Prefects, appointed on grounds of character rather than academic ability, operated as the headmaster's agents in a Lugardian system of indirect rule— a 'knightly order of masters and menials' in which prefects were responsible not to any constituency but to the all-powerful headmaster" (Sicherman 1996:13).

As I now recall the relevance of all of the above in smaller beginnings and quieter imports, three ships of the Elder Dempster Line, the *M.V.*s *Apapa*, *Accra* (softly mottled gray) and the *Aureol* (flagship and white in color) once plied the waters between Liverpool, England and the coast of Britsh West Africa. Complemented by cargo ships, they provided transport that fort-nightly took in Freetown (Sierra Leone), Takoradi in what was then the Gold Coast, and Nigeria's Apapa wharf—by way of landfall in the Canary Islands.

Inward bound from England, they carried imports in their holds and cabins that were on at least one occasion red double-decker buses, and in consequence of which "Welcome to Sierra Leone, / Double-decker buses!" became a *highlife*, and thus a song and a dance of the 1950s. Other cargo included English apples and trousers with, by the late fifties, zippered flies—even though the ones we identified as French remained stubborn with buttons. (I recall a brand of buttons that melted, with a briefly acrid smell, on contact with hot iron.) There were large newspaper-sized editions of *The Daily Mirror* in which the sensationalized dailiness of English folk had been compiled, inside yellow covers, for delivery overseas. The *London Illustrated News* was no less frequent; but this was a rather more continent affair. A softer sheen of sorts came, too, from Portuguese-brand pomade, and from nylon turned into affordable merchandise, especially shirts, that dried very easily in the extravagant August through October of our rainy seasons. Much later, and across "an empire's zones," we would come to recognize certain affinities in latitude and import as they "lay spilled from a small tea-chest" in the epic memory that Derek Walcott's *Omeros* makes of "absent war," "empire's guilt," and "fabulous quilt" (1990:263); so, too, of the convergence of certain terrains and types—

> Provinces, Protectorates, Colonies, Dominions,
> Governors-General, black Knights, ostrich-plumed Viceroys,
> deserts, jungles, hill-stations, all an empire's zones—

with their "post-red double-deckers" and "sweat-soaked kerchiefs" and "whistling kettle"; their "spit-and-polished leather" and the transport of "biscuits [that] break with grief" (261-262).

In our time, whole cabins and cargoes of such goods came freighted with "the good" that the logic of empire and the transport of colonial education also required. And here, the import of it all was especially manifest in Royal Quink Ink (blue) and the white foolscap paper on which, in our fifth and seventh years in secondary school, we wrote out answers that were now rewarded with, now denied The Cambridge University School Certificate and the Cambridge University Higher School Certificate, respectively. The con/texts of our imperial curriculum ranged from the seventeenth century of John Milton (*Samson Agonistes*) to the nineteenth century of the physics of the Faraday Effect—a matter, this, of what magnetic fields will do to light beams, as I now recall but did not then for Cambridge University. Besides which, and rather more accessibly, the said (Michael) Faraday also played some role in designing, so we thought, the bunsen burners that we shook (lightly and at an angle) over blue flames in our own laboratory. A German, Robert Wilhem

Bunsen, had produced the glass burner in 1855, the text pointed out. There was, too, the seventeenth-century chemistry out of which Robert Boyle generated the mnemotechnic "BOVIP" (1662) for us, and which had something to do, we were told, with the fact that at a certain constant temperature the volume of a gas is inversely proportional to its pressure. This "sceptical chymist" was a member of the Royal Society of London for the Improvement of Natural Knowledge (1660). And if it was not this Boyle who was member to that body, then a person who certainly mattered there was Isaac Newton, that physicist of gravitational pull and of equal and opposite action and reaction. About this we were on the whole rather convinced, and we could, if called upon to do so, indeed make assurance doubly sure.

We also developed some testable awareness of maps and of the "dawn of modern navigation"; but we never quite worked past or through the cluster of details which had helped to account for a parallel "time for empire." That would come much later, with knowledge of the fact that in 1714, for example, "Queen Anne's government offered [twenty thousand pounds] to anyone who could devise a way of fixing a ship's longitude to within 30 nautical miles, after sailing for six weeks across the Atlantic." We learnt, also later, that "the official jury for the award—the Board of Longitude—was as august as it could be." For its members "included the speaker of the House of Commons, the first lord of the admiralty, the astronomer royal, the president of the Royal Society, the first commissioner of trade, and the Savilian, Lucasian, and Plumian professors of mathematics at Oxford and Cambridge." Of course, in our time we did know about James Watt, and about the force of the steam engine to come. However, we did not quite know that in 1775 Watt had also explained it all to King George III in these terms: "Sir, we sell what the world desires: power." Only much later (as with *The Economist* and the Board of Longitude) would an Alain Peyrefitte explain in *The Immobile Center* that this adage was, in part, "a play on words: *power* in the dual sense of energy and political might" (1992:14).

Now and then, the odd exercise in Americana found its way into the Englishness of our colonial library and imperial curriculum. In later years, this disjuncture would occasion some surprise, given the ease with which we came to recognize the gravitational pull of and against Europe and belatedness in certain manifestations of American identity. "The head monkey at Paris puts on a traveller's cap, and all the monkeys in America do the same," New-Worlder Thoreau had once complained; but we did not know this, then. Our schedule of affiliations no more required such knowledge of us than it did the note of reversal that Edward Wilmot Blyden sounded when he wrote: "Pagans of discernment know that the blackman among them who calls himself a Christian and dresses himself in clothes adheres to European habits and customs with a reserved power of disengagement." But then, Blyden had been born in the then Danish Island of Saint Thomas in 1832; and he had resettled, with much intellectual turbulence, in Sierra Leone and in Liberia, beginning in 1852.

All the same, it needs to be acknowledged that there were those among us who rummaged in strange footnotes; and who, because they did so, could mention one Mr. Morse, a man whose first name was Jedidiah—a resonant Sierra Leone *krio* ("creole") name if ever there was one. This Morse was a North American who, so it seemed, had written a 1793 *American Universal Geography*. "Americans," he was reported by the rummagers to have said, "seldom pretended to write or think for themselves. We humbly received from Great Britain our laws, our manners, our books, and our modes of thinking; and our youth were educated as the subjects of the British king, rather than as citizens of a free and independent republic." In time to come, echoes of such import would be eerie because quickly familiar (to us) when we came upon F. Scott Fitzgerald visiting his "Owl Eyes" and "ghostly laughter" on a certain James Gatz of North Dakota. We also noted, and quite readily, too, that the particulars of Fitzgerald's charge sheet included a "Merton College Library" of uncut books which had somehow come to be housed in the extravagance of a Long Island, New York, mansion: "On a chance we tried an important-looking door, and walked into a high Gothic library, panelled with carved English oak, and probably transported complete from some ruin overseas." Here, then, was a knowable enough fellow: an American "poor son of bitch" who, in a "Platonic" transfiguration of himself into "The Great Gatsby," had engaged in the "vast, vulgar and meretricious beauty" and "business" of being both cut off from and measured for European ancestry. We could hear, so we believed, a certain relish and resonance in his saying: "I lived like a young rajah in all the capitals of Europe—Paris, Venice, Rome—collecting jewels." In the end, this "old sport" would sink, of course, weighed down by the "accidental burden" and "accidental course" that his embrace of awkward affiliations required.

That being the case, we could later sense, perhaps we did recognize, a bemused high-colonialist or hill-station tolerance in George Steiner's judgment that "the dominant apparatus of American culture is *that of custody*." Steiner would of course come to this conclusion in the face of an American "prodigality of conservation and retransmission" that was "brimful of classical and European art"; of "European and antique edifices [that] have been brought to the new world stone by literal stone or mimed to the inch"; so, too, by America's "appetites" for and its "devouring" of "the treasures and bric-a-brac of the medieval, the renaissance or the eighteenth-century past" (1996:280). In any case, Americana of such rather familiar vintage resonated with us. For example, given the high culture and great expectations that attended our curriculum at the Grammar School, it was relatively easy—and a frisson of delight, even—to discover affinities in the report-card earnestness of a letter written by one Charlotte C. Eliot (Mrs Henry W. Eliot) to a Mr. Cobb, for all that the letter was dated 4 April 1905, and addressed from 2635 Locust Street, St. Louis. "His teacher informs him," Mrs. Eliot had written, "that in the Harvard preliminaries he received credit in French and English. He has always been a student, and read extensively in English literature, especially Shakespeare. He has read practically all of Shakespeare, whom he admires, and retains much in memory" (Eliot 1988:6-7). In time, earnest preoccupation of this sort would be reflected in the "tight tether" that anchored our East African cousins in *their* imperial curriculum. It would also transpose the University College of East Africa at Makerere (Uganda) into a 1950s constituent college of the University of London. The evidence lay, famously, in the Honours literature curriculum. In it, the readings "spanned Chaucer—defiantly taught in the original despite a London University 'ban on Middle English'—to T. S. Eliot."

> Jonathan Kariara's arch essay on preparing for the English exmaination indicates an Honours curriculum that was dense and demanding for anyone, far more so for non-native speakers: *Emma* ("humorous and lovely to read"), *Cry the beloved Country* ("my Bible, noble book," the only "African" work studied), *Hamlet* ("good for my soul"), Synge's lovely Plays," *Great Expectations*, *Joseph Andrews*, *Antigone*, the "odious" *Odyssey*, and two other disliked works, *Typhoon* and *Much Ado About Nothing*. (Sicherman 1996:15-16).

At this English East African residential college, the staff adopted "an Arnoldian, Leavisite approach" to con/texts. Signally, in his inaugural address as first Professor of English, *Shakespeare in the Tropics*, Alan Warner did in fact explain "the underlying premise: African students would study English literature in order to 'become citizens of the world'" (Sicherman 1996:16). There were reasons enough, it would seem, for the latter-day prophetic thought—in one Jeremy Gavron—that Adewale Maja-Pearce recalls in *Who's Afraid of Wole Soyinka?* "Africa itself has a little bit of Caliban in it," Gavron declared. "Europe taught Africa language and its profit is to know how to curse." Notwithstanding this mark of the beast, "sweet sounds" and "grace hereafter" (*Tempest*) loom. "Give Africa time," Gavron prophesied, "and one day it may even write poetry," for all that any such unburying of Shakespeare in the native could require "fifty years, or a hundred, or even two hundred" (Maja-Pearce 1991:91).

Meanwhile, in the days of our own secondary (school) life at the Grammar School, it was quite the odd Americana that actually came our way. And when it did, the con/text was not the Herman Melville of *Benito Cereno.* Our Melville was, instead, the inexplicably various *Moby Dick,* with its "insular Tahiti" and "Virginia's dismal swamp" and the whiteness of Captain Ahab's very large whale. We found it easy to recall—indeed, to frolic in— certain conceits of Melville's according to which, for example, a face was like the "complicated ribbed bed of a torrent when the rushing waters have been dried up." There was resonance, too, in the fact that the text of some preacher's sermon in the narrative was about "the blackness of darkness, and all the wailing and gnashing of teeth there." But then, we were not at all invited to find this note an especially compelling one: there was, after all, no denying the signal quickness with which—uttering the words, "Wretched entertain- ment at the sign of 'The Trap'"—Ishmael had removed himself from what seemed "the great Black Parliament sitting in Tophet." Now, this last was a phrase, we thought, that certainly filled the mouth! Still, it was one that we did not need to look into, there being no real need to do so for our Cambridge University examinations.

Insofar as terrain and type involved other places overseas, the Europe that was Spain came to us through, but filtered in, Pierre Corneille's *Le Cid.* This dramatic context produced a Euro-Christian nation that was being fashioned for us out of the conquest of a Spain that had been Muslim, Moor, and Jew. Needless to say, in due time we did reach back to the Armada of 1588, in which context England certainly did that nation in, notwithstanding the riches which, as Shakespeare's *Comedy of Errors* put it, the Indies had "declined" (that is, surrendered) to the "hot breath" of Spain. In any case, "*Differo et dispero*" ("I scatter abroad; I overwhelm") was, we learnt, one of the phrases with which the English had celebrated the triumphant making of a certain "Elizabethan world picture." Meanwhile, in addition to being Corneille, France was also (several times for us) the *Tartuffe* of Molière, although there was one occasion when it was the Alfred de Musset of *On ne badine pas avec l'amour* (*You can't gamble with love*). Elsewhere—and this we got out of a geography lesson on "The Map as Conceit"—the country's "hexagonal" shape folded itself up into the nineteenth-century recesses of Charles Baudelaire's *Les Fleurs du Mal* (*Flowers of Evil*). But not before the laughter and the masque which Molière's *bourgeois gentilhomme* occasioned when he believed himself ready to be father-in-law to the son of the Sultan of Turkey. This was especially the case when that French bourgeois took lessons in a Turkish language (*"acciam croc soler ouch alla moustaph gidelum amanahem varahini oussere carbulath"*) that would make him worthy of so auspicious an embrace of East and West. Of course, we did have some parenthetical evidence of other constellations of such terrain and type—in the Orient, for example. However, these were so bound to the gravitational pull of "Black Hole of Calcutta" and "Boxer Rebellion"—not to speak of Ingrid Bergman and *The Inn of the Sixth Happiness*—that they remained areas of darkness, and caught in a density that could never be much illuminated. That being the case, we could hardly not have known about Thomas Babbington Macaulay and that Minute of February 2, 1835 which famously advocated the creation of a type that would be "Indian in blood and color, but English in tastes, in opinions, in morals and in intellect." It seems significant that I cannot now remember if we did or not.

What did remain well-lit in our lives then was transport that came in the poetry of John Masefield's "Cargoes," with its "Quinqueremes of Nineveh from distant Ophir," its "stately Spanish galleons," and its "dirty British coaster with a salt-caked smoke stack." Shakespeare was there, of course. But here, no infidel Turk or Ottoman moved with "mighty preparation," to the great discomfiture of the citizens of Venice. And the Turk's being a "circumcized dog" provoked no fateful consequence for some mercenary Moor who had been born with "gross clasp," "thick lips" and "sooty bosom" in a place that must have been little more than a hole in the horizon of Europe. The English playwright who counted with us raised no difficulty either for some visiting Duke of Morocco who, so he claimed, was well-liked by all the well-regarded virgins of his clime; but who needed to apologize for his "complexion" when he showed up in Belmont to woo Portia, a woman who was fairer than the word itself. In addition, ours was a world that could never quite conceive of projects that were as willed to detour or wedded to revision as, say, Emi Hamana's would be in a Shakespeare Society of Japan's *Shakespeare Studies* (1988). Unlike ours, Hamana's way with Shakespeare would require considerations of a certain kind. For in its light, and by way of a dissenting recourse to Ophelia's treatment in Victorian painting, the real drama in *Hamlet* would come from having to contend with Ophelia's entrapment in the "traditional image of female passivity and vulnerability." Briefly put, re-vision, as such, neither registered with nor beckoned to us. And so, curiously enough, given the complexion and the prideful politics that *The Tempest* and *Othello* have assumed in (post)colonial Shakespeare, the drama- tist was quite otherwise with us. His import was much greater in the toil and bubble of *Macbeth*; so, too, in that untroubled "quality of mercy" and act of dispossession which *The Merchant of Venice* played out into a moon-lit happy ending at Belmont, having taken rather clever care of an extravagant alien with an alien's taste for flesh. There was representation enough, elsewhere, in Hamlet's yearning to count himself king of infinite space in a nutshell, if only he could keep from being troubled by bad dreams. In *Julius Caesar*,

Marc Antony certainly commanded attention with his willful version of Brutus and other murderously honorable men, all of them marked, so it seemed, by "lean and hungry" looks. And then, there was our Richard III, who, by some unexamined alchemy of memorization, capered "nimbly in a lady's chamber, to the lascivious pleasing of a lute." The display of extravagance and appetite in the Falstaff (that "huge hill of flesh") and Hotspur of *King Henry IV, Part I* was a matter of great import, too. After all, these were qualities that we knew would be crowned in the next school year by the triumphant exceptionalism with which the whole-entire English nation in *Henry V* would once more put paid to the French at Agincourt, on St. Crispin's Day.

Pace Caliban and his "profit on't," if at all we learnt "language" in which to curse, and we once did so for the Cambridge University Higher School Certificate, it was in two contexts from *King Lear*. First, there was the "high-engender'd" anger in which Lear cursed his daughter, Goneril; in which he invited Nature, that "dear goddess," to convey sterility into her womb and "dry up in her the organs of increase." And then, there was the word-spinning tempest of Kent's way with Oswald:

> A knave; a rascal; an eater of broken meats; a base, proud, shallow, beggarly, three-suited, hundred-pound, filthy, worsted-stocking knave; a lily-livered, action-taking whoreson, glass-gazing, superserviceable, finical rogue; one-trunk-inheriting slave; one that wouldst be a bawd, in way of good service, and art nothing but the composition of a knave, beggar, coward, pandar, and the son of a mongrel bitch.

There were subtler occasions, of course; for when "the good" was not some "month of May-ing / when merry lads are playing," it was some other English "air"—for example, "Blow, blow thou winter wind / Thou art not so unkind / As man's ingratitude. . . . / Thy tooth is not so keen"—with lyrics by W. Shakespeare. In the end, and as I have put it in the "Juju" of *Highlife for Caliban*, "the alphabets of empires met / outside, in the dry seasons of our windows: / the tambourines of Byzantium / moist skulls under Rome [and] / the bonedust" of Vergil's Sicilian mountains (1995:36). With notations that were variously "round as rosetta stones/ and heavier," we were quite set (up) and scored for palimpsest as for pandemonium.

There was a great deal in our experiences that no doubt explains the deftness with which James Turner, say, makes the point in *The Politics of Landscape* that the history of *topographia* cannot be written (off) as a "simple increase in actuality"; that there really cannot be much of an excuse for taking "topoi" or its "mystifications" at face value (1979:xii-xiii). Still, it was remarkable the connections that did not then follow for us. Isolated from emergent African literatures, education at Makerere, for example, would become, "in David Rubadiri's apt phrase, a 'pot plant'—able to grow in its own confined boundary, but failing to take root and nourishment from mother earth itself"; besides which, "the focus on isolation and alienation discouraged any challenge to British cultural hegemony" (Sicherman 1996:19). On the other hand, it was true enough that those among us who read long and irrelevantly *in* the endnotes and footnotes of our imperial curriculum did make a point of revealing that their excursions made for startling recognitions. They said, for example, that in those "under-cellars" of our colonial library even Sierra Leone was now and then mentioned. Come see, they would say, pointing to a Christopher Columbus as he sailed off in May 1498 on a third voyage that would take to him no less a place than the Terrestrial Paradise: "When I sailed from Spain to the Indies . . . and reached the parallel of Sierra Leone, in Guinea . . . I found the heat so intense, and the rays of the sun so fierce, that I thought we should have been burned." Such rummaging among other people's marginalia and parentheses also produced the Thomas Jefferson of a letter of January 21, 1811. It had been written from Monticello to one John Lynch; and in it the Euro-American once again confirmed his view that Sierra Leone (or else "some of the Portuguese possessions in South America") would be a good place to which to ship out "the people of color" in the United States. Other such dispensations of our descent laid bare the fact that "savage Timme tribes" of Sierra Leone had contributed a necessary quota of hordes—and insight—to the S. Freud of *Totem and Taboo* and the J. G. Frazer of *The Golden Bough*. It turned out, too, that our place in the scheme of things—the evidence for arrested evolution that we embodied—had been a matter of inspiration and consequence in the "outposts of progress" that so preoccupied Joseph Conrad:

> The third man on the staff was a Sierra Leone nigger, who maintained his name was Henry Price. However, for some reason or other, the natives down the river had given him the name Makola, and it stuck to him through all his wanderings about the country. He spoke English and French with a warbling accent, wrote a beautiful hand, understood bookkeeping, and cherished in his innermost heart the worship of evil spirits. (1963:75)

In another of its encounters with the "gigantic tale" (Conrad) of discovery, Sierra Leone had been thrice-visited on slaving raids by that Elizabethan sea dog *par excellence* John Hawkins; for he had learned that "Negroes were very good merchandise in Hispaniola, and that store of Negroes might easily be had upon the coast of Guinea." Our terrain and its types had also provided a moment of fierce parenthesis, we learned, in the fulsome anger of Daniel Defoe's eigthteenth century "Reformation of Manners." About Hawkins, Sylvia Wynter would later write in "The Poetics and Politics of a High Life for Caliban" that he visited Sierra Leone three times in the 1560s, visits made notorious by his kidnapping and enslaving of the inhabitants to sell them in the West Indies. Wynter's remembrance of things past produces a Hawkins whose value lay in his readiness to be nothing if not "thief, merchant, mariner":

> He sailed to Africa in a seaworthy ship; and got black slaves partly by the sword, partly by trade; he sailed [then] to that other point of the triangle, islands and a continent gotten by storm, with his prey; and there threatened to cut the throat of the Spanish colonists if they did not trade. To traffic in men would call down God's vengeance, Queen Elizabeth had first said. But she profitted largely; knighted bold enterprises right and left. (1995:86)

In this world-(un)making convergence of latitude and import, Borges is as ironic as he is instructive. There is a signal reach for transport, and a subversion of import, too, in his "Everything and Nothing" profile of Shakespeare. The same is true of that reflection in Tlön that "Copulation and mirrors are abominable"; or else, of the larger "sophism" that "Mirrors and fatherhood are abominable because they multiply and disseminate" a "visible universe" that is nonetheless "an illusion" (1964:4). About the imbricated Shakespeare that multiplication and dissemination entails, James Irby makes the helpful point that Borges's "Everything and Nothing" leads us to "a realm where fact and fiction, the real and the unreal, the whole and the part, the highest and the lowest, are complementary aspects of the same continuous being." It is in this "realm where 'any man is all men' [that] 'all men who repeat a line of Shakespeare *are* William Shakespeare'" (1964:xix). As happens with Tlön, this discovery of terrain and type becomes an act that Borges associates with "a history of laborious creation over the centuries by anonymous scholars, first in Europe, then in the New World" (Irby 1973:36). Whether produced from between the covers of "weighty tomes," by "venture-some computation," or in the "vertiginous moment of coitus," this genre of discovery provides us with a world that could very well be suspended between "the luscious honeysuckle and the illusory depths [of] mirrors" (Borges 1964:12; 20). The "postscript" to the encounter with Tlön is no less telling, especially so, insofar as it may be related to that torn-off "postscriptum" for separation ("Exterminate all the brutes!") with which Conrad rounded off Kurtz's version of "the dreams of men, the seed of commonwealths, [and] the germs of empires." In Borges, the postcript to the brave new world of Tlön is contraindicatively associated with a slave-owning North American "millioniare eccentric" whose view is that "in America it was absurd to invent a country, and [instead] proposed the invention of a whole planet. To this gigantic idea, he added another, born of his own nihilism—that of keeping the enormous project a secret" (31).

What happens, Edward Brathwaite once asked helpfully, "if we define culture as a complex of voices and patterns of exclusiveness held together by geography, political force and social interaction?" Under these terms, he explains, each culture becomes definitive not only in itself, but in relation to others on which it impinges" (1969:6). In this view, West Indian culture, say, ought really to be "identifiable in relation to the cultures of Latin America, of North America, of West Africa, of Western Europe." But then, there are a culture's own "deposits of history"; and these require singular recognition, pointing as they do to life and structures that are "separable" (7). Whether pursued in the pathologies of the Madagascar of Mannoni's *Prospero and Caliban* (1950) and Fanon's *Black Skin, White Masks* (1959)—or else in the complex edge that Lamming brings to *The Tempest* in *The Pleasures of Exile* (1960)—there are grounds for other such measures of dis/affiliation in the itinerary in contexts that follows here. Consider, say, the "Brazil" that Paule Marshall's *Soul Clap Hands and Sing* (1961) plays out through and beyond the "mostly slapstick" accommodation, so it seems, that binds her Caliban— "aging in body" but "overwhelmned by [r]age"—to a Miranda who dances with "mincing steps" to his feints and dodges at being a boxer (1988:134). "Incongruous and contradictory," this nightclub of a relationship is between a New World Black who speaks Portuguese and a Miranda who is "one of those Brazilians from Rio Grande do Sul who are mixed German, Portuguese, native Indian, and some times African." It all makes for a tempestuous *pas de deux* that is as opaque and full of deposits of history as it is apparently transparent. So, too, for the "frightened, tearful voice" that Miranda gives to separation with her "Caliban! Caliban! Where are you going? The show! Are you crazy—what about the show tonight? Oh, Mary, full of grace, look what the bastard's done. The place! He's killed me inside. Oh, God, where is he going? Crazy bastard, come back here. What did I do? Was it me, Caliban? Caliban, *meu negrinho*, was it me. . . ?" (177). But then, *pace* this *meu negrinho* arrangement that holds "O Grande Caliban e a Pequena Miranda" together, at least one of the bodies in question reaches out and into a difference that is quite beyond the utopian bent with which latitude and import have otherwise converged in the "Casa Samba." Absent the antique drama of accommodation, the "destruction of the apartment" had been "swift and complete":

> While Miranda stood transfixed, a dazed horror spreading like a patina over her face (and she was never to lose that expression), [Caliban had] hauled down drapes and curtains, overturned furniture, scattered drawers and their frivolous contents across the floor, broke the figurines against white walls, smashed the mirrors and his reflection there—and then, with a jagged piece of glass, slashed open the silk sofas and chairs so that the down drifted up over the wreckage like small kites. Finally, wielding a heavy curtain rod as if it were a lance, he climbed onto a marble table and swung repeatedly at the large chandelier in the living room, sending the glass pendants winging over the room. With each blow he felt the confusion and despair congested within him fall away, leaving an emptiness and despair which, he knew, would remain with him until he died. He wanted to sleep suddenly, beside his wife, in the room with the Madonna (*ibid.* 176).

My interest in such occasions of difference and imbrication also gives a relevant edge to Cemal Kafadar's introduction to *Between Two Worlds*, to a context in which he proposes a counter to the "lid model" of historiography whereby certain dominant structures are conceived as "lids closing upon a set of ingredients that are kept under but intact"—that is, until the lid is toppled and those ingredients (peoples, for example), "unchanged, simply reenter the grand flow of history as what they once were" (1995:21).

Yet another inspiration for "discovery" and dis/affiliation in the pages that follow lies in the amazing conceit that Newton's *Thoughts Upon the African Slave Trade* (1788) once made of transport, text, and being. "The slaves lie in two rows, one above the other," he wrote, "like books upon a shelf." It was *John* Newton, of course, not the Isaac that we first knew, who then proceeded to inform us that he had known the bodies of slaves to lie "so close that the shelf could not, easily, contain one more." Now, had there been room enough in those Grammar School days and physics of ours to align our con/texts in certain ways, we might have crafted a fascinating heuristic out of Rabelais. I refer, of course, to that crisis in writing, reading, and interpretation which *Pantagruel* plays out so elaborately in the episode titled, "Letter Brought to Pantagruel by a Lady of Paris." The letter, it is worth remembering, contained no obvious inscription, "only a gold ring with a flat-cut diamond." Faced with this refusal of sign and sentence to appear, much less to signify,

> [Pantagruel] called Panurge to explain matters to him. Whereupon he said that the leaf of paper was written on, but in such a subtle way that no one could see the writing. Therefore, to bring it out, he put the letter before the fire, to see if it was written in sal-ammoniac soaked with tithymal juice. After that he held it up in

front of a candle, to see if it was not written with the juice of white onions. Then he rubbed a part of it with walnut oil, to see if it was not written with fig-wood ash. Then he rubbed a part of it with the milk of a woman suckling her first-born daughter, to see if it was not written with bull-frog's blood. Then he rubbed a corner with the ashes of a swallow's nest, to see if it was written in the dew that is found in the winter-cherry. Then he rubbed another corner with ear-wax, to see if it was written in raven's gall. Then he soaked it in vinegar, to see if it was written in whale sperm, which is called ambergris. Then he put it quite gently into basin of fresh water, and drew it out quickly, to see if it was written in feather-alum. (246)

Further research by Panurge into "invisible writing" and methods of encoding does dislodge signs. And when these were translated, from the Hebrew, as things turned out, they yielded meaning, the thrust of which was: "Say, false lover, why have you abandoned me?" But then, the contract of decipherment (Steiner) and the attendant urge to surrender to its uncoverings is countered by a greater urgency: a threat of danger to the "city of birth." The return to the native land requires the abandonment of the "Parisian lady, whom [Pantagruel] had kept as his mistress for some time." Moving within and yet against encrypted codes of seduction and alienation, Pantagruel embarks upon an instructive *retour au pays natal* (Césaire). He is driven by "full sails" and "open sea" into a *retour aux sources* (Senghor) in which the landfalls include the Fairy Isle, the Canary Islands, and the West Coast of Africa; so, too, it is worth noting, the port of Utopia (247).

Conceived of as a commerce in the good(s) of grammar school and cargo ship, the chapters that follow make for an echo-chamber of sorts within which master texts and their sub/versions converge in a contract of decipherment. In this regard, George Steiner's "A Reading Against Shakespeare" contributes a relevant thought when he notes that Goethe once "remarked in awe and, one has licence to suppose, a rival testiness: 'Shakespeare and no end'" (1996:110). Insofar as the thought is preoccupied with the problematic import of belatedness and "secondary material," there is additional relevance in that 1994 Oxford University Inaugural Lecture of Steiner's, "What Is Comparative Literature?," in which he makes the point that even "extreme originality begins, as we enter into questioning dialogue with it, to tell of origins." There is, he adds, "no absolute innocence, no Adamic nakedness," in the "perception of response to intelligibility"; for "interpretation and aesthetic judgement, however spontaneous or even misguided, arise from an echo-chamber of historical, social, technical presuppositions and recognizance. (Here, the legal sense of this term is pertinent: a certain contract of eventual decipherment, of informed evaluation underwrites the encounter between our sensibility and the text or work of art)" (1996:142).

Given assumptions about or claims upon things original and utopian in the Americas, Steiner does well when his "Archives of Eden" refers us to "the contagion of history" (268) in the thought of those who have been "less sanguine" about the transport and the import of cultures. The *caveat* lies, here, in the suggestion that "even if the New World was, or was to be, 'earth's other Eden', it was the Old Adam who had come to it through 'the swelling seas'" (*ibid.*). That being the case, he could not but carry with him certain layers of primary materials, among them, the "contagion of history." That granted, it is a matter of some importance that the host of world-making premises is considerably more appeasable in the Americas than it is in Conrad, for whom travelling through vast seas to "earliest beginnings" in Africa assuredly leads to a place of no memories. Conrad's Marlow does come to a knowledge of terrain and type, of course; but what he most recognizes is a "darkness [that] deepened" (1963:34). This discovery of a "mysterious arrangement of merciless logic for a futile purpose" (71) resounds against the lay of the land in Derek Walcott, even where the evidence is shot through—as it is in *Sea Grapes*—with the irony with which the Caribbean recognizes a "New World" that was "wide enough for a new Eden / of various Adams." Given this "mechanism of the Adamic" (Steiner), the "worst crime is to leave a man's hands empty," Walcott assures us in *Omeros*; for men "are born makers, with that primal simplicity / in every maker since Adam." *Omeros* also provides us with other registers of the contradictory embrace of goods and the good when it refracts and grounds that neon sign with which Ma Kilman's NO PAIN CAFE, ALL WELCOME displays its endorsement of Coca-Cola (1990:17). Here, the empire of signs signifies a new corporate reality, or presumes to do so—all the while that, "subdued in the rivers of her blood," the woman also contains "unburied gods, for three centuries dead, / but from whose lineage, as if her veins were their roots, / her arms ululated, uplifting branches / of a tree carried across the Atlantic" (242).

This foraging for signs of appropriation and difference is a helpful one, given the points of departure from and of arrival in the round earth's imagined corners that the works of Shakespeare and the lands of America provide here. Now monumental, now slip-sliding, my itinerary in contexts therefore ranges as it does, from "(wo)manchild in the (com)promised land" to "the length of Prester John's foot"; and from the explorations in "immoral thrusts under the act?" to the vernacular force with which a conceit of Wole Soyinka's in *The Road* ("*aksident store—all part availebul*") embraces even as it subverts latitude and import.

Chapter 1

Whatever Happened to Caliban's Mother? Or, The Problem With Othello's

(wo)Manchild in the (com)Promised Land

> Is so I set down so to substance
> and to sum, but, seduced, think
> to be elf with printless foot
> is admiration and nice.
> "Calypso for Caliban"
> (from *Carnival of the Old Coast*)

Comprehensive and pointedly vigorous as his 1960 reading of *The Tempest* was and remains in *The Pleasures of Exile*, it is to good effect that George Lamming anticipates one emphasis if not quite the orientation of what I intend to explore here by raising the issue, "Whatever Happened to Caliban's Mother? Or, The Problem With Othello's." Still, the connection with Lamming is an implicit one, primarily because his "take" on a mutual sense of native—and deficit—motherhood comes in a parenthetical thought. All the same, it does lead him to speculate on the relevant consequence: the failure of a potential alliance between Miranda and Caliban to materialize. Lamming focuses on the fact that "it has taken Prospero twelve years to tell the child one or two things which any decent parent of his diligence would have passed on long ago. When she asks him: Are you my father? he talks about the chastity of her mother; and we realize—with some knowledge of his type—that he is taking refuge in the lesson of chastity in order to invoke or obscure any talk about the woman who is supposed to be his wife" (Lamming 1992:115).

With Prospero's "Thy mother was a piece of virtue, and / She said thou wast my daughter," says Lamming, "we are left to wonder, who was really Miranda's mother? And what would she have had to say about this marvellous monster of a husband who refuses us information?" The (gendered) act of disrespect fails, however, to reach across the racial/class divide that separates Miranda's mother from Caliban's, Sycorax; and so does not create an alliance of these subjugated natives of Prospero's person. Lamming notes that "in

17

some real, though extraordinary way, Caliban and Miranda are seen side by side: opposite and contiguous at the same time. They share an ignorance that is also the source of some vision. . . . In different circumstances they could be together in a way that Miranda and her father could not." Moreover, the man appears to harbor and articulate an especially corrosive memory of the woman who is Caliban's mother—a memory which "for some reason arouses him to rage that is almost insane. For all that he is a Duke and noble, Prospero can't conquer that obscene habit of throwing the past, turning your origins into a weapon of blackmail. In Caliban's case it takes the form of his mother being a so-and-so" (Lamming 1992: 116; *also* Orgel 1984 ["Prospero's Wife"]; Orgel, ed. 1987 [*The Tempest*]; Vaughan and Vaughan 1991; and Saldívar 1991. See, too, Marshall's Caliban and Miranda in "Brazil," as above).

It is a decisive, because recalcitrant, matter, then, that on that island— and beyond it in the Europe of Naples and Milan and the Africa of Tunis and Argier—the politics of identity which ties the Duke to his daughter and both of them to their (European) adversaries could not inhabit the same ideological space as that which defines their rebellious (native) servants. Not even when these servants are constrained in their roles as "wicked dam" and "foul witch . . . grown into a hoop"; of "most lying slave . . . and filth"; of "moody" even if "airey spirit." Contraindications remain throughout, notwithstanding evidence of sycophantic or otherwise attendant postures in their "hail, grave sir"; "my noble master"; "pardon, master"; and "I thank thee, master." And it remains the case even in that "I'll be wise hereafter / And seek for grace" of Caliban. "Twixt such regions / There is some space," says Sebastian (II.i.260-61). He is as right as he is terse, for the utopian bent to be free of one another is in each case expressed in mutually exclusive, even if mirrored, categories. And sycophancy no less than grace may in fact be driven by an agenda like Caliban's—who, incidentally, does appear to respond correctly to Prospero's own fetishization of The Book. "Burn but his books," Caliban insists; for as Prospero well knows, no in-the-light-of-common-day book will coerce intercourse with spirits or with the graves of the dead (V.i.48-57) or "from toe to crown . . . make [people] strange stuff" (IV.i.233-34). Having first seized Prospero's books, Caliban tells Stephano, "thou mayst knock a nail into his head / . . . mayst brain him, / . . . or with a log / Batter his skull, or paunch him with a stake / Or cut his wezand with thy knife" (III.ii.69;96-100). So opposed, then, are the contexts for Caliban's retreat into "grace" and Prospero's high miracle of restoration, and so distant would both of them be from Ariel's preference:

> Where the bee sucks, there suck I:
> In a cowslip's bell I lie;

> There I couch when owls do cry.
> On the bat's back I do fly
> After summer merrily. (V.i.88-92)

The burlesque pathos in Gonzalo's efforts to re-constitute the ideal ("Had I but plantation of this isle [and the power by contraries to execute]. . . . / All things in common nature should produce / Without sweat or endeavor") only serves to measure ironic distances between and within *The Tempest*'s competing attempts to fashion an *eu-topos* (place of happiness) out of an *ou-topos* (no place). No less significant is the degree to which the drama plays on—or with—the fear of what can result whenever degree, caste, and race are tempestuously confused. The issue becomes a matter of some urgency when tempest of weather, and an inexplicably "sweet marriage" entered into with the Africans of Tunis, pose the threat of reducing the next heir of Naples to Claribel:

> She that is Queen of Tunis; she that dwells
> Ten leagues beyond man's life; she that from Naples
> Can have no note, unless the sun were post—
> The man i' the moon's too slow...
> A space whose every cubit
> Seems to cry out, "How shall that Claribel
> Measure us back to Naples?" (II.i.248-63)

This is the context in which Gonzalo's conjuration of the ideal commonwealth fails, for all that it seems to hold the promise, even if fatuously, of a resolution by way of utopian transcendence. But then, he is not Prospero; and he does not control the means of producing new worlds, or braves ones, for that matter. As a result, the "honest old councilor's" subsequent and attendant-lord celebration of a return to power that Prospero alone can engineer is as oracular and giddy as it is a transparent calculus of the value in and the certainty of European succession:

> Was Milan thrust from Milan that his issue
> Should become king of Milan? O, rejoice
> Beyond a common joy, and set it down
> With gold on lasting pillars. (V.i.205-209)

Parenthetically, what Gonzalo also exalts on these lasting pillars is an old-world polity that is even more removed from the utopian distortion to which he had been inspired by the Michel de Montaigne (1533-1592) of "The Cannibals." Montaigne's "real utopia" was one in which "the very words that import lying, falsehood, treason, dissimulation, covetousness, envy, detraction, and pardon were never heard of." Signally, it laid claim to no "politic superiority" nor "succession" (Brooke *et al.* 1935:930). Even more correctly, then, than Antonio could have meant, "the latter end of [Gonzalo's] commonwealth forgets the beginning" (II.ii.158). But then, the old councillor had declared himself ready to govern his version of utopia to a perfection that would excel the golden age that Montaigne had conceived of in both the excitement of discovery and the *mal de l'âme* of desperate hope (Leschemelle 1994:186-90). In *The Tempest*, meanwhile, Shakespeare maps aspirations to power and governance—or to Miranda's naively "brave" new world—in variously contraindicative ways. As a result, the only new-world order that Gonzalo can be assured of is very much constrained by the Politics of the Same. It is one in which the relative positions of Milan's and Naples's European castaways and restored penitents—and of the island's captive and latter-day rebels ("savage and deformed")—remain unchallenged. So assured are the circumstances in which Gonzalo's ideal plantation will remain lazily quixotic and subversive of its utopian bent. Thereafter, the commonwealth becomes one in which there would be "No occupation; all men idle, all"; the women, too, "but innocent and pure," of course:

> All things in common nature should produce
> Without sweat or endeavour: treason, felony,
> Sword, pike, knife, gun, or need of any engine
> Would I not have; but nature should bring forth,
> Of it own kind, all foison, all abundance,
> To feed my innocent people. (II.i.159-64)

In sum, given the closed economy that binds all to one, it is fatefully the case that, structurally adjusted or not, debt-burdened or not, the "island evidently belongs to Prospero: whitely Christian" (Aers and Wheale 1991:12). There is thus very much of an apt inadvertence to the economic speculation of Sebastian's teaser of a parting shot, when he says, "I think he will carry this island home in his pocket and give it to his son for an apple." So, too, the hegemonic expansion that marks Alonso's addition: "And, sowing the kernels in the sea, bring forth more islands" (II.i.88-92). Principal and bit players thus persist at their stations, so decisive are *The Tempest*'s unequal ratios of exchange and power.

Appropriately, the impression that Ferdinand and Miranda are engaged in some lyrical and utopian union—as against the supposition that they are being deployed for reasons of (European) tribe and state—originates in and is sustained primarily by the happy credulity of the politically innocent and untouchably high-stationed lovers; and they celebrate themselves in due fashion. For there is, famously, that conceit of Ferdinand's, with its exuberant "Admired Miranda! Indeed the top of admiration! Worth / That's dearest in the world! . . . O you, / So perfect and so peerless, are created / Of every creature's best!" The exchange of affection is no less engaging when, admired *and* ripening, Miranda makes an offering of herself in "fair and holy innocence," since she "dare not offer [yet] / What I desire to give, and much less take / What I shall die to want." There is transport here, and enough to engage Prospero himself: "Heavens rain grace / On that which breeds between 'em!" (III.i. 37-39; 82). Of course, he does remain aware of his own helping hand: "I must / Bestow upon the eyes of this young couple / Some vanity of mine art" (IV.i.39-41). Needless to say, the vanity and the art work to sustain Ferdinand at the top of his admiration. With "Temperance" made over into "a delicate wench" (II.i.36-42), Ferdinand is ready to be confirmed in and by Prospero's illusions. Parenthetically, the ex-Duke of Milan's expansionist politics does make for delicious irony when Alonso fears for his son: "O thou mine heir / Of Naples and of Milan, what strange fish / Hath made his meal on thee?" (II.i.111-13). In any case, fully captivated Ferdinand celebrates his enchantment:

> Let me live here;
> So rare a wonder'd father and a wife
> Makes this place Paradise. (IV.i.122-24)

Appropriately, the "fair encounter / Of two most rare affections!"—to which Prospero also summons a goddess who will pronounce it "a contract of true love" (IV.i.84)—is as much cold calculation as it is grace. After all, Prospero's "engine" and aim in all this are, inescapably, restoration to and of hegemonic continuity in the face of upstarts in Europe, and of filial awakening and restlessness. And in the face, too, of increasingly strained relations with foreign bodies eager for independence—gently, as in Ariel's hint, "Let me remember thee what thou hast promis'd / Which is not yet performed me;" or vehemently, as in Caliban's outbursts of exasperation: "This island's mine!"

It must register, then, that Prospero's return to civil(ized) society is set to take place in ways that will be seen and understood to be in pointed contrast to those of his fellow European sovereign, Alonso of Naples. For this Alonso it was who, though "kneeled to and importuned / By all of us," did not "bless our Europe" with his daughter, Claribel. What he has done is "lose her to an African" instead. It is Alonso who, for reasons that resist clarity, has left "the fair soul herself / Weighed, between loathness and obedience." He has left her "there," at the very edge of human habitation. And the puzzling nature of this negotiated abandonment can only be further deepened when one recalls

Brabantio's response to his daughter's even more unfathomable—*because voluntary*—"losing" of herself to yet another African, with "thick lips" and "sooty bosom," besides: "For your sake, jewel, / I am glad at soul I have no other child; / For thy escape would teach me tyranny" (*Othello* I.iii.195-97). In Prospero's case, meanwhile, any and all "overtopping" attempts at violation by native or other dangerous even if low-comedy types ("Caliban and his confederates") are to be well and truly "trashed." Situated as this father believes himself to be under a more "auspicious star," the ex-ruler of Milan is remarkably clear-headed about the twin urgencies of protocol and power. Thus, no matter where he is or imagines himself to be, from his "poor cell" on the island to his place of retirement in Milan, where "every third thought shall be my grave," he aims at and works toward a ceremony that will assure the ascendancy and the purity of a Euro-Christian bloodline: "In the morn / I'll bring you to your ship, and to Naples, / Where I have hope to see the nuptial / Of these our dear-beloved solemnized" (V.i.300-09).

To have so much "business appertaining" is no easy matter. For one thing, what so urgent a need forces on Prospero is unambiguous recognition of the fact that, regarding Caliban especially, Miranda is a dangerously seductive even if unbargainable advantage. The situation provokes in him a benign but wary response to eruptions of male sexuality—in Ferdinand, that is; in contrast, that is, to his horror-filled shock of recognition that Caliban can be sexually aroused by Miranda. The somewhat conflicted, because half-pandering, move to which he resorts thereafter is not surprising. Assured of the shipwrecked Ferdinand's readiness—or (better) compulsion—to provide service, he invites Miranda to position her ripening fertility where it can be displayed to productive advantage: "The fringed curtains of thine eye advance / And say what thou seest yond," Prospero asks of Miranda. In sum, the man's "take" on the situation, "So glad of this as they I cannot be," is throughout quite the appropriate one for someone who, faced with the need to admit impediment and (state) craft to coupling and copulation, "must uneasy make" any "swift business." Prospero is very much persuaded, besides, that it is his "prescience" to recognize "a most auspicious star whose influence, / If now [he courts] not but omit[s]," his fortunes "will ever after droop" (I.ii.181-183). For which reason, and measure for measure, there needed to be much ado in the making of *The Tempest*'s new world order. Far from it all being a *laissez-faire* matter of what you will or of as you like it, the situation demanded that Book, Transport, and Body be managed into a "most high miracle" of restoration; so, too, was it necessary to commerce with and yet nuance the "rough magic" of Prospero's coercive relationship with Caliban and Ariel, not to speak of his occult alliance with graves, for these must be made to "wake their sleepers" and serve his purpose. As a result there is a quite ironic shade, a thing of darkness indeed, to Prospero's preoccupation ("lest too light winning / make the prize light") when applied to his own efforts at restoration.

It does appear, all the same, that in at least one (gendered) respect the kingdom to come cannot be radically reconstituted, perhaps because of what seems to be the nature of a certain generosity in Miranda:

> How many goodly creatures are there here!
> How beauteous mankind is! O brave new world
> That has such people in't! (V.i.183-185)

Suggestive as her words might be of a frisson of something innately and irremediably sexual, the response that its exuberance provokes in Prospero ("Tis new to thee") is as mocking, even if gently so, as one might expect. Earlier, erotic heat had been barely held in check when he explained to the young woman the figure that Ferdinand cut: "No wench, it eats, sleeps and hath such senses / As we have, such" (I.ii.412-3). The appeal of the erotic suffuses Miranda's talk about the "jewel in my dowry"; so, too, when she responds with "No wonder, sir; / But certainly a maid" (III.i.54) to Ferdinand's wondering if she is maid or no. But then, stationed as she is to be "so brave a lass," Miranda cannot but be subject to *the* condition which ideal succession demands. And with her "no bed-right shall be paid / Till Hymen's torch be lighted" (IV.i.96-97), the goddess Iris is wonderfully succinct about the tension between the sacred politics of restoration and the incontinent urgency of erotic heat. As for Ferdinand, he had earlier, and in short but right order, declared his intentions: "If a virgin, / And your affection not gone forth, I'll make you / The queen of Naples" (I.ii.445-47). Given the importance that Prospero attaches to his "rich gift," and to the need for his prospective son-in-law's "acquisition" to be "worthily purchased," he is, if anything, even more explicit when he couples bed-right and ceremony:

> If thou dost break her virgin-knot before
> All sanctimonious ceremonies...
> .... barren hate,
> sour-eyed disdain, and discord shall bestrew
> the union of your bed with weeds. (IV. v. 6-21)

Still, notwithstanding the resonant quality of sexual ripening in *The Tempest,* it is Miranda's (virginal) provenance, all the same, to imagine the brave new world in the unnuanced way that she does; for as Peter New (1985) has observed, it is instructively the case that the man who describes the island of Utopia has two names, one of which means "Messenger of God, and the other Distributor of Nonsense."

Meanwhile, because it is all so near and yet so far in kind and consequence, the parody of such exchanges in the affairs of Caliban and Prospero provides counterpoint to *The Tempest*'s reach for high miracle and meaning. The reverberations are especially strong whenever the principals are knotted and crossed up in a fit of issues that has to do with inheritance and succession, and thus with the provocations of desire and anxiety, and the resulting circulation of sexuality on so tight an island. Rather less delicately put, the play must contend with a fit of issues that has to do with the exercise of power and with commodification of virginity—be it Miranda's, where signification is safely to be locked (up) in a European economy of taste; or in the awkward import of Claribel's, she "who is so far removed / [we] ne'er again shall see her." And so, notwithstanding (or perhaps precisely because of) the balance-of-trade calculation in Sebastian's "Twas a sweet marriage, and we benefit well in return," Claribel is more persuasively experienced as victim of a trafficking with the truly foreign "beyond" that "Afric" represents. Besides which, the apparently disastrous aftermath of "tempestuous noise" and shipwreck, Alonso says, now makes the words "daughter's marriage" resound like words "crammed" into his ears and "against the stomach of [his] sense." "Would I had never / Married my daughter there!" he says then (II.i.106-111). On the other hand, Tunis "was never graced before with such a paragon to their queen," so we are told. At least, this had not been the case since a certain "wand'ring prince" (Aeneas) engaged and then abandoned to fire the affections of a Queen of Carthage, "the widowed Dido," at a time when "This Tunis, sir, was Carthage" (II.i.72-73).

No less involved is the distracting value that *The Tempest* invests in the circumstances of Sycorax's maternity, "hither brought . . . to litter here / A freckled whelp hag-born—not honour'd with / A human shape." Sign and surplus in his own right, her son also contributes his various registers of experience. "You taught me language," Caliban grants Prospero/Miranda. "And my profit on't / Is, I know how to curse," so he says in an angry and apparently complete recognition of the absoluteness of Prospero's claim on "language." But the claim is an intriguing one. Caliban says: "You taught me *language* . . . The red plague rid you / For learning me *your* language" (I.ii.362-363; the emphases are mine). Prospero is unambiguous, of course, in his contention that it was *he*—or in some versions of the drama, his daughter—who took pity on and taught the "native islander" and "demi-devil" to speak a language; or who, in a more radical understanding of the claim, introduced the islander to "language" at a time

when thou didst not, savage,
know thine own meaning, but wouldst gabble like
A thing most brutish.

This account of dis/articulation is fascinating, and invites speculation. One wonders, for example, about the relationship between Sycorax and Caliban. How was it that he came to believe that, as he put it, "This island's mine, by Sycorax, my mother"? In short, whatever happened to "language" between Sycorax and her son? It is reasonable to assume that she communicated in Argier; that she successfully commanded the elements; that she issued (disobeyed) orders to Ariel. How?

Caliban's dis/articulation is one that Kamau Brathwaite explores in *Middle Passages* (1993). The occasion is recorded in the vernacular register of the "Letter Sycorax" that Caliban writes to his mother. This Caliban does so, we note, in telling shades of "prospero ling. / go"; and with them he translates the import of "pascal & co./balt & apple & cogito ergo sum" no less than "de rice & fall a de roman empire"; so, too, his interest in "how capitalism & slavely like it putt / christianity / on ice." He is thus full of archives and new discovery, and of a mocking and report-card satisfaction when he writes,

> **Dear mamma**
> i writin ya dis letter/**wha?**
> guess what! pun a computer **o/kay?**
> like i jine de mercantlists!

Import and dis/articulation in "The Letter Sycorax" relate well enough to a certain understanding of native voice and translation in Evelyn O'Callaghan (1984). For, so she explains, one of "the facts contributing to the growth of West Indian literature is that for a long time our writers have *not* been using English the way they used to" (1984:125).

At any rate, *The Tempest*'s Caliban is centrally, and recalcitrantly, involved in several dramas of restoration—given his own claims to patrimony in registers that are now angrily burlesque (I.ii.330-43), now maddened (II.ii.1-14), now the product of his drunken and "thrice-double ass'd" identity as "Cacaliban" (II.ii.161-92). But then, at once romantic *independentista* and cargo-cultist, the "moon calf" can conjure up, and ever so exquisitely, an isle that is full of "sounds and sweet airs that give delight and hurt not":

> Sometimes a thousand twangling instruments
> Will hum about my ears; and sometimes voices
> That, if I then waked after long sleep,
> Will make me sleep again; and then, in dreaming,
> The clouds methought would open and show riches
> Ready to drop upon me, that when I waked,
> I cried to dream again. (III.ii.140-14)

Thus conceived, *The Tempest* is pregnant with Shakespeare's slip-sliding, but sustained, concern with the limit(ation)s of identity and the contagion of difference. Terrain and type thus converge in "one Englishman's tribute to a sea-haunted age when his countrymen explored the round earth's imagined corners. Setting his scene in the Mediterranean, he had his eye," Russell Fraser writes, "on places farther from home, Patagonia, for instance, where savage natives adored their great devil Setebos" (1992: 240). The issue of alterity thus intrudes, and with studied topicality. The implications are no less consequential, of course, in the mutant, but comic, malice of Trinculo's way with Caliban: "What have we here? A man or fish? Dead or alive? A fish: he smells like a fish; a very ancient and fish-like smell; a kind of newest Poor-John. A strange fish! Were I in England now ... there would this monster make a man; any strange beast there makes a man" (II.ii.23-35). Remarked upon in other latitudes, as in *Carnival of the Old Coast* (1995), the con/fusion of identity will make for the self-caressing erasure with which, "not ariel-spirit / not daughter-flesh," Caliban must contend "when the wind breaks / in derelict places." "Be present," he says then, "while and still I am ready / if the revel end / to wake and cry to dream again" (66). Elsewhere, this time in Brathwaite's season of "Drought" in *Black + Blues* (1977), transgressive recognition of Self and Import soon confronts us with a Caliban who is "blind ... tortured ... twisted and bent," a victim of, among other things, "skin and trinket," and of wasted motion: "papernapkins soiled with sperm" (22).

Immoral Thrusts Under The Act?

> I therefore apprehend and do attach thee
> For an abuser of the world, a practicer
> Of arts inhibited and out of warrant.
>> Brabantio, to Othello (I.ii.78-80)

> [T]here remained, out of the destruction that had engulfed so large a portion of Blake's copperplates, ten plates, making sixteen impressions (a few having been engraved on both sides) of the *Songs of Innocence and of Experience*. The gentleman [Fredrick Tatum?] from whom they were obtained had once the entire series in his possession; but all save these ten were stolen by an ungrateful black he had befriended, who sold them to a smith as old metal.
>> Alexander Gilchrist, *Life of William Blake* (1863)

The esthetics and ethics involved in the collecting of (other) people's cultural property can be a complicated business. The rites and the rights of such collections are complexly explored by various hands in, say, Phyllis Mauch Messenger's *The Ethics of Collecting Cultural Property* (1989). So, too, incidentally, in what might be called Jeannette Greenfield's *l'autre face du royaume* volume, *The Return of Cultural Treasures* (1989). For his part, the George Steiner of *No Passion Spent* negotiates his way past a "desolate and impudent supposition" to press home his point, all the same, about the import of one such constellation of "monuments of unageing intellect" in "the archives of Eden": "Here hang the finest Stradivirus violins, violas, cellos on earth. They hang each millimetre restored, analysed, recorded," he adds. For which reason, they have been made "safe from the vandalism of the Red Brigades, from the avarice or cynical indifference of dying Cremona." Steiner also imagines ceremonies of preservation in which, once a year, "unless I am mistaken," they would be taken down "from their cases and lent for performance to an eminent quartet," thus allowing Hadyn, Mozart, Beethoven, Bartok to once again "fill the room. Then back to their sanctuary of silent preservation." And it is both against and through this prism that "Americans come to gaze . . . in pride [and] Europeans in awed envy or gratitude [at] instruments that have been made immortal. And stone dead" (1996: 283). In effect, the import of any master(ing) text or instrument can therefore become occasion for faith or else for agnosticism, if not for outright apostasy—and this within as well as across cultural boundaries. In what follows here, *both* sites and their way with Shakespeare (or Shakespeare's with them) will matter. For which reason, Jorge Luis Borges's "Everything and Nothing" view of Shakespeare will be of some heuristic significance; so, too, that signal articulation of "The West" that Octavio Paz derives from *The Tempest* in his *Conjunctions and Disjunctions*: "For the Christian West," Paz writes, "foreign societies were always the incarnation of evil. Whether savage or civilized, they were manifestations of the inferior world, the body. And the West treated them with the same rigor with which ascetics punished their senses. Shakespeare says it straight out in *The Tempest*" (1974:110). Meanwhile, Renaissance enthusiasms and nationalist geo-politics resound to other relevant effects in the "bow of Ulysses" within which James Anthony Froude's *The English in the West Indies* (1888) re-memorialized the Caribbean as epic "training ground" for the Elizabethan Englishmen who destroyed the Spanish Armada in 1588. No less signal, however, is the disaffiliating move of that Afro-Brazilian retreat from Shakespeare ("What have I got to do with Othello, for God's sake?") with which Abdias do Nascimento ends his *Sortilege*. All in all, the acts that interest me here have to do with encounter and dis/affiliation, or else with patterns of accommodation which, in her Latin

American context, Doris Sommer (1990) once identified as "plagiarized authenticity." My own itinerary in contexts will be variously mapped: as much through Oxford and South Africa and the Caribbean as on the popular stage in Bombay and along the ways of Turkey and Sierra Leone. There is, too, the no less instructive drama of belatedness, and the rivalry by mimesis, with which Euro-America has variously sought to negotiate its putative European ancestry, especially in light of a Matthew Arnold's monitoring judgment of "civilisation" in the United States, or else in a Paul Bourget's *Outre-Mer: Impressions of America*. If not in such places, then there is, as above, the high-stationed mode in which Steiner's *No Passion Spent* provides us with a problematic summary of the utopian reach for "newborn knowledge" and "innocence of intellect and sensibility": "This, then, is my surmise: the dominant apparatus of American high culture is *that of custody*. The institutions of learning and of the arts constitute the great archive, inventory, catalogue, store-house, rummage-room of western civilization." It is in this context, with its oscillation between a dialectic of "the frontier and the archive," that Steiner also makes the point that "Again and again, the impetus of American modernism, most particularly in poetry, has been paradoxically antiquarian." The perspective is a helpful one for my purposes here, and serves to position "antinomies" as well as a "spectrum of intermediate positions between them [that] turn on the primary trope of 'felt time', of the chronological." Here, the question of pre-text and dis/affiliation is played out with some instruction against the question of whether the New World was indeed "the *mundus novus* promised by St. John and proclaimed by Spanish ecclesiastical chroniclers almost immediately after Columbus's journey?" If we map, or insist on, terrains and types here that are "an authentic vestige of the Garden set aside for the re-entry of the new Adam," then we engage sites and consciousness that "had no 'history'." There is the alternative premise, of course; and it derives its force from the view that the originality of the *novus mundus* was always ancient business; that it was therefore "no more intemporal and immune from the inheritance of the fall than were [any other or older] lands" (1996:266, 281-282). There is the relevant issue all the same of how belatedness, whether assumed or real, relates to monuments of "unageing intellect" (Yeats), and to the "homeland" of consequence to which they point, be it Shakespeare, the Koran, or the Bible; or else those pieces of the Acropolis that were sold to the British Museum in 1816 as the Elgin Marbles.

For reasons that are therefore as much colonizing and "center" as they are imperial and "margin," let me anticipate certain conclusions about the esthetics of copy-writing, the economy of copyrighting, and the politics of re-constituting cultural icons and monuments. We engage in such activities under the *threat of an erasure of identity* that a Jean Franco might link to absence of density of specification and an Edward Said to existential weightlessness. We do so on a *gradient of dissimilarity* (Midgley 1988) along which we are forever falling away from or else toward each other. Finally, we engage in attempts at transfiguration in (the perhaps desperate) anticipation that some measure of *parity of esteem* among cultures would at least be seen to have taken place. In the end, whatever the issues are, their import is likely to be rather urgently textured wherever one is inclined to find value in that "philosophy of history" thesis of Walter Benjamin's: that "cultural treasures" form part of "the triumphal procession in which the present rulers step over those who are lying prostrate," since "there is no document of civilization which is not at the same time a document of barbarism" (Benjamin 1969:258). Obviously, it is one such document—"perhaps not a whole chapter but a reasonable paragraph"—that Chinua Achebe grounds in the mind of his District Commissioner in *Things Fall Apart* (1959): "He had already chosen the title of the book, after much thought: '*The Pacification of the Primitive Tribes of the Lower Niger*'." In Ngugi wa Thiong'o's east Africa, meanwhile, the title of the master text that we get in *A Grain of Wheat* (1967) is "*Prospero in Africa*."

Consider within this embrace of master text and dis/affiliating transport the sudden eruption against "those who deprecate all works of dead Anglo-Saxon white males" in Maynard Mack's *Everybody's Shakespeare* (1993:1). The outburst ends the paragraph of reasonable enough justifications with which Mack begins his approach to Shakespeare. But then, there is a certain easiness in Mack's sleight-of-pen assumption of pedigree that elides rather more engaging questions. One such comes in the cluster of issues—"burden of the past" and "artist moved by the grandeur of ancient ruins"—with which Goethe once circumscribed the figure of the English dramatist in W. Jackson Bate (1970). Steiner is no less instructive when, by way of Wittgenstein, he refracts his "Reading Against Shakespeare" in light of the proposition that "In our culture, taboos and prescriptive reverence hedge Shakespeare's work." In Bate's *The Burden of the Past and the English Poet*, Goethe had duly called attention to the commingling of anxious pedigree and alienating affinity that interests me: "Had I been born an *Englishman,* and had those manifold masterworks pressed in upon me with all their power from my first youthful awakening," the German observed, "it would have overwhelmed me, and I would not have known what I wanted to do! I would never have been able to advance with so light and cheerful a spirit, but would certainly have been obliged to consider for a long time and look about me in order to find some new expedient" (Bate 1970:5-6; my emphasis). Of course, the problematic nature of any "new expedient" at all is further

compounded by Goethe's readiness to believe that when Shakespeare wrote
he had given "us golden apples in silver dishes." By careful study, he
proposed, we may acquire the silver dishes; but then, we also run the risk of
discovering that we have "only potatoes to put in them" (5). In Steiner,
meanwhile, what Wittgenstein asks Shakespeare, "in the name of an urgent
and tragic moral need, in the name, finally of music, is this: is language
enough?" He does so after granting that the poet is "not only matchless
artificer and imaginer, but the beneficiary, the communicant with and
communicator to his fellow-men of a high, articulate religious-moral-philo-
sophical vision and criticism of life." Steiner thus holds out a near-apostate
notion of "western literacy in which Shakespeare would have the suspect
status consequent upon Wittgenstein's views"—when once we move beyond
the temptation to label such a view as "an historical curio, as an aberration
somewhat like Socrates' marriage." It is a thought that Steiner's "reading"
almost surrenders when it concludes that "Plato was wrong when he banished
the poets" and that "Wittgenstein misreads Shakespeare. Surely, this must
be so. And yet" (*ibid.*).

In 1895, Member of the French Academy Paul Bourget had grounded
his impressions of America, of its belatedness and new expediency, in what
proves to be complex sub/versions of things European. As much *outré* and
outre-mer, his landmarks involved a virtual monumentalization of the central
image that Bate uses in *The Burden of the Past* to contextualize pedigree and
misalignment in the architectures of the First, Second, and Third Temples.
"Flaubert wrote to one of his pupils: 'If you cannot construct the Parthenon,
build a pyramid'," Bourget asserted. "All America seems to be instinctively
repeating to itself in other words this stern but stimulating counsel" (1895:47).
First impressions to the contrary, Bourget's treatment of this misprision is
actually quite supple. For it manages to suggest categories that range from
heretic mimetism to that "rewriting of imitation as voracity" which, Brazilian
New-Worlder that he was, Oswald de Andrade embeds as the central premise
("cultural cannibalism") in his 1928 *"Manifesto Antropófago"* (Bary 1991:96-
97). Bourget's configurations include an overseas class of copying which,
so it seems, does not consist of "weak imitations, pretentions and futile
attempts, such as in every country bring ridicule upon braggarts and upstarts.
No. In detail and finish they reveal conscientious study, technical care." Still,
Outre-Mer also explains Euro-American reproduction in terms of mimicry
and mimic men; and here, the French Academician's approach to the ways of
the *mundus novus* recalls the monitoring censorship of Arnold's travels in
North American culture. For it is also Bourget's judgment that presumption
and belatedness had engendered "caprices [which] take for granted such
quantities of [money] that after a walk [in the Newport, Rhode Island of the
1890s] from cottage to cottage, from chateau to chateau, you half fancy that

you have been visiting some isle consecrated to the god Plutus, whose most modern incarnation is the god Dollar, [and who] neither enervated or enfeebled [is determined] to make itself manifest, spread itself, 'show off,' to use the real Yankee word" (Bourget 1895:46).

Evidence of the consequent rivalry by mimesis, or of plagiarized authenticity, is variously grounded; and one such—the delicious cloister of Magdalen—is fortuitous and apt. After all, the ghost of Oxford does haunt that simulacrum of a library in *The Great Gatsby*; so, too, American involvement in attempts to fix definitively the identity of the English dramatist known as "Shakespeare" (as, for example, Edward de Vere, Earl of Oxford). Rather more directly consequential, Oxford University will intrude in the alienating genesis and ethnography of the foreign text that we get in Laura Bohannan's "Shakespeare in the Bush." In sum, the reasons in Bohannan relate as much to the precarious and secondary nature of colonial enthusiasms as they do to the cult of authenticity. In Bourget, meanwhile,

> One of these [North American] men has spent some time in England, and it has pleased him to build for himself on one of these Rhode Island lawns an English abbey of the style of Queen Elizabeth. It rises up, gray and stern, so like, so perfect, that it might, without changing a single stone, be transported to Oxford on the shores of Isis, to make a pendant to the delicious cloister of Magdalen or the facade of Oriel. Another man loves France, and he has seen fit to possess in sight of the Atlantic a chateau in the style of the French Renascence. Here is the chateau; it reminds you of Azay, Chenonceaux, and the Loire, with its transparent ribbon of water winding idly in and out amid the yellow sand of the islands. A third has built a marble palace precisely like the Trianon, with Corinthian pillars as large as those of the Temple of the Sun at Baalbek [site of Roman ruins in Lebanon]. (*ibid.* 46)

Needless to say, wherever transport and appropriation are distended by the gravitational pull of "the sun at Baalbek," affiliation and disaffiliation assume even greater "overseas" complexity. They become especially awkward in contexts that have to do with "Africa proper," as in Hegel's philosophy of world history; or else—as in Conrad's *Heart of Darkness*—with some metahistorical invitation to conceive of kinship and transport in terms of "some implacable force brooding over an inscrutable intention." In part, so Mudimbe explains in *The Invention of Africa* (1988), the problem lies "with the idea of History with a capital H, which first incorporates St. Augustine's notion of *providentia* and later on expresses itself in the evidence of Social

Darwinism" (1988:16). As a result, "Evolution, conquest, and difference become signs of a theological, biological, and anthropological destiny, and assigns to things and beings both their natural slots and social mission." The same is true of appeals to the "inherent superiority of the white race, and, as already made explicit in Hegel's *Philosophy of Right*, the necessity for European economies and structures to expand to 'virgin areas' of the world" (*ibid*. 17). At any rate, compared to Oxford's cloister and to the Yankee's *show-off*, the gravitational pull of matters that relate to "Africa" is apt to ground alterity in exceptionally cardinal ways, be it via the "natural history" of the exotic in Pliny's "*ex Africa semper aliquid novi*" (II.iii), or in the compass of the self within which Sir Thomas Browne (1605-1682) reached for rapprochement in *Religio Medici*. Pliny's measure of difference, Mudimbe's *Invention* further indicates, includes the specifics of a certain "black river which has the same nature as the Nile (N.H.v,viii,44). Strange beings live there"; among them, "people who do not have individual names" (*ibid*.71). For his part, Browne, so his *Religio Medici* explained, could "never content [his] contemplation with those generall pieces of wonders, the flux and reflux of the sea, the encrease of the Nile, the conversion of the Needle to the North" and other "more obvious neglected pieces of Nature" (15). And yet, "There is all *Africa*, and her prodigies in us . . . in which he that studies wisely learnes in a compendium what others labour at in a divided piece and endlesse volume." Understood in/continently, we are a "Cosmography of [the] selfe"; and "wee carry with us the wonders, we seeke without us" (*ibid*.).

There are circumstances, of course, in which "Africa" is rather more vernacular in the measures of its import. For which reason, transport and mastering text may converge as they do in Sierra Leonean Thomas Decker's 1972 *krio* version of *As You Like It* (*Udat Di Kiap Fit—If the Cap Fits*); or else in the assurance that his 1964 *Juliohs Siza* offers, with its "*Padi dem, kohntri man, una ohl wey dey / na Rom. Meyk una kak una yes ya!. . . / A noh want foh pwell weytin Bra Brutus say* (Friends, countrymen, you, all of you who are here / in Rome. Set up your ears well. Please! / I do not want to spoil what Mister Brutus has said) (Decker 1988:54-55). *The Invention of Africa* enlightens too when—in response to the question, "What then should we do with the problem of transhistoric thought?"—Mudimbe considers a criterion according to which "experiential authority" invents itself in the processes of translation and exegesis. "From the rhetorical margins of history," *Invention* concludes, such a process "opens upon a paradox: something like the pure reflection of consciousness" (Mudimbe 1988:199). Mudimbe thus identifies orders of knowledge that "enlarge and universalize regional archives"; he also grounds their "invention" in a certain dynamic of history and of the colonial experience. As a consequence, the *l'ordre de choses* that results does not negate "the truth of social forms as expressed and generated by the dialectic between *Leben* (living and sharing with others) and *Gemeinsamkeit* (a permeating community). On the contrary, a permanent recapitulation of this dialectic should remain as an endless task of reading, commenting upon the permanent production of cultural legends and '*une parole pour-soi*'" (*ibid.*). Given such configurations of sign and surplus, Walter Mignolo's explanation of his intentions in *The Darker Side of the Renaissance* (1995) is especially relevant when he proposes that "historically" he had looked at "colonial expansion as the darker side of the European Renaissance." In addition to which,

> Theoretically, [he] attempted, first to displace questions related to the representations of the colonized with questions related to the performances at both ends of the spectrum (colonizer and colonized) as well as in between (colonizer in exile, colonized in adaptation). . . . Theoretically, [such moves require] a pluritopic hermeneutics; ideologically, [they imply] the creation of loci of enunciation parallel and opposite to the loci of enunciation created in the field of anthropology: instead of looking at marginal societies from the perspective of academic centers [the objective is] to look at cultural and political centers from the academic margins. (Mignolo 1995:311-312)

Conceived of within and against such constellations of latitude and import, the volatile nature of investments in "Shakespeare" may help to clarify why and how a 1995 Oxford University Press catalogue could hardly be averse to informing us that in his new edition of *Shakespeare's Lives* (1993) Samuel Schoenbaum "once again shows how we have reshaped Shakespeare . . . from the Bard's contemporaries (who didn't praise him as much as we think) to Malcolm X (who denied he existed)." And why, elsewhere, Grace Ioppolo's 1991 editorial ways in "revising Shakespeare" are expansive and relevant, since her discussion of theories of revisions, from 1623 to 1990, follows through to culminate in the premise that Shakespeare's texts maintain their greatest meaning not through attempted restoration to original editions but instead through understanding and continuation of their multiplicity. There is, too, the strategic splicing of observations (from Samuel Johnson) with which Arthur Sherbo introduces his *Birth of Shakespeare Studies* (1986) and *Shakespeare's Midwives* (1992): "The compleat explanation of an author not systematick and consequential, but desultory and vagrant, abounding in casual allusions and light hints, is not to be expected from any single scholiast, [for] a commentary must arise from the fortuitous discoveries of many men, in devious walks of literature" (1992:11). Furthermore, and for Bill Overton this anticipates the provisional nature of the *texts* themselves, "in the freedom of the Elizabethan *theatre*, when there was little time for group rehearsal and no director to coordinate, variety [in performances] would have been even greater" (1987:11-12). Overton makes an exemplary point of underscoring the fact that the apparent particularity of Shylock's "Jewish garberdine" refers in fact "to no known garment and probably means an ordinary cloak." And, parenthetically, the "garberdine" in Trinculo's "my best way is to creep under his garberdine" is, in fact, Caliban's (*Tempest* II.ii.39-40). In any case, Overton points out that Portia's "Which is the merchant here? and which the Jew?" (IV.i.171) certainly "suggests that there is no obvious difference in appearance between Antonio and Shylock." However, there is the ever-present interplay of licence and instability; for which reason, Overton warns, "I quote the line as it appears in the Quarto and Folio texts" since "most modern editions, like the Penguin, obscure the point by starting a new sentence at 'and', which slows the line down." Authoritarian clarification is familiar enough in the textual history of Shakespeare; but then, so too are the implications of Overton's reminder that in this case it occurs in a play in which "it is only recently that two characters, Salerio and Solanio, have been distinguished from the three characters of earlier editions." Discoveries and re-figurations of this sort should serve "to underscore once again the provisional nature of Shakespearean texts." However, they also demonstrate just "how easy it is to assume details for which there is no explicit and little implicit textual authority"—but details, all the same, that have been known to strongly influence staging of and import in Shakespeare (11-13).

Inflection and multiplicity are no doubt at work in the 1994-95 "Message From The President" (of The Shakespeare Association of America) in which Bruce R. Smith sees his own "cultural poetics" study, *Homosexual Desire in Shakespeare's England* (1991), as a legitimate measure of the view that "Shakespeare" stands as a reference for the multiple cultures of North America; that the phenomenon is, *tout court*, "public property" (1). In which case, Gary Taylor's *Reinventing Shakespeare: A Cultural History from the Restoration to the Present* (1989), even if brash (especially in its survey of "The Present"), is hardly surprising in its view that "most histories of Shakespeare's reputation belong to the genre of academic romance" (373). Examples of such "romance" may therefore be indexed as much to A. L. Rowse's dismissive "roaring homo" response (1992) to Oxfordian claims on the "real" Shakespeare as to the passion with which Charlton Ogburn persists in *The Mysterious William Shakespeare* (1984). The genre that Taylor identifies is in fact a rather capacious one. The protagonist in its stories is now "honest ghost," now shadow of a glove-maker's son. In other versions, he is very much the incarnation as well as the implausible exercise of genius.

"Thus hounded, he ceased to be Ferrex or Tamerlane and became no one again," Borges (1960) had written about a Shakespeare who, as an *hacedor*, was "everything and nothing"; but then, Shakespeare also took "to imagining other heroes and other tragic fables. And so, while his flesh fulfilled its destiny as flesh in the taverns and brothels of London, the soul that inhabited him was Caesar, who disregards the augur's admonition, and Juliet, who abhors the lark, and Macbeth, who converses on the plain with witches who are fates." In figure and in sum, Borges notes, "No man has ever been so many men as this man, who like the Egyptian Proteus could exhaust all the guises of reality. At times he would leave a confession hidden away in some corner of his work, certain it would not be deciphered; Richard affirms that in his person he plays the part of many and Iago claims with curious words 'I am not what I am'" (248-249).

All in all, Shakespeare can be "public property" almost to the point of seeming incoherence—and in ways that do seem to have been prescient. Consider the suggestive relevance of that transfiguring dream which Cleopatra has of Antony, in which, with "his legs [bestriding] the ocean" and "his rear'd arm [cresting] the world," the man had a voice that "was propertied as all the tun'd spheres" (V.ii.81-83). We learn, too, that "his delights were dolphin-like" for "they show'd his back above / the element they liv'd in."

> in his livery
> Walk'd crowns and crownets; realms and islands were
> As plates dropp'd from his pocket. (V.i.82-92)

"Shakespeare would have been amazed," Borges also wrote, if people had tried to tell him to limit himself to English themes; "if they had told him that, as an Englishman, he had no right to compose *Hamlet*, whose theme is Scandinavian, or *Macbeth*, whose theme is Scottish" (*ibid*. 181-182).

But then, how exactly does an "original" template mean when its parts are so promiscuously authorized; or when, in Mudimbe's language, "regional archives" are enlarged and universalized? And where does individual signature lie in relation to boundary and transgression—especially so if, as *Hamlet* suggests, "borrowing dulls the edge of husbandry"? Or else if, to borrow from *Measure for Measure,* identity and import lie in some "cold obstruction"; or are "blown with restless violence round about / The pendent world"? After all, when authorship so capaciously harbors itself—from the "sledded Polacks on the ice" of *Hamlet* and the "palm trees" of *As You Like It* to that "Puritan" in *The Winter's Tale* who, says the Clown, sings "psalms to hornpipes"—it invites complicated questions about creativity among (other) peoples' spheres and crownets; within their realms and islands, be they "in mearly the west of England"; among the gum trees of Arabia; or elsewhere when, in appreciating a horse in *Henry V*, we learn that "his colour is of nutmeg / and his heat that of the ginger." Of course, one could very well grant that this overseas invocation of the round earth's imagined corners does yield the quality of transport and goods that W. B. Yeats once celebrated when he observed that "Shakespearean fish swam the sea, far away from land / Romantic fish swam in nets coming to the hand. / What are all those fish that lie gasping on the strand?" (1989:240). Still, such celebration need not be the response when the preoccupation is with hegemonic shifts. *Pace* Yeats, it is not unreasonable to suspect that fishing may entail "the experiential authority of 'inventing'" (Mudimbe) or of usurpation as much as it does academic romance (Taylor). As a result, and this happens to be the case when Shakespeare himself uses the verb in *The Winter's Tale* (I.ii.196), "to fish" in certain ways and beyond certain limits is to conjure up the specter of "chaste treasures" opened to "unmaster'd importunity" (*Hamlet* I.iii.32-32). Here, the thought of bodies private and public being expropriated may therefore provoke anxieties that textual emendation or editorial mediation alone, as below, will not fully resolve. "When does metaphor become harmful?" Michael Gorra asks in "Tact and Tarzan" (1991): "Is a writer ever entitled to see a place that's not his own in metaphoric terms? Shakespeare may have had nothing like the actualities of colonial settlement in mind when he wrote *The Tempest*, for all that he drew on the Bermuda pamphlets. But you can argue that he should have—and that his seeing the New World as metaphor, as land of enchantment, marks a degree to which he shared in the colonialist rhetoric" (Gorra 88). The playwright would thus be complicit in develop- ments that Eric Cheyfitz contemplates in *The Poetics of Empire*; that Peter Hulme explores in *Colonial Encounters*; which Paz recognizes in *Conjunctions and Disjunctions,* and that Al-Tayyib Salih teases out into the circumstances of *Mawsim al-Hijrah ila al-Shawal* (*Season of Migration to the North*).

In effect, when, like some "hot love on the wing" (*Hamlet*), a mastering text operates somewhat beyond the lie of the land that Yeats's Anglo-Irish map accounts for, its transports may compel rites of return to or from some bush of ghosts. Love is, after all, not always a thing upon which to look "with idle sight" (*Hamlet*). And so it is that in heuristic illustration of one measure of the unmastered importunity that Laertes fears, I borrow from Amos Tutuola's *The Palm-Wine Drinkard* the allegory of "THE FULL-BODIED GENTLEMAN REDUCED TO HEAD" (1953:21-25). It is, parenthetically, no casual matter that in both the Nigerian's novel and in the service to which it is being put here, the Allegory of Re-turn is complexly worked into the dominant narrative: the drinkard's determined quest for the return of his dead palm-wine tapster from Deads' Town. The drinkard does get to down quaffs of palm-wine in Deads' Town where, parenthetically, "both whites and blacks were living" and to which he had come, the tapster explains, after he spent two years in training" elsewhere, "in a certain place." It was "after he had qualified as a full dead man, then he came to this Deads' Town" (99-100). In any case, the drinkard departs from his bush of ghosts with compensation of a telling kind: a regenerative "EGG" (120-122). He thus returns from this imagined corner of the world with a version of what Tutuola has identified elsewhere, in *My Life in the Bush of Ghosts,* as "Invisible Missive Magnetic Juju which could bring a lost person back to himself from an unknown place, how far it may be" (154). This return to a *parole pour soi*, with its translation of manifest form (back) into "EGG," is an important one. In heuristic terms, the authority of textual import is as starkly tapped out as it is in fact regenerated by its translation into the vernacular origins that "EGG" promises. Besides which, the economies of scale that the exchange involves are of some consequence. Consider the loss, the native *a priori*, if you wish, for which the palm-wine drinkard seeks transport and compensation. It once spanned a period of 15 years and an acreage of 500,000 palm trees. It had been possible, then, for the tapster to express a vintage two hundred and twenty five kegs of wine a day—one hundred and fifty every morning ("but before 2 o'clock p.m.") and another seventy five in the evening. And with consequences of note for self and community: "So my friends were uncountable by that time and they were drinking palm-wine with me from morning till a late hour in the night" (7).

The reach for and the celebration of such an exchange notwithstanding, the cautionary tale remains. It focuses on the problematic nature of callow attraction in a young maid's wits, as *Hamlet* might put it; so, too, on its readiness to conceive of some "brave new world, that hath such beauteous people in it" (*Tempest*). Tutuola's narrative introduces its "creature"—he was a phenomenally "beautiful 'complete' gentleman"—in a context of strained affinities and alien(ating) romance. Beginning with the description of the "'curious' creature," the tale is vivid with the shot and danger of desire, with an apparition that was *sui generis* in its capacity to captivate. Indeed, its every property did seem to be tuned to all the spheres, and to be full, too, of "hairbreadth scapes i' th'imminent deadly breach" (*Othello*). "If I were a lady," Tutuola's drinkard declares, "no doubt, I would follow him to wherever he would go, because if this gentleman went to the battle field, surely, enemy would not kill him or capture him and if bombers saw him in a town which was to be bombed, they would not throw bombs on his presence, and if they did throw it, the bomb itself would not explode until this gentleman would leave that town, because of his beauty" (25). But this is transport that is also very much refracted by the cautionary sign, "DO NOT FOLLOW

UNKNOWN MAN'S BEAUTY." Its full exposition, "RETURN THE
PARTS OF THE BODY TO THE OWNERS; OR HIRED PARTS OF THE
COMPLETE GENTLEMAN'S BODY TO BE RETURNED," produces
disarticulation, and of course disaffiliation. For, soon enough, the erstwhile

> complete gentleman was reduced to head and when they reached
> where he hired the skin and flesh which covered the head, he
> returned them, and paid the owner, now the complete gentleman
> in the market reduced to a "SKULL."

"Keep you in the rear of your affections," *Hamlet* had in any case thought it
fit to warn Ophelia, "out of the shot and danger of desire" (I.iii.34-35). It is
new to you, Prospero had been laconic in that response of his to his virgin
daughter's easy conception of how "beauteous" an appearance could be. In
the end, the lady of Tutuola's *The Palm-Wine Drinkard* remained a lass
"with only 'SKULL'" whom, so she thought in the marketplace, she once
knew well (21). She thus provides proof of just how much she had indeed
been something of "a green girl / Unsifted in such perilous circumstances,"
as Polonius once put it. "You should not have believ'd me," Hamlet says, "for
virtue cannot so innoculate our old stock" (III.i.118-120). As for the drinkard,
in the larger frame of Tutuola's concerns he turns his attention to a recuperative "INVESTIGATION [OF] WONDERFUL WORK IN THE SKULL'S
FAMILY HOUSE" (26).

Concerned as we then become with *textual matters*, the relevant
"interpretation" of import and latitude now develops out of a world in which
David Womersley (1995) identifies not a Tutuola but an Edmond Malone
(1741-1812) in the Shakespearean space between academic romance and
bush of ghosts, even where the editorial significance of that space is under-
stated in Peter Martin's "opportunity fumbled" literary biography of Malone.
Womersley reviews Martin in such a way as to emphasize the compensatory
point that Malone lived his editorial life within a certain aftermath of
Shakespeare, and "at the very centre of eighteenth-century literary and
scholarly world." In 1790, Malone produced an edition of Shakespeare's
plays which, together with "the preliminary publications which led up to it,
such as the essay of 1778 on the order in which Shakespeare's plays were
composed, are events of some magnitude in the history not only of
Shakespearean scholarship but of editorial scholarship generally, because
there we find certain protocols of annotation, explanation and authentification
deployed for the first time" (5). The significance of the protocols may be best
summed up according to the editions in which "Shakespeare" has been
variously contained or generated, whether in Francis Meres's 1598 "household of Pallas" (*Palladis Tamia*) or in the specifics of Caincross's *The*

Problem of Hamlet: A Solution (1936); or else in, yet again, Tucker Brooke's review of the *Hamlets* in *Hamlet*:

> [The] first quarto of *Hamlet* is the most puzzling of all early representations of Shakespeare's work, but the modern texts of the play owe practicaly nothing to it. It is now generally agreed that it is based upon rough short-hand reports of the speeches as they were delivered on the stage, eked out perhaps by the text of the old pre-Shakespearean *Hamlet*. In this quarto are found little over half the number of lines in the authoritative versions; several passages are so confused as to be quite meaningless; and in a number of cases both the incidents and the names of the characters differ from those of the standard text. . . . Modern texts of *Hamlet* are made up from the second quarto edition, printed in 1604, and from the folio version of 1623. . . . The 1604 text contains over two hundred lines not found in the Folio. The Folio, on the other hand, is the only authority for about eighty-five other lines, mainly of a local nature which it would doubtless have been injudicious to print in 1604. (Brooke 1935: 519; see also Aers and Wheale 1991)

Meanwhile, in his expression of "confusion worse confounded" over approaches to Shakespeare, Bernard Grenabier makes the point in *The Heart of Hamlet* that "To make one's way through the conflict [of opinions] is to understand (*durch Mitleid*) perfectly Lucifer's hazardous voyage through Chaos," that "dark / Illimitable ocean, without bound, / Without dimension, where length, breadth, and height, / And time and place are lost" (1960:55-56). It is the view of David Bevington, for his part, that the text of *Richard III* "is one of the most perplexing in all Shakespeare [since it] is generally regarded as a memorial reconstruction of a peculiar kind, one in which the acting company banded together to reconstruct a play of which the copy was missing. The reconstructed version may later have been cut, perhaps for provincial performance. This defective text was the basis for the 1597 quarto, which was reprinted in 1598, 1602, 1605, 1612, 1622, 1629, and 1634." Each reprint was "successively more error-laden than the previous one." Bevington's (1988: 147) summary judgment on the First Folio text is that it had been fashioned from the quartos of 1602 and 1622, errors and all. Meanwhile, about the implications for *Othello*, R. A. Foakes makes the point that "it is the habit of criticism to attend to the chronology of Shakespeare's plays in general ways, usually in terms of convenient groupings, such as the dark comedies, the central tragedies, the late plays, and so on." He invokes *Othello* to make the point that "to the extent that we take the dating of the plays for granted, and think of them in conventional groupings, we are liable to ignore details that are both surprising and significant." Thereafter, Foakes makes this the opening premise from and through which he examines "the descent of Iago" by way of the thrust of satire in Ben Jonson and in *Othello* (1986:16).

Still, registers of the "rugged and defective" notwithstanding, there are occasions when "Shakespeare" does coincide tidily enough with a certain emphatic understanding of *Shakespeare*. Thus, and with regard to *Pericles, Prince of Tyre*, Russell Fraser's biography of the playwright's later years picks its deliberate way past a "minefield" of scholarly opinion that "Shakespeare 1) wrote all of it, 2) wrote only the last three acts, assigning most of the rest to somebody else, 3) revised the finished work of others" (1992:217). "Eighteenth century editors reversed the relation, laying the work as a whole to 'some friend whose interest the 'gentle Shakespeare' was industrious to promote." In this view, "improving the dialog, [Shakespeare] augmented the 'catastrophe,' and was 'most liberal of his aid' in Act V." However, "this picture of the master adding 'a few flowery lies'" to the play, Fraser concludes, "offends sensibility. From the stunning first scene straight to the end, the design of *Pericles*, a grand conception, is Shakespeare's" (*ibid.* 216; 217). For his part, Kazuaki Ota moves by other measures to identify the possibility that "Shakespeare most probably wrote [his earliest Romances, *Pericles* and *Cymberline*] primarily with the Court, rather than the Blackfriars or the Globe, in mind" (1989:10). And here, in a Shakespeare Society of Japan *Shakespeare Studies* essay, Ota's calculation derives as much from "the 1604 payment [that] was made to 'Richard Burdag. . . *for the mayntenance and releife* of himself and the rest of his company being prohibited to p'sente any playes publiquelie' because of the plague" as it does from the proposition that "James's patronage would have made considerable difference to the King's Men theatrical business" (*ibid.* 9).

All in all, Shakespeare's texts and their polymorphous import, and the man himself, converge as they do in apparent justification of the Taylor and Jowett contention that "Shakespeare" re-shaped or in shape is ever a collective industry of the imagination; that he is as much immaculately *das-Ding-an-sich* as he is the consequence of "legislated expurgations, theatrical innovation, and posthumous adaptation." In effect, offstage or centered, the figure coincides with but also exceeds the total of its sum; and this appears to be true as much for "The Stranger in Shakespeare" (Fiedler 1973) and "Everybody's Shakespeare" (Mack 1993) as it is where the questions have been "Who wrote Shakespeare?" (Henderson 1887) and "Was Shakespeare Shakespeare?" (Martin 1965). Elsewhere, there are enough misalignments of affinity to remind one of "the Leaning Tower of Pisa" (Amphlett 1955:1), and to account for a collective industry in which, as in Wallace Stevens, Sarah Bernhardt will weave "a small circle" out of *Hamlet*. In another constellation of sign and surplus, the erotic "helix" that Frankie Rubinstein (1995) makes of the works is consummately designed to turn the spotlight on a Shakespeare in whose *Merchant of Venice* Portia *would* respond with "Fie, what a question's that, / If thou wert near a lewd interpreter!" when Nerissa asks, "Why, shall we turn to men?" (III.iv.78-80). Meanwhile, the playwright is "velluminous" indeed when his *Hamlet* tacks East-West in Salman Rushdie's"strong vellum" (1994). Like the earth upon which it is supposed to exist, "this noble stuff," the narrative explains, "endures—if not forever, then at least till men consciously destroy it, whether by crumpling or shredding." The reality, *East,West* assures us, is that "men take an equal pleasure in annihilating both the ground upon which they stand while they live and the substance (I mean paper) upon which they may remain, immortalised, once this same ground is over their heads instead of under their feet" (63).

Rubinstein explains that she deploys her figure to recuperate sites of silence and expurgation that have survived "generations of annotated volumes of Shakespeare, untold numbers of glossaries and analytical works, countless performances of the plays in virtually every major language of the world." Her dictionary of puns and *double-entendres*, and of tools and wordplay, makes an issue of sexiness and the erotic in Shakespeare and his time. Her contention is that "the blinders of mores, taboos, censorship, fear of censorship, biases, blockages and the like have been perpetuated by scholars, directors and audiences of Shakespeare's plays" (1995:ix); and her aim is to restore "significant meanings and insights into the human condition not seen, ignored, lost—these simply because of their sexual or bawdy content" (*ibid.*). The bard and such bawd are briskly shaded and turn "velluminious" in "YORICK," Rushdie's short story version of *Hamlet* in *East,West*. Here, Shakespeare and his characters quite (un)become themselves as "undead phantasms" and "Will-o'-the-Wits." For this is the context in which "one Master YORICK took to wife [a] toothsome goldhair [and extravagantly foul-breathed] waif, by name 'Ophelia'." (After all, Shakespeare's Hamlet *did* advise his Ophelia: "if thou wilt need marry, marry a fool"). Now, proof that something may indeed be quite out of joint comes in "the rottenest-smelling exhalation in the State of Denmark; a tepid stench of rats' livers, toads' piss, high game-birds, rotting teeth, grangrene, skewered corpses, burning witchflesh, sewers, politicians' consciences, skunk-holes, sepulchres, and all the Beelzebubbing pickle-vats of Hell!" This, so we learn, "is Ophelia's breath" (Rushdie 1994:66). In this East-West Shakespeare, "dusty-faced and inky-fingered, lurk beautfiful young wives, old fools, cuckoldry, jealousy, murder, juice of hebona, executions, skulls; as well as a full exposition of why, in the *Hamlet* of William Shakespeare, the morbid prince seems unaware of his own father's real name" (64). The result is a "truly, velluminous story!—which it's my present intent," we are told, "not

merely to explicate, annotate, hyphernate, palatinate & permaganate—for it's
a narrative that richly rewards the scholar who is competent to apply such
sensitive technologies" (64).

The Shakespeare in *Hamlet* appears to be even more hyphenated to all
the tuned spheres when we come upon the complex of relationships that make
up the "impure 'impure impure history of ghosts'" in Jacques Derrida's
*Specters of Marx, The State of Debt, the Work of Mourning, and the New
International* (1994). Here, a conjuration of affinities binds the playwright in
a "whither Marxism?" relationship to, among other terrains and types, George
Hani's apartheid South Africa and Paul Valery's Europe. Derrida thus
confronts the "deafening disavowal of Marx" and other attempts "to exorcise
his ghost" in the face of the disintegration of Soviet-style Communism and
the corollary end-of-history "*neo-evangelistic* rhetoric" of a Francis Fukuyama
(59-65). But then, Derrida also makes what, according to his publishers,
Routledge, is his "definitive entry into social and political philosophy" by
conjuring up a "spectropoetics" and by crafting a logic of "*hauntology*" out
of Marx, refigured, and the *Hamlet* of "Mark me . . . I am thy Fathers Spirit";
"What, ha's this thing appear'd againe tonight?" and "Thou art a Scholler—
speake to it, Horatio." Indeed, the book's epigraph is Hamlet's "The time is
out of joint" (4-13; 95). Furthermore, the "whither Marxism?" thrust of
Specters is also limned suggestively against the absent presence of Yorick, to
which Derrida appeals with: "That Scull had a tongue in it, and could sing
once" (9).

> Oh, Marx's love for Shakespeare! It is well known. Chris Hani
> shared the same passion. I have just learned this and I like the
> idea. Even though Marx more often quotes *Timon of Athens*, the
> *Manifesto* seems to evoke, or to convoke, right from the start, the
> first coming of the silent ghost, the apparition of the spirit that
> does not answer, on those ramparts of Elsinore which is then the
> Old Europe. (10)

The times of Apartheid and the Age of Shakespeare are rather more thickly
shaded in the resonances that we get (below) from Alex La Guma's *Hamlet*-
haunted seven stories of Cape Town, *A Walk in the Night* (1967), and in Lewis
Nkosi's *Home and Exile* (1965), with its invocation of the English dramatist
and his contemporaries. In chronicling "the fabulous decades: the fifties,"
Nkosi will make the point that the catalogue of excess in those years could
only be fully captured by and in "the cacophonous, swaggering world of
Elizabethan England." It was that world which provided "the closest parallel
to our own mode of existence: the cloak and dagger stories of Shakespeare;
the marvellously gay and dangerous time of change in Great Britain came
closest to reflecting our own condition." Here was what made it possible for

an "African musician returning home at night to inspire awe in a group of thugs surrounding him by declaiming in an impossibly archaic English: 'Unhand me, rogues!'" (Nkosi 1965:18).

Hamlet had elsewhere (en)gendered suspension of disbelief of another kind in the "long ago" that Wallace Stevens recalls in *The Necessary Angel* (1951). The drama had been played out then with Sarah Bernhardt (1844-1923) in the role of the Prince of Denmark. It was when this Hamlet "came to the soliloquy 'To be or not to be,'" Stevens recalls, that "she half turned her back on the audience and slowly weaving one hand in a small circle above her head and regarding it, she said, with deliberation and as from the depths of hallucination: 'D'être ou ne pas d'être'." And, Stevens grants, "one followed her" (56-57). This is transport of no mean consequence, and invites elaboration. For one thing, Stevens's willing suspension of disbelief responds to the question—"Do we [ever] come away from Shakespeare with the sense that we have been reading commonplaces?"—with which *The Necessary Angel* moves to counter the suggestion that "the 'thoughts' of Shakespeare or Raleigh or Spenser were in fact only contemporary commonplaces and that it was a Victorian habit of mind to praise poets as thinkers." There is the figure of Bernhardt herself, of course; and she brings with her a surrounding noise of dis/affiliation, so to speak. It is one that anticipates my interest in the alien-within cluster of issues that Linda Nochlin and Tamar Garb have anthologised in their collection of essays on modernity and the construction of identity, *The Jew in the Text*. Thus, and like Shakespeare's Jessica in Venice, the "Jewess on stage" provokes consideration of identity and dis/affiliation that rather more directly preoccupy the Carol Ockman and the Sander Gilman in Nochlin and Garb. There is, too, the no less consequential alignment of parvenus and palimpsests that underlies Adrian Rifkin's approach to "nation" and "alterity" in the same collection of essays. In sum, whether in relation to *The Merchant of Venice*'s "ancient grudge" or to the Jewess and modernity, there is a useful enough preoccupation with alien(ated) identity here. It accounts for the point of departure—"Why do they hate us so?"—with which Nochlin introduces us to a "plethora of hostile, denigrating, and debasing representations" (1996:7). More about the disaffiliating import of all this later. For now, it is with relevance of another variety that Stevens lowers the curtain on Bernhardt's representation of Shakespeare. He does so in *The Necessary Angel*'s involuted but instructive appreciation of an "intricate metamorphosis of thoughts." What Stevens foregrounds here is the mind responding to import and latitude "with a gallantry, an accuracy of abundance, a crowding and pressing of direction which, for thoughts that were both borrowed and confused, cancelled the borrowing and obliterated the confusion" (1951:57).

Given such configurations of Shakespeare and strange vellum, it is no surprise that, offstage, the English playwright has also circulated in North America as the property of bench and bar. For he does indeed do so in a genre that has been variously at work in those benign courtroom exercises with which American Bar Associations (in Boston and New York, for example) have long found occasion to explore not only the "real" identity of Shakespeare but to also ponder the weight of the evidence in favor of Hamlet's sanity. Out of one such demonstration comes the news—from Boston, Massachussetts—that "on Sunday, May 26, 1996, at twelve noon, the C-SPAN 1 cable network will broadcast *The Trial of Hamlet*, a unique cultural event which was presented earlier this year by the Huntington Theatre Company [the professional theatre in residence at Boston University] and the Boston Bar Association's Senior Lawyers Section. Supreme Court Justice Anthony M. Kennedy presided over a trial which was to determine whether Shakespeare's Hamlet was guilty or not guilty by reason of insanity for the murder of Polonius" (*The Huntington* 1996:1). Elsewhere, Shakespeare has been quite "on location" at the American bar, and engaged in claims of intellectual property, no less. Briefly: the appropriation of the playwright here involves erstwhile North American collaborators, "young scholar" Mary Ann McGrail and "Hollywood producer" Dr. Steve Sohmer who have engaged in contending proof of their shared (or parallel) belief that *Hamlet* "has buried within it an ingenious and highly subversive reading of Martin Luther's rebellion against the Catholic Church" (Remnick 1995:68). In their claims on *Hamlet* McGrail and Sohmer appeal to the biography of Martin Luther (1483-1546) that we get in the Foxe (1516-1587) of the *Book of Martyrs*. They also foreground such matters as Hamlet's education at an otherwise inexplicably "provincial" Wittenberg University and his punning interest in "a certain convocation of politic worms" that are "e'en now at their diet." Predictably, McGrail and Sohmer also argue that such references must have resonated with special effect; that Elizabethans would very likely have heard and responded to "diet of worms" *qua* the Diet of Worms (70). The proposition is, in the end, strongly commonsensical. After all, the 1521 Diet in the German city of Worms had been an occasion of great geo-political and Christian drama. Besides which, there had been other convocations of note in that city, among them the rights and sovereignty Diet of 1122 ("The Investiture Controversy") and that of 1495 (Maximilian's *Ewiger Landfriede*). Parenthetically, it is worth recalling here that Ogburn and Ogburn (1947) had earlier identified the year 1598 as a "momentous one" for Edward de Vere, Earl of Oxford, whom the Oxfordians have identified as the real Shakespeare. It was in that year that the Earl's patron William Cecil (Lord Burghley) had died "quietly at the age of 78." Although the actual year of his birth was 1520, Lord Burghley was wont "to speak jocosely of having been born during the

Diet of Worms" (Ogburn and Ogburn 1955:34). The Ogburns also recalled "that Hamlet, in talking of Polonius's death, says, 'A certain *convocation of politic worms* are e'en at him. Your *worm* is your only emperor for *diet*'" (*ibid.*). The convocation of 1521 had resulted, of course, from Luther's refusal to disavow the theological and antipapal implications of his reformist theses, about which Church and State authorities (among them the Emperor Maximilian in 1518) had been already apprised. A copy of the same, perhaps apocryphally, had been posted on a church door at Wittenberg. Against such a background, and to judge from the panoply of persons and estates that James Macaulay records in *Table-Talk and Anecdotes of Luther* (1885), it would have been most intriguing indeed for *Hamlet not* to resonate to some recognizable effect when its protagonist carries on so about that "convocation of politic worms" where "your fat king and your lean beggar is but variable service." According to Macaulay,

> Luther mentions in his letter that he had appeared before the Emperor [Charles V] and his brother, the Archduke Ferdinand. But in truth there had seldom if ever been seen so great and august an assembly. The six Electors of the Empire, whose descendants almost all became kings; eighty dukes, rulers of large territories; thirty archibishops and other Romist prelates; many princes, barons, counts, and knights of good estate; seven ambassadors, including those of France and England; the Pope's nuncios; in all above 200 notables, such was the imposing Court. (43)

Meanwhile, in the overseas of Limon and Halio's eastern and central European studies of Shakespeare (1994) as well as in Dirk Delabastita and Lieven D'hulst's *European Shakespeares: Translating Shakespeare in the Romantic Age* (1992), heuristic—when not directly nationalist—assumptions about "the afterlife of Shakespeare and his works" (Davidhazi 1992:147) are no less illuminating in their migratory and anchoring tendencies. The preoccupation here with translation and import is properly underscored when, from elsewhere, Octavio Paz considers the less obvious (as against Graeco-Roman classics) but still just as powerful influence of Shakespeare: "The translations of [Shakespeare's] poetry into German and Russian are indeed works of pure poetry, and the result has been his acclimatization in Germany and Russia, whereas in France and Italy, where he has been far less fortunate in his translations, his popularity and influence have been correspondingly less" (1973:20). In their introductory chapter, "Once Again, 'Shakespeare in Europe'," Delabastita and D'hulst raise issues that are worth keeping in mind. Coincidentally, they do so by way of the John Drakakis view in *Alternative Shakespeares* (1985) that "the protean values which subsequent generations of critics have discovered in the texts themselves can be demonstrated to be in large part the projection of their own externally applied values" (Delabastita and D'hulst 1993:24). *European Shakespeares* covers its ground accordingly, from Scandinavia's discovery of the English playwright to the way in which he has been integrated into West Slavic literatures and cultures. Other readings explore complexities in the English playwright's reception within the "comic matrix" of German translations and, in the Portugal of Maria da Rocha Afonso, by way of the textual history of Simao de Melo Brandao's *O Mourou de Veneza*. Afonso writes about this find that "In 1940, Jorge de Faria, a scholar and drama reviewer published a short note in the *Mundo Grafico* about a manuscript he had found and bought and which was probably the first Portuguese translation of Shakespeare's *Othello*." All the same, "for further versions of [this play] Portugal had to wait until 1820 for the unpublished translation of an excerpt of Ducis' *Othello* by Almeida Garrett . . . and until 1856 for Luis Augusto Rebello da Silva's 'Imitation' *Othello, ou O Mouro de Veneza*" (*ibid*.: 134; 143). Delabastita and D'hulst approach and negotiate the variousness of Europe's Shakespeares with the summary observation that "Shakespeare's remarkable capacity for serving the most diverse functions is implied in the positions of critics as wide apart as Ben Jonson ('not of an age, but for all time') and Jan Kott (Shakespeare as 'our contemporary'), even though, significantly enough, more often than not the full epistemological and ideological implications of this have escaped being spelled out or weren't even perceived" (9).

In a concluding chapter in which the focus is on versions of *Hamlet* in the Netherlands of the late eighteenth and early nineteenth centuries, Delabastita explores the "shifting poetics of translation." He works a theoretical path into a complex history of Shakespeare's reception, and settles for the value of abandoning any "strictly diachronic viewpoint" of source texts and translations. In the process Delabastita rehearses the view that "those versions of Shakespeare which allegedly failed to make an important 'contribution' to an 'authentic' appreciation of the 'real' Shakespeare can on further examination be observed to take us straight into the heart of complex networks of functional relationships" (231). It is the case, after all, that the reception process with which *European Shakespeares* had all along been engaged "does not in the least resemble a linear progression or an organic 'growth' with an immanent dynamic towards an 'ideal' response" to the works of the English dramatist (220). And, parenthetically, it bears keeping in mind an irritation which Shakespeare himself had once provoked in Samuel Johnson. Johnson's rather unadventurous complaint was that the playwright had a practice of giving "to one age or nation, without scruple the customs, institutions and opinions of another, at the expense not only of likelihood, but of possibility" (Cunliffe 1935:90).

All in all, this criss-crossing of synchronic and diachronic re-visions within and across cultural boundaries makes it easy to appreciate the logic of the position adopted by the editors of the Clarendon *Complete Works* (1988). The economy and latitude in their conclusion—that "theatre is an endlessly fluid medium"—is as exfoliative as it is an instruction in particulars:

> It is likely that in Shakespeare's time, as in ours, changes in the texts of the plays were consciously made to suit varying circumstances: the characteristics of particular actors, the place in which the play was performed, the anticipated reactions of his audience, and so on. The circumstances by which Shakespeare's plays have been transmitted to us mean that it is impossible to recover exactly the form in which they stood either in his own original manuscripts or in those manuscripts, or transcripts of them, after they had been prepared for use in the theatre. Still less can we hope to pinpoint the words spoken in a particular performance. Nevertheless, it is in performance that the plays lived and had their being. Performance is the end to which they were created . . . and we have devoted our efforts to recovering and presenting texts of Shakespeare's plays as they were acted in the London playhouses which stood at the centre of his professional life.(Wells *et al.* 1988:xxxix).

There is similar value in Michael Mullin and David McGuire's "Purge on Prettiness" (1989). For they make a point of emphasizing innovation and transition in their review of the costumes that the Motley team (Elizabeth Montgomery, Margaret Harris, and Sophia Devine) produced for the Shakespeare Memorial Theatre's 1954 *A Midsummer Night's Dream*. "More and more Shakespeareans," Mullin and McGuire claim, "have come to recognize the importance a seminal production can have in the *evolving* interpretation of Shakespeare's plays" (65; my emphasis). They conclude, then, that although 1954 was unprepared for unorthodox interpretations of the *Dream*, "it is reasonable to see with hindsight that Motley's costume designs . . . anticipated substantially greater departures from tradition by Peter Hall in 1966 and Peter Brook in 1970" (76). Evidence of departures into and from other traditions abounds, of course. This much is suggested when Abiola Irele frames Wole Soyinka's *A Dance of the Forests* within *A Midsummer Night's Dream*; it is also true of the pattern of responses to the Teatro do Ornitorrinco Caca Rosset's Brazilian *Sonho de Uma Noite de Verão* at the 1991 Central Park Shakespeare Festival in New York. In any case, whether they are located overseas or not, such refractions in the cult of authenticity turn the spotlight on the contingent Shakespeare (as against a transcendent

one) that Richard Burt, for one, argues into relevance in *Licensed by Authority*
(1996) : "It would therefore be a mistake to conclude, as have some modern
critics, that Shakespeare's self-consciousness about his art . . . enables it to
transcend history and ideology; rather, as Louis Montrose (1980) suggests,
we should see [in a play like *The Winter's Tale*, for example, an instance of]
'autotelic deceptiveness' employed by Shakespeare 'to legitimate his art'"
(96).

　　　Given this history of dis/affiliating encounters with Shakespeare, there
should be no real cause for conservationist alarm when, from even farther afield,
and in a Shakespeare Association report titled "Shakespeare in India" (1926),
C. J. Sisson wrote the following about popular adaptations of the English
dramatist on the Bombay stage: "It is of the highest interest to realise that
Shakespeare's plays are here living, dynamic forces still. They are being used
with equal respect and disrespect, if one may phrase it so, even as our ancestors
used the classics, and they may yet bring about a renaissance of great drama in
the popular vernacular theatre." Sisson's flexibility leads him to the view that
a "wise" as against the "orthodox" Shakespearean "would therefore be com-
forted . . . with the thought that the great dramatist was fulfilling . . . in the far
corners of the earth, his essential function of delighting men with the picture of
life in the form of a work of art" (19; 8). This story about the delighting of men
could have been more politically nuanced, of course; after all, the importation
of Shakespeare's "picture of life" and "work of art" also worked in concert with
imperial convictions of the variety that defined the viceroyalty (1899-1905) of
George Curzon when he declared that the "sacredness" of the *mission civilisatrice*
in India "haunted [him] like a passion": "To me the message is carved in granite,
hewn in the rock of doom: that our work is righteous and that it shall endure."
This Viceroy endorsed Edmund Burke's theory of imperial trusteeship, and
believed in England's mission to rule the Subcontinent. He acknowledged being
"an imperialist heart and soul"—but "very far indeed from being a Jingo," caring
"not a snap of the fingers for the tawdry lust of conquest." A "most superior
person," Curzon assumed that "the empire was justified by the benefits it
conferred" (Gilmour 1994:165). For his part, Sudipto Chatterjee tells a story of
imperialism and theater that is relevantly shaded when he discusses "the Bengal
Renaissance," that is, the period "from 1795 to the last quarter of the nineteenth
century." It was during this "Orientalist" and "Anglicist" phase of the Raj that
Chandra Girish Ghosh proved to be "one of the best translators Shakespeare has
had in the Bengali language" (1995:34). Ghosh's 1893 *Macbeth*, Chatterjee
judges, "is undoubtedly the finest Bengali version of the play to date"—for all
that thus translated it "lived through only ten performances and died an untimely
death" (*ibid.*). Still, there was "one achievement [that] the natives could be proud
of" in the circuit of terrain and type during the decade of the 1840s. This was the
1848 appearance of a Bengali, Vaisnav Caran Adhya, in a professional English

production of *Othello*. As a result of this staging at the Sans Souci Theatre, "one of the few professional European theatres in the white quarters of Calcutta," Vaisan Adhya, "or Auddy as he was better known was probably the first person of color to play the tragic Moor" (20).

The sometimes ironic import of so much transport and translation is highlighted in closer quarters when, in an *Othello* "returned" to Italy, Giuseppe Verdi's librettist for *Otello* (1887), Arrigo Boito, works to "spare us the necessity of speculating on Iago's motives—disinterested malignity, resentment . . . the suspicion that 'the Moor between my sheets hath done my office' . . . or as one American commentator believes, an unrequited passion for the Moor himself." To allow Iago to reveal himself, as Boito does, not by way of Shakespeare's own "enigmatic soliloquies," but in that astonishing *Credo in un Dio crudel che m'ha creato/simile a sè e che nell'ira io nomo* (I believe in a cruel God, who has created me/in his image and whom, in rage I call upon) of Act 2, Scene 2 is to re-present Shakespeare in rather exceptional "articles of faith." Though Julien Budden thinks that they are "in the last analysis meaningless," they certainly make for a poetry that is "dark, nihilistic"—with its "cruel God . . . primordial mud . . . the worm . . . Death . . . Nothingness. *Truly Shakespearean lines'*, Verdi called them" (emphasis added):

> I believe I am evil
> because I am man. . . .
> I believe the honest man is a mocking buffoon,
> and both in face and heart,
> everything in him is a lie...
> Death is nothingness.
> Heaven is an old wives' tale. (Budden 1986:24)

All things considered, and given the subversive roles that Kamau Brathwaite (below) assigns to Sycorax and her "curser" of a son, there are reasons enough for me to acknowledge here that it was as pre-text no less than as prelude that I positioned recognizably (de)colonizing markers in my excursus into *The Tempest*. The point is that I did so in some anticipation of the kind of sub/version that marks Brathwaite's "Letter Sycorax," with its "pun a computer o/kay / like i jine de mercantilists!" and its "fe we / fe a-we" refiguration of "prospero ling. / go. . . inna / libraria / [with] all a dem brooks of the dead":

> ### Dear mamma
> i writin yu dis letter/**wha?**
> [even if] nat one o we shd response if prospero get
> > curse
> > wid im own
> > > curser   (1993:95-116)

Against the invitation not to "response," my choice here is to "jine" a palaver that "have key an board / an / evva / ting." For it is a palaver that has much to do with two currents of thought about Shakespeare and the early modern period; so, too, with the corollary granting or revoking of liçence across cultures in a world in which, as Caliban now recognizes, "pascal & co. / balt & apple & cogito ergo sum / come to h/invent all these tings since / de rice & fall a de roman empire" (100-101). One set of reasons is thus grounded in what presumably happens when the empire writes, or reads, back; or when, in somewhat of an oblique counterpoint, a master text produces a critique whose post-colonial transpositions resonate the way that they do in Ben Brantley's "*Tempest* Deepens As It Goes Indoors" (1995). Brantley's appreciation of what happened to George Wolfe's "wild" *Tempest* when it moved into New York City's Broadhurst Theater celebrates the fact that the "bold-stroke fierceness" of the 1994 Central Park version of Shakespeare's drama gave way to "a more civilized spirit," a "richer ambiguity," and "an increased refinement of theme and character." Thus re-imported, the production acquired a "greater eloquence [guaranteed] to draw tears from all but the stone-hearted." Brantley's summary of the noisier post/colonial agenda that the Broadhurst stage had thus domesticated into "infinitely more modulation [and a] sense of the complexity of human understanding" is as follows:

> In [first] putting over his reconception of *The Tempest*, with its emphasis on gnawing anger bred by political rivalry and the colonial bonds between master and servant, [Wolfe] often required his actors to scale up their performances and italicize their delivery in ways that would soar in the open air. The words "slave" and "master" were hit like gongs by Prospero (Patrick Stewart) and his other-wordly assistants, Ariel (Aunjanue Ellis [a female and black, incidentally]) and Caliban (Teagle F. Bougere). (B1)

It is Brantley's view that Wolfe had lived with Shakespeare's "complicated work" to improved effect, resulting in a display of "new intricacies and feelings." For which reason, even if "Prospero ultimately loses his powers of sorcery, those who have brought his world to life have only increased theirs." Furthermore, and this is relevant in Lamming and in Wynter (below), Brantley is persuaded that the Broadhurst production is marked by "an enhanced awkward sweetness in Prospero's dealings with his daughter (the delightful Carrie Preston)" (B5).

Whether by way of the "Letter Sycorax" or in the "archives of Eden," or else through Wole Soyinka's approach to Shakespeare "the living dramatist," I anticipate being able to "jine" the transport-and-licence palaver in rather more complex ways than seem to have been possible in the ethnography of the foreign text that we get in Laura Bohannan's "Shakespeare in the Bush," that 1966 "classic" of cultural anthropology. For in Bohannan, condescension and a perhaps casual ethnocentricity remain distinguishing features, notwithstanding the caution-edged relativism in her reception-theory attempt at literary and cultural criticism. She oscillates between a reductive tolerance of "bush" people (Africa's Tiv) and a high-culture ambivalence about the legitimacy of her own American relationship to Shakespeare. Her approach picks and crops in ways that never quite escape the unbearable lightness of her origins as an anthropologist of a certain stripe.

As I have already suggested, it is signal that Bohannan's difficulties with pedigree and belatedness had been prefigured in the "first and last impressions" of Matthew Arnold's *Civilization in the United States*: "What really dissatisfies in American civilization is the want of the *interesting*, a want due chiefly to the want of the two great elements of the interesting, which are elevation and beauty" (1977:190). Elsewhere, it is the European Bourget's *Outre-mer* that compounds the issue when it asserts that "for all that the word *art* trembles on the lips of the North Americans, . . . if a word may some day characterize their taste in art, it will be a word that negates art itself: the grossness of affectation, the ignorance of all that is subtle and exquisite, the cult of false grandeur, the *sensationalism* that excludes the serenity that is irreconcilable with the pace of feverish life." The point is tellingly appreciated, parenthetically, in the Euro-Latin-American arielism of José Enrique Rodó's *Ariel* (1988:81). For the Uruguayan Rodó confirms Bourget's censorious exercise of taste when he cites *Outre-mer*'s conclusion that it is in "such sycophancy [that] the hearty and righteous heroes of *self-help* hope to crown by assimilating refinement, the labor of their tenaciously won eminence" and to put on display "a trophy for their vanity" (*ibid*. 81). Meanwhile, it is from within the belly of the beast, so to speak, that "We covered some thirty thousand miles." The voice is that of Margaret Webster (1975) writing about her "Shakespeare on Wheels" endeavor to stage the English dramatist over the length and breadth of the United States between 1948 and 1950. Webster, born and raised in New York but the daughter of Dame May Whitney and Ben Webster, themselves noted English actors, records the following, perhaps insufferably benign, observations about the difficulties she encountered when, beginning in February 1937, she directed *Richard II*, "a play virtually unknown to American audiences," for Maurice Evans in New York. Though the production, and others following, found eager enough audiences, it was also the case that several actors went so far as to refuse parts on the grounds that they could not "speak English" or "were afraid that by so doing they would endanger their chances of future employment as gangsters." In the end, Webster explains, "we tried to attain some homogeneity of speech that was neither dude English nor localized American, pertaining neither to Oxford University nor to Akron, Ohio" (14-15).

Confronted, and at Oxford, no less, with latter-day notions of this deficit in Euro-American sensibility —in relation to Shakespeare's Englishness, this time—Bohannan's protest is that

> human nature is pretty much the same the whole world over; at least the general plot and motivations of the greater tragedies would be clear—everywhere—although some details of custom might have to be explained and difficulties of translation might produce other slight changes. To end an argument we could not conclude, [my English friend] gave me a copy of *Hamlet* to study in the African bush: it would, he hoped, lift my mind above its primitive surroundings, and possibly I might, by prolonged meditation, achieve the grace of correct interpretation.
>
> It was my second field trip to that African tribe, and I thought myself ready to live in one of its remotest sections—an area difficult to cross even on foot. I eventually settled on the hillock of a very knowledgeable old man, the head of a homestead of some hundred and forty people, all of whom were either his close relatives or their wives and children. (1977:13)

There are, I should think, rather more productive, because less exotic, ways of getting into and out of a quandry about dis/affiliation, and about the transport of master texts beyond the horizons of Oxford and Euro-America. Still, "what is an anthropologist to do," Nancy Scheper-Hughes asks in the context, this time, of evaluating field trip and master(ing) text in Clifford Geertz's *After the Fact, Two Countries, Four Decades, One Anthropologist* (1995), "when, after four decades of involvement in the daily 'goings-on in two provincial towns, one a Southeast Asia *bend in the road*, one a North African *outpost and passage point*,' he wants to say something definitive about each place, to compare and contrast their recent and at times *unspeakably* violent postcolonial histories, and finds that the ground has shifted under his feet?" (Scheper-Hughes 1995:22; my emphasis). The question is perhaps not quite the right one to ask here. For one thing, Bohannan is much too unselfconsciously circumscribed in her contradictions; for another, the cardinal points in Scheper-Hughes's language rather too quickly encourage thoughts of an immense exercise of (anthropological) power on considerably reduced and exotic folk. One readily imagines attributions of great knowledge/power to the singular figure of *memsahib* Bohannan in Tiv-land and to a be-striding *bwana* Geertz in two countries and across four decades. Vincent Pecora's "The Limits of Local Knowledge" is, I should think, a trenchant enough exercise in containing such fantasies of latitude and insight (1989:243-276). There is, too, the summary conclusion to which George Marcus comes in *Writing Anthropology*, with its contextualization of fieldwork and university settings; and its awareness of the nature of the "ethnography that most anthropologists must write" in response to circumstances that include the turning of a dissertation into a published monograph or series of articles. For such arrangements are not unrelated to the granting of professional credentials and therefore to angles of ascent or descent in the profession (1986:265).

Meanwhile, to the degree that "classics" like Bohannan's contribute their share of "Africa" to the reception history of Shakespeare, or to the genealogy of master texts in Africa, there is relevant instruction in Irele's considerably less anxiety-ridden view that when the likes of Harold Bloom pronounce "with such solemnity on the centrality of Shakespeare to the Western canon, he is not merely barging into an open door, as the French say—for it cannot be said that the point has ever been seriously in dispute." More telling is the fact that such a pronouncement "displays a singular lack of awareness of the tremendous investment of other contemporary peoples and cultures in the work of the English bard." The scope and intensity of this investment as regards Africa are demonstrated, Irele points out, in, for example, Alamin Mazrui's essay on Julius Nyerere's translation of *Julius Caesar* as *Juliasi Kaizari* in 1969—and of *The Merchant of Venice* in 1972 as *Mabepari wa Venisi* (*The Bourgeoisie of Venice*). These translations, "along with other workings of Shakespeare's plays in the language, provide an example of a process of imaginative engagement with Shakespeare in Africa already evident in Thomas Mfolo's integration of the character of Macbeth into his portrait of Chaka in his classic Sesotho novel, and Wole Soyinka's deployment of *A Midsummer Night's Dream* as the organizing intertext for the symbolic elaboration of his play *A Dance of the Forests* [commissioned in recognition of Nigeria's Independence from Great Britain in 1960]" (1996:1-2). Soyinka's later "homage to Shakespeare in 1988 comes as an explicit celebration of a debt acknowledged even earlier by J. P. Clark-Bekederemo, whose internalization of what he calls 'the example of Shakespeare' has determined the expressive idiom of his own plays" (Irele 1996:2). Meanwhile, and even if in somewhat of a counterpoint to Irele's tolerance, Handel Kashope Wright's "What Is Shakespeare Doing in My Hut?" (1993) generates insights that "Shakespeare in the Bush" is not quite positioned to recognize. For Wright's interviews and analysis make contested terrain of imperial expansion and colonial curriculum in Sierra Leone—by way of Shakespeare's *Coriolanus* and Wole Soyinka's *Death and the King's Horseman*. "What Is Shakespeare Doing in My Hut?" makes the disjuncture the basis for a radical if exploratory pedagogy of the local, one that engages "schema theory," cross-cultural studies, and the colonial legacy (72;79).

Wright and Irele manage to inflect literary reception in ways that Bohannan's classic anthropology does not quite recognize; and Mudimbe's ordering of knowledge and praxis in *The Invention of Africa* suggests why this would be so. "Both imperialism and anthropology took shape," he explains, in contexts that encouraged "the reification of the 'primitive'." They were therefore constrained by paradigms that required the "inherent superiority of the white race," and by a philosophy of right that accounts for Hegel's being persuaded of "the necessity for European economies and structures to expand to 'virgin areas' of the world" (1988:17). It is the case, granted, that any and all such hegemony-seeking "anthropologies of the bush" could benefit from the nuancing that Talal Asad introduces in "From the History of Colonial Anthropology to the Anthropology of Western Hegemony." There is, first, Asad's premise that "the role of anthropology in maintaining structures of imperial domination has, despite slogans to the contrary, usually been trivial" since the knowledge they produced was often too esoteric for direct governance. It was also marginal in comparison to routine accumulations by, for example, merchants, missionaries, and administrators (1991:315). All the same, and as Mudimbe also proposes when he relates imperialism to primitivist anthropology,

> The process of European global power has been central to the anthropological task of recording and analyzing the ways of life of subject populations, even when a serious consideration of that power was theoretically excluded. It is not merely that anthropological fieldwork was facilitated by European colonial power . . . ; it is that the fact of European power, as discourse and practice, was always part of the reality anthropologists sought to understand, and of the way they sought to understand it. (*ibid.*)

And here, Yambo Ouologuem's representation of "fieldwork" in *Bound to Violence* (1968) merits being attended to, given the ironies of its approach to the invention of the native text and to the subversions that follow from its alienated translation. This is famously the case, of course, when his narrative's thinly-disguised "Shrobenius" ("that human crayfish with a groping mania") and his "shrewd anthropologists" began taking notes from and about the natives. For all that the enterprise then became "harnessed to the vapors of magico-religious, cosmological, and mystical symbolism," a certain flock of men did follow in the wake of what was apparent esoterica. And "what men!" They were "middlemen, adventurers, apprentice bankers, politicians, salesmen, conspirators—supposedly 'scientists,' but in reality enslaved sentries mounting guard" (1971:87; 95-96). Given Ouologuem's mockery, there is actually a good measure of relief in what Gorra represents as an "anticlimax" of a conclusion when Geertz's *One Anthropologist, Two Countries* is driven to acknowledge that anthropology has become "'so indefinite a quest' that he can't offer any 'sense of closure' beyond the assurance that it remains 'an excellent, interesting, dismaying, useful, and amusing, [way] to expend one's life'" (147). In addition, and not unreasonably, I might add, Deborah Root's discussion of "art, appropriation, and the commodification of difference" in *Cannibal Culture* leads her to call for the decolonization of the anthropological eye. We need, she remarks, "to carefully examine cultural and aesthetic phenomena we have been taught to find interesting" (1996:204).

Still, there are other anthropological ways of being instructed in such matters; and one such comes in Arjun Appadurai's "Global Ethnoscapes: Notes and Queries for a Transnational Anthropology," with its interest in "fluid, irregular shapes." Appadurai is productive and useful, too, for the emphasis that he places on the "global ethnoscapes" within and across which deeply "perspectival constructs" and "historical, linguistic and political situatedness of different sorts of actors are inflected" (1991). The perspective in "Global Ethnoscapes" sits well with the rather more fussy and Bakhtin-inflected *The Dialogic Emergence of Culture* in which Dennis Tedlock and Bruce Mannheim make the point that

> To propose that language and culture are dialogical to their core is to relocate them in the interstices between people, [and] to see language and culture as emergent qualities of action, "as a result of thousands of life-changing dialogues that call into play the affective and corporeal energies of the particpants in the history of their times.". . . This is the ontological sense of dialogue, discussed earlier. It does not require that linguistic and cultural patterns and social relations be generated anew with every interaction. Rather, every interaction takes place within specific social, institutional, and historical coordinates, all of which color the interaction at the same time as they are reshaped, to greater or lesser extent, by that interaction. (1995:8-9)

But then, ethnoscape and dialogism notwithstanding, there is a relevant *caveat* in Gananath Obeyesekere's *The Work of Culture* (1990) about what happens when "anthropologists take over the model of the theatre" (288). The thought merits some consideration, especially so to the degree that Obeyesekere is ready to ground his view in the proposition that "current anthropology is like the modern funeral parlor or, better still, like a bourgeois bathroom:

everything is tidy, everything smells clean, and the shit is flushed into the dark, rat-infested sewers that line the belly of the city" (*ibid.*). Given our concern with Shakespeare, the skepticism is especially resonant when Obeyesekere emphasizes the point that the "theatre *is* an analogy or a fringe model; it is not a theoretical model. It breaks down soon: there is a sufferer or patient, not an actor; there is a priest, not a director; there is a congregation, not an audience; there are sacred words, not a secular script; there is a willingness to believe, not a willing suspension of disbelief" (*ibid.*). This is helpful commentary, but it is one that may be nuanced, too, by historicist literary criticism that chooses to argue that when we locate literary texts in a "differential field" we are better able to observe how such texts "underwrite or confront other constructions of reality, and how they function in relation to other discursive practices." There is a certain representation of things here that has been ready to insist, with some profit, that "literature participates in constructing a culture's sense of reality, that it is not simply reflective but helps actively to constitute the larger symbolic order by which a culture imagines its relation to the conditions of its existence" (Matus 1995:5). For which reason, it seems to me that Mignolo's approach to the Renaissance is worth re-situating here, given its reach for import and latitude. To recapitulate: theoretically, *The Darker Side of the Renaissance* moves in ways that require "a pluritopic hermeneutics"; ideologically its approach implies the creation of loci of enunciation parallel and opposite to the loci of enunciation that result from considerations of difference, of representations of other-ness. As a result, instead of looking at marginal societies from the perspective of academic centers, Mignolo chooses to do so by exploring cultural and political centers from the academic margins (1995:311-312). Meanwhile, about the mapping of such terrain and type, Edward Said makes for useful summary when he calls attention to parts and constellations that are "hybrid, heterogenous, extraordinarily differentiated, and unmonolithic" (1993:xxv).

A hermeneutics of the exceptional and of the pluritopic allows for productive engagements with Shakespeare and the currency with which he circulates, if for no other reason than the one, from T. S. Eliot, which Frankie Rubinstein uses as an epigraph for the slip-sliding measures of the bawdy in her Shakespeare: "About any one so great as Shakespeare it is probable that we can never be right; and if we can never be right, it is better that we should from time to time change our way of being wrong" (1995:ix). Moreover, as things turn out, political violence and literary esoterica no less than commerce in racial difference do converge in self- and tribal-fashionings of what is parvenu and palimpsest in Shakespeare—whether in Laura Bohannan's "Bush" and Alan Warner's "Tropics" or in the Shakespeare that Phillip Zarrilli produces by way of South India's 1989 *Kathakali King Lear* (below).

The dis/play of such "jumbled identities" (Zarrilli 1992:36) provides us with inference and material with which to account for that 1936 all-black "voodoo" *Macbeth* which Orson Wells set in 18th-century Haiti, and which he staged with a gigantic mask as Banquo, a Hecate armed with a 12-lb bullwhip, and an on-stage band of drummers. Similarly, a generic and "overseas" otherness helps to frame Mark Rylance's recent excursion into a "cult" *Macbeth* at London's Greenwich Theatre. To judge from John Mullan's "Look on't again I dare not," this was a *Macbeth* in which the medieval Duncan and his tribe of aristocratic thanes become "shaven-headed, saffron-robed Hare Krishna devotees who are all the same "allowed furry-hooded anoraks when they have to go out into all that 'fog and filthy air'." Mullan's conclusion was that "rarely could a Shakespearean tragedy have suffered a worse fate from a company's efforts to find for it 'an equivalent modern world'"—and to do so, Rylance made bold to claim, without intending "to condemn alternative religious communities, any more than Shakespeare intended to condemn the Scottish aristocracy" (Mullan 1995:21).

Appadurai's ethnoscapes, Mignolo's pluritopic hermeneutics, and Ouologuem's preference for sub/version also bring a wide-angled clarity to Stephen Rayne's metaphor-of-the-90s "African" *Macbeth*, a 1995 playbill for which was prefaced, incidentally, by Director of the Royal Shakespeare Company Terry Hands's 1990 conviction that "to many peoples, in many nations, *Shakespeare is still our greatest living author*" (emphasis in the original; qtd. in Agbaw 1996:103). The Rayne production featured yet another "all-black" diaspora cast, this time from the RSC and the Royal National Theatre. To this ensemble fell the task of playing out the English playwright's representation of murder, vaulting ambition, and witchcraft in medieval Scotland as a drama of modern Africa's political history of military coup-d'etats, and its seemingly incorrigible investment in under-development and in the occult (Rayne, Kaplan, and French, as qtd. in Agbaw 1996). Under Rayne medieval and post-World War II geo-politics meet in mutual illumination of each other when, for example, Malcolm mourns the fact that "Each new morn, new widows howl, new orphans cry, new sorrows / Strike heaven on the face, that it resounds / As if it felt with Scotland and yell'd out / Like syllable of dolour" (IV.iii.4-8; Agbaw 1996:104). In the end, the logic of and the affect in the RSC "Africanized" *Macbeth* move obliquely across the ironies of Cameroonian critic S. Ekema Agbaw's review of one Pennsylvania, U.S.A., performance. For all that the world may indeed be a stage, Agbaw concluded, "what I, probably the only African in the audience found most disturbing was the historical, political and cultural implications of presenting a medieval Scottish murderer as a contemporary African dictator. It does seem to be quite a 'down-fall'n birthdom' indeed" (108-109).

Politicized or otherwise engaged dispensations of *The Tempest* have rather more famously engendered readings in which, as Francis Barker and Peter Hulme once recognized, "Nymphs and reapers [do indeed] heavily vanish" from this last of Shakespeare's plays. As a rule, the "vanishing" has been especially urgent whenever the drama is explored in terms of the treament of its overseas native who had "suffered by a thunderbolt," and in the light of Prospero's obsessive need to annul the consequences of his expulsion from power in Europe (Hulme 1986:112-115). Even if at some cost in utopian and sexual romance, this understanding of *The Tempest* rightly focuses on the play's interest in the politics of subversion and usurpation. Unattended to, or severely underplayed, one could very well conceive of Shakespeare's drama as a pastoral romance; as a comedy of restoration that is above all concerned with "marriage-blessing" and "long continuance and increasing, / Hourly joys"; so, too, with celebrating an ideal planting in which there would be "earth's increase / foison plenty" and "vines with clustering bunches growing" (IV.i.106-110). However, this "majestic vision" of "fancies" and sensuous increase is sustainable only to the degree that Shakespeare's very political Prospero "had forgot that foul conspiracy / Of the beast Caliban and his confederates" (IV.i.139-140). It is when the politics of power is engaged that Prospero starts suddenly, that he speaks with an urgency that is quite other than romance or giddy pageant. It is then that, to a strange, hollow, and confused noise, fancies vanish, and abruptly bring the curtain down on "reapers, properly habited" and on "Nymphs in a graceful dance." This rupture in the pastoral and its cancellation of utopian transcendence very much matter. "Never till this day," Miranda tells Ferdinand, "Saw I him touch'd with anger so distemper'd." True enough; for now, with his "fancies" interrupted, Prospero's rage against Caliban is urgent and remarkably bitter:

> A devil, a born devil, on whose nature
> Nurture can never stick; on whom my pains,
> Humanely taken, all, all, quite lost;
> And as with age his body uglier grows,
> So his mind cankers. I will plague them all,
> Even to roaring. (IV.i.188-90)

This site of roaring, plague, and canker is an important point of departure into "the School of Caliban" that Barker and Hulme identify; that Césaire highlights in his Caribbean adaptation of *The Tempest*; and that José Saldívar privileges in his study of "genealogy, cultural critique, and literary history" in *The Dialectics of Our America* (1991). Saldívar's moves identify him with "engaged writers, scholars, and professors of literature who work under a common political influence, a group whose different (imagined) national communities and symbologies are linked by their derivation from a common and explosive reading of Shakespeare's last (pastoral and tragicomic) play, *The Tempest*" (123; also Cartelli 1987; Vaughan and Vaughan 1991).

Not unreasonably, the pastoral site—with its "baseless fabric" and "insubstantial pageant" of goddesses, reapers, and nymphs—is precisely the place into which Césaire introduces the disruptive presence of Eshu in Act 2, Scene 3 of his *Tempest*. The Martinican's *adaptation pour un théâtre nègre* (1969) thus re-incarnates one of the figures in Prospero's pageant of "*dieux et déesses*" (of gods and goddesses). Signally, Césaire's representation of "*The Lords Back There*" is incarnate in that most un-boundaried of gods, Eshu Elegbara, "the very embodiment of the crossroads." For in both the Old Worlds of the Yoruba and the New one of the Americas, whether in Brazil or in Cuba and Haiti, Eshu has remained the messenger of the gods. He not only carries sacrifices, deposited at crucial points of intersection, to the goddesses and to the gods, but he is sometimes the bearer of the crossroads in verbal form, "in messages that test our wisdom and compassion ('Is this true; shall I help him; what larger purpose opens up beyond this message?')." In addition, he also wears the crossroads as a cap, colored black on one side, red on the other, provoking in his wake foolish arguments about whether the cap is black or red" (Thompson 1984:19). In Césaire's *Tempest*, Eshu's contraindicative presence is duly remarked upon by Miranda, and with the appropriate measure of discomfort: "But this one! Who is this one? He certainly does not look benevolent. If I weren't afraid to blaspheme I'd even say he looks more devil than god." Prospero wonders, meanwhile, whether Ariel had made some mistake; whether "*aurait-il quelque chose qui grince dans ma magie*"—if his magical powers had been a bit off. As is clearly the case with Césaire's Miranda and Prospero, there are those for whom this intrusion into the *magie* of icon and monument constitute an undisciplined busy-ness. For it represents yet another measure of the lunge toward the barbarism of an especially unworthy "Caliban and his confederates" who are bent on estranging the Renaissance; or else engaged in mis-educated mappings of the "darker side" of the Renaissance. This *quelque chose qui grince* engenders anxieties and disapproval whether in Césaire's outpost of civilization or, closer to the "center," in Leo Steinberg's way with "the sexuality of Christ in Renaissance art and in modern oblivion" (1983). Canonical iconography is on exhibit in Steinberg, but its display is one in which "the genitalia of the Christ Child or of the dead Christ [are shown to be] the unmistakable objects of revelation or of demonstrative emphasis." In the event, Steinberg's study collates a heretofore unaccounted-for rummaging of fingers and groins and halos that shed new light, so the appreciations on the dust jacket announce, on "an unrecognized represssion" (Arthur Danto); on "evasive theology" (Arthur Cohen); and on ways of "reimpowering [our] senses" (Richard Howard).

The collection of essays in H. Aram Veeser's *The New Historicism* (1989) is summarily helpful here; so, too, his introductory remark that the "arrival of [such a] poetics of culture was neither unscheduled nor unwelcome." Veeser calls attention to studies of Renaissance texts that have worked "to show connections between cultural codes and political power"— before anyone thought to give the approach a polemical label, such as "new historicism" (xiii). It is instructive that Veeser's explanation focuses on "circulation of social energy," of the variety that undergirds Stephen Greenblatt's pivotal *Shakespearean Negotiations* (1988). It very much matters, then, that Veeser's own culture-in-action project, *The New Historicism*, makes a point of taking off from Greenblatt's "I began with the desire to speak with the dead" (Veeser 1989: i). The working out of tribal and other political agendas in the poetics of such colloquys is productively illustrated, I am sure, when John Gross privileges four hundred years in the life of a certain ethnicity as the basis for his study, *Shylock: A Legend and Its Legacy* (1992). In the eighteenth century, Thomas Doggett, an actor who excelled in low comedy parts at the Drury Lane Theatre, had chosen to reduce the Jew, and with the aid of George Granville's "appalling adaptation" (Webster 1975:146), apparently succeeded in making a comic figure out of Shylock. More recently, though, Joseph Shatzmiller's contemporary approach has produced a recognizably thick description of the condition in which Shakespeare's Jewish merchant found himself; for the focus in *Shylock Reconsidered: Jews, Moneylending and Medieval Society* (1990) is on trials, litigations, and Jews, with Marseilles as the representative location. As a result, Shatzmiller sheds comparative light on Shakespeare's transformation of debtor and creditor relations in *The Merchant of Venice*, and on the problematic coherence of the play's investment in tribal abuse and wit, its catalogue of legal escape clause and romance, and its treatment of the alienation of property.

He thus helps to reinforce the premise that accounts for the telling circumscription of the fear that Shakespeare's alienated character acknowledges when he says, "There is some ill a-brewing towards my rest, / For I did dream of moneybags tonight" (II.v.17-18). All the same, the over-riding interest in Money and Scripture certainly focuses on the "suit" of issues that bind Christian merchant and Jewish merchant to and against each other. In Act 1, Scene 2 of *The Merchant of Venice*, Shakespeare sets up an equilibrium of sorts that is destined to implode, granted. Still, before the structure collapses, there are apparent grounds for a certain parity of esteem. On the one hand, the Jewish moneylender makes an offer that cannot be refused, promising as he does to "Supply your present wants, and take no doit / Of

usuance for my money [since] you'll not hear from me. / This is a kind offer."
For his part, the Christian borrower responds and seals the bond with, "Hie
thee, gentle Jew. / The Hebrew will turn Christian; he grows kind." Far from
pointing in the direction of a world that is perilously perched on uncertainties
that extend from Mexico to India, and on Portia's *dea-ex-machina* cleverness,
the rate and tempo of exchange confirm, so it seems, the sober realism that
accounts for the ways of the Rialto; so, too, for a certain accommodation of
difference within and among bodies politic:

> The Duke cannot deny the course of [this] law
> For the commodity that strangers have
> With us in Venice, if it be denied,
> Will much impeach the justice of the state,
> Since that trade and profit of the city
> Consisteth of all nations. (III.iii.26-31)

It is to relevant effect, then, that Diana Schaub's *Erotic Liberalism* summarizes Montesquieu's representation of Jews, Judaism, and commerce in *The
Persian Letters* (1721) as well as in *The Spirit of the Laws*'s consideration of
"How Commerce Broke through the Barbarism of Europe" (1748). Schaub
makes the point that "Montesquieu had acknowledged—and in his under-
stated way, celebrated—the Jewish role in the advent of modern capitalism."
For he "credits Jews with the resuscitation of commerce in its revolutionary
modern form" since,

> As a result of the proscription of lending upon interest, common
> to both classical political philosophy and medieval Christianity,
> commercial activity became the despised province of the Jews.
> Such wealth, in hands unsecured by the privileges of citizenship,
> was too much for the greed of princes to resist. Throughout
> Christendom, the Jews were plundered, tortured, killed, and
> exiled. Earthly salvation came in the form of letters of exchange,
> for by this Jewish invention "commerce . . . became capable of
> eluding violence, and of maintaining everywhere its ground."
> [And] once the bill of exchange had rendered commerce safe for
> the Jews who engaged in it, the Church found it difficult to
> maintain the ban of Christian involvement. (1995:127-128)

Of course, a residual tension remained attached to any and all such transactions, as much for reasons of hegemonic shift as for "ethnick superstition" and
religious sanction. After all, no less a person than Aquinas had been a "zealot"
on this score, for he had left "no room for a prudential decision to allow usury

in order to prevent greater evils." John Hood thus traces Aquinas's various strictures, from the *Summa Theologiae* to *De Regimine Iudaeorum*, to their culminating argument against "spoilation": "If it is argued that princes would suffer from such a policy, we must reply that they have brought this suffering upon themselves. It would be better to compel Jews to work for a living, as is done in parts of Italy, than to allow them to live in idleness and grow rich by usury. If rulers suffer loss, it is only because they have been negligent" (1995:105).

When, elsewhere, Edward Andrew makes Shakespeare's play the occasion for an even deeper and theoretical excursus into the social sciences, his "unorthodox manner" results in a re-presentation in which Shylock becomes a "possessive individualist" whose circumstances serve the heuristic purpose of illuminating the grammar in Lockean claims about human rights. In *Shylock's Rights*, Andrew explains, "I interpret *The Merchant of Venice* as if it were presenting the arguments for and against human rights. Rights, we have said, emerge from the distinction between charity and justice, represented in the play by the unity of opposites, Antonio and Shylock, matched as 'two gelded users of money.' Natural rights in the person of Shylock confront Christian duties in the person of Antonio" (1988:34-35). The particulars of *The Merchant of Venice*'s actual dealings in and its disruption of currency and romance, and of tribal rights and election, are perhaps nowhere more concentrated than when Shylock's experience confirms Schaub's observation that "throughout Christendom, Jews were plundered, tortured, killed, and exiled" (1995:127): "[Antonio] hath disgraced me, hindered me half a million; laughed at my losses, mocked my gains, scorned my nation, thwarted my bargains, cooled my friends, heated mine enemies. And what's the reason? I am a Jew" (III.i.55-56).

In sum, the fact that "the Jew" is conceivable as "a creature that [bears] the shape of man," the urgent commerce that accounts for Antonio's letter, the bills of exchange on the Rialto, and the haunt of biblical prophecy, all these identify points along that gradient of dissimilarity where I propose to dis/affiliate Ethiope and Irish, circumcized Turk, and Moor with sooty bosom, thick lips, and gross clasps. Collectively and yet differentially, they trace out contours of the "other and the not-other"; they also generate the sub/versions of representation that result from their being "'always and already' in each other's presence" (Rifkin 1995:276). *The Merchant of Venice*'s Bassanio had been well-positioned to be transfixed, so to speak, by the convergence of such forces and modes of narration. At the end of Act 3, Scene 2—just after he had chosen the right casket in a world of apparent *magie*, and thus become lord of a "fair mansion" and of the even "fairer" Portia—Bassanio receives a letter from Antonio that is made up, so he tells Portia, of "a few of the unpleasant'st words / That ever blotted paper" (III.ii.251-252). "Few" plays against "unpleasant'st" in just the right degree: the dispensation of latitude and import is far-reaching indeed in Antonio's short letter. It maps a commerce that extends from Tripolis, Mexico, and England to Lisbon, Barbary, and India, and accounts for their import with telling succinctness: "Sweet Bassanio, my ships have all miscarried, my creditors grow cruel, my estate is very low, my bond to the Jew is forfeit" (III.ii.315-318). Simply put, the romance of Belmont needed to be underwritten by transport to and bills of exchange from the Rialto, as mediated by the Jew and "moneybags." But then, the Jew "transacts" in the bitter recognition that "the fawning publican" that the gentile merchant is "hates our sacred nation"; that Antonio had in the past railed at and spat upon his "Jewish garberdine," and all this, "even where merchants most do congregate." In the end, Christian abduction embraces Jewish ducats, only to be somewhat dis/confirmed in the moonlit romance of Jessica in Belmont. I say "dis/confirmed," because the consummation is embedded in a lyricism that is marked by Medea's disruptive shadow, and by the image of "Troilus mounted [upon] the Troyan walls, / [sighing] his soul toward the Grecian tents, / Where Cressid lay that night" (V.i.4-6).

Mudimbe also proposes a reading of differentiation and "cosmography of the selfe" (Browne) that bears being kept in mind here, in this itinerary in contexts. His *Parables and Fables* makes the point by way of Merleau-Ponty's observation that "Myself and the other are like two nearly concentric circles which can be distinguished only by a slight and mysterious slippage. . . . Nevertheless the other is not I and on that account difference must arise" (1991:xix). Elsewhere, it is Dympna Callaghan's view, in her re-reading of Elizabeth Cary's *The Tragedie of Mariam, Faire Queene of Jewry*, that "Paradoxically, the stark coloration of virtuous femininity as white and licentious femininity as black is destablized by the fact that these polarities are set in relation to one another amid Jews, peoples of an allegedly compromised ethnicity" (1994:170). There is a relevant focus on such slippage when Adrian Rifkin argues the point that "'other' is not necessarily illuminating as a concept":

> For 'other,' in even the subtlest of its gradations, normally asks for a line that will be neat—even though the reason why the line is drawn may not be clear and though what lies on either side of it not be clearly different. On the contrary, it is bound to be over-determined. The same line may be drawn around more than just one 'other'—something all too often forgotten in the articulation of the 'being-other' that is being a Jew. The other and the not-other are 'always and already' in each other's presence with all the difficulty of knowing what it is, this self made of presence and of lack. (Rifkin 1995:276)

Johannes Fabian has proposed, reasonably enough, that "encountering the Other in shared time is what anchors anthropological discourse in this world" (1991:59). On the other hand, when Howard Eilberg-Schwartz surveys the problematic question of "the savage in Judaism" (1990:6-7), he introduces us to a telling instance of exceptionalist resistance to contact and shared time. Eilberg-Schwartz marks out his terrain succinctly: "The argument of this book is contained in its title: *The Savage in Judaism*"; for which reason, it is concerned with the presumed irrelevance of the "discipline of anthropology or comparative inquiry" for "understanding the religion of the Jews" (ix). In his account of strenuous disaffiliation Eilberg-Schwartz identifies four types of "defensive strategies " that have been "deployed during and beyond the Enlightenment to cope with the savage presence in Judaism: denial, marginalization, excision, and temporization." He notes that when "comparisons are tolerated, they are almost all of the metonymic variety, that is, between cultures and religions that are in a single geographical area and hence 'in contact.' But there is a lack of interest in, and even hostility toward, metaphoric comparisons, comparisons that are drawn between religions and cultures that are similar in some respect but are separated in place and perhaps also in time" (*ibid.*).

Robert Bonfil's nuanced grounds for conceiving of the Jew as the "alien within" (1995) adds yet other contours to the map of the "other and the not-other" that interests me, and it merits some thought here, as does the greater impatience with which Robert Michael works his way through and past any such nuancing to make the point that "the exalted concept of 'Judeo-Christian' tradition has often been simply a mockery of the cruel realities that lay beneath" (1994:101). The coexistence of Jews and Christians in Europe, Bonfil points out, involved "a complex process of continuous adaptation"; and the fact that Jews were tolerated cannot be adequately explained by looking at "theoretical formulations, such as the Augustinian justification of tolerance of Jews as witnesses to Christian truth." The "inertial persistence of Roman legal traditions" does not quite suffice either. Furthermore, "careful quantitative researches make less plausible than before the idea that tolerance can be traced to the fiscal opportunism of Christian rulers." Bonfil suggests

> the existence of some hidden mechanism inherent in the psychol-
> ogy of Christian religiosity as a determining factor in shaping the
> destiny of the Jews. The fact that antisemitism did not disappear
> in countries where there were no Jews at all may indicate that
> Christians, more than reacting to the presence of Jews, consid-
> ered Jews and Judaism as a necessary part of their Christian
> endeavor to define their own cultural religious identity. (265)

"In the days of Titus, and afterwards in every nation and pincipality of Europe," Elmer Stoll recalls, Jews "were *servi camerae*; and, in return for the slight protection they thus received, they were pillaged and plundered, legally or illegally" (Myrick 1987:165). In the complex of issues that is at work in *The Merchant of Venice* Christian romance is indissolubly bonded to commerce and "rich gift." By the same token, sword-point conversion of the alien parallels the nationalist preference that marks the triumph of the local hero (Bassanio) over the "death's head" of Morocco, the "blinking idiot" of Spain, the "vilely drunk" German, and the motley figure that Portia identifies as an Englishman. Of course, this being Shakespeare, there is a great deal of irony in the way of "sufferance by example": "The villainy you teach me," Shylock promises, "I will better the instruction" (III.i.76). When Gratiano exults in court, he does so in a language of dis/affiliation that owes its present and past genealogies to Shylock: "A second Daniel still say I, a second Daniel! / I thank thee, Jew, for teaching me that word" (IV.i.339-340). There are limits, of course, to such sub/versions of terrain and type: witness the sharp tilting of the gradient of dissimilarity when Shylock emphatically rejects the "smell of pork, [that] habitation which *your* prophet the Nazarite conjured the devil into!" (My emphasis). That being the case, famously,

> I will buy with you, sell with you, talk with you, walk with you, and so following; but I will not eat with you, drink with you, nor pray with you. (I.iii.31-34)

Shylock's "and what's his reason? I am a Jew" certainly underscores the "ancient grudge" in all this; and it does so according to the terms of the complex affiliations that link Shakespeare's gentile and Jewish merchants, be it in the rambuctious genealogy of some ballad about "the murtherous life and terrible death of the riche jew of Malta," or in that learned vision of massive dispossession—"*Judaeus vero nihil propium habere potest, quia quidquid acquirit non sibi acquirit sed regi, quia non vivunt sibi ipsis sed aliis, et sic aliis acquirunt et non sibi ipsis*"—which we get in Henry de Bracton's thirteenth-century volumes on the laws and customs of England (*De legibus et consuetudinibus*). Summarily put in the words of Aquinas, the Jews were condemned "to perpetual servitude"; for which reason, "the lords of the earth may use their goods as their own" (*ibid*. 164 [Stoll]). Ballad and latin judgment also account for the dramatic pedigree that links Shakespeare's play to Marlowe's *The Jew of Malta* and its view that "To undo a Jew is charity, and not sin" (IV.v.76). All the same, John Munro's discussion of "patterns of trade, money, and credit" in the early modern period does well to call attention to the contraindicative embrace of economic gain and article of faith which the ecclesiastical ban on Jewish usury provoked in many a Christian merchant. "I am as like . . . / To spet on thee again, to spurn thee too," Antonio tells Shylock; for which reason, "If thou wilt lend this money, lend it not / As to thy friends . . . / But lend it rather to thine enemy" (I.iii.127-132). The interdiction against "a breed for barren metal" was a constraint, Munro explains—a bond, if you will—that merchants "did devise various means of evading." On the other hand, the effort also succeeded in extracting "higher transaction costs, including death-bed restitutions," from those "fearing the mortal peril to their souls" (Munro 1995:152). Francis Bacon's awkward recognition makes the necessary point that usury was "the certainest means of gain, though one of the worst, as that whereby a man doth eat his bread '*in sudore vultus alieni*,' and beside doth plough on Sundays" (Brooke 1935:201). Of course, due weight was given to such insight as may be found in Psalm 15, where the Elect that are fit to dwell in God's tabernacle and upon his holy hill include him "that putteth not out his money to usury, nor taketh reward against the innocent."

"Moneys" was thus a "bondman's key" with which to conjure and contend, as in *The Merchant of Venice*. The "moneys" suit had also been at work in *The Jew of Malta*, but in a considerably less nuanced way, when Marlowe's Barabas counters gentile exclusion with the defiant roll call of "a scattered nation" that has "scrambled up / More wealth by far than those that brag of faith":

> There's Kirriah, Nones in Portugal,
> Obed in Bairseth, some in Italy,
> Many in France, and wealthy every one (I.i.125-29)

"Moneys is your suit," Shylock tells Antonio. That being the case, any number of apparent contraindications surface in Shakespeare's presentation of the case: "What should I say to you? Should I say, / 'Hath a dog money? Is it possible / A cur can lend three thousand ducats?'"

Meanwhile, Sir Thomas Browne may be counted among those that "brag of faith,"given the self-congratulatory recognition of difference with which he anchors himself in the "Religion of [his] Countrey." The author of the *Religio Medici* had written thus about being in a position "to enjoy that happy stile [of Christian], then maligning those who refuse so glorious a title" (1898:I.i.15-21). It was also Browne's judgment that the "Jew is obstinate in all fortunes [since] the persecution of fifteene hundred years hath but confirmed them in their errour: they have already endured whatsoever may be inflected, and have suffered, in a bad cause" (*ibid*. 26). He was, for his part, properly "ashamed at the Rabbinicall Interpretations of the Jews, upon the Old Testament, as much as their defection from the New" (*ibid*.). The author of the *Religio Medici* was also greatly puzzled, finding it "truely [beyond] wonder, how that contemptible and degenerate issue of *Jacob*, once so devoted to Ethnick Superstition, and so easily seduced to the Idolatry of their Neighbours, should now in such an obstinate and peremptory beliefe, adhere unto their owne Doctrine" (*ibid*). Needless to say, the "grudge" and the disaffiliation that it occasioned are all the more telling for being rooted in a common Scripture. There was authority in it for recognizing the likes of the Moor as infidel and for imputing a crucial degeneracy to the Jew, as is well illustrated in the encyclopaedic antagonism with which the likes of Raymond Marti, a Dominican contemporary of Thomas Aquinas's, wielded his "dagger of faith" against Moors and Jews in *Pugio Fidei* (1272). Meanwhile, John Hood's *Aquinas and the Jews* relates the "grudge" to a view that identified and situated Jews and their history in two periods: an Old Testament "time of Law" and a Christian "time of grace"; and the "hinge" that joined them was Christ, "or more specifically, the Crucifixion," Hood explains (1995:xii). In both dispensations and in the "pivotal event of Jesus's death, theology demanded the Jews play a dual role." In consequence, "no medieval theologian doubted the Jews were the chosen people of God"; that their "history was a preparation for the coming of Christ. . . . At the same time, however, theologians were prepared to explain "the Jews' rejection of Christ by tracing a steady spiritual decline from the faith of Abraham and Moses to the malice and hypocrisy of the Pharisees" (*ibid.*). For Hood, Aquinas's signal contribution to all this lay in the systematic clarity that he brought to bear on this traditional apprehension of the alien-within: "He made an effort to explain how it was possible for Jews to be at the same time chosen *and* rejected, ignorant *and* malicious Christkillers, damned *and* destined for salvation" (*ibid.*).

There is a clear enough history of justification here. It runs from Pauline judgment to patristic theology, and is echoed in that view of Browne's that it was his good fortune to own a "zeale" that would not "so farre make [him] forget the generall charitie" that he owed "unto humanity, as rather to hate then (sic) pity Turkes, Infidels." "Jewes," for their part, provoked a need to account for degeneracy and recalcitrance; and for these "Ethnick Superstition" and "Rabinnical Interpretations [upon] the Old Testament" could be blamed. "Mark what Jacob did: / When Laban and himself were compremised / . . . the ewes being rank / In the end of autumn turned to rams . . ./ Who then conceiving . . .," Shakespeare's Shylock once tried to explain. However, impatient with the fulsome note in the Jew's attempt at an exegesis on Jacob's "way to thrive" and to be blest, Antonio had countered with a rather abrupt "hand of heaven": "Mark you this, Bassanio, / The devil can cite Scripture for his purpose," like "an evil soul producing holy witness"

(I.iii.71-100). Stoll provides the relevant information that shortly before *The Merchant of Venice* was written, Elizabeth I's "perjured and murderous Jewish doctor" Lopez had provoked disregarding laughter when he "protested from the scaffold [in 1594] that he loved the Queen as he loved Jesus Christ. Such words 'from a man of the Jewish profession,' says Camden, 'were heard not without laughter'" (Myrick 1987:160). Conflicted and still pregnant with dis/affiliation, this *factor judaicus* surfaces in various gradations in the latter days, be it in Trollope or in that popularizer (with his sister, Mary) of Shakespeare, Charles Lamb. "I confess that I have not the nerves to enter their synagogue," Lamb would write. His reasons included the frisson of medieval horror of not being able to "shake off the story of Hugh of Lincoln." There remained, as ever, the puzzling persistence of Jewish degeneracy and defiance in the face of Christian revelation and election. Lamb therefore wondered: after "centuries of injury, contempt, and hate, on the one side—of cloaked revenge, dissimulation, and hate on the other—Why [do they] keep up a form of separation, when the life of it [Judaism] is fled?" (Schweitzer 1994:165).

In the end, I find it significant that early-modern studies and contemporary politics coalesce in Stanley Wells's rather cautious formulation of features that have since worked to situate *The Merchant of Venice* in its nexus of competing allegiances: "The response of twentieth-century audiences has been complicated by racial issues; in any case, the role of Shylock affords such strong opportunities for an actor capable of arousing an undercurrent of sympathy for a vindictive character that it has sometimes unbalanced the play in performance" (1988:485). Bill Overton (1987) is more explicit when he identifies one of two sets of reasons "why Shylock is a problem": "One lies in the history of the Jews. Dispossessed from their homeland and scattered among other nations, victims of all forms of oppression to the dreadful extreme of pogrom and holocaust, their story should permanently warn against the appalling dangers of all racial prejudice." Especially so because, and this is hardly surprising, under the Nazi regime *The Merchant of Venice* was produced to incite racial hatred. "If in any way the play encourages prejudices, those taking part in producing it carry heavy responsibility" (Overton 1987:24). The play's "moral scheme is not entirely clear cut," Wells concludes. "The Christians are open to criticism, the Jew is true to his own code of conduct" (485). It was possible elsewhere for a David Anderson to be certain that he could "see no reason, why the Jewish race should be ashamed of Shylock" (Brooke *et al.* 1935:166). But then, as though in response, Overton juxtaposes production contexts when he counterpoints the following views. "For Patrick Stewart, who played the role in 1978, 'Shylock is an outsider who happens to be a Jew'," Overton reports. However, "David

Suchet, who played Shylock in 1981 and is himself Jewish, rejects this proposition: 'as Shylock I'm not an outsider who *happens* to be a Jew but *because* I'm a Jew'" (53). At any rate, Wells and Anderson and Overton exercise a benign option which, it is clear, Marlowe's considerably less nuanced *Jew of Malta* had made impossible, at least in the summation that we get in T. W. Craik (1983), for whom the play's several devices, from its prologue to its machiavellianism, "serve to correct the . . . wrong inference that the Jew has been turned into a monster by the Christians' injustice." To be sure, "the injustice gives him ground for revenge, but he was selfish and deceitful before his wealth was thus confiscated." For this "usurer," with his self-advertized "extorting, cozening, forfeiting, / And tricks belonging unto brokery" that had "fill'd the goals with bankrupt," death in his own cauldron was in fact "poetically just" (Craik 1983:xi-xii).

In the end, the Shakespearean Jew that surfaces in the creole/Caribbean world of *Highlife for Caliban* is a man of "when all has been said and done." By the creolized date of "Shylock, After" Shakespeare's character has been comprehensively assaulted, Sylvia Wynter explains, "in the ghetto of his Jewish being, [and] dragged into an alien universe [to be made] the scapegoat for its self-condemnation; to find himself cramped against the night, condemned, [and] against his will baptized to Christian life, his true being able to survive only by the direst cunning." Wynter thus "creolizes" the Jew's alien-within category to make the point that Shylock is caught in the simultaneity of terms that have both dislodged and lodged him "*in nomine* / by name the jew / *sed semper* / the jew / golem in yellow / gold *pax tecum*" (Wynter 1995:102). Thereupon, the character becomes a man of memories who is trapped in the self-caressing insufficiency of memories of disaffiliation and torment:

> jessica
> jessica keep
> the windows
> that the pipes
> and the recorder
> and the flute
> whistle only
> against the seamed
> edges of my skull
> cap O jessica keep
> hold against the windows. (*ibid.* 44)

Still, and *contra* the Ethiope "blackamoor" and the Ottomite "infidel," the inclusionary category that the hyphen in Judaeo-Christian assumes remains a crucial one, and is elsewhere reflected when Nelson Vieira identifies the "contradictory or indeterminate image" of the "outsider within," associating it with "far-reaching and reveberating features linked to Jewish thinking and writing" (1995:30). The problem of the other and the not-quite-other is measured in similar terms when Bryan Cheyette's "Neither Black Nor White: The Figure of 'the Jew' in Imperial British Literature" turns its attention to the Jewish protagonist of Anthony Trollope's *Nina Balatka* (1867). "He was very dark—dark as a man can be and yet show no sign of colour in his blood," Trollope wrote. "No white man could be more dark and swarthy than Anton Trendellsohn" (*ibid.* 31). Sander Gilman provides us with a summary view of this approach to the "Jew's body" when he writes,

> Jews had been classified as an inclusionary category with a status analogous to that of woman. (The Jew is always defined as masculine.) As long as Christians viewed themselves as the extension and fulfillment of the Jew, they still needed the Jew. The "Synagogue" was thus old, while the "Church" was young. But even this theological model always proposed the female Jew as inherently different from male Jews, yet also different from the ideal feminine. Chateaubriand in *Essays on English Literature* (1825) wrote that "Jewesses have escaped from the curse of their race. None of them were to be found in the crowd that insulted the Son of Man. . . . The reflection of some beautiful ray will have rested on the forehead of Jewesses." "I hate Jews because they crucified Christ," said the anti-Dreyfusard Paul Bourget at the end of the nineteenth century, "I adore Jewesses because they wept for him" (1995:99-100).

For which reason, *The Merchant of Venice* once declared, "If e'er her father come to heaven / It will be for his gentle daughter's sake" (II.iv.33-38). Justification for hating the Jew and loving the Jewesss was thus allied with a "testamental antagonism to Jews and Judaism" that was as much Saint Paul's as it was that of Saint John Chrysostom whose view it was that Jews "grew fit for slaughter" (Michael 1994:105;115). By the same token, Christian election could not come into its own without an exemplary embrace of the alien-within. Witness Saint Vincent Ferrer (1350-1419) for whom it was necessary to accept, indeed to celebrate, the fact that "Jesus Christ was Jew, and the Blessed Virgin was Jewess; [so, too, that] this circumcised God is our God." But then, the Jew's rejection of revelation required the Dominican monk's pronouncement that damnation awaited anyone "who dies a Jew" (Schweitzer 1994:164).

It is Leslie Fiedler's understanding (1973) that by the age in which Shakespeare conceived of Shylock and Jessica, "there had begun to grow both in him and in his audience a longing . . . for a representation of the female principle in Jewish form more human than the Blessed Virgin, yet, unlike the Jew's daughter [in the medieval ballad *Hugh of Lincoln*], benign and on the other side" (Callaghan 1994:171). Callaghan adduces one such manifestation from Thomas Adams's "defense" of women published in 1629, in which context we learn that "though Christ honoured our sex, in that he was a man, not a woman," it was the case, all the same, that "the worst and greatest crime that ever was done, was committed by a man, not by woman; the crucifying of our Lord Jesus; not a woman had hand in it" (Callaghan *ibid.*). With Shakespeare, such representations add a peculiar sense of pathos and treachery to the issue of dis/affiliation. *The Merchant of Venice* and its conflicted ensemble play a relevant "Jewess" note, so to speak, and we hear its resonance in the wonder that Jessica—that "most beautiful pagan" and "sweet Jew"— could indeed have been "issue to [the] faithless [but wealthy] Jew" when she is so near to being Fair.

That being the case, there is, *tout court*, the Jewess's need to be saved from tribal affinity; for this is clearly the point of her response to Launcelot's "bastard hope" that "your father got you not—that you are not the Jew's daughter." "Our house is hell . . . Alack what heinous sin is it in me / To be ashamed to be my father's child!" The voice is Jessica's, of course. As the "fair" Jewess puts it elsewhere, "though I am daughter to his blood / I am not to his manners" (II.iii.19-20). Her father's rejoinder gives back measure for measure: "I have a daughter; / Would any of the stock of Barabbas / Had been her husband, rather than a Christian" (IV.i.292-294). But then, her husband, Jessica declares, had made her a Christian, and had thereby redeemed her into the gentile/gentle ranks of the Fair Maid of the West. Of her "love-news" letter, Lorenzo does indeed say that "'tis a fair hand, / And whiter than the paper it writ on / Is the fair hand that writ" (II.iv.12-14). Salerio celebrates her redemptive abduction from Jewish paternity in terms of a divide between black and white, an unbridgeable one insofar as far as it involves the male Jew, Shylock. "I say, my daughter is my flesh and blood," Shylock insists; however, the Christian's reply to this is: "There is more difference between thy flesh and hers than between jet and ivory; more between your bloods than there is between red wine and rhenish" (III.i.40-45). Meanwhile, for all that he is a clown, Launcelot registers affection for Jessica in due form when he addresses her as "Most beautiful pagan, most sweet Jew" (II.iii.10-11). And Lorenzo is, as he should be, quite beside himself about her:

> So you are, sweet . . . .
> Beshrew me but I love her heartily!
> For she is wise, if I can judge of her,
> And fair she is, if that mine eyes be true,

And true she is, as she hath proved herself;
And therefore, like herself, wise, fair, and true,
Shall she be placed in my constant soul. (II.vi.44; 52-57)

Jessica-on-stage leads me to a second set of particulars in this study's preoccupation with latitude and import, with differentiation and sea-change into something rich and strange. "Ethnick superstition" and gradient of dissmilarity in what follows are very much gender-inflected, and the concommitant politics is sexual/textual indeed. Given the particulars that are now at hand, I have tried to contain and yet anticipate a certain attitude in the formulation, "Whatever happened to Caliban's mother? or, the problem with Othello's?" I am thus set to engage contexts of consummation that do not now involve Jewess and European man. Instead, and as John Peale Bishop's anguished disrelish would put it, "The ceremony must be found / that will wed Desdemona," she who is "fair and delicate as a grasshopper," to the "*huge* Moor" (my emphasis). The facts of the matter here are unambiguous, at least they are to Bishop: "though [Desdemona] may pant again in his black arms / (his weight resilient as a Barbary stallion's) / she will be found / when the ambassadors of the Venetian state arrive / again smothered." Simply put, "These things have not / been changed / not in three hundred years." No less consequential, then, is the *querelle de femmes* (woman palaver) recognition that incontinence in Caliban or Caesar threatens to be nakedly exhausting of female presence, as is suggestively the case when Emilia makes the point that "They eat us hungrily and when they are full / they belch us" (*Othello* III.iv.101-103).

Granting the above contours, I also mean to register something of the discomfort that we feel when, foregrounding his sister, the Clown in *Twelfth Night* says: "Sir, her name's a word, and to dally with that word might make my sister wanton. But indeed words are very rascals" (III.i.22-24). This is a matter of some consequence: for there is a certain density to the denigrated matter—to that *womanshenegro*—into which being female and black collapses when words are "very rascals" indeed with a certain kind of woman. The coinage is William Faulkner's, of course, in *Light in August*—a novel about which, parenthetically, Mario D'Avanzo has suggested that Byron Bunch's first name "alludes to Shakespeare's voice of love and good sense and natural feeling, the Biron of *Love's Labor's Lost*" (Ruppersburg 1994:24). Rather more consequential for my purposes is the fact that Faulkner's protagonist, Joe Christmas, looks "down into [the negro woman as though into] a black well"; and that what he sees "at the bottom" were "two glints like reflections of dead stars." For then, "He kicked her hard, kicking into and through a choked wail of surprise and fear. She began to scream, he jerking her up, clutching her by the arm, hitting at her with wide, wild blows, striking at the voice perhaps, feeling her flesh anyway, enclosed by the womanshenegro. ... Then she fled beneath his fist" (Faulkner 1990:156-57). The likes of such a body is elsewhere caught in the dialectic of fair and foul with which Joseph Conrad's *Heart of Darkness* divides Kurtz between the precarious ideal of the Fair Maid of the West, his European Intended—who came forward dressed all in black but with fair hair, pale visage, and pure brow that seemed surrounded by an ashy halo (1963:75-6)—and the extravagant display of his womanshenegro in the Congo—of that "gorgeous, wild apparition" who stands out in all the "jingle and flash of [her] barbarous ornaments" on the bank of a river in the heart of Africa:

> [Her] hair was done in the shape of a helmet; she had brass leggings to the knees, brass wire gauntlets to the elbow, a crimson patch on her tawny cheek, innumerable necklaces of glass beads on her neck; bizarre things, charms, gifts of witch-men, that hung about her, glittered and trembled at every step. (61-62)

As I hope to show by way of *Antony and Cleopatra*, the appeal of the vision derives from a certain unholy and somewhat generic magic, shaded as it all is by "unspeakable rites." The vision is, at bottom, one of "overpowering, carnal women located in dark and remote corners of the world" (Sanders 1992:104). Womanshenegro is, needless to say, not quite as available for redemptive abduction as is the "lovely garnish" ("Now by my hood, a gentle and no Jew!") that *The Merchant of Venice* makes of Lorenzo's Jessica. Wherever such women surface, as the gift of some witch-man or gauntleted with wire, they provoke disturbing resonances that may be very quickly heard, I trust, in Abena Busia's and Sylvia Wynter's preoccupation with the "unvoiced female" that Sycorax is presumed to embody, beyond Miranda's meanings; so, too, in readings of women, "race," and writing of the sort that we find in Margo Hendricks and Patricia Parker (1994). Theirs is a collection in which "Renaissance" and "postcolonial" studies are conjoined in variegated encounters, as is the case when when Jyotsna Singh discusses Othello's identity and postcolonial theory in light of contemporary African rewritings of Shakespeare's play (*ibid*: 287), and when Ania Loomba explores early-modern representations of women by way of her interest in subaltern revisionism. This is the vantage point from which Loomba begins her treatment of "The Color of Patriarchy," and in which context she underscores both "the difficulty and the especially pressing concern [with] respect to the female subject" (*ibid*:17).

Meanwhile, in "Silencing Sycorax: On African Colonial Discourse and the Unvoiced Female," Busia (1989) sets out to recover and to re-constitute identity. She is especially preoccupied with what Trinh T. Minha (1989), in "writing postcoloniality and feminism," has suggestively configured as "woman, native, other." Elsewhere, Clarisse Zimra's "In the Name of the Father" opens its exploration of "chronotopia, utopia, and dystopia" with a brisk situating of the likes of Christopher Columbus and Tvzetan Todorov in an enduring "blur of ethnocentric and phallocentric myopia" (1993:59). The oscillations of "fair" and "dark" women in Arabo-Islamic literature contribute their share of such representations, as is evident when Fedwa Malti-Douglas's *Woman's Body, Woman's Word* cites the example in which the poet "al-Bahili recounts that he said to a black slave girl, 'Heat in you is greatest,' to which she replied, 'He knows the heat of the bathhouse who has entered it'" (1991:34). Here, too, "Al-Jahiz, the great ninth-century prose literateur, relates: 'I inspected a slave girl and said to her, 'Do you play the *'ud* well?' She replied, 'No, but I can sit on it well.' The Arabic word *'ud* not only refers to the famous stringed musical instrument but can also mean a stick, a rod, a pole: a clear allusion to the male sexual organ" (*ibid.*). This dispensation of womanshenegro is one to which Nawal el Saadawi's Egyptian narrative also calls attention. Saadawi's *She Has No Place in Paradise* casts a contemporary reflection on the tradition that *Woman's Body, Woman's Word* examines. Not so parenthetically, Malti-Douglas associates her project (subjecting "the most quasi-sacred texts of the Arabo-Islamic sphere" to the "gender microscope") with *Rewriting the Renaissance* (1986) and its "discourses of sexual difference in early modern Europe." It is her view that its editors and contributors provide eloquent demonstration of the fact that re-examination of "cherished texts from different angles, principally feminist ones" can be "a most enriching experience" (Malti-Douglas 1991:6). At any rate, Saadawi re-examines the premise by way of a trenchant re-vision of a certain "silk-curtained, wide bed" in paradise. On top of that bed, fair and recently dead, sat Zainab's husband; he sat "like a bridegroom. On his right was a woman. On his left another woman. Both of them wore transparent robes revealing skin as white as honey, their eyes filled with light, like the eyes of *houris* [virgins of Islam]." This is the context in which womanshenegro is nothing if not *the* (wo)man-child in the (com)promised land:

> [Zainab's] husband's face was not turned towards her, so he did not see her. Her hand was still on the door. She pulled it behind her and it closed. She returned to the earth, saying to herself: There is no place in paradise for a black woman. (Saadawi 1989:156)

Meanwhile, and as befits her bemused "reflections from a black-eyed squint," the Sissie of Ama Ata Aidoo's *Our Sister Killjoy* is somewhat more sardonic about such representations; indeed, she finds herself driven to make the observation that "Sometimes when they are hotly debating the virtues of the African female, I ask myself: 'But who am I? Where did I come from?'" (1977:117).

Sylvia Wynter's elaboration (1990) is characteristically dense in its concern with paradigm and particulars. Following Zimra ("Righting the Calabash" 1990) and Philip ("The Absence of Writing, or, How I Almost Became a Spy" 1990), she explores the implications of "image-making" in the "discarding of the power of the logos of the Father." She is, however, very much invested in "the Silent Song of the [native] Mother." Both concerns engender issues that Wynter finds "powerfully re-enacted in the plot-line of *The Tempest*" (1990: 358). Her focus on Sycorax results in Wynter working at the unhoned edges of the in-house patriarchy that is Claudine Herrmann's concern in *The Tongue Snatchers* (1989): "The woman who seeks to understand her condition immediately finds herself struggling with a cohesive group of concepts that are both suspect and well-organized, a complicated network that crisscrosses all the givens of culture," and which "unerringly" reflect a man-observer (Hermann 1989:5). Significantly, in "Beyond Miranda's Meanings: Un/silencing the 'Demonic Ground' of Caliban's 'Woman'," what Wynter emphasizes most within such a network of terrain and type in *The Tempest* is the absence of Caliban's physiognomically complementary mate.

> For nowhere in Shakespeare's play, and in its system of image-making—one which would be foundational to the emergence of the first form of a secular world system, our present Western world system—does Caliban's mate appear as an alternative sexual-erotic model of desire; as an alternative source of an alternative system of meanings. Rather there, on the New World island, as the only woman, Miranda and her mode of physiognomic being is canonized as the "rational" object of desire as contrasted with Caliban's mate—of another population of human, i.e., of a "vile race" "capable of all ill," which "any print of goodness will not take," a "race" then extra-humanly condemned by a particular mode of Original Sin which "deservedly" confines them to a "rock," and reduces Caliban to a laboring machine as the new "massa damnata" of purely sensory nature—"He does make our fire, / fetch in our wood, and serve in offices / that profit us." (Wynter 1990:360).

Still, as will be evident (in Soyinka and Richardson, and in Bronte, Conrad, and Lawrence, below), an exceptionalist paradigm may be needed for the erotic model, and for the voice, that *Antony and Cleopatra* confers upon

Cleopatra, for all that she is native woman and invaded. So, too, for the remarkable effect of the burnished light that Shakespeare sheds on a creation who, in "her infinite variety," is also the paragon of native and dark seduction. For there is much here that exceeds the antiphon of mere verbal conceits with which, in *Love's Labour's Lost*, the King insists that a "black as ebony love" is the "badge of hell" and "the style of night" while Biron mounts a dark-lady rescue with "No face is fair that is not full so black. . . .And therefore is she born to make black fair" (IV. iii.245-95). Counterpointed as the spectacularly alien Cleopatra is to the "good and beautiful" Octavia—she that is "fair," and a Roman "whose beauty claims / No worse a husband than the best of men"— our "rare Egyptian" makes for and is made over into "dish" and "cookery" and "triple-turned whore" whose giving only famishes taking; and who, "riggish," "makes hungry where she most satisfies." Not even Antony can resist a certain thrust and cut during a lovers' quarrel (and on the woman's birthday, besides!):

> You were half blasted ere I knew you, ha!
> Have I my pillow unpressed left in Rome,
> Forborne the getting of a lawful race,
> And by a gem of women, to be abus'd
> By one that looks on feeders? (III. xiii.105-09; 185-86)

In Agrippa's sauntering lasciviousness, Cleopatra is the "Royal wench! / [Who] made great Caesar lay his sword to bed; / He ploughed her, and she cropped" (II.ii.233-34). "If she is dark," writes A. C. Bradley, bent upon, and betrayed so by, *his* rescue mission, "it is because the sun himself has been amorous of her" (Everett 1988:237). For a distinction of some significance is already under way here, between this bedazzling *dark* lady—a "blazing exception . . . a law unto herself [and] elusive as mercury" (Webster 1975: 74), and that *black Other* which Pandarus conjures up in *Troilus and Cressida*, in the insouciant posturing with which he declares that the fairness of a fair Helen, even in her Sunday best, would not matter: "What care I? I care not an she were a blackamoor; 'tis all one to me" (I.i.73-76). This dis/play of the blackamoor is recognizably at work in *Much Ado About Nothing* and in *A Midsummer Night's Dream*; it is in the former that Claudio takes the measure of his interest in Hero when he responds to Leonato's query with: "I'll hold my mind, were she an Ethiope" (V.iv.38). When Lysander's eyes are wrongly juiced by Puck's negligence in *A Midsummer Night's Dream,* he rejects his erstwhile love Hermia with "Away you Ethiope!" and with "Out, tawny Tartar, out!" (III.ii.257; 263), until, that is, the error is corrected when Oberon instructs Puck to crush a "herb into Lysander's eye, / Whose liquor hath this virtuous property, / To take from thence all error . . . / And make his eyeballs roll with wonted sight" (III.ii.367-69).

Beyond her "salad days," but beggaring all description as she rushes into "the secret house of death," Cleopatra, meanwhile, remains "morsel fit for a monarch." But then, to the degree that when the very "air" had gone to look upon Cleopatra it had "left a gap in Nature," the "wonderful piece of work" that this native woman is also serves to measure the danger that the bloodline of the conquistador courts, be he Caesar or Pompey. Or Mark Antony—who had himself "gone to gaze on Cleopatra" and then been transported into such a state! "Let Rome in Tiber melt, and the wide arch / Of the rang'd empire fall! Here is my space" (I.ii.33-34). Thereafter, "he fishes, drinks, and wastes / The lamps of night in revel," Octavius learns (I.iv.4-5). In Scarus' eyes, Antony is emptied of "experience, manhood, honor," having become "the noble ruin" of the woman's "magic" (III.x.18-23). It is possible, true, that this degrading of things Roman may be explained by the premise, as in *A Midsummer Night's Dream*, that "lovers and madmen have such seething brains"; that "The lover, all as frantic, / [will see] Helen's beauty in a brow of Egypt" (V.i.10-11; 4-5).

But then, "burnished" Cleopatra is nothing if not *the* measure of the "Inappropriate/d Other who moves about with always at least two/four gestures: that of affirming 'I am like you' while pointing insistently to the difference; and that of reminding 'I am different' while unsettling every definition of otherness arrived at" (Minh-ha 1986:9). Furthermore, and as Plutarch wrote about the original character, "her tongue was an instrument of music to divers sports and pastimes, the which she easily turned to any language that pleased her. She spake unto few barbarous people by inter-preter, but made them answer herself, or at least the most part of them: as the Ethiopians, the Arabians, the Troglodytes, the Hebrews, the Syrians, the Medes, and the Parthians" (Everett 1988:196). Not unexpectedly, Cleopatra is especially particular about how, being woman, she is to be undervalued, or "esteemed for nothing"; for "catching but the least noise of this, [she] dies instantly. I have seen her die twenty times upon far poorer moment. I do not think there is mettle in death, which commits some loving act upon her, she hath such a celerity in dying" (I.ii.141-49).

> Rather on Nilus' mud
> Lay me stark naked, and let the water-flies
> Blow me into abhoring! (V.i. 52-7)

she declares, particular in her "thoughts of horror" about being native-woman-other in Rome, and intolerably held up "to the view"—be it plebeian, among "mechanic slaves / With greasy aprons, rules, and hammers . . . in their thick breaths, / Rank of gross diet" (V.ii.209-212), or patrician:

> Know, sir, that I
> Will not wait pinion'd at your master's court;
> Nor once be chastis'd with the sober eye
> Of dull Octavia. Shall they hoist me up
> And show me to the shouting varletry
> Of censuring Rome? . . .

When in the end she does decide to untie "this knot intrinsicate / Of life" by applying snakes to her breast and arm, she proves to be again exceptional. For even as she makes her exit this woman sets herself up in sub/versive refiguration of an entire cluster of tropes, from the geo-political "Give me my robe, put on my crown" to the transcendent "I have immortal longings in me"; and from the erotic consummation of "Husband, I come!" to the final irony of the nurturing posture in which she feeds away her life: "Peace, peace / Dost thou not see my baby at my breast, / That sucks the nurse asleep?" (V.ii.; 282-109; 303-305). And Octavius's response to seeing her dead is to remark that "She looks asleep, / As though she would catch another Antony / In her strong toil of grace" (V.ii.345-346)—as no doubt befits one that "hath pursued conclusions infinite / Of easy ways to die" (V.ii.354-355).

Still, insofar as this "eastern star" and "lass unparalleled" is dark at all, she is neither Helen nor Miranda; nor is she Octavia, *sister* to Caesar and *Roman wife* to Antony. She is not even the accessible Desdemona; or the Tamora who opens up to Aaron in *Titus Andronicus*. The deliberate nature of the insult that Antony hurls at Cleopatra bears re-contextualizing here: "Ha! / Have I my pillow unpress'd left in Rome, / Forborne the getting of a lawful race, / And by a gem [Octavia] of women?" So, too, the fact that for all that he is himself deeply involved, he cannot forget that other Romans have cropped the woman. It makes for a remembrance of things past that drives him to identify the Egyptian as a "triple-turned whore." But then, "The beds in the east are soft," Antony had once told Pompey (II.vi.46) when he sought to explain his dalliance away from Roman discipline and domesticity, in the arms of a woman who had once been "queen to Caesar in the mattress," as Enobarbus recalls the matter (II.vi 71). Of course, there had been the plain enough thrust with which that "ass unpolicied" (Cleopatra's final estimation of Octavius Caesar) once measured the frontier of what is permissible with the certain kind of woman that she could not *not* be, after all: "Let us grant, it is not / Amiss to tumble in the bed of Ptolemy" (I.iv.714). Her being an invaded native-woman-other, not a redeemable Fair Maid of the West (as is *The Winter's Tale* Hermoine, for example), is thus refracted in (dis)plays of concupiscent energy, for all that she is, so she proclaims, "fire and air; my other elements / I give to baser life." Not even Antony can resist the thrust of the repressed with which he points out to Cleopatra: "I found you as a morsel cold upon / Dead Caesar's trencher; nay, you were a fragment / Of Cneius Pompey's; / besides what hotter hours, / Unregister'd in vulgar fame, you have / Luxuriously pick'd out; for I am sure / Though you can guess what temperance should be, / You know not what it is" (III.xiii.115-22). Antony speaks from and into a genre in which the woman had been made available to being "cropped" by a succession of Roman generals. And Pompey is, in this context, positioned to remember that Cleopatra was "fine Egyptian cookery" and that "Julius Caesar grew fat with feasting there," enough to produce a son. With his "O ho, O ho, would't had been!. . . / I had peopled else/ This isle with Calibans," this is the genre in which Caliban had sought to participate, when native, male, and invaded he had sought enlargement by cropping Miranda (I.ii.348-350). He is, needless to say, not a successsion of Roman generals in Egypt; besides which, witness Aaron and Tamora in *Titus Andronicus*, if actually "ingendered" the coupling of Caliban and Miranda would only deliver "monstrous birth to the world's light" (*Othello* I.iii. 396). For consummation between the fair Desdemona and the huge Moor does not help *people* the outskirts of empire with the sons of conquistadors, even if bastards. All in all, then, the volatility and dis/play of the native woman's body in *Antony and Cleopatra* do stand in some ironic counterpoint to the monumental will that we get at the end when Cleopatra says: "I have nothing / Of woman in me: now from head to foot / I am marble-constant" (V.ii.238-240).

The sex-and-conquest implications of such encounters and the "getting up of the bellies" of invaded women are inflected in yet other ways in Shakespeare. The thrust of what may be lost and gained is recognized by no less a character than Richard III, that diffused infection of a man, and the shame, besides, of his own mother's heavy womb. He invokes pillage and rape to relevant effect when, before the battle at Bosworth Field, he calls for "men of sound direction" that "lack no discipline." He also arouses by invoking the familiar specters of patriarchy at war: ownership of lands and being "blessed with beauteous wives." That being the case, why should "scum" and "base lackeys" "vomit[ted] forth to desperate adventures" be allowed to "enjoy our lands? Lie with our wives? / Ravish our daughters?" (V.iii.314-336). In several other instances, it is the coupling of Dido and Aeneas that shapes and shades the import of such narratives of invasion and consummation.

With Europe's Claribel left off in marriage on the African coast of Tunis, *The Tempest*, for one, belabors the appeal of the model. Though the connection is on the whole made by way of somewhat dimwitted, perhaps self-comforting, references to "widow'd Dido" and "widower Aeneas," Gonzalo will confirm that "This Tunis, sir, was Carthage" (II.i.73-85).

Elsewhere, Hamlet's interest in Dido makes of her little more than a listening (out)post when the Prince of Denmark requests from his troupe of players a recitation of Aeneas's tale to Dido. Because the native woman and her self-immolating grief over the loss of her European lover are being set up as a foil for Gertrude, it is obvious that the reference to its being "chiefly loved" is transparently strategic. The narrative that interests Hamlet involves Priam's slaughter, an act of murder to which Hecuba, his wife, responds with proper and wifely horror (IV.ii.468), a response that Dido rightly appreciates in Aeneas's telling. In *Henry VI*, Part II, meanwhile, Queen Margaret works up a guilt-ridden connection between her circumstances ("ay to be a queen and crowned with infamy") and Dido's: "how often have I tempted Suffolk's tongue . . . / To sit and witch me, as Ascanius did, / When he to madding Dido would unfold / His father's acts, commenced in burning Troy! / Am I not witched like her?" (III.ii.116-20). The transgressive intercourse that Claribel-in-Africa harbors is more directly at work, even if inverted, when *Titus Andronicus* plays out its sub/version of Dido and Aeneas. Tamora, Queen of Rome, invokes the couple in her eagerness to surrender to her "lovely Aaron," the North African. "Rome" thus takes in "Africa"; but this sexual coupling is a reversal of Dido and Aeneas, since, complex irony, it was when he was on his way to found Tamora's "race" that the eponymous hero of Virgil's epic had taken in his African queen and port of call. At any rate, given the turbulent politics that undergirds *Titus Andronicus*, Tamora's surrender ends up being considerably more than sexual intercourse in a "counsel-keeping cave." When Tamora delivers a son who is both "shame and stately Rome's disgrace!" (IV.ii.63-64), she brings about cause for even more palace turmoil and racial disturbance, and this occurs, it should be noted, in the context of that already turbulent politics of "drums and colours"—with "friends and factions" and "followers and favourers" all set to "plead . . . successive title" by sword should "pure election" fail (I.i.1-19). It is in the thick of this challenging noise of rivalry and election that, anxious for rendezvous, Tamora invokes Aeneas and Dido in hot love and idyllic consummation::

> Let us sit down and mark their yellowing noise,
> And after conflict such as was supposed
> The wand'ring prince and Dido was enjoyed
> When with a happy storm they were surprised,
> And curtain'd with a counsel-keeping cave,
> We may, each wreathed in the other's arms,
> Our pastimes done, possess a golden slumber. (II.iii.10-26)

For his part, when Aaron-Aeneas contemplates the invitation to "mount her pitch," he is not at all wreathed in romance. Instead, Tamora's own climb to

"Olympus' top" in the turmoil of Roman politics leads him to calculate and to anticipate: "I will be bright," he thinks, "and shine in pearl and gold, / To wait upon this new-made empress." He then corrects himself: "To wait, said I? to wanton this queen" (II.i.1-20). *Pace* Tamora's reading of Virgil, her own sexual encounter involves anything but post-coital and golden slumber. Her giving birth to a potential heir to the Roman throne, and a dark one at that, only intensifies the political turmoil—as Aaron soon enough hears: from Demetrius's "hellish dog, thou hast undone her" to Chiron's "Rome will despise her for [her] foul" delivery. Meanwhile, the "blackmoor child" produces a not at all surprising "caterwauling" from the nurse. The pretender-creature is, after all, one that she identifies as "a joyless, dismal issue." It is "loathsome," too, "as a toad," and this among "the fairest breeders of our clime." It is all enough for Tamora herself to turn matricide, to invite Aaron to "christen it with [his] dagger's point." Aaron conceives of another plan: he would introduce into the royal household the lighter-skinned child of a countryman of his, and "let the emperor dandle him for his own" (IV.ii.158-163). It all comes to naught, of course. The Moor in *Titus Andronicus* is neither the hero of a founding epic nor is he in a romance of restoration. His production and celebration of a first-born son and heir will lead him into nothing but the play's final act and sentence:

> See justice done on Aaron, that damn'd Moor,
> By whom our heavy haps had their beginning:
> Then, afterwards, to order well the state,
> That like events may ne'er it ruinate. (V.iii.200-204)

There is some irony, no doubt, in the fact that when Dido is again invoked at the end of a play that is filled with so much ruination in Rome, she is once more the "love-sick" native woman, "sad with attending ear" as she listens to Rome's "erst ancestor" recite to her the beginnings of the "sons of Rome" at the fall of Troy (V.iii.80-85).

In my view, transgressive union of this variety is nowhere more intriguingly lulled into service than in the moon-soaked lyricism, complete with Aeneas and Dido, with which *The Merchant of Venice* hovers at the edge of a consummation that would wed a *converso* Jewess to a Gentile, but in a world that remains resonant with Shylock and his dream of "moneybags"; with the language of his difference from and exile among "Christian fools" and "Hagar's offspring" (II.v.43). "It was my turquoise; I had it of Leah when I was a bachelor," he says about one of his losses, graphic with dishonor. "I would not have given it for a wilderness of monkeys" (III.ii.113-115). The principals at Belmont are, of course, Lorenzo and a by now complexly limned Dido-Jessica-Medea-Jewess, recently abducted, but willing. Here, then,

Leah and Jessica, Dido and Cleopatra, Medea and Cressida converge in quite
an embodiment of the "in/appropriate(d) other":

> Lorenzo: In such a night
>   Stood Dido with a willow in her hand
>   Upon the wild sea banks and waft her love
>   To come again to Carthage.
>
> Jessica: In such a night
>   Medea gather'd the enchanted herbs
>   That did renew old Aeson. (IV.i.9-14)

In providing us with an answer to the question, "Who was Dido?"—and thus
with a genealogy of overpowering, carnal women located in some suitably
dark and remote corner of the world—the *Carthage* that we come back to in
Soren, Khader, and Slim (1990) presents us with a story that is at once African,
Roman, and Phoenician, that is at once ancient and modern. Dido was, so we
learn, "a Phoenician royal beauty to be sure, as beautiful as Jezebel, to whom
she was related. To Virgil she was a competent, mature and strong woman"
who first appears in Book I of *The Aeneid* "in all her beauty." Embedded in
popular fantasy no less than than in Graeco-Roman culture and patrician
politics, the evolution that follows is suitably giddy and disciplined.
Shakespeare coincides with Hollywood and Virgil in *Carthage*'s re-presentation of its "in/appropriated she." There are echoes, too, of that pre-text of
Plutarch's, "The Life of Marcus Antonius," and the template that it provides
for "the last and extremist mischief of all other (to wit, the love of Cleopatra)
[that] lighted" on Mark Antony (Everett 1988:194):

> When we try to conjure up an image of this extraordinary creature
> [Dido] in our minds, we think of Elizabeth Taylor as Cleopatra or
> perhaps even Ursula Andress as H. Rider Haggard's "She Who
> Must be Obeyed." But this may not be a twentieth-century error
> on our part. Virgil composed his epic in the age of Cleopatra. The
> story of an exotic foreign queen whose beauty, charm and wiles
> tempt both Julius Caesar and Mark Antony from their proper
> duties was still fresh in the Roman mind. . . . Was the image of
> Dido . . . colored by the Cleopatra story? . . . It was consistent with
> the way Romans traditionally thought . . . . Phoenician women
> were thought of as beautiful but dangerous. (Soren *et al.* 1990:
> 21-22)

The stereotype endures, and is recognized as such in Jill Matus's *Unstable
Bodies* (1995:131-148) when "Cleopatra" is re-troped as *the* sign of incontinent desire in Charlotte Bronte. Matus calls attention to a central chapter in

Bronte's *Villette* where Lucy Snowe(!) focuses "on an ostentatious painting entitled *Cleopatra*, which depicts a voluptuous, semi-recumbent figure." Lucy Snowe's scrutiny of the painting leads her to conclude that her "desiring self" would be "spoiled, grow greedy and monstrous like Cleopatra," unless it is hidden or stifled (144):

> Charlotte Bronte supposedly based the painting she describes on a "real" picture which she saw at a Brussels salon in 1842, but this picture was not named *Cleopatra* at all and differs in significant ways from Bronte's fictional painting. Her "recognition" of an ordinary Orientalist painting as a version of Cleopatra illuminates how discurses of sexuality and race converge and overlap through longstanding western stereotypes of the Egyptian Queen and the burgeoning nineteenth-century fascination with the East and Oriental exoticism. By loosening the knot of associations that the painting provokes, we can think about *Villette* in relation to mid-Victorian representations of female sexuality and their articulations in terms of race and class. (131-132)

The knot of associations is older than Lucy Snowe, of course; and it has since endured reproductions and resisted diminishment in high art and in low, as is clearly the case in D. H. Lawrence's "The Man Who Died" (1925) and in Cecil B. DeMille's *Cleopatra* (1934). It is in the latter context that Claudette Colbert's Egyptian says of her Roman Antony, "I've seen a god come to life! I'm no longer a queen; I'm a woman!" The figure repeats itself, and to quite pregnant effect, this time, in Lawrence's version of native woman and seminal visitation. In a certain sense, this presentation of the female self is common enough, and may be recognized as such in the Wilson Knight of *The Crown of Life* (1947) when, in eerie affinity with Milton and Lawrence no less than with the screenwriters for DeMille, Knight declares that "Cleopatra is not one, but all, woman, waiting for man." In addition, "She is another Dido, as Vergil writes down the story; or as Milton's Eve—'He for God only, she for God in Him'." When Cleopatra "waits with her girls for Antony at Alexandria," they "are as the Eternal Femininity waiting for Man" (Knight 1987:297). Meanwhile, it is A. C. Bradley's view that many "unpleasant things can be said of Cleopatra; and the more that are said, the more wonderful she appears." Signally for Bradley, the "exercise of sexual attraction is the element of her life; and she has developed nature into a consummate art" (Everett 1988:236-237).

For his part, Lawrence abandons undirected sexuality; so, too, the sanction of Milton's God. Instead, he chooses to celebrate the consummation under the aegis of "all-tolerant Pan," on a "sacred little peninsula" in Lebanon where the "temple [faced] south and west, towards Egypt" (Lawrence 1953:185). His "rare" woman has tarried there across but also above religious transitions and political dispensations. *In hoc signo*, she awaits impregnation by the Man Who Had Been Crucified, but who, turned apostate, now seeks to escape from his erstwhile Word and its greedy virginity. In their exceptionalist copulation lie the seed and flowering of a new testament of the body meta/physical. And over it all hovers the Cleopatra that Lawrence's recapitulation of things generates: "When she was young, the girl had known Caesar, and had shrunk from his eagle-like rapacity"; there had been, too, the "golden Anthony [who] had sat with her many a half-hour, in the splendour of his great limbs, and glowing manhood, and talked with her of philosophies and gods, though he mocked at them. [The] big bright eyes of Anthony [had] laughed down on her, bathing her in his glow." It is true enough that she had "felt the lovely glow of his male beauty and his amorousness bathe all her limbs and her body erotic." However, "the very flower" of this woman's womb "was cool, was almost cold, like a bud in shadow of frost," notwithstanding the man's "flooding sunshine." Anthony had left; and she had waited for fulfillment that lay beyond "the golden brief day-suns of show such as Anthony" and beyond "the hard winter suns of power, such as Caesar" (189-90).

In the famous aphorism that Michiko Kakutani invokes in a review of Lucy Hughes-Hallet's *Cleopatra: Histories, Dreams and Distortions*, Blaise Pascal once made the observation that had Cleopatra's nose been shorter, the face of the world would have changed. "In other words, if Cleopatra had been less beautiful, Caesar and Antony would not have fallen in love with her, and the course of history would have been fatefully altered" (1990:B2). Perhaps so; ironically, however, there is very little in any and all such "preparation" and "most absurd intents" that had not been anticipated by Shakespeare's Cleopatra herself, down to even the necrophiliac extravagance of Gustave Flaubert in Egypt (1850), with his "Oh, how willingly I would give up all the women of the world to possess the mummy of Cleopatra!" and its "Like the ocean, [the Nile] sends our thoughts back almost incalculable distances; then there is the eternal dream of Cleopatra" (1966:11; 98). "Nay, that's certain," Shakespeare's Egyptian had assured her attendant, Iras. Notwithstanding Octavius's pledge that he was "no merchant, to make prize with you / Of things that merchants sold," it was Cleopatra's prescient fear that

> Saucy lictors
> Will catch at us, like strumpets; and scald rhymers
> Ballad us out o' tune; the quick comedians
> Extemporally will stage us, and present
> Our Alexandrian revels; Antony

> Shall be brought drunken forth, and I shall see
> Some squeaking Cleopatra boy my greatness
> I' the posture of a whore. (V.ii.215-220)

Quite so, and licensed by authority, besides. Which is why, to speak in a borrowing from Sheila Cavanagh's *Wanton Eyes and Chaste Desires*, "the importance of being fairest" has always been a telling one (1990:75). After all, the "wide world" cannot be ignorant of the worth of so "fair" a one as Portia, for example—especially when she is, in fact, "fair and fairer than that word," as Bassiano well knows. "For the four winds blow in from every coast / Renowned suitors" to where "her sunny locks / Hang on her temples like a golden fleece" (I.i.167-170). With the dark Duke of Morroco (that "shadowed livery of the burnished sun [and] a neighbor and near bred") this attraction of the "fair" was enough to command worship and confession: "I would not change this hue," he says to Portia, "Except to steal your thoughts, my gentle queen" (II.i.1-12).

It matters, then, *how* Thomas Heywood expands the latitude and the import of his *The Fair Maid of the West* (from being merely the west of England). For his play has the Moor, Mullisheg, trafficking and trading in types of the maid, making them all his objects of desire: "Find us concubines," he commands,

> The fairest Christian damsels you can hire
> Or buy for gold, the loveliest of the Moors
> We can command, and Negroes everywhere.
> Italians, French, and Dutch, choice Turkish girls
> Must fill our Alkedavy. (IV.iii.27-33)

Heywood's coupling of "fairest Christain damsel" and Moor re-figures the problem-plagued relationship between Othello with Desdemona. But then, from Iago to Thomas Jefferson, from Samuel Coleridge to the latter days of Charles Lamb and of Frantz Fanon and James Baldwin (below), this dark reach for the Fair Maid has invariably provoked a fairly unbroken body of assumptions. Jefferson provides us with a useful summary when he observes in his *Notes on the State of Virginia* (1787) that "[the males of the negro species] are more ardent after their females: but love seems with them to be no more than an eager desire, than a tender delicate mixture of sentiment and sensation" (1972:139). Besides which, the "first difference which strikes us is that of colour," Jefferson wrote. "And is this difference of no importance? Is it not the foundation of a greater or less share of beauty in the two races? Are not the mixtures of red and white, the expressions of every passion by greater or less suffusions of colour in the one, preferable to the eternal monotony [and to] that immovable veil of black which covers all the emotions of the other race?" (138). Moreover, Nature itself was complicit in torrid zone and color; so, too, in the gravitational pull of species and libido; for as white is to black so is black to ourang-outang. "Add, [then, to the fine mixtures of red and white], flowing hair, a more elegant symmetry of form, their own judgment in favour of the whites, declared by their preference for them, as uniformly as is the preference of the Oran-ootan for the black women over those of his own species" (138). This line of descent in Jefferson's preoccupation with the esthetics and the color of the sexual helps to explain the aptly titled *Black Face, Maligned Race* in which Anthony Barthelemy reviews early-modern European representations to make the point that "legitimately [the black woman in the drama of the early modern period] functions in the community solely as a waiting-woman, illegitimately as a bawd and whore." On the whole, she is "unusually libidinous"; and in ways that are both *sui generis* and which serve as counterpoint to the Fair Maid, she generates disruptive heat, from that rising up of her negro belly in *The Merchant of Venice* to the character of Treasure in *The Triall of Treasure* (1567) and into the "hyperbolic exemplum" that Beaumont and Fletcher make of Lucifera, the "black succubus," in *The Prophetess* (Barthelemy 1987:125).

Given the hugely libidinous nature of the Blackamoor, to contemplate the surrender of the Fair Damsel to his type is to intensify the threat to and the "ardent" exhaustion of any female, and thus to provide evidence of just how preposterous it would be for nature so to err, as Brabantio once concluded with regard to Desdemona. Murray Carlin's drama, *Not Now, Sweet Desdemona* (1969), makes a heuristic point of taking as its epigraph Coleridge's unambiguous disrelish: "It would be something monstrous to conceive of this beautiful Venetian girl falling [in] love with a veritable negro." Any such erring of nature would serve—as Iago well knows—to "awake the snorting citizens with the bell," fearful as indeed they should be that "the devil" would make grandsires of "citizens"; that they would have "nephews neigh" to them; "coursers for cousins; and gennets for germans." For which reasons, and

> for shame, put on your gown;
> Your heart is burst, you have lost half your soul;
> [For] even now, now, very now, an old black ram
> Is tupping your white ewe. (I.i.86-91)

According to John Peale Bishop (1940), the implications, or the thrust, if you will, of any such "tupping" have not "changed in three hundred years," notwithstanding that quest for a "ceremony" that would indeed wed Desdemona to her huge Moor. But then, no quest for what *The Tempest*, relying on Ferdinand and Miranda, refers to as a "solemnized" union could be more futile. In Bishop, *Othello*'s "fair Venetian" [was] noble to her fingertips," and "delicate," besides, "as a grasshopper." However, given the Moor's pedigree, "tupping" would forever be nothing but "tupping," Bishop concludes, even if that word itself is "obsolete." In this rendezvous of "other" with "not-other" there are large issues and small points, all of them "indicative." In Bishop, the reach for consummation ends as it must: in a darkness that falls upon the door of the nuptial room, and on things that are "ancient as the metaphors in dreams; / strange, with never before heard music; continuous until the torches deaden at the bedroom door." This could hardly have been unexpected:

> For though Othello had his blood from kings
> his ancestry was barbarous, his ways African,
> his speech uncouth. It must be remembered
> that though he valued an embroidery—
> three mulberries proper on a silk like silver—
> it was not for the subtlety of the stitches,
> but for the magic in it. Whereas, Desdemona
> once contrived to imitate in needlework
> her father's shield, and plucked it out
> three times, to begin again, each time
> with diminished colours. This is a small point
> but indicative.

Whether in the latter days, or in the early modern period of the likes of William Strode (1602-1645) or Thomas Campion (1567-1620)—or else in the mock-Petrachanism of William Dunbar's "Of Ane Blak-Moir" ("Of a Blackamoor") and in Shakespeare himself—such oscillations of foul and fair no doubt carried, and can still deliver, a complex charge. " I do not intend to suggest," Ania Loomba has relevantly explained, that a negative critique is the only kind of pleasure that canonical texts make available to traditionally marginalized students/readers." For, she adds, "to respond from the fullness of one's specific situations is also to discover *new and different sources of textual pleasure* or issues to identity with: I certainly find that I enjoy *Antony and Cleopatra* and *Othello* a great deal more today than I did as a student when I wasn't allowed to comment on the racial difference of their central figures" (1994:24). There is instruction, too, in the thought that early-modern representations of "virtuous femininity as white and licentious femininity as black" (Callaghan) occur toward the end of what was in effect the first century of English experience with the Negro. They include the horrific "courtly love" that William Dunbar makes of it all—in what is possibly the earliest

attempt in British literature at representating the "negro" woman. Dunbar's
"Of Ane Blak-Moir" is a "bit of Renaissance horseplay," Ronald Sanders
explains; it had been apparently written to celebrate a jousting contest held
at the Court of King James IV of Scotland in 1506 or 1507. Having before
made poems "of ladyes quhytt" ("ladies white"), Dunbar undertook to write
one the refrain for which would be "My ladye with the mekle lippis" ("My
lady with the big lips"). With its cluster of images—"She who has a
protruding mouth like an ape, / And is like a toad in her gape; / And whose
short cat's-nose turns up; / And she who shines like any soap"—we get in
"Black-Moir's" "ladye" a measure of what, Sanders writes, was "by and large
a moment of unformed relationships" and "lack of sophistication." In the end,
its re-cognition of difference settles into an embrace of the familiarly
monstrous:

> And quhai infelde receaves scahem,
> And tynis thair his knychtlie naem,
> Sall cum behind and kis hir hippis. . .
> My ladye with the mekkle lippis. (Sanders 1992:213)

For now "the atmosphere takes on a hint of the witches' sabbath, in which the
kissing of the hind parts was a regular feature of the ritual." Whoever receives
"shame in the field," Dunbar writes, "And there loses his knightly name /
Shall come behind and kiss her hips." (*ibid.*).

It is clearly the case that the early modern period also witnessed a re-
figuration of "fair" and "foul"; and that this involved a process in which
"Ethiope" and "dark" were in transition from values that had been attached
to them in, say, the Patristic symbology of an Origen (c. 185-c. 254) and of
a Saint Ephraem Syrus (c. 306-373). Although the terrain and type could still
be as flat as they were in the eleventh-century *Chanson de Roland*—with its
"cursed race / Black as ink and whose faces / Have nothing white except the
teeth," as befits men from "Ethiopia, a damned land / Of . . . big-nosed and flat-
eared black people" (C. H. Sisson 1983:72-73)—Renaissance maps of
blackness in human form were being drawn at the edges of the imaginative
chiaroscuro of Christian thought; so, too, according to the politics and profit
of nationalist expansion. Whether in Origen or in *The Epistle of Barnabas* the
terms of reference had once served to justify a Saint Jerome (c. 347-c. 420)
in his contention that "we" were all Ethiopians once, "made so by our sins and
vices. How? Because sin had made us black. But then we heeded Isaiah (Isa.
1:16)—'Wash yourselves, be clean'—and we said, 'Thou shalt wash me, and
I shall be made whiter than snow' (Ps. 50[51]:9). Thus we, Ethiopians that
we were, transformed ourselves and became white." More matter of fact was
Jerome's observation, elsewhere, that his "skin, being dirty, recalled the

scruffy look of a Negro's epidermis" (Devisse and Mollay 1979:27). Of course, such exegeses on light and dark—and their cross-racial symbolism—had been embedded even more anciently in *The Book of Numbers* when Moses allied himself with Ethiopia by taking an Ethiopian wife. He had thereby provoked the dis/affiliation as well as the fair-is-foul irony of the punishment visited on his brother Aaron and, especially so, on his sister Miriam "when they spake against Moses because of the Ethiopian woman whom he had married: for he had married an Ethiopian woman." The brother and the sister's disapproval had "kindled" the anger of the Lord who came down "in a pillar of cloud, and stood in the door of the tabernacle, and called forth Aaron and Miriam" in reproach. At the end, "the cloud departed from off the tabernacle; and, behold Miriam *became* leprous, *white* as snow and Aaron looked upon Miriam, and behold *she was leprous.*" Upon which Aaron beseeches Moses: "Let her not be as one dead, of whom the flesh is half consumed when he cometh out of his mother's womb" (*Numbers* 12: 1-16). It is the reach of such exempla from the Church Fathers that helps to account for the views that Jean Devisse and Michel Mollay's *The Image of the Black in Western Art* summarizes in "The African Transposed." They note that "from St. Jerome and fourth-century Christianity the Occident inherited two basic lines of thought and reflection. The first regarded Africa as a distant land, the home of heretics and schismatics. . . . The second theme of meditation had to do with blackness as color. Due to lack of actual contact with Africa, blackness was available as an element in the visionary domain of theology and metaphysics, and as such was the opposite of light; [and was in fact] the refusal of light" (II. 2: 299; 255).

It was true, of course, that the question whether the leopard could lose its spots or the Ethiopian his color did not provoke answers that were invariably negative. Miracles of conversion were no doubt possible. As a result, Shakespeare's early modern period did in fact inherit registers of "Ethiope" identity in which the "metanoia of absolution" was of some consequence. After all, "metanoia" presupposed spiritual awakening as well as fundamental transformation of mind and character; and one such conversion of and from darkness explains why a *Book of Hours* that belonged to Charles V (and dated 1519) highlighted the Baptism of the Ethiopian Eunuch in one of the miniatures. Thus emblematized, and notwithstanding the loudness with which Iago and his aroused kinsmen remain puzzled about how it was possible for "nature so preposterously to err," the *Book of Hours*, so it seemed, had once welcomed the black into "the elect without reticence or mental reservation" (Devisse and Mollay 1979:237). Elsewhere, in that other and most lyrical of her origins, and from among the daughters of Jerusalem no less, the Ethiope could and did exfoliate into the *nigra sum sed formosa* (black but beautiful woman) of *The Song of Songs*. In this regard, the figure has been most lyrically even if somewhat contraindicatively invoked in the exquisiteness of Ephraem Syrus's *The Pearl, or Seven Rhythms on the Faith*:

> Very glistening are the pearls of Ethiopia. . . . And the dark Ethiopic women became pearls for the Son; He offered them up to the Father, as a glistening crown from the Ethiopians.
>
> The Queen of Sheba was a sheep that had come into the place of wolves; the lamp of truth did Solomon give her, who was also married her when he fell away. She was enlightened and went away, but they were dark as their manner was. The bright spark which went down home with that blessed [Queen] held on its shining amid the darkness, till the new Day-spring came. The bright spark met with this shining, and illumined the place. (*ibid.:* 29)

All the same, by the time that Thomas Wright gave his 1601 coloration to the "passions of the minde in generall," with accompanying admonitions, it seems clear that such a word as "foul," in addition to its original meaning of only "putrid," "rotting," and, by extension, "dirty," was beginning to take on a particular visual connotation (Sanders 1992: 246). For which reason,

> To a red man reade thy need;
> With a brown man breake thy bread;
> At a pale man draw thy knife;
> From a black man keep thy wife.

Meanwhile, the "Ethiopia" in the likes of the Iberian Jaoa de Barros (1552) is in transit away from Jerome but still hedged about with things dark and foul: for "it [did seem] that for our sins, or for some inscrutable judgement of God, in all the entrances of Ethiopia that we sail along, he has placed a striking angel with a flaming sword of deadly fevers, who prevents us from penetrating into the interiors to the springs of this garden, whence proceed rivers of gold that flow to the sea in so many parts of our conquest" (Pratt 1992:69). There is, elsewhere, the oscillatory dynamic that we get in the 1613 of *The Triumphs of Truth*: Thomas Middleton's erstwhile "sweet fac'd devil" King of the Moors watches a re-cognition of himself in the "amazement [that] set upon the faces of [the] white people" because "being a Moor . . . in opinion's lightness / [He is held to be] as far from sanctity" as is his "face from whiteness."

   It being Shakespeare, there is a recognizably aphoristic flair to the way in which the issue of color and its conventions is raised in *Titus Andronicus—*

literally so, given the illegitimate child that the Moor fathers on the Queen of Rome: "Where the bull and cow are both milk-white," we learn, "They never do beget a coal-black calf." Shakespeare thus situates himself in the chiaroscuro effect of bodies "fair" and "foul" with subversive and teasing effectiveness, most famously perhaps in *Macbeth*. The Shakespeare of *Twelfth Night* seems prepared to be bemused, from "the east to western Ind," by the "false gallop of verses" according to which "No jewel is like Rosalind . . . / All the pictures fairest lin'd / Are but black to Rosalind. / Let no fair be kept in mind / But the fair of Rosalind" (III.ii.97). In *The Tempest* Prospero recalls that the conspirators "painted their foul deeds" of usurpation "with colours fairer" when they embarked upon the business of setting him and his three-year old daughter adrift in the "rotten carcass" of a boat (I.ii.143). In *Measure for Measure*, Lucio identifies the "fair sister" and "gentle Isabella" to relevant, even emblazoned, effect with "Hail, virgin, if you be, as those cheek-roses / Proclaim you are no less" (I.iv. 16-17). Convent-bound as Isabella is, and obviously no Tamora *(Titus Andronicus)*, the salutation sits well—especially in a play in which the "gettting up" of the bellies of women is pivotal to the plot. In Sonnet 127, meanwhile, Shakespeare notes that "In the old age black was not counted fair, / Or if it were, it bore not beauty's name, / but now is black beauty's heir." The (de)generative context of Sonnet 18 acknowledges the fact that "every fair from fair sometime declines;" however, in the "miracle" of Sonnet 65 "in black ink . . . love may still shine bright." Elsewhere, it is clear that there is a studied thrust in *Othello*'s swift, and reasons-of-state, translation from black to fair. "Your son-in-law is far more fair than black," the Duke tells a Brabantio who has come to court filled with denigrating horror (I.iii.290). The translation allows the state to discount the Senator's complaints about a bewitched and stolen daughter, and to rush the accused Moor into battle against a Turkish fleet that was ranged against Venice, some distance away in Cyprus.

In the likes of Thomas Campion (1567-1630) and William Strode (1602-1645) the importance (and the seduction) of being fairest had been called upon to serve rather more conventional ends, which they do within the compass of this familiar "Garden" and "breast." In the "fair" vision that Strode makes of his "Gentlewoman Walking in the Snow," "the wanton snowe" flies to her "faire" breast "like little birds into their nest" (Dobell 1907:47). It is in the nature of the conceit that the snow is "overcome with whiteness there"; so, too, that it would lose its place in that bosom of privilege and fall to her "garment's hemme" where "for greife it freez'd into a gemme" *(ibid.)*. The work of the conceit is more extravagant, but remains racially in-house, so to speak, when the suitor in Strode's "A Lover to His Mistress" undertakes to explain to her "how the Rose did first grew redde" and " whence the Lilly whitenesse borrowed."

You blusht and then the Rose with redde was dight:
The Lillies kissde your hands, and so came white:
Before that time each Rose had but a stayne,
The Lilly nought but paleness did containe:
You have the native colour, these the dye;
They flourish only in your livery. (Strode 1907:48)

"Lilly" and "stayne" are more contraindicatively embraced in Campion's "Garden" where "Roses and white Lillies grow." It is true, of course, that things do seem to be formulaic enough when

Those Cherries fayrely doe enclose
  Of Orient Pearle a double row,
Which when her lovely laughter showes
  They looke like Rose-buds fill'd with snow.
           (Davis 1987:174)

However, this "enclosing" is rather more sexually charged, grounded as it is in cold continence and concupiscent heat, although it is not race but class that stokes the fire. When Campion moves to guard the ripening "cherry," he does so in a sanctuary that is as much exalted desire ("where none may buy") as it is commerce and intercourse in plainsong ("cherry ripe! themselves doe cry"). Walter Davis has rightly called attention to the fact that the music beneath the words "Cherry ripe" comes from a London street seller's cry. "With its earthy commercialism," the sexual urge undercuts "the high Petrarchan style of the rest of the song" according to which

A heav'nly paradice is that place,
Wherein all pleasant fruits doe flow.
  Till "Cherry ripe!" themselves doe cry. (Davis 1987:174)

Yet another dimension of the Fair Maid is introduced in David Farley-Hills's judgment of Ophelia who, so we are now told, "appears out of an insufficient past." All the same, what we do come upon is "a 'real' and sympathetic girl whose love is mysteriously sacrificed to unknown gods. The dramatic effectiveness of Shakespeare's method is nowhere more vividly illustrated than in the scene where the rejected girl sings in her madness of a sexual fulfilment that has been denied her forever" (1990:31). The Ophelia role is complexly re-figured in *Othello* when, on the night of her death at the hand of her husband, Desdemona finds herself haunted by the memory of *her* mother's maid, Barbary. When this maid's love proved false, "She had a song of 'Willow,'" Desdemona recalls: "An old thing 'twas, but it expressed her fortune, / And she died singing it" (IV.iii.28-30). Not surprisingly, it is this punishing return of the repressed that Emi Hamana emphasizes in her "feminist re-vision" of Ophelia in "Let Women's Voices Be Heard" (1988:23). In the process, she invokes Peter Erickson's "Rewriting the Renaissance, Rewriting Ourselves" (1987) and its attempt at a rapprochement between "feminism" and "new historicism"; so, too, Kathleen McCluskie's approach to *King Lear* and *Measure for Measure* in "The Patriarchal Bard, Feminist Criticism and Shakespeare" (1985), and Claire McEachern's "Fathering Herself: A Source Study of Shakespeare's Feminism" (1988). Crucial to the oppositional reading that Hamana works through is the proposition that flashes of female revolts do occur in Shakespeare, only to be finally held in check. As I have indicated above, the implications are clear enough in the terseness with which, in *Othello*, Emilia makes the point that men are all stomach; that they "eat us hungrily and when they are full / they belch us" (III.iv.101-103). But then, men had better be wary. Given the villainy that they teach, "Let husbands know / Their wives have sense like them," Emilia points out; "they see, and smell,/ And have palates both for sweet and sour / As husbands have. What is that they do / When they change us for others?" That being the case, "have not we affections / Desires for sport, and frailty, as men have? / Then let them know, / The ills we do, their ills instruct us so" (IV.iii.93-103). In Hamana's impatient reading of what all this implies in *Hamlet* and for Ophelia, "*Shakespeare is thus fundamentally a patriarchal playwright*"; "Let Women's Voices Be Heard" is prepared to be emphatic about what this arrangement of things allows for: it "*does not prevent contemporary feminist readings of him because his texts still contain possibilities for subverting patriarchy*" (1988:23). There is a certain Logic of the Same elsewhere, in the Elsinore of *Highlife for Caliban*, for example; and it accounts for the frisson of delight, and for the horror of consubstantion, too, that undo Ophelia when

> A cylinder of mud rots
> in the space between ophelia's thighs
>   and rotten rots
> the place where the prince of denmark
> thought to lay his head. (Johnson 1995:65)

Ophelia is here the "beautified" Fair Maid of the West who comes to her "muddy end" because "God deprived her of wisdom"; because, so we now read, "when God walked on water" he did not do so "wearing the petticoats of crazy spinsters" (*ibid.*). Meanwhile, back in *Hamlet*, "Affection! pooh! ...Tender yourself more dearly; Or.../ You'll tender me a fool," Shakespeare's Polonius had cautioned his daughter. However, as things turn out when Hamlet's "sweet bells [are] jangled out of tune and harsh" (III.i.166),

Polonius fears needlessly. After all, Ophelia will find consummation only in the grotesque epithalamium that Gertrude makes of her garland of flowers and waterlogged garment. But then, this is all as it should be. For the girl had been representatively victimized by the extravagance of female devotion which— from *Othello*—Emilia once underscored when she referred Desdemona to "a lady" who would have walked "barefoot to Palestine" for the "taste" of Ludovico's "nether lip." And all this takes place in a patriarchal dispensation in which, it bears remembering, even an Ophelia can suspect enough to ask Laertes not to be as some "ungracious" pastors are who point out "the steep and thorny way to heaven, / Whiles [like] a puff'd and reckless libertine," they themselves "tread the primrose path of dalliance" (*Hamlet* III.i.47-50).

Meanwhile, the points of departure into such *querelle-de-femmes* matters in Sheila Cavanaugh's *Wanton Eyes and Chaste Desires* (1990) and in Mary Ellen Lamb's sexualization of the act of writing in *Gender and Authorship in the Sidney Circle* (1990) are equally relevant. "'How will you have your discourse' said she, 'without you let my lips alone?'" With these opening words, *Gender and Authorship* explains, "Philocea protests the prevention of her narrative by the kisses of her beloved prince Pyrocles in Sir Philip Sidney's *The Countess of Pembrokes's Arcadia*." Lamb thus introduces her perspective in strategic fashion, with a focus on a "project of containment" that is masked, she explains, by a "strategy of sexualization" (1990:3). Cavanaugh begins with a no less strategic counterpoint. For *Wanton Eyes and Chaste Desires*, "Lo I the man" is a crucial and resonant opening move in Spenser's *The Faerie Queene*. In Cavanaugh's judgment, "The gendered foundation of [*The Faerie Queene*'s] opening conventions" emphasizes a set of relationships in which, among other consequences, "anatomy is clearly destiny; gender is repeatedly more than deeds." Predictably, "female sexu- ality remains intertwined with images of danger, actual or potential" (1994:1); in figure and in sum, it is "often encrusted with myth and symbolism, restrained within close quarters, and made available for (k)nightly edifica- tion" (34).

Shakespeare is of course capaciously anchored in latitudes that are quite other than the thresholds of in/tolerance that the Fair Maid and Cleopatra, with her "infinite variety," complicate in the ways that I have outlined above. Related and yet differently oriented explorations of terrains and types account for the way in which the Benedick of *Much Ado About Nothing* maps the thought that Beatrice had indeed turned "harpy" when she misused him "past the endurance of a block." For which reason, he declares, rather than endure another encounter with her, "I will go on the slightest errand to the Antipodes. I will fetch you a toothpicker now from the furthest inch of Asia, bring you the length of Prester John [King of Ethiopia]'s foot, fetch you a hair off the great Cham [Khan]'s beard, [or] do embassage to the

Pygmies" (II.i.271-80). That being the case, and given the "pendent world" and the "round earth's imagined corners" that the English playwright populates with versions of Ethiope and Turk, and of Irish, Moor and Jew, whenever I am confronted with too bounded a Shakespeare, I find myself very much inclined to orient matters even more contentiously than *Cymbeline* does with its "Hath Britain all the sun that shines? Day, night / Are they not but in Britain? . . . There's livers out of Britain" (III.iv.136-141).

Of course, there are aspects of this reach for latitude that bear being kept in mind, and Mudimbe's *The Invention of Africa* suggests as much when it makes the point that "we are not only dealing with a potential imaginary museum but with concrete constraints produced by two major orders: a topographic dimension which explains how and why discourses on the Same and the Other are expounded, and a cultural order which, in the disorder of what today seems to be a common humanity, indicates clear divisions, subtle frontiers, and sometimes the so-called openings to one-ness" (1988:22). In fact, Shakespeare is himself especially teasing in *Antony and Cleopatra* when Antony conjures up that response of his to Lepidus's question, "What manner o' thing is your crocodile?" What is neatly instructive in the reply, *a la* Mudimbe, is the calculated dis/play with which sign fails to signify; with which apparent substance collapses into a simulacrum of itself:

> [It] is shaped, sir, like itself; and it is as broad as it hath breadth;
> it is just so high as it is, and moves with its own organs; it lives
> by that which nourisheth it; and the elements once out of it, it
> transmigrates. (II.vii.46-51)

Shakespeare adds import to latitude in other such ways, as happens to be the case when a spirited appreciation of the Dauphin's horse in *Henry V* produces the observation that "He's the colour of nutmeg" and "of the heat of the ginger" (III.vii.16-18). Consider, too, in *As You Like It,* the ease with which Rosalind moves from "palm-tree" to "Pythagoras' time"; with which she invokes "berrhymed Irish rat" (that is, the belief that Irish witches could destroy rats with rimes); and the span of great curiosity that she measures with the expression: "One inch of delay more is a South-sea of discovery" (III.i. 207). In Act 3, Scene 3 there is also the map of difference with which she mocks that "giant rude invention" of a love letter, for it is a document in which she recognizes the "Ethiope words" of a "boisterous, cruel style"—a "style for challengers": "like Turk to Christian" (31-35).

It was perhaps inevitable, given Shakespeare, that this reach for latitude would soon encompass that dark commerce in which *Macbeth*'s witches, no less, concoct their multi-species and multicultural brew out of "the ports" and "all the quarters [in] th'shipman's card." The English playwright's fair-is-foul and foul-is-fair Scotland is thereafter not only measured by "scale of dragon, tooth of wolf, / [and] Witches mummy," and by the social rupture that is implicit in the "finger of [a] birth-strangled babe / Ditch-delivered by a drab." The world is also landmarked, so to speak, by "liver of blaspheming Jew," and by "Nose of Turk, and Tartar's lips" (IV.i.22-29). There is, elsewhere, the "potential imaginary museum"—as fond-foolish as it is cold invention—that we get in *The Tempest*, especially in Prospero's way with the "great globe itself" and "such stuff as dreams are made on." Here, and with an openly manipulative Prospero on top and invisibly deploying strange shapes and salutations, Sebastian is ready to be persuaded that "there are unicorns"; that "in Arabia / There is one tree, the phoenix' throne, one phoenix / At this hour reigning there." Here, too, spellbound Antonio declares that "travellers ne'er did lie / Though fools at home condemn 'em" (III.iii.20-26). But then, with Shakespeare we ride on the ironies of a "never-surfeited sea": "When we were boys," Gonzalo rightly asks, "Who would believe that there were mountaineers, / Dew-lapp'd, like bulls, whose throats had hanging at 'em / Wallets of flesh?" Or else, that "there were such men / Whose heads stood in their breasts?" (III.iii.43-47).

My point of departure then: in the degree that the early modern period presumes upon forms of the Ethiope, the Turk, and the Jew—and of Christian man and berrhymed Irish rat—I find myself quickly impressed by how unmanageable Brabantio-like notions of boundaries and proprietorship ought really to be, with their "O thou foul thief. . . I'll have it disputed on" (*Othello* I.ii.61-75). For which reason, I borrow terrain and type from Steven Mullaney's *The Place of the Stage* (1988) to tease at the implications of the fact that when Brabantio is opposed to kinship with "bondslaves and pagans," he exalts coherence by exclusion in an *Othello* in which the Ottomite is already at the gates of Venice; in which the city-state, whose boundaries extend into Cyprus, is beholden to an "extravagant and wheeling stranger / Of here and everywhere"—and with thick lips. My interest in Mullaney lies in the symbolic topology that he makes of the Renaissance City and its Liberties (that is, the "domain traditionally reserved for cultural phenomena that could not be contained within the strict or proper bondaries of the community"). Within the walls, granted, the city's "ideals and aspirations of commmunity were staged in an extensive repertory of rituals, ceremonies, and cultural performances." However, so Mullaney explains, "the inscription of ideological values on civic space, the ritual creation of the social topology, did not halt at the boundary of the city walls." The margins were also the staging ground for "incontinent hopes, fears, and desires" (viii). We thus arrive, this time by way of Edward Tetsuya Motohashi's summation of "The Surburbs of Your Good Pleasure," to a re-cognition of the separation and of the convergence of "official authorities" and "popular communities"; to an awareness that the two were not only "complementary" but that they were also "prone to a reversal" (1988:46).

Granting their imminent translation into domestic tragedy, foreign relations in *Othello* therefore reach across boundaries in such signal ways, especially when they invite us to consider the "importancy of Cyprus to the Turk / And [to] let ourselves again but understand" (I.ii.20-21) the imperial need to sustain Venice's colonial expansion into Cyprus (historically, from 1451 to her expulsion by the Turks in 1571). For the state, there is a *realpolitik* issue here, and it is one which requires that, Desdemona'd or not, the Moor be commissioned to act upon the knowledge that the "Turk with a most mighty preparation makes for Cyprus" (I.iii.221). There is, too, the anxious arithmetic with which the State Council measures and calculates, caught up as it is in "warlike brace." We learn that there is a major but, so it seems, diversionary fleet headed for Rhodes: about this force, "My letters say a hundred and seven galleys"; "And mine a hundred forty"; "And mine two hundred." There are questions that relate to the appearance of an "after fleet": "How many, as you guess?"; and here, the response is that there are "thirty sails" and that "now they do restem / Their backward course, bearing with frank appearance / Their purposes toward Cyprus" (I.iii.1-39). Now, there really could be no place in all this dead reckoning for some "mangled matter" about a "fair lady" and a "sooty bosom"; about "rules of nature" and suitors that should have come from among "the wealthy curled darlings of our nation"—matters that so preoccupy Desdemona's father. Of course, he does fail to get a hearing for them; besides which the urgency of the *state's* foreign relations quickly makes his son-in-law "more fair than black." It is at this point that Brabantio falls a dramatic distance into the "liberties" of Venice, so to speak—given the hysteria of great expectations ("My daughter! O, my daughter!") with which he first responds to the Duke's apparently solicitous "Why, what's the matter?" Consider in Act 2, Scene 3 the degrees of visibility that the Ottomite threat confers on the Venetian magnifico and the foreign general, even when the Turkish fleet appears to be steering away, "with due course toward the isle of Rhodes":

> *Enter Brabantio, Othello, Cassio, Iago, Roderigo, and Officers*
> Duke: Valiant Othello, we must straight employ you
>   Against the general enemy Ottoman.
>   *(To Brabantio) I did not see you.* Welcome, gentle signior
>   (My emphasis)

When Brabantio insists as he does on an exaltation of borders, it is as though, turned amnesiac, a Europe-Shakespeare-Venice so capacious in fancy, so vested in details near at hand, but so presumptuous in its appetite for the extramural, should somehow escape being re-configured according to the incontinence of its own occupation of Cyprus; its "discourses on western planting"; its "declarations of the Indies"; its "true reports of the late discoveries" of foreign clime and folk! Besides which, nationalist amplitude and pride very much mattered; and they accounted as much for Venice's deployment of its mercenary Moor as for the encomium with which the Michael Drayton (1563-1631) of "Voyage to Virginia" (1606) once exhorted England's "brave heroic minds / Worthy your country's name" to "Go and subdue!"; and to "be frolic" with "fowl, venison, and fish [and] useful sassafras." Here, triumphant nationalism and studied topicality blend in a poetry in which only "loit'ring *hinds* / lurk . . . at home, with shame" while overseas there were "the pearl and *gold*," and "Virginia, / Earth's only paradise," that were all ready to be "ours to hold" (*ibid.*; my emphasis). As did others of his compatriots, Drayton paid tribute to the foremost chronicler and enthusiast of Elizabethan England's principal voyages, Richard Haklyut (1552-1616):

> Thy voyages attend,
> Industrious Haklyut,
>> Whose reading shall enflame
>> Men to seek fame. (Hardin 1973:139)

Percy Adams (1983) underscores this "fame" and "enflaming" when he identifies a "Protestant Haklyut" for whom "travel was not only a pilgrimage to a religious shrine." It was also "a sermon read in the greatest of cathedrals—for travel taught the wonders of God's creation." The "Mappe," Haklyut was certain, did bring him to the Bible where, turning to Psalm 107, verses 21-24, he could read that "they which go downe to the sea in ships, and occupy by the great waters . . . see the works of the Lord, and his woonders in the deepe."

> But even this pious motive for traveling became thoroughly sublimated as other motives expanded and absorbed not only Haklyut but all the merchants, warriors, diplomats, adventurers, and explorers whose accounts he published. (Adams 1983:185)

Still, as Michael Foss puts the matter under the Shakespeare-inspired title, *Undreamed Shores: England's Wasted Empire in America*, "Poetry guided the spirit of discovery as strongly as the compass" (1974:11). There were, in addition, the pedigree and the sanction for such matters that God and the Classics provided. For like the prophet Isaiah it was known that Seneca had once spoken of a time when "Ocean will undo the chains of things, and the great world will be revealed, and a new mariner, like Jason's pilot Tethys, will discover a new world so that Thule will not be the farthest land" (Foss *ibid.*).

It is often the case, then, that in Shakespeare "affections" of record are shown to be ever so anchored, and suspectible, to value invested in "hopes abroad." Quite so; for there are always "those [who] like merchants venture trade abroad," as Canterbury puts it in *Henry V* (I.ii.192). I make the point, for all that a King Henry VI may insist that "My crown is in my heart, not on my head / Not decked with diamonds and Indian stones" (**III**—III.i.62-63). Still, and as is suggested when *Measure for Measure* encompasses the globe, it is no casual thing to be in "thrilling region of thick-ribbed ice" or to be "blown with restless violence round about / The pendent world" (III.i.123-125), what with wind-blown commerce and, as Shylock claims to know, swarming varieties of predatory land rats and piratical water rats. "Ships are but board, sailors but men; there be land rats and water rats, water thieves and land thieves—I mean pirates—and then there is peril of waters, winds, and rocks." (I.iii.21-25)

There are other constellations of terrain and type in Shakespeare's early modern period in which a nationalist geo-politics (with England unnegotiably on top) resonates, for all that one grants the *caveat* that E. A. J. Honigman *et al.* raise about the degree to which "increasing unease" with the period's political culture—as in *Richard III*—compromises that representation by Tillyard of the Elizabethan "world picture" (1986:x), according to which the "Elizabethans pictured the universal order under three main forms: a chain, a series of corresponding planes and a dance" (Tillyard 1943:23). In this regard, a Michael Drayton's celebration of "Virginia"—with its "Go, and subdue"—and a Walter Ralegh's "discoverie" of and readiness to open up the "madenheade" of Guiana all matter as indices of the now eurocentric, now expansionist enterprise that interests me here. Nationalist "extra-territoriality" is no less defining a consideration in Shakespeare, for all that one grants satirical digs which, as in *The Tempest*, work to blur the line between monster and Englishman. It is here that we learn about England that "Any strange beast there makes a man." The same is true of the composite mockery that *The Merchant of Venice*'s Portia makes of the young English baron and suitor at Belmont. In her estimation, what England has produced in Falconbridge "hath neither Latin, French, nor Italian." For all that he is a "proper man's picture," he remains no more than a "dumbshow; and, alas, who can converse with him?" Besides which, "How oddly he is suited! I think he bought his doublet in Italy, his round hose in France, his bonnet in Germany, and his behavior everywhere" (I.ii.67-75). Now, one grants this slip-sliding judgment of European terrain and type; so, too, the apparently comic geography of body parts that we get in *The Comedy of Errors* (III.ii.95-146).

There are, all the same, the reach for latitude and the celebration of import that provoke Tillyard's "world picture," and which, elsewhere, result in the tidy summation that we get in Wilbur Abbott's view that what "the court of

Lorenzo de Medici had been to letters, what the court of Ferdinand and Isabella had been to war and adventure a hundred years before, the court of Elizabeth now became to both letters and adventure." In short, with the "defeat of the Armada, after so many years of travail England . . . stood forth triumphant and rejoicing in her strength." And so, strong in the prestige that the Spanish overthrow meant, "enriched by the trade and plunder of the oceanic world, inspired by the new learning of the Renaissance and the spirit of the Reformation, skilled alike to wield the sword and the pen, the brilliant circle" that England then ranged about, its "English queen touched the high level of courtly achievement in action and intellect alike" (I. 1918:342). In effect, the triumphalist geo-politics that is discoverable in the likes of Ralegh, Shakespeare, and Drayton is not unusual; and Francis Bacon (1561-1626), for his part, was being arch but transparent enough when his "Of the True Greatness of Kingdoms and Estates" proposed that "the kingdom of heaven is compared, not to any great kernel or nut, but to a grain of mustard-seed; which is one of the least grains, but hath in it a property and spirit hastily to get up and spread. So are there states great in territory, and yet not apt to enlarge or command; and some that have but a small dimension of stem, and yet apt to be the foundations of great monarchies." Bacon thus spoke about matters which "hath been no where better seen, than by comparing of England and France; whereof England, though far less in territory and population, hath been, nevertheless, an overmatch" (1826:314). In the complex of relationships that all this entails, "Kings have to deal with their neighbours; their wives; their children; their prelates; their nobles; their second nobles or gentlemen; their merchants; their commons; and their men of war," Bacon wrote; and from "all these arise dangers"—especially so, "if care and circumspection be not used" (*ibid.* 288). Elsewhere in Bacon's *Essayes*, "On Empire" had therefore begun on a finely tuned and aphoristic note: "It is a miserable state of mind to have few things to desire, and many things to fear" (288; 285). And it soon enough works its way to the *realpolitik* argument for *Lebensraum*, for strategic territoriality:

> There can be no general rule given . . . save one, which is that princes do keep due sentiment, that none of their neighbours do overgrow so, by increase of territory, by embracing of trade, by approaches, or the like, as they become more able to annoy them, than they were. . . . And the like was done by that league (which Guicciardini saith was the security of Italy) made between Ferdinando of Naples, Lorenzius Medici, and Ludovicus Sforza, potentates, the one of Florence, the other of Milan. (288)

In this respect, the early-modern urge to acquire "marvelous possessions" (Greenblatt 1991)—to map terrain where Ralegh's "sledges" could dig into

Guiana's "madenheade" and Drayton commerce with "Fowl, venison, and fish . . . and useful sassafras"—this urge had been pursued in word and deed that anticipated the more familiar recrudescence of expansionism in the nineteenth century. For example, the "mere motion" of a set of letters patent that Elizabeth I signed in 1584 had been a signal moment in the charter myth of "discoverie" and "planting." "Know ye all that of our especial grace, certain science and mere motion," the Queen's document had proclaimed, "we have given and granted to our trusty and well-beloved servant, Walter Ralegh Esquire, free liberty and license from time to time to discover, search, find out and view such remote, heathen and barbarous lands, countries and territories not actually possessed by any Christian prince nor inhabited by Christian people; the same to have, hold, occupy and enjoy to him, his heirs and assigns forever" (Nicholl 1995:25). It was in standard conquistadorial cum latter-day colonial governor-general guise, then, that Ralegh spoke, through an interpreter, to a native Trinidad of the sixteenth century:

> I made them understand that I was the servant of a Queen, who was the great *cacique* of the north, and a virgin, and had more *cacique* under her than there were trees in their island; that she was an enemy of the *Castellani* in respect of their tyranny and oppression, and that she delivered all such nations about her as were by them oppressed; and having freed all the coast of the northern world from their servitude, had sent me to free them also, and withal to defend the country of Guiana from their invasion and conquest. (Nicholl 99)

Of course, Elizabeth's own gesture replicated—and countered—the nationalist privilege with which the Spaniards Ferdinand and Isabella had earlier launched Christopher Columbus toward the Indies. But then, the glory that that enterprise produced, and the armada that it launched, had been wrecked off the coast of Elizabeth's England in 1588. Duly celebrated in poem and engraving, "*differo*" and "*dissipo*" ("I scatter abroad"; "I overwhelm") were quite the words, indeed, with which to top the memorialization of the event when George Carleton engraved his 1624 *Thankful Remembrance [of] Church and State in the reigns of Elizabeth and James I* (Brooke and Cunliffe 1935:12). Quite so; for by 1595 commerce and calculation had already brought Ralegh to that argument of his that the "large, rich, and bewtiful Empyre of Guiana" (meaning, incidentally, territory that is mostly modern Venezuela) needed to be penetrated and taken. The place "hath yet her Madenheade," he wrote, in making the case to his Virgin Queen. She, Guiana, that is, had never been "sackt, turned, nor wrought, nor the vertue and salt of the soyle spent by manurance, the graues haue not been opened for gold, the mines not broken with sledges" (Ralegh 1968:96). It very much mattered, of course, that Guiana's "madenheade" was thought to be much too adjacent to El Dorado, that chimera of the Americas which so haunted Spain's gold-driven and cross-sanctioned conquistadors. In effect, given England's major rivalry with Spain, to the sensual urgency of Ralegh's new economics was added a reasons-of-state and balance-of-power issue. We get more of this triumphalist orientation when, in the Drayton of "The Ballad of Agincourt" (1619), "fair stood the wind for France" on Saint Crispin's Day. It was a time when "English men / with such acts [filled] the pen":

> Warwick in blood did wade
> Oxford the foe invade
> And cruel slaughter made
>   Still as they ran up;
> Suffolk his ax did ply,
> Beaumont and Willoughby
> Bare them right doughtily,
>   Ferrers and Fanhope. (Hardin 1973:145)

When such matters are engaged through what Margaret Webster (1975) calls the "studied topicality" of Shakespeare's plays, it becomes even more clear why and how the urge "to enlarge" rises to play itself out as manifest destiny. This is the case, famously, in *Henry V*'s flourishes against France when, what with Agincourt and Saint Crispin's Day (October 25, 1415), "all the youth of England are on fire" and charged with that "Cry [of] 'God for Harry, England, and Saint George!'" (II.i.33-34).

Shakespeare thus contributes in signal ways to the insular as well as the expansionist politics of *Lebensraum*, notwithstanding his invocation, as in *The Tempest*, of a concommitant, and subversive, geography of "baseless fabric," "thin air," and "insubstantial pageant." Despite certain incongruities, then—such as, famously, the impossibly free navigation that *The Winter's Tale* assumes between Sicily and the deserts of Bohemia, or the "fancies" that account for Prospero's, or Othello's, way of mapping the "great globe itself," Shakespeare and his Renaissance were not unresponsive to an imperative of the age: "to add amplitude and to sow greatness to [its] posterity and succession" (Bacon). The *Lebensraum* advantage of holding one's own is elsewhere echoed in the materialist level-headedness with which *Richard II* refers to an "England so wont to conquer others" (II.i.56). The concommitant England-on-top theme is more celebrated, of course, in *Henry V* and at Agincourt. However, and as it will matter here, the extra-territoriality of consequence is nowhere more resonant than in the final *flourish* and *exeunt* that we get in *King John*. For it is here that Philip the Bastard, illegitimate son of King Richard (Coeur-de-leon) and later knighted as Sir Richard Plantagenet, brings the play to a close with the nationalist satisfaction and challenge of the lines: "This England never did, and never shall / Lie at the proud foot of a conqueror. . . . / Come the three corners of the world in arms, / And we shall shock them" (V.vii.115-17). That being the case, and notwithstanding the Elizabethan playwright's invocations of Nilus's mud and mythic gardens, of rivers of gold and Ethiope-places, he does resonate, too, with "This England's" *realpolitik* investments in virgin lands and other forms of undreamed shores. In effect, the threat of "merchant-marring rocks" notwithstanding, it is rarely the case in the plays that a "brave vessel, / Who had, no doubt, some noble creature in her, [is ever] Dash'd all to pieces" (*Tempest* I.i.6-8) in ways that wholly efface the political thrust, the cultural anthroplogy, and the economics in Shakespeare's Elizabethan mode of circulation abroad.

There were, besides, those other contemporaries of Shakespeare's and their pursuit of "discoverie" and "plantation." For it was in one such that that Elizabethan sea-dog *par excellence* Sir Francis Drake (he of the decisive defeat of Spain's Armada of 1588) would die of fever and dysentery off the coast of Panama in 1596. A year earlier, Ralegh had brought fancy and cold calculation to bear on the "madenheade" of Guiana and had thus provided occasion for the apparently satirical reference which Shakespeare makes to the enterprise in *The Merry Wives of Windsor*—protege that the dramatist was of Ralegh's rival at Court, the Earl of Southampton (Sanders 1992:252). 1595 was also the year in which Sir John Hawkins had died off the coast of Puerto Rico after slave-trading raids and other peregrinations that had taken in Sierra Leone: "He visited Sierra Leone three times in the 1560s—visits made notorious by his kidnapping and enslaving the inhabitants to sell them in the West Indies" (Fyfe 1964:34). In Sylvia Wynter's reading, Hawkins is nothing if not representative "thief, merchant, mariner"—especially when she situates his type in the context of "The Poetics and the Politics of a High Life for Caliban":

> He sailed to Africa in a seaworthy ship; and got black slaves partly by the sword, partly by trade; he sailed [then] to that other point of the triangle, islands and a continent gotten by storm, with his prey; and there threatened to cut the throat of the Spanish colonists if they did not trade. To traffic in men would call down God's vengeance, Queen Elizabeth had first said. But she profitted largely; knighted bold enterprises right and left. (Wynter 1995:86)

It is clearly the case that such imperial rites of passage, of Renaissance "frolic" (Drayton) in colonial expansion, justified the template that James Anthony Froude's *The English in the West Indies, or, The Bow of Ulysses* (1888) would make of the Elizabethan world picture. Froude's epic remembrance of things past harks back to an age when, far from being "casual seedlings," the West Indies had been regarded as "precious jewels" and the Caribbean Sea as "the cradle of the Naval Empire of Great Britain."

> [On that Sea] Drake and Hawkins intercepted the golden stream which flowed from Panama into the Exchequer at Madrid. . . . In those waters the men were formed and trained who drove the Armada through the Channel into wreck and ruin. . . . If ever the naval exploits of [England] are done into an epic poem—and since the *Iliad* there has been no subject better deserving it—the West Indies will be the scene of the most brilliant cantos. For England to allow them to drift away from her because they have no immediate marketable value, would be a sign that she had lost the feelings with which great nations always treasure the heroic traditions of their fathers. (Froude 10)

The reverberations of this "tradition" explain the extra-territorial enthusiasm with which, in the latter days of 1947, G. Wilson Knight would celebrate *The Tempest* as "a myth of the national soul." Knight would transform Prospero into a "Philosopher-King" who, *avant la lettre*, had been engaged in a triumphalist affirmation of *Rule Britannia*, the aim of which was no more and no less than a civilizing mission that would "raise savage peoples from superstition and blood-sacrifice, taboos and witchcraft and the attendant fears and slaveries, to a more enlightened existence" (Cartelli 1987:108). For his part, the Joseph Conrad of *Heart of Darkness* would limn the River Thames to relevant effect. "It had known and served," he wrote as a prologue for Marlow's descent into the Congo, "all the men of whom the nation is proud, from Sir Francis Drake to Sir John Franklin, knights all, titled and untitled—the great knights-errant of the sea. It had borne all the ships whose names are like jewels flashing in the night of time, from the *Golden Hind* returning with her round flanks full of treasure, to be visited by the Queen's Highness and thus pass out of the gigantic tale, to the *Erebus* and *Terror*, bound on other conquests—and that never returned" (1963:4).

Given the recurrent details of this gigantic tale in Shakespeare, it was inevitable that imperialist or colonial interests would be duly exported from, or imported into, the patriotic enthusiasms of *Henry V* and the "mighty preparation" that the Ottoman compel in *Othello*. The same is true of the circulation and vexations of race, money, and power in *The Merchant of Venice*; of the discovery of the "native" who had "lately suffered by a thunderbolt" in *The Tempest*; so, too, the political and military dispensations that seek to define the world(s) of *Antony and Cleopatra*. It is not unreasonable, then, to propose that the plays engage in moves that are as expansionist and insular in their cast as they can be suggestively anti-colonial. After all, the

Elizabethan playwright does move about so: sometimes the plays do so with, ironically, the intensity of arrested motion through which we learn in *King John* that the "tackle of my heart is cracked and burn'd, / And all the shrouds wherewith my life should sail / Are turned to one thread, one little hair" (V.vii.52-54). Elsewhere, *Pericles* will cut "long leagues short, / Sail seas in cockles," and thus "take imagination / From bourne to bourne, region to region" (Sc.18.1-4). In *Henry IV*, Part II, theological import and geographic distance neutralize each other in the benign irony with which the King anticipates, indeed reaches for, death. "Doth any particular name belong to the room where I first did swoon?" the King asks *in extremis*. The response that he gets, "'Tis called Jerusalem, my noble Lord," makes for Christian relevation and punning discovery, a convergence that the King duly appreciates with "Laud to God!" For it had been prophesied that he would die "but in Jerusalem; / Which vainly [he] supposed the Holy Land." His journey is thereafter a foreshortened pilgrim's progress in which he asks to be borne to "that chamber"—for in "that Jerusalem shall Harry die" (IV.v.232-243). There is, meanwhile, that rather more salacious geography in *The Merry Wives of Windsor* where, with his "greedy intention" and "appetite of desire"—they "scorch [him] up like a burning glass"—Falstaff maps out the promise of the New World in Mistress Page and Mistress Ford. "She is a region in Guiana, all gold and bounty," he declares about Page's wife who, so he believes, had given him "good eyes," just as the latter had offered him a "leer of invitation." Aroused by their "course o'er [his] exteriors" and by other "most judicious oeillades" that "gilded [his] foot" and "sometimes [his] portly belly," Falstaff decides that he can and will be "cheaters" to the two women. For which reason, "They shall be exchequers to me, they shall be my East and West Indies, and I will trade them to them both" (I.iii.61-64). Elsewhere, and with his "I go, I go, look how I go / Swifter than arrow from a Tartar's bow" the Puck of *A Midsummer Night's Dream* (III.ii.100-101) can, like Ariel in *The Tempest*, "put a girdle about the earth in forty minutes." Quite so. After all, *Totus mundus agit histrionem*—all the world's a stage (*As You Like It* II.vii.139)—proclaimed the motto over the Globe Theatre where Shakespeare played out such matters and their suppositions. Thus, in a work like *The Merchant of Venice*, lovers and money lenders, no less than ship owners and quick-thinking lawyers, know the extra-territorial to be a matter of consequence. For often, like "manna" dropped "in the way / of starved people," sea lanes and latitudes beyond Europe lent themselves, even if precariously, to "better news in store" in a world of "gold and silver"; of "usances" and "bondman's key." Not surprisingly, there is the comedy of restoration that a Portia can make of investments abroad when she has the apparently bankrupt Antonio unseal a letter which contains the news that "three of [his] argosies had richly come to harbor suddenly" (V.i.275-277).

The political economy of desire in such a play as *The Merchant of Venice* is in fact rather more realistically anchored. For its principals quite appreciate the anxiety involved in "plucking grass to know where sits the wind, / Peering in maps," as they do and must, "for ports and piers and roads" (I.i.18-20). It is in this dispensation of things that Salerio recalls his having "reason'd with a Frenchman yesterday, who told me," he says, that in the "narrow seas that part / The French and English, there miscarried / A vessel of our country richly fraught" (II.viii.27-30). There is a global dimension, too, to this sea-borne economy, and it is one that can haunt Antonio ("Thou know'st that all my fortunes are at sea") and worry Bassanio, citizens as they are of the trading state that Venice was. "What, not one hit?" Bassanio asks in anxious disbelief about the state of Antonio's investments overseas. "Hath all his ventures fail'd?. . . / From Tripolis, from Mexico and England, / From Lisbon, Barbary and India?" It is all enough to generate "a few of the unpleasant'st words / That ever blotted paper!"—and thus to push Shylock toward his impossible brand of revenge when the merchant of Venice's "means are in supposition" and his "argosy" bound up in "ventures...abroad." Still, we are in world in which such ventures can make a man "sufficient" for three thousand ducats, and a bond (I.iii.15-26). Contract and "forfeiture," so it seems, can hold; for "the commodity that strangers have / With us in Venice, if it be denied, / Will much impeach the justice of the state, / Since that the trade and the proifit of the city / Consisteth of all nations" (III.iii.25-31). All in all, *The Merchant of Venice* calculates and worries with good reason: the poetry of the moon-lit garden of Belmont, the scales of exchange at the Rialto, and the public places and magnificos of Venice very much depend on argosies that are bound to the narrow sea of the English Channel; so, too, to the wider ones that lead to North Africa and to the New World of "the Indies" (II.ii.270-273).

In Act 3, Scene 2 of *The Comedy of Errors*, and thus somewhat closer to home, Shakespeare's Antipholus of Syracuse had asked, "Where . . . the Netherlands?" To this inquiry, Dromio's famously clever and topical reply was, "Oh, sir, I did not look so low." Shakespeare's England did in fact look into the Dutch "golden age" with deep interest, of course. Ralegh, for one, did turn his attention to such matters; and, in doing so for James I, produced those "Observations" of his "touching trade and commerce with the Hollander, and other nations, wherein is proved, that our sea and land commodities serve to inrich and strengthen other countries against our owne." The assessment of where the Netherlands stood in relation to English interests led to a studied preoccupation with "the causes of the magnificency and opulency of cities," and with the "safety for defence of the people and their good." Equally defining were the "series of miniature engagements" that pitted the Dutch against the English in Africa, the East Indies, and the Caribbean. These were engagements that served as prelude to the major confrontation of 1665, and which would attract the attention of the likes of John Dryden in England (Schama 1988:233). In the war of commonwealths and plunder of fleet that all this involved (Schama 1988:235), the Age of Dryden found occasion to contribute a brand of poetry in which, as James Fenton puts it, "everything [would be] at the disposal of the imperial purpose: teacups, chronology, spices, mythology" (1996:60). That being the case, imperialist poetry was never more apologetic about its intentions than in, say, the argument for and account of the Battle of Lowestoft that Dryden published in his *Annus Mirabilis*. Here, porcelain shatter, odors fly, "and some by Aromatic splinters die" when "amidst whole heaps of Spices light a Ball"; here, too, Dryden complained that in "thriving Arts long time had Holland grown, / Crouching at home, and cruel when abroad; / Scarce leaving us the means to claim our own." We learn here that there was hindrance of this sort because, among other things, the Dutch "aw'd" what Dryden refers to as "our merchants." But then, the Dutch themselves found proof enough that England was nothing if not a "sea-scouring island" that was "constant only in its will to subjugate the Netherlands. . . / [For we are] the lead in its heart, the thorn in its foot" (Schama *ibid*. 235).

The commerce and social changes that came with the power to thus scatter abroad and to colonize made it possible for Europe's early modern period to both crown itself with Indian gem stones (as in *Henry VI*) and to "breathe Indianly" as well. Crucial to the latter was Europe's experience of tobacco in the northern hemisphere of the "still-vex'd Bermoothes." It was possible to "breathe indianly" in England because the augmentation of the Virgin Queen into Virginia did not result only in the poetry and warmth of Drayton's encomium. For Englishmen of means, it also opened up vistas to which tobacco's heat contributed, "without their having to leave the comforts of home" (Nicholl 1995:146). This augmentation of the Indies brought to the English and European elite and to their merchant classes the appeal of what Francis Beaumont (1584-1616) called the "indian sun." It also also attracted the interest of no less a figure than James I who railed against the noxious extravagance that he considered tobacco to be. The king's response was to produce a "counterblast"—to which a certain Dr. Edward Maynwaringe added information that tobacco was "a procuring cause of the scurvy," and Dr. George Thompson a "treatise of bloud" that warned against the habit of smoking.

In any case, it is in the context of values that were attached to this "indian sun" that Allison Blakely's *Blacks in the Dutch World* frames yet another representation of the Moor in early modern Europe: the *rookende*, or Smoking, Moor. Blakely does so in a study of racial imagery in the Netherlands and its provinces, be they in the New World of the Antilles or in the slave castles on the west coast of Africa. *Blacks in the Dutch World* and its orientation of the Moor merit citation here, if for no other reason than that there is virtually no reflection on the figure in the "embarrassment of riches" with which Simon Schama represents the "golden age" of Dutch culture. The assymmetry holds for all that Schama's "integration of tobacco into the 'home life' of the country" does take in the measure of long-stemmed clay pipes; Sephardic families like the Diases and Fonsecas who dominated the earliest phases of the processing industry; the West India Company's supplemental imports of the leaf from Brazil, Venezuela and Virginia/Maryland; and Dutch cigar exports even to the Turkish Levant. In this regard, the difference between Blakely's *Blacks* and Shama's *Embarrassment* is instructive, especially so where Schama illustrates instances of the belief that tobacco could "induce dangerously stupefied trances" (212). For he does so by way of the "sexually insulting jest" in a Jan Steen painting, *"Man Blowing Smoke at a Woman,"* and in Jan van de Vlier's *The Sense of Smell*, an etching which also shows a man blowing smoke in a woman's face. Shama also includes an engraving in the series *Groote Tafereel der Dwaasheid* (Shama 195-197; 206-207). It is an uncommented-upon detail, a *rookende Moor*, in the last illustration, that Blakely foregrounds when he calls attention to the tropological synthesis that tobacco and the black figure allowed Dutch culture to make:

> The Smoking Moor in the Netherlands, who had similar relatives all over Europe, was a fusion of history and fantasy which captured uniquely well the nebulous response in Europe to the exposure to new worlds and new sensations. With respect to the image of blacks it brought another example of the growing interchangeability of the terms "Negro" and "Moor," which persisted into the eighteenth century. At the same time, the odd figure of the Smoking Moor often showed mixtures of black African, American Indian, East Asian, and Middle Eastern physical traits. The indistinctness of this symbol for the tobacco trade suggests that the main prerequisite was that it be exotic, with little importance placed on accuracy or precision. It was enough that it seemed from another world. The Moor had long been the main symbol of trade contacts with the outside world. The black African could be associated with tobacco both because African slaves in the new world cultivated it and because African peoples were thought to be highly sensual. (Blakely 1993:58-59; also, Jones 1965; Devisse and Mollay 1979)

The injunction "Go and subdue!" did not only manifest itself in expansionist politics and commerce. Given the likes of smoking moors and of native islanders that "hath lately suffer'd by a thunderbolt" the Renaissance could not avoid contact with difference that was quite beyond the *alien-within* that the Jew represented. And this was so notwithstanding the kind of liberties that the Jew allowed Portia's cleverness, or Launcelot's low comedy when he decides to seek employment outside Shylock's home; "for I am a Jew if I serve the Jew any longer." The play harps on this degree of difference:

> I should stay with the Jew my master who (God bless the mark!) is a kind of devil; [but then] to run away from the Jew, I should be ruled by the fiend who, saving your grace, is the devil himself. Certainly the Jew is the very devil incarnation; and in my conscience, my conscience is but a hard conscience to offer to counsel me to stay with the Jew. (*Merchant of Venice* II.ii.23-30)

Elsewhere, the nature of Jewish alienation is enough to remind Solanio to say his prayers: "Let me say Amen, lest the devil cross my prayer, for here he comes in the likeness of the Jew" (III.i.19-20).

Still, the farther reaches of Renaissance "travells" and "plantations" did increase the sample of human stock in ways that intensified puzzlement, quite beyond Solanio's calculated mis-recognition of Tubal: "Here comes another of the tribe. A third cannot be matched, unless the devil himself turn Jew" (III.i.73-74). Much farther from the European home, there were places with "a very ancient and fish-like smell" (*Tempest*); so, too, "savage natives [who] adored their great devil Setebos" (Fraser *ibid.*). "What have we here? A man or fish? Dead or alive?"—one man of the age would ask in the dramatic turbulence of Shakespeare's play. Margaret Trabue Hodgen shades her survey of "early anthropology in the sixteenth and seventeenth centuries" (1964) to relevant effect when she makes the observation that it has often been said that the Renaissance discovered man; and that the perplexities associated with that discovery were profound, for all that the man who was brought center stage was, in fact, a "familiar fellow, a white European."

> When, at about the same time, the explorers threw the spotlight of publicity upon backward, darker-skinned, non-Europeans, when they brought home and told their stories of naked cannibals, there was something more involved than the enlargement of the European sample of the genus *Homo*. Here, or so it seemed, was a different kind of man. Or was he a man? There were those to say he was not. (1964:353)

Ronald Sanders's approach to the "origins of American racism" in *Lost Tribes and Promised Lands* suggests something of the complex re-cognition that contact of such magnitude entailed. For it provides us with a telling example of a heretofore unattached "dark notion" that needed to find a "local habitation and a name, and an unfortunate flesh with which to invest it" (1992:106). It may seem a truism, Sanders writes, that the Devil has now been black for many centuries; a truism, that is, "until we realize that Satan has no color in any of his appearance in the Old and New Testaments, except for Chapter 12 of the Revelation of John, where he appears as a serpent that is quite *red*" (*ibid.*). It was according to such dispensations of difference, then, that the discovery of "liberties" overseas helped to re-incarnate certain manichaean tendencies. In effect, and as Partha Mitter explains in his *Much Maligned Monsters* treatment of the issue, "classical monsters and gods, Biblical demons and Indian gods were all indiscriminately lumped together with congenital malformations under the all-embracing class of monsters" (1992:10). Richard Eden's contribution to the "principal navigations, voyages, traffiques and discoveries of the English nation" (1598-1600) could thus make observations about a people of "beastly living" without God, law, religion, or commonwealth, and who are so "scorched and vexed with the heat of the sun, that in many places they curse it when it riseth" (*ibid.* 214).

In "Montaigne's 'Of Cannibals': The Savage 'I'," Michel de Certeau offers a reading of the 1580 essay that is very preoccupied with such questions as "Who is a 'barbarian'? What is a 'savage'?" He provides a framework within which one may focus on that gradient along which, as "native islander," "hag-seed" and "moon calf," the likes of Caliban approach and fall away from the Rest. The thought rescues from low-comedy and mere carnival profit the import of Trinculo's cluster of questions: "What have we here? A man or a fish?" "Where the devil should he have learnt our language?" (II.ii.23-35). It adds nuances, too, to Prospero's conviction that Caliban was a "thing of darkness"; a vile race "which any print of goodness will not take"; and a "slave" who, "savage," could not know his own meaning, but wouldst gabble like / A thing most brutish" (I.ii.351-360). For here, or so it seemed, was a different kind of man. Or was he a man? Obviously, there were those to say he was not. De Certeau positions his Montaigne within the "status of the strange" and of the "circularity of the textual fabrication of identity." This is the context in which he writes suggestively about the relationship between *"representation of the other"* and "the fabrication and accreditation of *the text as witness of the other*" (120-121). De Certeau's terms of reference thus allow for a response to *Othello* that would focus on the ways in which the Moor of Venice encourages surplus identities of himself; in which he is complicit as a witness against himself. That being the case, whether by cold calculation or in grandiloquent self-advertisement, there is telling irony in the fact that Othello does bear witness against himself with that "traveller's history" of his life, in a Venice that was already predisposed to a certain understanding of his racial and sexual type. For he does embroider and carry on so: about Cannibals and Anthropophagi; about rocks whose heads touch heaven; and about men whose heads do grow beneath their shoulders. The awkwardness of Othello's place in the scheme of things and his "'dilated' traveller's tale," Patricia Parker observes, thus re-opened "to Venetian (and English) eyes exotic worlds beyond the direct reach of vision." In addition to which there is Iago and *his* "close dilation" of a European world to which the Moor is alien; especially when he passes himself off as "a Venetian informer on the secrets of Desdemona's 'chamber'" (1994:94).

These ironic openings into secret places combine "to chart the crossing in [Shakespeare] of domestic and exotic, 'civil' and 'barbarian' explicitly within the register of fascination and the vicariously visual" (*ibid.*). In effect, Othello feeds the "European appetite or hunger for report (synecdochally by its reference to the 'greedy ear' of Desdemona that did 'devour [it] up'," and he does so in ways that lend aboriginal authenticity to the view that it was indeed possible for "Nature so preposterously to err." Parenthetically, it is according to other such savage-pictures, and when he is turned "deboshed fish" by "celestial liquor," that Caliban goes on so with his "I'll fish . . .; I'll bring . . .; I'll show . . ."; and his "I'll kiss thy foot" [and] "With my long nails will dig thee pig-nuts" (II.iii.133-165). In *Othello*, meanwhile, and for all that the reverberations are initially muffled by the "loud reason" and "more stubborn and boisterous" noise of impending war, the Moor also speaks himself into "liberties" (Mullaney) or "surburbs" (Motohashi) that justify the practice of "Geographers [who] in Afric-Maps With Savage-Pictures fill their Gaps," as Daniel Defoe would write in the eighteenth century of "The Reformation of Manners" (1702).

Savage-pictures of a parallel sort, about the Irish this time, account for the fact that in the 1324 witchcraft proceedings against Dame Alice Kyteler in Ireland it was revealed that the Devil had appeared to her "sometimes in the form of a cat, sometimes in that of a shaggy black dog and sometimes in that of a kind of Ethiope" (Sanders 1992:107). In effect, from Euro-Christendom's Aethiope to Shakespeare's "berrhymed Irish rat" in *As You Like It*, there is enough of a familiar politics of conquest and an anthropology of difference to justify Humphrey Tonkin when his poetics-of-empire Edmund Spenser (1552-1599) leads him to conclude that in its "every line, *The Faerie Queen* epitomizes [a] double vision, in which Virgil and Faerie Land, Gloriana and Venus share our attention in happy if incongruous decorum" (1989:20). Post/colonial attitudes provide the lens through which Tonkin reads Spenser. He does so with some persuasion, notwithstanding suggestions of excess in, for example, his chapterful of "epic and empire" assertions that "*The Faerie Queen* is a poem about empire," given the fact that the "programme of [England's] cultural independence" with regard to Spain or to Ireland was fundamentally "expansionist." It was the case, moreover, that the "centuries-old aspiration to Anglicize Ireland" had involved the brightest and the best of the age. Ralegh was among those who had been preoccupied, as Spenser put it, with the "reducing of that savage nation to better government and civility" (Sanders 1992:226-227).

There is a compelling familiarity in this and other colonial contextualizations of Ireland, so festooned upon the Irish are tropes of a recognizable kind. As a consequence, in the "more remote parts of the country, the 'wild Irish' often seemed as primitive and exotic in English eyes as any heathen people overseas" (Sanders 1992:227). Evidence of this is clear in the anthology that Andrew Hadfield and John McVeagh's *Strangers to that Land* (1994) makes of propositions that "England's territorial domination supposedly depended upon a religious and civilizing mission to reclaim the Irish church and people for European Christendom." There is elsewhere a generic quality to the dismissive interest with which Fynes Moryson (1566-1630) produced the Ireland that we get in his 1617 "itinerary" of "travell through twelve dominions." For according to this gone-primitive and heart-of-darkness jaunt, the Irish "wander about slovenly and naked, and lodge in the same house (if house it may be called) with their beasts." We also learn that "nothing is more common among them than for the men to lie upon the women's laps on green hills till they kill their lice, with a strange nimbleness, proper to that nation" (qtd. in Brooke *et al*. 1935:1). Imperial wanderlust and the colonial eye thus reproduce the lie of the land in ways that Mignolo has associated with "imaginary constructs" and "loci of enuniciation" in *The Darker Side of the Renaissance*. And here I invoke Wittkower's "Marvels of the East" to reinforce the thought that it is thus that "much-maligned monsters" make "their way into natural science and geography, encyclopaedias and cosmographies, romance and history, into maps, miniatures and sculpture"; that they gradually become "stock features" in representations of reality (Mitter 1992:6-7).

In their *Strangers to that Land*, Hadfield and McVeagh provide us with an anthology of such exotic interests and settler expropriation, from before "the Reformation to the famine." The anthology presents truths about the native in predictable measures, whether the politics is in Ralegh or in the psychology of the Giraldus Cambrensis of *Expugnatio Hibernica* (1189), with its conquest-of-Ireland declaration that the Irish temperament is "innately unstable." Spenser's own "A View of the Present State of Ireland" was no less representative, and the same may be said for an anonymous "Discourse" which called upon Elizabeth to make a profitably cleansed plantation of the place: "And for providing for all parties her Majestie may give 1.s. in England for a gaine of 5.s. in Ireland. Allwaies provided that cleare riddance may be made of the Irish bloud and stirpe there as neare as shall be possible. Whereby her Majestie shall make Ireland profitable unto England or mearely a West England" (Hadfield and McVeagh 1994:52). It is all of one piece, then, that in 1562 William Camden recorded an arrival at Court of folk out of Ireland upon whom "the English people gazed at with no less admiration than nowadays they do them of China and America" (Sanders 1992:227). We are on terrain, after all, where estranged and estranging people "do that which heaven hath forbid," as Othello himself once put it (II.iii.170-171).

Through it all, the early modern period cast its eye overseas on the Turk only in certain ways. As above, it is instructive that in seeking to deny murderous culpability, no less a character than Shakespeare's Richard III, that "diffused infection of a man" and the "slander of [his] mother's heavy womb," poses the question that he does: "What, think you we are Turks or infidels?" (III.v.40). It is equally consequential that, as the Herald puts it in *Othello*, any and all "tidings. . . importuning the mere perdition of the Turkish fleet [put] every man into triumph, some to dance, some to make bonfires, each man to what sport and revels his [addiction] leads him" (II.ii.1-6). By the same overseas token, there is the "archive" of such matters that we get in Orhan Pamuk's *Beyaz Kale* (*The White Castle*). "We were sailing from Venice to Naples when the Turkish fleet appeared," so we read at the beginning of the Turkish counter-narrative. And there, Othello or not, "We lost our nerve . . . [but] our oarsmen, most of them Turks and Moors, were screaming with joy." With the "dream-like blue of its delicate, marbled binding" shining among the faded documents of "that forgotten 'archive'. . . in Gebze," *Beyaz Kale* is the fictional memoir in which Pamuk's captured Italian records Turkey's enlargement through to its collapse at the gates of Vienna (13). Meanwhile, Aziz Nesim's 1977 autobiography, *Boyle Gelmis Boyle Gitmez* (*That's How It Was But Not How It's Going To Be*), picks up the remnants of Othello's countrymen and women, by-products too of Turkey's amplitude. They are bound to service, still, although engaged in considerably less violent duty than Othello's mercenary-proud killing of some "circumcised dog" of a Turk who had once beat a Venetian and "traduced" that European state. Nesim cites Ahmet Rasim remembering the blackamoor's kind in 1924 as "a dwindling group":

> At one time in Istanbul there was an entirely different group of blacks, with the names *baji* (nurse), *dadi* (child's nurse), *sutnine* (wet-nurse), and *mama dadi* (nanny). I know that I was raised at almost the end of the black and white slave trade. In Istanbul's Atpazar (in the Fatih area) and the Tophane quarter were found a number of slave houses which traded especially in blacks from Egypt, Tripoli, Abyssinia and Yemen. (Nesin 44)

Culturally and politically, the Euro-Ottomite recognition and deployment of difference was always a matter of great urgency during the early modern period. It was in due fashion that Sir Thomas Browne's *Religio Medici* had tilted at the gradient of dissimilarity that separated Euro-Christendom from Jew and Moslem. "The religion of the Jew is expressly against the Christian," Browne declared, "and the Mahometan against both; for the Turke, in the bulke hee now stands, he is beyond all hope of conversion; if he fall asunder there may be conceived hopes, but not without strong improbabilities" (26). The Duke in *The Merchant of Venice* measures this dissimilarity very much *comme il faut* when he asks Shylock to "pluck commiseration of [Antonio's] state." For in thus "glancing an eye of pity on his losses," Shylock would show himself sensitive to a disaster that would move even "brassy bosoms and rough hearts of flint, / From stubborn Turks and Tartars never trained / To offices of tender courtesy." We all expect, the Christian Duke concludes, "a gentle answer, Jew" (IV.i.27-34).

Whether as "moiety" or "principal," religious antagonism certainly ran through records of the relationship of Christianity with the stubborn Turk. Consider in this light the clarifying brutality with which, for example, Dante's *Divine Comedy* set itself to the task of identifying as schismatic the founder of the religion that was indissolubly associated with the Turk and the Moor. For Dante lodged him to telling effect in *Inferno* (Canto XXVIII): with "splayed / Trunk [and] spilled entrails [that] dangled between his thighs." The Christian poet had thus confined the Islamic prophet in the Ninth Chasm of self-mutilation where, because Mohammed is "split open from his chin / Down to the farting-place,"

> I saw his organs, and the sack that makes the bread
>
> We swallow turn to shit. Seeing my eyes
> Fastened upon him, he pulled open his chest
> With both hands, saying, "Look how Mohammed claws
>
> And mangles himself, torn open down the breast!
> Look how I tear myself! And Ali goes
> Weeping before me—like me, a schismatic, and cleft."
>   (Dante/Pinsky 1995: 295-297)

The Turk/Moslem is caught in somewhat of a transition when, in the 1550s of his *Defense of the Indians*, Bartolomé de Las Casas inveighed against the brutality of Spain's conquistadors, overadvertized the virtues of the Indian and, with the fateful suggestion that if necessary negro slaves could be brought from Castile to the Americas, undersubscribed to the humanity of the African. The Turk and the Moor, Las Casas was convinced, were the "truly barbaric scum of the nations." They, and the Arabs, are "a people said to be well-versed in political affairs. But how can they be honored with this reputation for uprightness when they are an effeminate and luxury-loving people, given to every sort of sexual immorality? The Turks, in particular, do not consider impure and horrible vices worthy of punishment" (Las Casas 1992: 51). Until its ill-fated crusade against the Moors at El-Ksar-el-Kebir in 1578, Portugal had also mapped and trafficked in Moslem alterity. And here, "one exploit, this time to the west [of Japan], deserves particular mention. In 1541 Ethiopia was delivered from her Moslem enemies, 'saved', as Gibbon placed on record, by 450 Portuguese" (Atkinson 1987:14). Meanwhile, Luis Vaz de Camoes's epic *The Lusiads* (1572) had been dedicated to Portugal's "Great King, whose far-flung dominions greet the sun's gaze alike when it rises, when half-way through its course, and when it sinks to rest." Camoes had of course celebrated Euro-Christian triumph and nationalist pride in recognition of a sovereign power "at whose hands we look to see Arab, Turk, and Indian shamed" (40). All in all, from Dante to Bacon, and from Las Casas to Sir Thomas Browne, there is, I should think, much that helps to account for that flourish with which, quite apart from his mercenary interests, Othello is driven to identify himself as nothing if not Venetian and Euro-Christian. How else are we to account for that vaulting ambition, indignant rebuke, and autobiography of conversion with which Shakespeare's Moor exalts himself into European design: "Are we turned Turks, and to ourselves do that / Which heaven hath forbid the Ottomites?" (II.iii.170-172).

"For empire and greatness," Francis Bacon wrote with some diminished concern, "it importeth most, that a nation do profess arms as their principal honour, study, and occupation"; he also observed that, even "though in great declination," the Turks "have it at this day" (*ibid*. 317). However, interest in the Turk had been less cavalier in Hartmann Schedel's 1493 "world chronicle," the *Liber Chronicarum* (also known as the *Nuremberg Chronicle*). For Nuremberg was then critically located in eastern Europe, and Turkish power was not in any great declination. The alignment therefore "weighed heavily upon the profitable relations existing with the Danubian area and Venice" (Devisse and Mollay 1979:222). Still, and as Brandon Beck points out in his tracing of literary representations of the Ottoman Empire in the later years of the seventeenth century, faultlines of European schism also clarify Daniel Defoe's recalling in 1715 the contents of a pamphlet that he had published in 1683. In it, Defoe had recorded the fact that when the Turks besieged Vienna, the Whigs in England, generally speaking, were for the Turks' taking it, for all that the Turks had a "History of Cruelty and Perfidious Dealings" and had "rooted out the Name of the Christian Religion in above Threescore and Ten Kingdoms" (Beck 1987:97). Defoe thus called attention to European factionalism and its role in dividing perceptions of the Turk. An "abundance of people had," he noted, "so much zeal for the Prostestant Religion in Hungaria, that they wish'd every day the Turks should take Vienna" (Beck *ibid.*). Such inflections aside, Euro-Christian antagonism to Ottoman identity and power was unassuageable. As happens in *Othello*, anxious geopolitics and emergent shifts in commerce and political power help to account for the perspectives that Bacon, among others, brought to bear on a figure whose every "mighty preparation" could loom as it did to catalytic effect in the Venice of Shakespeare's play. Appropriately so; since, as Cemal Kafadar explains,

> Mehmed's toughest opponent was Venice, against which he waged war from 1463 to 1479 in the Aegean and the Peloponnese, where the Most Serene Republic held several towns and forts. Venetian fleets also raided the Anatolian coasts, hoping to link up with eastern rivals to the Ottomans, such as the Katamanids, and, when they were reduced to Ottoman subjection, the Akkoyunlu (the White Sheep). But Mehmed defeated the Akkoyunlu in 1473, and in 1479 he forced Venice to make peace. [And when, later,] in 1480 Mehmed's gaze extended beyond the Venetians' empire, his chief target was not Naples, whose king had backed Venice and Hungary against him, but Rome. (1994:596)

Kafadar's "The Ottoman and Europe" opens on a note that underscores the stubborn longevity of the countertext. It is telling that it does so in what amounts to a concluding prologue in which the narrative is ostensibly about the 1992 summer bidding by various cities for the right to host the Olympic games of the year 2000. The Turkish delegation arguing the case for Istanbul was astounded, Kafadar writes, "to hear their Central Asian cousins defend the case of Samarkand as the capital of Timur" ("Tamerlan" 1336-1405) who "saved Europe from the Turkish menace"—and thus made the European Renaissance possible. "So powerful has the European world hegemony rendered western public opinion, and so normative western historical experience, that such references are by now common. In reality, of course, Timur had no such thing in mind, for when he invaded western Asia in 1402, he aimed only to punish the upstart House of Osman" (589). However, the generic view has never quite ceased to consist of "uncritical readings of early modern political writers: Niccolo Machiavelli ('they are all slaves'), Jean Bodin ('when the [timariots] die, their heirs can inherit only their moveable goods'), and Francis Bacon ('nobility attempers sovereignty') (Kadafar 616). Even in the far reaches of the new lands of America—specifically on the little rocky bastion of St. John, in Bridgeport, Barbados—Euro-Christian and Ottoman meet in the generic romance that Alejo Carpentier's *El siglo de las luces* (*Explosion in a Cathedral*) makes of a certain person whose "name bore a crushing weight of historical association." It was all embodied in

> the remains of Ferdinand Paleologue, descendant of the last Emperor of Greece—Priest of this parish—1655-1656. . . . The first time he visited the house in Havana, Victor Hugues had spoken at length about this tomb of the unknown grandson of the Ecumenical Patriarch who had been killed during the final resistance of Byzantium, having chosen to die rather than fall into the sacrilegious hands of the conquering Turk. (306)

Given the reach and resonance of the early modern world that I have outlined above, Jack Jorgens writes with due logic about its principal playwright; for he makes the point that Shakespeare was in a position "to intuit the shattering impact of protestantism, empiricism, capitalism, nationalism, and the explorations of the New World which gave birth to the modern world. [He was therefore] an epitome of the dynamic, questioning age which produced Montaigne, Cervantes, Bacon, Galileo, and Machiavelli" (1991:107; *also* Ann Mackenzie 1990). This is amplitude writ large, even if on rather European terrain and terms. But then, given the round earth's imagined corners, there does remain to be considered that native who had suffered by a thunderbolt, and whose articulation of his experiences once provoked the question: "Where the devil should he learn our language?" (*Tempest* II.ii.68-69).

"The Length of Prester John's Foot"

> I sit with Shakespeare and he winces not.
>> W.E.B. Du Bois, *The Souls of Black Folk*

> Ah teyk pamishohn frohm Bra Brutohs dem
> For kam tohk na Bra Siza in berin.
>> Thomas Decker, *Juliohs Siza*

I enter the lists here fully cognizant of latitude and import in that cartographic conceit which Maria once made of Malvolio's face in *Twelfth Night; Or, What You Will.* "He does smile his face," she had remarked then, "into more lines than is in the new map with the augmentation of the Indies" (III.ii.84-85). For much the same reason, I am unpersuaded, although intrigued, by the remarkably white-eyed squint (due apologies to Aidoo 1977) in J. D. Rogers' corollary discussion of voyages and explorations in Shakespeare's England. The map, drawn in 1600 by Edward Wright, with the assistance of Richard

Haklyut and John Davis, was the first one to be produced in England according to Mercator's principles of projection. And it does make that signal appearance in Shakespeare's play. Rogers notes this, elaborately. However, his altogether transfixing conclusion is that

> in spite of maps Shakespeare did not write of the new-found new world and the new-found old world as momentous additions to the world in which his characters lived and moved. . . . Europe fascinated [Shakespeare] with so powerful a spell that what was not Europe was mere dust, possibly gold dust, but mere dust in the balance in comparison with Europe. (Brooke 463)

There is an especially unimaginative narrowness in Rogers, for all that, elsewhere, a Ben Jonson too had once exulted in a certain kind of Shakespeare: "Triumph, my Britain, thou hast one to show / To whom all scenes of Europe homage owe." Rogers's way would obviously underestimate the capacious import of how Shakespeare makes Cleopatra respond, for all that she is "fire and air," when she is offered a choice the stark realities of which are death or humiliation in Europe: "Rather a ditch in Egypt / . . . Rather on Nilus' mud / Lay me stark nak'd . . . / Rather make / My country's high pyramides my gibbet" (*Antony and Cleopatra* V.ii.57-62). To be persuaded by Rogers is to dull the hearing, too, of that—granted—noisy extravagance with which Aaron rejects the invitation, in *Titus Andronicus*, to reduce black to dust: "Ye white-lim'd walls! ye ale-house painted signs! / Coal-black is better than another hue. . . ./ For all the water in the ocean / Can never turn the swan's black legs white" (IV.ii.97-101). That being the case, "Zounds! is black so base a hue?" (IV.ii.71).

By contrast, the way in which Wole Soyinka (1988:211) understands "local colour" in Shakespeare provides us with an astute counterpoint to what Rogers appears to represent:

> When one examines the majority of Shakespeare's plays very closely, there really is not much overt respect paid to "local colour." If anything, the colour is not infrequently borrowed from elsewhere to establish a climate of relationships, emotions or conflicts: "Her bed is India; there she lies, a pearl" (*Troilus and Cressida* I.i.99). Where we encounter a localized immediacy we are wafted instantly away on a metaphoric bark to nowhere:
>
>> Between our Ilium and where she resides
>>   Let it be call'd the wild and wand'ring flood;
>>   Ourself the merchant, and this sailing Pandar
>>   Our doubtful hope, our convoy, and our bark. (I.i.100-3)

Soyinka's response is a generous one. Its esthetic scope cuts across a certain mapping of the cultural politics of nation and race in Great Britain which has at one time or another engaged the likes of Members of Parliament Craddock, Enoch Powell, and Margaret Thatcher (Dabydeen and Wilson-Tagoe 1988: 80-82); and which has been subjected to Paul Gilroy's discriminating judgment in *There Ain't No Black in the Union Jack* (1987). Coincidentally, its all-consuming import also threatens so, at the outskirts of empire, in Austin Clarke's *Growing Up Stupid Under the Union Jack* (1980):

> In the Shop we saw advertisements, technicolour paintings and photographs printed on tin. The tin was always peeling off. . . . But always, the message, as if through spite, would be left. I first saw those five white girls, the Dionne sisters in this Shop. They bathed in bubbles with *Palmolive Soap*. And everybody stopped using *Pears Soap* and other English soaps. *Palmolive* made you beautiful and fertile. And all the women [married or single] who were pregnant, closed their eyes and wished . . . as they bought "a cake o' *Palmolive* please." . . . [Myself] I was in an English countryside. I was a dreaming fool. And my dreams found me writing poetry. They were copies of English poetry. What other poetry would I know? (82)

There are, I should think, any number of reasons for de-monumentalizing Shakespearean imports, notwithstanding the iconic certainties of Wilson Knight, or of J. D. Rogers, for that matter. The reasons have as much to do with riots and risings, with politics and history, as they do with the volatile art of making artefacts. Besides which, being human does involve the security of standing monument-still even as it does the instability of change and (dis)play—whether "by indirect or forced courses"—to use words with which a certain Venetian First Senator once expressed his puzzlement over the how and the why of Desdemona *and* Othello.

There is licence and latitude in such penetrations of the domestic by the foreign. In fact, they make for a certain goodness-of-fit when Ania Loomba begins her discussion of critical and cultural difference in a nexus of apparent coincidence and contradiction. For she does so with what she describes as the "feel [of] a giddy turning" that is "occasioned by an oscillation from Renaissance to postcolonial studies." But, she adds, "thanks to the pedagogic and cultural hangovers of colonialism, these seemingly disparate areas occasionally intersect and make the giddy turnings worth while" (1994:17). Quite so; for there is a historical sense in which transports of the imperial Book, as Scripture, Ledger, and Artefact, are inextricably bound up in the making (up) of the Americas no less than of Africa and the India of the Raj or of the subaltern. "There is but one country in the world . . . except Germany, where the plays of Shakespeare have of recent times formed the safest and surest attraction to the indiscriminate masses who attend popular theatres, where the proprietor of a theatre could count on a profit on a Shakespeare production. That country is India." So writes C. J. Sisson, in 1926, about performances of Shakespeare, in the vernacular (Marathi, Gujarati, Hindi, and Urdu) in the 1900s (6).

It remains all of one piece that in Loomba's version of India's varie-gated encounters with Shakespeare, this time among what Sisson would no doubt have referred to as the cultured classes, *Hamlet* should become for many male postgraduate students in Delhi "the ultimate representation of "the human condition"; and that it should also be "the name of a prize-winning variety of mango developed recently in Trivandrum in South India" (17). Consider, though, that in Phillip Zarrilli's "For Whom is the King a King?" Trivandrum's "Victorian styled V.J.T. Hall" (16) proved to be no less of a relevant stage for yet another encounter with Shakespeare, in a July 28, 1989 South Indian *kathakali* (dance-drama) version of *King Lear*. Zarrilli's subse-quent "anthropology of interculturalism" exegesis, much like Appadurai's ethnoscaping, is an elaborate description and theorizing of the production. Accordingly, he identifies the encounter with *King Lear* in its Western content; situates it within the highly conventionalized *kathakali* mise-en-scene and techniques; and reconstitutes the whole as an unusually collabora-tive (Australian, French, and Indian) process of conceptualization and real-ization. The ensuing *Kathakali King Lear* performances in continental Europe, Edinburgh, Singapore, and Kerala therefore served to illustrate and to be an encounter which approximate, Zarrilli proposes, "a more ambiguous 'Caribbean' experience . . . reconceived as an inventive process or creolized interculture" (16-7; 36).

There is a kindred edge to the disjointing congruence of the Shakespeare that we get in Vikram Seth's *A Suitable Boy* (1993), his monumentally ambiguous and yet precise novel of the India of the 1950s. Its 1,474 pages are devoted to chronicling the contradictory politics of nation-building. No less foregrounded is the wounding, even if comical, psychology and cultural politics of Brahmpur University's Department of English Literature, at a meeting of whose syllabus committee ("The point was the inclusion of James Joyce on the syllabus of the paper on Modern British Literature") we learn that Dr. Pran Kapoor "regarded the head of the English Department, Professor Mishra, with a loathing that almost made him ill." Shakespeare is of course present in Seth's calculated references to *As You Like It* (1019); and to *Julius Caesar*, in which context we learn that "so few parents wanted their daughters to act on stage" but that, given this drama's emphatically masculine cast, "the themes of violence, patriotism and a change of regime" made for "freshness" and "historical context" (76). Similarly, there is little that is casual in Seth's

use of casting and rehearsal sessions of *Twelfth Night,* especially his arrangement of the "mixed marriage" roles of Olivia and Malvolio which he assigns
to the novel's adolescent Muslim and Hindi protagonists. The narrative thus
delivers a palpable hit in the passage which, given Kabir, caused Lata
"particular difficulty":

> Olivia: Wilt thou go to bed, Malvolio?
> Malvolio: To bed? ay, sweetheart; and I'll come to thee.
> (845-47)

Of course, Shakespeare in India has been perhaps most famously re-configured in *Shakespeare Wallah* (1965). He is there culled to our attention, so to
speak, in the cinematography of Subrat Mitra, the music of Satyajit Ray, and
the writing of James Ivory and Ruth Prawer Jhabvala—as edited by Amit
Bose and produced by Ismail Merchant—all this to a "simple, poignant"
effect. At least, Leonard Maltin comes to this judgment in his synoptic view
that the film is one in which a Playboy, Shashi Kapoor, who has an actress-
mistress, Madhur Jaffrey, romances the white-woman member (Felicity
Kendall) of a two-bit English theatrical company touring Shakespeare in
India (Maltin 1990:1029). All the same, and in yet another oscillation between
Renaissance and postcolonial studies, it is not unreasonable to propose that
the template for the film's cross-over love story may well be Othello's
readiness to believe that in the "entire and perfect chrysolite" of Desdemona
he had discovered a "pearl richer than all his tribe." After all, the implications
had been quite "hot, hot and moist" (III.iv.39) when, at the Shakespearean
heart of the matter, Othello kneels in "due reverence of [his] sacred vow" of
"perdition" and "chaos" to come—

> Like to the Pontic Sea,
> Whose icy currents and compulsive course
> Nev'r feels retiring ebb, but keeps due on
> Even so my bloody thoughts, with violent pace,
> Shall never look back, nev'r ebb to humble love,
> Till that a capable and wide revenge
> Swallows them up. (III.iii.450-457)

There are other resonances, of course: notwithstanding the suggestion of
some ascent to equivalence in the Anglo-Indian title, it may be argued that the
conjunction "*Shakespeare-Wallah*" cannot be entirely innocent of a certain
well-serviced yoking. It is recognizable enough in the jungle-*wallah* and
punkah-wallah and *tonga-wallah* that attended the British Raj's passage
through India; and which the *Oxford English Dictionary* condenses into the
restrained clarity of the following building-block entry:

wallah wo(hook).la. Anglo-Indian. Also wal(l)a, wollah. a. Hindi -*wala*, a suffix, forming adjs. with the sense "pertaining to or connected with" what is denoted by the sb.; hence forming sbs., as in *nao-wala* boatman, *Dilli-wala* inhabitant of Delhi. The suffix in this function may be compared to -er; Europeans have commonly apprehended it as a sb. equivalent to "man", "fellow".

Freighted thus, both the vehicle of and the tenor in the *wallah*'s descent into Shakespeare may lead from (and back into) the kind of division that Mulk Raj Anand plays out in "Third-Class Khadi-Clad Rabble and Anglo-Indian Top Dogs," the title that he gives to the first letter of thirteen, plus prologue and five postscripts, which make up his epistolary novel, *Caliban and Gandhi, Letters to "Bapu" from Bombay* (1991).

Import and sub/version are thus sharper in Anand; so, too, is the concommitant call for a re-figuration of Caliban *without* Prospero. This need is apparent in the historicized pages of "Letter Ten" in which Anand works out the implications of the fact that Mr. Jinnah's intended insult of Bapu, "Oh Gandhi! That Caliban!," was instead "an unintended compliment"—the revisionist point being that "Mr. Jinnah did not realise what a compliment he was paying you.... If he had read Shakespeare's *Tempest* he might have seen you as arch rebel of the 20th century, as Caliban was of the 15th century." Still, it signifies that Gandhi's nationalist agenda has him moving beyond Caliban's impatient and "primitive instinct of revenge against Prospero." Anand's "Bapu" thus "seek[s] to conquer anger and hate, as did Buddha and Mahavira Jina in the 6th century B.C." (93-94). Ironically, any such move was one which a nervous British imperialism was quite prepared to identify and respond to as subversive alterity and foul conspiracy. As reported in the *Calcutta Weekly Notes*, the 1918 Sedition Committee report had no hesitation at all in coming to such a conclusion. For it reported that it could not "overlook the lamentable fact that the revolutionary literature brought to light . . . does suggest that [the] religious principle of absolute surrender to the Divine Will" can in fact be employed "by designing and unscrupulous people to influence and unbalance weak-minded persons and thus ultimately bend them to become instruments of nefarious crimes from which they might otherwise recoil with horror" (Kar14-15). Ellen Gainor has well summarized this volatile relationship of theater and politics. "The theater has always been a locus of political force," she writes; and this for reasons that have to do with its role as "the disseminator of a dominant ideology and/or the place for colonized revolt." There are, in effect, those "historical moments . . . in which theatrical performance can be the primary conduit for lessons of vital social and personal import" (1995:xiv).

It is no surprise, then, that whenever "Shakespeare" can be pressed into imputations of disservice, or deployed as monumental shibboleth, the undertaking does settle, sooner or later, into dense collocations of "signs, symbols, language, bits of quotes, fragments of allusive references, clusters of associations, sounds and the structuring of sounds with which to fabricate" a biography or a politics (Wynter 1995:94). A concommitant question haunts approaches that harp so on mastering texts and their import: is sub-versionness [the Politics of the Same], as against *subversiveness*, at all avoidable whenever the empire writes back? What degrees of translation and interpretation are involved when we raise the issue of whether the empire's readings-back are practices and arts inhibited and out of warrant; of whether they bring with them that inherent illicitness which, Brabantio suspects, cannot *not* be at work whenever and wherever Othello engages in things Venetian. This is suggestively the case both in Brabantio's perspective on Othello and his thievery and in, once again, that astonishing rise to equivalence that The Moor thinks he is entitled to when he says, "Are *we* turned Turks, and to *ourselves* do that / Which heaven hath forbid the Ottomites?" This very estrangeable man had then gone on to complete his exercise in unwarranted affiliation with the admonition, "For *Christian* shame, put by this *barbarian* brawl" (II.iii.170-72; my emphasis). But then, Jean Franco is elsewhere sufficiently sustained in the unruly ways of Puerto Rico's Edgardo Rodríguez Julía to rework the issue of warrant, affiliation, and identity. She observes then that "what used to be a source of embarrassment to the intelligentsia—the imitation of the metropolis, the recourse to pastiche—has now come to be seen as an irrepressible process of appropriation and defiance" (1989: 212).

In sum, quite other wor(l)ds converge to generate answers to the question that Kenneth McClellan had once posed when he asked, "whatever happened to Shakespeare?" (1978). That being the case, the reach and range of any response to the question must always be inflected by an "implicit network of peculiarly cultural associations between forms, statements, and other aesthetic elaborations, on the one hand, and, on the other, institutions, agencies, classes, and amorphous social forces." Such a network, Randall Johnson writes (Johnson 1991:102) in a further elaboration of Edward Said, "anchor[s] writers and their texts in a complex system of relationships which include, in Said's words, the 'status of the author, historical moment, condition of publication, diffusion and reception, values drawn upon, values and ideas assumed, a framework of consensually held tacit assumptions, presumed background, and so on'." Said thus foregrounds a notion of affiliation that is similar, Johnson notes, to what Pierre Bourdieu identifies as "the configurations of the literary 'field,' understood as a system of agents or as 'forces which, by their existence, opposition or combination, determine its specific structure at a given moment in time'" (*ibid.*). A good measure of this conflation of agency and dis/affiliation has been famously articulated in refigurings of *The Tempest*, as in Anand. This is very much the case in

Barbados's George Lamming and Mexico's Octavio Paz. The same is true of Octave Mannoni's Prospero in Madagascar; so, too, in that "Prospero in Africa" through which Ngugi wa Thiong'o's *A Grain of Wheat* (1968) passes judgment on colonialist pacifications of savage tribes. It is worth recalling here that in *Shakespeare in the Tropics*, Alan Warner's inaugural address as first Professor of English at the University of East Africa, the Professor had clearly identified this "underlying premise"; its thrust was that "African students would study English literature in order to 'become citizens of the world'" (Sicherman *ibid.* 16).

Elsewhere, revolutionary no less than craven understandings of the Americas have followed in the wake of investments in the Caliban of Roberto Fernández Retamar (Cuba) or in the Ariel of José Enrique Rodó (Uruguay). Phenomenal Shakespeares have also been generated by other "mis-readings" from the Caribbean—Martinique and Puerto Rico, respectively—of Aimé Césaire and Rosario Ferré. In Césaire's *Une tempête*, as adapted *pour un théâtre nègre*, Shakespeare's Caliban is as much Haitian as he is Hegelian. He is there presented as a counter figure to "the complete totalitarian" that Prospero is. Césaire keeps his Caliban, so we are told, "close to beginnings [so that he] can still participate in the world of marvels" at the same time that he is represented as a historically conscious rebel and positive hero. In Césaire's optimism Caliban thus becomes, "in the Hegelian sense," an incarnation of "the slave who makes history" (Nixon 1987:571). Of course, when Césaire-Caliban thus hitches a ride into History he is being remarkably liberal with Hegel, given the German philosopher's *Lectures on the Philosophy of World History* in which "Africa proper" is the site of a recalcitrant alterity that is characterized by "great muscular strength, good-naturedness, and completely unfeeling cruelty." In consequence, it "has no historical interest of its own, for we find its inhabitants living in barbarism and savagery in a land which has not furnished any integral ingredient of culture. From the earliest historical time," Hegel adds, "Africa has remained cut off from all contacts with the rest of the world; it is the land of gold for ever pressing in upon itself, and the land of childhood, removed from the light of self-conscious history and wrapped in the dark mantle of night" (1980:172-173).

In a somewhat unhappy review of South African J.M. Coetzee's *Waiting for the Barbarians*, George Steiner (1982) identifies the salient features of that "most famous of all modern political allegories," Hegel's "The Master and the Servant" (in *The Phenomenology of Spirit*), the allegory in which Césaire initiates and justifies Caliban's insurrection. In Césaire-Caliban the seeds of sub/version are productively embedded in Prospero's own "This thing of darkness I acknowledge mine" and in his "We cannot miss him: he does make our fire, / Fetch in our wood and serves in offices / That profit us" (I.iii.311-13). Steiner's summary of Hegel's "dialectical model" is as elegant and quiet as Césaire's adaptation is revolutionary and urgent. But then, given the European tribal politics, not to speak of the power of the occult, within which Shakespeare safeguards Prospero's return to power, the clarity of Steiner's exposition also serves to measure the distance that Césaire needed to cover to transform Caliban into the slave who "makes history" that can overthrow Prospero:

> The master needs the servant—intimately, compellingly. It is only the servant who can underwrite the master's self-recognition. Moreover, in economic and technical terms the master grows less and less productive, less and less independent precisely to the degree that he relies on the servant. It is the servant, not the master, who embodies the positive impulses and capacities for renewal in the community. Becoming more and more aware of his indispensability (more self-aware), the servant will seek with other servants bonds of solidarity which masters, in their tragic autism, cannot entertain. It is, in consequence, the servant who is the carrier of historical evolution and the explorer of new modes of human interaction. (Steiner 1982:103)

It is the impossibility, or the precariousness, of any such transformation that Sylvia Wynter condenses into her observation that "it is the neo-colonial event that finally divests Caliban of that which had kept him whole—a dream of revenge against Prospero. But how shall he now revenge himself upon himself?" (1995:92). She does so moreover in the context of a political history that has "spread like a blood-red stain" and been worked out as much in Sierra Leone as in the "terrible centuries of Haiti and Latin America":

> Christophe of Haiti, whose fact and alienated French Court, complete with dancing master, could not be oudone by Césaire's fiction; then the peculiar terror of an Estrada Cabrera of Guatemala, of a Trujillo, of Duvalier; a peculiar "underdeveloped terror." (*ibid.*)

Eustace Palmer is clear about the pathological dialectic that is at work in such a political culture: the post-independence and neo-colonial Caliban is now one who, "once liberated by Prospero, assumes the latter's dictatorial powers; forgetting his erstwhile thraldom and the implications of his colour and cultural background, tries to adopt his erstwhile tormentor's lifestyle. In Sylvia Wynter's words, '[what we get] is Caliban Agonistes, blinded by the white bone of instant power, tossed to him when he had once snapped and growled'" (857; also Nixon 1987:576; Bruner 1976:248). In Rosario Ferré's re-figurations, meanwhile, rebellion comes in a climax in which, as we shall see, Desdemona anticipates her Moor by engaging in a feminist and pre-emptive response to Shakespeare's configuring of race, gender, and subordination in *Othello*. It is easy enough to detect two sets of impulses in the oscillations that link master text to sub/version here. First, there is the suspicion that engaging master(ing) texts will only deepen into second-order approximations, further confirming the condition of being yoked to an alien (and alienating) master metaphor—the consequence of ignoring Tutuola's warning sign: "DO NOT FOLLOW UNKNOWN MAN'S BEAUTY."

The fear of comparative disadvantage can be a defining one, for there are contexts in which the meeting of native *wallah* and colonial icon can only be interdictory. In this view, Shakespeare's passage through India—and rooms for his lodging there—cannot be disengaged from British imperialism and the logic of its colonizing curriculum. The two coincide in the readiness of Hill Station, Raj, and British Council to be hegemonic about English culture; and to discover the seditious (or the unworthy) in native behavior. Chatterjee's study of theater in the Bengali Renaissance thus identifies a nicely conjunctive moment in the first quarter of the nineteenth century, when "Bengali newspapers started voicing the need for native theatres" (*ibid.* 20). But then, the theater which emerged "concentrated, by general concensus among the organziers, on producing plays in the English language—not only English plays but also English translations of Sanskrit plays." In the end, the "one achievement the natives could be proud of during this decade was the appearance of a Bengali, Vaisnav Caran Adhya, as Othello in a professional English production of the Shakespearean play at the Sans Souci Theatre, one of the few professsional European theatres in the white quarters of Calcutta, in 1848." The Bengali Adyha, or Auddy as he was better known, was probably the first person of color to play the tragic Moor (1995:20). Outside this, so to speak, *sans-souci* affiliation, stagings of imperial import were more properly framed by the latitude that British Censorship Acts in India assumed, from as early as 1867. Those Acts could not have been unrelated to the opportunities that Shakespeare had to extend into India what C. J. Sisson could then transmute into "essential function."

The consequences for bard and wallah may be deduced from the reach of the documents that are referenced in, say, Hiranmoy Bhattacharya's *Raj and Literature: Banned Bengali Books* (1989)—a study of censorship in India that begins with what amounts to a review essay of such titles as *Banned Controversial Literature in British India, 1907-1947; Proscribed Bengali Books; Patriotic Poetry Banned by the Raj*; and *Persecution of Drama and Stage* (21). Alien control over native theater had been no less crucial in the British rule that Sisir Kar discusses in *Banned Bengal* (1992). Manuscripts had to be deposited with the relevant authorities for approval, and vigorous action could be and was indeed taken against (native) drama. Kar estimates that in the course of time a "few hundred" such manuscripts found their way into the Lalbazar Police Headquarters in Calcutta. In effect, three types of moves were made against offending or potentially subversive theater: drama books were proscribed according to the Press Act; staging of drama could be banned under the Dramatic Performances Act; and, finally, performances could be cancelled by executive order (172). Interestingly, Sisson (1926) had in fact broached these developments. He did so, however, only to re-orient the politics of their implications. He had cited Professor Legoux's "*La révolte de l'Inde contre Shakespeare*" (1925), but primarily to regret the fact that by 1912 "it cannot be gainsaid" that "the decline of the vogue for Shakespearean adaptations on the popular Bombay stage, and the more exclusive preoccupation with themes of indigenous origin in the *Mahabharata* and allied sources," were partly due to a "querulous nationalism" and its "conscious reaction against European culture and, especially, English culture" (17). What was potentially at stake, of course, was that celebrated Minute of February 2, 1835 in which Thomas Babbington Macaulay had advocated the creation of a type that would be "Indian in blood and color, but English in tastes, in opinions, in morals and in intellect" (Chatterjee 1995: 22).

Taste, transport, and translation are rather more dynamic matters in the "irrepressible process of appropriation and defiance" that Jean Franco ("The Nation as Imagined Community") discovers in the unruliness of Edgardo Rodríguez Juliá. For it is Juliá's claim that "We live in a period of ghostly intentions and unburied gestures [where] tradition breaks up into a thousand conflicting fragments." That being the case, "How can so much volatility be reconciled with such depth of feeling?" (Franco 1989:211). There is instruction, too, in another nuancing of the cult of authenticity through the "surfeit of camels" argument with which Borges once showed himself quite prepared to accommodate latitude and import, even to seeming self-effacement. Needless to say, the thesis and its elaboration in "The Argentine Writer and Tradition" are vintage Borges. For he re-cognizes "authenticity" by way of the observation in Gibbon's *Decline and Fall of the Roman Empire* that in that "Arabian book *par excellence*, in the Koran, there are no camels." This very absence of camels, Borges declares, clearly proves the authenticity of the Koran, if there were any doubts about the Arabian-ness of the work. "It was written by Mohammed, and Mohammed, as an Arab, had no reason to know that camels were especially Arabian; for him they were a part of reality, he had no reason to emphasize them; on the other hand, the first thing a falsifier, a tourist, an Arab nationalist would do is have a surfeit of camels," on every page; but "Mohammed, as an Arab was unconcerned: he knew he could be an Arab without camels. I think we Argentines can emulate Mohammed, can believe in the possibility of being Argentine without abounding local color" (1964:181).

In his 1928 "Manifesto Antropófago," meanwhile, Brazil's Oswald de Andrade provides us with yet another problematic conflation of import and latitude. Here, in confronting European cultural hegemony and the limits of the (South American) local, Andrade conceived of "a universalizing and modernist project" for which "cannibalism" provided the explanatory category (Bary 1991:96). Andrade's "rewriting of imitation as voracity" is an instructive one, whether it is a ludic, and thus sub/versive, display, or else a third-world fetishization of the "hegemony of the metropolis." Bary summarizes the complex of issues that follows from Andrade's "cannibalism": "The phrase 'a transfiguracão do Tabu em totem' [the transmutation of taboo into totem], which functions in the text [of 'Manifesto Antropófago'] as a kind of refrain, crystallizes [the text's] cultural program: the uprooting of catachresis, that body of theory and practice through which the Portuguese first 'civilized' Brazil, and of subsequent Western cultural models that Brazilians have uncritically internalized." This is a presumably calculated (re)turn to "instinct and rejection of the paternal authority," a move whose "internalization" the Freud of *Totem and Taboo* had designated "as the origin of civilization." The assumption is one that "enables Oswald to claim as positive the colonialist construction of Brazil as 'primitive.' Similarly, the embrace of totemistic cannibalism releases him from any need to assert '*brasilidade*' by a rejection of all things foreign, as it allows him to transmute the negative characterization of Brazilian culture as derivative into a positive value" (*ibid.* 96-97).

In effect, "querulous nationalism" (Sisson) no less than "surfeit of camels," and "cultural cannibalism" help to account for hegemonic shifts and political dis/affiliation. Their interpretive acts and expropriative consequences are variously significant in Mudimbe's cycles of "invention" (1982); in the dynamics of affiliation with which Susan Handelman turns to "hebraic" or "heretic hermeneutic" (1987; 1982); and in G. Douglas Atkins's (1980) discussion of the "dehellenization" of contemporary literary criticism. The same is true of the "variegated garbs of ancient theologies and philosophies" within which Moshe Idel discusses an earlier, and conflicted, synthesis of Jewish Kabbalah and Christian hermeneutics during the Renaissance (1988:263). There is relevance of a perhaps more recognizable sort in that announcement, "A specter is haunting criticism," with which Edward Pechter's "The New Historicism and Its Discontents: Politicizing Renaissance Drama" (1987:292) so signally heralds his season of his "discontent" (1987) with a poetics of culture that H. Aram Veeser *et al.* otherwise celebrate. It is a celebration from which, in turn, Judith Lowder Newton demurs with "History as Usual? Feminist and the 'New Historicism'" (1987); and about whose "gargantuan gloss" Jane Marcus is skeptical in "The Asylums of Antaeus: Women, War, and Madness" (1989:132). In this regard, similar preoccupations undergird Preston King's "Historical Contextualism: The New Historicism?" (Talmor and Talmor 1995:212) and Arac and Ritvo's focus on the "macropolitics" difficulty involved in having "to contextualise the context of the context . . . of the context" (1995).

Clearly, the grounds for all such engagements are both strategic and substantive. Pechter duly asks, "What is the value of the new-historicist contextualization? Are its versions of texts and of history useful and interesting? Why or why not? Who gain from them, and what is the gain?" (295). These are questions that foreground problematic issues of authenticity and appropriation. Reasonably enough, Pechter advances a genealogy for his own likes and dislikes. "My complaint earlier about the way the new historicists ignore theatrical impressions was itself based on contextualization, a theatrical one," he explains. "I was marching under the banner of Morgann ('in Dramatic composition the *Impression* is the *Fact*'), but it is only when we agree that the theater is the right context (and, indeed, a particular notion of theater) that these impressions are there to become facts" (*ibid.*). Meanwhile, in *The New Historicism* telling reverberations of hegemonic shifts (counterattack and gun; domain and noninterference) can be heard in the introductory chapter where Veeser celebrates his preferred methodology and its territorial expansion:

> As the first successful counterattack in decades against [the ethos of conventional scholars], New Historicism has given scholars new opportunities to cross the boundaries separating history, anthropology, art, politics, literature, and economics. It has struck down the doctrine of noninterference that forbade humanists to intrude on questions of politics, power, indeed on all matters that deeply affect people's practical lives—matters best left, prevailing wisdom went, to experts who could be trusted to preserve order and stability in "our" global and intellectual domains. . . . In response, the platoons of traditionalists have rushed to their guns. (ix)

It goes without saying that for the unpersuaded, among them a Director of the (USA) National Humanities Center, W. Robert Connor, what the likes of Veeser celebrate is symptomatic of disturbing tendencies "within the humanities today." For it betrays little more than a decline-and-fall dedication to mere "epiphenomena." There is much in Connor to suggest that this "betrayal" would involve the mismeasuring of "high literature" and "popular genres" beyond which, in *The Classics and Trash* (1990), Harriet Hawkins has attempted to synthesize the meanings attached to "tradition" and "taboo." The same would be true, I presume, of Jonathan Crewe's recent preoccupation with "so hurtful a topic as race" in "Out of the Matrix: Shakespeare and

Race-Writing." It is within this epiphenomenon that Crewe recognizes complex shades of England and English-ness, and of what he somewhat gingerly identifies as "proto-racial" features in the early modern period (1995:13).

Given the degree to which Connor's "Milton as Misogynist, Shakespeare as Elitist, Homer as Pornographer" (1990) mans the ramparts against barbarism under the aegis of thoroughly non-American icons (shades of Matthew Arnold and Paul Bourget, and of Margaret Webster, perhaps), the Euroamerican that he is is of particular interest to me. For looked upon as an "overseas" and colonial phenomenon, there is irony in the hagiographic belatedness of Connor's turn to Milton. His genuflection to high English culture may thus be related to the suspicion that Burt voices in *Licensed by Authority*: that recent deployments of such icons in North America seem to be driven by a need "to provide fuel for the already incendiary legitimation crisis" of what he refers to as "postmodern political criticism" (168). By the same token, Connor's assumption of colonial pedigree is a recycling of Sensabough's reception history of the English poet in early America. Connor thus harks back to a somewhat evacuated world in which Milton had once "quickened ideals and values" and "even shaped dreams of an American Millenium" (Sensabough 305). Still, nineteenth century Euroamerican concerns—these included alternative visions of what constituted "manifest destiny" as well as questions about the orthodoxy of the controversial *De Doctrina Christiana* (an 1825 publication)—had converged to diminish the appeal of the erstwhile much-celebrated English poet.

> [A]mong the great names of the past acclaimed in that early day Milton ranged more variously over moral, spiritual, and intellectual life of the country than any one man. Schoolmaster and poet, statesman and prophet and priest, he spoke with singular effectiveness on countless occasions to Americans of widely differing talents, interest, and tastes. Few authors in any age have moved so pervasively over the sensibilities of a nation, and odds argue that Milton himself will never do so again with the same sweep and power. Milton idolatry, national ambition, and paradoxes born of the Enlightenment converged to make his imprint in early America unique. (*ibid.*)

In sum: whether at "home" or "overseas," such anxieties of influence, or else insurrections of subjugated and belated knowledges, have been variously associated with "existential weightlessness" (Said) and "arrested decolonization" (Jeyifo); with moral victory (Greenblatt) and the migratory profit of "hybridity" (Bhabha)—or else with that "promiscuous pluralism" into which Salman Rushdie conflates "hybridity, impurity, intermingling

. . . and mongrelization" (Hollinger 1995:119-120). All the same, identity formation need not be as oscillatory as it tends to be in such interpretive strategies, not even when Caliban is driven to insist that all he ever learnt in the language of the master was how to curse. This much is evident in the kind of nuancing that Greenblatt offers in *Learning to Curse*; and is especially the case when " lines refuse to mean" that they are as reductive as one might assume:

> Caliban enters in Act 1., cursing Prospero and protesting bitterly, "This island's mine, by Sycorax my mother." [And then], "You taught me language, and my profit on't/Is, I know how to curse." . . . Caliban's retort might be taken as self-indictment, even with the gift of language, his nature is so debased that he can only learn to curse. But the lines refuse to mean this; what we experience instead is a sense of their devasting justness. Ugly, rude, savage, Caliban nevertheless achieves for an instant an absolute if intol- erably bitter moral victory. . . . In the poisoned relationship between master and slave, Caliban can only curse; but we know that Caliban's consciousness is not simply a warped negation of Prospero's. (24-25; 31)

Elsewhere, licence to perform interpretive (or expropriative) acts on master texts has been represented as the carnivalesque specialty of the margin. Here, "borderlands" provide the ground from and within which to rewrite "from a subversive, 'Calibanic' typology, in opposition to the . . . ruling 'center'" (Saldívar 1991:17). The peculiar virtue of thus writing from the margin lies in the "signifying" (Gates 1986) or "triple play" (Baker 1988) escape that it can effect from otherwise imperializing or totalizing gestures.

Translations or transpositions of rabbinical exegeses, and thus a "hebraic hermeneutic," provide other typologies of and shifts in hegemony. They engender or historicize constellations in which "the book tends to become either a book of defection or a book of reconciliation," and then possibly "a knot" (Bakan 1991:8). This much is clear when Handelman and Atkins develop, respectively, the implications of their "heretic hermeneutic" and "dehellenizing literary criticism." Of course, a rather explicit counterpoint to all this lies, in part, in Matthew Arnold and his various delimitations of the boundaries of sweetness and light. "It is time to Hellenise, and to praise knowing," the Arnold of *Culture and Anarchy* had written; "for we have Hebraised too much, and have over-valued doing" (1869:37). For him, a signal instance of the necessary *euphuia* lay in "Greek art . . . Greek beauty," with its "fidelity to nature,—the *best* nature" (147). As I have already indicated, this conversation in Euro-Christianity about Athens and Jerusalem involved ancestry of various kinds, some of them epic. Milton's *De Doctrina*

Christiana was relevantly persuaded that "on the introduction of the gospel, or new convenant through faith in Christ, the whole of the preceding covenant, in other words, the entire Mosaic Law, was abolished." Such conviction was not missing in *Paradise Lost*, of course:

> So the Law appears imperfect, and but giv'n
> With purpose to resign them in full time
> Up to a better Cov'nant, disciplin'd
> From shadowie Types to Truth, from Flesh to Spirit,
> From imposition of strict Laws, to free
> Acceptance of large Grace, from servil Fear
> To filial, works of Law to works of Faith. (XII, 300-306)

A similar thought resounds in Hegel when, rescuing Jesus as an instance of "Jews of a better heart and head who refused to become lifeless machines," he pointed to "the burden of statutory commands" that overwhelmed Judaism, "providing a rule for every casual action of daily life." According to Hegel, then, the result was that by Jesus' time "the service of God and the [call to] virtue, was ordered and compressed in dead formulas and nothing save pride in this slavish obedience to law . . . was left of the Jewish spirit," (Dickey 1989:175).

Moshe Idel, meanwhile, outlines an instance of dis/affiliation from the period of the Renaissance when "Jewish Kabbalah . . . found its way into the Christian world as a 'philosophy.'" It was "highy appreciated both as a style of speculation and as a repository of extremely important hermeneutics. [However], from the beginning, Christian Kabbalah overemphasized this aspect of Jewish mystical lore. Time and again Christian Kabbalists explained the significance of *gematria, notarikon*, and *temurah,* fascinated by the new exegetical avenues opened by Kabbalistic hermeneutics" (*ibid.* 263). Tishby (1994) cites Rabbi Judah Aryeh Modena's *Sefer Ari Nohem* (1690) to relevant effect. But now, the focus is on the danger from and in hegemonic shifts that have to do with "Christian supremacy" and "heresy." "One of the reasons why I have refrained from [kabbalah]," the Rabbi had explained, "is my experience, from my youth onward, of the arguments of apostates. . . . I know that you have among your Christian books a certain work written by Pico della Mirandola, who was the first Christian to study the kabbalah" (Lachower and Tishby 1994:35). No less consequential for the "Roaring Lion" had been the likes of "Giovanni of Quilini and others who wrote about the kabbalah [so that it] spread among them, as the sloping beam that supports the roof of their religion" (Lachower and Tishby *ibid.*). Not quite so parenthetically, it is worth relating all this to the book-of-defection and book-of-reconciliation premises that David Bakan (1991) foregrounds when he introduces *Maimonides on Prophecy.* For Bakan leads *The Guide of the Perplexed* into a quite relevant knot of dis/affiliation when he addresses the implications of approaching the book "with the assumption that Maimonides understood Judaism and Greek philosophy to be a priori alien to each other" (Bakan 1991:8). If one does so, *The Guide* becomes "extraordinarily difficult." For then "the book tends to become either a book of defection or a book of reconciliation, and then a knot."

> Some [Bakan observes] have taken the book as evidence of a kind of intellectual and spiritual disorder in Maimonides in his later years, as evidenced by his friendliness to Greek thinkers. Others take Maimonides to have sought to put Jewish—or even Judeo-Christian—thought together with Greek thought. But all who deal with him find knots that do not unravel. (*ibid.* 8)

These are knots that do not come unraveled even in the simultaneity with which, say, Leo Strauss posits dis/affiliation when, in "two consecutive sentences," he wrote about *The Guide* that "it is not a philosophic book—a book written by a philosopher for philosophers—but a Jewish book: written by a Jew for Jews." But then, Bakan notes, "as though Strauss may have had a key in his hand and dropped it, he states: '[The Book's] first premise is… that being a Jew and being a philosopher are two incompatible things'." The conclusion in *Maimonides on Prophecy* is that "This is not Maimonides' premise. Accepting this as Maimonides' premise makes it virtually impossible to open the door" (*ibid.* 9).

The cultures and transport of note here are not South American anthropophagy or Tutuola's cautionary tale or South India's *Kathakali* dance theater. Instead, dis/affiliation involves affinity with or defection from Athens; so, too, shifts within Jerusalem. As do Aizenberg and Atkins—in their preoccupation with "hebraic" and "de-hellenizing" strategies—Nelson Vieira contributes to the debate over this emergence of rabbinic interpretation in modern literary theory (Handelman) by way of readings in which the emphasis is on "the prophetic discourse of alterity." Taking his "cue from Derrida," Vieira identifies "a hermeneutics that derives from Jewish tradition but is neither rigidly fixed nor restricted to Jews" (1995:30). He quotes David Theo Goldberg's *Jewish Identity* as proposing that a "nomadic quest across ceaseless duration of history has become so set in the historical consciousness of Jews that Israel becomes just one more resting place. Jews, then, epitomize the peripatetic condition of the postmodern person" (*ibid.* 30-31). Vieira also recognizes the legitimacy of the connection that Handelman's *The Slayers of Moses* and "Jacques Derrida and the Heretic Hermeneutic" seek to establish with the rabbinic tradition and its marginal "rebellion" or textual "heresy." Nevertheless, he adds, "she overstresses the argument, claiming that this mode of interpretation was 'born of the tension between continuity and rebellion, attachment to the text and alienation from it'" (*ibid.* 45). Vieira's conclusion is that Handelman's thesis is enriched, "despite the ensuing academic dispute, by her exposition of Derrida's dialectic of scripture versus logos, of Hebrew versus Greco-Christian modes of thinking. . . . Handelman cites the Hebrew *davhar*—meaning 'thing/word,' 'deed,' and 'act'—as opposed to logos, linking word or ordered meaning to divine reality" (*ibid.*). In "Dehellenizing Literary Criticism," meanwhile, Atkins identifies "Hebraists," among them Geofrey Hartman, Jacques Derrida, and Harold Bloom, who have worked to further reshape an "already de-hellenized" literature which "long ago threw over classicism and its valoration of decorum, linearity and centering." Aizenberg has elsewhere summarized the "hebraism of contemporary literary theory" thus: "What the 'Hebraists' propose to do is to effect the same kind of revolution in critical language as has been effected in literary language. (Indeed, the distinction between the two is one of the things they want to obliterate)" (1991:250). Aizenberg also notes that in Handelman this "heretic hermeneutic" aims at "dislodging the Greek-Western logos" (Aizenberg *ibid.*). Only by so doing, its "critical iconoclasts believe, only by freeing hermeneutics from logocentrism and making commentary continuous with the literature it seeks to read, can the interpretive endeavor or work be led into alternatively productive ends" (*ibid.* 249-250).

Mudimbe offers a similar—but more complexly grounded—approach to hegemonic shifts; it holds, for example, that re-inscribing may in fact be re-constitution, but only into an oddly liberating yet watchful circulation within the Logic of the Same. The view is related to dis/affiliation that differs in being the thought of an African who is alienated-within rather than that of an alien-within. In Mudimbe's, as it were, mobius-stripped formulation of the contin-gent nature of "speech from within versus speech from without" (1991:7), if we are ever to arrive at *l'autre-face-du-royaume* it may be *le nom du père* alone that will effect the necessary exorcism of *le non du père,* of his *odeur.* In which case, "truly for Africa to escape the West involves an exact appreciation of the price we have to pay to detach ourselves from it. It assumes that we are aware of the extent to which the West, insiduously perhaps, is close to us; it implies a knowledge, in that which permits us to think against the West, of that which remains Western. We have to determine the extent to which our anti-Occidentalism is possibly one of the tricks directed against us, at the end of which it stands, motionless, waiting us" (Ngate 1988;11-12). So freighted, and *entre les eaux,* between tides, indeed are import and licence (Mudimbe 1991a).

I am very much persuaded that Biodun Jeyifo helps bring a disciplined clarity to bear on the nexus of power and interpretation that may well be at the various hearts of the matter here—given the apparent tendency to conflate premise with strategy and authority with simulacrum; and given the degree to which, in Veeser's summative formulation, "every expressive act is [necessarily] embedded in a network of material practices"; and that "every act of unmasking, critique, and opposition uses the tools it condemns and risks falling prey to the practice it exposes" (Veeser 1989:xi). "What gives [any] critical discourse its decisive effectivity," Jeyifo writes in a re-thinking of "arrested decolonization," is "the combination of historical, institutional and ideological factors that make the discourse a 'master' discourse which translates the avowed will-to-truth of all discourses into a consummated, if secret, will-to-power" (Jeyifo 1990:34).

Needless to say, when it is not Homer or Milton but Shakespeare himself who is thus "enskied and sainted" and consumed in "place and greatness," legitimation and shifts in hegemony involve even greater commerce in sign and surplus. The panoply of effects is especially unavoidable, I suppose, to the degree that

> millions of false eyes
> Are stuck upon [the Bard]; volumes of report
> Run with false, and most contrarious quest
> Make [him] the father of their idle dream,
> And rack [him] in their fancies.
> (*Measure for Measure* IV.i.58-64)

I propose, then, that far more than the usual degree of elegance and cleverness was staked out when, in 1940 and variously elsewhere, Borges resorted to that "Everything and Nothing" parable about Shakespeare. I offer the view notwithstanding its apparent affinity with the "contrarious quest" and "idle dream" and "fancies" that are suggested in such titles as *Everybody's Shakespeare* (Mack 1993), "Was Shakespeare Shakespeare?" (Martin 1965), and *Shakespeare, In Fact* (Matus 1994). "There was no one in him," Borges wrote; for "behind his face (which even through the bad paintings of those times, resembles no other) and his words . . . there was only a . . . dream dreamt by no one" (1964:248-249). It is worth recalling here that faced with that face which resembled no other (as in the Martin Droeshout engraving in the 1623 Folio), Ben Jonson had been struck by the poetic insufficiency of the image, but not quite as audaciously as Borges. "This figure that thou here seest put," Jonson wrote, "It was for gentle Shakespeare cut, / Wherein the graver had a strife / With nature to outdo the life." However, could the engraver "but have drawn his wit / As well in brass as he hath hit,

> His face, the print would . . . surpass
> All that was ever writ in brass!
> But since he cannot, reader, look
> Not on his picture, but his book.

Jonson had been moved to fashion a "memory" of William Shakespeare in which the Master becomes "a monument without a tomb /. . . alive still" and able to "shake a stage."

Borges does not quite allow for a Shakespeare that can be so satisfyingly contained in spectacle and text. Given his figure and its sum, it is perhaps worth making the point that in 1972 Borges recalled that someone had told him that it was "impossible to translate Shakespeare into Spanish"; and that he had responded with the observation that the playwright was equally impossible to translate into English. "Because if we were to translate Shakespeare into an English which is not the English of Shakespeare, a great deal would be lost. There are even sentences of Shakespeare's that only exist if pronounced with those same words, in that same order and with that same melody" (Sorrentino 1982:38). But then, in a commemorative poem about Shakespeare Leonard Digges (1640) had rather more succinctly conceded the exceptionalist point that to get it right at all, "Some second Shakespeare must of Shakespeare write," notwithstanding pretenders or heirs apparent (Wells 1988:xlix; Pechter 1986:75-76). In the end, neither Jonson nor for that matter William Basse who had urged Shakespeare to so "possess as lord, not tenant, thy grave, / That unto us or others it may be / Honour hereafter to be laid by thee" (1604), prove to be quite as ready to invest in the ghostlier demarcations within which Borges opts to situate the life and afterlife of his Shakespeare:

> History adds that before or after dying [Shakespeare] found himself in the presence of God and told him: "I who have been so many men in vain want to be one and myself." The voice of the Lord answered from a whirlwind: "Neither am I anyone; I have dreamt the world as you dreamt your work, my Shakespeare, and among the forms in my dream are you, who like myself are many and no one." (248-249)

About Shakespeare, the Argentinian and God have the advantage of us, in the divinely totalitarian gesture with which the interpretive circle is left open, even as it is closed off. For it is in "God's Script" (1949) alone that "a single word" could have such "absolute fullness" since "no word uttered by him can be inferior to the universe or less than the sum total of time." In such a con/ text, "Shadows or simulacra of the single word equivalent to language and to all a language can embrace are the poor and ambitious human words, *all, word, universe*" (Borges 1964:171).

But then, "Neither am I anyone," "absolute fullness," and "forms in my dream" are all just as likely to intensify the problem of Shakespeare and the anxiety of being influenced; and to authorize closure that will bring an end to continental drift, so to speak. Given the right circumstances, then, an all-embracing "Shakespeare" will be as de-formed in fact and fiction by the hegemonic pull of the "High Renaissance" as by the subaltern preoccupations of a post-colonial *wallah*. "Whoever he was," Mulkh Raj Anand asserts in *Caliban and Gandhi*, "William Shakespeare was a prophet of the emergent imperial sway" (1990:94). In this regard, that magic of Prospero's in *The Tempest* "anticipates, symbolically, the machines with which the Europeans subjugated the Black and Brown communities of Africa, [the] Americas and Asia." All the same, even as Shakespeare asserts the "will of the hero-prince to prevail" in such "royalist" plays as *King John, Richard II, Henry VI, Henry VIII*, and *Richard III*—and in the Rome of *Antony and Cleopatra, Julius Caesar*, and *Coriolanus*—the Renaissance dramatist also "anticipates revolts by those prevailed upon." That being the case, Anand concludes, Caliban's revolt against Prospero can be seen as a "cathartic anticipation of the slave's urge for freedom from imposition" (*ibid.*).

Be that as it may, Shakespeare and his import also "translate" according to vernacular agendas; and the particulars involved may be traced, Harriet Hawkins's *The Classics and Trash* notes, "from *King Lear* to *King Kong* and back" (1990:103-131). Anand therefore makes much of the fact that for all that Gandhi is suggestive of Caliban, this nationalist's Indian-ness involved consequential affiliations with a 6th-century B.C.E. world of Buddha and Mahavira Jina (*ibid.*). Elsewhere, Femi Ojo-Ade's reflections on culture, commitment, and construction engage in a "squint-eyed" and "centers-of civilization" framing of African literaure in European languages. In the process, he deals with terrains and types in which, "[n]ot surprisingly the colonial master, the symbolic Prospero, has given the magic of language to only a few chosen Calibans, who have used it in various ways" (1991:7). Such then is the trajectory along which Ojo-Ade works his way through "Afrikana" and certain of its master(ing) texts, beginning with a vernacular sub/version in which we get a "Once upon a time when the hen used to have teeth and before humanism began to die, when Africa was still free and the center of the universe." He conjures up the likes of Nobel laureate Wole Soyinka, Mongo Beti, and Es'kia Mphahlele, and of Buchi Emecheta and Ama Ata Aidoo, to make the point, *inter alia*, that to be "compelled to communicate in languages imposed from the outside is a true tragedy" (15). For which reason, he writes, "I saw and still see the literature with the squint of a killjoy, albeit an African killjoy" (20) In other circumstances, it is the krio of Sierra Leone and the Swahili of Tanzania that provide us with the measure of two other "Afrikana" attempts at transport and translation by way of Shakespeare. It is in one such context that Thomas Decker explains what his aim was in translating *Julius Caesar (Juliohs Siza)* and *As You Like It (Udat Di Kiap Fit—If the Cap Fits)* into krio in the 1970s. It was, he said, "first to make propaganda for the krio language by proving that the most serious things can be written and spoken in it, and secondly to make it possible for people who did not have the opportunity of reading Shakespeare at school to taste this great writer by seeing one of his most popular plays staged in their own language" (1988:xv). About his Swahili renditions, *Juliasi Kaizari* (1969) and *Mabepaari wa Venisi* (tellingly, *The Bourgeoisie of Venice*, 1972), Julius Nyerere's observation was that he would be very happy if [the translations] will assist his fellow students in advancing their Kiswahili studies so that they could speak and write it more proficiently. Kiswahili is a rich and beautiful language. But its beauty and richness can be augmented only if put to novel uses":

> nitafurahi sana ikiwa tafsiri hii itawasaidia wanafunzi wenzangu kuendelea kujifunza Kiswahili zaidi ili waweze kukisema na kukiandika kwa ufasaha zaidi. Kiswahili ni lugha tamu na pana sana. Laikini utamu na upana wake hauna budi utumiwe zaidi ndipo utakapoongezeka. (Mazrui 1996:71)

Whether because of the *ujamaa* sociology that justifies Nyerere's translation of *Merchant* as *Bourgeoisie,* or in the high culture of the Euro-American academy, the regimes of truth under which we discipline or otherwise transport the Elizabethan may require the canonical tidiness of an "authentic" Shakespeare, as in Orgel, or of "an essential" one in nine plays and the sonnets, as in Fraser. Of course, bard and body of work may be tempered, too, by the consolation of Margaret Webster's "Shakespeare without tears." Still, Borges suggests, in matters that touch upon the English dramatist, defining boundaries or keeping heresy at bay cannot be easy.

Consider the mix of irreverent sub/version and meticulous editorial scholarship that distinguishes the pages and drawings of the "complete, illustrated" texts of "The Cartoon Shakespeare Series." Its *Twelfth Night*, for one, promises, and delivers, a "most original treatment with characters in costume from all ages, motorbikes, jazz sessions, and limousines. And for the first time, a 6-page glossary is provided, so that none of the wit, ribaldry or innuendo is missed." Oval Projects Limited, with editorial and printing offices in London, Singapore, and Hong Kong, thus presented "the most popular of all Shakespeare's comedies" which, in 1985, joined cartoon editions of *Macbeth, Othello*, and *King Lear*—since followed by *The Tempest, The Merchant of Venice, The Taming of the Shrew, A Midsummer Night's Dream*, and *Hamlet*. In them, Shakespeare re-appears in language that is as folio-scrupulous as the comic-book medium is, one suspects, *épater le bourgeois* revisionist. The consequent admixture of "taste and distemper" may be said, with due licence from the Olivia of *Twelfth Night*, to be "generous, guiltless [but] of a disposition [to] take those things for birdbolts that [others] deem cannon bullets" (I.v.98-100).

Still, gunboat and bard meet in at least one studied exercise in can(n)on formation of recent vintage. I refer here to *The Economist*'s "Queen Margaret, or, Shakespeare Goes to the Falklands" (1982-83). This geo-political satire sought to compensate, the editors wrote, for the "exclusion of W. Shakespeare from the Task Force press corps" that chronicled Britain's Falklands and Argentina's Malvinas War. With "the nation bereft of its traditional record of British heroic victories [and in virtual proof of Borges's view of the malleability of the man], W. Shakespeare had to work within the economy of existing material", to which *The Economist* had obtained "exclusive rights." The playwright had inevitably to change most proper names and a few pronouns to reflect the 1982-83 Cabinet of Margaret Thatcher's Conservative government. The text of "Queen Margaret" is accordingly "made-up" of lines from twenty-four plays, and reconfigured as 213 extracts or broken extracts the origins of which range from *All's Well That Ends Well* through *The Taming of the Shrew* to *Pericles*. The architecture of the whole is also grounded, and armed, in the scholarship of a scrupulous endnote:

> None [of the extracts] is shorter than a line, almost all are couplets or longer. Only proper nouns have been altered, together with the relevant pronoun, plus a very few titles with capital letters (e.g. Backbencher for Nobility). Quotes from the more obvious scenes, such as *Coriolanus* IV vi, are sometimes indicated by a *passim*. The references are sequential for each scene and the key is: title point, act and scene point, line. The line reference is either from the Riverside Shakespeare or Bartlett's Concordance and should therefore be treated by readers as a rough rather than precise indication. (106)

When Shakespeare circulates thus, "as cultural capital within the voracious patterns of social consumption" (Aers and Wheale 1991:3), even more specialist productions are predictable, as is arguably the case in Eric Partridge's *Shakespeare's Bawdy* (1947). Evidence of an even more "distempered appetite" is apparent, I should think, in the three hundred and eight pages of *Shakespeare's Insults, Educating Your Wit* (1994) where Wayne Hill and Cynthia Öttchen (of Queen's College, Cambridge, no less) promise "the smartest stings ever to snap from the tip of an English-speaking tongue." Theirs is a context in which Shakespeare becomes "a treasure . . . a richly colored stone to throw . . . in genuine generosity" (ix). Meanwhile, in the mid-Manhattan context of Bauman Rare Books, located in New York's Waldorf-Astoria, Shakespeare is rather more elaborately "propertied." Extravagantly "velluminous" (Rushdie), he is there advertized in *The New York Times Book Review*, by way of a "magnificent limited gift edition [of] *The Tempest*, signed and superbly illustrated by Edmund Dulac, special copy number 0000 of 500, presumably intended for Dulac himself, and with original vellum binding and slipcase," which may be had for $2500 (10/1/95).

In and with all this readiness to stake claims through and about Shakespeare we risk a surfeit of visitations, of course—as was the case, apparently, on 11 February 1756, when there took place what was "infinitely the worst alteration of *The Tempest*." Montague Summers (1922) cites Theophilus Cibber to make the point that Shakespeare's play was thereupon "castrated into an opera" (lv). More recently, Thomas Quinn Curtiss's (9/17/90) review of the Paris production of "Peter Brooks's Inventive *Tempest*" catalogued a re-vision and sub/version in which Sotigui Kouyate, an African actor, played "with August dignity . . . the grievously wronged Prospero," a man persecuted, deprived of citizenship, position and fortunes, and sent into exile to triumph over adversities in a foreign land. An Asian, Shantal Malhar-Shivalingappa, was his Miranda; another African, Bakary Sangare, played Ariel. Brooks's Caliban was David Bennent, European and white. Usually seen as a monster, Caliban is here a "small and quicksilver acrobat." Interestingly, Bakary Sangare's Ariel is "lively, but less elf than earthbound funnyman" (Curtiss 10/17/90:10).

Whatever the reasons for such re-casting, we no doubt risk justifying a Lesley Aers and Nigel Whealey (1991) response to the question, "Where is Shakespeare now?" Their answer is, in essence, a mocking recognition of the discipline-and-punish arsenal that can(n)on formation engenders. Out of it comes a "Shakespeare" that then becomes "the great Shibboleth of Eng. Lit," and thus a phenomenon that is several times made over into subjugating contortions of itself as *Sashpierre*: "a word used for detecting foreigners"; as *Shaxbee*: "a secret password identifying members of a party or cult"; and as *Shakeschafte*: "a mode of speech characteristic of a profession or class." The playwright's family name is recorded, we learn, in over eighty variants during the medieval and early modern period. For Aers and Wheale the variants—from Willm Shagspere through Wm Shaxpere to Shaxberd—mark yet another instance of the radical instability among many more which encourages us to question every aspect of the reputation which attaches to so unstable a name. Notwithstanding, or perhaps because of, its status as an "insecure shibboleth," the idea of the plays and poems grouped under the generic heading "Shakespeare" has come to represent or to serve the interests of "a national totem; a rite of passage that has to be negotiated within education; and, having demonstrated competence in the mystery, the name becomes a fetish which identifies an elite" (1991:2-3).

The consequences can be infectious, even in putatively oppositional contexts. So Richard Burt (1996) claims in his "challenging" reading of Shakespeare and Ben Jonson. For which reason, Burt's aim is to modify certain key premises in otherwise revisionist New Historicist or Marxist accounts of "the theater as social institution" in which "Shakespeare has been regarded as the central poet of the nation, a representative of the progressive, popular voice" while Jonson "has been relegated to the margins" (79). Burt's preference is to restage matters, and on that ground he confronts arguments in which Shakespeare's "cultural centrality is reaffirmed" by the assumption that his is a "universal vision of experience [that should remain] secure [and] essentially unshaken because he had access to the fully developed techniques and values of a popular theater turned into a national institution" (*ibid.*).

Given the amplitude of the commerce in Shakespearean shibboleths, it could hardly have been possible to exorcise the perception, or the fact, of incontinence from the 1991 New York City Central Park Shakespeare Festival—at least, insofar as it involved the staging of the Brazilian Caca Rosset's *Sonho de Uma Noite de Verão (A Midsummer Night's Dream).* Presumably taking his cue from the fact that Titania is the queen of the Amazons, Rosset had staged his Teatro do Ornitorrinco Shakespeare on a set that represented an Amazonian rain forest, "but one defoliated by an unspeci-fied calamity [as a result of which] trees have been reduced to stumps," according to the studied calm of *New York Times* critic Mel Gussow. The calm belies the temptation to excess which Rosset otherwise provoked in, say, the Anglo-American synopsis that we get in *Newsweek*'s, "Shakespeare-as-a-Second-Language." For in it, so we are told, "A man in Elizabethan dress, wearing an ass's head, spouts Shakespeare in Portuguese while borne aloft by seven nearly naked women. . . . The only thing missing is Shakespeare" (8/12/91). Meanwhile, "Bared Bard: To Peel or not to peel," graced by a photograph of a white female straddling a black male, effectively captures the graphic thrust of the precis that *Time* produced (8/5/91).

Elsewhere, the imputation of incontinence in a Shakespeare production would come in Samuel Schoenbaum, and provoked when "imperialism . . . called the shots" in Tony Richardson's 1987 Los Angeles staging of *Antony and Cleopatra.* "The time frame was updated to the Fascist 'thirties," Schoenbaum writes, "with Octavius a bare-skulled Mussolini caricature with a personal guard of Blackshirts; Cleopatra was a royal black African (shades of the Duce's conquest of Ethiopia!) with hip-length tresses, just going gray in cornrows, and black attendants, while Antony wore Khaki and jodhpurs" (Everett 1988:288). The impression of there being an edge to this expression of doubt about the legitimacy of cornrows and jodhpurs in Shakespeare might be instructively tested against the degree of tolerance that Christopher Michaud records in his *Reuters* summary of reviews of The Royal National Theatre's 1992 *Richard III.* Michaud cites *USA Today* critic David Patrick Stearns to the effect that Sir Ian McKellen "strides toward the audience in 20th-century military garb [reminiscent of the regimes of Hitler and Stalin] and issues his 'Now is the winter of our discontent' speech like marching orders." But, here, all the same, was a "bold, startling interpretation" in which the play presents a 1930s England with a fascist frame of reference.

Michaud reports, too, that *New York Times* critic Frank Rich found McKellen's "frightening insidious portrayal of a Machiavellian politician" to be "a stunning antiheroic alternative to the archetypal Olivier image;" and that at *The New York Post* Clive Barnes highlighted the drama of McKellen's playing Richard with a "brahmin-like accent," thus reflecting director Richard Eyre's feeling that "so much of the play is about class, in which the characters are "very conscious of whether they are old or new money." Barnes notes, in appreciation, that McKellen "turns Richard into a caricature of a Hollywood . . . version of a British World War Two officer and gentleman, barking out his poetry in Sandhurst's rasping bombast, relishing his insolence and glorying in his class villainy." Thus re-cast and re-positioned, *Richard III* was a "stunningly chilling performance," with a "transcendent star performance," even if, for Frank Rich, as was the case, incidentally, for most of the other critics, the export-to-America supporting cast was "far below the high National Theatre standard visible right now at its home base" ("Sir Ian McKellen Wins Raves for His *Richard III*" *Reuters* 06/12/92).

The North American weeklies, *Time* (06/22/92) and *Newsweek* (06/22/92), also provided commentary, in "Made Glorious Summer" and "A Power-Hungry Psycopath in Any Era," respectively. *Time*'s William A. Henry writes of "an arrestingly cruel and humorless, all chill and absolutely no charm" representation of Richard, in a production that "has won raves from London to Cairo to Tokyo." And Jack Kroll, of *Newsweek*, noted that "like a rock star, Ian McKellen has toured the world since 1990 in Shakespeare's Richard III. . . . [That he has turned] the dangerously familiar opening speech ('Now is the winter of our discontent') into a sinister manifesto, a mini-*Mein Kampf* that flaunts Richard's physical deformity and proclaims his intent to get the crown at any cost." Deformity and re-vision meet in happy congruence when "The modern military garb gives Richard's useless left arm, limping gait and twisted back the look of battle traumas. He is a soldier-Satan, underscored by McKellen's dazzling dexterity as he dons a glove one-handed, his fingers working into it like five sibling snakes slithering to their lair." The climax comes in a fitting death by mutation: "At the end, sprawled on Bosworth Field like a stomped beetle, McKellen emits a bloodcurdling death rattle—the sound of . . . evil energy escaping like toxic waste into the dark." We do not need to wonder at the imagery in which Howard Kissel, of the *New York Daily News*, finally grounds his view of the actor's virtuosity: "McKellen minimises Richard's hunch and maximises his arm—'like a blasted sapling, withered up.' At one point, brandishing it in an enemy's face, he makes you believe the arm has no bone and is soft as a large soggy fungus" (Michaud *ibid.*).

Still, *The Village Voice* did publish a review, "Fawlty Tower" (6/23/

92), in which it registered a terribly unhappy reaction to what it saw as the production's sheer incontinence. Unimpressed to the point of extravagance, Michael Feingold objected to the undisciplined "excuse for Sir Ian McKellen to show off." He also offered advice—in the spirit of his discontent: "If you elect to stay past the intermission of this shoddy travesty, I suggest walking out—loudly and noisily if possible—just after [Charlotte Cornwell as Queen Elizabeth's] exit." For as a sample of the Royal National Theatre of Great Britain at work, this production-for-America, in which "the catch-as-catch-can costumes suggest the fascist '30s," is "a near total disgrace—a production that has no coherent vision, no imagination, no depth, no sense of shape or pace, no imaginative strokes that aren't weary from overuse, no rapport with either the text or the world outside, and for a capper, the most shockingly inept supporting cast." Meanwhile, on its *Headline News*, CNN's Sylvia Thornquist cut across latitude and protocol to report, under "A Renowned British Actor Makes the Move to the Big Screen," that the "openly gay" and recently knighted McKellen had performed to such effect that in Leipzig "they thought we were making a comment on Hitler; and in Cairo they thought it was some comment on Saddam Hussein" (06/12/92).

The variousness of the Shakespeare that is thus put on display reinforces Borges's parable of indeterminate sign and surplus. It allows us room, yet again, for some thirteen other ways of looking at a blackbird. We may reflect, then, upon the androgynous "hobgoblin" of a character that Caliban becomes in John Dryden's reading of *The Tempest*, where "the copiousness of [Shakespeare's] Invention" produced a creature, "begotten by an Incubus on a Witch," who is shown to have "all the discontents, and malice, of a Witch and of a Devil." He has also been "most judiciously furnished with a person, a Language, and a character which will suit him both by his Fathers and Mothers side" (Dryden 1984:239-240). But then, should we choose to deny the relevance of Dryden, eighteenth-century and Englishman that he was, there is Houston A. Baker, twentieth-century African American, and game enough. For with the latter we may marvel, if nothing else, at the panache of "Caliban's Triple Play," with its anti-dualist, "three-personed-god" interpretation of Caliban as a master signifier and liberating tactician whose bases are in "Third World geographies" (1986:395). It is from within this "School of Caliban" that Saldívar elsewhere recognizes Baker's "unabashedly political" celebration of the thought that Caliban performs a 'powerful drama of deformation'" because he is very much "like a maroon in Jamaica, or Nat Turner in the U.S. South" (Saldívar 1991:147).

Meanwhile, liberating tactics in W.E.B. Du Bois had been somewhat more canonical in the "Of the Training of Black Men" chapter of *The Souls of Black Folk* (1903). Du Bois—whose maternal grandfather was named Othello Burghardt (1791-1872)—had earlier conceived of a high culture of translations "across the color line" in which it would be possible to "move arm in arm with Balzac and Dumas"; to which Aristotle and Aurelius would be summoned and respond "with no scorn or condescension." Here, "smiling men and welcoming women glide in gilded halls"; and here, too, Du Bois had declared, "I sit with Shakespeare and he winces not" (1996:157). But then, the commensurability of so marvelous a proposition with the momentous struggle between "barbarism" and "civilization" in the lands of America was always a matter of some contestation. This was especially true in the nineteenth century, given the nature of its double-dealings in European ancestrality and *pureza de sangre* (purity of blood). Consider the implications in Henry James, for example, when he wrote; "If [Nathaniel] Hawthorne had been a young Englishman, or a young Frenchman of the same degree of genius, the same cast of mind, the same habits, his consciousness of the world around him would have been a very different affair; however obscure, however reserved, his own personal life, his sense of the life of his fellow mortals would have been almost infinitely more various. One might enumerate," James added, "the items of high civilization, as it exists in other countries, which are absent from the texture of American life, until it should be a wonder to know what was left. No State, in the European sense of the word, and indeed barely a specific national name. No sovereign, no court, no personal loyalty, no aristocracy, no church, no clergy, no army, no diplomatic service, no country gentlemen, no palaces, no castles, nor manors, nor old country houses, nor parsonages, nor thatched cottages or ivied ruins; no cathedrals, nor abbeys, nor little Norman churches; no great Universities nor public schools—no Oxford, nor Harrow; no literature, no novels, no musuems, no pictures, no political society, no sporting class—no Epsom nor Ascot!" (James 1987:133).

The imputation of belatedness may be understood as Bourget and Arnold do, above; so, too, in light of the satirical urgency with which Alejo Carpentier limns his terrain and type when, in *Los pasos perdidos (The Lost Steps)*, he confronts us with a "scenography" that "defied ubication." This New-World "ship of ours," Carpentier writes, "made one think of Bosch's *Ship of Fools*"—what with its "its cargo of bellowing bulls, coops of chicken, pigs running about the deck under the hammock of the Capuchin and getting tangled up in his rosary of seeds, the song of the Negress cooks, the laughter of the Greek diamond-hunter, the prostitute in her mourning nightgown bathing in the prow, the guitar-players making music for the sailors to dance" (1956:119). In addition to which, "in the humidity of this world, the ruins were more ruins, the vines pried loose the stones in a different way, the insects had other tricks, and the devils were more devils when the Negro dancers groaned beneath their horns" (*ibid.*). Here was difficult terrain, indeed, in which to map cultural formations where Shakespeare and Balzac, or Milton and Dumas, would not wince.

The invention of categories with which to translate and accommodate, or else contend with, such indices of Old-World—meaning European—hegemony has always been an obsessive affair in "the dialectic of our America" (Saldívar). The consequences resonate in the reach for inclusiveness that we get in a Simon Bolívar (1783-1830) and a José Martí (1853-1895); so, too, in the "cultural cannibalism" that Andrade emphasizes in "Manifesto Antropófago." Elsewhere, hierarchies of culture and dis/affiliation preoccupied the Domingo Faustino Sarmiento of *Facundo, o la civilización y la barbarie* (1845). In his time, Sarmiento had engaged in a "double-dealing logic," Doris Sommer (1990) explains. Endorsed as he was by European exoticism, Sarmiento "begins by announcing programmatic oppositions between civilization and barbarism." Sarmiento's was a "logic" which "allegedly glorifies [a] Land" that had resisted domestication; but the reasoning also exposed a duplicity in which Sommer's "Plagiarized Authenticity" implicates *The Tempest*:

> To whose authority would the virtuous, or stubborn Land yield? Whom would she allow to inscribe his name, to produce a landmark? Certainly not the Indians. They had had their chance and were obviously unequal to the challenge, mostly because they had been cast as nomads in the discourse of the Americas ever since the sixteenth century settlement of Roanoke and Shakespeare's *The Tempest*. (141-42)

The Arielism of the Uruguayan José Enrique Rodó (1900) was no less involved in racial and cultural mappings of the Americas. Rodó's agenda and his Shakespeare required that an "exquisite bronze of *The Tempest*'s Ariel" be privileged; and it sits accordingly, "like the presiding spirit" over an "exquisite yet austere decor" made up of Prospero's classroom and books. This "ethereal" creation, Rodó proposes, "symbolizes the noble, soaring aspect of the human spirit." The figure stands thus, in contrast to "the clinging vestiges of Caliban [who is] the play's symbol of brutal sensuality" (31). In Rodó the Americas were at a historical juncture in which "barbarism no longer unleashes its often heroic and regenerative hordes to attack the beacons of civilization." For that very reason, "high culture [Euro-Latin American Arielism] must be on guard against the mild but equally destructive effect of different peaceful, even educated hordes: the inescapable hordes of vulgarity," precisely the horde that was gaining the upper hand in that "Cyclopian nation" in the making, the United States (1988:31). "We have our *USA-mania*. [However], it must be limited by the boundaries that our reason and sentiment jointly dictate" (71). For where "Caliban casts out Ariel," the Euro-American Ezra Pound of "Hugh Selwyn Mauberley" (1920) would later agree, the "dead art" of "the sublime / in the old sense" is invariably supplanted by "accelerated grimace" and "tawdry cheapness" (1957:61-2).

Although the differences are instructive, there is a related framing of the politics of *The Tempest* when Cuba's Fernández Retamar (1989) notes Jan Kott's irritation at the utopian stubbornness of French philosopher Ernest Renan's 1878 *Caliban, Suite de "la Tempête"*: "Renan saw Demos in Caliban; in his continuation of *The Tempest* he took him to Milan and made him attempt another, victorious coup against Prospero. [It marks an interpretation that is] flat and [that does] not do justice to Shakespeare's Caliban" (114). Incidentally, Rodó shares a similar, though more directly partisan, discomfort with Renan's "enthronement of Caliban" (Rodó: 1988:58; 98). Of course, the discomfort is one that is not shared by members of the "School of Caliban," among whom Retamar and Lamming are of seminal importance. *Their* revolutionary Caliban is one who would, and with good cause, see in Ariel's accommodationist postures little more than the attributes of a mimic-man. *Pace* Rodó, this Ariel is exactly what Caliban calls him, a "jesting monkey" (III.ii.52) whose penchant for accommodation—"Sir, all this service / Have I done since I came" and "Was't well done?" (V.i. 226; 240)—does show him to be unbearably "correspondent to command" (I.ii.297).

There are echoes here of Juan Zorilla de San Martin's rejection of Arielism—however without embracing Caliban—in the "Ariel y Caliban Americanos" chapter of *Las Américas*. According to this reading, Rodó had invested in the insubstantial and in a not-quite relevant pedigree: "*Pero bien ese Ariel, geniecillo del aire, inglés de nacimiento y de lengua, es demasiado instable, impalpable, y muy poco o nada afirmativo para poder constituir...una fe comun*" [That Ariel of his, a sprite, English by birth and in speech, is far too unstable, too unsubstantial, and lacks any truly positive attributes around which a bond of community could be fashioned] (1945:33). Octavio Paz is inclined, for his part, to be impatient with the minutiae of dis/affiliation, given what he takes to be manifest in Shakespeare's play. In consequence, identity and allegiance are sharply drawn in the Mexican's *Conjunctions and Disjunctions*. "For the Christian West," Paz asserts, "foreign societies were always the incarnation of evil. Whether savage or civilized, they were manifestations of the inferior world, the body. And the West treated them with the same rigor with which ascetics punished their senses. Shakespeare says it straight out in *The Tempest*" (1974:110). Saldívar reads Baker to similar effect: "In Baker's view, *The Tempest* is especially significant for vernacular 'racial' writing because it contains 'the venerable trope of Prospero and Caliban—figures portrayed in terms of self-and-other, the West and the Rest of Us, the rationalist and the debunker, the colonizer and the indigenous people" (1991:146). We get an even more naked representation of the view from Frantz Fanon when he roots Mannoni's psychology-of-colonialism reading of Shakespeare's play in the Logic of the Same: "Prospero, as we know, is the main character of Shakespeare's comedy, *The Tempest*. Opposite him we have his daughter, Miranda, and Caliban. Toward Caliban, Prospero assumes an attitude that is well known to Americans in the southern United States. Are they not forever saying that niggers are just waiting for the chance to jump on white women?" (1967:107; but see, too, the Caliban and Miranda of Marshall's "Brazil").

Meanwhile, along the equatorial line and across from Brazil, the 1986 Nobel Laureate Wole Soyinka reaches back to craft, in "Shakespeare and the Living Dramatist" (1988), a rather more genial display of Shakespeare's re-rootings. It is in relationship to the dramatist's Arab co-practitioners that the Nigerian ponders "the phenomenal hold" and "universal puzzle of Shakespeare's evocative power"; that he weaves "universalism" into "local colour" in response to Sean O'Casey's question, "Was Shakespeare at Actium and Philippi?" The English dramatist, with "his limitless universal themes," shows himself to be quite at home in matters "congenial to the Arabic epic—or narrative—tradition." He may thus not be unrelated to Ahmad Shaqui's struggle-for-Egyptian-independence drama, *Masra' Kliyupatra (The Fall or Death of Cleopatra)*, for "between 1899 and 1950, some sixteen plays of Shakespeare had been translated and/or adapted by Arab poets and dramatists, [among them]—need I add?—*Antony and Cleopatra*" (206).

"Shakespeare and the Living Dramatist" is a weave of patterns that are as fine-pointed as they are elaborate. With them Soyinka proceeds to implicate, for example, the cult of Isis and the *Islamic Book of the Dead* in those final house-of-death lines from Shakespeare's Cleopatra. For him, the Egyptian Queen speaks figuratively of the house of death, but then again, perhaps she does much more; especially if the "awesomeness" of her words "can only be fully absorbed by an Egyptian, or one steeped in the esoteric cults of Egypt and allied religions, including Islam." By appealing to the provocations of fantasy and the staging of facts, and by "evoking tones, textures, smells, and even tastes which were so alien to the wintry climes of Europe," Soyinka explores latitude and depth in *Antony and Cleopatra*. Having etched, as Shakespeare did, the conflict between Egypt and Rome on so realistic a canvas, how—*pace* that Irishman O'Casey—how can it be at all reasonable that the English playwright never "sailed up the Nile and kicked up sands in the shadow of the pyramid" (207). Indeed, how resist the urge to be less than content merely "to adopt or reclaim" Shakespeare?

M. M. Badawi, in an article in *Cairo Studies* (1964) titled, "Shakespeare and the Arab World," states that the matter goes much further. Apparently it was not simply that Shakespeare stumbled on to an Arab shore during his unpublicized peregrinations; he was in fact an Arab. His real name, cleansed of its anglicized corruption, was Shayk al Subair, which everyone knows is as dune-bred an Arabic name as any English poet can hope for. (206)

On such a point, Soyinka is inclined to be tolerant: "That Shakespeare may turn out to be an Arab after all is less alarming a prospect than that he should prove to be Christopher Marlowe." Still, licence and import notwithstanding, the truth remains that "no one has yet begun to ransack the sand-dunes of Arabia, shovelling aside the venerable bones of Bedouins in the hope of disinterring the bones of the author of *Antony and Cleopatra*" (220). So, too, incidentally, is there comfort and companionship for Wole Soyinka in the fact that the *European Shakespeares* of Dirk Delabastita and Lieven D'hulst (1992) records no evidence of disinternment in the wake of, say, Brigitte Schultze's encountering in Jerzy Sito's "Shakespeare, Poland's National Poet" another summary claim in yet another history of Shakespeare's reception (63).

And "from toe to crown... / make us strange stuff"

Rosario Ferré's project, in *Fábulas de la Garza Desangranda (Fables of the Bleeding Heron)* (1984), involves quite radical re-articulations of the female—Ariadne, Dafne, Ismene, Antígona, among them—into full-voiced presence and plenitude. The figures that Ferré thus metamorphoses stand in some resolute contrast to the self-destructive paralysis, or implosive rage, heretofore visited upon the heroines of Ovid's *Heroïdes*, to which she calls explicit attention. It is in Ovid that Ariadne, for example, tells Theseus that since being abandoned by him she has "either roamed about, like a Bacchante roused by the Ogyian god, or, looking out upon the sea, [or] sat chilled upon the rock, as much a stone [herself] as was the stone [she] sat υ pon." And it is in Ovid, too, that she says, "Straight then my palms resoun led upon my breasts, and I tore my hair, all disarrayed as it was from sleϵp" (Kestner 1989:57). Meanwhile, in the *sola, perduta, abbandonata* subplot of Shakespeare's *Measure for Measure*, "poor Mariana" cuts quite the appropriate figure when she is abandoned by Angelo. Left in tears, not one of them dried with his comfort, and accused, besides, "of discoveries of dishonor," Shakespeare's "wronged" and "dejected" maid sits "at the moated grange" where, before it all ends well, she listens to—and is limned into—"one of the loveliest songs" in all Shakespeare (Bald 1987:106):

> Take, O take those lips away,
>   That so sweetly were forsworn;
> And those eyes, the break of day,
>   Lights that do mislead the morn;
> But my kisses bring again, bring again,
> Seals of love, but sealed in vain, sealed in vain. (IV.i. 1-6)

In the Shakespeare of *The Rape of Lucrece* the condition of the wronged maid is irredeemably consequential and dramatic: "He, he ... tis he," says Lucrece when she identifies Tarquin as her violator. Thereafter, she acts but only to make herself a "self-slaughtered body":

> Even here she sheathed in her harmless breast
> A harmful knife, that thence her soul unsheathed. . . .
> And bubbling from her breast it doth divide
> In two slow rivers, that the crimson blood
> Circles her body in on every side. . . . (1723-38)

Equally relevant, I should think, is the patient virtue with which Anne, "so young, so old widowed" into a "meanly matched marriage" with Richard III, anticipates her fate. Her "woman's heart," she tells Queen Elizabeth, "Grossly grew captive to his honey words" and thus "proved the subject of [her] own soul's course." As a result,

> Never yet one hour in his bed
> Did I enjoy the golden dew of sleep,
> But with his timorous dreams was still awaked.
> Besides, he hates me for my father Warwick,
> And will, no doubt, shortly be rid of me.
>   (*Richard III*, IV.i.78-86)

Making the difference dazzle in any such consummation is what the Puerto Rican writer Ferré does when she engages in a re-writing of Ovid and Shakespeare no less than of Saint Paul. This last is an object of concern in "Cuando las mujeres quieren a los hombres" ("When Women Love Men"), with its Caribbean "flow of consciousness" and the vituperative climax that further divides Ferré's two Isabels—on the one hand, Isabel Luberza, the late Amborisio's white, middle-class wife, and, on the other, Isabel la Negra, his black prostitute mistress (Olmos 1983:82-84). Meanwhile, with her Shakespeare, Ferré's interest in "a different ending" re-figures the assumed genius of women for dying. The Puerto Rican New Worlder assumes an identity here that stands in some intriguing relationship to that "Renaissance Woman," Helisenne de Crenne, and the *querelle des femmes* that *she* attended to in her 1539 *Les Epistres de familières et invectives*. "It is clear," Mustacchi and Archambault write, that "Helisenne is conscious of the 'Heroides' tradition in writing the invective letters: she had surely read some or all of Ovid's twenty-one *Heroïdes,* most of which are long complaints in verse attributed to famous mythological women and intended for their unfaithful lovers" (1986:9). More contemporaneously, Ferré inflects the continuum that Ovid represents in ways that are also reinforced in Margaly Martínez Gamba (*Restos y cenizas*). With her *Restos y cenizas* treatment of seven *Heroïdes* women and seven modes of existence that have been inscribed in art and contained in history, Gamba works her own revisionist way through the "wreckage and ashes" of a controlling *mito de varón* (man-centered myth). She thus re-figures "Euridice, Electra, Clitemnestra, Antígona, Medea y Helena"; for they are the *"siete nombres, siete modos de estar en el mundo, siete formas de entrar en la historia y en el arte, siete mitos* [y] *siete mujeres convertidas en mito a la sombra de un varón"* (Fiscal 1990:54). Like Ferré, Gamba has a clear agenda: *"Es un llamado para que de entre restos y cenizas ... emerja un ser humano en plenitud"* (*ibid*. 55). Her call is for moral attention and restoration to plenitude.

The tradition of *plenitud* within which Ferré thus re-designs and re-figures cannot but impose telling strains on perspectives about women who, like Othello's Desdemona ("Your wife, my lord; your true / And loyal wife"), are very much at home in their "ability to endure misfortune without complaint, [an ability believed to be so] consonant with the passivity associated with women from the time of Aristotle, who allowed women excellence [only] in the 'imperfect' or passive virtues of *continentia, verecundia,* and *tolerantia,* or chastity, modesty, and long-suffering." Never too far behind, of course, was the corollary excellence of women in regard to *ars moriendi,* the art of dying—agreeably, well (Lamb 1990:127). It matters, too, that this is an art that can be even worse compounded—as happens when, in revisiting Shakespeare, Tayeb Salih embeds the genre in the *Othello* of his Sudanese *Season of Migration to the North* (1970). In the spectacular incontinence of the drama that Salih's Desdemona makes of her Night of Nights, "She continued to look at the blade-edge with a mixture of astonishment, fear and lust. Then she took hold of the dagger and kissed it fervently. Suddenly she closed her eyes and stretched out in the bed, raising her middle slightly, opening her thighs ['that repository of secrets, where good and evil are born'] wider: 'Please, my sweet,' she said moaning: 'Come ... I'm ready now'" (1970:164).

Constellation of such "virtues" will in fact produce any number of dangers, Ferré's revisionist perspective insists—as much to others as, worse, to self. This much is clear in *Richard III*'s Anne and in *The Rape of Lucrece.* Violence and violation are no less consequential in *Hamlet,* where yet another instance of living in chaste containment so as to die agreeably and well results in the (un)making of an Ophelia. The play's urgent appeals to and investment in her chastity are framed in terms of fear; she is constrained throughout by narrow lessons in virginity and by the amplitude of princely privilege. She is variously warned that as far as female companionship is concerned, her apparent suitor is a prince, and therefore incarnate as reasons-of-state. From her brother she receives lessons in the virtue of fear. "Fear it . . . dear sister," Laertes urges, as he warns her against "too credent" an ear, and against opening her "chaste treasure" to "unmaster'd importunity." Be wary, he tells her in parting, for "contagious blastments are most imminent" in the liquid dew of youth. "Best safety [therefore] lies in fear" and in being "in the rear of your affection, / Out of the shot and danger of desire." It is, after all, the case that "The chariest maid is prodigal enough" (I.iii.10-50). No less constricted and constricting is the father's fear that some bastard birth would follow consummation of the shot and danger of desire. "Not to crack the wind of the poor phrase," he says, "you'll tender me a fool." Laertes's sober intensity is reinforced by the mockery that comes with Polonius's investment in education by belittling assault: "Affection! pooh! you speak like a green girl, / Unsifted in such perilous circumstance." For which reason, Ophelia is to "be somewhat scanter of [her] maiden presence." In plain terms, the father would have her preserve what Prospero would call her "virgin-knot" lest too light winning make the prize light. His order is therefore that "from this time forth / [she not] slander any moment leisure / As to give words or talk with Lord Hamlet." Her response is a very satisfactory, "I shall obey, my lord" (I.iii.90-136).

Not unreasonably, it is Juliet Dusinberre's view in *Shakespeare and the Nature of Women* (1975) that under such tutelage the woman is allowed "no independent identity"; that it is "a condition which makes her incapable of coping with a world in which [the likes of her father and brother have] no real part—the world of her relation to Hamlet" (Hamana 1988:27). In the end, the more persuasive evidence is that Ophelia has all along been caught in a madness-inducing repression of desire; in the strain of Hamlet's "antique disposition"; and in her father's misapprehending and fatal decision to traffic and trade with his daughter into a brave new world of royal blood ties. Ophelia sinks into and under the weight of the contradictions. She also re-constitutes them in the insights of her songs when she goes mad and is full of talk about "Quoth she, 'Before you tumbled me, / You promised me to wed'" (IV.v.60-66). In my view, this return of the repressed in Ophelia is nowhere more transparent than in the briskness with which a virgin loses her virginity in one such song:

> Tomorrow is Saint Valentine's Day,
> All the morning betime,
> And I a maid at your window,
> To be your Valentine.
> Then up he rose, and donn'd his clothes,
> And dupp'd the chamber door;
> Let in the maid, that out a maid
> Never departed more. (IV.v.48-58)

Consider in this light the dissheveled entry into and exit from Ophelia's chamber that Hamlet had made earlier, "with his doublet all unbrac'd, / no hat upon his head, his stockings foul'd, / Ungart'rd, and down-gyvved to his ankle." All his "bulk and being" notwithstanding, he had "long stayed" to no real purpose: "That done, he lets me go" (II.i.75-95). Consider, too, the charged I-get-the-point-thank-you brevity of her exchange with Hamlet in Act 3, Scene 2. There, to his "Lady, shall I lie in your lap?" her reply had been "No my lord." His explanatory double-entendre, "I mean my head upon your lap," had allowed her to agree, "Ay, my lord." But she had thereafter retreated from the thrust of his "Do you think I meant country matters?" with "I think nothing," and had withdrawn even further with her "What is, my lord?" response to Hamlet's "That's a fine thought to lie between maids' legs" (III.ii.107-114). The give-and-take is pointed enough, but is "still better, and worse," when in response to her "You are keen, my lord, you are keen," Hamlet had assured her that "It would cost you a groaning to take off mine edge" (III.ii.236-238).

There is, finally, the *ars moriendi* context of the "weeping brook" in which this woman sinks to her end in mud. Gertrude's narrative is, effectively, a garland of sexual confections and insight; so, too, a record of the return of the repressed. She recalls that Ophelia's flowers included those "long purples" which "liberal shepherds give a grosser name," but which "our cold maids do dead men's fingers call." Wreathed in this way, her garments full of drink, Ophelia sinks in her "melodious lay" to a "muddy death." That the whole should end thus, in a complexly embedded sexuality, is hardly surprising—given the structure, "not around a focal point but as in a helix," with which Frankie Rubinstein has identified the capaciousness of Shakespeare's sexual puns (1995:xi). Appropriately, in Gertrude's version of the same, Ophelia's sinking is as much lyrical pathos as it is graphic-grotesque (IV.vii.168-184). In Hamana, there is a quasi-volitional dimension in a "suicide" that was "intended not as a mere desperate return to the peace of nonbeing but as a more positive meaning" (1988:36). The experience of this death by water is rather more grounded, so to speak, in *Highlife for Caliban* where Ophelia's end comes with knowledge of "mud in the holes between her thighs"—

> where under the hair she [had] waited to be
> dead in a place into which
> a voice, politely impolite, leaned
>   once, to say,
> "lady, shall I lie in your lap?" (66)

To suggest that "the most beautified" Ophelia's story is a *Heroïdes*-like fable about yet another naked exhausting of female presence is to move us directly into the transforming urgency that we get in Ferré's fables of bleeding herons and endangered women. Read both for itself and within other narratives of wreckage and ashes, the Puerto Rican's *fábulas* reinforce the concerns of her 1976 *Papeles de Pandora (Pandora's Papers)* and the revisionist postures of the 1971-1976 *Zona de carga y descarga (Loading and Firing Zone)*. "When I was working on my book fables," Ferré explains, "I read the *Iliad* and Sophocles. The character of Antigone is very important to me. . . . The idea was to give a new history of women, interpreted as it should have been and given a different ending: Desdemona kills Othello, Ariadne leaves Theseus. . . . If you read the *Iliad* from a feminine point of view and take into account the female characters as well as the goddesses, it's truly a dazzling work" (García-Pinto 1991:98).

There is an Ophelia-like figure who shadows those who seek to excel in the passive virtues only to surrender their identity in lines like Ophelia's "And I, of ladies most abject and wretched, / That sucked the honey of his music vows" (*Hamlet* III.i 158-159). In *Othello* the figure is, of course, Barbarie—"her hand on her bosom, her head on her knee." Dutifully, bizarrely appropriate, given the barbarian echo of her incarnation in *Othello,* she haunts Shakespeare's Desdemona as she, too, prepares to die well:

> My mother had a maid call'd Barbarie:
> She was in love, and he she loved proved mad
> And did forsake her: she had a song of "willow;"
> An old thing 'twas, but it express'd her fortune,
> And she died singing it: that song tonight
> Will not go from my mind; I have much to do,
> But to go hang my head all at one side,
> And sing it like poor Barbarie. (IV.iii.26-33)

There is a cluster of ideas and a continuum of representations in all this that Ferré is bent on dislodging when, in re-visiting Othello and Desdemona's Night of Nights, she steers "Banquete de Bodas" into a difference that is ironic, activist, and barbarian (non-*tolerantia*). As a result, even though to quite opposed effects, it is hard to imagine a re-plotting of *Othello* that could be any closer to Iago's conjoining of the couple into "erring barbarian and supersubtle Venetian" (1.iii.361-362). In Ferré, the mismatched couple's "habitación ceremonial" is, at first, and ominously, a setting in which Desdemona appears, "vestida del rojo primario" [dressed in red]; where she is, at first, "perdidamente enamorada del Moro y del Amor"—hopelessly in love with the Moor and with Love. It is there, however, that Ferré's woman is also forwardly, ambiguously, aroused: "atrapa entre el índice y el pulgar/ las cocolias huidizas del sexo," in the hold that she has, between her thumb and forefinger, of the sexual. Consummation follows, apparently. But the climax in Ferré comes when Othello falls asleep and is poisoned by Desdemona: "Piel de palisandro" and "sigilosa se inclina sobre el Moro / deja caer una perla de veneno / al fondo de su copa de cobalto" (1984:58-59). In sum, transfigured into a pearl-white drop of poison that is set down inside a cup of black cobalt, Ferré's Desdemona thus decides against taking the chance for which Shakespeare's had been groomed. The re-figuration must have been, one suspects, an especially nuanced one for this Puerto Rican fabulist, among whose memories of her hometown, Ponce, is a beautiful theater that was burnt down, and later rebuilt. It was called La Perla (García-Pinto 1991:81).

Ferré thus re-values the original "pearl" that was "richer," so The Moor had believed, "than all his tribe." But in a pre-emptive strike, it would not be *her* Desdemona but Shakespeare's who, when confronted with the ominous solicitousness of The Moor's "Have you prayed tonight?" and his "I would not kill thy unprepared spirit / . . . I would not kill thy soul," would reply with the pathos of "These are portents; but yet I hope, I hope, / They do not point to me;" with "O, banish me, my lord, but kill me not!" and with "Kill me tomorrow: let me live tonight!" (V.ii. 26; 30-31; 45-46; 78; 80).

Ferré thus rejects self-slaughtering *tolerantia* in a way that is even more resonant when one comes upon the incarnation of the "virtue" that we get in Al-Tayyib Salih's *Mawsim al-Hijrah ila al-Shawal* (*Season of Migration to the North*). For it is in this version of *Othello* that the Desdemona character, Jean Morris, actually embraces a "hell-fire" of "murderous consummation"; and that she does so with: "Come with me. Come with me. Don't let me go alone" (1970:164). She surrenders thus—for all that the "moments of ecstasy were in fact rare, [since] the rest of the time we spent in murderous war in which no quarter was given" (161). *Migration's* "Desdemona" tore up "books and papers"; and this response, so we are told, was "the most dangerous weapon she had." Not unexpectedly, "every battle would end with her ripping up an important book or burning some piece of research" (*ibid.*). But then, this woman cannot *not* succumb, notwithstanding gestures that here and there orient the drama of her life toward the resistance that Ferré foregrounds. For her part, Ferré insists; and she pushes through to re-situate

Shakespeare with an alert rebelliousness that heightens the irony of other—and increasingly impatient, even quirky—considerations of Othello's fate.

The "quirk" is especially intriguing in the near-emergence of an andronygous Desdemona-Othello in Simi Bedford's *Yoruba Girl Dancing* (1994), a fictionalized memoir of a Sierra Leone-ancestored Nigerian girl's arrival by ship, the *Ariel* (47), into the race-resistant upper reaches of English society. Thereafter, a posh all-girl boarding school becomes the heart of a complex in which, the only black among otherwise perfectly white schoolmates, Remi Forster navigates a labyrinth of race, caste, and culture. The result is an experience of estrangement by seeming inclusion. She finds it to be one which *Othello* had once and so persuasively served to illustrate. Desdemona and Othello thereupon coincide in *Yoruba Girl Dancing*'s quite remarkable con/figuring of Shakespeare. What the complex means, Forster explains, is that "because of my public school education and upbringing, I have grown up thinking of myself as an Englishwoman, one of you, Desdemona."

> But now that I'm becoming an adult I suddenly discover that I am in fact Othello. . . . Othello was destroyed . . . because his marrying Desdemona was seen as an attempt to become a Venetian, and the Venetians could not tolerate this in a black man. It has become increasingly obvious to me that if I do the same thing by trying to become one of you, I am likely to receive the same treatment. All this time I've been living in a fool's paradise and now I don't know who I am. It's a tragedy." (173)

Yet another "climbing the metaphor" to survey its tragedy occurs in *The European Tribe*, the 1987 "traveller's history" by Caribbean-born, England-based Caryl Phillips. For his part, Phillips borrows from Frantz Fanon to read Othello into an "abandonment-neurotic" predicament, and into its defining and "zebra striping" surge of "desire to be suddenly white." And who, then, "but a white woman can do this for me? By loving me she proves that I am worthy of white love. I am loved like a white man. I am a white man. . . . I marry white culture, white beauty, white whiteness" (Fanon 1967:63). For Phillips, this deficit condition is especially at work when the Moor is most full of "heroic posturing and powerful oratory." Evidence of its fatal attraction is nowhere more compelling than when it leads Othello "too far and [he] secretly woos and marries the daughter of one of your leading citizens." Matters escalate into tragedy at that moment of "triumph" which, for Phillips, is when "Othello begins to forget he is black." In *The European Tribe*'s brisk telling, Shakespeare's now ex-colored man seems at first to be a "black European success" story, the "Jackie Robinson of his age." However, this fundamentally estranged and quite incomplete man is soon forced into a paralyzing anxiety "not to love in order to avoid being abandoned." Phillips's stark conclusion is that Othello "had fallen for a white girl, married her, and tried to achieve equity in the society through her. Society wreaked a horrible vengeance on them both" (45-51). Arguably, this happens with something of the cold dedication with which F.R. Leavis advanced the "modernist" and "realistic" view which influenced the 1965 Stuart Burge-John Dexter *Othello*— but which Robert Hapgood thinks Laurence Olivier was able somehow to temper, according to Jack Jorgens. "In analyzing Othello's character, Leavis wrote deflatingly of his 'obtuse and brutal egotism,' his 'ferocious stupidity,' his 'habit of self-approving, self-dramatization,' the shallowness of his love for Desdemona, and the lack of 'tragic discovery' in the end where all is self-idealization and pride." So then, "in molding a context for Othello, John Dexter had told his cast, "Othello is a pompous, word-spinning, arrogant black general" (Jorgens 1991:203).

Elsewhere though, in the Othello-sequence of *Carnival of the Old Coast* (Johnson 1995), Othello is, in fact, made to call his Desdemona's attention, in "Magic," to their condition, as being one in which they are "attached . . . to the poisonous / fondness of kinship and fools." However, in surrendering, as he then does, to the urge to pull himself in "to the very tailbone," he fails to heed the thrust of an earlier lesson, in "Othello, laid, beside himself." Simply stated, "they all should have stayed home." The Moor, for certain, should have stayed home. Failing that, "he should have kept aim / tacked hard to war at her father's / table (kept the point unmixed / and to the point)." After all, it was predictable enough that this

> our brother will murder one that counts.
>
> we have seen him,
> our brother, unbuttoned
> too to the very hip...
>
> there is too ponderous a weight
> at the groin: it shames us all
> now, this itch for alabaster
> he wants in marble. (15)

Meanwhile, even though she appears to be still betrothed to *ars moriendi*, *Carnival*'s half-awakened Desdemona wryly suspects, in "Romance, for Desdemona," that "a temptation of taste / improvised into a sweetness" is "never the sign sufficient." For there is a certain irony to "flames / that burn us back to Paradise." It is one that is manifest when

Our apparitions return to us,
to grin like death at our doors...

it must be then we are moved
to think, too, of adam's will—
prick figure on stick,
(godfat so with gesture and clause)
and the hidden joylessness of choice. (17)

In the season of Tayeb Salih's migration to the North, meanwhile, "I am no Othello, I am a lie" is, finally, the double-edged, courtroom epiphany to which Othello is led, this time in his incarnation as the Sudanese Mustafa Sa'eed Othman. He is a man implicated in the suicides of two white women and on trial for the murder of a third, his wife. His epiphany is pedigreed, of course. Shakespeare's character, by then the murderer of a white woman, had divorced himself from himself to reply, "That's he that was Othello: here I am," to Lodovico's question, "Where is this rash and most unfortunate man?" (V.ii.283-84). But in Salih's season of discontent it is betrayal that brings about Sa'eed's near-containment in Othello, a man denied the aggrieved memories of *victimization* by imperialist aggression: "the rattle of swords in Carthage and the clatter of Allenby's horses desecrating the ground of Jerusalem" (1970:94-5). That being the case, Sa'eed's going the Othello-way with white women is very much a failure to respond appropriately to the stunning arrogance of colonialist assumptions and actions, as happened when the Englishman Lord Kitchner had made himself at home in Sa'eed's Sudan: "When Mahmud Wad Ahmed was brought in shackles before Kitchner, the intruder [meaning Kitchner!] said to him, 'Why have you come to my country to lay waste and plunder?' It was the intruder who said this to the person whose land it was, and the owner of the land bowed his head and said nothing" (94).

By name Mustapha Sa'eed Othman, born in Khartoum 16 August 1898, father Mustafa Sa'eed Othman (deceased), mother Fatima Abdussadek, Salih's character had begun life thus. Thereafter, by "long story" and by the train that deposits him at Victoria Station, London, he had moved to become more Moor than Man. From that eponymic, and imperial, station, Sa'eed moves into and through the beds of white women whose obsessions with the "orientalist" East more than match, and confound, his own obsessions with the occident. For how else could he better exfoliate, so to speak, into that "I am *like* Othello—Arab African" in response to the question, "What race are you?" And all this in a world where Oxford again looms large (58; 93; my emphasis).

It is Salih's brief that Sa'eed is in the condition that was Othello's because each man had seduced, and then been emptied into being "jungles where non-existent animals called to each other." And if not that, then, a trading and trafficking confection of orientalist fantasies: "sandalwood and incense; ostrich feathers and ivory and ebony figures; the paintings and drawings of forests of palm trees . . . suns setting over the mountains of the Red Sea . . . baobab trees in Kordofan, naked girls from the tribes of the Zandi, the Nuer and the Shuluk. . . . Arabic books . . . in ornate Kufi script" (144-146). But then, fundamentally deprived of substance as he is, there comes the day when he is driven into the wretchedness of his alter ego. The reason is, he tells us, that "once I found a handkerchief that wasn't mine." He could hardly have been worse, or done better. "I saw the handkerchief in's hand / . . . I saw the handkerchief," Othello had himself insisted (V.i.62; 66). It is all enough to poison the delight of the Moor and the Sudanese. Afflicted thereafter with what he calls the "smell of infidelity" in his whole house, Mustapha Sa'eed Othman engages in a dead reckoning consummation that becomes his Night of Nights when "We were a torch of flame, [and] the edges of the bed tongues of Hell-fire, [and] the universe, with its past, present, and future was gathered together into a single point before and after which nothing existed" (164). "'Here are my ships, my darling,' his Desdemona had said then, her thighs wide open, 'sailing toward the shores of destruction.' I leant over and kissed her," he recalls. "I put the blade-edge between her breasts and she twined her legs round my back. Slowly I pressed down. Slowly. She opened her eyes. What ectsasy was in those eyes!. . . 'Darling,' she said painfully, 'I thought you would never do this. I almost gave up hope of you.' I pressed down the dagger until it had all disappeared between her breasts. I began crushing my chest against her as she called out imploringly, 'Come with me. Come with me. Don't let me go alone" (164-165). For this act of consummate penetration he will spend seven years in prison, return to a degraded quietness in his native land, and disappear in a narrative to which the conclusion is

> I entered the water as naked as when my mother bore me. . . . When I first touched the cold water I felt a shudder go through me, then the shudder transformed into a sensation of wakefulness . . . . Though floating on the water, I was not part of it. I thought that if I died at that moment, I would have died as I was born— without any volition of mine. . . . Now I am making a decision. I choose life. . . . I shall live by fire and cunning. I moved my feet and arms, violently and with difficulty, until the upper part of my body was above water. Like a comic actor shouting on stage, I screamed with all my remaining strength: "Help! Help!" (168-169).

"An impression of colour-madness" is the subtitle of Leonard Barnes's *Caliban in Africa* (1930) about South Africa in the early twentieth century. The book, as is obvious, derives a template of sorts from Shakespeare, and is strongly indicting of white "anti-native sentiment." It is also remarkably complacent in its own tolerance for the natives, and makes a point of noting their "rather childish sense of fun," their being "psychically" blessed with "an indomitable eupepsia"—and with the "unsophisticated faith and loyalty to life, which is the secret of the charm of the race" (72). Two of the book's epigraphs are particularly apt. The first is from *The Tempest*: "What have we here? a man or fish? dead or alive? A fish: he smells like a fish; a very ancient and fish-like smell; a kind of not of the newest Poor-John. A strange fish!" The second, from Lady Anne Barnard, appears at the head of the opening chapter; it reads, in part, "This place is not wholly governed by wisdom, ability, or elevation of mind."

Some half a century later, Janet Suzman's Shakespeare would be fashioned into a powerful expression of the anguish and exasperation of The Republic of South Africa's experience of Apartheid, so cued-to-the-bone is Suzman's 1988 Johannesburg Market Theater stage and film *Othello*. Her resort to Shakespeare is akin in its theatrical context to her countryman Lewis Nkosi's when, in *Home and Exile* (1964), he appeals to the English dramatist and his contemporaries in chronicling "the fabulous decades: the fifties." The catalogue of excess in Apartheid could only be fully captured, he wrote, by and in "the cacophonous, swaggering world of Elizabethan England." It was that world which provided "the closest parallel to our own mode of existence: the cloak and dagger stories of Shakespeare; the marvellously gay and dangerous time of change in Great Britain came closest to reflecting our own condition." Here was what made it possible for an "African musician returning home at night to inspire awe in a group of thugs surrounding him by declaiming in an impossibly archaic English: 'Unhand me, rogues!'" (18). Of course, the South African admixture in Nkosi's world of home and exile, no less than in the underground one of Peter Abraham's *Mine Boy* (1946) and in Alex La Guma's apocalyptic *Time of the Butcherbird* (1979), also involved oddly syncopated rhythms of violence and urgency: a "new kind of kinship and love"; "a new kind of fear and hatred called apartheid" (La Guma 107).

Nkosi and Suzman, Abrahams and La Guma—and Coetzee—thus foreground certain dimensions of the Renaissance playwright that Jack Jorgens gives us in *Shakespeare on Film*, especially in the "Chimes at Midnight" chapter, in which context the English dramatist is represented as "an artist writing for an increasingly secular, urban audience, for a kind of theatre and company unknown to London before the 1590s, and in a language just beginning to rival Latin in subtlety and range. [But he was one who also saw] that change was not always for the better, that things were being destroyed which were precious and irreplaceable, and that the new forces which were being unleashed might bring the time, as Albany says in *Lear,* when 'humanity must perforce prey upon itself, like monsters of the deep'"

(107). La Guma's own "walk in the night" (1962) is circumscribed as much by Shakespeare as by the Cape Town of District Six—that inferno of "dark corners and unseen crannies." In its "fetid heat and slippery dampness the insects and vermin, maggots and slugs, 'roaches in shiny brown armour, spiders like tiny grey monsters carrying death under their minute feet or in the suckers, or rats with dusty black eyes with disease under the claws or in the fur, moved mysteriously" (34-35). It is into this midnight at the ramparts that La Guma leads us by way of his epigraph, from *Hamlet* (I.v.9-13):

> I am thy father's spirit
> Doom'd for a certain time to walk the night,
> And for the day confined to fast in fires,
> Till the foul crimes done in my days of nature
> Are burnt and purged away.

There is little to be surprised at, then, that Caribbean Murray Carlin brings Shakespearean template and Apartheid into dramatic union in *Not Now, Sweet Desdemona*, his "duologue for Black and White within the realm of Shakespeare's *Othello*." There is also not much of a reason to be appalled at the apartheid esthetics of the work's epigraph, provided by Samuel Taylor Coleridge (1818): "It would be something monstrous to conceive this beautiful Venetian girl falling in love with a veritable negro." *Not Now* was first performed in July 1968 by the Ngoma Players at Makerere University College, Uganda, with its episodes made up of circumstances that are played out as and through a rehearsal of *Othello*. Eschewing Suzman's tragic heat and Nkosi's extravagance, or perhaps because he manages to combine them, Carlin transforms and foregrounds the heart of the matter in a theater of the absurd. Its "nuclear" features are condensed into a parable about the politics of race and sexual desire. It is in their duologue, as it negotiates meaning out of the parable, that Carlin fleshes out his principals, a West Indian Negro (prone to exhibitionist bitterness) and his white South African lover (given to an annoying callowness). Thus situated, Carlin confronts attitude and circumstance with a defining *reductio ad absurdum*: Apartheid's Law of sexual circulation as codified and enacted in the Immorality Act.

In what I take to be the play's nuclear fable, the Law's prime exhibit is none other than the Prime Minister of the Republic, who has been hurled into court because he had changed, with no apparent warning, from apartheid-white to kaffir-black. He had changed all over: "every crease of him"; "at 0200 hours, precisely." His wife knew; because, compounding the issue, the "transmorgrification" had taken place during the act of sexual intercourse in, unavoidably, a Whites Only residential area. All this happens, moreover, under circumstances that are charged with the usual "index and prologue to the history of lust and foul thoughts" (Iago) associated with white-black sexuality. This is sexual bait that Nkosi and Suzman well understood, and that South African novelist J. M. Coetzee allegorizes into yet another "waiting for the Barbarians" (1980): "There is no woman living along the frontier who has not dreamed of a dark barbarian hand coming from under the bed to grip her ankle, no man who has not frightened himself with visions of the barbarians carousing in his home, breaking the plates, setting fire to the curtains, raping his daughters" (8). Iago had of course counted on just such a voyeuristic disrelish when he went public in Venice: "Call up her father, / Rouse him," he had urged. "Make after him, poison his delight, / Proclaim him in the streets, incense her kinsmen" (I.i.64-65).

This brutal mix of racial anxiety with sexual titillation and comic malice is, at bottom, what shapes and drives Carlin's parable of the absurd in *Not Now, Sweet Desdemona*. His South African whiteblackman is formally pronounced a "Bantu Male," after a comprehensive examination—"hair, nails, buttocks, intelligence test." He is then jailed, of course, having become immediately guilty of whole categories of offenses—though "at first they weren't quite sure which jail to put him in." At the trial the judge asks, critically, about the exact timing of the man's denigration, so to speak, of the affair twixt-the-sheets. He asks, in essence, to uncover its relationship to the moment of "the decisive, husbandly action—the establishing Marital Thrust." If consummation came "afterward," then "the Marital Thrust is no longer Marital Thrust [but] becomes an Immoral Thrust under the Act." Cross-examined, the wife's complicating testimony is that the change in her ex-husband, the then citizen and Prime Minister, had occurred "during"—at a point that might be called "Halfway House" (54).

The case ends with the ex-Prime Minister and ex-whiteman hung on a petard of the Law's erection: "The Court found her innocent and him guilty, of course." Carlin-Othello explains, patiently, the logic of the absurd:

> **Desdemona:** Innocent . . . . and guilty . . . of love . . .for each other? How did they do that?
> **Othello:** The Judge was a very great Judge, and wise. . . . He reasoned as follows: A woman, in bed, in the dead of night, with her husband—and having no reason to expect anything extraor-dinary—cannot be held responsible, in the case of sudden trans-formations, until she had turned on the light. . . . But [as for] the defendant . . . his mysterious translation could not have been a matter of appearances only. For these ultimate differences, as everybody knows, are matters of spirit and soul, as well as body. The ex-Prime Minister—voter—husband and—European must have been aware, in the instant of turning black, that he was black. Because, of course, his whole psychology must have changed. In

that instant he must have felt like a Shangaan. . . . The defendant, being in a state of legal intimacy with his then wife, and becoming suddenly aware of his change in nature and status, should immediately have apologized, and respectfully have withdrawn. (55-56)

Carlin's Actress-Desdemona and Actor-Othello are left to ponder so carnivalesque a confusion of the power of mask and eros; to contemplate its rehearsals as condition of existence; and, finally, to reach toward an optimism in which to raise glasses "to a theatre without ghosts" (62).

It is a forlorn hope, perhaps; and it is certainly nothing else if Shakespeare's Othello is left foregrounded as "horned man" and racialized "monster." The sexual anxiety that runs through *Not Now, Sweet Desdemona* is a long-memoried one. There is considerable evidence, of course, that Shakespeare was always one to play on its "horn-mad" or "cuckold-mad" conceits, as in *The Comedy of Errors* where "many fond fools serve mad jealousy" (II.i.56-60; 115). He often worked too on the torments, linking them to the "contagious fogs" and "forgeries of jealousy" (*Midsummer Night*)— that "monster / begot on itself; born on itself" (*Othello* III.iv.158-59). "There are millions now alive / That might lie in those unproper beds / which they dare swear peculiar," Iago knows this. There's many a man, *The Winter's Tale* claims, "even at this present, / Now, while I speak this, holds his wife by th'arm, / [And] little thinks she has been sluiced in's absence, / And his pond fished by his next neighbour" (1.ii.193-196).

The ever-present fear of being "fished" generates elsewhere in Shakespeare the lyrical malice with which the playwright ends *Love's Labour's Lost* by undercutting, in the cuckoo's call, what appears to be an unmitigated celebration of Spring. There is, besides, a certain proposition about the ways of women to contend with: "You jig, you amble, and lisp, you nickname God's creatures, and make your wantonness your ignorance" (*Hamlet* III.i.138-140). Still, attempts at fishing are sometimes as cheerful and tolerable as Falstaff's circumstances will allow them to be in *The Merry Wives of Windsor*. The power of this "strange misprision" does work its way into being, finally, a case about nothing (*Much Ado* IV.i.187). All the same, the path to its proving that it is indeed much ado about nothing is rather less benign when Claudio is persuaded that Hero had "fallen / Into a pit of ink, [and] that the wide sea / Hath drops too few to wash her clean again, / [and] salt too little which may season give / To her foul-tainted flesh." Predictably, the result is Beatrice's realistic, even if melodramatically succinct, "She's wronged, she's slandered, she's undone" (IV.i. 141-45; 312). No less predictable is Leonato's dis-honored reaction: "Hence from her! Let her die!" And *ars moriendi*, the woman, in this manner accused, in this manner refused, "upon the grief [had] suddenly died" (IV.iv.64-65), so we are led to believe. Fortunately, although full of sound and fury, the imputation of incontinent behavior, which Charles Gildon (1709) had found "too shocking for either tragedy or comedy" (MacCracken 1935:374), does turns out to signify nothing. At the end, the pipers strike up, and there is "*dance, and exeunt.*"

In *A Midsummer Night's Dream*, meanwhile, male torment and its corollary threat of female erasure are likewise contained in a terrorizing (and ultimately benign) fear of cuckoldry, occasioned here by Titania's infatuation with "a lovely boy stolen from an Indian King." Her involvement is one that parallels, by the way, Oberon's with his "warrior love," that "bouncing Amazon" and "buskin'd mistress" (II.i.70-71). Containment of the forgeries of jealousy is very nearly *not* the case, however, in *The Winter's Tale*; for here the special terror of Othello's case is pre-figured in Leontes' seething and fevered mind; in the "intensity of poetic suffering with which he expresses his irrational jealousy" (Wells *et al.* 1988:1101):

> . . . Is whispering nothing?
> Is leaning cheek to cheek? is meeting noses?
> Kissing with the inside lip? . . .
> Skulking in corners?. . . . Is this nothing?
> . . . The covering sky is nothing, Bohemia nothing,
> My wife be nothing, nor nothing have these nothings
> If this be nothing. (I.ii.286-98)

So persuaded, then, is this husband of the fact that "it's a bawdy planet . . . from east, west, north, and south"; that his wife is a "bed-swerver"; that "physic for't there is none." And because he "has drunk" deep from the cup, "and seen the spider" at the bottom, he orders her to "look for no less than death." And her response shows, *ars moriendi* again, that she is indeed prepared to do so agreeably and well: "Now, my liege, / Tell me what blessings I have here alive, / That I should fear to die" (III.ii.90-107). But here the Delphic Oracle itself, in the absence of Wynter and Busia, Aidoo and Emecheta—or Rosario Ferré—does intervene to prevent this woman-wife-mother from being un-voiced and erased. It all ends well. Sixteen years into "the wide gap of time" since she was "dissevered," Hermione is called back to life: "Tis time. Descend. Be stone no more." "Oh, if this be magic," a repentant Leontes says, "let it be an art / Lawful as eating"(V.iii.99; 109-11).

Signally, Henry MacCracken is persuaded that the "ennobling of the queen's character, from the shows and conventions of grief to the majesty of true grief in an emperor's daughter," is chief among the dramatic transforma-tions that Shakespeare effected on his source for *The Winter's Tale*—Greene's 1588 *Pandosto, The Triumph of Time*, also titled, *The Fortunate Lovers*. MacCracken believes, too, that "in the queenly serenity with which

[Hermione's] spirit meets injuries, she stands as a worthy companion to the portrait of Katherine in *Henry VIII*' (1935:855). On the whole, then, "of Leontes's queen no critic has ever expressed himself in terms of less than superlative eulogy. One may cite as an example Hudson's 'her proud submission, her dignified obedience; with her Roman firmness and integrity of soul, heroic in strength, heroic in gentleness, the queenliest of women, the womanliest of queens.' Her gentleness and serenity give tone" to a play which, MacCracken concludes, "a critic of our day has called the most gentle of all Shakespeare's dramas" (856). The judgment is a telling one for a sad tale, "best for winter," which had seemed for quite a while to be irredeemably beset by "goads, thorns, nettles, tails of wasps"; and ready to "give scandal to the blood" (I.ii.328-30).

When, by way of contrast, Marvin Rosenberg's *The Masks of Othello* explores blood, scandal, and "fishing" in racial waters over the three centuries during which actors and critics have been called upon to "fill out the mighty Moor's image," there is an almost perverse refusal to scant the play of difference, and the temptation of the illicit, in the ensemble that we get in Othello, Iago, and Desdemona. The survey makes for a rich and varied history that, elsewhere, an Eldred Jones (1964) or a Virginia Mason Vaughan (1994) would review to more studied conclusions. Rosenberg is committed to being rather more vigorous: *Othello* "is the most erotic, the most sensual of the great tragedies, and the time came when Anglo-Saxon culture, grown strenuously refined, tried to drive from the text its 'offensive' words and sexual atmosphere, and even threatened the form of the play" (1961:viii). On this issue, Margaret Webster is emphatic to the point of indelicacy. A thin actor playing Falstaff certainly faces a challenge, she asserts. But even more of a challenge faces the white actor playing Othello: for he "must blacken the very marrow of his bones." It very much matters, Webster insists, that "Othello is repeatedly described, both by himself and others, as black; not pale beige, but black; and for a century and a half he was so represented on the stage. But after this the close consideration of nice minds began to discern something not quite ladylike about Desdemona's marrying a man with thick lips."

All in all, then, more than "a difference of pigmentation" is involved (Webster 1975:178-79)—as is concentratedly the case in the title of Michael Neill's stellar critique, "Unproper Bed: Race, Adultery, and the Hideous in *Othello*" (1989); and as is incontinently the premise in the prurient, but clarifying, noisiness of Michel Cournot's

> The black man's sword is a sword. When he has thrust it into your wife, she has really felt something. It is a revelation. In the chasm that it has left, your little toy is lost. Pump away until the room is awash with your sweat, you might as well just be singing. This is

> *goodby.* . . . Four Negroes with their penises erect would fill a
> cathedral. They would be unable to leave the building until their
> erections had subsided; and in such close quarters that would not
> be a simple matter. (Fanon 1967:169)

Bodies private and politic are thus threatened with an utter ravishment that is born of "foul disproportion" and "thoughts unnatural," as Iago had claimed all along. *Pace* Gonzalo's utopian transcendence which would "by contraries / execute all things," no "high miracle" is possible in the sexual tempest in which we now find ourselves. This, then, is the stuff of quite "another country" from which returning were as tedious as going over; and in illustration and perverse confirmation of which the African American James Baldwin writes in *Another Country*:

> Her breath came with moaning and short cries, with words he
> couldn't understand, and in spite of himself he began moving
> faster and thrusting deeper. He wanted her to remember him the
> longest day she lived. And, shortly, nothing could have stopped
> him, not the white God himself nor a lynch mob arriving on
> wings. Under his breath he cursed the milk-white bitch and
> groaned and rode his weapon between her thighs. She began to
> cry. *I told you*, he moaned, *I'd give you something to cry about*
> . . . A moan and a curse tore through him while he beat her with
> all the strength he had and felt the venom shoot out of him,
> enough for a hundred black-white babies. (Baldwin 1993:24)

Measure for measure, "corruption [does indeed] boil and bubble / Till it o'erun the stew" here. We have entered into regions, to borrow from Hamlet, of "enseam'd bed" that is "stew'd in [enough] corruption" to make one "thought sick at the act" (III.iv.50; 92-94). It is all of one piece, then, that in such regions Brabantio *will die* of his daughter's marriage to a Moor (V.ii.204-206); that the simple clarity of Charles Lamb's disrelish will find "something extremely revolting in the courtship and wedded caresses of Othello and Desdemona" (Singh 1994:287). That being the case, some larger import and profit might have been derived therefore from the Clown in *Twelfth Night*; for he did, after all, point out that "Many a good hanging prevents a bad marriage" (I.ii.20). Failing that, corrupting heat and degeneration are inevitable whenever, as Hamlet claims to know, we leave "fair mountain" "to feed, / and batten on . . . moor" (III.iv. 65-66) that ought to be alien, and alienating. "What devil was't / That thus hath cozen'd you at hoodman-blind?" Hamlet would demand of a Gertrude gone incontinent and astray. As I have indicated, it is deeply significant that Brabantio *dies*, horror-struck, at his daughter's unproper mating.

This father's anxieties coincide with and link his own sixteenth century with the nineteenth of Samuel Taylor Coleridge and of Charles Lamb. So, too, with that twentieth-century Euro-American poetry of John Peale Bishop (1892-1944), according to which, even if the word is obsolete, "tupping is still tupping" insofar as it means a conjoining of Othello, "his weight resilient as a Barbary horse," and Desdemona, "small and fair, / delicate as a grasshopper." For which despairing reason, the "ceremony must be found / that will wed Desdemona to the *huge* Moor" (1960:15; my emphasis).

> Mayst thou never want sweet water to wash
> Thy black face in, most mighty Morocco,

Thomas Heywood had written in his (circa 1604) *The Fair Maid of the West* (V.ii.64-5). Notwithstanding, Bishop remains persuaded that certain things "have not been changed / not in three hundred years," making assurance doubly sure that Desdemona will be found "when the ambassadors of the Venetian state arrive / again smothered." Small wonder then that Bishop's anxious ambiguity, "The ceremony must be found," ends as and where it does—when "the torches deaden at the bedroom door" (15-16).

In *The Merchant of Venice* Shakespeare had, in fact, broached the transgressing of such boundaries, but there the consequences of so dangerous a liaison had been teasingly skirted. Thus, for all that "the best-regarded virgins of [*his*] clime" had never seen anything wrong with his color, Morocco does travel to Europe to make that florid, and apologetic, entrance into Belmont: "Mislike me not for my complexion" (II.i.1). In a fortunate turn of affairs, the Moor had chosen wrongly; but had succeeded all the same in confirming his identification with "carrion Death" and "empty eye." Portia's discriminating, even jolly, cleverness had gotten it just right: "Let all of his complexion choose me thus" (II.viii.79). She gets it right in a way that effectively counterpoints the infectious giddiness with which she celebrates the "continent" choice that her Bassanio had made:

> O love! be moderate! allay thy ecstasy!
> In measure rein thy joy, scant this excess!
> I fear too much thy blessing! make it less
> For fear I surfeit. (II.ii:111-115)

She acknowledges boundaries, Morocco and Aragon, that Desdemona will transgress. But then, Portia is "fair and fairer than that word"; is "richly left [in Belmont and is in] nothing undervalued to Cato's daughter, Brutus' Portia" (I.i.161-166). Such women do not leave fair mountain (as in *bel monte*) to feed and batten on alien moor. And, of course, they do not get "transported . . . to the gross clasps of a lascivious Moor" (I.i.125), as Roderigo says of Desdemona.

With Othello placed thus, at center stage, what we get is the certainty of an undeflected racial dangerousness. We commerce here in the shade of antique and "hideous" consequences (Neill 1989; Parker 1994:93). It is all a matter of high and "post-haste" drama, of course; and one that is especially played out when The Moor acts out the truth of the fact that "Chaos is come again" (II.iii.92-93); of his being "one not easily jealous, but being wrought / [is] Perplex'd in the extreme." Besides which, early in Shakespeare—by the end of Act 2, Scene 1—what with Desdemona surrendered to the Moor, with the Turkish fleet bearing down on Cyprus, and with Marcus Luccicos away in Florence, Othello does threaten to become the base upon which Venice's corporate culture is poised. The state of affairs certainly threatened to become a "mangled matter" of "bondslaves and pagans" putting the "free condition" of Venice's social hierarchies in "circumscription and confine." Still, Ben Okri makes the point that, in the final analysis, "it doesn't really matter that Shakespeare didn't, and quite possibly couldn't get Othello fully in focus, nor looked at him closely enough. What matters is that because of Shakespeare's genius Othello haunts the English stage. He won't go away. He is unable to hide on stage but is always there, a reminder of his unexplained presence in white consciousness, and symbol of the fact that black people and white are bound on a terrible bed of history"—and doomed to "his relentless cycle" (1987:564). Othello's sexually-charged blackness-in-human-form identity, stands apart, a singular figure "on a stage overflowing with white people, talking about him—and her" (Carlin 1969:32-33). Small wonder that he is obsessed into asking Iago that question of questions about his whitewoman wife and her white countryman being together, alone, in a world of so much whiteness: "Naked in bed, Iago, and not mean harm!" (III.i.5). The frenzy is a defining one, and helps to drive the volatile stranger into a second epileptic fit in two days: "Lie with her! Lie on her! We say lie on her, when they belie her. Lie with her! 'Zounds, that's fulsome.—Handkerchief—confessions—handkerchief!—To confess, and be hanged for his labour; first to be hanged, and then to confess. . . . It is not words that shakes me thus. Pish! Noses, ears, and lips.—Is't possible?—Confess—handkerchief!—O devil!" (*He falls into a trance*) (IV.i.34-43). There is, elsewhere, the telling rupture with which the incontinent breaks into Othello's ceremonial and formal welcome of Lodovico. He says, then: "You are welcome, sir, to Cyprus—Goats and monkeys!" Not surprisingly, Lodovico is driven to ask, "Is this the noble Moor whom our full Senate / Call all in all sufficient?" (IV.i.263-264).

Anxious for Rendezvous

> . . . the first . . . that leap'd
> [into the foaming brine] cried,
> "Hell is empty
> And all the devils are here."
> **Ariel**, *The Tempest* (I.ii.211-15)

Crude and disturbing as the likes of Iago make cross-racial "tupping" in *Othello*, its eruption does not quite fill a cathedral; a lady's chamber, perhaps. This is because the transgressive sexuality is very much contained in a city and on a street of whites who, unlike Othello, are at home in the public *and* private spaces of Venice. "Indeed, it might be claimed," R. A. Foakes observes, "that Othello's habituation to 'glorious war' has incapacited him for domesticity" (1986:22). He is thus not "merely an alien black man of mysterious origins in the white world of Venice [but more signal is the fact that] he has no intimates," cut off as he is from "the play's private relationships, and the scenes in which characters engage in small talk" (*ibid.* 23). The color of this isolation is a feature that Ben Okri emphasizes in his "Meditations on *Othello*": "I find it strange that Othello is the only black man in the universe of the play. He is isolated by colour." Moreover, "his position in society makes his isolation deeper," among "people who could see him as their worst nightmare" (1987:563). But then, the fact remains that The Moor is one nightmare, and surrounded. Foakes makes a point of setting in relief the fact that "Othello has no *private* scene alone with Desdemona until the murder in Act V" (22). Iago thinks it all out to a hungry Cassio: "He hath not yet made wanton the night with her; and she is sport for Jove" (II.i.16-17). What we have instead are moments and gestures of erotic heat and desperation (emphasized in Suzman's *Othello*). Or else we get suggestions of *coitus interruptus* and hints of "unproper bed" activity, as happens when Iago himself flames into an uncertain lust for Desdemona (II.i.262-63), and into his sudden "wife for wife" (II.i.293) revenge motive: "I do suspect the lusty Moor / Hath leap'd into my seat" (II.i.289-90); that "it is thought abroad, that twixt my sheets / He has done my office" (I.iii. 386-388).

In effect, for all the sexual anxiety rampant within, and outside, the drama, intercourse is teasingly on hold. Othello is kept (off) at strategic bay by the State's foreign relations. Soldier and stranger that the Moor is, when he is not closetted off, he is citadelled; or strategically honey/marooned on Cyprus. His grandiloquent illusions notwithstanding, his "unhoused free condition" is in fact "put into circumscription and confine" (I.ii.26-27). Besides which, in the singularity of his barbarian blackness and thick lips and sooty bosom, Othello is visibly locked out of the common run of humanity, which is signally white. With or without Iago's extravagance, the Moor is invariably limned out of the Man: "These Moors are changeable in their wills. ... [T]he food that to him now is as luscious as locusts, shall be to him shortly as bitter as coloquintida" (I.iii.345-47). In some essentialist way—and again, Iago helps him along—he is very open to being persuaded that Venice can only be natively known by—and in—its whiteness. "I know our country disposition well," Iago tells him; and all along, the talk of others seems to be full of gestures of exclusion, of "our" and of "her" and of Venice's custom, father, way, nature, complexion, credit, degree; of "the wealthy curled darlings of our nation" who, for sure, are neither "lascivious Moor" nor "bond-slaves and pagans." Away from the Turkish threat, the general antici- pation seems little different from Iago's: Desdemona's "delicate tenderness will find itself abused, begin to heave the gorge, disrelish and abhor the Moor." Besides, "if she had been blessed, she would never have loved the Moor" (II.i.248-249; 229-231). There had been, too, that telling moment when Desdemona herself had embraced attraction and recognized difference, before Othello turned "hint" to advantage: "She thanked me, / And bade me, if I had a friend that loved her, / I should but teach him how to tell my story, / And that would woo her. Upon this hint I spake" (I.iii.163-166). Even more telling, perhaps, is the parting shot from, and abandonment by, the woman's own father: "Look to her, Moor, if thou hast eyes to see. / She has deceived her father, and may thee" (I.iii. 292-93).

As for Othello, even though he had once actually said, and no doubt believed, "Her father loved me, oft invited me"; even though he had heard the Duke tell him, as defender of the State, "we have a substitute [defender] of most allowed sufficiency, yet opinion, a more sovereign mistress of effects, throws a more safer voice on you" (I.iii.128; 223-25), the Moor in him cannot *not* soon undermine him. Under pressure, Emilia will frame *the* question: "Hath she forsook so many noble matches / Her father and her country and her friends, / To be call'd whore?" (IV.ii.124-27). Later, she will descend into a telling reduction: "The Moor hath kill'd my mistress!" (V.ii.166). Brabantio may never, as he claims, have heard it said that "the bruis'd heart was pierced through the ear" (I.iii.219-20), but then he is not Othello. He is certainly not Othello ambushed by Iago's "I have told thee often enough, and I'll re-tell thee again and again, I hate the Moor" (II.i.363-64).

Nor is he Othello cornered into the estrangement, the "chromatic tension," where Ben Okri (1987:562) finds him. Under the cumulative weight of his distress, Othello is driven to the realization that Lewis Nkosi intended when he observed that Black consciousness really begins with the shock of discovery that one is "not only black but also *non*-white" (44). The Man inside the Moor soon gets to be pretty much well-trashed, and self-trashing, in spite of his services, his demerits, and a proud fortune. In spite, too, of the panache with which he rejects Iago's suggestion that he should worry about the complaints of a certain "magnifico" whose daughter he has married on the sly: "Let him do his spite: My services which I have done the signory / Shall out-tongue his complaints" (I.ii.18-19). He is right, of course, given the Turkish fleet. After all, Brabantio does surrender, "So let the Turk of Cyprus us beguile . . . I humbly beseech you, proceed to the affairs of state" (I.iii. 210; 219-20).

Still, faced with a marshalling of forces that have nothing to do with wars with which he is familiar, Othello does collapse. The simplicity of the five words that set him spinning, Iago's "Ha! I like not that" (III.iii.35), is telling. The Moor's obsession with the signs and signatures of his badness-of-fit are thereafter marked out, again and again: "I am black"; "I am declined / Into the vale of years"; "Why did I marry?" (III.iii. 247-70). He confirms Brabantio's sense of the unnatural: "And yet, how nature, erring from itself . . . ." He cannot resist corrupting images of his color, and the effect registers in the self-denigrating conceit into which he identifies Desdemona: "Her name, that was fresh / As Dian's visage, is now begrimed and black / As mine own face" (III.iii.391-93). Elsewhere, there is the disorienting self-pity of "I have a pain in my forehead"; so, too, the (self-crucifying) language of his rage, "Arise, black vengeance from thy hollow cell!" Evidence of pain contained, "my heart is turned to stone: I strike it, and it hurts my hand," (IV.i.177-79) is countered when he authenticates barbarian excess, "I'll tear her all to pieces"; "I will chop her into messes" (IV.i.195). Although the irony in his choice of an audience is awful, the man is right about the condition that his condition is in: "but yet the pity of it, Iago. O Iago, the pity of it, Iago!" (IV.i.191-92). In the end, driven like a stake into the Man, the Moor kills his white Venetian woman. When, finally, Othello does see Iago, it is in a fog of utter incomprehension: "Will you, I pray, demand that demi-devil/Why he hath thus ensnar'd my soul and body?" (V.ii.301-02).

This, then, is the world into which Othello invokes and appeals to his mother, his father, too, when he turns belatedly to kith and kin for memory, and for *juju*. "I fetch my life and being / From men of royal siege," he had once said. True, perhaps; but who can tell so far from home? Besides, by the time Othello looks homeward again, the man will not (or cannot) keep his relations and their ties in order. Further, because he can now conjure with only a "handkerchief / spotted with strawberries" that Iago claims he saw Cassio wipe his beard with (III.iii. 431), the Moor is clearly beyond the reach and rite of return that Tutuola (*My Life in the Bush of Ghosts*) commands with his "Invisible Missive Magnetic Juju which could bring a lost person back to himself from an unknown place, how far it may be." Terribly alienated and alienating, when Othello goes to work on his handkerchief story in Act 3, Scene 4, it goes from Egyptian charmer to mother, subdues the father, then is bequeathed to the son. "Make it a darling like your precious eye," so, he says, his mother had told him about that *juju* of a handkerchief: "there's magic in the web of it" because some "sibyl in her prophetic fury sew'd the work." Besides which, the thing "was dyed in mummy which the skilful / Conserv'd of maidens' hearts" (II.iv.69-75). But then, later, in the numbing shock of Act 5, Scene 2, an "act that shows horrible and grim," the story sheds all echoes of his noisy dilations on cannibals and quarries and "hairbreadth scapes i' th' imminent deadly breach" (I.iii.128; 169). The handkerchief story thereupon drops its embroideries, and shifts the mother's position: "It was a handkerchief, an antique token / My father gave my mother" (V.ii.16-17). However, Othello soon discovers that not even this *juju* of a handkerchief will do the trick where he now finds himself. Furthermore, the trouble with the man's last-minute appeal to the mother is that she is, by then, really a no-thing; or, if anything at all, no more than an anxiety-ridden, perhaps guilt-edged, simulacrum. By the time this blackamoor of Europe thinks of looking her up he is too deeply enmeshed in Venetian embroidery to be anything but the butt end of a cautionary tale. Ben Okri writes, "Frantz Fanon might have been thinking of the long nightmare at the end of Othello's sleep when he wrote in the closing sentences of *Black Skin, White Masks*, 'O my body, make me a man who always questions.'" Just such a view fashions Okri's own conclusion: "Trapped in ambition, marked by his colour, refusing to confront his predicament, [Othello] is the authentic self-betrayer. He is also the white man's myth of the black man. But he is also a negative myth for black people in the West. Signposts along roads that can lead to hell also have their own peculiar value" (1987:619).

It is "value" that has since justified Ama Ata Aidoo in the black-eyed squint to which "our sister killjoy" resorts when confronted with stories about black generals and their sojourn in places with rocks whose heads touch the sky. So, too, when they go on so about mothers to whom they owe some *juju* of remembrance. Sissie notes it all, with weary impatience, "It was the mother thing. Everybody claimed that he wanted to make sure he did something for 'My Mother.' 'My Mother has suffered.' Awo, Mama, Ena, Nna, Emama, Iyie. . . .[But] just look at what's been happening to her children over the last couple of hundred years. . . . Her sons were conscripted into imperial armies and went to die in foreign places, all over again or returned to her, with maimed bodies and minds." And she wails then for "Lost Black minds;" for all those "Beautiful Black Bodies . . . / Buried in thickets and snow / Their penises cut."

To look down on Othello's final act with Aidoo's squint-eyed weariness with being charitable is to be tempted with an alternative truth about the Moor: that he chooses to erase himself among and for strangers; and that the valedictory speech in which he does so is remarkable for two things. First, for its graceless, and mercenary, pride; second, for its denial of kith and kin—believing, as the man does, that he had found, then lost, "a pearl richer than all his tribe." In this respect, the moment is indeed one of "exorcism," of a "decisive self-separation from the turbaned and the circumcized," as Sanders proposes it to be. However, the consequences may not be as benign, and as complexly Moses-in-and-contra-Egypt, as Sanders wishes when he is moved to ask, "Who could doubt the fullness of his identification with the Christian cause?" (1992:250). Not when this speech is "heard" with a certain black-eyed squint:

> And say besides that in Aleppo once
> Where a malignant and a turbaned Turk
> Beat a Venetian and traduced the state,
> I took by th' throat the circumcised dog
> And smote him—thus. [*He stabs himself*] (V.ii.360-65)

Consider, again, the traducing (display of) irony in the fact that this same Moor had elsewhere thought he could rise to equivalence, and more, with his European employers: "Are we turned Turks, and to *ourselves* do that / Which heaven hath forbid the Ottomites? / For Christian shame, put by this *barbarian* brawl" (II.iii. 170-172; emphasis added). "'Ah, there's the erase' Us." Not the "rub," merely, Maya Angelou would write (1993:154) when in her turn she situates a caged bird (one Henry Reed, valedictorian) inside the outrageous fortune of erasure and yet of being asked to be "nobler in the mind." Angelou's response catches the ironic import at just the right moment of tension: "To Be or Not To Be." Yes. But. Hadn't there been evidence, earlier, of the apparent pointlessnes of a project to memorize the whole of Shakespeare's *The Rape of Lucrece*? "It was for nothing" (152). "Hadn't [Henry] heard the Whitefolks? We couldn't be. So the question was a waste of time. . . . I feared to look at him. Hadn't he got the message?" (154). In this light, there is instruction of a certain variety in the Brazil of Abdias do Nascimento's play, *Sortilege* (1978). For when his Emanuel returns to the "black waters of Yemanja" (to the mother of the waters and of all the *òrixas* of *candomble*) he begins the rite of return in a gesture that promises to be a familiar one when he checks the blade of his sword. However, he comes to a quite distinct recognition of how to be or not to be:

> Put an end to it. . . . A small stab. . . . A well honed blade. Make it like black Othello. Remember? But . . . Desdemona was innocent. And Othello? . . . What have I got to do with Othello, for God's sake? He killed, he murdered out of jealousy. Or for charity. Not me. My hands are clean. My hands and my soul. I'm not a black man with a white soul. Why white? Who has ever seen the color of a soul? (33)

A Conclusion: The Murder Of All Mothers

How the mother-thing (un)becomes in the tongue-snatched incarnation that we get in Moroccan Tahar Ben Jelloun's *The Sacred Night* bears some pondering here:

> My mother, who had opted for silence and resignation, out of calculation more than fatalism, said to me one day when my father's harsh words had hurt her deeply: "Pray with me my daughter, that God or Fate let me die before you, but that I be granted just a month or two after your father's death! How I would love to be able to breathe for a few days or weeks in his absence. That is my sole desire, my only wish. Were I to die before him, I would go doubly battered, horribly laid waste, humiliated. I am resigned to living in silence, my voice stifled by my own hand. But may I be granted some time, however short, to utter just one scream from the depth of my soul, a scream that has lurked deep in my breast for so long, since before you were born. That scream is waiting, eating at me, ravaging me, and I want to live so that I do not die with it still inside me. Pray for me, my daughter, you who know life from both sides, you who can read both books and the hearts of saints. (1989: 39)

The issue is, precisely, that of the "unvoiced female"—of that woman-native-Other in Ama Ata Aidoo and Buchi Emecheta; in Busia and Wynter—who always remains at the risk of being used worse. It is also more; for to "unvoicing" is now added the threat of the erasure. Wynter identifies its operations when Caliban is "soldered on to Miranda as the only symbolically canonizable genitrix" (1990:361) and is thereafter circumscribed in a context in which only in further estranging the mother can he remember her: "I never saw a woman, / But only Sycorax my dam: and she [Miranda]; / But she as far surpasseth Sycorax / As great'st does least" (III.ii.108-11). Elsewhere, the erasure is a fulsome one, its context being the memory- and flesh-dissolving hurricane of agony with which Othello recalls Desdemona, freshly murdered for failing to give him proof—by way of his mother's handkerchief: "Blow me about in winds! roast me in sulphur! / Wash me in steep-down gulfs of liquid fire! / O Desdemona! Desdemona! dead! / Oh! Oh! Oh!" (V.ii.279-83).

To my mind, all this entails a dismembering which has been most acutely remembered in the unmaking of the maternal which Nnu Egu incarnates in Emecheta's *The Joys of Motherhood*, where we are made to understand that "what actually broke her, was, month after month, expecting to hear from her son, and from Adim too who went to Canada, and failing to do so. It was from rumours that she heard Oshia had married and that his bride was a white woman." The "pity of it all" is one over which Emecheta rejects compromise. Her choice is to underscore the cruelty of *retour aux sources* rituals in which appeals to "the mother thing" are little more than empty re-figuration: "When her children heard of her sudden death they all, even Oshia, came home. They were sorry she had died before they were in a position to give their mother a good life. [And so] she had the noisiest and most costly second burial . . . ever seen" (1979:224).

As with Caliban and Othello, it is a remarkable thing in all this that the daughters of Venice and of Prospero are denied mothers. Lamming speculates on and dramatizes the effects in the sixth chapter of his novel about the beginnings of colonialism in the Americas. *Natives of My Person* (1971a) is a third text, along with *The Pleasures of Exile* and *Water With Berries* (1971b), in which this Caribbean re-figures Shakespeare and the early modern period in a complex crossfire of issues. In the process, Lamming re-maps a t(ri)angle which, in *Natives of My Person*, is made up of the Europe of England (Lime Stone, with its House of Trade and Justice), Spain (the Kingdom of Antarctica), and Africa and the Americas. This last is "soil that is new and freely chosen, namely the Isles of the Black Rock, more recently known as San Cristobal." However, with their fabulous mines empty, and "offering little else but fruits of nature and the broken skeleton of the ancient Tribes who celebrate their slow but certain extinction," San Cristobal is also a cross-eyed attempt at utopian expiation: "For I have seen men of basest nature erect themselves," the Commandant of the ship *Reconnaisance* says, "into gentlemen of honour the moment they were given orders to seize command over the savage tribes of the Indies" (1971a:17).

Lamming concentrates the mismeasure of this tempest of vision and murder in a "necklace of pure silver," with a "large cameo of rubies" pendant—the whole gleaming like a "firmament of stars." With this, the Commandant has returned to the Lady of the House, she whom he conceives of as "a colony of joys given over entirely to his care" (65). "You were the reason I took them, he said." And the woman, who had wanted to ask about San Souci, the Demon Coast, the flight of the Tribes, "was blinded from the sparkle that scurried like rats' feet over the glass. . . . She was speechless with wonder when she saw her throat imprisoned with such splendour." He insists all the while on the mirror that he holds up to her, in which burnished surface "she saw [herself] a firmament of stars" ablaze. However, this Lady soon wears "the necklace like a chain of nails." "Souvenirs of you," he said. . . 'Souvenirs of your conquest,'" she answers back, acknowledging thus the "catalogue of miseries" in the climax to which she is being brought.

Because hers is a consciousness that is prone to read subversively, rather than through Miranda's readinesss to be submissive—"Sir, are you not my father?"—Lamming's Lady of the House is alert to the priorness of an "emptying" in Prospero's dominion, one that has since made "the scene" of the tempest "an uninhabited island," and especially unreceptive of the maternal. Evidence abounds too of some aboriginal violence and violation; and it dominates talk among Prospero ("tyrant" and "sorcerer"), Ariel ("jesting monkey"), and Caliban ("poisonous slave"). The circumstances had to have involved an "emptying" at which that pregnant woman from Argier, Sycorax, was critically positioned, she who was "A witch, and one so strong / That she could control the moon, make flows and ebbs, / And deal in her command without her power" (V.i.268-71). In Ariel's Prospero-impelled memory, the sprite had been imprisoned by her "a dozen years" (I.ii.270-79). Also, according to Prospero, though how he knows is unclear, Sycorax was "banish'd" from Africa. But then, "for one [never-explained] thing she did / They would not take her life" (I.ii.267-268). Sign and signified in Sycorax have thus settled into something of that image-resisting-image effect which, in another context, Mary Ann Doane (1991) limns into "a figure of a certain discursive unease, a potential epistemological trauma [whose] most striking characteristic, perhaps, is the fact that she never really is what she seems to be. She harbors a threat which is not entirely legible, predictable, or manageable" (1).

Of this complex weave of circumstances, Shakespeare's Miranda shows no awareness. Nothing in Prospero's daughter suggests the slightest recognition of Sycorax—except for that entirely apt colonizer *memsahib* outburst against Caliban, "Abhorred slave and vile race. . . I taught thee/When thou did'st not, savage / Know thine own meaning / But would'st gabble like / A thing most brutish" (I.ii.352-58)—which, however, some editors insist on assigning to Prospero, on the grounds that it is inappropriate in Miranda. Further, except for that vague "dream than an assurance" of "four or five women" servants,

> I do not know
> One of my sex; no woman's face remember,
> Save, from my glass, mine own; nor have I seen
> More that I may call men than you, good friend,
> And my dear father; how features are abroad,
> I am skilless of. (III.i.48-53)

Miranda's conception of Woman is thus very much contained in the father's interdictory memory and refracted in his gaze. It was inevitable, then, that she would consummate her father's restoration in good order, not as the pregnant burlesque that Caliban had offered to Stephano: "She will become thy bed, I warrant, / And bring thee forth brave brood" (III.ii.113-14), but as a "solemnized" exchange commodity that will make the patriarchal dominion and "contract grow." So much, then, is this young woman circumscribed into being nothing if not her father's daughter. "More to know," she had said, "Did never meddle with my thoughts" (I.ii.23-4).

Not so with Lamming's Lady of the House in *Natives of My Person*, who must contend with a "long and desolate struggle inside her skull" (83). We also learn in the narrative's "Excerpt from the Voyages of Marcel, A Fisherman and Native of Lime Stone" that this daughter's father, Master Cecil, was "a man of infinite avarice and crazy no less." It was he who "against all reason [did] bring his only daughter out on a voyage. . .a girl of exceeding beauty and great spirit; after which the young woman went almost mad what with living so near the blasphemies of the savage Tribes under her father's command. She took to melancholy ways afterwards" (37-40). "I was there," she now says in an agony of moral clarity, "talking to the stones on the mantelpiece. 'Ten thousand women died in a single month. They had not yet seen their men after my father took them away. Ten thousand in one month.'" She had been thus positioned to be more than touched—as were Miranda and Desdemona but, in their cases, to little enlightenment. Lamming's Lady of the House is "afterwards" bonded to less easily resolved allegiances. Her Commandant lover and husband ("who had not known the face of [tempestuous] weather until she came into his life") and Master Cecil *had* dowried her with "a catalogue of miseries." One recalls too the "vengeance of destructive generosity" with which the Ship's Steward says of his wife: "Jewels, silks; name it and she will have it. That's my last plan. To make the rest of her life the most luxurious mourning in history" (189).

In any case, when the Lady of the House finds out that there is to be yet one more voyage to the Demon Coast or to the Islands, her dismay is focused, first, on her being deserted again: her "horrible passages of waiting" to come; those "one thousand eleven miles of days." But then, chronic loneliness is soon re-constituted into a fiercely gendered outrage. "Go feed on your humans," she declares. "That's your work. . . . A human eater is what you are. . . . With a butcher's skill." This she says to a man "who couldn't cope with rage"; whose view of "his need" was that "the ocean had chosen him for the Kingdom; [that] he had a destiny across the seas, a duty that the future would purify. And yet she let her rage denounce him as a common criminal" (82). Lamming re-produces and re-figures and imbricates, collapsing fictional identities (Prospero-Othello-Ferdinand; Miranda-Desdemona; Father-Lover-Husband; Master Cecil-Gabriel de Tate Lysle of the House of Trade and Justice) into the likes of Ralegh, Drake, and Hawkins, Elizabethan sea-dogs; of William Cecil (Lord Burghley), principal advisor to Elizabeth I (96-98) and Lord High-Treasurer. When the daughter in *Natives of My Person* accuses her Ferdinand-Commandant of genocidal excess, a Prospero of composite proportions works his way into the foreground: "A voice leapt from his throat against his will. 'And your father? . . . Do you feel the same about your father?'" But this daughter knows full well what she responds to with, "My father was in command of the Demon Coast." Throughout, echoes reinforce Lamming's import. The Commandant, says the Lady of the House, is "a cannibal"; "he might have been a foreigner she discovered on the moors." Faced with an invitation to be be-dazzled and silent, Lamming's Lady implodes, first, retreating into the domestic particulars of "'I must talk with you. . . . About us, . . . about you and me'"; of "If you prefer a murderer's work to me . . . then you must murder me." But this soon gives way to an expanded and gendered politics of identity; to "the mother thing." "Their punishment was worse than mine," she says. The transgressive extension of her sympathy to encompass the murdered mothers of her Father-Lover's adventures leads her past enraged certainty ("You will sail, I know.") to dead-reckoning outrage: "So answer me now. Whose women will you murder next? Tell me, answer me, before you sail. Whose children will you strangle next?" She sets herself the task of forcing answers to questions the climax to which comes in a "wild arithmetic" of murder. First: "Now, tell me how you do it. Tell me"; and then, "What are you?"; "And the women of the Tribes . . . are there any families left on the Demon Coast?" And then she asks, "How many of us are there in Lime Stone? . . . Here in Lime Stone, how many are we? . . . How many? . . . How many are we in the North?'. . . . 'People,' she said briskly, 'how many people in the North?'" When he finally answers, "One million and a half, his voice firm and clean, his tone exact," Lamming writes that "She sat still, repeating syllables she couldn't calculate. Million and one month, one hundred months, ten thousand. How many? How many are we left? How many would we be?" In the end, the rage and anguish in her politics of identity echo something of the terrible ironies of the joys of motherhood in Emecheta; so, too, the catalogue of abuse in Aidoo.

> "What do you mean?" he said again. "Tell me, my darling, what can you *possibly* mean?"
> "Mean, mean, mean, you know well what I mean." She wheeled her body around and boxed the air with her fist. "Imagine ten thousand mothers died each month. With twice as many children buried. Imagine that here in the North. Ten thousand by the month. It would bring the region to an end. And in less years than you have been at sea. Can you imagine this Kingdom without the North? Can you? But ten thousand mothers dead. And in a month!" Extinction was now real as the air she breathed. . . . "Ten thousand mothers died on the Demon Coast. Ten thousand in one month." (73-87)

The equations in this arithmetic of murder would appear to resolve the question of the unvoiced female in a cross-cultural politics of identity. But

Lamming pushes the matter deeper, into the ironic twist with which he concludes his narrative's apparent move into unambiguous empathy. There are limits, after all, to such a move, and to the latitude of its rage. In the final analysis, no infinite variety will re-figure the Lady of the House into womanshenegro; into any one of the ten-thousand-a-month mothers of the Demon Coast. Nor can she be Caliban's mother, or Othello's, for that matter. "You fail to recognize that, as women," Audre Lorde would observe in Mary Daley, "[the nature of] those differences [expose] all women to various forms and degrees of patriarchal oppression, some of which we share, and some of which we do not" (1981:97). In *Natives of My Person,* the play of difference re-inscribes the Lady of the House in the sub/version that she cannot not be. In the end she does retreat into a tribal union of same to same with her Commandant, for all that she had once heard the wind: "'You're mad,' the wind was warning. 'Love has driven you mad'" (73). But then, "that summer of his fifth Voyage out she came back to her little cabin of space where she would store fresh leaves and watch the days accumulate in her crystal jar. There was fever in her eyes, and a wish that reconciled her to his going. 'Whatever you are, I love you,' she said. 'I love you. It is you I love'." There is passionate irony, all the same, in the cluster of images that the narrative embraces here—from colonial governor-general's plumed hat to native woman invaded as though from overseas. And all this, moreover, in a narrative in which the title, *Natives of My Person,* so effectively suggests sub/version of John Locke; of the utopian premise that persons are owners of themselves; and of that consent theory in which light, Locke declared, "every man, that hath any possession, or enjoyment, of any part of the dominions of any government, doth thereby given his *tacit consent* [to a conjunctive relationship that] reaches as far as the very being of any one within the territories of that government" (Herzog 1989:182).

> She was [Lamming writes] a colony of joys given over entirely to his care. Some tyranny of love had condemned her to his need. . . . She felt him come massive and firm as mast inside her; weighing her slowly with his loins, and thrusting her gently forward; until she heard and felt the wash and lather of the ocean spread over her. . . . The plumes of his ostrich feathers had taken her by the hair and launched her body like a sail before the wind. She made a noise like a wounded bird. (1971a:65)

The penalty of shipwreck in which Lamming then grounds *Natives of My Person* deepens the irony. The narrative's Chorus of Women finds itself stranded in a new-world cave, the consequence of a failure to stave off the collapse of a utopian—and patriarchal—assault on the paradisiac. The conflation of insight with delusion is writ large, into a Platonic parable of sorts that is suffused with "the same smell of absence" and "the familiar waiting." The women's cave seemed "to shrink and close like a skull [while] they gazed toward the mouth." The Surgeon's wife asks, then, "Why did we follow them here?" And the Steward's wife asks, too, "Yes, why follow them there?"

> Lady of the House: Because we are a future.
> Steward's Wife: A future, you say?
> Lady of the House: A future, I repeat. We are a future they must learn. (351)

On this note, the narrative ends, with a chorus of women in full voice but stranded in a reality that is untranslatably utopian. For which reason, then, the women remain, like so many shipwrecked natives of Prospero's person, as much haunted by as hoarding the import of his meanings.

It was a signal and the other instruments quickly followed, the drums exploding into the erotic beat of a samba, the bass becoming a loud pulse beneath the shrieking horns—and in the midst of the hysteria, a voice announced, first in Portuguese and then in English, "Ladies and gentlemen, the Casa Samba presents *O Grande Caliban e a Pequena Miranda*—the Great Caliban and the Tiny Miranda!"

      Paule Marshall, "Brazil"

The vessel had been beset by all the contrary winds that on allegorical maps puff out the cheeks of perverse genies, the enemies of sea-faring people.

      Alejo Carpentier, *Concierto barroco*

Is Heaven a Place—a sky—a Tree?
  . . .
Unto the Dead
There is no Geography
      Emily Dickinson

Chapter 2

"The Still-vex'd Bermoothes":
The Lands of America and The Topography of Utopia

Soundings

> Surely it is no accident that the *roof* of Pandemonium is made of
> the same material as the *pavement* of Heaven.
>> B. Rajan, *"Paradise Lost" and the 17th Century Reader*

> In that case... I rearrange, rotate, turn upside down, sketch and
> redraw all the known maps....It would be better to turn to poets
> who sometimes made acccurate prophecies in the best metered
> verses. I open the book of Seneca's *Tragedies* [and] linger over
> the tragedy of *Medea*.
>> Christopher Columbus, in
>> Alejo Carpentier's *The Harp and the Shadow*

In what follows, my interest in "the irretrievable wealth of Prospero's
cup" (Lamming) and its aftermath in the New World derives from the
several cultures of "discoverie" that *The Tempest's* and *The Harp and
the Shadow's* early-modern geographies are meant to suggest, with
their "What have we here? Man or fish?" and "Brave new world, and all who
dwell in it"; their "*Something*, another thing" and "optical illusion, like the
West Indies were for me." The same is true of the fact that in them some
"native islander . . . hath lately suffer'd by a thunderbolt" and that other such
natives "carried green parrots that did not speak, perhaps from fright." Given
Carpentier's rotating and rearranging of all such maps, *The Harp and the
Shadow* also introduces us to pre-texts for and sub/versions of the genre of
"augmentation" with which the early modern period variously attached
"undreamed shores" (*Measure for Measure*), "What manner o' thing is your
crocodile?" (*Antony and Cleopatra*), and other measures of import to an
England which, in *King John* and *Richard II* and *Henry V*, say, was in the
process of greatly transforming itself into a sea power and colonial empire,
from being merely an island that was separated from the coast of Europe by
"narrow seas" (*Merchant of Venice*). The concommitant expense of spirit,

waste of shame, and "profit on't," reached out across a great variety of latitudes, of course. In 1493, for example, it had involved the Spanish Ambassador at the Papal Court announcing the discoveries of Columbus on behalf of his monarchs by observing that no less an authority than Christ had placed the Fortunate Isles under Spanish sovereignty. Other dispensations of the same account for the fact that, since Manuel I of the early sixteenth century, the official title of all Portuguese monarchs had been "King of Portugal and Algarves, both here and yonder in Africa, Lord of Guinea, Lord of the conquest, navigation, and commerce of Ethiopia, Arabia, Persia, and India." In yet others of its soundings, the "material" (Rajan 1967:45) and spirit of "discoverie" that interest me here ranged from conceiving of fetching "dew" from the "still-vex'd Bermoothes" at midnight in *The Tempest* to a certain occasion when *Hamlet* and *Richard II* were performed on an East India Company flagship as it lay anchored off the West African coast of Sierra Leone in 1607 (Levin *et al.* 1974:5). In 1753, the revelation of God ("How Sweet the Sound of Jesus's Name") would come to Captain John Newton at the mouth of the Sierra Leone estuary, when a sudden storm threatened to send the ship, the *African*, and all on board to the bottom, with losses that would undercut the trade in rum and slaves, cloth and knives, and sugar, tobacco, and molasses that linked England, Africa, and the Indies of the New World (Galeano 1987:25).

There is, elsewhere, the Quest motif and the "juggernaut" of dis/ affiliations that Malcolm Lowry's *Under the Volcano* (1947) will make of its Mesoamerican geography, and of its negotiating of whence and thence and meanwhile. For it is here, and with import that will surface later, that the narrative's Hugh thought: "the *S.S. Noemijolea*, 6,000 tons, leaving Vera Cruz on the night of November 13-14 (?), 1938, with antimony and coffee, bound for Freetown, British West Africa, will proceed thither, oddly enough, from Tzucox on the Yucatan coast, and also in a northeasterly direction: in spite of which she will still emerge through the passages named Windward and Crooked into the Atlantic Ocean" (1971:103). The real theme of *Under the Volcano*, Octavio Paz will explain in *Alternating Current*, is the age-old one of "expulsion from paradise" (1973:14-15). This is a reasonable enough conclusion to derive from the utopian bent of a New World narrative in which the final words do make a capital issue of the question: "*Le gustan este jardin / que es suyo? / Evite que sus hijos lo destruyen!*" (Do you delight in this garden / yours entirely as it is? / Do not then permit others of your kind to destroy it.) (376).

With Sierra Leone I introduce a "coastal" note that will be of some ideological consequence and, I hope, heuristic value, in what follows. Because I plan to organize certain "fashionings" of self and other around it, it is worth acknowledging that my map of "discoverie" shades off here and there into a counter-genre of "discoverie" in which "Africa proper" (Hegel) is *the* outpost of *ultima thule*. "The fact remains that I have smoked a pipe of peace at midnight in the very heart of the continent of Africa and felt very lonely there"—Conrad will duly note about this collapse of an erstwhile utopian genre at Stanley Falls, in September of 1890 (1963:118). "Dearest and best of Aunts!" he would later write from Kinshasa in the same year, "As a crowning joy, my health is far from good. *Keep the secret for me*, but the truth is that in going up the river I had the fever four times in two months, and then at the Falls (its native country) I had an attack of dysentery lasting five days" (*ibid.* 119). This is a world upon which, not quite so parenthetically here, *Heart of Darkness* descends by way of one of its two prologues at Gravesend, some twenty-six miles outside London. I am especially interested in the one which celebrates the "tidal current" and the "unceasing service" of the Thames for having in the past borne a special breed of men, from "Sir Francis Drake to Sir John Franklin, knights all, titled and untitled." They had surfaced, we learn, in a "gigantic tale" of departure and conquest, with great expectations of returning with "round flanks full of treasure"—on ships whose names "are like jewels flashing in the night of time," from the *Golden Hind* (visited by "Her Queen's Highness") to the *Erebus* and the *Terror* (1963:4).

Shakespeare's several constellations of the New World of "the Indies" in such places as *Twelfth Night*, *The Merry Wives of Windsor*, and *The Comedy of Errors* offer a great many figures with which to advance the premise that is explicit enough in my "paradise-lost" epigraph: the sweetness-and-curse proposition that Utopia is the commonwealth of (im)plausible facts. This much is evident in the summary of philosophical, economic, and *Lebensraum* matters that we get when Roger Garaudy's *Alternative Future* makes the point that "The birth of capitalism and the sudden broadening of man's horizon's during the Renaissance directly influenced Thomas More to situate his *Utopia* (1516) in Cuba, Campanella his *City of the Sun* (1623) in Peru, and Bacon to write *The New Atlantis*" (1974:107). Whether in Renaissance experiences of "exile and change" (Giamatti 1984) or of "self-fashioning" (Greenblatt 1984), there is the corollary view that the "reader of a work like Fernand Braudel's *The Mediterranean and the Mediterranean World in the Age of Philip the Second* will appreciate how deep and fundamental are the distinctions that [the] Utopians" in More seem bent on overturning. For his *Utopia* was apparently aimed at "sweeping away of centuries-old accumulation of local and particular culture, marked seemingly indelibly in all the varieties of [its] dress, speech, architecture, behavior" (Greenblatt 1984:41). We may perceive in this utopian bent, Greenblatt concludes, an oscillation between a cleansing away of "clutter" that resists human improvement as well as a failure to appreciate the "opacity" of human social existence (*ibid.*). In yet another augmentation of issues that will be relevant here, consider the extravagance of "incompassing" and the "imitation of all heroick spirits" which, under the pseudonym R. B., Nathaniel Crouch (1632?-1725?) so fully exhibits in *The English Hero, or, Sir Francis Drake reviv'd: being a full account of the dangerous voyages, admirable adventures, notable discoveries, and magnanimous achievements of that valiant and renowned commander: as I. His voyage in 1572 to Nombre de Dios in the West Indies, where he saw a pile of bars of silver near seventy foot long, ten foot broad, and twelve foot high. II. His incompassing the whole world in 1577, which he performed in two years and ten months, gaining a vast quantity of gold and silver. III. His voyage into America in 1585, and taking the towns of St. Jago, St. Domingo, Carthagena and St. Augustine. IV. His last voyage into those countries in 1595, with the manner of his death and burial.* The material would later be "revised, corrected, and beautified with pictures," as printed in 1687; the fourth edition in 1695 would be an "inlarged" one. This remembrance of things past resonates, too, in that 1888 publication of James Anthony Froude's, *The English in the West Indies*, with its "bow of Ulysses" re-memorialization of the Caribbean Sea as "the training ground" for the Elizabethan Englishmen who had destroyed the Spanish Armada in 1588.

Of course, there had been similar reverberations in *The Lusiads* (1572) that Luis Vaz de Camoens (1524-1589) made of Portugal's presence on the high seas and along the coasts of Africa and Asia. *The Lusiads* had accomplished its epic "incompassing" according to the "new and burning zeal" with which Camoens had responded to the "Nymphs of the Tagus." This post-Homeric odyssey, and post-Virgilian re-constitution of imperial grandeur, celebrates a "noble Lisbon" that is "beyond all others / [and] Princess of the earth." She is invited to "Look on [her] Argonauts as they plough the angry waves." As for the rest of the world, "Let Africa and the seas beyond begin to feel the weight of your armies and their exploits, until the whole world tremble." For his part, the Moslem is called upon to fix "his eye on [Portugal] in terror—recognizing the symbol of his destruction." Elsewhere, so we are told, "the barbarous heathen at sight of you bends his neck to the yoke" (1987:41). In the figures of this expansionist nationalism we come upon pre-texts enough to account for the fact that, "built up from 1415 onward, the Portuguese empire in 1580 was practically intact, having reached the peak of its extension and prosperity. Only in Morocco had the Portuguese decided to abandon several towns and fortresses that were more costly than productive. Yet Ceuta, Arzila, and Mazagan and Tangiers remained Portuguese." From a certain "ecumenical standpoint," then, "no other country, not even Spain, had such a worldwide system of human and commercial relations" (Marques

1985:4;8). On the other hand, and from quite a *riverso* portrait of the late sixteenth century by an anonymous Italian, in parts a "terrible libel," the Portuguese were "unpolished, lazy, silly, and proud" (*ibid.*). Although somewhat jaundiced in its overall portrayal, the *Ritratto et Riverso del Regno di Portogallo* (*Portrait and Reverse of the Kingdom of Portugal*) did have occasion to take note of a relevant convergence of latitudes and of import, of the "unbelievable" amount of spices that came into Portugal: "The ships are loaded with pepper without using any sacks, in the way corn is loaded in Sicily. The transparent porcelain all come from there, and so do rubies, diamond, pearls, and all the other precious stones. All the merchandise that arrives in Alexandria, Egypt, from the same countries by another way is not a millesimal part of what arrives here, and from where all the world is supplied" (4-5).

There is, meanwhile, the early-modern amplitude and influence of the "Dutch World." As I have indicated above, its augmentations are ones which Simon Schama configured and illustrated as, by and large, an internal "Golden Age" in *The Embarrassment of Riches* (1987), but which documents of the West India Charter Company, Allison Blakely's *Blacks in Dutch Culture* (1993), and Derek Walcott's *Omeros* have extended into terrains and types of the still-vex'd Bermoothes—or, if you wish, into that "fresh green breast of a New World" that had "flowered once for Dutch sailors' eyes" at the end of Fitzgerald's *The Great Gatsby*. In Blakely, imports from that flowering entailed significant ties that bound the Netherlands to the Dutch East Indies, Cape Colony, Surinam, the Dutch Caribbean islands, Dutch Brazil, and New Netherlands. Also relevant is the "coastal" map that we get of Dutch slave-trading fortresses, and missionary activities, along the West African coast (3). In the event, by the seventeenth century, Dutch *mundus novus* and African *ultima thule* had entered into commerce that manifests itself as it did in certain documents of the General Charter West India Company. These included a "Proposal of merchandise drawn up by the General and counsellors in Guinea, 27 December 1653, [and] sent with the *Roode Leeuw*"; so, too, a "debet done upon the orders of General J[acob] R[uychaver] by various factors on the Gold Coast and in Benin, the Bight and Angola between 1 January and 31 December 1652, in Guinea." We learn from the "debet" that Africans had been bound for Brazil and other places in the Americas, and that they had been exchanged for such items as *blaue negros cleede* (blue negro-cloths), *kan pr. leckagie p. attest* (84 jugs faulty as per attestation), and 99 dozens *bootsmans als andre messen* (boatswains' and other knives) (Jones 1995:178; 152-154). In the latter days, *Omeros* would recall the import of such transports to the New World through which "The Dutch" and the "Dutch road [grossed] / a fortune in the Northern Antilles" with their "tonnage, direction, and mass / of Dutch merchantmen, the arms they shipped in reserve / to American colonies through St. Eustatius" (1990:79).

Any and all such meridians and latitudes converge and disaffiliate to richly antecedent effects when Carpentier positions his Columbus to "speak plainly" in *El arpa y la sombra* (1978) about the "*Something*, another thing" that his experience of world-making had proved to be. Why did you, then, encourage a second voyage, he asks a skeptical Isabella. "To screw Portugal," she replies, what with the kinds of messengers that Portugal had been sending to the Pope, and its representation of itself in certain kinds of ways (Carpentier 1990:105). Scatologically clear-sighted, religiously suffused—and very much embittered—Columbus's circumstances in Carpentier are not quite Miltonic or Shakespearean or Camoens, of course, though not unrelated. Couched as the self-regarding confession of an unshriven Last Messiah of Christ, *The Harp and the Shadow* is, at one level, a novel about a burnt-out ancient mariner of the Ocean Sea. The narrative also provides us with meticulous cullings from and sub/versions of pre-texts of the Discovery—chiefly from Columbus's own writings: from the journal entries of the first voyage through the *Book of Privileges* to the haunted hermeneutics with which the *Book of Prophecies* justifies itself through Classical Antiquity and according to Biblical authority. But first, and by way of explanation, here: I put "pre-text" to work in what follows in both its unhyphenated sense as well as according to what Edith Hall intends when she observes in *Inventing the Barbarian* that one of the functions of the tragic performances at the City of Dionysius was to provide "cultural authorization for the democracy and inter-state alliances of Greece." She makes the concommitant point that the "enormous interest in the barbarian" manifested in the performance, or display, of that alliance can "partly be explained in terms of the Athenian and Panhellenic ideology which the poets both produced and reflected." In this sense, their pre-texts created a "whole new discourse of barbarism," a complex system of signifiers that served to denote, indeed, to anticipate, "the ethnically, psychologically, and politically 'other'." It did so in "terms, themes, actions, and images" many of which were to be of lasting influence on western views of foreign cultures; for example, of Asiatic peoples as effeminate, despotic, and cruel" (1989:2). It is no surprise, then, that "The beds in the east are soft" in Shakespeare's *Antony and Cleopatra*, or that in Columbus's Scythia there are "people with ears so large that they can wrap themselves in them, to keep themselves warm." Elsewhere in *The Harp and the Shadow* "the very name of the *Grand Khan* resonates of gold," producing "celestial music" that clatters "onto a "banker's table" (88;43). Rich in such pre-texts and their templates, Carpentier's "great compass" directs our travel into the still-vex'd Bermothes from here on, though *The Harp and the Shadow* does so in full sail and with cross winds (85). Columbus is, so he tells us, "sound in mind and memory"; however, he is already "stiffening" under "the woolen wrapping that envelops [his] defeated body like that first box" (36). There is instruction in his being thus boxed in; for this image of (un)becoming derives its heuristic value from a curiosity that Columbus had been shown by some tradesman at a fair on the island of Chios: "It was a sort of box, in the shape of a man, which contained a second box, similar to the first, which in turn encased the body of a man, who almost looked alive" (36).

Not surprisingly, Carpentier sets Columbus's "quill" to work in an instructive con/fusion of registers. The voice ranges from mere talk about "three ugly sirens, with the faces of men" to the "gleaming, glistening, glittering, dizzying, dazzling, exciting, inviting image in the hallucinatory vision of a prophet [that] came unbidden to my mouth as if impelled by a diabolical interior energy" at the Great Spectacle in Barcelona (102). As Columbus points out, "Not only have I studied Marco Polo, whose stories of his travels I have annotated with my hand and mark, but I have also read Juan de Monte Corvino" (79). *The Harp and the Shadow* puts on exhibit a Columbus who is enchanted by even as he disarticulates the *"Idea"* of discovery through multiplicities of pre-texts and "centuries of theologies." He is soon enough ready to surrender, though not without considerable elaboration, to the thought of having pursued a "country never found that fades away like a castle of enchantments each time you sing your victory song." For, so it seems, the reach for such stuff as dreams are made on has become little more than a "following of vapors," a seeing of things that never did become "intelligible, comparable, explicable, in the language of the *Odyssey* or in the language of Genesis." In effect, Columbus had (mis)translated and (un)made his way into and among "Islands, islands, islands" that included a "large one, a tiny one, a harsh one, a mild one; a bald island, a hairy island . . . an island within an arc of fish and parrots. . . an island surrounded by foam, like a little girl in a lace skirt" (109). For the rest, he explains, "I say that the blue mountains I can see in the distance are like those in Sicily, though they are nothing like those of Sicily. . . . I allude to the fields of Castile, here where not a single thing recalls the fields of Castile" (87). Columbus, Thomas and Carol Christensen conclude somewhat extravagantly, "lacks the words to understand or to convey most of what he has discovered; in this sense he has failed to discover anything" (1990:xiii). Still, there had been reasons enough, as *The Harp and the Shadow* recognizes, for Columbus to doubt discovery, for him to stumble his way into articulation. After all,

> To designate a *table*, it's necessary that there be, in the mind of
> the one who hears, a *table-concept*, with the appropriate qualties
> of *table-ness*. But here, before this admirable landscape that I
> gazed upon, only the word *palm* had a referential value, since
> there are palms in Africa, palms—though different from the ones
> here—are found in many places, and, consequently, the word
> *palm* is accompanied by a clear image—and especially for those
> who know the religious significance of Palm Sunday. (86)

Granted, figures like the girl in lace skirt and the palm of Palm Sunday give
referential value to and stabilize New World landscape and material. In this
regard, chronicles like Gonzalo Fernández de Oviedo y Valdes's latter-day
Historia natural y general de las Indias and *Sumario de la historia natural
de las Indias,* and before them Hernán Cortés's *Cartas de relación de la
conquista de México* (1519), had been no less able to reproduce their versions
of a stabilizing *Zeitgeist*. They did so by way of appeals to "innumerable
riches" in *spice* and "innumerable treasures" in *pearls*. In effect, notwithstanding the disruptive *tropicalismo* of Oviedo's preoccupation with the
Devil and debauched native women, there had been politics enough, and
"profit on't" all, to justify the *Veedor*'s (Overseer's) assuring translation of
his New World material to his Spanish monarch. "Certainly," he wrote, no
other Prince could claim "such a quantity of *gold* coin as in your Majesty's
kingdom"; for nowhere else but in the Indies "could there be such a quantity,
of millions and millions in *gold*" (Merrim 1989:189; my emphasis).

A "swimmer between two waters," and now "shipwrecked between
two worlds," Carpentier's Columbus sounds out notes of excited alarm about
"a world that played tricks on him," throwing him off course, and leaving him
"neither *here nor there*." He is compelled to wrestle with the problematic
nature of the pre-textual and other loops of correspondence; so, too, with
himself as someone who "today will die, or tonight, or tomorrow, like a
protagonist of fictions" (126). *The Harp and the Shadow* re-constitutes the
whole in a narrative in which the "Discoverer-discovered, uncovered" (125)
declares himself to be "astonished" by his "natural talents as an actor, as a
wielder of illusions, in the style of the mountebanks of Italy [who go] from fair
to fair." He knows himself to be nothing if not, so he tells us, "an impresario
of spectacles" who took his "Pageant of Marvels from throne to throne." He
had set sail suffused with thoughts of Solomon, and with very good pre-texts
indeed for doing so. Solomon had been wiser than "Heman, Kalkol, and
Darda"; he had been the embodiment, too, of so much of the stuff of dream
and discovery: "from the cedar that is from Lebanon" to "the hyssop that roots
in the wall." In addition, hadn't Solomon been "informed about everything by
his messengers, ambassadors, tradesmen, and seamen? From Ophir and

Tarsus they brought him shipments of gold. In Egypt they bought his chariots, and in Cilicia they procured his horses." The man knew "an infinite variety of things—virtues of plants, relationships of beasts, and lewd and lascivious acts, and the contumelies, ignominies, and sodomies of different peoples." He had been in a position to know, too, from his women: Moabite, Ammonite, Edomite, Sondian, not to mention the Egyptians. In addition to which—and the "secret dream of all true men!"—that "very fortunate [and] wise, depraved man [in] his marvelous palace" had been able to choose, "according to his whim, from seven hundred principal wives and three hundred concubines, not counting guests, travelers, unexpected visitors, the woman from Sheba, for example, who paid him to have her" (42). There is some irony, of course, in the identity of the son of Solomon that Columbus later assumes "*over there*"—in the West of the still-vex'd Bermoothes; for then, he finds himself "rocking like Absalom hanging by the hair, between dream and life, without ever learning where the dream began and the life ended" (125). He also articulates the collapse of his great expectations in the unadorned vernacular that we get in "Cities they call them!"—when all that he had actually found were "ten Indian huts covered with bird shit" (*ibid.*).

The vexation is no doubt understandable, given the elaborate point that he had made of his departure in his journal entries. For he had set out in resonant fashion: "*In the Name of Our Lord Jesus Christ*," and under the "Most Christian, exalted, excellent, and powerful princes, King and Queen of the Spains and of the islands of the seas, Our Sovereigns." Moreover, it was "in this year of 1492," he observed, "that Your Highnesses concluded the war with the Moors who reigned in Europe. On the second day of January, in the great city of Granada, I saw the royal banners of Your Highnesses placed by force of arms on the towers of the Alhambra" (Fuson 1987:51). But then, the Columbus of *The Harp and the Shadow* had not been unacquainted with the vagaries of men who had sailed off in "phantasmal ships through hyperborean nights without dawn [to] discover islands, unknown lands, which had been mentioned in a treatise entitled *Inventio fortunata*." A certain German sailor named Tyrkir, and member of the party of Leif the Lucky, had been something of a landmark in this regard. The fellow had gone missing for a season; then, he had returned, "drunk as a lord," with stories about a land of enormous grapes and powerful wine ("Well, just look at me"). This Tyrkir had also been quite prepared, "just like Beowulf," to "lop the heads off" any one who denied that he could be king where he now found himself. All the same, he soon "fell flat on his face and vomited and wailed that all Normans are sons of bitches. . . . But from that day on the Normans knew that past Green Land lay 'Vinland'" (48-49).

The "overflowing cornucopia" of what Carpentier's dispirited but productively vexed Genoan presents from his deathbed makes for quite a constellation of world-(un)making material. They will prove to be variously clarifying, I hope, in my handling of Conrad and Naipaul no less than Camoens, Shakespeare, and Cortés; so, too, the nineteenth century of Pope Pius IX and the twentieth of Borges and Walcott, as I hope to illustrate. It matters, too, that, in a postille to his copy of d'Ailly's *Epologue mappae mundi* Columbus had made a point of underscoring his "coastal" experience, of his having sailed frequently south from Libson to Guinea. In those days, he had purposefully studied the course, as captains and mariners do; and he had become adept, too, at taking the altitude of the sun with the quadrant and other instruments (West and Kling 1991:11). Consider, then, some of the "natively" generic material with which his discovery of the Indies manifested itself. "For green parrots, with sly little eyes, that never learned to say a single word in our language," and for such things as crude red caps and cat-bells and dog-bells—and while the natives looked funny, and burst out laughing, patting themselves on the belly—the Admiral of the Ocean Sea had been able to take possession of lands without the natives being aware of a thing. "And what was worse, without my *I claim thee* in the name of the etcetera, etcetera, etcetera" (92).

In others of these "etceteras" *The Harp and the Shadow*'s material was "Golden Calf" and "Promised Land." It had also been "shit-assed Spaniards" who claimed that Columbus had "gravely underestimated the earth's circumference." But then, among the figures that truly counted here was Queen Isabella; she was a woman of some mettle and seduction still, for all that she had been betrayed by an unworthy Aragonese of a husband who, when he wasn't mounting a maid of honor, was occupied "with some converted Moor, hot-blooded Jew, or woman of the troops, if there was no better flesh in which to sink his teeth" (65). She it was who would send him beyond the "stone bowl" of the every day world (Rushdie 1996). In this regard, the *East, West* story that Salman Rushdie makes of his "Christopher Columbus and Queen Isabella" provides us with a "plausible scenario," even if its circumstances make for a more anxiety-ridden, sexually teased, and considerably less heroic character. This Columbus's years of lobbying and of courtship, so to speak, had not been quite as modulated by sublime choruses and conjuring dexterity. Instead, foreplay and frustration, and maddening alienation, had marked his reach for "consummation" in that fateful year of 1492. Granting the obvious measures of desire—preferment, hopes of cash, three tall ships—when Columbus first arrived at the court of Spain, "Consummation" ("*Yes. I'll come.*") had really been what most mattered to him, according to Rushdie. Thus, when the Queen asked him what it was that he desired, Columbus had bowed "over her olive hand and, with his lips a breath away from the great ring of power, [had] murmured a single, dangerous word. 'Consummation'" (1996:107). He does so in a narrative that is "dream of a dream" and "sexual appetites," in which "ways and meanings" are bound to an "unknown and perhaps even unknowable world beyond the Edge of Things, beyond the stone bowl of the every day." Myth-making and myth-mocking disssonance is acidly etched in the chorus of xenopobic voices that swirl about an equally unregenerate ancient mariner in Rushdie: *See him, the drunkard, his huge, shaggy head filled with nonsense! A fool with his glittering eye dreaming of a golden paradise beyond the Western Edge of Things*" (109). And this chorus of insults, *The Harp and the Shadow* confirms, is indeed what "shit-assed" Spaniards say "who always consider you a foreigner. And that is because you have never had a homeland, mariner: that is why you had to search *over there*—in the West" (125). For there was the gravitational pull, always, of the "still-vex'd Bermoothes": "I just wanted to get *over there*"; to be fitted out with "solid ships, broad-waisted, with experienced pilots and men with hair on their chests," even if from the galleys (*The Harp and the Shadow* 56). And so, in Carpentier's version Columbus had spoken to the Queen as he always did "before the great and the powerful." Once again, he declares, "I displayed my bag of wonders, my hallelujahs of dazzling geographies, but [then], as I began my recitation of possible marvels, a new idea began to take shape" (66-67). Thereafter, and the queen's *machisma* notwithstanding, there could only be "one woman for me," Columbus realized: "the world that still waited *for me* to be fulfilled" (66-67). Besides which, the Castilian had taken to being self-indulgent in her teasing of him; for in the evening she would make him promises of the final million maravedis that he needed, only to take back her assurances at daybreak. "Pig!" she had screamed at him once, in Carpentier, that is. "You're nothing but a pig!" And he had shouted back, "Pig yourself! [And] you know better than anyone what I am and what I have been!" (68).

Utopian and bent on the Indies, Columbus had gone from court to court in an age impatient to fulfill itself, with himself the most impatient of them all. "Chosen One, was I," he would declare in Spain, winding up a path that had been long and difficult, in which he had once tried to play off Isabella's Spain against the King of France who had a wife on whom certain praises could be heaped. "Pig! Filthy swine! You would betray Christ for thirty denarii!" Columba had screamed at him then (68):

> *Seven years have I been in your Royal Court and everyone who heard of my enterprise said it was a mockery. [But] Now even tailors apply for discovery.* (121)

The "etceteras" of *The Harp and the Shadow*'s discovery are elsewhere delimited by portentous "tales of men like Jonah, who spent three days and three nights in the belly of a whale, with his forehead plastered with sea weed." In others of his pre-texts, the self-baptized Torchbearer of Christ (*Christo-phoros*) reached for world-making material that was both from and opposed to the "*Lord* of Abraham and Jacob, the one who spoke to Moses from the burning bush—the *Lord* before his Incarnation," even though his Matthew, Mark, Luke, and John, "to tell you the truth," had been left behind in Spain on the first voyage. Plainly put, "they hadn't crossed the Ocean Sea" to a certain "*over there*" of "islands, islands, islands," where the still-vex'd Bermoothes was as yet a sea of islands that were in "such tight and sunny constellation"—he had counted a hundred and four—that, thinking what to call them, Columbus "named them *Gardens of the Queen*" (109). But then, with "death hovering over him," the Admiral of the Ocean Sea re-examines the yellowed pages of his journal of that first voyage only to discover that on the twenty-fourth of December when, as a Franciscan, he should have been meditating on the divine event of the Nativity, he had written the word "GOLD five times in ten lines that could have been taken from the grimory of an alchemist"—as if influenced by "witchcraft" or some "infernal vapor" (94). All the same, "*I required that Cuba be a continent and a hundred voices rose to say that Cuba was a continent*," Columbus declares (123).

Consider in this light the Columbian exchange that the islands of *The Harp and the Shadow* would become "amidst a growing economy of Cre-ation" in the eighteenth century of *Explosion in a Cathedral*. Esteban would there re-cognize the "tangible image, a ready—and yet so inaccessible—configuration of a Paradise Lost, where trees, barely named as yet by the torpid, hesitant tongue of the Man-Child," would be endowed with "apparent immortality" as well as with the "flux," the "trace," and the "arabesque" of a "world of symbiosis" (176-177). Familiar soundings come our way, too, out of that isle of *The Tempest* that's "full of sounds, and sweet airs, that give delight, and hurt not," and which Wilfred Cartey makes the prologue to the world that he once anthologized as "whispers from the Caribbean," with its "I going away, I going home" (1991). They do so, too, in Lamming's *The Pleasures of Exile* where the circum-Caribbean is a "sea that is cobalt, changing frivolously to green, bright semicircles of foam along the coast that stretches and contracts like arms in a gymnasium"; in a world in which "the tide seems to encourage those exiled pieces to turn to islands. [For] they prolong themselves in a squad of green surfaces; [then] narrow into brief mounds of vegetation, entirely silenced by the ocean. Then they reappear, tiny islands in a heroic effort to resist the total embrace of the sea; [making of themselves] an illogical geometry on the blue-bright screen of the morning, appearing almost suspended between sea and sky. An enchanting exchange of blues turning to green and back again" (17). On this strand of discovery, Esteban would marvel at, and *conceptualize* for us, just how much the language of these islands of the New World has had to make use of "agglutination, verbal amalgams and metaphors to convey the formal ambiguity of things which participated in several essences at once" (*Explosion, ibid.*).

Once upon a time, moreover, as Jules Verne declares in the St. Peter's Basilica "Morality Play" that also lies at the heart of *The Harp and the Shadow*, "*The truth is that a group of facts, systems, and doctrines was being developed during Columbus's era. It was time for a single intelligence to come and propound and assimilate them. All these disparate ideas came together in the mind of a single man who possessed, in the highest degree, the genius of perseverance and of audacity*" (144). But then, it was also at this point that the ghost that Columbus had by then become saw Victor Hugo lean on the bar to make the counterpoint that "*If Christopher Columbus had been a good cosmographer, he never would have discovered the New World*" (143). It bears recalling that there is a decidedly ecclesiastical framing of the "etcetera" of discovery in *The Harp and the Shadow*; and that it is a form of its ritualized debate that accounts for Carpentier's blending of Verne's and Hugo's voices, among those of other historical figures in the narrative—all this within the "hearing" of a quite dispirited Columbus. The Scriptures, it turns out here, had not descended on the New World with quite the investiture that they could have. This much becomes clear in the latter-day preoccupations of a certain Signior Mastai— of the family of Mastai-Ferretti—who, on the fifth of October, 1823, had in fact boarded a ship, the *Héloise* this time, and weighed anchors to set sail for the New World. "Better Abelard's Héloise than Rousseau's," mused this Mastai, Pope Pius IX as of 1845, and obsessed with the idea of a Saint Christopher, of a "Porter of Christ" (a *Christo-phoros*) between the Old World and the New (15;28). Sailing from Genoa ("It had been a native of Genoa who launched the extraordinary adventure that gave man a consummate vision of his world."), the Pontiff-to-be had indeed reached the Americas on the *Héloise* in an entourage that included the Delegate Giovanni Muzzi, his personal secretary, Don Salustio, the Dominican Raimundo Arce, and the Archdeacon Cienfuegos, plenipotentiary minister from Chile—by recent appointment of Bernardo O'Higgins—to the Holy See. There, he had observed with some productive disquiet "the power of spreading philosophical and political ideas that were oblivious to the boundaries of seas and mountains" (5). A measure of the facts, and of the swirl of fictions, that had made the Vatican visit necessary may be gleaned from the nature of reports that represented the Chilean Church as a sanctuary for intriguers of every stripe—from cloaked Carbonari and pentitent renegade priests to Voltairean ex-curates; so, too, deserters from the Lodges, "ready and willing to sell the secrets of freemasonry for thirty denarii" (12). O'Higgins, Director General of the Chilean Government, was bent on seeing the church reformed and brought under the direct charge of the Vicar of the Lord on Earth ("A masterstroke, however you looked at it!"). He was reputedly

> quite friendly with a formidable Venezuelan, mentor of Simón Bolívar and general of the French Revolution, whose worldly exploits would make a fantastic adventure novel; they even say— "deliver me, God, from impure thoughts," thought Mastai—that he slept with Catherine the Great, when "her lover Potemkin, worn out by the excessive ardors of the sovereign, decided the handsome hot-blooded Creole might be able to satisfy the ourageous appetites of the Roman Empress, who may have been getting on in years, if you know what I mean, but was still termendously fond of. . . ." "Enough, enough, enough," said Mastai to his informer [then]. (13).

From out of such "confused, choatic times." there had emerged at least one elaborate papal consequence; and the opening "Harp" section of the *The Harp and the Shadow* is virtually bound up in the challenge of a relevant sentence, in Latin, from His Most Eminent Prince Cardinal Donnet, the Archibishop of Bordeaux. This prince of the Church had four years before earnestly beseeched the Pope that the cause of that servant of God and illustrious personage, the faithful Christopher Columbus, be advanced for canonization by special procedure (29). "The ideal, the perfect way to join the faithful of the old and new worlds," Pope Pius IX had himself come to believe, "was to find a saint whose acceptance was ecumenical, a saint whose fame was unlimited, incontrovertible, a saint of planetary wing span, a saint so enormous . . . that he could have one foot on the shores of this continent and the other on the banks of Europe" (28).

It is this attempt to beatify Columbus at the Basilica, with its *pro introductione illius causae exceptionali ordine*, that gives *The Harp and the Shadow* another one of its several myth-mocking, myth-making frames. Here the con/texts oscillate between a historicist, but *leyenda-negrista*, descent into *ou-topos* and a juridico-ecclesiastical reach for utopia. Needless to say, any such *"venerationem fidelium erga Dei Christophorum Columbum"* called for strictly prescribed actors. For example, it required that there be at one end of the table, the Postulator of canonization, and at the other, the promoter of the critic of canonization, the Devil's Advocate ("that subtle and intimidating Minister of the Republic of the Inferno"). *"Proceed without fear,*

Christopher. If what you are looking for has not yet been created, God will make it appear in the world, from nothing, to justify your audacity" (143). Quoted from Schiller, the words are those of the Postulator, and invoked in a proceedings at which Columbus can only moan, "I'm screwed, [now] I'm really screwed" (144), when Bartolomé de las Casas is summoned to testify at a Basilica proceedings where his own record of the discovery had already sentenced him to be an "absent/present protagonist." It is from within its framing of Columbus that the Devil's Advocate "imperturbably" argued that, among others of the candidate's demerits, "If there had indeed been cannibals among the Indians in America," that was "twice the reason Columbus had for not bringing the Indians to Spain, because the cannibals would present a constant danger to the children playing in the public gardens. And it could have meant some Indian would get a craving for the loins of a pretty little girl" (138-139;7;145). All the while, Columbus hovers over his own (un)becoming, constrained by pre-texts and plain-speaking that make him a proximate enough witness against himself. He is in no position to avoid hearing the Devil's Advocate's quick response to an objection of the Postulator's. To withdraw the last remark about "the loins," the Advocate tells the president of the proceedings, would be to leave the pretty girl "with a bone" (146).

Carpentier fashions *The Harp and the Shadow* into a narrative that is instructively preoccupied with being the chronicle of an actual discovery, with the mapping of an "optical illusion," and with the ties that bind both of these experiences to "web[s] of fabulous stories." *Pace* the recalcitrance of the theological debate at the Basilica, there was a great deal of imbricated material in any such enterprise—and from "the Revealer of the Planet! How exciting!"—to transform the latter days of "some poor country estate"into "a veritable Palace of Marvels." After all, the Discoverer's mind had been several times "inflamed" with a plausible enough scenario:

> Surely even Ulysses's tales in his allies courts could not have matched the splendid tales of adventure that emerged *that afternoon* from the mouth of Columbus who would discover the mysteries of death before nightfall, just as, in life, he had discovered the mysteries of a geographic *beyond*, previously unknown, which men had imagined since the happy age and happy times that Don Quixote spoke of in his discourse to the goatherds, "the happy age and the happy times on which the ancients bestowed the name golden." (31)

Columbus thus acknowledges in Carpentier that he had been unable "to open a book without trying to find in it" a "background, a verse, a portent of [his] mission." He could not *not* seek "presages, applying oneiromancy to the interpretation of [his] dreams." The gravitational pull of so many con/texts had, in turn, led him to consult yet other memories of the future, among them "the Pseudo-Joseph and the Alphabetic Keys of the Pseudo-Daniel, and, therefore, the tract of Artemidorous of Ephesus." His catalogue of pre-texts had translated his life into a feverish and "disturbed obsession" with "designing more or less fantastic plans." All the same, it was *he* who had succeeded in taking (in) the full measure of GOD and GOLD; *he* who had played out Seneca's drama and Isaiah's prophecy to the full, so he believed. On the other hand, for all that he had "shouldered his bag of tricks," that prophetic moment in Seneca—*"venient annis . . . quibus Oceanus vincula rerum laxet"*—had never quite become flesh "in the flesh of the one who [was now] sweaty and ailing, defeated in body, waiting for the Franciscan confessor to tell him everything, everything. . ." (58). All the while, though, such memories of the future involve him in "another trip and then another, [now] remembered, on the verge of leaving on the journey from which there will be no return. . . . Another trip and another trip, and still he had not found the *one good deposit of gold*" (118).

       In this respect, Columbus was as god-intoxicated as he had been transfixed when he first saw *Indians* who wore small bits of gold in their noses. He recalls being "Shaken, sweating, determined, crazed, [and] peppering [them] with sign-language questions" to find out how they had obtained it, where it was found, how it was mined, how it was worked" (84). This was all so much *Zeitgeist* business, of course—and reductively charged, too, with an obsessive "money-changer's language, the language of a Lombard banker." But then, the Indies never did fulfill the great expectations in god and gold that that it provoked. For which reason Columbus had had to measure out the triumphs of his enterprise in quite other ways, as "a tremendous and unabashed fake," for example (55). This is the spirit in which he recalls being undone on the Feast Day of Saint Stephen, a worthy one for thinking about the apostle's transfiguring death by rocks and stones. What he had done instead was write the word "GOLD" a dozen times in an account in which he "mentioned the word Lord God only once—and only as part of a secular expression" (94). And then, there had been that great celebration of "the Discovery" before Their Highnesses in Barcelona, with its "suffocatingly warm" and "sour smell of sweat-soaked silk, satin, and velvet"; its "red carpet" on which the green parrots of the New World had "started to vomit cheap red wine"; and his abducted Amerindians who, when they were not on exhibit with the parrots of the Spectacle and Marvels of Indies, bent down and howled—or else shivered to an embittered death on the docks (102). There was, needless to say, a good deal of sub/version in all this, never mind the *Te Deum* to come, and the sourness, too, as below, in Bartolomé de las Casas's remembrance of things past. At any rate, further instigated as Columbus was by and in Barcelona, perhaps, by an "almost imperceptible wink ("*Quosque tandem, Christoforo?*") from his Columba, he had known enough to play the actor and to be nothing if not *the* Admiral of the Ocean Sea. In short, he had made much of what little he had actually accomplished, "through Your Highnesses," of course:

> I was the one who opened, I was the one who led the way to new horizons, making the world round, like a pear, like the breast of a woman with a nipple in the middle—and my eyes quickly sought those of my Mistress—the world that Pedro Aliaco, the illustrious chancellor of the Sorbonne and Notre Dame de Paris, had seen as *almost* round, a*lmost* spherical, creating a bridge between Aristotle and me. With me, the prophesy in the Book of Isaiah is fulfilled. Now it has achieved reality: "Their land is filled with silver and gold, and there is no end to their treasures, in a place of broad rivers and streams, where galleys with oars can go, and stately ships can pass." (103)

The dissonances of discovery, or else the treachery of its pre-texts, soon caused Columbus to "substitute, for gold and flesh, words. Great, beautiful, weighty, juicy rich words" (118). He had then set about and indeed done much to accomplish this feat of translation, especially with the third voyage. "All right!" he had not found the Indies of spices and gold. But, "shit!", Columbus insists, he "had found nothing less than the Earthly Paradise!" There it was, just south of the island that he had named Trinidad, never mind a history of imaginings in which "deceivers" or otherwise "worthy scholastic masters and theologians" had located the place anywhere from the source of the Nile in Ethiopia to somewhere in the Orient, *"etcetera"* (119-120). Quill in hand, Carpentier's protagonist thus "speaks" from a somewhat querulous deathbed—one with a tell-tale mirror at the foot—and to which, traveling as he must from four leagues away by mule ("fit only for women and clerics," in any case), the confessor will not quite arrive in time (35;127).

Carpentier's besieged but self-regarding Admiral and Governor had been quite the "New Burnisher" who fashioned the politics and the art of world-making out of, and then back into, "a workshop of marvels, like those the goliards make in Italian fairs." *The Harp and the Shadow*'s optical illusions and sensual excitement, its antique prophecies and Amerindians with green parrots, had been grounded, too, in the mercantile and *Lebensraum* logic of "gold, lots of gold, as much gold" as could be made commensurate with a "mirage" which—"thanks to me," Columbus declares—had "created a vision of Colchis and the Golden Chersonese." But then, the character had been caught (up) in his cross-purposed genres of discovery. The voice that we get in *The Harp and the Shadow* is as fulsome in its transports as it is disconcerting in its disclosures when Columbus identifies himself as "the

promoter of a sacred representation"; as the man who had carried out for the
Spaniards who sent and came with him "the great act of Taking Possession of
Islands that did not even consent to be known." He recognizes with some
irony that he has ever since become "the Conqueror-conquered" who only
really began to exist for himself and for others "the day [he] reached *over
there*." As he puts it, "it is those lands that have formed me, sculpted my
shape" to no real purpose (122). Soon enough, he hears the Bachelor de
Mirueña and of Gaspar de la Misericordia on the stairs as they arrive with the
confessor to raise "the curtain on the final scene. The moment of truth, the
final reckoning. But there will be no reckoning." In the end, Columbus's only
desire is to extricate himself "from the labyrinth" in which he has since found
himself: "I wanted to gird the earth, but the earth was too large for me. It is
for others to clear away the transcendental enigmas the earth still holds," he
concludes. For which reason, "May the heavens have mercy upon me, and
weep upon the land" (127;129).

The note of resolution here is as beguiling as had been the Latin pre-
texts and Indian nose rings, the graphic sensuality and pious arithmetic, too,
with which Columbus had set out in his "imitation of the heroick." For after
all had been said and done, the man dies in a con/fusion of attributes that
apparently justified his extravagant and yet bitter view of himself as *Christo-
phoros*—as the protagonist in what Carpentier's *Explosion in a Cathedral*
would play out in its "century of lights" as a "great all-embracing, sacramental
drama" that had promised to make an "immense stained glass window" of the
Caribbean and its sea of islands. Meanwhile,

> I am who I am, like the Lord of Wrath, [we read in *The Harp and
> the Shadow,*] and from this moment on I can call myself *Don*,
> because from this moment on—all must recognize and say it—
> I am the Grand Admiral of the Ocean Sea and viceroy and
> Perpetual Governor of All the Islands and Terra Firma that I have
> discovered and that henceforth, following my command, will be
> discovered and won in the Ocean Sea. (78;108)

In explaining so congeneric an encompassing of latitude and import, Carpentier
has Columbus conjure up a richly cross-purposed analogy. From it we learn
that the "farmer who has shaken the fruit from his neighbor's olive trees is
almost as innocent as he stands before the Throne of God, as the whore
(pardon my language. . .) who, for want of a better occupation, plies her trade
on her back with a sailor in port, while above her hangs a picture of Mary
Magdalene, whose effigy in Paris graces the banner of the Brotherhood of
Rakes, which is recognized as a public treasure—signed and sealed by official
decree—by King Louis of France" (35).

All in all, *The Harp and the Shadow* dis/closes its terrains and types in ways that make it easy to invoke, as I do below, certain configurations of the round earth's imagined corners, from Argentina to the Congo. The details of the map that follows will therefore include that far-south *orbis tertius*—Tlön, Uqbar—the instructive discovery of which Jorge Luis Borges's protagonist will famously announce that he owed to the "conjunction of a mirror and an encyclopaedia." Yet other versions of the brave new world—for sure a "garden of forking paths" (Borges)—would be limned in such con/texts as the Iberian *comedia americana*, the Mesoamerican *auto sacramental*, and the baroque opera which, respectively, Lope de Vega, Sor Juana Inés de la Cruz, and Antonio Vivaldi produced in *El nuevo mundo descubierto por Cristóbal Colon* (1598), *El divino Narciso* (1690), and *Montezuma* (1773). Given my heuristic, because anchoring, interest in its implications, there are straightforward enough reasons to also "discover" *The Harp and the Shadow* and its protagonist in narratives of "Africa proper." The womanshenegro (Faulkner) *tropicalismo* of Columbus's sensuality is, for example, recognizably imprinted in Conrad's latter-day descent when his Marlow encounters that "savage and superb" woman of the Congo. "Wild-eyed and magnificent," she had stood there with all those innumerable necklaces of glass beads on her neck; "bizarre things, charms, gifts of witch-men, that hung about her, [that] glittered and trembled at every step" (62). Columbus's own African pre-text merits citation here, given the great and "coastal" lengths to which it goes in *The Harp and the Shadow* to make the point that "man does not live by flesh alone." True enough, Carpentier's protagonist concedes. But then, he had also sailed along and made landfall on the African coast, and there he had known

> the dark-skinned women—always darker—until [he] reached
> the darkest ones of Guinea, of the Gold Coast, with their knife-
> inscribed cheeks, adorned with pearls threaded through their
> eight braids, woolly hair sticking out, and abundant buttocks,
> whom the Portuguese and Galicians so rightly favored—and I
> say "rightly," because I seem to remember that if King Solomon
> was wise in allying himself with the woman--*nigra sum* [I am
> black...]—whose breasts were like clusters of grapes, of the
> black, swollen grapes ripened at the foot of the mountains, in sea
> breezes, and made into heavy, fragrant wine that, when it is
> drunk, leaves its savorous imprint on the lips. . . . . (40-41)

A concession: in thus crossing meridians and constructing plausible scenarios—in "shaking the fruit from [a] neighbor's olive trees," if you wish—I am not unmindful of the exceptionalist claims in Octavio Paz's *Alternating Current*, in which context he identifies his Latin American New World as a unique, borderline situation, one in which conquest and domination by the

Spanish and the Portuguese bear little resemblance to that of Asia, and even less to that of Africa, as conquered by other European peoples. It is Paz's view, for example, that, contra the gravitational pull of Mohammedanism or Buddhism or Hinduism in those places, "the stepping stone to modernity for Latin America is Christianity." In his New World, "Christianity is a path rather than an obstacle, one that involves a *change*, not a *conversion*, as it does in Asia and Africa." This a plausible scenario, of course; and it is one that encourages the thought in Paz that what "we really are is an eccentric backward part of the West" (199). There is another plausible scenario, again from Paz; and this time it involves the disruptive unearthing of material that makes Euro-Christian translation, or Euro-Amerindian embrace, even more awkward. For Paz now introduces the fabric of "American" sensibility through the unsettling proposition that Mesoamerican Coatlicue's "unearth-ing" is "a repetition, on a reduced scale, of what the European mind must have experienced at the time of the discovery of America." Cycles of discovery and consciousness are thus refracted against this figure's "changing fortunes"— from "goddess to demon, from demon to monster, and from monster to masterpiece"—ever since it was first unearthed on August 13, 1790.

> Whether on top of the pyramid or buried among the ruins of an old *teocalli*, whether hidden behind a screen or placed in the center of a museum, the Coatlicue always causes astonishment. It is impossible not to linger and look at her, if only for a moment. The spirit is caught in amazement: the enigma of the block of stone paralyzes our sight. The exact nature of the sensation that overcomes us in this moment of stillness is unimportant: admi-ration, horror, enthusiasm, curiosity. Without ceasing to be what we see, the work of art once more reveals itself as that which lies beyond what we see. What we call a "work of art"—an ambigu-ous name, especially when applied to the works of ancient civilizations—is perhaps no more than a configuration of signs. (1990:18)

My point then: Carpentier's fractious grounding of the signs of discovery and (un)becoming in Columbus raises issues that interest me for being so apparently moveable. "Do you get the story?"—Conrad's Marlow asks in the context in which he, too, must contend with the "notion of being captured by the incredible," for all that he is, granted, rather severely disadvantaged in pre-texts (27). "Burn but his books," Caliban had once advised his "confeder-ates" about how to rein in Prospero's way with the great globe itself in *The Tempest*, and how to then cut the man's "wezand" (his windpipe) with a knife (II.ii.95). By the time we get to Marlow's way with discovery, Columbus's discursive style and imperializing library sound thin and make for things parodic. In Conrad's "Africa proper," we are at a rather considerable, and thus telling, remove from the New World of Walcott's "Seven Seas" in *Omeros* (1990) and of *The Harp and the Shadow*'s "*Something*, another thing." As a result, we glide past "like phantoms" (36) in a "weary pilgrimage" through a "God-forsaken wilderness" (13). We do so "amongst hints for nightmares" (14), or else in the low comedy of "names like Gran' Bassam, Little Popo, names that seemed to belong to some sordid farce acted in front of a sinister back-cloth" (13). *Pace* Columbus, in such a world hard usage of the book only results in comically diminished import; and departure from the "world of straightforward facts" into the *Heart of Darkness* (14) only plays itself out in the rhetorical anxiety with which language fails to signify when the surface, much less the uncertain depth, of some *terra* refuses to be *cognita*. We are several degrees removed from the richer con/texts, and the promise of translatability, with which the Columbus of the *Book of Prophecies* had once lugged himself off into discovering the New World with Isaiah and Baruch, Augustine and Seneca; or, yet again, with a Nicholas of Lyra who, in an example of "twofold literal meaning" derived from the Old Testament of the eighth chapter of the Book of Daniel, had been able to speak "figuratively of the war between the Greeks and the Medes" (West and Kling 103-104).

"Fancy a man lugging with him a book of that description into this nowhere and studying it—and making notes—in cipher at that!" The title and text that provoke this "extravagant mystery" in *Heart of Darkness* is "*An Inquiry into some Points of Sea-manship*, by a man Towser, Towson—some such name—Master in His Majesty's Navy" (38). In what reads like a sub/ version of the postilles (handwritten notes) in Columbus's collection of books, Marlow records his thought that "such a book being there was wonderful enough; but still more astounding were the notes pencilled in the margin, and plainly referring to the text. I couldn't believe my eyes! They were in cipher! Yes, it looked like cipher" (39). It fits, of course, that this instance of the book in the wilderness should end in the *reductio ad absurdum* discovery that the "cipher" was, in fact, the Russian scribbles of that "harlequin" creature and "admirer" of Kurtz. "I looked at him in astonishment," Marlow informs us later. "There he was before me, in motley, as though he had absconded from a troupe of mines, enthusiastic, famulous (sic)" (55). Elsewhere, all that we get from the attempt to re-constitute the world as narrative is resistance. We are left to contend with the fact that there was "no sign on the face of nature of [the] amazing tale that was [being] not so much told as suggested [by way of] desolate exclamations, completed by shrugs, in interrupted phrases, in hints ending in deep sighs. The woods were unmoved, like a mask—heavy, like the closed door of a prison—they looked with their air of hidden knowledge, of patient expectation, of unapproachable silence" (57).

Granting the necessary exceptions, then, the dispensation of pre-texts in the New World is instructive for being variously the same and mobile—insofar as it dis/confirms, say, the gravitational pull toward chaos that so distinguishes the tropics, even when they are sited within "the West." In the event, and with its "phoo!" and "ough!" and "complaining clamour modulated in savage discords" (40), the "opaque air" of "Africa proper" will parallel, but then pull away from, that "epilogue and bibliographical notice concerning Chaos" which Antonio Benítez-Rojo appends to *La isla que se repita* (1985) and its "heteroclitic" embrace of things rich and strange. There is a recognizable but obviously recalcitrant density to the African material, and it counters the constellation of forces that dis/attract matter in the America of *The Repeating Island*: "If I have seized hold of certain models belonging to Chaos," Benítez-Rojo explains, "it has not been because I think that these can manage to signify fully what's there in the archipelago; rather it's because they speak of dynamic forms that float, sometimes in unforeseen and scarcely perceptible ways within the Caribbean's huge and heteroclitic archive" (1992:269). By contrast, in the "form of ultimate wisdom" that surfaces in Conrad's narrative—one that "seemed to shape itself without human lips" (28)—we come "within a hair's breadth of the last opportunity of pronouncement" only to find ourselves faced with the "humiliation" of there being "probably nothing to say" (72). Here, the experience of dis/order that "landmarks" *The Harp and the Shadow*'s "*Something*, another thing" is rather less mysteriously related to the experience of "sane men" who, "wondering and secretly appalled," had been "cut off from the comprehension of [their] surrounding" (29). Unpoliced, and perhaps utterly unpoliceable, the experience of Africa intensifies the suspicion of being "kept away from the truth of things," and induces thoughts about "the very end of the world [and] the fascination of abomination—you know." Properly understood, "end times" in Africa is not at all invested with the millenarian geoeschatology that allows Columbus to re-discover the Garden of Genesis, and Mather's *Magnalia* to promise "golden candlesticks," in the New World. With Congolese declension, the "mind of man" risks thorough annihilation, and finds itself at the vanishing point of heroic impulse and prophetic revelation. A true domain of things cancelled or fatally illegible, this is terrain that negates even the ambiguous material that Rajan makes of the roof of pandemonium *and* the floor of heaven. "I was also buried," Marlow explains, "in a vast grave full of unspeakable secrets. I felt an intolerable weight oppressing my breast, the smell of damp earth, the unseen presence of victorious corruption, the darkness of an impenetrable night . . . ." (63).

Meanwhile, there is a quite useful exchange of sub/versions in the con/texts through which *The Harp and the Shadow* reads its (un)making of the "still-vex'd Bermoothes." It sets us up, of course, for the imbricated "memories of the future" that Carpentier's *real maravilloso* accents and profiles in the New World of *The Lost Steps, Concierto barroco,* and *Explosion in a Cathedral*. Elsewhere, the congeneric notes will shade off into Naipaul and his belief that "Conrad's darkness" was profound in the degree to which it invented nothing: because stories of "lonely white men going mad in hot countries" were familiar enough; because the "African back-ground—the demoralized land of plunder and licensed cruelty" may be taken "for granted." No less consequential is the concommitant discovery of "the world's half-made societies—places which continuously made and unmade themselves, where there was no goal." In Naipaul such places include, famously, "that island in the mouth of a great South American river, the Orinoco, one of the Conradian dark places of the earth" where there was always "something inherent in the necessities of successful action [that] carried with it the moral degradation of the idea." (1977:49;57). This "dismal, but deeply felt [kind] of truth and half a consolation" helps to account for the import of the "flag" that Naipaul raises thereafter over his "dot" of a colonial island and its mimic, because irredeemably belated, men: "The society I came from was colonial, and was originally a slave society to which, later, people like myself, from Asia, went. There was [thus] a double inferiority about it: the slave society which created nothing, which depended for everything on the master society—and the Asiatic living in this closed society of myth. . . .The people I saw there were little people who were mimicking upper-class respectability. They had been slaves, and you can't write about that in the way that Tolstoy wrote about even his backward society—for his society was whole and the one I knew was not" (Hamner 1977:49). Meanwhile, there is the no less consequential "alchemical plateau" that latitude and import become in the Walcott of *Omeros*. With its curtain of beads that tinkled each she came through it, there is, too, the threshold of the vernacular across and within which we enter Ma Kilman's NO PAIN CAFE, ALL WELCOME, in both *Sea Grapes* (1986) and *Omeros*.

"This is how, one sunrise, we cut down them canoes. / Once the wind bring news." From Book One, Chapter One of *Omeros*, the voice is that of "foam-haired" Philoctete whose unhealed, and apparently unhealable, sore was "radiant like anemone" on his shin. For all that Philoctete "smiles" the opening line "for the tourists, who try taking / his soul with their cameras" (3), the composite figure that he is effectively introduces us to the con/fused worlds of the seven books and sixty four chapters that make up the odyssey of re-discovery in *Omeros*. With its pre-texts and templates Walcott embarks "all over again" on a memories-of-the-future epic of "diaspora, exodus" and re-constitution (207). He does so with the likes of Hector, who was there, Theophile also; so, too, Placide, Pancreas, Chrysostom, Maljo, even if "in this light, they have only Christian names" (9). Meanwhile, the "altar piece of the

Roseau Valley Church" in Saint Lucia hangs in a chapel in *Sea Grapes* that is both a vernacular and syncretist "pivot of the valley," around which "whatever is rooted loosely turns—men, women, ditches, the revolving fields / of bananas, the secondary roads." Here, in a reprise which, curiously enough, "nobody yet sees or adores," we come upon a man and a woman "who could be Eve and Adam dancing." For as much as it is a "cursed valley of broken mules" and "swollen children," of "dried women" with their "gap-toothed men," the New World of Roseau is also a "rich valley [and] fat with things" (46-47). Walcott's lines of descent succeed each other thus: according to a design which, having followed the "sea-swift to both sides of the text" is "like the interlocking / basins of a globe" (319). The epic's "I sing our wide country, the Caribbean Sea" (320) is as much the point in the Homer and Vergil of *Omeros*'s "epilogue" (321) as it is the genesis of "abrupt fishermen cursing over canoes" (14-15). Succinctly put, we are in a "reversible world" in which

> The clouds turned blank pages, [proving]
> The New World was wide enough for a new Eden
> of various Adams. (181)

Philoctete variously works his way through world-making material that reflects "the scar made by a rusted anchor" and which, "for some extra silver," he is ready to identify "under a sea-almond." But then, there is also the "corolla of [the] sea-urchin"; and the root of its import, of its "cure," is something that he does not offer to explain: "It have some things—he smiles—'worth more than a dollar'" (4;242).

Needless to say, sub/version looms, as *Omeros* is ready to acknowledge: "You're right, Homer and Virg are, by now, New England farmers"; besides which, these days all that the "winged horse guards" is a "gas-station" in some undistinguished corner of New England. All the same, because he is bent on transmutation, Walcott harks back to—even as he hacks at—"the limbs from [some] dead god, knot after knot, / wrenching the severed veins from the trunk." And while the "height rang with axes," *Omeros* informs us, Achille "swayed back the blade" and "prayed silently": "Tree! You can be a canoe! Or else you cannot!" (6). The response is suitably, transformingly, epic; under Achille's "tapping chisel," and with their "hollows exhaling to touch the sea," the "nodding prows" of the canoes "soon" agree "with the waves to forget their lives as trees," and thus to serve (8). By such moves we enter a "reversible world" (207) in which an eponymous "Seven Seas [would] try to tell Achille the answer / to certain names"; would "describe snow"; name "impossible mountains," while "Sybils sweep the sand of our archipelago" (164) in yet another constellation of discovery and pre-texts. In sum, Walcott's "overlapping wharves" make for a "hurricane season" of possibilities which, with its "disasters" and "goddamned party," explain the "increase in the faithful" at Ma Kilman's NO PAIN CAFE, ALL WELCOME. "Is a prophecy," Ma Kilman's dead husband had explained, for the NO PAIN of the neon sign (advertising Coca-Cola) had been his idea, not her own (17). For all that all sorts of things may be very much "consubstantiated and imbricated before [their] time"(Carpentier), there is template and material here with which to account for other such New World places as *The Hills of Hebron* (Wynter) and the Puritan evangelism of the *Magnalia Christi Americana* (Mather). The same is true of Nancy Morejón's Cuba, where "the island sleeps like a wing"; so, too, in the "making of more Americans" that we come upon in Maxine Hong Kingston's *China Men* as well as in the Brazilian-Japanese transport that Karen Tei Yamashita records in *Brazil-Maru*.

Juxtaposed or jostled, this "world of symbiosis" *and* "theater of Universal Voracity" (Carpentier) explain the heuristic tool that I make of that conceit—AKSIDENT STORE—ALL PART AVAILEBUL"—with which, quite before *Omeros*'s "no pain, all welcome cafe," Wole Soyinka's *The Road* (1965) once marked the limits of utopian transcendence. Soyinka again informs my practice here by way of the "determinate negation" (Hegel) with which *The Road*'s Professor remains convinced that "the truth" of things *lies* with ambiguous clarity in "the sleeping chrysalis of the Word." This guide into our consciousness of things therefore embraces signs of the contraindicative with a conviction that later accounts, in Soyinka's *Madmen and Specialists* (1971), for his Old Man's inviting us to "practice" on the "'cyst' in the system" and to acknowledge the "dog" that "dogma" so patently anticipates. Needless to say, the same sub/version holds for the "mar of marxism" and the "mock of democracy"; so, too, for the "ass in the mass" and the "peepee of perfect priesthood" (1991:275). Whether in Columbus, Shakespeare, and Ralegh, or else in Cortés, Conrad, and Walcott, such has been, presumably, the nature of world-making material that we get when it is simultaneously the *floor* of Heaven and the *roof* of Pandemonium (Rajan).

In summary *défense y illustration* of the real and the imagined corners of my "still-vex'd Bermoothes" here, it is worth illustrating again the degree to which Carpentier allows Columbus to tell all by pretext and to show by invention; to (un)do as much with the left hand as the right one. This sleight of hand is one which the "Discoverer-discovered, uncovered" of *The Harp and the Shadow* is indeed prepared to demonstrate, almost. But then, the "glory [of being] Magnifier of the World" required nothing less than so adept a "repertoire of illusions" (77-78). That being the case, he knows enough to "Open [his hands], show them, move them with the dexterity of a juggler, with the delicacy of spun gold, or instead, be dramatic and raise them in prophesy, quoting Isaiah, invoking the Psalms, lighting Roman candles, exposing the forearms as the sleeve falls back, suggesting the invisible, signaling the unknown, scattering riches, holding up treasures as numerous as the imaginary pearls that still appeared to slip through my fingers, falling to the ground and bouncing in an oriental play of light from the amaranth of the rugs" (57). And in further illustration, Columbus recalls that there had been a certain once upon time on his third voyage *over there* when, seeing that the Indians on one island appeared mistrustful, he had improvised a plausible scenario, by ordering his Spaniards to dance boisterously to the sound of tambourines in the poop castle, to show that "we were a merry people, pleasant in nature" (122). There had been that other occasion of "the greatest misery," this time on a beach in Jamaica, when he had nonetheless become "Astrologer and Miracle Monger." For it had occurred to him to consult the *Efemerides* of Abraham Zacuto ("which I always carried with me"), and which, as matters turned out, predicted an eclipse of the moon that February. Columbus thus had with him quite a pre-text with which, "gesticulating like a necromancer," he proceeded to announce an approaching darkness that would spread over the skies of the New World, to the great discomfiture of the Amerindians (*ibid.*).

The making of the Indies in *The Harp and the Shadow* is, all in all, a matter of Papal Bull and Holy Office of the Inquisition; of popular witchcraft and charms from the Clivicula de Salomon (56). It is no less a consummation of the intrigues of pimps and madames. It is in due fashion, then, that Columbus once "got astride" a handsome Biscayan woman who would give him another son—and without any thought of marriage to her either (the woman was not related to the Braganzas or the Medinacelis). The moment that he mounted her, Columbus recalls, he could tell that she had been down that "road" as often as he had. "Which didn't stop" the Admiral of the Ocean Sea "from following where other men had been before, on that pearl-white filly, without bridle or stirrups" (62). Columbus had stayed on this material course, so to speak, while Bartholomew went off to advertize his brother's plans to, among others of the monarchs of Europe, the "first Tudor king of England"—that is, to Henry VII (1485-1509), and thus to the world just before Shakespeare and Ralegh and Drake moved in their various ways into the Indies. In any case, with his errand Bartholomew was carrying out what Columbus himself had once threatened Spain with: that because he was fatigued with Isabella's teasing, he would deliver his proposition to the king of France, "who was anxious to finance it, because he was a king who had an intelligent wife, a queen who was drawn to the sea like a good Breton, worthy descendant of Helene of Armorica, daughter of King Clohel, wife of Constantine the Elder, who had been chosen by the Lord to exhume the Cross, which was buried twenty hands underground in Mount Golgotha in Jerusalem." It was this declaration of intent, deliberately couched to arouse passions of a certain kind, that had earned him that "Pig! Filthy swine! You would betray Christ for thirty denarii!" (69). Such, then, was the logic of the circumstances and the nature of the material with which, Columbus explains, "I played my theatrics before dukes and monarchs, financiers and friars, rich men, clerics and bankers, the great men from here and there."

With *The Harp and the Shadow*'s "Predestined One, Unique and Necessary Man" we head into the "Bermoothes" with reasons enough to "sail like [a] pinnace" to "golden shores, and into a "region in Guiana" that is "all gold and bounty," as Falstaff would informe Robin in *The Merry Wives of Windsor* (I.iii.57-70). The global primacy of this material, conceived of as nothing short of GO(L)D, also explains why Columbus once digressed in a letter of his, about his fourth voyage in 1503, to make the point that Josephus had been of the opinion that Solomon had found his gold in Aurea. "If so, I declare that those mines of Aurea are a part of these in Veragua which . . . are at the same distance from the pole and at the equator." In his will, Columbus added, David had left Solomon "3000 quintals of gold from the *Indies* to aid in the building of the temple." According to Josephus, it was these same regions that had provided that gold; for which reason, Jerusalem and Mount Zion were now in a position to be rebuilt by "Christian hands" (West and Kling 70). Columbus's thought of conversion under "Christian hands" was no idle matter, given the religious crusades and commercial transactions and "money suits" of the times. For example, as in that courtroom scene of Shakespeare's where, parted from his ducats and daughter, Shylock must "presently become a Christian" (*The Merchant of Venice* IV.ii.387), the world of *The Harp and the Shadow* was one in which Columbus found it easy enough to come upon a certain Luis de Torres who "used to be" a Jew—for "this used to be" was often heard in those days (72).

In several respects, Carpentier's narrative is prologue to and epilogue for an early modern period during which, as in *The Merchant of Venice*, whole argosies of ships would be bound to Tripolis and the Indies, to Mexico and the rough waters of the Goodwins that separate England from Europe, or the "Narrow Seas that part the French and English." The period and its principals took serious account of certain concommitants to so much sea-borne discovery and traffic and trade—for there be "land-rats and water-rats, water-thieves and land-thieves," by which Shylock means, so he explains, "pirates, and the perils of waters, winds, and rocks" (I.iii.15-25). Reasonably enough, transport and the "profit on't" required that a certain world-order be introduced and respected, with regard to contractual agreements in a globalizing economy. And so, for all that he is apparently bankrupt and in mortal danger, Shakespeare's Antonio recognizes that his Duke of Venice "cannot deny the course of law, / For the commodity that strangers have / With us in Venice, it if be denied, / Will much impeach the justice of the state, / Since that the trade and profit of the city / Consisteth of all nations" (III.ii.26-31). While it is true that not all that "glisters" in such a world is gold, the metal, or some such other dream of "money bags," will make a man master of the fairest of fair women, among them one that's already richly left on Shakespeare's fair enough mountain (at *bel monte*) (III.ii.165-174). In others of its con/texts, the early modern period seemed "ready to lift the moon out of her sphere" (*The Tempest* I.i.183); to hold the promise of a brave new world and beautous people; and, in at least one embittered and quite drunk Caliban, to promise "freedom" from European discovery—and therefore the coming of "high-days" in which, "No more dams I'll make for fish, / Nor fetch in firing, / At requiring,/ Nor scrape trenching, nor wash dish" (II.ii.180-186).

For reasons that have to do with the reach of the cultural geographies in what follows, consider the degree to which "abiding memories" from the "august light" and "principall voyages" of the Elizabethan Age frame latter day journeys to "outposts of progress" in "African proper." And here, I refer to the Renaissance pre-text that accounts for one of the two prologues with which Marlow embarks upon his genre-annihilating encounter with the Congo in *Heart of Darkness*. The narrative had been a consequential "imitation of the heroick" when Ralegh used it to translate Guiana into a "rich, large, and bewtiful" New World whose virginity was ripe for the taking. The richness of its material had counted, too, in that *relación* which, dated July 10, 1519, Cortés had addressed from Veracruz to the extravagant majesties of the Emperor Charles V and his mother—to the "*muy altos y muy poderosos excelentísimos príncipes, muy católicos y muy grandes reyes y señores, la reina doña Juana y al emperador Carlos V, su hijo.*" In the event, with its "gauzy fabric" and "diaphanous folds"(Conrad), Ralegh's and Cortés's early-modern "discoverie" had mined quite other veins than those that are exposed in the "shocking hullabaloo" of the Congo. "Phoo! I can sniff it now," Conrad's Marlow reports about his experience of what, in another version of the same, Perry Miller's *Errand into the Wilderness* (1962) represents as "barbaric tropics." Given the orientation of their hyperbolic responses to landscape, Conrad's "sordid farce" and Miller's "tawdry adven-ture" make for narratives that deviate sharply from the utopian bent in the Americas—even where this dialectics of the possible is preoccupied with a certain "darker side of the Renaissance" (Mignolo) during which the New World's "green age" was a "rotting lime / whose stench became the galleon's text," and thus associated, Walcott writes, with "ancestral murderers and poets" of the likes of "men like Hawkins, Walter Raleigh, Drake" (1986:20). After all, ambiguous conquests resonate in, say, Ralegh's *History of the World* (1614) where it was always possible for "Indian discoveries" and "so many misadventures and miseries" to lead to "so many goodly provinces as [to] bury the remembrance of all dangers past" (Clendinnen 1995:3). Here, discovery and being marvelously possessed will lead us back to the prophecy-haunted and extravagant beginnings that Carpentier's *The Harp and the Shadow* fashions out of Columbus's "workshop of marvels" (56). By contrast, huge deposits of "Africa proper" make any such exaltation of design impossible on an earth where "big trees were kings" and "vegetation rioted," virtually annihilating all creation into a green thought in a green shade—except for the hopelessly reduced humanity that glimpses of "rush walls" and "peaked grass-roofs" imply. This far from even the ruins of the Brazilian *casa grande*, as in Freyre, or from the Caribbean great house, even if ruined, as in Walcott and Cliff, what we get is a counter-narrative that is "an invasion, an infliction [and] a visitation." Here, the reach for utopia is measured by an "elevation" in the course of which "a donkey [carried] a white man in new clothes and tan shoes" (30). Moreover, past a certain "bend in the river," Marlow will be encouraged to consider himself *the* "mind of man," one with reasons enough to believe that it was toiling on the edge of a "black and incomprehensible frenzy." His discovery of terrain and type cannot be at all restrained by, say, any one of the fifteen "most outstanding features" that contribute to even the disconcerting aboriginality with which Coatlicue's Mesoamerica could emerge in Paz as an integral part of a "fourth continent," one whose "full and palpable presence" embraced "city states with a military and theocratic social system, in which the trading class held an important position." It also had "an art that had already provoked the amazement of Dürer before it astonished Baudelaire, an art that has found recognition in temperaments as diverse as the Surrealists and Henry Moore" (20).

Consider, in this light, the atavistic map of the tropics that Columbus skirts in Carpentier but which Boris de Rachewiltz is quite prepared to re-draw and to foreground in *Eros Nero* (1963). For Rachewiltz guarantees the reader of his *Black Eros* "an insight into the African mind through a study of the role of eroticism in African life from the days of earliest history down to the present." The assurance is, presumably, not an unreasonable one. "African eroticism" is, after all, the "primal force in African society and religion as well as in [its] magic and folklore" (1968:5). Such is the understanding of terrain and type that accounts for *Black Eros* being wholly persuaded, *inter alia*, that "the vagina of the negress is generally narrower than a European woman's but deeper: six inches instead of four, and is 'premingent' [so that] a woman can urinate standing up like a man" (120). Equally consequential is Rachewiltz's certainty that although "convention-ally classified [as] primitive" by the "colonial mind," present-day African societies ought to be "more accurately defined as degenerative forms of ancient societies that many ages ago sprang up throughout the Black Conti-nent. Over the course of centuries their solar-oriented psychology gradually degenerated to a point where all that now survives is the lunar magic of the witch-doctor, while the originally highly developed individualism of the African has become submerged in a collective unconscious" (*ibid.*). As Eugene Redmond remarks about the "sociological nightmares" that Conrad embodied in the "nigger" of *The Nigger of the "Narcissus"*, there is discovery of a predictable sort in the likes of Rachewiltz; and it makes for a genre of narrative that is a "threshing floor" for "all the hearsays, stereotypes, guilts, fears, resentments, ignorances, malignities, and conscience-evoking dramas played out within the broader arena of race and color" (1979:361). "The African setting," Edward Said once wrote about Conrad's way, "is superbly set forth in all its strange, menacing incomprehensibility" (1970:xii-xiv). As result we find ourselves in "an inextricable mess of things decent in themselves" but which, so Marlow informs us in *Heart of Darkness*, "human folly made to look like the spoils of thieving." There is material here, of course, with which to also limn "a quarrelsome band of footsore sulky niggers" as they trod on the heels of donkeys, carrying with them "a lot of tents, camp-stools, tin boxes, white cases, [and] brown bales" (30).

Cut off from regular notions of being, and denied participation in the dialectics of World History, "Africa proper" confirms a state of continual fear and of danger of violent death, one in which life is nothing if not poor, nasty and brutish, indeed. This far from the New World's way with the archives of Eden—and from excavations of Coatlicue's Mesoamerica or of the Andean heights of Macchu Picchu—consider the difficulty of conceiving of the human, much less the surplus category of what art could be. In its Congolese declension, what Conrad once identified as "just simply the conversion of nervous force into phrases" (Said 1970:x) is especially threatened by the "high seat" of the "devils of the land," all the more so because at the heart of it all lie "unspeakable rites"; so, too, a profound, quirky absence of "rivets." It is here that Marlow is several times driven to ask: "Do you understand this?" He does so in the telling absence of "rivets" with which to "stop the hole" in his material. About this, he is emphatic: "What I really wanted was rivets, by Heaven!" "Rivets," Marlow repeats, "To get on with the work—to stop the hole. Rivets I wanted" (28). Consciousness and representation (un)become themselves with "the terrific suggestiveness of words heard in a dream, of phrases spoken in nightmares," none of which involved "arguing with a lunatic either" (67): so close do any and all contracts of intelligibility come to being completely annulled.

> Do you see the story? [Marlow asks]. Do you see anything? It seems to me I am trying to tell you a dream—making a vain attempt, because no relation of a dream can convey the dream-sensation, that conmingling of absurdity, surprise, and bewilderment in a tremor of struggling revolt, that notion of being

captured by the incredible which is the essence of dreams. (27-28)

Now, it was in just such a Congo that André Gide wryly acknowledged European men, himself among them, playing "the part of great white chiefs with much dignity, saluting with our hands and smiling like ministers on tour"—and being attended to by "one huge fellow, ridiculously dressed up in skins [and beating] on a gigantic xylophone, which he carried slung round his neck." He was, so we learn, the conductor of a women's dance group which, "singing and uttering savage yells, swept the ground before us, waved great stalks of manioc or broke them under our feet by beating them noisily on the ground" (1957:59). We are on terrain that is *the* site of the "geographical unconscious," and encysted with the extravagance of race, besides. And here, I borrow from Robert Hughes's *The Fatal Shore* to thus identify an "imagined country" that is irremediably home to the "inscrutable otherness" that "affronts to normality" *will* produce (1986:ii). Gide, for his part, quotes John Keats's "As if of hemlock I had drunk" to recall losing all notion of time, place and self; of "every day" sinking "further and deeper into strangeness" (93). There is some irony, no doubt, in this invocation of the richly sensuous poet in a *voyage au Congo* during which, "as a rule," the eyes travelled "over a joyless stretch of green dullness, under a sky with no promise in it, over a landscape uninhabited by god, or dryad, or faun—an implacable landscape, with neither mystery in it nor poetry" (111).

At one end, narratives of discovery make for "radiant fabric" and "benign immensity of unstained light" that are suffused with nostalgia for what Conrad's "Elizabethan" narrator recalls: his "Queen's Highness" and "knights-errant"; so, too, the "gigantic tale" of an age in which the names of ships, from *Golden Hind* to *Erebus* and *Terror*, had been "like jewels flashing in the night of time" (4). Conrad narrates his way into the "heart of darkness" through and past other far-flung pre-texts and their echoes, among them "band of Pilgrims" and "Eldorado Exploring Expedition" (32). They tease out ironic traceries of an "Indies" in which, as in Sozina's *En el horizonte esta El Dorado* (1982), many soldiers of fortune penetrated remote terrains where they sought El Dorado, that *over there* where "the four winds meet and all colors and pains mingle, but [where they had also] found nothing" (Galeano 1987:4). All the same, it was in pursuit of this brave new world that "Spaniards, Portuguese, Englishmen, Frenchmen, and Germans [had spanned] abysses that the American gods dug with nails and teeth; [had violated] forests warmed over by tobacco smoke puffed by the gods." The likes of such men had "navigated rivers born of giant trees the gods tore out by the roots; [and tortured] Indians the gods created out of saliva, breath, or dream" (*ibid.*). Meanwhile, at the other, and Congolese, heart of the matter there would be talk of a certain kind about the collapse of "immense plans"; and about the absence of any really "readable report" when discovery is a confection of "horror" and "imbecile rapacity"; of "unpardonable sin" and "thump"; so, too, of "blow on top of the heart" and "being hot and cold all over" (35). There is the blinding illumination, too, of Kurtz's torn-off "postscriptum" ("Exterminate all the brutes!"). In effect, what we get at the end is the "unearthly glow of [a] triumphant darkness" (77), from out of which "the manager's boy [suddenly] put his insolent black head in the doorway, and [announced] in a tone of scathing contempt: 'Mistah Kurtz—he dead'" (71).

Such then is the undercurrent that dis/affiliates "Africa proper" from the genre of epic pre-texts in the likes of Cortés and Pizarro, of Camoens and Shakespeare. The rupture that interests me here is nicely framed when *The Harp and the Shadow* limns Columbus within and yet against the "prophetic significance" of Seneca's *Medea*. On the one hand, "*Tiphys [had] dared to spread his venturous sail, the hidden lessons of the breezes learning*"; but then, the same *Tiphys, tamer of the deep, [had] abandoned to an untrained hand his vessel's helm.*" As a result, "*on a foreign shore, and far from his native land he died, and now within a common tomb, 'midst unknown ghosts, he lies at rest. . .*(158). Latter-day Tiphys that he is, Conrad's sailor re-embodies this moment of wreckage and erasure, for all that, or perhaps because, his narrative is actually anchored some twenty six miles west of London, where, framed by "The Director," "The Lawyer," and "The Accountant," he rides the "tidal current" of the Thames estuary on the cruising yawl *Nellie* (1963:3). Disassociated from Columbus's extravagant reach for "consummation," and no longer any one of the flashing "jewels" of the Renaissance, all that pounds its way into the foreign shore of Conrad's "night of first ages" is a "battered, twisted, ruined, tin-pot steamboat." From and through it, Marlow chronicles what amounts to mere "instalments" of the "loot of innumerable outfit shops and provision stores." With the *Niña*, *Pinta*, and the *Santa María* long gone—and so, too, the *Terror* and the *Golden Hind*—a quite different vessel rings under our feet like an "empty Huntley & Palmer biscuit-tin kicked along the gutter," although the thing was, in fact, "nothing so solid in make, and rather less pretty in shape" (29;30).

Conrad is actually quite helpful when he underscores the argument that I am making here; he is especially clarifying when he traces the origins of the genre in which Marlow will be disillusioned and Kurtz destroyed back to a certain "boyish boast." "When I was a little chap," Marlow explains, "I had a passion for maps. I would look for hours at South America, or Africa, or Australia, and lose myself in the glories of exploration" (8). But then, from among the display of all the "colours of [the] rainbow" on the world's map, this sub/version of adventures on the high seas had played itself out in "the yellow" of Africa," and "Dead in the center," no less. "And the river was there—fascinating—deadly—like a snake. Ough!" The world's "large shining map," with its promise of transport and "profit on't," had ended in "sordid farce" (10). Destiny had turned out to be a "droll" thing, indeed. All the same, insofar as it involved "Africa proper," there could not really be any "circumventing" of the how and the why of Kurtz's "exalted and incredible degradation." It had not been a "boyish game" at all. Not when it was clearly "the heavy, mute spell of the wilderness" that had drawn "him to its pitiless breast"; that had "awakened forgotten passions" and then "driven him out to the edge of the forest, to the bush, towards the gleam of fire, the throb of drums, the drone of wierd incantations." For "this alone had beguiled his unlawful soul beyond the bounds of permitted aspirations." In effect, "Confound the man!": he had "kicked the earth to pieces," a deed that was certainly possible for any one European man to do, all by himself, in Africa proper (66; 67).

Shadowed as he is by epic gestures, Marlow had "wrestled with death," of course. However, the experience had proved to be "the most unexciting thing you can imagine," and grounded in a "cropful of inextinguishable regrets" (71). That the disenchantment is as much intimate biography as it is extravagant fiction is evident from reading Conrad at Stanley Falls (1890). "This is the very spot of my boyish boast," Conrad wrote in his notebooks when he did get *over there*. "Yes, this was the very spot." And yet,

> a great melancholy descended on me. There was no shadowy friend to stand by my side in the night of the enormous wilderness, no great haunting memory, but only the unholy recollection of a prosaic newspaper "stunt" [that involved Livingstone and Stanley] and the distasteful knowledge of the vilest scramble for loot that ever disfigured the history of human conscience and geographical exploration. What an end to the idealized realities of a boy's daydreams! I wondered what I was doing there, for indeed it was only an unforeseen episode, hard to believe in now, in my seaman's life. Still, the fact remains that I have smoked a pipe of peace at midnight in the very heart of the African continent, and felt very lonely. (1963:118)

Because world-making has become so rickety an affair, insight into its operations is several times couched as it no doubt must be: "You can't breathe dead hippo waking sleeping, and eating, and at the same time keep your precarious grip on existence" (41). This all as it should be in the heart of darkness. Denied such "stuff as dreams are made on" (*Tempest*), "man's untrammelled feet" now lead him into a "region of the first ages of a man's solitude—utter solitude without a policeman" (50). Time in the days of Congolese declension is ultimately measured back to "earliest beginnings" where "splashes" and "snorts" recall "an ichthyosauraus" taking a "bath of glitter in the great river." Once again, there is that low comedy of an epiphany in which "we must put up with sights, with sounds, with smells, too, by Jove!—breathe dead hippo meat, so to speak, and not be contaminated" (3; 50). The African tale is not at all inclined to rescue, much less exalt, any such experience into design. It is no surprise, then, that the Congo cancels the utopian design according to which "knights all, titled and untitled," had sailed from Deptford, from Greenwich, from Erith bent on privateering and national glory in the "gigantic tale" of the Renaissance (4). Hunters for "gold or pursuers of fame," they had "followed the sea" from the Thames estuary, "bearing the sword, and often the torch, messengers [that they were] of the might within the land, bearers of a spark from the sacred fire" (4). For all that Kurtz is a type to whose making all of Europe had contributed, and for all that he is therefore "prodigy" and "emissary of pity, and science, and progress, and devil knows what else," his *reductio ad absurdum* descent from the "spark of sacred fire" into a world without rivets and into a bush that howled does not quite fit the bill (5;50). "Oh, he struggled! he struggled!" alright, Conrad writes about a Kurtz whose "voice" unceremoniously disppears into "something" that is buried "in a muddy hole" in the middle of Africa, notwithstanding the "magnificent folds of eloquence" and its "occasional utterances of elevated sentiments," among them the likes of "My Intended, my station, my career, my ideas" (69-71). But then, his command and terra firma were "mould of primeval earth" and "hollow sham"; "primitive emotions" and "lying fame" (69-71).

We are latitudes and quite some registers removed from Seneca and his Argonauts, and from Carpentier and the Columbus of *The Harp and the Shadow*; so, too, from language and deeds that had once been dedicated to *Díos Nuestro Señor* and to an *Invíctisimo César* in Cortés's Mesoamerica. Unlike the Columbus of *The Harp and the Shadow*, this voyager of the latter days is denied pre-texts of the right sort, be they Seneca and Augustine; or else the amplitude of Ovid's golden age in *Metamorphoses* (89-112), or the one in Homer's Odyssey in which context the ideal voyage would lead to "Elysion, with golden Rhadamanthos at the world's end, / [and] where all existence is a dream of ease." As heralded by the Menelaus of Book Four, the dispensation to come would be one in which

> Snowfall [would never be] known, [nor] long
> frost of winter, nor torrential rain,
> but only mild and lulling airs from Ocean
> bearing refreshment for the souls of men—
> the West Wind always blowing. (Giamatti 1969:16)

The pursuit of such terrains and types in the "Indies" are complexly affiliated in the itinerary in contexts that follows. They range from that "alchemical plateau" upon which Walcott reconstitutes the Mediterranean and Caribbean worlds in *Omeros* back to an early modern Europe that had been very much preoccupied with, and often hell-bent for, El Dorado. There is a certain logic, for example, in the sub/version of Montaigne's Amerindian utopia of "Cannibals" that we get in the fractiousness with which *The Tempest* deals with Gonzalo's longing for a "plantation" that could be governed "with such perfection as t'excel the golden age." The same is true of the problem of belatedness in Walcott's odyssey and its determined effort to "sing the wide Caribbean." As compared to so vexed a "Bermoothes," Ovid's new world had only been "lately sundered from high heaven." It was therefore innocent of certain anthropological or racial equations that a 1632 translation of *Metamorphoses* assumed. The Cyclops were indeed "a salvage people"; but even "more salvage," we now learn, "are the West-Indians at this day" (Kermode 1986:xxxvi). By contrast, and because it was truly fresh from creation, Ovid's golden age fully justified a panegyric in which "Ether [still] retained some seeds of cognate heaven." Recused from internal contradiction as that new world was, warm breezes *mulcaban natos sine semine flores*—that is, "they soothed flowers born without seeds" (Ovid *ibid.*)

Pace the nature of governance and metamorphoses in Ovid and Homer, the Renaissance had to contend with a rather more turbulent, because contingent, politics. Traffic and trade during the period had been compelling enough to require of one Spanish Ambassador that he announce, as above, that Spain's discovery of and sovereignty over the Indies had been sanctioned by Jesus Christ himself. Consider, too, the readiness with which Cortés had assured his emperor that there were country and mines enough between the northern coast of Mesoamerica and the province of Mechuacan, and natives to work them. "*Entre la costa del Norte y la provincia de Mechuacan hay cierta gente y población que llaman Chichimecas; son gentes muy bárbaras y no de tanta razón*" (299). Should such folk be unwilling to serve, Cortés was prepared to declare war on them on behalf of his emperor, and to make *esclavos* (slaves) of them: "*porque sacaron oro de las minas*" (*ibid.*). All this made for a violently competitive politics of territoriality; so, too, for great expectations that ships would return with "round hulls full of treasure" (Conrad). For all that Shakespeare apparently mocks the reach for utopia in Gonzalo, other such dreams of ideal "commonwealth" and "plantings" did abound. *The Tempest*'s own conflation of serendipitous landfall, profit, and isle that's "full of sweet sounds and hurt not" helps to further contextualize the *mappamundi*, whether it be to frame it against Montaigne's utopia or else to have it benignly assume the contours of certain pre-texts from Antiquity (Ovid; Homer). The Age was after all one in which a compilation like Samuel

Purchas's *Haklyutus Posthumus, Purchas his Pilgrims*, with its "continuing history of the world, in sea voyages and lande travells, by Englishmen and others," also laid out crucial premises about the "lawfulness of discoveries'." Especially so when "discoverie" involved land populated by some race upon which no stamp of goodness will take—misbegotten as it must have been by the devil on a witch. As Frank Kermode notes, there is in Purchas a "somewhat sophistical argument for the propriety of usurping the rights of native populations," to which is added an "insistence, half-mystagogic, half-propagandist, on the temperate, fruitful nature of the New World" (Kermode 1986:xxxi). But then, Purchas is also grounded in the "natural assumption" of a European prince's right to expand and exercise dominion. Therefrom the logic of, for example, Prospero's right "to be lord" on the island of *The Tempest*. Like the conquistadors in Mesoamerica, Shakespeare's Prospero is fully prepared to exercise such a right; and to articulate degrees of difference in the worth of native and person: "Shrug'st thou, malice? [that is, Caliban] / If thou neglect'st what I command, I'll rack thee with old cramps, / Fill thy bones with aches, make thee roar / That beasts shall tremble at thy din" (I.ii.367-371). It is a matter of some importance here that, notwithstanding the "rotten carcass" of the "butt" in which he had been cast adrift by his European compatriots, Prospero had achieved landfall in the new world with material evidence of degree and estate: with "rich garments, linens, stuffs, and other necessaries," among them volumes of the books that he had once prized above his dukedom (I.i.164-168). As for the natives who would suffer this "history of [European] travaile" (Eden 1577), as "by a thunderbolt," they were worth *some* trouble, of course. Even if, like Caliban, "they had no rational language, they did not lack certain mechanic arts, like the building of dams for fish" (Kermode, *ibid.*). Witness, then, the resonance that we get in that countertext of Caliban's in which he moves as he does to celebrate the return of a future when he would neither build dams nor wash dishes for the foreign masters who have descended on his island. Shakespeare's "brave monster" thus oscillates between the rebellious service of his first words to Prospero, "There's wood enough within," and the utopian bent of his drunken reach for liberation: "Freedom, high-day!"

The slip-sliding terrains of discoveries that follow will be as much the productions of Columbus, Cortés, and Carpentier as those of Vivaldi and Borges. "Native" re-discovery of contact and consequence will also matter here, as implicitly driven by Shakespeare's Sycorax, and explicitly so by Ariel's and Caliban's claims on the still-vex'd Bermoothes. The concommitant refigurations will be featured in the North American southwest that we get in Leslie Silko's *Ceremony* as well as the Peruvian *Ríos profundos* (*Deep Rivers*) of José María Arguedas; so, too, I might add, in other measures of the cultural geography before and after the *Quinto Sol* that Gordon Brotherston maps and anthologizes in his *Book of the Fourth World*.

> How many worlds define this planet? Where is the heart of each, and its frontier? According to the *mappamundi* invented by the Babylonians and later adopted by the Romans and medieval Europe, there were once three worlds. Within the surrounding ocean, Asia, the first and greatest, occupied the upper eastern half-circle; below to the west lay the Second and Third Worlds Europe and Africa. Numerically, in this Old World scheme, America then came to occupy the fourth and final place, as the *quarta orbis pars* of post-Columbian cartography. This fact has the advantage of estabishing for the fourth world an identity analogous to those of the other three. It has the disadvantage of the numerical series as such: When translated into time, it militates in principle against the notion of "New World" antiquity. (1992:1)

Asian American notions of utopian space and surrounding ocean, as in Karen Tei Yamashita's *Brazil-Maru* and Maxine Hong Kingston's *China Men*, will be no less consequential here. It is in the latter context, for example, that Kingston teases out the thought that the "making of more Americans" could indeed have been affiliated with a boatload of mandarins in March of 1603. But then, suggestions of our slip-sliding terrain—with its contraindicative "*Something*, another thing"—surface here, as they do in that "utopics' instance in which, according to Louis Marin, "noise" interrupts the transmission of information about the exact location of Thomas More's Utopia. The notion and consequence are just as telling, so to speak, in *China Men*—since whether because of "midnight" or "accent" Kingston's narrator could not quite hear, so we learn, if her Filipino scholar was really saying "that looking for Gold Mountain was like looking for a needle in a haystack. 'No. No,' he said. 'A gold needle.' To sew sails, was it? A compass needle, was it? The mandarins asked for ships, which they would fill with gold, some to give to the Filipino king, some to take back to the Queen of Spain, and some for the Emperor of China" (1980:307).

In summary illustration of such a *mappamundi*, consider, if you will, the "juggernaut of affiliations" with which Malcolm Lowry's *Under the Volcano* situates its Quauhnahuac on a hurricane and a bridge, for all that "a bell speaks" the language of Dante ("*Dolente . . . dolore*") in the rhythms of a medieval text that seems set to identify the Mesoamerican world of the narrative as primarily a "Hell of Christian damnation"—or as "Purgatory, surely" (Spender 1971:xxix). "Two mountain chains traverse the republic roughly from north to south," Lowry wrote, "forming between them a number of valleys and plateaus" under the volcanoes Ixtaccihuatl and Popocatepetl.

> Overlooking one of these valleys, which is dominated by two volcanoes, lies, six thousand feet above sea level, the town of Quauhnahuac. It is situated well south of the Tropic of Cancer, to be exact on the nineteenth parallel, in about the same latitude as the Revilagigedo Islands to the West in the Pacific, or very much further west, the southernmost tip of Hawaii—and as the port of Tzucox to the east on the Atlantic seaboard of Yucatan near the border of British Honduras, or very much further east, the town of Juggernaut, in India, on the Bay of Bengal. (3)

Orbis pars dis/affiliates here in response to the dipsomaniac transports of the British Consul (306-308) as it does because of the unstable reprise that a tourist-folder makes of the "SEAT OF THE HISTORY OF THE CON- QUEST"—with its Tizatlan (in whose ruins "could still be appreciated the stone blocks where were offered the sacrifices to their Gods"), its Matlalcueyatl ("on this place, young Xicohtencatl harangued his soldiers, telling them to fight the conquistadors to the limit, dying if necessary"), and its Ocotelulco ("In that place, according to tradition took place the baptism of the first Christian Indian") (295-301). Quauhnahuac is "a bridge" from which, true, it was "too dark to see the bottom, but here was finality indeed, and cleavage!" In this respect, the place was like the times: "wherever you turned the abyss was waiting for you round the corner. Dormitory of vulture and city of Moloch! When Christ was being crucified, so ran the sea-borne, hieratic legend, the earth had opened all through this country, though the coincidence could hardly have impressed anyone then!" All the while, that Mesoamerican god of storm, "huracan," hovers over the con/fusion of relationships, and with good reason. "No natural phenomenon was more open to the interpretive skills" of the early modern period, Hulme has written. By the middle of the sixteenth century, the Arawakan word (*hurakan*) had been readily adopted into Spanish; and as early as 1587 and 1555 the word was in use in Richard Eden, in the forms "Furicanos" and "Haurachanas," respectively (Hulme 1986:94). Therefrom, the importance of a a document like *The True Reportory of the Wracke of the Sea Adventure* (1609), details of which help to account for the nature of the "still-vex'd-Bermoothes" in Shakespeare's *Tempest*. As *Under the Volcano* observes, Huracan's tempest of a name thus works "so suggestively" to identify the nature of the "intercourse between opposite sides of the Atlantic" (15-16).

Elsewhere, "glittering excrescence of sugar" and therefore "sugar- coated Empire" help to account for the *orbis pars* and *mappamundi* of the New World in Sylvia Wynter's *The Hills of Hebron*. Hers is a vexed

"Bermoothes" in which Governor Eyre's "innumerable crucifixions" once made the sea-shore look like a line of strange coconut palms. Parenthetically, in the reduction that takes place in the Congo, this kind of extravagance would be "symbolic," and the heads of the "done-tos" food for thought; so, too, for ants and for vultures, had there been any in the sky. As seen through the heart of darkness—and without much of a shock, really—Kurtz's fence of skulls was a collection of heads that looked like knobs. And these were heads that did not hold much in the way of "trade secrets," either. In the event, Conrad has Marlow train his "glass" on the collection in due fashion: "Black, dried, sunken, with closed eyelids," they seemed to be sleeping, except that the "shrunken dry lips [showed] a narrow white line of teeth [that seemed to be] smiling continuously at [some] endless and jocose dream of eternal slumber." "I want you clearly to understand," Marlow explains, "that there was nothing exactly profitable in the heads being there. They only showed that Mr. Kurtz lacked restraint in the gratification of his various lusts" (58). *The Hills of Hebron* rather more elaborately grounds its "done-tos"—those who "live only in the blank spaces between commas, semicolons, colons—in the microcosmic shadow world between full stops." They are the vanishing point "between the interstices of every page, imprisoned in mute anonymity," precisely because they are "the done-tos who had made possible the deed." Wynter grounds the thought in the relevant pre-texts of empire and dominion:

> On such and such a date, Hawkins founded the slave trade, laid the corner-stone of the empire on which the sun will never set as long as Britannia rules the waves and the Englishman is the foremost of all men. One or two of the New Believers who had had a brief schooling in Cockpit Center before their exodus, had once recited a borrowed welter of charms, stood in the hot sun waving flags, gleaming new pennies clutched in their hands as they rejoiced for the birthday or coronation of some heir to Queen Elizabeth, during whose reign they had first been enslaved, made to till the soil, breed and die to manure the earth that sprouted forth a glittering excrescence of sugar. And when the sugar-coated Empire was crumbing away, Queen Victoria bestowed upon them a freedom that was more shadow than substance. They cried out to her that hunger was darkening their eyes so they could not see this feedom, and she told them to make bread from their sweat. And black Deacon Bogle led them in a rebellion, but the Lord was not on their side, and Governor Eyre hanged them in their hundreds, so that along the sea-shore the coconut palms were as innumerable crucifixions against the sky. (1962:53-54)

These and other measures of dis/affiliation make for quite an array of myth-making and myth-mocking appeals to the utopian bent in the Americas. They will further clarify, I hope, the heuristic value of an early modern period whose economic realities Lamming underscores when his *Natives of My Person* makes the point that however much "People might praise the daring and industry of the nation's parliament" in Lime Stone, it was the "House of Trade and Justice which received their ultimate obedience" (13). There is the no less consequential fact that in 1714 Queen Anne's government would offer a prize money of twenty thousand pounds to anyone who could devise a way of fixing a ship's longitude to within 30 nautical miles, after sailing for six weeks across the Atlantic. The official jury for the award—the Board of Longitude—had been as august as it could be. Its members included the speaker of the House of Commons, the first lord of the admiralty, the astronomer royal, the president of the Royal Society, the first commissioner of trade, and the Savilian, Lucasian, and Plumian professors of mathematics at Oxford and Cambridge (*The Economist* 1993:121). Now, in the making of such a world, Shakespeare's Trinculo may doubt discovery, but he knows enough about his times to recognize that a "monster" could make a man a "piece of silver"; that men in Europe would, in fact, "lay out ten [doits]" to see "a dead Indian" (II.ii.23). He knows all this because of "fancy" and some "vanity of art"; he also does for reasons of state and matters of commerce. "When we were boys," Gonzalo recalls, who would have believed that there were mountaineers, "Dew-lapped, like bulls, whose throats had hanging at 'em / Wallets of flesh?, or that there were such men / Whose heads stood in their breasts?" He knows better now, of course, given the returns of commerce and travel. For never mind that Prospero is *invisibly on top*, "we now find / each putter-out of five for one will bring us / Good warrant of such things" (III.iii.43-49). After all, by 1616—the year of Shakespeare's death, and some ten years into *The Tempest*—the British Empire had been pretty much on its "destined way," and the "profit on't" had already produced "forks and carriage from Italy, silks from the Orient [and] tobacco from America" (Cunliffe 1935:23).

Where *The Harp and the Shadow* and *The Tempest*, or else the Board of Longitiude and *The Hills of Hebron*, are not the pre-texts for my "still-vex'd Bermoothes," versions of the same surface (in some detail later) in the Carpentier of *Concierto barroco*, *Explosion in a Cathedral*, and *The Lost Steps*; so, too, in the "Scene of Adventures that lies in *America*, called *Surinam*, in the *West-Indies*" that we get from Mrs. Aphra Behn's *romance bárbaro* about a "*Gallant Slave.*" Her 1688 *Oroonoko, or the Royal Slave* is a narrative about a still-vexed South America that had begun in the Africa of a "*Coramantien*" country of "*Blacks* so called," that "had no king." In that country, so we learn, Oroonoko had once "softly waken'd *Imoinda*, who was not a little surprised with Joy to find him there; and yet she trembled with a thousand Fears. I believe he omitted saying nothing to this young Maid, that might persuade her to suffer him to seize his own, and take the Rights of Love. And I believe she was not long resisting those Arms where she so long'd to be; and having Opportunity, Night, and Silence, Youth, Love, and Desire, he soon prevailed; and ravished in a moment what his old Grandfather had been endeavouring for so many Months. 'Tis not to be imagined the satisfaction of these two young lovers; nor the vows she made him, that she remained a spotless maid till that night" (23-24). Soon enough, Behn's African romance heads into the lands of America, to a "Place where all the slaves received their Punishments of Whipping"; where, bound to two stakes, they were "whipped in a most deplorable and inhuman fashion, rending the very flesh from their Bones." It was here that Oroonoko, a "Ceasar" from the Gold Coast, "Strove not to break his Fetters; though if he had, it were impossible; but he pronounced a Woe and revenge from his Eyes that darted Fire, which was at once both awful and terrible to behold" (67). Meanwhile, it was in the neighboring and considerably vexed Guianas—quite unlike Ralegh's "madenheade" or Falstaff's "golden shores"—that Captain J. G. Stedman's *Narrative of a five-years expedition against the revolted Negroes of Surinam* reduced its New World of 1772-1777 to "retreating wives and children" and "ascending flames, and unfathomable marsh." Along with "the continued noise of the firing, shouting, swearing, and halloing of black and white men mixed together," there was also "the shrill sound of negro horns from every quarter, and the crackling of burning village[s]" (Price 1979:307). The Brazil of Gayl Jones's *Song for Anninho* and of Richard Price's *Maroon Societies, Rebel Slave Communities in the Americas* (1979) accounts, too, for the February of 1694 when some two hundred *palmaristas* fell or "hurled themselves [from] a rock so high that they were broken to pieces." Hand-to-hand combat during this encounter took "another two hundred *palmarista* lives." Eventually, "over five hundred of 'both sexes and all ages'" would be captured and sold outside Pernambuco. My context here is, of course, the fall of Palmares, and it provides the epigraph that I make, below, of Jones's *Song* in "Shaped Something Like a Woman's Nipple."

For now, yet other contexts of "discoverie-uncovered" blend in ways that both anticipate and reflect the oscillations with which Ariel and Clarence embrace form and deformation in *The Tempest* and *Richard III*, respectively. Ariel helps us identify a context of (un)becoming in which "nothing" remains that does not suffer a "sea-change" into "something rich and strange," in a brave new world of ambiguity that is caught between "ancient grudge and new mutiny," as the prologue to *Romeo and Juliet* rather conveniently puts it for me. "Full fadom five," Ariel provides us with a con/fusion of form and deformation in which symbiosis is, famously, "jewel" that (un)becomes itself as "skull." He is teasingly and benignly aw(e)ful about Ferdinand's "drown'd father": of his bones coral are made; those are pearls that were his eyes; "sea-nymphs hourly ring his knell" in a transmutation in which "nothing of him doth fade, / But doth suffer a sea-change into something rich and strange" (I.ii.397-404). Considerably less ambiguous subversion looms, of course, in *Richard III*'s less accommodating tempest. With *its* "tumbling billows of the main" and the completeness thereafter of Clarence's terror-stricken knowledge of "what pain it was to drown," Shakespeare's sea-borne imagery of the times maps the outer limits of encounter and translation. Clarence presents us with an experience of death by water that marks the vanishing point of utopian consubstantiation, to which it appends, just in case, a grotesque pickling in which, says the First Murderer, if "that" and "that" and "all this" (stab wounds) will not do, then, "I'll drown you in the malmsey-butt within" (I.iv.269-270). "What dreadful noise of waters in my ears!" Clarence dreams in anticipation, "What sights of ugly death within my eyes!"—and all of them "mocked the dead bones that lay scattered by" in the "slimy bottom of the deep."

> Methought I saw a thousand fearful wracks;
> Ten thousand men that fishes gnawed upon;
> Wedges of gold, great anchors, heaps of pearl,
> Inestimable stones, unvalued jewels,
> All scattered in the bottom of the sea.
> Some lay in dead men's skulls, and in the holes
> Where eyes did once inhabit there were crept,
> As 'twere in scorn of eyes, reflecting gems. (I.iv.20-33)

The world of *The Tempest* is, granted, principally the Mediterranean one of Milan and Naples; so, too, the Barbary Coast of Tunis and Argier. Its setting, witness Sylvester Jourdain's *A Discovery of Bermudas, Otherwise Called the Isle of Devils*, apparently invites being represented as some generic *terra incognita*, whose familiar strangeness would indeed make it an "Isle of Devils" that was "esteemed and reputed as a most prodigious and enchanted place." About this *ou-topos*, or no-place, by wandering sailors never seen, some have rightly said that "'tis buried deep / Beneath the sea, which breaks and roars / Above its savage, rocky shores / Nor e'er is known to sleep" (Cunliffe 1935:900). But then, *The Tempest* does offer us particular lines about "the great globe" itself—among them the invitation to historical narrative that we get in "I long / To hear the story of your life, which must / Take the ear strangely" (V.i.311-313). And these are lines which justify yet other ways of recognizing "the still-vex'd Bermoothes." Jourdain, for one, had been a crew member of the *Sea Adventure*, flagship of a transport of the Virginia Company bound for Jamestown in North America on June 2, 1609. The ship had disappeared in a storm and was presumed lost; but then, on May

23, 1610, two small pinnaces showed up in Jamestown with Admiral Somers, Sir Thomas Gates, first governor of Virginia, and their men. "Bermoothes," pronounced as three syllables, was an attempt, John Cunliffe explains, "to reproduce phonetically the name of the Spanish discoverer of the islands, Bermudez" (899). They had been little known until the appearance of publications about the *Sea Adventure*, like *The True Reportory of the Wracke and Redemption of Sir Thomas Gates*, by William Strachey, and "Rich's 'News from Virginia', a ballad of 1610 by "one of the Voyage." The accident of the island's discovery had been immediately followed by English occupation and settlement (899). It was from this experience of shipwreck, then, that a number of survivors returned to England in 1610 with those much noised-about tales of survival. And indeed there is persuasion of a rather immediate sort in *The Tempest* when Francisco responds to Alonso's fear that "some strange fish" had made a meal of his son and heir, Ferdinand:

> Sir, he may live.
> I saw him beat the surges under him
> And ride upon their backs. He trod water,
> Whose enmity he flung aside, and breasted
> The surge most swoll'n that met him . . .
> 'Bove the contentious waves he kept, and oared
> Himself with his good arms in lusty strokes,
> To th' shore . . . I not doubt
> He came alive to land. (II.i.115-120)

Shakespeare's play appeals to ear and eye with a turbulent realism that echoes contemporary accounts of the wreck. Its still-vexed notes resonate as *The Tempest* opens in a confusion of "noise[s] within": with a record of voices that presents us with "Mercy on us! We split, we split!"; with "Farewell my wife and children!"; "Farewell, brother!"; and with a final toll in which "We split, we split, we split!" (I.i.65-67). There are echoes of the same, too, when Gonzalo takes the measure of the tempest and of their survival. "But for the miracle, I mean our preservation," he says, then, "few in millions / Can speak like us" (II.ii.6-8). Strachey's graphic description of "the most dreadful Tempest," especially its "St. Elmo's Fires," adds substance to Ariel's explanation of how he "flam'd amazement" in "every cabin"; why "sometime [he would] divide, / And burn in many places; [or] would flame distinctly, / Then meet and join" (I.ii.195-201). Elsewhere in *The Tempest*'s reach for the New World, and thanks to Richard Eden's way with its far-south regions, the "great devil" of the Patagonians surfaces to become the play's Setebos. This is the guise in which he plays god to that "foul witch" from North Africa, Sycorax. It is the guise in which he is also subject to domination by European man. For the play's native "monster-servant" and "foot-licker" is soon enough called upon to confirm this order of things. Prospero's "art is of such pow'r / It would control my dam's god, Setebos / And make a vassal of him," Caliban acknowledges (I.ii.371-373). In effect, contentious realism, utopian expectations, and counter-hegemonic arguments cluster around the latitudes and the import of the play's "still-vex'd Bermoothes."

The overlapping agendas account for the precision with which Prospero asks about the condition of Alonso's fleet; so, too, for the giddiness—"All hail, great master, grave sir, hail! I come / To answer thy best pleasure; be it to fly, / To swim, to dive into fire, to ride / On the curl'd clouds"—with which Ariel is prepared to serve. It is equally telling that quiet calculation ("Thou didst promise to bate me a full year") accompanies his informing Prospero that "the king's ship" is "Safely in harbour"; that it lies

> in the deep nook, where once
> Thou call'dst me up at midnight to fetch dew
> From the still-vex'd Bermoothes, there she's hid. (I.ii.227-229)

It is in *The Tempest*, of course, that Ariel identifies "the still-vex'd Bermoothes" as the terminus for a seemingly capricious exercise of power by Prospero. He once needed "dew," and imperiously, Ariel reminds the ex-Duke of Milan, "thou call'dst me up at midnight to fetch [it]" (I.ii.228-29). Ariel's subsequent reference to a point of departure ("deep nook") is a helpful mapping of Prospero's investment in power; so, too, of Ariel's hopes of liberation. The ship carrying Alonso—he is King of Naples and on his way back to Europe after marrying off his daughter to an African in Tunis—has found safe anchorage in the "nook," Ariel assures Prospero. It is therefore sequestered from the rage of the storm that Prospero has had Ariel whip up. On Alonso's side, the tempest had been thorough enough to raise fears of a total dynastic collapse, and (finally) an expression of regret about trafficking in daughters and Africans. In the apparently disastrous aftermath of "tempestuous noise of thunder and lightning" and of the shipwreck, "daughter's marriage" had come to sound like words "crammed" into his ears and "against the stomach of [his] sense":

> Would I had never
> Married my daughter there! For, coming then,
> My son is lost and, in my rate, she too,
> Who is so far from Italy remov'd
> I ne'er again shall see her. (II.i.106-111)

There is no relieving his "trespass" either in the fact that "thunder / that deep and dreadful organ pipe pronounc'd / The name of Prosper" (sic) (III.iii 96-100). Still, for all that Alonso believes himself to be hopelessly grounded, the king's ship is in fact safely tucked away in Ariel's nook. The arrangement assures Prospero's return to Milan, and to the enlargement of his dukedom; one that will be "solemnized" by the marriage that he has engineered between his daughter Miranda (Milan) and Ferdinand (Naples). In turn, the wholesale departure of the Europeans would mean the removal of foreign resistance to Caliban's claim to patrimony, to ownership of the island. For Ariel, it would mean unfettered access to an ideal world of "bees" and "cowslip's bell"; of flights "after summer merrily" while cradled "on the bat's back."

That said, a host of proximate issues obviously accounts for Lamming's view in *The Pleasures of Exile* that he "cannot read *The Tempest* without recalling the adventure of those voyages reported by Haklyut"; and when, he adds, " I remember the voyages and the particular period in African history, I see *The Tempest* against the background of England's experiment in colonisation" (13). Furthermore, with its "If I can recover him, and keep him tame, and get to Naples with him" (II.i.68-69); its "What have we here? Man or fish? Dead or alive?"; and its "What's the matter? Have we devils here . . . with salvages and men of Inde?" (II.i.57-58), Shakespeare's play resonates with *attitudes* enough (from "demi-devil" to "vile race"; from "thing of darkness" to "bastard one"). They account for the succinctness with which Paz's *Conjunctions and Disjunctions* raises what is certainly a crucial matter in a Caribbean that Hulme (1986) refers to as the "crucible" and "historically archetypal" meeting place of cultures (107;94). "For the Christian West," Paz declares, "foreign societies were always the incarnation of evil. Whether savage or civilized, they were manifestations of the inferior world, the body. And the West treated them with the same rigor with which ascetics punished their senses. Shakespeare says it straight out in *The Tempest*" (1974:110). Since Lamming's "pioneering essay," Hulme adds, approaches to *The Tempest* have moved colonialism, and therefore the New World Atlantic material, to the very center of Shakespeare's play (106). Consider, in this light, the circum-Caribbean Calibans that have become variously articulate in Roberto Fernández Retamar, in Kamau Brathwaite, and in Fanon, or else in the Madagascar of Octave Mannoni's *Prospero and Caliban, The Psychology of Colonialism* (1950). For his part, Rodó opted for a discovery of Euro-Latin American privilege in Shakespeare's drama. *Ariel* (1900) does so when, "at the end of a year of classes" taught by a "venerable old teacher, who by allusion to the wise magician of Shakespeare's *Tempest*, was often called Prospero," Rodó's essay gives pride of place to a "regal" bronze statue of Shakespeare's "airy spirit" at the very moment, so we are told, "when Prospero's magic sets him free, the instant he is about to take wing and vanish in a flash of light" (1988:31).

As I have already indicated, the Renaissance's seed of commonwealths and germ of empire *are* the material of the "tale" against which which Conrad

launches Marlow on his *reductio ad absurdum* version of the same in the
Congo (1963:4-5). In the world of the circum-Caribbean, meanwhile,
Carpentier's *Explosion in a Cathedral* sets its sights on what is clearly a sub/
version of such "discoveries" when Victor Hugues's transport of three ships,
L'Espérance, *La Thétis,* and *La Pique,* return to the Caribbean in self-
congratulatory style during *el siglo de luces,* the "century of lights." They do
so as vessels of Revolution and Enlightenment, proclaiming themselves to be
"We the cross-less, the redeemer-less, and the god-less" (125). Although
liberated from the symbol that Columbus's *Niña*, *Pinta*, and *Santa María* had
painted on their sails, Hugues's eighteenth-century transport plies waters that
remain vexed with the Euro-Christian imperialism and profiteering that were
very much at work in the early modern period of *The Tempest*. The English
are in Guadeloupe and St. Lucia, the ships discover, because England had
captured "the islands when [Hugues and his transport] were leaving France"
(130). Now, to avoid "the British peril" would entail deviating off course to
a degree that risked encountering "the Spanish peril." As a result, witness the
"Bermoothes," Hugues's ships could very well "end up in the area of the
Bahamas at the worst possible time of the year." It is here, Carpentier writes,
that Esteban recalls "some lines from *The Tempest* which spoke of the
hurricanes in the Bermudas" (*ibid.*). Meanwhile, Prospero's preoccupation
with power and ursupation resonates in *The Harp and the Shadow* when, with
"pen flying," Columbus recalls a "desperate effort" to initiate moves that
would "erase the failures of [his] enterprise," and "stem the tempest that,
having cast [him] onto this island, could just as well fly back across the ocean
and demolish the statue that [he] had managed through [his] labors to erect—
although as yet unfinished and still somewhat shaky on its pedestal—on the
Great Stage of Barcelona" (113). Equally suggestive dispensations of *The
Tempest*'s sea-change—those are pearls, after all, that were his eyes—surface
when Columbus deals in his "repertoire of illusions," the particulars of which
include his having spoken of "pearls, many pearls, merely because [he saw]
some mussels that signal their presence" (87). Not unlike the tempests of its
first centuries, then, such recognizable patterns in the discovery of terrain and
type have made the latter days of the Indies "loop of correspondences" and
"radiant, self-circling sunstone"; a place of "moss" that "feather[s] the mute
roar / of the staved-in throat / of the wreck" as well as a "five-knuckled
peninsula" that bars "the heartbreaking ocean" *(Sea Grapes* 54-55). In the
Pablo Neruda of *Song of Protest*, to whom Walcott dedicates the eponymous
poem from which I cite, the Caribbean is a "waist where two oceans marry,"
and the "gathering place," too, for "the tears of two oceans."

     "I dreamt I awoke with one dead seeing eye and one living closed eye,"
Wilson Harris writes as his protagonist sets off on "dreaming feet" in *The
Palace of the Peacock* (1981:13-14). The narrative deals out of terrains and

types with which Harris identifies what he refers to in "Tradition and the West Indian Novel" (1967) as "the subtle links, the series of subtle links which are latent within [the West Indian, and which constitute] the latent ground of old and new personalities." Harris develops his world-making material on apparently familiar ground, and out of circumstances that have involved "the most bitter forms of latent and active historical diversity." He invokes a variousness that allows us, Kenneth Ramchand claims, to "visualize a fulfilment," a set of "wider possibilities and relationships" out of an apparent "uncertainty of design" (Harris 1981:3-4). *The Palace of the Peacock*'s reach for "substance and universal meaning" is as much a hard physical-geography counter to the fabulous Guianas of the Renaissance's Ralegh, Falstaff, and El Dorado as it is idiosyncratic and suffused with the numinous. For it is here that Harris's protagonist aims at nothing less than the "IT" that would end all "frustration" in "a new functional inspiration and beginning and erection in living nature and scaffolding." Succinctly, he "longed to see [that] atom, the very nail of moment of the universe" and thus of the "indestructible nucleus and redemption of creation" (*ibid*:130). Elsewhere, dis/affiliations compound the "belt of circumnavigation"—the language is Herman Melville's in *Moby Dick*—along which Walcott's "Names" indentures and transfigures the "goldsmith from Benares, / The stone-cutter from Canton, / The bronzesmith from Benin" (*Sea Grapes* 1976:32). In *Omeros*, the challenge is re-viewed from that "alchemical plateau" upon which Walcott re-constitutes the "whirr" of "memory's engines" in the New World; so, too, the apparent extremes of its "lectern" and "auction block" (94). In *The Star-Apple Kingdom*'s "The Schooner 'Flight'" (1979), Shabine's "I met History once, but he ain't recognize me" highlights a corollary preoccupation with bastardy and belatedness. But then, the same Shabine's "Sir, they say I'se your grandson!" and his "I am either a nation or I am nobody" underscore an equally emphatic, even if fractious, insistence on recognition. Shabine—a word for "red nigger"—also recognizes himself as inhabiting a circum-Caribbean that is both a whole "fucking island" and the memory of a time when "these islands were Paradise." *Sea Grapes* records the gravitational pull of similar forces in "Names," on an American strand on which "the sky [had] folded, / as history over a fishline," and where "the foam foreclosed / with nothing in our hands" but a "stick with which to trace our names on the sand" and this in the path of an "indifferent sea." Being thus stranded in the Americas warrants wondering whether "we [have] melted into a mirror / leaving our souls behind" (32).

Of course, the issue of affiliation and belatedness has been variously raised as a concomitant of any identity in the New World. It is as present in *The Harp and the Shadow* as it is in the "ecclesiastical history"of Mather's *Magnalia Christi Americana* and in the "Natural History" that Walcott accounts for in *Sea Grapes*, especially. "What have we here? Man or fish?"

The Tempest had wondered in its time, before settling for native islander and man-monster, struck by a thunderbolt. Walcott's way is to opt for a "Natural History" which takes as its pre-text a "stunned" shape across the bay, one that is ambiguously Shakespearean in being a "huge fish" or "a man / like a huge fish" (31). However, the evolutionary history that we get cuts across its complex of affiliations to give us "The Walking Fish," "Frogs," "Turtles," and "Butterflies." The process grants fissures and discontinuities: "Dragons no longer fly" here; "the mastodon's gone down in the brea of muck" while "the tiger's sabres [have] turned to coral." Here, too, the "ocean god rages, at a loss for words," and frogs (un)become in an economy of "famine, genocide [that is] as natural as moonlight." In sum, "the sea breathes" and "the Atlantic remembers." They do so against a terrain upon which mutant turtles have been lit by the politics of "the bomb's fountaining" new word: "Let there be light!" (31). There is a "natural history" of becoming here which, "as [it] / paddle[s] this air, breathe[s] this new sea," cannot help wondering if it is "still swimming through one gigantic eye" (30). In the end, the fish-frog's "cataracted eye" stares "past panic"; the mutant turtle teaches "adaptability"; and, consubstantiated, the "Walking Fish" is prepared to name "this foothold, with a grateful croak, / earth" (*Sea Grapes* 29-31). Mather's *Magnalia*, for its part, had staked out its claims on "the strands of America" according to an immigrant and wholly Euro-Christian theology. The threat of belatedness and mutation was contextualized accordingly: the devil is doomed to disappointment if he entertained "any expectation, that by the peopling of America, he should deprive Europeans of two benefits," literature and religion, that had been conferred upon an otherwise "miserable world" (*ibid.*). Granted, the place was "altogether unknown to the penmen of the Holy Scriptures"; indeed, before a certain "Neapolitan stumbled" upon it, it was obviously a pre-Christian "*regiones exterae*" and "*tenebrae exteriores.*" Mather was nonetheless prepared to assert that it was altogether unimaginable that "the brave countries and gardens [that now] fill the American hemisphere" could have been created to be "nothing but a place for dragons." Besides which, no less a figure than "the learned Joseph Mede" himself had ascertained that the American hemisphere would "escape the conflagration of the earth, which we expect at the descent of our Lord Jesus Christ from Heaven" (18). For which reason, the *Magnalia* was prepared to announce to the "European churches" the appearance on "the American strand," not the evolution of some Man-Fish, but a fully emblematic pre-text: "golden candlesticks (more than twice seven times seven!)" (5).

This millenarian understanding of the discovery of the Americas had been a matter of some consequence in *The Harp and the Shadow* when, "with venom concealed beneath his smiling mask," Columbus was quite sure, Martín Alonso had asked: "Where have we arrived, Admiral?" Alonso had asked this question of the *Magnalia*'s misidentified "Neapolitan." He had done so knowing full well the layered implications of the fact that there stood before them "people who were naked, with barely even a handkerchief to cover their shame." Decidedly other than Cathay and Cipangu, and quite unlike persons who could be associated with the Grand Khan and thus with quantities of gold with which to restore Jerusalem to Christian hands, these natives were hopelessly stranded, it seemed clear enough, outside History and Religion. For Columbus on his deathbed, Alonso's query rankled even more, for it could not *not* resonate with malice of theological proportions. (It bears remembering that the said Alonso was the pilot who had earlier sent off a letter to the king and queen about the Indies enterprise, a letter "that was filled to the brim with infamies." For which reason, "may the soul of [the] miserable little bastard be consumed in the flames of hell!" (97)). *The Harp and the Shadow* thus consigned Alonso to damnation in the context of the first voyage. Equally relevant is the pious arithmetic that the third voyage and the *Book of Prophecies* had by then made of the year of Columbus's discovery of the original Biblical garden of Eden on the strands of America, in "the middle of the lands" of the New World. The interfering presence of naked natives and green parrots notwithstanding, the Terrestrial Paradise had all along existed "outside the known world, in the unknown ocean surrounding all the land masses." It was a real location, and discoverable as such, but only eschatologically, near the end of time—and by none other than Columbus.

> Beginning with Adam, [Columbus listed] the antediluvians for a total of 1,656, followed by the patriarchs, adding 400 years of captivity in Egypt, then 480 years to the completion of Solomon's Temple, next 410 to the destruction of the Temple, followed by 70 years of Babylonian captivity, then 400 years continuance of the second temple until it was destroyed. [He also] summarized that from the birth of of Abraham until the destruction of the second temple were 1,088 years; then, according to the Jews, from the destruction of the second temple until now, 'being the year of the year of the birth of Our Lord 1481,' are 5,241 years. Twenty years later, [Columbus] presented another chronology, according to the calculation by King Alfonso, "which is considered to be the most exact," listing 5,343 years from Adam until "the Advent of our Lord Jesus Christ," making the new total for the year 1501 [the date of the writing of the *Libro de las profecías*] to be 6,845 years. (West and Kling 1991:90)

Given the weight of so much calculation, what could it mean that natives now stood naked before them with green parrots that did not speak, with "balls of [not very fine] cotton thread." That is, with items that they then "exchanged for some things that weren't worth a fig": like "small glass beads, hawks' bells—hawks' bells that they especially liked to hold to their ears to hear them better—rings of brass, along with many colored caps." After all, these were trifling things which, Columbus records, "I had bought in the markets of Seville, when I remembered on the eve of weighing anchor, that the mannikins of Vinland were extremely fond of colored cloth and fabric" (82-83). But then, traffic and trade of this variety could only make for subversions of portents. There had been the occasion, for instance, when "five, six, seven 'kings' of [some] island came to render tributes." They were kings "like those we'd seen already; kings who, instead of dressing in imperial purple robes, wore a tiny codpiece for every celebration. And this procession of naked 'majesties' forced me to speculate that we were still quite some distance from the fabulous Cipango of the Italian chronicles" (92-93). In the end—and thus the bitter intrusion of Alonso's question—far from being ready to produce any number at all of golden candlesticks, Columbus was readier to accommodate the thought that all he had done was rend "a veil of the unknown and entered a reality that surpassed [his] understanding," For, as he puts it, "there are discoveries so momentous—though possible—that by their very immensity they annihilate any mortal who dares to enter them" (158). In this regard, the Columbus of Walt Whitman's "Prayer of Columbus" (1874) had been luckier—for all that at first he is himself "a batter'd, wreck'd old man / Thrown on [the New World's] savage shore." He is "far, far from home," and "pent up by the sea and dark rebellious brows"—on terrain upon which he is quite ready to believe himself hopelessly grounded, his "voyage balk'd, the course disputed, lost." However, unlike his avatar in *The Harp and the Shadow,* the sails of other ships rise to justify him in his assumption of "new better worlds," even if their "mighty parturition" still mock and perplex. By the same token, and *pace* the voices at St. Peter's Basilica in *The Harp and the Shadow,* the "miracle" of his transfiguration is justified when he hears "anthems in new tongues" saluting him (1950:329-330).

There is a mosaic of imaginings in all this that is very much invested in the aw(e)ful plausibility that matter and mind can be reconstituted in ideal forms. A concern to mediate between ideal forms and the inadequate provisions of experience lies at the center of all utopian writing. This characteristic feature derives, Baker-Smith explains in *Between Dream and Nature,* from "the effort to reconcile ideal possibilities with the recalcitrance of the known" (1987:8). George Steiner (1996) leads his pre-texts and "archives of Eden" into the requisite zone of instability when he emphasizes the fact that from the outset the ambiguities "in the theology and sociology of the Edenic" were "formidable" ones. How could matters be otherwise? If the "Great Migration was to escape from the blackness of Goshen and take possession of the New Canaan," Steiner adds, "it could only do so in the (literal) light of a newborn knowledge, of an innocence of intellect and sensibility" (267). For his part, Louis Marin makes a point of calling our attention, in *Utopics: Spatial Play,* to a certain transmission in Thomas More's *Utopia.* Its apparent aim had been to disambiguate the "thalassographic" con/fusion that More embeds in the signs—*ou-topia* (no-place) and *eu-topia* (place-of-happiness)—with which he fashioned a name for the island that his narrative locates somewhere between Europe and the Americas. "Where is the island of Utopia to be found?" More's correspondent records the fact that Raphael had been asked the question, and that he had indeed answered it. However, the response had been obliterated by a servant's unfortunate fit of coughing; and the question had apparently never been asked again (1984:115; Kingston 1980:307). According to Marin, the fact that "noise" intercepts "transmission" here is no accident. It was inevitable in a narrative of "utopic practice[s]" and "sudden distance[s]" in which "contiguities and continuities" create ruptures in historical time and geographic space. "It is by this fracture," *Utopics: Spatial Play* concludes, "that we catch a glimpse—as if illuminated by lightning—of the free force of unlimited contradiction" (xxii). Utopia is, *tout court,* an already compromised harnessing of desire, a "place of rupture where the dogma of original sin must be inscribed—but 'invisibly'," and as much as is possible according to a "libidinal economy" of "perverted pleasures" (170-171).

Consider, then, the dystopian thrust of Alonso's question, Columbus's pious arithmetic, and the "contagion of history" that Steiner re-discovers in the Americas. When he calls attention, that is, to "less sanguine" views about how "new"—and thus about how utopian—the New World could ever have been. Succintly: "Even if the New World was, or was to be, 'earth's other Eden', it was the old Adam," Steiner's reprise points out, "who had come to it through 'the swelling seas'." As a consequence, no Destiny in and of the Americas could ever become Manifest without the "contagion of history." The thought infests with cynicism, or tempers with a *caveat,* any answering of the question about whether America was "young" or "old"; about its being an "authentic vestige of the Garden set aside for the re-entry of the New Adam"; and about its being the "*novus mundus* promised by St. John and proclaimed by the Spanish ecclessiastical chroniclers almost immediately after Columbus's journey" (*ibid.*). Meanwhile, and full of ironic "set-asides," it is in a tellingly reduced theological dispensation that Walcott maps one such contagion of history in the *novus mundus.* Re-entry into the "vestige of the Garden" is played out into quite "another life," in *Omeros* when the focus is on the "spike" that the coming of the railroad "hammered / into the heart of their country as the Sioux looked on" with "their stunned, anachronistic faces" (175). In effect, when "My face is frozen in the ice-cream paradiso /

of the American Dream, like the Sioux in the snow," the *novus mundus* is called upon to surrender to the recognition that "Manifest Destiny was behind me now"(174).

Whatever the pre-text, it encouraged the predictability of the myth-making and myth-mocking reprise that we get in Eduardo Galeano's *Faces and Masks* volume (1987) on the Americas. Its "memory of fire" and "vast mosaic" present us with "pursuers of hallucination" who had set out from the wharves of Europe for lands where "beggars" would be "avenged" and "vendors" become "dowried debutantes"; where "nobodies" would "turn into marquises, scoundrels into saints, [and] gibbet-fodder into founders" (5). And there was, too, that eighteenth century in which that drawer of "exact maps of the earth and the heavens," Guillaume Deslile, still wrestled with the import and latitude of El Dorado, into whose "golden waters princes—were they undulating golden fish or actual flesh and bone?—plunged and swam by the light of torches." For which reason, Deslile wondered in the Paris of 1701 whether to "paint in the mysterious lake, as [had] become custom, somewhere in the upper Orinoco." After all, Ralegh had proclaimed in his 1595 "discoverie" of the "large, rich, and bewtiful empyre" of Guiana that the place existed; that it was comparable in size to the Caspian Sea (Galeano, *ibid.*). All in all, there is much in such *terre-sans-mal* (Clastres 1975) and e*n-el-horizonte-esta-El-Dorado* (Sozina 1982) narratives that explains Peter New's succinctly pointing out (1985) that the man who describes the island of Utopia in Thomas More's *Utopia* has two names, one of which means Messenger of God, and the other Distributor of Nonsense.

Martín Alonso's spirit of skepticism in *The Harp and the Shadow* thus infects the dialectics of the possible. The sub/version of pre-texts and templates that it aimed at—its view of the "old Adam" surfacing from "the swelling seas"—is perhaps nowhere more pointedly identified than in Walcott's insistence in *Sea Grapes* that "When Adam was exiled / to our New World in the ark's gut the coined snake coiled there for good / fellowship also." As a matter of fact, "That was willed" (1976:12). What counted even more was the fact that the snake on its "forked tree admired labor"—and that Adam himself "had an idea":

> He and the snake would share
> the loss of Eden for a profit.
> So both made the New World. And it looked good. (*ibid.* 12)

There is a related exercise in world-making in the *Lebensraum* logic and utopian bent of the Simon Bolívar that we encounter in the slip-sliding ironies of Gabriel García Márquez's *The General in His Labyrinth* (1991) and, earlier, in the baroque inventions of José Joaquín Olmedo's "La victoria de

Junín: Canto a Bolívar" (1825)—if not quite in Bolívar's own "Letter from Jamaica" (1815) and in his address at Angostura (1829). Drawing his inspiration from the sweep of Bolívar's success at Junin, the Ecuadorian Olmedo had celebrated that making of the New World with a great deal of antique enthusiasm. It was one from whose con/fusions Bolívar had found it necessary to extricate himself, when he pointed out to Olmedo that he had made "a Jupiter of [him]; a Mars of Sucre; an Agammemnon of Lamar; an Achilles of Cordoba." Because Olmedo's panegyric had shot "where not a single shot was fired," there is mockery, and instruction, too, in Bolívar's observation that "all the heat of the torrid zone, all the fire of Junín and Ayacucho, all the thunderbolts of the Inca Manco-Capac have never produced a more intense conflagration in the mortal mind." As a result, "the earth [had been] set aflame with the burning sparks of Achilles's chariot—which never rolled in Junin" (Torres-Rioseco 1970:51).

At the Congress of Angostura (1819), meanwhile, Bolívar himself had formulated a dialectics of "emanation," "dissimilarity" and "transcendence" with which he sought to make a synthesis of so much terrain and so many types. Rather more substantively, of course, the 1824 Battle of Junín had routed the best of Spain's colonial armies. Tellingly, the Spain that Bolívar recognized in all this is one which, somewhat like the one in *The Harp and the Shadow*, had become "neither European nor North American, but a composite of Africa and America rather than an emanation of Europe"; for she "fails as a European people because of her African blood, her institutions, and her character" (Retamar 1989:5). The imperfectly differentiated spaces that Bolívar thus sought to illuminate in the "bigger idea" of a "total integration of the Americas" (Saldívar 1991:272; 26) are recognizable as such in the registers across which Márquez's *The General in His Labyrinth* makes an ironic tale of manifest destiny. The techniques of composition derive as much from extravagant imbrications as they do from the studied "quicksands of voluminous, contradictory, and often uncertain documentation" with which Márquez returns us to an important premise in Bolívar: the insistence, for all that "the greater part of the native peoples had been annihilated," that the Americas represented "the human race in miniature." There was his equally important and "ultimate hope" of realizing "the fantastic dream of creating the largest country in the world: one nation, free and unified, from Mexico to Cape Horn" (Márquez 1991:77;48). The "General" in his "labyrinth" articulates his vision in "raw" and "prophetic" sentences that would later be published in a Kingston newspaper, and which, Márquez reminds us, "history would consecrate as "The Jamaica Letter" (*ibid.*).

Lamming's approach to such dispensations of the utopian bent in *The Pleasures of Exile* is to take their measure in several cycles. In one such, it is a "sad and hopeful epic of discovery and migration" as a result of which, today, lines of succession "exist in an unpredictable and infinite range of custom and endeavour, people in the most haphazard combinations, surrounded by memories of splendour and misery, the sad and dying kingdom of Sugar, a future full of promises. And always the sea!" (Lamming 1992:17). New World disaffiliations and composites push and pull in other "heteroclitic" (Benítez-Rojo 1995) directions when *Omeros* makes the New World's story an odyssey of re-discoveries in which "Kings lost their minds" and a "Jesuit mission / burned in Veracruz." It is also one in which—because there *had indeed* been that *circa* 1492 *"Hey, Jews, better pack your bags"* of Carpentier's *The Harp and the Shadow* (46)—"fleeing the Inquisition,"

> a Shephardic merchant, bag locked in one elbow,
> crouched by a Lisbon dock, and in that position
> was reborn in the New World: Lima; Curaçao. (Omeros 155)

Undocking from similar positions also explains the Jewish voices that Nelson Vieira (1995) anthologizes in Brazil; and the same is true of the "tropical diaspora" that Robert Levine (1993) contextualizes on a Cuban island where, unlike most other Latin American places, Levine observes, the indigenous culture had been eradicated. Thereafter, the culture on the island would be the experiences of foreigners, among them, Jews:

> Spain authorized Jews to enter its Cuban colony for the first time in 1881, although non-Roman Catholic worship services were not permitted until after the Spanish-Cuban-American War of 1898. A tiny group of families of Jewish origin—between fifty and one hundred—was present in Cuba, including the Maduros, Brandons, Marcheans, Machados and Dovelles. Some were linked to families with the same name elsewhere in the circum-Caribbean, in Panama, Curaçao, the Virgin Islands, and Surinam. (Levine 1993:2)

New World latitudes dis/affiliate into yet other instances of cultural mis/ alliances, from the "frontier" of the American West to Nicaragua. For example, a conflation of racial election and territorial expansion accounts for the contagion that infects John O'Sullivan's vision of the coming of a "Great Nation of Futurity" whose fate it was "to overspread [a] continent allotted by Providence" (Wald 1995:109-110). The absurd spectacle and Anglo-Saxon cast that this expansionist premise assumed in the Nicaragua of 1856-57, under that other "gray-eyed Man of Destiny," William Walker, would lead his apologist, William Wells, to declare that "The term 'Manifest Destiny' is no longer a myth for paragraphists and enthusiasts; the tide of American population, stayed on the shores of the Pacific, seeks new channels and already the advancing steps of the blue-eyed race is heard among the plains and valleys of Central America" (Slotkin 1986:251). In Karen Tei Yamashita's *Brazil-Maru*, meanwhile, Asia re-converges on "a small inconsequential dot on a virtually unmapped area," somewhere slightly north of the Tropic of Capricorn, "in the middle of a country that covered half of the South American continent." "We were," Yamashita's narrator recalls, "the tiny seed of a small beginning, [and] one story among many." Stories, that is, about Japanese second sons without rights of inheritance; about many who had been left homeless by the 1923 earthquake of Kanto; and about the 1918 Rice Rebellion in which 25,000 peasants had protested the high price of rice; so, too, about "others like us. Christians with the same conviction" (1992:6). To the degree that they were all convinced that the "future is in Brazil" and that "most of Brazil is virgin forest," *Brazil-Maru*'s protagonists had followed "a route around the earth, sailing south from Japan through the South China Sea to Singapore, then on to Ceylon and the Cape of Good Hope." The transport had eventually reached Sao Paolo, 1925, on a train—by way of a ship that had also docked "on the coast of India and the tip of Africa" (3).

There is an especially apt, because extravagant, summary of the utopian bent in *The Pleasures of Exile*, recalling as it does the ways of Columbus in *The Harp and the Shadow*. Optical illusion and pageantry, commerce in substance and simulacra root themselves only to exfoliate into strange fruit. But then, this had been the case right from the start when, so he thinks in Lamming, "Columbus went in search of Ophir":

> [B]ut the result was a different kind of grain. The gold grew tall green; and the lady Sugar, seductive as Josephine, increased the dowry of the anonymous slave. It sweetened, hot and black, the irretrievable cup of Prospero's wealth. One corner of the Caribbean, was a kitchen rich with hands that could never again claim their original landscape. "It was," says [C. L. R.] James, ". . .the greatest colony in the world, the pride of France, and the envy of every other imperialist nation. The whole structure rested on the labour of half a million slaves" (1992:151)

When Lamming returns us to this "fantastic migration" and to knowledge of the "mischievous gift" that sugar was, he does not quite lead us to a world of sweetness and light. We are led, instead, to a special site of seduction in the proliferous and epicene Indies that the *novus mundus* is. The same is true of the amplitude with which, in *Abeng* (1984), Michelle Cliff maps out the cultural economy of all the "connections and disconnections" that followed when sugar became "a necessity of western civilization." Of course, Fernándo Ortiz's *Contrapunteo cubano del tabaco y el azuchar* (1940) had famously played out the import as allegorical romance and economic history. He had done so on a cultural map in which he identified tobacco and sugar ("energy and dream"; "sensuality and thought") as "the two most important personages in the history of Cuba." "Sugar is she; tobacco is he," *Cuban Counterpoint* declared. "Sugar cane was the gift of the gods, tobacco of the devils; she is the daughter of Apollo, he is the offspring of Persephone" (Ortiz 1947:6).

It is easy enough to recognize in all this a pre-text that *The Harp and the Shadow* embeds in one of Columbus's unfulfilled objects of desire: spice. Granted, there had been "fruits" from his encounter; for example, there had been "that one, with a drab brown rind and a red flesh, with seed like carved mahogony; that one, with violet flesh, its seeds inside a gelatin past; that other, larger, smaller, never the same a the one next to it, with a gelatin paste; that other, larger, smaller, never the same as the one next to it, with a fragrant, white, bittersweet center, always fresh and juicy even in midday heat...." However, what they all lacked was the "rich dance of Doña Cinnamon with Don Clove." Desire and lack are even more fully on exhibit thereafter in the allegorical pageant of commerce and consummation that Columbus then makes of "Doña Cinnamon, Doña Nutmeg, Doña Pepper, and Doña Carda-mon entered on the arm of Don Ginger and Don Clove, to the beat of a tune whose musical harmonies resonated with the color of saffron and the smell of malabar and the names Cipango, Cathay, the Golden Colchis, and all the Indies—which, as everyone knows, are many—the numerous, proliferous, epicene, and beautiful Indies" (57).

Meanwhile, other forms of the strange growth that Lamming's "mis-chievous gift" of sugar assumes would be embedded in the lusotropical and *droit du seigneur* satisfaction with which Gilberto Freyre returns to the "happier days" of the Brazil of "Plantation Boy" (1924); to a time, that is, when there was "always a farm hand / who'd cut him a fine juicy joint to suck"; so, too, to a certain "*conhecer negras nuas*"—a knowing of black women—in the form, especially, of a "naked black slave girl" who would "launch the plantation boy / on his first adventure in love" (Johnson 1984:239-240). For his part, Galeano is considerably less decorative in *Las venas abiertas de America Latina* when he concludes that it was the fate of the "sugar islands—Barbados, the Leewards, Trinidad-Tobago, Guadeloupe, Puerto Rico, Haiti, and Santo Domingo—to be incorporated one by one into the world market" (1973:77). Sugar also forges the chain of events that helps to account for the nature of Thomas Carlyle's insights in "The Nigger Question," that nine-teenth-century context in which he undertook to offer proof of the fact that he did not "dislike the negro"—for all that he recognized the commercial importance of the crop in the British West Indies. After all, while "all manner of Caribs and others pine into annihilation, the black African alone, of all wild-men, can live among men civilized" (1940:311). However, what Carlyle most abhorred in the "yonder" of the Indies was the ruination of the sugar plantation. (Had he but governance, indeed...). But, there lay sugar and all the profit on't; and there, too, lay "our beautiful Black darlings with little labour except to the teeth, which surely, in those excellent horse-jaws of theirs, will not fail." Carlyle thus put his "niggers" on exhibit, "with their beautiful muzzles up to the ears in pumpkins, imbibing sweet pulps and juices; the grinder and incisor teeth ready for ever new work," while the "sugar-crops rot round them" (305).

Ortiz had in any case been insightful enough to recognize the limits of pretext and translation. For he had observed that it "would be impossible for the rhymesters to write a 'Controversy between Don Tobacco and Doña Sugar'" in the style of Juan Ruíz (1283-1350) and his *Libro de buen amor* (1330): as just "a bit of friendly bickering, which should end, like the fairy tales, in marrying and living happily ever after." In the New World of the Indies, a somewhat more problematic place than that benignly scabrous and roguish Archipreste de la Hita could conceive of, the "marriage of tobacco and sugar, and the birth of alcohol, conceived of the unholy ghost, the devil, who is the father of tobacco, in the sweet womb of wanton sugar" (Ortiz 1947:93). This consubstantial growth is clearly the issue when sugar becomes the "necessity" that Cliff delineates in the call-and-response narrative of *Abeng*. She maps out a "necessity" that forged ties between

> tea-drinkers of England and coffee-drinkers on the continent, those who used it to sweeten their beverage, or who laced these beverages with rum. Those who took these products at their leisure—to finish a meal, begin a day, to stimulate them, keep them awake, as they considered fashion or poetry or politics or family, sitting around their cherrywood tables or relaxing in their wingback chairs. People who spent afternoons in the clubs of Mayfair or evenings in the cafes on the rue de la Paix. People holding forth in Parliament. The Rathaus. The Comédie Française. People who talked revolution or who worried about revolution. They took their coffee and tea, their sugar and rum, from trays held by others, as their cotton was milled by others, and their lands were kept by others. The fabric of their society, their civilization, their culture, was an intricate weave, at the heart of which was enforced labor of one kind or another. (1984:27-28)

"*At this price you eat sugar in Europe; No barrel of sugar reached Europe that is not stained with blood.*" Such echoing voices had before ranged from that of Voltaire's Candide, in Surinam, to Helvetius's—whether in Louis Doucet's version of what happened when the French sought to make their fortune in the Caribbean (*Quand les français cherchaient fortune aux Caraïbes*) or else in the anthropology and history of the "*siglo de las luces*" that we get in Michèle Ducet (Galeano 1987:40).

Meanwhile, "mosaic of imaginings" is the foundational thought upon which Patrick Chamosieau's *Texaco* (1997) re-configures a Martinique upon which Columbus had experienced landfall in the Indies. In this regard, there is a certain symmetry in the thought that before that "consummation" of his with the New World, Columbus had once "cast his lot with those who pledged pilgrimages," and in that context had "promised Saint Mary of Guadalupe that he would bring her a Pascal candle made from five pounds of wax" (*The Harp and the Shadow* 96). Chamoiseau begins his novel with a circum-Caribbean preface in which he identifies "Milestones In Our Attempts to Conquer the City." Its second item is from "The Age of Longhouses and Ajoupas," and is listed as "1502: Christopher Columbus arrives in Martinique." Thereafter, and as Rose-Myriam rightly points out, "multivoicedness, collage, and foreign smatterings" account for terrains and types that have since become the Caribbean through Ages of Straw, Crate Wood, Asbestos, and Concrete (1997:395; 3-5). *Texaco* is therefore the "mosaic of imaginings" that it is; one whose proper articulation requires, so a protagonist informs us, "a Cervantes who has read Joyce" and is fluently creole, to boot (327). This is not surprising, of course. Yet another example of a mischievous gift in the Indies, and thus an *aksident store—all part availebul*, "TEXACO" is "shanty-town" and alien/ corporate body. Its "poetics of hutches" is Adamic and Babelic: for it is "Fort-de-France's mess" as well as the "poetry of its Order" (181;220;224). In one of his several notes to the "Word Scratcher," the novel's "Urban Planner" explains that Marie-Sophie Laborieux's founding of "TEXACO" (the squatter township) had taught him "how to re-read our Creole city's two spaces. For there is, on the one hand, the historical center, living on the new demands of consumption"; on the other, there is the "suburban crown of grassroots occupations, rich with the depth of our stories." It is between the two places that "humanity throbs":

> In the center, memory subsides in the face of renovation, before the cities which the Occident inspires. Here on the outskirts, one survives on memory. In the center all dissolves in the modern world; but here people bring very old roots, not deep and rigid, but diffuse, profuse, spread over time with the lightness of speech. These two poles, linked by social forces, mold the faces of the city with their push-and-pull. (170)

It is in the far-south world of just such a network of dis/affiliations, meanwhile, that Borges's compatriot Margo Glantz expresses that preference of hers for a New World "pluralism that [would allow] for a thousand distinct forms." With it she embraces difference and lines of descent in a Buenos Aires that remains as productively *bábelico* as it had been when, in 1936, Borges used the occasion of the four hundredth anniversary of Buenos Aires to identify a "corner of America" in which "men from all nations had made a pact to disappear for the sake of the new man which is none of us yet." For her part, Glantz delimits an American Antipodes that justifies her 1989 *No pronunciarás*'s being marked by a "cosmic preoccupation that includes the religious and the sacred." Its pluralism reflects the fact , Glantz explains, that "I have the heritage of Jewry I denied for such a long time, but it is my heritage. I'm forever linked with the Bible, with the prophets, which is where the title of *No pronunciarás* comes from: "Thou shalt not take the name of the Lord thy God in vain" (García Pinto 1991:118).

"I have always been (and always will be) in Buenos Aires," Borges had written in "Arrabal" (1921) about the extraordinary concretion of things in a city which he has consistently represented as his past, present, and future—"*mi pasado [que] es mi porvenir, y mi presente.*" As Emir Rodríguez Monegal further notes, Buenos Aires is the "sordid background" for the "parodic transcription" that we get in "The Monster's Celebration," just as it is the city that Borges "transcribed phantasmagorically and under European names in 'The Death and the Compass'"—in a narrative in which the real city is separated from its imagined figuration by "only a thin disguise of chess board geometry and Chestertonian paradox" (Monegal 1973:18-19). Rather more ominously, the Buenos Aires of "The Wait" is a "gray nightmarish" place where a man waits for his enemies to kill him (*ibid.*). With its suburban quarters, general stores, and pink corners; its local gangsters covered with white soft hats; and its twilights and streets that were once open to the "invading pampas," Borges's New World city turned labyrinth is a telling map, Monegal concludes, of dreams and political disenchantments. It recalls, too, the "*something*, another thing " that Chamoiseau makes of Marie-Sophie Laborieux's "TEXACO" and Walcott of Ma Kilman's NO PAIN CAFE, ALL WELCOME.

Notwithstanding the utopian bent with which the languages of Adam and Babel push and pull only to embrace each other in such contexts, there are other narratives, of course, where bastardy and orphanhood—or worse things, genocide would be one—make for disaffiliation that is final. Granted, "a schooner beating up the Caribbean / for home" *could* be Odysseus, or Omeros, if you wish, "home-bound on the Aegean." All the same, there are con/texts, Walcott once wrote in *Sea Grapes*, in which "The classics can console. But not enough" (3). What Walcott refers to elsewhere as "that cry / that terrible vowel, / that I" must then contend with a history of the New World in which a stick traces names on sand that the sea will again erase, even if "to our indifference" (*ibid.* 33). That being the case, there is a quite ironic con/fusion of aboriginal uprooting and immigrant renovation in the "curious article" from Mato Grosso with which *Brazil-Maru* brings its epilogue of arrival in *eu-topos* to a conclusion:

> Three days ago, the so-called Indian of the Lost Tribe was found dead, killed probably while helping himself to someone else's food or store of hidden goods. He was described as a very slight, bowlegged, unkempt man with long dirty black hair, thin strands falling in a tangled beard from his face. He was found shot through the head and clutching a rusty old carbine, empty except for the red earth pushed into the tip of its disintegrating barrel. (248)

Brazil-Maru grounds itself here in an ancient enough narrative of dis/ articulation in the New World. For, needless to say, the subtext in Yamashita's afterword is native alienation and alien renewal. In this regard, its origins had been legible enough in other graphic signs of erasure, among them the smallpox which had once given the advantage to Cortés and his men against other tribes of lost Indians in Mesoamerica. And when Pizarro landed on the coast of Peru in 1531, and with about 200 men set about the conquest of the Inca Empire, he had been aided by "similarly grim luck." Fortunately for "Pizarro and unfortunately for the Incas, smallpox had arrived overland around 1524, killing much of the Inca population, including both the Emperor Huayna Capac and his son and designated successor, Ninan Cuyoche" (Crosby 1973:72). Succinctly put, the Indians of the New World died "in droves of diseases the Europeans, Africans and Asians had accommodated themselves to long, long ago. As one indignant Spaniard put it, Indians 'died like fish in a bucket'" (*ibid*. 21).

The "laceration of [such] shame" notwithstanding, cultures could only be re-created, Walcott's "The Caribbean: Culture and Mimicry" (1974) argues, out of a certain "knowledge of nothing, and in deeper than the superficial, existential sense, we in the Caribbean know all about nothing. We know that we owe Europe either revenge or nothing, and it is better to have nothing than revenge. [For] revenge is uncreative" (12). There is, too, the corollary initiative which, in a borrowing from the Carpentier of *Los pasos perdidos*, Walcott's *Another Life* identifies as "Adam's task of giving things their names" (44), even if the context is that regretful one of ruination in which we come upon "the Indian turning green, the Negro's smile gone, and the white man more perverted": all of them more and more "forgetful of the sun they left behind"; all of them "trying to imitate desperately what came naturally to those whose rightful place is in the net" (*ibid*.). Strategically as well as substantively, Walcott's "What The Twilight Says" (1970) had also sought to recognize the New World as a constellation of *uncopyrightable* discoveries, precisely because "[we] were all strangers here." For which reason,

> The claim which we put forward now as Africans is not our inheritance, but a bequest, like that of other races, a bill for the condition of our arrival as slaves. Our own ancestors shared that complicity, and there is no one left on whom we can exact revenge. That is the laceration of our shame. Nor is the land automatically ours because we were made to work it. We have no more proprietorship as a race than have the indentured workers from Asia except the claim is wholly made. By all the races as one race, because the soil was stranger under our own feet than under those of our captors. Before us they knew the names of the forests and the changes of the sea, and theirs were the names we used. (11)

Somewhat more bravely, Paz's *Alternating Current* (1973) identifies a "dialogue of masks, [a] double monologue of the victimizer and the victimized" from out of which "Latin America is [nonetheless] beginning to have a face" (202).

For his part, Naipaul is not quite so ready to be forthcoming, so to speak. The New World pre-text that he discovers in Conrad's "Karain" effectively reproduces the "colonial," "mixed," and "secondhand" reality to which he condemns the Caribbean. Deeply embittered as he is, this con/textuality justifies him in his view of the islands as trapped in an "ominous sequence of days" in the course of which no highly organized society could ever be produced, one from and about which a great novelist could create. "And really," Conrad had himself explained, "looking at that place, [Karain], landlocked from the sea and shut off from the land by the precipitous slopes of mountains, it was difficult to believe in the existence of any neighbourhood. It was still, complete, unknown, and full of solitude; of a life that seemed empty of anything that would stir thought, touch the heart, give a hint of the ominous sequence of days" (Naipaul 1977b:59). With an imagination that has ever since been both fired and constrained by Conrad, Naipaul has been fertile with narratives in which, so he insists, those born in the colonial backwaters of the Caribbean remain "curiously naked, [and therefore] lived purely physically." Out of all this comes the "naked neurosis" of the "done-to" that so preoccupies Naipaul. Summarizing a critique of Gordon Rohlehr's, Sylvia Wynter has associated the condition with Naipaul's being indentured to the experience of being "a minority in a majority culture to which one is doubly marginal as man and as writer" (1972:13).

> To explain this neurosis in the specific Trinidadian context is to explore the "resentful consciousness" of Naipaul—or a [Kenneth] Ramchand—growing up to find himself despised by a brown and Creole middleclass, who, as successful mimics of Western culture, looked down on East Indians as "coolies" who lacked "culture." However, once the latecomers, the East Indian immigrants, began to enter the educational system, to take their place in the Creole class, they not only claimed their full share in Western "culture," but also pointed to the "high" culture of India to give them one more point in the game of oneupmanship between themselves and the blacks. Yet the real counter in the game was, and is, the ability to "acquire" Western "culture." (*ibid.*)

Infected by stories in which, as in *Guerrillas*, "No one will make a fresh start or do anything new," Naipaul's dissenting imagination has been most at home being alienated by the "elusiveness of the quest object" and by "bitter knowledge of placelessness" (Ramchand 1984:80; 66). In the event, he has written out his circumstances into disturbed and disturbing patterns of unbecoming affinities. "Nobody ain't listening to me," Mrs. Baksh declares in *The Suffrage of Elvira*. "Everybody just washing their foot and jumping in this democratic business. But I promising you, for all the sweet it begin sweet, it going to end damn sour" (Ramchand 1984:67). The view finds its pre-text in Conrad where it had appeared "to us like a land without memories, regrets, and hopes; a land where nothing could survive the coming of the night, and where each sunrise, like a dazzling act of special creation, was disconnected from the even and morrow" (Naipaul 1977b: 58). For his part, Ricardo Forster leads us to quite the vanishing point of all this with his "Dialogue Along the Margins." Here, the New World's variously hyphenated *Alpha-Omega* and hallelujahs of dazzling geographies complete their surrender to patterns of disorder and areas of darkness. The promise of renovation ends in what, borrowing from Quevedo, Borges would represent as *la utopía de un hombre que esta cansado*, as the utopia of an exhausted man. In Forster, the Americas are, quite simply, "no longer a promise, nor [the] hallucinating dream of another continent." They are, instead, the site of a post-*encuentro* "silence" in which "The bastard has no parents who will recognize him" (Tomassi, Jacob, and Mesquita 1994:35-40).

Inga Clendinnen limns a relevant *aksident store* of dis/articulations in *Ambivalent Conquests* when she makes the point that "Colonial situations breed confusions"; that "a favourite metaphor for the tangled miscommunications between native and outsider is a 'confusion of tongues'" (1995:127;36). *Ambivalent Conquests* thus embeds its preoccupation with pre-text and template in "the dangerous business of translation from one meaning system to another." She illustrates the point in a Yucatan where "depleted populations [and] forced migrations must have fractured social life, and frighteningly disrupted the reassuring pulse of collective ritual activity" (*ibid.*). Consider, in this light, the Mesoamerican turbulence that lies at the heart of Borges's "The God's Script." Tzinacan, his magician of the pyramid of Qaholom, is imprisoned in a post-*encuentro* governance that has reduced his world to a "stone prison." He is also transfixed by memory of a "God's Script," one in which there had once been "absolute fullness," and in which "every word [could] enunciate and sustain an infinite concatenation of facts" (1964:171). However, the substance of conquest and the simulacra of translation have since made for distortions; and they intercept Tzinacan's attempt to "return" to the aboriginal "formula of fourteen random words," to rearticulate his way back to his "god's script" from "poor and ambitious human words [like] *all, world, universe*." His Mayan attempt at translation is not much helped, of course, by his experience of European "discoverie." The present tense of his aboriginal condition is effectively delimited by a narrowness that is "deep and of stone; its form, that of a nearly perfect hemisphere." The figure only aggravates the sense of "oppression" and the "vastness" of what has been lost. Once upon a time, the magician's utopian and bent world of Qaholom had been a place of the jaguar and the tiger where, "with the deep obsidian knife," he had "cut open the breasts of victims." That world had been wholly unmade by Pedro de Alvarado, who had tortured and "devastated [it] by fire" in a determined search for "the location of hidden treasure" (169; Díaz del Castillio 1963:362-382).

Such, then, is the context in which Borges's magician preoccupies himself with wondering how import could disappear so completely in the god's script. His circumstances lead him to an epiphany of sorts, in which "Someone said to me: *You have not awakened to wakefulness, but to a previous dream. This dream is enclosed within another, and so on to infinity, which is the dream of grains of sand. The path you must retrace is interminable and you will die before you ever really awake*" (Borges 1964:172). In the end, this Amerindian magician surrenders his remembrance of things past, as surrender it he must, to the *ou-topos* into which Alvarado has turned his world. The cancellation of his magical pre-text is quite telling, of course; since to utter the aboriginal syllables "in a loud voice" would suffice, so it had seemed, to unmake the world of "discoverie." It would suffice

> to abolish this stone prison, to have daylight break into my night, to be young, to be immortal, to have the tiger's jaws crush Alvarado, to sink the sacred knife into the breasts of the Spaniards, to reconstruct the pyramid, to reconstruct the empire. Forty

syllables, fourteen words, and I, Tzinacan, would rule the lands
Moctezuma ruled. But I know I shall never say those words,
because I no longer remember Tzinacan. [Besides which], whoever has seen the universe, cannot think in terms of one man, of
that man's trivial fortunes or misfortunes, though he be that very
man. That man *has been he* and now matters no more to him.
What is the life of that other to him, the nation of that other to him,
if he, now, is no one. This is why I do not pronounce the formula,
why, lying here in the darkness, I let the days obliterate me. (173)

For its part, the far-south mirror-and-encyclopedia world of Borges's "Tlön,
Uqbar, Orbis Tertius" invents even as it disarticulates New World con/texts.
It does so in an especially studied design, one in which pre-text and template
are grounded by and into an "idea of proliferation" that requires "endless
rivalry and replacement" (Irby 1973:37). With Tlön, and in his role as new
magician for an unknown planet, Borges famously sets out to *re-discover* a
new world in which "numismatics, pharmacology and archaeology have been
revised" (1964:7). We gather, too, in this reprise that "biology and mathematics are awaiting their avatar." About the role of the "mirror" in the genesis of
such a world, Borges explains that it "worked to trouble the depths of a
corridor." The authority of the encyclopedia was, for its part, an awkward pre-
text of things past and to come. It was "a literal but delinquent reprint" that
was both "fallaciously" and "in fact" called *The Anglo-American Cyclopaedia*
(New York:1917). Not surprisingly, a reading of its pages of "rigorous prose"
in the National Library only generated a "fundamental vagueness" (3-4).

Borges effectively produces a *terra in/cognita* that had been conjured
into being by "a history of laborious creation over the centuries by anonymous
scholars, first in Europe, then in the New World." Of course, in making (up)
his own "*something*, another thing," Columbus had had occasion to resort to
Isodoro and Ambrose and Scott, "true theologians, to screw the mediocre
Spanish theologians" who had always opposed him." He had needed, too, the
science of Pliny, Aristotle, and, once again, the prophetic significance of
Seneca, who had all helped to endorse him in a role which, like Virgil's, was
to announce a New Age out of which will surface a New World (*The Harp and
the Shadow* 120). Borges conjures up the texts of an "undocumented" but
"brave new world"—*The Tempest* is directly invoked—that is then
"[a]rticulated, coherent, with no visible doctrinal intent or tone of parody." Its
parts cohere into just the kind of constellation that could be suspended
between "the luscious honeysuckle and the illusory depths [of] mirrors"
(7;12; 20). It degenerates and engenders material (Rajan) from the proposition that "*Copulation and mirrors are abominable*"; or, as corrected, from the
"gnostic" premise in a "heresiarch," whose "name was not forthcoming," that
the "*visible universe was an illusion or (more precisely) a sophism.*" For

which reason: "*Mirrors and fatherhood are abominable because they multiply and disseminate*" (4).

In effect, any and all re-affirmations of whatever becomes manifest is grounded in "the word" and its inter-textual (enyclopedic) ways. After all, a good measure of the world and its pre-texts lie in "weighty tomes" and "venturesome computation." But then, Borges also notes that engendering is nothing if not the climactic experience of the "vertiginous moment of coitus"; of a certain moment of embeddedness in which "all men [are] the same man" (*ibid.* 12). Signally, the footnoted assurance here is that "all men who repeat a line from Shakespeare *are* William Shakespeare." The proposition carries with it the clarifying explanation, or the comforting New World thought, that the "concept of plagiarism does not exist" (*ibid.*). Not unexpectedly, this invalidation of copyright effectively cancels the awkwardness of belatedness, and with it the anxieties of bastardy and orphanhood. Somewhat more benignly, Borges's vertiginous moment of consummation recalls Carpentier's in *Explosion in a Cathedral*, with its "fluid unity, where like was eaten by like, consubstantiated and imbricated before its time"; so, too, its "language that made use of material that allowed for verbal amalgams and metaphors that conveyed the formal ambiguity of things which particpated in several essences at once" (178-179).

Borges's *orbis tertius* is, in the end, a coincidence of refracted arrivals and imprisoning departures, where naming is as much an arresting as it is an alchemy of locations and identities. For instance, notwithstanding "the scrupulousness of cartographical indices"—and the exhaustion of "all imaginable spellings: Ukbar, Ucbar, Oogbar, Ookbar, Oukbahr"—this new world is a "rich" presence, but only because it is full of "enticing allusion and ellipsis" (Irby 1973:37). The slip-sliding templates of its much-fissured material make for layers of archeology and for cycles of dis/affiliation. "Already a kind of palimpsest, a many-layered paraphrase of other paraphrases," the genre and topography of discovery here make "critical resume and commentary both desperately tautological and inaccurate, for at every turn one is also faced with sly reversals and subversions" (Irby *ibid.*). It is no surprise, then, that this vexed *orbis tertius* is, finally, a "vast methodological fragment" whose particulars, as "written in English," lie in a certain document of (what else?) "1001 pages" (Borges 1964:7). In the end, it is from so Adamic *and* Babelic acting out of the "God's script" that "an unknown planet's entire history" looms on the horizon. It does so, *all part availebul:* "complete with its architecture and quarrels, with the terror of its mythologies and the uproar of its languages, its emperors and seas, its minerals and birds and fish, its algebra and fire, its theological and metaphysical controversies" (*ibid.*). It is also the product of the no less *aksident-store* premise that "a book which does not contain its counterbook is considered incomplete" (7;13). Equally telling, as in Conrad, though somewhat differently enchanted by erasure, there is that matter of the "postscript" in Borges's *orbis tertius*. Traceable to a certain "millioniare eccentric," and former slave owner, it declared that "in America it was absurd to invent a country, and proposed the invention of a whole planet. To this gigantic idea, he added another, born of his own nihilism—that of keeping the enormous project a secret" (31).

Carpentier is suitably elaborate when his *Concierto barroco* (1988) re-orchestrates the variety of accents and notes with and around which Antonio Vivaldi produced in *Montezuma* (1733) the hero of "the first serious opera" inspired by the discovery and conquest of the Americas. Although complexly successful, Vivaldi was of course not really exceptional in being impressed. Witness the intensity with which, in the Brussels of 1520, the painter Albrecht Dürer had already responded to an exhibit of the gifts that Montezuma presented to Cortés:

> I saw the things that were brought to the King from the New Golden Land: a sun entirely of gold, a whole fathom broad; likewise a moon, entirely of silver, just as big. . . and all sorts of strange articles for human use, all of which is fairer to me than marvels. . . . I have never seen in all my days that [which] so rejoiced my heart as these things. For I saw among them amazing artistic objects, and I marvelled over the subtle ingenuity of the men in those distant lands. (Hanke 1979:460-461; Paz 1990:20)

The novel's over-arching context is, moreover, an age that had been very much impressed by the discovery of the Americas, and which had then expressed its fascination in a "rich literature [running] from Montaigne through Voltaire and Marmontel," and back to Columbus, of course. It had done so in compositions that included Vivaldi's opera and the earlier (1695) "pseudo-opera" or masque, *The Indian Queen*, which Henry Purcell had derived from a play by Sir Robert Howard and John Dryden. And all this had been achieved with something of the "baroque" energy that Paz summarizes when, writing about colonial Mexican poetry, he identifies a "derivative art" that tends "to exaggerate what it copies." Baroque art is not, in this reading, "an imitation of nature but neither is it pure invention. It aims not at reproducing or creating the world, but at counterfeiting it, recreating it, and, so far as [is possible], exaggerating it, transforming it into a swift and sumptuous game, rich in content and eloquence" (1973b:26).

The opening notes of Carpentier's *Concierto barroco* are, famously, that myth-making, myth-mocking acknowledgement of a Golden Age of Silver: "Of silver the slender knives, the delicate forks; of silver the salvers with the silver trees chased in the silver of the hollows for collecting the gravy of roasts." Of silver, too, were

> the triple-tiered fruit trays of three round dishes crowned by silver pomegranates; of silver the wine flagons hammered by craftsmen in silver; of silver the fish platters, a porgy of silver lying plumply on a seaweed lattice; of silver the saltcellars, of silver the nutcrackers, of silver the goblets, of silver the teaspoons engraved with initials . . . (Carpentier 1988:33)

Here was pure invention and mined material enough for men who had set out from Spain—"'their bottoms showing through their breeches', as the saying goes—to seek their fortune in the lands of America" (48). For which reason, a man could now make "the silver ring from time to time when he urinated with stately stream, copious and percussive [and] well aimed into a silver chamber pot, the bottom decorated with a roguish silver eye [that was] soon blinded by the foam which, reflecting the silver so intensely ultimately seemed silvered itself." In such a world, of silver were the "breakfast service, large cups and small"; so, too, the enema syringe, the writing case and the razor case. And no less consequentially, of silver were "the reliquary of the Virgin and that of Saint Christopher—protector of seafarers and travelers" (56).

The ensemble of enthusiasms in *Concierto barroco* is elsewhere, and quite appropriately, captured in a "grandiose painting" that had taken as its subject "the most transcendent event" in Mesoamerican history—as understood by some "European artist who might have passed through Coyoacan." The result was a "great theater of events" in which the Indians "seemed copied out of an account of travels in the kingdom of Tartary." In it, Cuauhtemoc had been transformed into a "vague-looking" Telemachus, with eyes that were slightly "almond-shaped." Meanwhile, "part Roman and part Aztec—a Caesar with quetzal-feather headdress," Montezuma sat on a throne carved in a style that was "a hybrid of Vatican and Tarascan Indian—beneath a canopy held aloft between two hallberds" (35). For the rest,

> Hernán Cortés [stood], a velvet hat on his head, sword in his belt—arrogant boot bestriding the first step of the imperial throne—[and] frozen in a dramatic tableau of the Conquest. Behind, Friar Bartolomé de Olmedo in the habit of the Mercederian Order, brandishing a crucifix with a gesture betokening scant friendliness, and Doña Marina, with sandals and Yucatecan *huitpil*, arms outstretched in dumb show of intercession, apparently interpreting to the lord of Tenochtitlan what the Spaniard has just said. (35-36)

Concierto barroco translates its profiles and accents from and into "bazaar" and "verbal fiesta" and "ark of the covenant"; and they all (un)become themselves in a snake-enchanted "decantation" that is also concierto for trumpet and jazz, latin liturgy and cantata, and baroque opera. We are in a fluid narrative, after all, in which "grapevine tracery" and "encrusted monstrances" converge in the shape of some "main-altar painting of a fabulous Jerusalem" (*ibid.*), and on terrain that is as much a "nostalgia [for] diaphanous mornings in Mexico" as it is sharply etched against volcanoes which created the illusion of "whiteness superimposed on the blue of an immense stained-glass window" (46; *Explosion* 245; Lowry 1971). Carpentier's baroque thus highlights the circumstances under which Antonio de Solis's seventeenth-century *Historia de la conquista de México* became, as above, that eighteenth-century opera of Vivaldi's. Solis, a poet and playwright, had been named royal chronicler of the Indies in 1684; 1684 was also the year in which he published his Livy-influenced *historia,* a work that reveals, Benjamin Keen writes, "a haughty aristocratic spirit, a fervent piety, and the same sombre *desengaño,* disillusionment with the things of the world, that pervades the plays of Calderón" (176). David Clark adds to all this the *real maravilloso* information that the "genesis of *Concierto barroco* reveals something even more intriguing: Carpentier's remarkable discovery of Alvise (referred to variously as Albize and Albise) Giusti's libretto to Vivaldi's first opera, *Montezuma,* which premiered in 1733. Further investigation led to Carpentier's documentation of a meeting between Vivaldi, Handel, and Scarletti which took place in Venice during the Christmas carnival in 1709" (1988:25). Signally, Carpentier anchors this convergence in the concierto's *negro* character, Filomeno, whose provenance is as reduced as it is contraindicatively epic. He was, the narrative indicates, "the great grandson of one Salvador, a black who a century before had been the hero of a deed so celebrated that a poet of the country, Silvestre de Balboa, sang of him in a long, well-rhymed ode entitled *Paragon of Patience*" (49).

Carpentier re-scores the *Concierto*'s several parts and bodies in an orchestration in which "cornetto" finds and mates with "viola, flautino with chitarrone, while the violini piccoli alla francese joined in quadrille with the trombones" (84). With "all the instruments [thus] scrambled together," canticle and "cannibal" music subvert each other, so it seems, into an apparent dissonance. By the very same token, their accents and profiles blend in concord of a striking sort when, "'*Kabala-sum-sum-sum*', chorused Antonio Vivaldi, out of ecclesiastical custom giving the refrain an unexpected inflection of Latin litany; and '*Kabala sum-sum-sum*', chorused Domenico Scarlatti. '*Kabala-sum-sum-sum*', chorused George Frideric Handel; so, too, '*Kabala-sum-sum-sum*', repeated the sixty-six female voices of the Ospedale." *Basso continuo* and ab/original agent, Filomeno leads this elaborate orchestration of what is at bottom an Afro-Cuban *cantar para matar una culebra* (ritual chant for killing a snake). His own *"Ca-la-ba-son-son-son"* therefore accented "the beat more strongly each time" (84) in a baroque formulation of New World "answers to problems in the irons of Ogun or along the pathways of Elegua, in the Ark of the Covenant or the casting out of the money changers, in the great Platonic bazaar of ideas and consumer goods of the famous wager of Pascal and Co., Underwriters, in the Word or the Torch" (130).

The profiles and accents in *Concierto barroco* are clearly plurivocal. In addition, its material is "heteroclitic" in ways that reinforce the readings of Carpentier that now follow. For he is one in whose *The Lost Steps* (*Los pasos perdidos*) dis/affiliation of symphonic proportions resonates. It does so in the wake of a complex return to the past of the Americas in which the protagonist is, so it seems, engaged in anthropological research into the origins of music. For John Brushwood, the "fullest appreciation of the novel evolves from its sense of history," representing as it does yet another instance of Carpentier's "placing history in a perspective that is larger than history itself." *Los pasos perdidos* representatively goes through stages that relate to the European conquest of the New World and the mythical *Odyssey*; it engages issues that have to do with the origins of art and its relationship to the "most elemental expression of feeling" (1975:87). In the process, Carpentier produces a 1953 narrative which reads, parenthetically, like a sub/version of that "world-on-the-wane" or *"tristes tropiques"* anthropology that Claude Levi-Strauss would choose to make of his own experiences of South America. Elsewhere in Carpentier, the *siglo de las luces* "material" of *Explosion in a Cathedral* is as privileged as it is cross-lit by a "century of lights" in which configurations of Renaissance "discoverie" are put on exhibit against certain rationalist presumptions about "exact significance" and "sublime enlightenment"; about why, for instance, "the Future City would not be situated in America, like those of Thomas More and Campanella, but in the cradle of philosophy itself" (99). It is typical of the embrace of the contraindicative that Esteban is also encouraged by the circum-Caribbean framing of the corollary Age of Revolution to think of himself as being in "the midst of a gigantic allegory of a revolution rather than a revolution itself, a metaphorical revolution, a revolution that had been made elsewhere, which revolved on a hidden axis" (95). It is here, too, that Barthélémy says ("drily"), "We live in an illogical world. Before the Revolution, a slave-trader sailed these seas, owned by a *philosophe* and friend of Jean-Jacques. And do you know what she was called? The *Contrat Social*" (189).

The organizing principle in Carpentier's gigantic allegories of the New World may be best summarized, then, by way of at least four of the operating premises in *The Lost Steps*: "inexhaustible mimetism of virgin nature" and "labyrinth of chronology"; "unremitting obsession with time" and "memories of the future." "Our truth" and "our goal," Carpentier once concluded about his reach for amplitude, is to fashion "an American accent" out of "the adaptation of the European conqueror" to a life that he has been "forced to lead in a continent subject to different telluric forces"; and where "one of the most extraordinary cultural events of history took place, since it became the crossroads in which, for the first time, races that had never met found each." The preface to *The Kingdom of This World* also identifies other "indelible marks" of what is involved here, and they range from taking due cognizance of seekers of the Fountain of Youth and of the Golden City of Manoa to the "stupendous Negro versions of the feast of Corpus Christi, which can still be seen in the town of San Francisco de Yare, in Venezuela." For his part, the Walcott of *Omeros* strikes a relevant chord when he writes of trying to see "the other side across the meridian." His is an attempt of some historic significance, since among other approaches, it involves revisiting Pope Alexander VI's 1493 division of the world of the Discovery. *Omeros* does so with a precision that clarifies the main, and hyphenating, role that the New World epic assigns to the sea-swift. The bird's task is to sew "the Atlantic rift with a needle's line," and thus to restore a "hyphenating horizon" to the "world's green gourd" that the Papal Bull had "once split like a calabash" when he gave one half and "the seeds of its races" to Lisbon, and the other half to Imperial Spain (191-193). It is worth remembering, the father tells his son at the end of Book Four of *Omeros*, that "in its travelling, all that the sea-swift does / it does in a circular pattern" (188). The epic of re-configuration nonetheless recognizes ruptures and dissonance, with their "boiling engines" and "fissures"; so, too, an imperative that is implicit in the conjoined and "deep indignation" of Hephaestus *and* Ogun grumbling "at the sins / of souls who had sold their race" (289). But then, Carpentier had rightly asked at the end of the preface to *The Kingdom of This World*, "What is the history of all of America if not a chronicle of marvelous realism?"

What I have tried to sketch out above is explicit in the figure and in the sum with which Gabriel García Márquez once identified the very sowing of "the seeds" of narrative about the Americas. His 1982 Nobel Lecture, "The Soltitude of Latin America," does so to relevant effect, using as its pre-text of choice a "short and fascinating book" by Antonio Pigafetta.

> [He was] a Florentine navigator who went with Magellan on the first voyage around the world, [who] wrote, upon his passage through our southern lands of America, a strictly accurate account that nonetheless resembles a venture into fantasy. In it he recorded that he had seen hogs with navels on their haunches, clawless birds whose hens laid eggs on the backs of their mates, and others still, resembling tongueless pelicans, with beaks like spoons. He wrote of having seen a misbegotten creature with the

head and ears of a mule, a camel's body, the legs of a deer and the whinny of a horse. He described how the first native encountered in Patagonia was confronted with a mirror, whereupon that impassioned giant lost his senses to the terror of his own image. (1982:4)

Graphic authenticity, optical illusion, and terror of the image all engender issues that will be further developed in Carpentier, and representatively invoked in the beginnings that surface with the Macondo of Márquez's own *Cien años de soledad* (*One Hundred Years of Solitude*) and in the "chimerical nation" that follows in *El otoño del patriarca* (*The Autumn of the Patriarch*). No less telling in this regard is the Guillermo Cabrera Infante of *La Habana para un Infante Difunto* (1979). For here, absent the pull of issues that play themselves out in *Tres tristes tigres* (*Three Sad Tigers*), *Infante's Inferno* makes a telling exhibit of transport and intercourse with the female body, among them that of a "nubile Nubian," a young streetwalker worth "a peso." At bottom, the exhibit is a familiar one. It will be variously on display, and climactically so, I believe, in that *guaracha* finale—with its "COLORED WOMEN HEAT ME UP"—to which Luis Rafael Sánchez brings "Bartolomé de las Casas's recruits" to the Americas, especially the women ("all the dark skin comes from there"), in *Macho Camacho's Beat*.

   This certain kind of woman and her *mulata* counterpart contribute a great deal of primitive sensuality to the contexts that I account for below, in "Shaped Something Like a Woman's Nipple." As things turn out, the ground that I approach there is very much implicated in the obsessions that Cabrera Infante embeds in his *Inferno*. Thus, although the inexperienced protagonist in the novel does not actually consummate his encounter with the *negra* (because of a premature ejaculation), the "Hottentot head" and "large, bulging buttocks . . . high and protuberant," and the "pubes" and "tits" of the *negra* are very much consubstantiated in the climax to which he comes elsewhere with Honey. She is "white-skinned, almost livid," but one could also see that she "had black blood"; that "Perhaps her African forefather was further back into the Dark Continent than that black-faced grandfather who peers out of the family tree" (1984:223). In any case, this *retour aux sources* is certainly invoked when Cabrera Infante's protagonist left off "caressing [Honey's] nipples (seizing her udders was like trying to utter the ineffable) and ran [his] hand down her stomach, past her nigger's navel, to her dark pubic zone—kinky with wild, woolly hairs."

   Later I was to learn [so he informs us] that the pubes (that singular word is plural) tends to have curly hairs, at least in Havana. [Not surprisingly], Honey's pubes disclosed the blackman hidden in the bush of her ancestors. Even the Havana blonde (true or false)

grew curls on her mount of Venus. I imagined Gulliver trying to
masturbate (he couldn't do anything else: his penis would be a
pin) a colossal Brobdingnag hag and having to make his way
through the acacia grove of dyed pubic hairs, each as tall as a false
acacia but entangled in a thick African thicket. (248-249)

Back in *The Lost Steps* Carpentier presents us with a protagonist who is
representatively besieged by but articulated through rather more complex
crises of allegiance and identity. Carpentier deploys his narrative's "tempos"
and "telluric symphony" in ways that produce volatile shifts, one in which
"years are substracted, melt away, in [a] dizzingly backward flight of time."
In the clarifying irony of one such move, "we have not yet come to the
sixteenth century." The time is soon enough "much earlier"—the Middle
Ages—and to telling effect. For, so *The Lost Steps* contends, it was not the
man of the Renaissance but "medieval man" who had embarked upon the
discovery, translation, and conquest of the New World. Such a man it was who
had marched off, "complete with pliers, nails, and lance," to do "battle against
those who, [one recalls Borges's Magician of Qaholom], employed similar
implements in their sacrifices." Not surprisingly, "the first churches beyond
the Ocean Sea" had been built on the "blood-stained foundations of the
teocalli" (177). *The Lost Steps* also accounts for its reach for sign and
substance by way of another conceit—that "quaint" sign, "memories of the
future"—around which the narrative refracts the utopian bent of discovery
(128;165). But then, "How could [such things] be otherwise?" Marin does
well to ask in the context of his *Utopics: Spatial Play*. "How can we repeat
the once, the only once? How can we repeat it in memory or represent it
without the event being forgotten?" (*ibid*. xxvi).

   The Lost Steps plays out—indeed, exhausts—the utopian grounds upon
which its protagonist tries to believe that he could find transport and
experience consubstantiation in Schiller's "*Töchter aus Elysium!*" and
Beethoven's *Ninth Symphony*, even if not quite according to the genealogy of
his father's taste: "'Joy! The most beautiful divine gleam, daughter of
Elysium, drunk with your fire we enter, O celestial one, your sanctuary. . . .
All men shall be brothers where you spread your gentle wings.' Schiller's
verses, with their unconscious irony, wounded me. They represented the goal
of centuries moving steadily toward tolerance, kindness, mutual understanding. The *Ninth Symphony* was the gracious, humane philosophy of Montaigne,
the cloudless blue of Utopia, the essence of Elzevir, the voice of Voltaire
raised in the Calas trial" (96). This was all resonant enough, but only as little
more than *pre-text*. Beyond that, the promise of transcendence proves to be
illusory. "The *Ninth Symphony* suddenly began to bore me with its unfulfilled
promises, its Messianic pretensions. . . . I turned off the radio. . . . A fruit fell

in the night" (97). That the *Ninth Symphony* should fail to signify as it does in *The Lost Steps* is peculiarly apt, of course. For one thing, it does so in a chapter that begins with an epigraph from the Yucatan *Book of Chilam-Balam*: "It will be the time when he takes the road, when he uncovers his face and talks and vomits what he swallowed and lays down his load" (76).

The *Ninth Symphony* and its romantic enlightenment apart, *The Lost Steps* is complexly embedded in other contexts of dis/affiliation, and these range from the esoteric *judería* of the signs of Kabbalah to the unearthing and the sexual archaeology of a certain clay object through which Carpentier's protagonist finds himself looking back into no less a figure than "the Mother of the Infant Gods, of the totems given to men so that they would acquire the habit of dealing with the divinity, preparing the way of the Greater Gods. The Mother, 'lonely, beyond space, and even time,' whose name, *Mother*, Faust twice uttered with terror" (1956:183). The invitation to dis/affiliate is especially emblematic when the "piping of a scissors-grinder strangely mixed with the melismatic call of a gigantic Negro carrying a basket of squids on his head" (42). There is a disruptive "*something*, another thing" here that lingers. Consubstantiated yet resistant, the image persists in Carpentier, and engenders that vision of a "huge man standing at the jetty, holding aloft an enormous squid he was trying to sell," and who was in this guise "transformed into Cellini's Perseus" (*Explosion* 86).

The nuclear fable that lies—Carpentier is deliberate—at the heart of *Explosion in a Cathedral* is that of the Discovery and variations of its utopian bent. Once upon a time, we learn, "two irreconcilable historical periods [the Totemic and the Theological had] confronted one another [in] a struggle where no truce was possible." In its wake, terrain and type converged to change their identity, and to be integrated into a "great all-embracing, sacramental drama" that promised to make an "immense stained glass window" of the Caribbean and its sea of islands. Witness, in this light, the canticle of praise that had been echoed when Rodrigo de Traina's cry of "Land! Land!" sounded "like the music of the *Te Deum* to the rest of us", in *The Harp and the Shadow*. In similar fashion, the introit to that Papal reconstitution of the Discovery at St. Peter's Basilica had opened with "the swelling voices of the pontifical choir as it sang out a triumphant *Te Deum*." There is, too, the canticle, yet again, the *Te Deum*, with which Bartolomé de las Casas records that he himself had responded to the Discovery. Of course, there would also be the Christ-sanctioned herald of Spain's claims upon the Indies that the Spanish Ambassador at the Papal Court proved to be in 1493. Rightly enough, the "first island discovered by the invaders from a continent inconceivable to the islanders themselves had received the name of Christ, and the first cross, made of branches, was planted on its shore." Carpentier embeds this allegory of the Discovery in E*xplosion* (241-248), making it the fulcrum in a narrative that grounds its accents and profiles in a "theatre of Universal Voracity," in a "fluid unity," where "like was eaten by like, consubstantiated and imbricated before its time" (179). Considered in this way, *Explosion* displays its "century of lights" across a circum-Caribbean that is complexly mis/aligned with things medieval and sacramental; so, too, with Renaissance "travells" and imitations of the "heroick" when, "with a leap of some thousands of years," the New World's "Mediterranean Sea had become the heir of the other Mediterranean, and received the Christian Laying of Hands" (244-245). The result is a recognizable but refracted Bermoothes in which

> a fantastic bestiary had arisen of dog-fish, oxen-fish, tiger-fish, snorers, blowers, flying fish; of striped, tattooed and tawny fish, fish which bit off testicles—cases had been known—another that was herbivorous; the red-speckled sand-eel; a fish which became poisonous after eating manchineel apples—not forgetting the vieja-fish, with its gleaming throat of golden scales; or the woman-fish—the mysterious and elusive manatees, glimpsed in the mouths of rivers where salt water mingled with the fresh, with their feminine profiles and their siren's breasts. (178)

To such exotic invocations and hyphenated accommodations of difference, the narrative adds categories of Enlightenment orders of knowledge. The *siglo de las luces* which *Explosion in a Cathedral* profiles was, after all, one whose principal testament lay in the empiricism of the *Encyclopedia*—that famously *Reasoned Dictionary of the Sciences, Arts, and the Profession*, in seventeen volumes and seven plates. Its appearance had been no less of "an epoch-making and very profitable venture in publishing": its 4,000 copies had circulated widely throughout France, even if the initial subscription price of 280 *livres* caused some hindrance, even among the affluent (Hampson 1968:86). In its pages, or else from its terrains and types, experimental science aided by new tools such as the telescope and the microscope—the relevance will soon be clear in *Explosion*'s *siglo de las luces*—revealed high magnifications of matter, from the house-fly and spermatozoa to botany. Such developments disclosed that there were more contours to the shapes of things in the heavens and on earth than had been dreamt of even in Cartesian doubt— not to speak of Scripture (*ibid.* 73). All the same, the abbé Pluche could still propose in his *Le spectacle de la nature* (1732-1750), that the divine show that nature was had been designed for the delight of man. In some still-resistant way, adherence to a principle of benevolence or *bienfaisance* animated man himself and the divine order around him, and this outlook "seemed to have been more or less co-terminous with the frontiers of the Enlightenment" (Hampson 1968:79-80). On the other hand, and by the end of the epochs (Discovery, Age of the Tree of Liberty, Age of the Scaffold, and Age of the Great Delirum) that Carpentier blends into one in his century of lights, the Marquis de Sade would have produced his sub/versions of material that was indeed germane to deist, *philosophe*, and scientist. His way would involve the catalogues and classifications of the "120 days of Sodom" that the body and its urges will accommodate; so, too, *Aline et Valcour, or the Philosophical Novel*, with its murder, incest, and travel-to-utopia settings, as well as the ultimately indifferent challenge of the voice of Zamé: "O just and holy God, of what concern to you are our systems and our opinions? What difference does the manner in which men invoke you make to your own majesty?" (105).

In the New World that Carpentier typically creates when he appeals with his usually meticulous precision to such signatures, it was indeed possible for any number of things to always become "dazzlingly evident." *Lo maravilloso* could, after all, inhabit the dailiness of *lo real*, and quite beyond "the tricks of the prestidigitator," the "banalities of 'committed' writers," and the "merry-making of . . . existentialists," as that 1949 preface to *The Kingdom of This World* once put it. Not surprisingly, embrace of the contraindicative and "fluid unity" best explain why it had been possible in 1780 for "some wise Spaniards to leave Angostura still in search of El Dorado; and why during the days of the French Revolution—long live reason and the supreme being!— Francisco Menendez from Santiago de Compostela should travel through Patagonia looking for the Enchanted City of the Caesars" (*ibid.*). That being the case, some island which had been named after San Domingo could indeed have been "Tarsis, Caethia, Ophir, Ophar and Cipango—in fact all the islands or regions cited by the ancients, and up till [then] wrongly located in a world enclosed by Spain" (*Explosion* 246). There was, too, the very nature of transport to and transposition in the Indies. For example, it was without his actually willing it, Columbus confesses in *The Harp and the Shadow*, that Hispaniola had been transfigured, as though by some "diabolical" interior energy in him. It was thus that "it grew, it swelled, until it achieved the fabulous heights of Tarsus, of Ophir or Ophar, and finally reached the borders, which I found at last—yes, found!—of the fabulous kingdom of Cipango" (102). Meanwhile, and as above, the parrots vomited and the Indians howled, while Barcelona and Seville resounded with joy and jubilation, with "the music of organs and trumpets of heralds" (98).

Carpentier thus teases at and in several registers. The crossroads effect that the circum-Caribbean brings to it all adds to the range of signatures that he uses in *Explosion in a Cathedral* to re-discover the new-ness of the New World in, for example, its "vast cemeteries of broken sea-shells" that had been "tossed, tumbled, triturated [and] reduced to powder so fine it seeped through one's fingers like water." Here, *Explosion* works within and yet against an order of knowledge in which the shell was secular discipline and thus justified in and by catalogue and classification. At the same time, symbol and shell merge to illustrate the sacramentalist premise that *liber naturae liber dei*, that the book of nature is the book of God. This process of de/emblematization had begun quietly enough in *The Harp and the Shadow* when Columbus reported that his crew "fished out of the water a little piece of wood that had been curiously worked by a human hand;" and when the men on the *Niña* "found a small stick covered with tiny seasnails" (76). *Explosion*'s rather more complex move is to imbricate disciplinary formation and sacramentalist exaltation, and then to make of them the elaborated menu that the narrative serves on "that branch of oysters which the sailors then brought in, after detaching a limb of the tree with their machetes [and producing thus] a plant made of shell-fish, with a root, branch and a handful of leaves, and the salty enamel of the shells, which offered the rarest and least definable of foodstuff to the human palate." There is numinous *ur-text* and sensuous property here. Because matter is latent morphology that hints at "all the baroquisms to come," *Explosion* could look to "a single snail"—or upon "the prickly husk of the sea urchin, the helix of the mollusc, the fluting of the Jacobean scallop-shell"—with much profit. It could do so and still be driven by the spectacle of nature to epiphany and canticle: "What sign, what message, what a warning is there in the curling leaves of the endive, the alphabet of moss, the geommetry of the rose-apple? Contemplate a snail—a single snail. *Te deum*" (180).

The *Te deum* appears to be genuine enough; for it does recall the fact that at two o'clock on a certain Friday morning in *The Harp and the Shadow* Rodrigo de Triana had indeed sung a cry "Land! Land!" that had been like "the music of the *Te Deum* to the rest of us. . ." (76). But then, given Carpentier's sleight-of-hand reach into the archives of the discovery, there are reasons enough to hear the inharmonious echo of another *Te Deum*. To attend to it is to confirm the suspicion that *Explosion* raises its canticle of praise in some ironic confirmation of that excitement with which Bartolomé de las Casas had reported on Columbus's stage-managed return with those parrots, Indians ("ready to receive to Faith"), and gold of the Spectacle and Marvels of the Indies to Barcelona and Seville in 1493 (*The Harp and the Shadow* 99-101). "I saw them in Seville," Las Casas had written:

> The King and Queen [received and heard all this] with profound attention and, raising their hands in prayer, sank to their knees in deep gratitude to God. The singers of the royal chapel sang "*Te*

Deum laudamus" while the wind instruments gave the response and indeed, it seemed a moment of communion with all the celestial joys. Who could describe the tears shed by the King, Queen and noblemen? What jubilation, what joy, what happiness in all hearts! How everybody began to encourage each other with plans of settling in the new land and converting people! (West and Kling 1991:43).

Needless to say, the dispirited Columbus of *The Harp and the Shadow* provides counterpoint: "I returned to the dockyard where the Indians were shivering under their wool coverlets, and where the parrots, having finished vomiting the wine they had gulped down, were lying with the feet in the air, with the glassy eyes of dead fish gone bad" (106). Meanwhile, all seven of the Indians "I had exhibited before the throne—some dying of a cough, some of measles, some of diarrhea"—would soon be dead. This Columbus also knows from Diegito that the Amerindians "neither liked nor admired us," finding that "our houses stank of rancid grease, our narrow streets of shit, our best horsemen of armpits" (*ibid.*). And as for that *Te deum laudamus* (we praise thee, O Lord) and "new land and converting people!" Well, "Our plan to inculcate them in the doctrines of our religion [had] come to nothing." Among their reasons: if God had created and pronounced everything good, they argued, then they could not see how Adam and Eve could have committed any offense; besides which, going perfectly naked could hardly be indecent. "Moreover, the idea of a serpent with an apple in its mouth made them laugh uproariously because, so they said, 'snakes don't eat fruit'" (*ibid.* 107).

Carpentier thus teases at registers; he also builds up and away from chronicles of the New World. In the process he fashions narratives that are as "unparalleled" as they are in fact palimpsestic. It is no surprise, then, that the complex of references that we get in Compostela and scallop shell, medieval *Te deum* and Renaissance Discovery all converge in *siglo de las luces* sub/ versions of the likes of Dominican monk (Las Casas) and English adventurer (Walter Ralegh). The Ralegh figure would by then have been re-formed from conquistador of Guiana's "madenheade" to the imprisoned and death-bound man of "Give me my scallop-shell of quiet, / My staff of faith to walk upon, / My scrip of joy... / hope's true gage." The Ralegh of "The Passionate Man's Pilgrimage" had set out thus, transported from the Renaissance's "gigantic tale" into the medieval iconography of a pilgrim to the Galician shrine of Saint James of Compostela, *Matamoros* (Slayer of the Moors). Of course, he now heads for a new and quite other world—"to the land of heaven / Over the silver mountains / where spring the nectar fountains"—by way of the scaffold. The affinities that I imply here are not at all extravagant, by the way. In figure and in sum, they are sharply etched out in "The Road to Santiago" (1963) where, with his scallop-shell and without "deviating from the straight road to Santiago," Carpentier's "Pilgrim tramped the road of France, grasping his staff in emaciated hands, wearing a cloak sanctified by beautiful shells sewn to the leather, and [carrying] a gourd filled with pure stream water" (1970a:20). It is appropriate, parenthetically, that the "Camino de Santiago" appears in a collection that bears the title, *Guerra del Tiempo* (*The War of Time*). Meanwhile, in *Explosion* itself Esteban does in fact follow "the old pilgrims's route to Santiago," where he duly contemplates "what for centuries had been contemplated by men singing canticles, men with pilgrim's badges, staffs and cloaks, men whose sandals had shuffled this road so often, feeling closer to the gates of Glory" (100).

Inexorably, any and all such transpositions (un)become themselves in ways that recall, once again, the siren (im)plausibility of Ariel's "those are pearls that were his eyes"; so, too, Clarence's death by water, with its "wedges of gold, great anchors, heaps of pearl, / Inestimable stones, unvalued jewels," and its "ten thousand men that fishes gnawed upon"—all of them "scattered in the bottom of the sea." Such, after all, is the architecture of virtually all "the baroquisms to come" (*Explosion*) when, as is his wont, Carpentier allows "the marvelous to flow freely from a reality closely followed in every detail" (Preface, *El reino*). As a result, the circum-Caribbean remains the still-vex'd Bermoothes that it has become, one in which a

> whole mythology of shipwrecks, of sunken treasure, buried without epitaphs, of treacherous lights burning on stormy nights, of portentous births—of Madame de Maintenon, a Sephardic miracle-worker, and an Amazon who finally became Queen of Constantinople—[would be] associated with these islands, whose names Esteban would repeat to himself in a whisper, delighting in the euphony of the sounds: Tortola, Santa Ursula, the Fat Virgin, Anegada, the Grenadines, Jerusalem *Caída* [Fallen]. (*Explosion*)

It is from and upon this "plurality of beaches" that, three centuries after Columbus, Carpentier further refracts the evidence of import in the New World. He does so, this time, through a prism of "pieces of polished glass— glass invented in Europe and strange to America; glass from bottles—from flasks, from demijohns, in shapes hitherto unknown on the New Continent; green glass, with opacities and bubbles; delicate glass, destined for embry- onic cathedrals, whose hagiography had been effaced by water; glass fallen from ships or saved from shipwrecks, polished by the waves with the skill of a turner or a goldsmith, till the light was restored to its extenuated colours, and cast up as a mysterious novelty" on the shores of the Caribbean Sea (176). The "century of lights" thus makes symbolic and mock romance out of unequal exchange and commercial debris; and it does so in that "theatre of Universal Voracity" where "like was eaten by like," and where each thing could also be "consubstantiated and imbricated" (179). Nothing of all this "doth fade," Ariel had in any case assured us, "but doth suffer a sea-change into something rich and strange." The "burthen" to all this matters, of course. It is a death knell, after all, and rung hourly—even if by sea-nymphs (I.ii.400-403).

In another instance of the proliferation of profiles and pre-texts that we get in *Explosion*, Carpentier puts on display a catalogue of instruments that appear to be mere exotica. As things turn out, however, the exhibit is a studied one, and made up of the delights of "discoverie" and the physics of mechanical force and motion. Like the single shell—and as he does with the orchestration of instruments in *Concierto barroco*—the catalogue reaches for and confirms affinities of a special kind in the making of the New World. Typically, Carpentier accounts for this convergence of latitude and import by way of "the oddest pieces of apparatus" as well as by sheets of instructions; so, too, when the narrative's young men eagerly exchange theories, impatient for "dawn to confirm the efficacy of a prism, and marvel to see the colours of the spectrum outlined on the wall" (25). Given the dis/play of "telescopes, hydrostatic balances, pieces of amber, compasses, magnets, Archimedes screws, model winches, speaking tubes, Leyden jars, pendulums, balance-beams and miniature cranes," and "a mathematical box, containing all the most advanced instruments," the exhibit is suffused with sign and surplus (24). We are at one and the same time grounded in a physics of optics and a geometry of space, in a conjoining that relates, too, to the history of "perspective" in Islamo-European thought.

The implied and overt signatures make even more transparent the importance that Carpentier attaches to paintings in his works, from variously Anonymous to Dürer and Francisco de Goya; and from a "mature beauty [that] was reminscent of some luxurious Leda in a Flemish painting" (*Explosion* 203) to Van Gogh, Tanguy, and the Cuban Wilfredo Lam (*The Kingdom of This World*). It is no casual matter, of course, that the central image in *El siglo de las luces* is a painting titled "Explosion in a Cathedral"—a significance that is rather too quickly given away by the English title. In this painting "perspective" is as much prophetic (but apostate) discourse as it is geometry and illusion. Furthermore, to the degree that painting adds import to discovery, the art form evokes the Leon Battista Alberti of that signal 1436 publication, *Della pintura* (*On Painting*); and also affiliates Alberti with the influential *Opticae thesaurus* (1270) of Alhazen (Abu Ali Al-Hasan Ibn Haytham). This is "joinery" that is in turn related to Columbus and the Indies.

For when Columbus set sail in 1492 he had done so, Francesco Ammannati proposes, with the map that Paolo dal Pozzo Toscanelli (1397-1482) had produced in collaboration with Alberti. A "*grande studioso fiorentino*" had thus played "*un ruolo rilevante*" in the "*scoperta dell'America*," especially "*dell'aspetto scientifico*" (1992:61; Hulme 1986:24; 37). Ammannati's "Toscanelli e Colombo" thus discusses "*l'immaginario geografico medievale*" and "*la cartografia delle grandi scoperte.*" He suggests, too, that the Indies enterprise was as much "*una gigantesca impresa individuale*" as it was a conjoining of due forces—"*quanto che i tempi fossero maturi per un simile evento*" (*ibid.*). Given Carpentier's palimpsestic narration of such events, it is appropriate that Ammannati also foregrounds relationships as he does. He sees in *impresa* and *evento* a conjoining of mathematics and faith, of reason and doubt. "*La raggione*" was thus "*solo una parte nell'impresa di Colombo, que fu condotta all'insegna del dubbio e della fede*" (*ibid.* 68).

Explosion in a Cathedral also takes the measure of instrument and discovery in an eighteenth century that Carpentier compounds into the fluid dis/unity of *dubbio* and *fede*. Telescope and mathematical box certainly suggest affiliations of a familiar sort with the "century of lights." With them the Age is recognizably "catalogued" in the way that, say, Alexander Pope (1730) had celebrated it when he wrote, "Nature, and Nature's Laws lay hid in Night. / God said, *Let Newton Be!* and All was *Light*." So, too, when, eager to "mark / The *Mathematic* Glories of the Skies, / In Number, Weight, and Measure, all ordain'd," Edward Young (1759) had exclaimed: "O for a Telescope His Throne to reach!" (Barfoot 1987:150). Carpentier's *Explosion* takes us latitudes deep into, even as it rides counter to, the century within which Young had engaged in such conjectures on original compositions. For Young, "so boundless are the bold excursions of the human mind, that in the vast void beyond real existence, it can call forth shadowy beings, and unknown worlds, as numerous, as bright, and, perhaps, as lasting, as the stars; such quite-original beauties we may call Paradisiacal." (*ibid.* 138)

In the end, Carpentier's periods, profiles, and ghosts are consubstantiated in typical fashion by the fact that Francisco de Goya (1746-1828) frames the canvas upon which *Explosion* displays its terrains and types. Segment by segment, through the Goya of the 1863 disasters of war (*los desastres de la guerra*), Carpentier both makes a palimpsest of and implodes his narrative's Ages of Revolution, Reason, and Discovery. He does so, that is, from an opening *siempre sucede* (it always happens) through the discomfiture of *extraña devoción* (strange devotion) and the (un)reason of *con razón o sin ella* to the finality of *asi sucedío* (and that was what did happen) (29;143;343). Century of Lights thus confounds itself in the Age of the Tree of Liberty, Age of the Scaffold, and Age of the Great Delirium (260). In the end, the last of the novel's protagonists disappears into that Goyesca explosion of the month of May in which "the entire population of Madrid had poured into the streets in an impromptu uprising as devastating as it was unexpected." The Goya in Carpentier is well-limned, indeed: "All over Madrid an atmosphere as of some great cataclysm or telluric convulsion prevailed—with fire, iron and steel, anything that cut or explode, in rebellion against their masters—amid a mighty clamour of *Dies Irae*" (348). *Explosion in a Cathedral* thus blends its insights with the dramatic conceit and political allegory that Rafael Alberti, say, made of *Noche de Guerra en el museo del Prado* (*Night and War in the Prado Museum*): a context in which the Author-character limns a world in which "Soldiers of the first days of the war, men of our town, [were] like those whom Goya saw toppling over in their blood under the fire of Napoleon's soldiers," in 1808. Here, in Alberti, the play's Beheaded Man rings down the curtain with lines from Antonio Machado:

> Madrid! Madrid! How lovely your name sounds!
> The bulwarks of all Spain today.
> The earth trembles, the sky thunders.
> You smile with bullets in your body. (Johnson 1969:238)

Carpentier's way with his instruments of the age remains various and therefore variously significant throughout *Explosion*. He re-focuses their import, for example, when, "making swimming motion with his outstretched arms," Carlos threw himself down on a set of low trestles on which rested sacks of birds' feather. Not so accidentally, he does so in a warehouse which the narrative maps as having come "from all over the world"—with its Flour Street and Wine Street; Tackle Street and Deerskin Street; so, too, its Spice District (with "ginger, laurel, saffron and cheese from Veracruz"). There are Andean blankets from Maracaibo and a pile of sticks of dye, and books of gold and silver from Mexico. Parallel lines of La Mancha cheese lead elsewhere to Oil and Vinegar Court. All the while, and with what really amounts to a studied call to attention, Esteban spun the hoops of "an armillary sphere" that stood like "a symbol of Commerce and Navigation" (21)—an instrument in whose wake a multiplicity of things and persons had arrived "by so many different sea-routes" to the Indies and their *real maravilloso* order of things:

> [I]t was a wonderful archipelago, where one came across the strangest things: enormous anchors abandoned on lonely beaches; houses fixed to the rocks with iron chains, so that the cyclones could not sweep them into the sea; a huge Sephardic cemetery in Curaçao; islands inhabited by women who lived alone for months

and years on end, while the men were working on the mainland;
sunken galleons, petrified trees, unimaginable fish; and, in Barbados, the tomb of a nephew of Constantine XI, the last emperor
of Byzantium, whose ghost appeared to solitary wayfarers on
stormy nights. (33)

Carpentier's way with the emblematic and the brutal also accounts for the
"terrifyingly aggressive symbolism" and the "bituminous darkness" with
which *revolución* and *luces*, guillotine blade and printing press finally
(un)become themselves in *Explosion in a Cathedral*. It also explains the
"Door" that *Explosion* opens upon and yet from inside its brave new world.
Given Carpentier, this contraindicative opening occurs with the dry clarity of
"sheets of instruction," according to a "thorough collation of date and
chronology." All the same, the procession of carpenters engaged in its
construction assumes the shapes of figures performing "some bloody and
mysterious rite." Soon enough, mathematical precision and occult ritual
converge in "a geometrical projection from the vertical, a false perspective,"
which began to emerge: it was "a configuration in two dimensions of what
would soon take on height, breadth and a terrible depth. With something of
the air of Aztec immolators, the dark figures [engaged in its construction]
toiled at their nocturnal joinery, taking parts, runners and hinges from coffin-
like crates" (124). In the end, "gaunt as a theorem," the "Machine" stood out,
"suddenly transformed into a symbolic figure." Thus it was that, together with
Liberty and the printing press, "the first guillotine was arriving in the New
World" (131).

As an allegory of discovery, the narrative deals with yet other degrees
of immanence and materialization, of course. This much is clear from the
"becoming-sign"—the "utopics, spatial play" (Marin 1984)—that *Explosion*
also makes a point of identifying as "enigmatic geometrical shape,"
"Pythagorean symbol," and "Stone of Mecca"; so, too, as the "slender
cathedral architecture of certain snails, which with their winged and needle-
pointed shells could only be seen in terms of the Gothic" (194). "It was
wonderful," Esteban records, to encounter "stuttering, budding, creeping"
form everywhere. There is a utopian latency that *Explosion* soon re-cognizes
into and as a circum-Caribbean pre-text—as a "gulf full of islands . . but with
the incredible difference that these were small islands, mere designs or ideas
for islands which had accumulated . . . just as models, sketches and empty
casts accumulate in a sculptor's studio." These forms occupy a space that
Marin implies when he writes about the "a-temporality of utopic representation and of its discourse of knowledge." They also allow the imagination a
certain "completion of mastery" and a fusion of "inside and outside, past and
future, fantasy and the possible" (Marin 1984:xxvii). In Carpentier, "comple-

tion of mastery" awakens in Esteban to a compelling urge "to give expression to these *things*"—for all that, in the absence of "the god's script," their being articulated by the "torpid, hesitant tongue of the Man-Child" will only lead to memories of the future that cannot *not* engender Gorgon Island and Staircase of Candles; Frowning Rock and Angel Island ("with those outspread Byzantine wings"). Elsewhere, Esteban passes "from Temple-Cave, consecrated to the adoration of a diorite Triangle" on to "Condemned Isle." There is a certain land-of-look-behind irony, then, to the fullness of this discovery of the islands. Not unreasonably, the genre recalls Columbus faced, as above, with the "Islands, islands, islands" of *The Harp and the Shadow*, among them "one with neither name nor history"; another with "the music of castanets"; and yet another one that lies within an "arc of fish and parrots" (109). Esteban makes the obvious enough connection when he "marvelled [and] realised that this Magic Gulf was like an earlier version of the Antilles, a blueprint which had contained in miniature everything that could be seen on a larger scale in the Archipelago" (194-195).

There is, finally, a considerably less esoteric, indeed, quite vintage, reprise of The Discovery in *Explosion in a Cathedral*. Here, its ambit and sign come in "a mahogany bowl in which the taste of must was combined with the scent of the thick, cool wood, that had a fleshy feel against the lips." In it was "the noble juice of the vine, which had nourished the proud and turbulent Mediterranean, now spread into this Caribbean Mediterranean, where the blending of characteristics had for many thousands of years been in progress within the ambit of the peoples of the sea." This genealogy of pedigree and taste is as accommodating as it is accommodated; it had been aged and textured into a heteroclitic smoothness, one in which

> after long being scattered, the descendants of the lost tribes had met again, to mingle their accents and their lineaments, to produce new strains, mixing and commixing, degenerating and regenerating, a temporary enlightenment followed by a leap backwards into the darkness, in an interminable proliferation of new profiles, new accents and proportions. In their turn they had been reached by the wine which had passed from the Phoenician ships, the warehouses of Cadiz, and the amphorae of Maarkos Sestos, into the caravels of the Discovery, along with the guitar and the glazed tile, and had landed on these shores so propitious to the transcendental encounter of the Olive with the Maize. (183)

Whether in Borges or Carpentier, commixing and propitious translation thus add dispensations to The discovery and its world-making materials that interest me here.

Arguably, it is all of one piece in the history of language and imperial power that 1492 was the year in which Antonio de Nebrija published and spelt out the "companion to empire" implications of the first study of Castillian grammar. Printed in Salamanca and dedicated to Queen Isabella, Nebrija's work was triumphalist Christianity, Spanish imperialism, and linguistic discipline all in one. He explained that he had written the work in recognition of "the scatterred members and pieces of Spain" who would be "consolidated and joined in a body and unity of kingdom." He also anticipated a future in which the Christian religion would have been purged, and its enemies vanquished. At which utopian point, "nothing [would be] left but the flowering of the arts of peace. Among the first ones is that which language teaches us" (Gómez-Moriana 1989:97-98). In certain "pre-textual" ways, then, Columbus's log entries for November 11, 27, and December 21, 1492 had been positioned accordingly, in a still-vex'd Bermoothes. In the first, a canoe with six youths came alongside the ship of the Castille-empowered Admiral from Genoa. "Five came aboard. These I ordered held and am bringing with me," Columbus wrote. He next ordered the seizure of "seven women, small and large, and three children." The men would be willing to undertake what was desired of them, he reasoned, "if I let them have their wives." Besides which, "these women will teach our people their language, which is the same throughout these islands of India" (107). The entry for Tuesday, 27 November 1492 registers difference; it also anticipates exercise of power, and Christian sanction:

> I do not know the language, and the people of these lands do not understand me, nor do I or any other person I have with me understand them. And these Indians I am taking with me misunderstand things many times; besides I do not trust them very much because they have attempted to escape several times. But now, Our Lord willing, I shall see all I can, and little by little I will investigate and learn, and will have this language taught to persons of my house because I see that the language is all one up to this time. Then the benefits will be known, and one will labor to make all these people Christian, since it can easily be done. (119-120)

The *Log* thus conceived of the function of language in openly hegemonic ways. The appeal is one that well anticipates the recognition that we get in *The Tempest*.

"We cannot miss him: he does make our fire, / Fetch in our wood and serves in offices / That profit us," Prospero will then say of his islander, Caliban (I.ii.310-312). Caliban's own profit on language is mapped somewhat diffrerently, of course. Hulme understands the protagonist of Defoe's *The Life and Adventures of Robinson Crusoe* to relevant effect when he observes that unwilling as Crusoe may be ever to call Friday "slave," he has "no qualms about adopting the other half of the dialectic: 'I likewise taught him to say Master, and then let him know, that was to be my name'" (205). Equally defining is the fact that Prospero and his daughter are so unnegotiably convinced that, what with being "poisonous slave" and "earth," and "tortoise," "hag-seed," and "puppy-headed monster," Caliban is a native on whom "any print of goodness [will] not take." With its "mythic" and "simplifying crucible" (Hulme 1986:186), Prospero's representation of native speech and cognition rather quickly resolves the kind of crisis that difference had provoked in, say, Manuel da Nóbrega, when he wondered whether Amerindians would "be able to confess through interpreters" (Rodrigues 1985:34). This was all a matter of some concern, of course, when, "like Christofer," the likes of Prospero bore "in speech mnemonic as a missionary's / the Word to savages" in the hope that "converted cannibals" and "good Fridays" would then "learn to eat the flesh of Christ," as Hulme puts it, citing Walcott's "Crusoe's Journal" (Hulme 1986:175). Antonio Vieira's seventeenth-century *Sermões Pregados no Brasil* well summarized the problem of language acquisition and cultural translation among such natives. Given Christian theology and the technologies of oral and written communications,"If it is difficult to hear a language that you do not understand," Vieira preached, "how much more difficult it must be to understand a language that you do not hear? The first problem is to hear it; the second, to understand it; the third, to reduce it to grammar and to rules; the fourth to study it; the fifth (and not the least, hurdle, one which obliged St. Jerome to wear down his teeth) is to pronounce it" (Rodrigues 1985:40). For its part, Inga Clendinnen's *Aztecs* re-thinks the issue of language and translation in ways that clearly temper the dismissive certainty of Prospero's thoughts about the latitude and import of native speech—that is, his, or his daughter's, declaration to Caliban: "Thou didst not know thine own meaning, but wouldst gabble like / A thing most brutish." *Aztecs* invites us to think otherwise when it suggests the range of anxieties provoked by the Nahuatl text of Sahagún's General History, "that indispensable text," but put together "a full generation after the conquest."

> Sahagún was unusual in his determination to use knowledgeable Indian informants, to realize that their statements would be collective, and to check those collective statements against similar statements of other equally knowledgeable elders from adjacent settlements. The statements were elicited in part by

presenting traditional pictographic material for elucidation, and in part by questions asked by his hand-picked and mission-trained Indian aides. (Clendinnen 1995a:282)

Meanwhile, when, complicating the picture, La Malinche/Doña Marina had first offered to endow Cortés's words with meaning and to make those of Amerindia known to the Spaniards, the now empowering, now accusatory liminality of the figure that she became may be seen in two significant portrayals. There is, first, the astonishing inconsequentiality with which Cortés refers to assistance from some "native Indian woman," to "una india desta tierra," in his 1519 *relación* (48). There is also that dramatic representation in which La Malinche holds on to the space—but is herself grounded—between Aztec warriors and Spanish conquistadors. The *encuentro* in the nahuatl pictograph is a study in collaborative tension; and what it captures is nothing if not perhaps *the* New World instance of (wo)man in the (com)promised land:

El encuentro (**The Florentine Codex, Bk 12**)

Clendinnen positions Sahagún's informants to relevant effect: the native mind in their context has been "lit by the brilliant but notoriously uneven retrospective light of catastrophe"; and there was the additional difficulty of inscribing "the spoken word" to contend with. As a consequence, some "dubious orthographies present painful problems." In "a particularly valuable colonial manuscript from 1558," we now learn, "a small 'ambiguity in the linguistic structure of the original' permits equally devoted translators to present the male hero either as deflowering and/or devouring the mythic female, or being himself assaulted and eaten; no small discrepancy" (*ibid.* 283).

Of course, Prospero's narrower agenda allows for a considerably less involved view of such matters. He is, after all, quite unnuanced when he denies in Caliban any capacity to think, speak, and mean *before* he taught him "language." He is unyielding in that contention of his that it was *he*—or in some versions of the drama, his daughter—who took pity on and taught the "native islander" and "demi-devil" to speak; or who, in a more radical understanding of the claim, introduced the islander to "language." *He* it was, the man insists, who "endow'd" Caliban's "purposes / With words that made them known" (I.ii.353-356). At any rate, disregarding any discrepancy or some demi-devil's curse, Columbus had logged his entry of choice on December 21, 1492. "Nothing is lacking," he wrote then, "except knowledge of their language in order to give them commands because they do whatever they are told without contradiction" (145). No doubt, he anticipated a native islander whose last word would approach Caliban's in *The Tempest*: "Ay, that I will; and I'll be wise hereafter / And seek for grace" (V.i.295-296). In figure and in sum, the 1492 *Log* thus articulates its preferences in ways that are better accounted for by the perspectives that cultural historians and literary texts have since brought to bear on the early modern period that matters here.

Paul Kristeller, for one, has identified it as one in which controversies about latitude and import "are partly due to national, religious, and professional ideals and preferences [which have in turn] influenced the judgment of historians, and to the great complexity and diversity that belongs to the period itself" (1972:111). Henry Kamen points to other re-alignments when he observes that the meeting of the Iberian peninsula and the Americas "changed the Spanish experience by offering new wealth and new mental horizons, and promoting social mobility" (1994: 475). Gerald Strauss has observed about the Europe of this period that "no other words carried the conceptual richness and emotive power of the pair *reformatio-renovatio* [and their satellite terms *instauratio, restauratio, reparatio*] which—as organizing language—resonated in nearly every segment of society" (1995:1). It was no idle note that was being struck when, in addressing the Fifth Lateran Council (1512-1517), "the noted scholar, orator and Augustinian vice-general Aegidus Viterbo had implored those present to recognize that "even as celestial and human beings, which are subject to motion, crave renewal," so the Church must be "restored to its ancient splendor and purity" (3). From cosmography to body politic, renewal was both desired and deemed necessary (*ibid.*). It was elsewhere the judgment of the historian Oviedo that "America was the greatest intellectual adventure of all time" since, so he pointed out, "what I speak of cannot be learnt in Salamanca or Bologna or Paris" (Kamen 1994:475). By the same token, and as Francisco Lopez de Gómora wrote, *"esta la experiencia en contrario de la filosofía*" (Pollard 1986:1). All the while, when import flowed back into Spain, it did so in forms of bullion of a familiar sort, and in ways that stimulated the economy even as it provoked theological debate. In the summation that we get from West and Kling (1991), this blend of contexts accounts for approaches to the Indies in which five sources of knowledge were obviously important: "scientific conceptions from ancient Greeks and Romans supplemented by works from Jewish and Arabic scholars; facts and prophecy from the Bible; teachings of the church fathers; interpretations of medieval theologians and cosmographers; and practical information gleaned from conversations with people from all walks of life" (9).

It is in one such unfolding that Menocal's *The Arabic Role in Medieval Literary History* situates and advocates its al-Andalusian Hispanism. She proposes, then, that if "hispanomedievalists help to make it clear that the twelfth, the thirteenth, or the fourteenth centuries and their literatures cannot be fully seen or clearly understood without looking first where others looked, to Spain," then the kind of Hispanism that she advocates would "certainly be central to European medieval studies. Just as al-Andalus once gave other Europeans so many of the means to decipher and unveil the heavens, such a newly defined Hispanism will uncover a long-obscured constellation of stars that once lit the skies of medieval Europe" (1987:153). As might be expected, New World affiliation with such skies is studiedly esoteric in the Borges of "Los traductores de las *1001 Noches*" (1936), and his signature is elsewhere recognizable in the Islamic philosophy, and the panache of demands, with which his 1949 "Averroes' Search" ("La Busca de Averroes") begins:

> Abulgualid Muhammad Ibn-Ahmad ibn-Muhammad ibn-Rushd (a century this long name would take to become Averroes, first becoming Benraist and Avenryz and even Aben-Rassad and Filius Rosadis) was writing the eleventh chapter of his work *Tahafut-ul-Tahafut* (*Destruction of Destruction*) in which it is maintained, contrary to the Persian ascetic Ghazali, author of the *Tahafut-ul-falasifa* (*Destruction of Philosophers*), that the divinity knows only the general laws of the universe, those pertaining to the species, not to the individual. (1964:148)

With rather more immediate relevance for the conjoining of Spain and the Indies in the early modern period, L. P. Harvey highlights the Islamic Spain of the years between 1250 and 1500; so, too, the decisive conquest of Granada (1490-1492) and the cultural formations that account for the "all Mudejars now" Spain of 1492-1500 (1990:307-339). As the voice of the Columbus of *The Harp and the Shadow* once put it: "I had seen the royal standard raised over the towers of the Alhambra; I had been present at the humiliation of the Moorish king, wrested from his vanquished city and made to kiss the hands of my monarchs" (68). Menocal and Harvey, like Carpentier's Columbus, identify a terminus from within which Anthony Pagden's *Spanish Imperialism and the Political Imagination* (1990) advances its discussion of property rights and "dispossessing [of] the barbarian" in Spanish America (13-36); the same is true of the "instruments of empire" with which he examines the criollo use of the Amerindian past to fashion syncretist "savage nobles" out of "noble savages" (91-116).

Notwithstanding such pre-texts for criollo primitivism, or for latter-day adjustments of native sensibility, it very much matters that halfway through his *Diálogo sôbre a conversão do gentio* (1557), the Jesuit Padre Manuel da Nóbrega gave succinct voice to a stubborn preoccupation when he asked, "*Estes têm almas como nos?*" (Do the likes of these have souls like ours?) (Sturm 1985:72). It was a question that endured, notwithstanding responses generated by gatherings such as The Fifth Lateran Council and Pope Paul III's Council of Trent (1545-1563). For to industriousness that provided evidence of audacious daring in commerce and speculative theology were added contacts in which "I" became "Other" in deeply problematic ways. In Carpentier's *Explosion*, the Caribs would hurl themselves against "enormous ships" that carried "unsuspected, unsuspectable invaders": "They clambered up the sides and attacked them with a savage desperation, which these new arrivals could not understand" (244). In quieter dispensations of the same, Caliban would remind his Prospero: "I lov'd thee / And show'd thee all the qualities o' the isle, / The fresh springs, brine-pits, barren place and fertile." In return, "Thou mad'st much of me, wouldst give me / Water with berries in't"; and there was talk, too, about which was the greater and the lesser light on the horizon (*The Tempest* I.ii 335-337). At any rate, whether unsuspected or unsuspectable, within a generation of Columbus, Portugal would be "inundated with blacks"; by 1565 Seville "was estimated to have 7.4% of its population as slaves, mostly blacks" (Kamen 1994:476). "All the places are full of slaves," the Flemish Clenardus wrote in intolerant fascination (1535): "Captive blacks and Moors perform all tasks. Portugal is so crowded with these people that I believe that in Lisbon there are more men and women slaves than free Portuguese.... Truly, when I first arrived in Evora I thought that I had come to some city of evil demons: everywhere there were so many blacks whom I so loathe that they may just be able to drive me away from here" (Saunders 1982:1).

Pace the profit and the pageantry of spice, land, and gold, the matter of human difference—naked and/or dark, especially—caused a great deal of epistemological disorder, further impressing the question that Columbus had provoked when he came upon and displayed Amerindians. Succinctly, how could there be creatures who so resembled men when no mention of them had occurred in the biblical narrative of how the sons of Noah came to inherit the earth? When the answers came, they did so, from conquistador to *sor presa*, with a certain conceptual economy. José de Acosta, for instance, settled for transportation by shipwreck and accidental tempest of weather, after dismissing two other possibilities: that the travels of Noah's Ark included an American port of call and that angels might have transported them across the ocean, "holding them by the Haire of the Head, like to the Prophet Abacuc" (Fell 1977:16). As with Mather's *Magnalia*, looking to the "penmen" of the Scriptures for a place within Euro-Christendom in which to identify the Indians of the New World had its signal moments. And these ranged from that venom in the voice of Martín Alonso (*The Harp and the Shadow*) to the *Religio Medici* of Sir Thomas Browne, where the matter touched on nothing less than the question of the Ark's bearings—"which must needs bee strange unto us, that hold but one Arke, and that creatures began their progresse from the mountains of *Ararat*." The whole rendered Scripture "more hard to comprehend," and "put the honest Father to the refuge of a Miracle" about, among other issues, "How *America* abounded with beasts of prey, and noxious Animals, yet contained not in it that necessary creature, a Horse"; so too "by what passage those, not onely Birds, but dangerous and unwelcome Beasts came over: How there bee creatures there, which are not found in this triple Continent" (23).

In the end, prophecy held its own, of course; for it variously allowed the sons of Noah to inherit the earth and to exercise what the Book of Genesis apparently intended: a European and Christian hegemony of the Elect that the signs and wonders of the lands of America themselves had sanctioned. "Now that I am old," Bernal Díaz recalled in *The Conquest of New Spain*, "I often pause to consider the heroic actions of that time. I seem to see them present before my eyes; and I believe that we performed them not of our own volition but by the guidance of God. For what soldiers of the world, numbering only four hundred—and we were even fewer—would have dared to enter a city as strong as Mexico, which is even larger than Venice and more than four thousand five hundred miles away from our own Castille and, having seized so great a prince, execute his captains before his eyes" (1963:250). In other versions of the prophetic, John Eliot's *Brief Narrative of the Progress of the Gospel amongst the Indians in New England in the Year 1670*, would espouse the view that Indians were descendants of the ancient Jews; since, among other similarities, their practices involved sequestration of women who were menstruating. A related "Christianography" (Mather) accounts for the map of conjectures in Thomas Thorowgood's 1650 *Iews in America, or Probabilities That the Americans Are of That Race.* Not only a map, Thorowgood's project was also an advocacy of missionary activity. Its preoccupation with Amerindia was grounded in at least two formulaic and millenarian imperatives. First, there was the persuasion that the Second Coming would be hastened by converting Jews to Christianity; and second, that the Christianographic expansion of the world which the discovery of America entailed confirmed the nearness of an end-time—witness, as above, the pious calculation of years and genealogies in Columbus's *Book of Prophecies.* The enterprise of the Indies was similarly called upon to serve the argument of Manasseh ben Israel, "a well-known rabbi from Amsterdam," who found grounds on which to argue that the ten lost tribes had managed to settle in the New World, and thus to influence the beliefs and practices of its inhabitants. In this positioning of Jewish identity, the rabbi did not only seek to address Puritan and Anglican messianic expectations; he also sought to make a case for the readmission of Jews into England. The prophetic, and strategic, calculation here was to encourage recognition of a certain kind: that "the readmittance of Jews into England, the last end of earth, was a final and necessary event prior to the Messiah's arrival" (Eilberg-Schwartz 1990:34-36).

An important, and earlier, rapprochement with Amerindia had involved the Fifth Lateran Council that Giuliano della Rovere (Pope Julius II) convened between 1512 and 1517, and whose charge was as much to map out the latitude of papal power as it was to delimit the immortality of the soul. The complex agenda that the Council faced may be guaged by the fact that it also needed to negotiate a theological path through swirls of Averroist Islamic philosophy, Thomism, and Platonist thought—and this against the gravitational pull of an emergent humanism. The intrusive impact of this clustering of ideas, writes Paul Kristeller, may "be seen in the decree by which the Council . . . condemned the unity of the intellect and formulated the immortality of the soul as a dogma of the Church" (1972:36; Menocal 1987; Harvey 1990). Appropriately, when the Council moved to accommodate the Amerindian in the scheme of things it did so with telling recognition of certain imperatives, among them, the rise of European nationalisms and the centrality of Euro-Christian man's election to grace. There was thus a certain conceptual economy to the map of Creation as a whole that the Council then produced (Fell 1977:16):

Adam and Eve

Sinful Babylonians	Noah the righteous & his spouse		
(Most destroyed in the Flood)	Shem	Ham	Japhet
(Some banished in the wilderness)			
Amerindians	Arabs, Hebrews, Syrians, given the semitic lands	Lybians, Egyptians, Africans	Peoples of Europe and Asia

Of course, the making and mapping of the Americas involved encounters which were other than Graeco-Roman Antiquity, African, and European. There was that compelling mis-recognition of Asia. After all, in its circum-Caribbean origins the Americas had first surfaced as "The Indies" because of Columbus's mis-mapped obsession with the Great Khan and the wealth of Cathay. As he acknowledges the issue in *The Harp and the Shadow*, "Without my willing it, Hispaniola was tranfigured by this inner music [a diabolic interior energy] into the fabulous kingdom of Cipango" (102); in addition, "The name of the *Grand Khan* resonated of gold . . . celestial music" (88). About Columbus and this gravitational pull of "The East" Edmundo O'Gorman writes in *The Invention of America* that there had been, *tout court*, a quite "Doric simplicity to the obsession." Columbus "intended to cross the ocean toward the west with the purpose of reaching, from Spain, the far eastern shores of the Island of the Earth and thus connect Europe with Asia." In this respect, and Carpentier's latter-day proddings notwithstanding, "Nothing was able to shake" the man's faith that "he had reached Asia, he was in Asia, and it was from Asia he had returned. No one, nothing, to the day of his death, ever made him relinquish this cherished conviction" (1961:78;74).

All in all, the "material" of Asia provided pre-text and template enough with which to embark upon various discoveries of the New World, whether in Yamashita's *Brazil-Maru* or in Kingston's *China Men;* so, too, in the Arabo-Portuguese implications of Gilberto Freyre's Luso-Brazilian geneal-ogy, about which more later (below), and in the residual Moorishness that Paz lodges in the Mexican consciousness of "the sons of La Malinche." Mean-while, "The sun of Asia creeps above the horizon / Into this haggard and tenuous air, / A tiger lamed by nothingness and frost," Wallace Stevens would write in "Like Decorations in a Nigger Cemetery" (1972:104). He does so "lamely," *pace* the exuberant New World testament into which the Walt

Whitman of "A Passage to India" had thought it possible to translate and thus "eclaircise the myths Asiatic." For this poet of the Americas who was so prepared to sound his "barbaric yawp over the rooftops of the world," Asia was an *antecedent*, therefore necessary, constellation of "far darting beams of the spirit," "unloos'd dreams," "deep diving bibles and legends," and "elder religions" (*ibid*. 339). Meanwhile, a quite dis/affiliating use of the "Asiatic" material in the Caribbean would involve Naipaul in *A House for Mr Biswas* and in the "abandoned, blighted cocoa estates" of East-Asian West Indian enclaves where Ralph Singh's father, in *The Mimic Men*, would speak about "the voyages, so recent but already in our strange hemisphere so remote, which the fathers and indeed some of the people we saw had made from another continent, to complete our own little bastard island" (122) .

Re-figurations of Arab and Japanese—and of Chinese, Jew, and Hindu —variously nuance or else historicize the "oriental" in the Americas. Such is the case in, say, Gabriel García Márquez's *The Chronicle of a Death Foretold* where the principals include those knife-wielding and honor-bound clans of Arab-Caribbeans, with their "colored cloth and bazaar trinkets." It is within this circle and cycling of consciousness that Márquez evolves his "chronicle," explaining that

> The Arabs comprised a community of peaceful immigrants who had settled at the beginning of the century in Caribbean towns, even in the poorest and most remote, and there remained, selling colored cloth and bazaar trinkets. They were clannish, hard-working, and Catholic. They married among themselves, imported their wheat, raised lambs in their yards, and grew oregano and eggplants, and playing cards was their only driving passion. The older ones continued speaking in the rustic Arabic they had brought from their homeland, and they maintained it intact in the family down to the second generation, but those of the third . . . listened to their parents in Arabic and answered in Spanish. (1982:93-94)

"A new civilization": this is how Karen Tei Yamashita further identifies that convergence of profiles in *Brazil-Maru*. "This perhaps sounds strange to-day," she explains, "but in those early years [of the twentieth century] that is the way we used to talk to about colonizing Brazil, especially about the particular Japanese colony located on the far northwestern corner of the State of Sao Paulo, founded by the Christian evangelist, Momose-sensei, and where my parents chose lot number thirty-three: Esperança" (1992:7). The larger question of import remains, of course: for many other Japanese immigrants had already experienced the "tepid heat of the port of Santos" and "the sheer green wall lifting into a mass of shifting clouds" since 1908, when "they had arrived at this same port in shipload after shipload until there were thousands of Japanese, the majority laboring on coffee plantations in the State of Sao Paulo" (3). This embrace of latitudes had been cardinal, indeed. It is in an appropriately named "New World Ranch," the narrator records, that "I heard my mother's low groan, and then saw my new brother—Koichi, my father would name him—emerging from my mother in a thin film of blood. My father said, 'Ah, it's a boy. It's a boy. Born in Brazil! Born in Brazil!'" (16).

Lo hebreo or *lo judío* constitutes another, and proximate, tradition from the Orient in the making of the Americas. There are cultural pre-texts and historical consequences in the fact that the hermeneutic, or otherwise esoteric, judaica that interests Borges and Carpentier evolved when and as they did during the period in which "The Indies" was discovered: *"Hey, Jews, pack your bags.* . . It may have been meant as a joke, but the joke could get rough," Columbus recalls remembering in *The Harp and the Shadow* (46). Yet other cultural productions of note include the Kabbalistic *ta'mey mizvot* whose "golden age" Moshe Idel has associated with the early modern period. In the "new-perspectives" context of his study, the age had borne fruit in an "immense number of folio" by the leading Kabbalists of Spain as well as in other elaborations that extended into and through the sixteenth-century "exegetical literature of commandments and prayer" (1988:iv-xv). Signally, "no elaborate and detailed survey of the nature and history of this religious movement is known . . . until the period of the Renaissance" (2). Besides which, the period from 1305 (the death of Moses de Leon/de Guadalajara) to 1492 (the expulsion from Spain) generated its share of contributions. This much is clear in *The Wisdom of the Zohar* when Isaiah Tishby summarizes the textual and reception histories of "The Book of Splendor": "The 'canonization' of the Zohar and its wider influence were consequent upon the expulsion from Spain, which shook the very foundation of Judaism. . . . This historico-spiritual transformation which brought kabbalah out of a closed circle of mystical initiates into the wider world and also into the homes of the Jewish masses, raised the Zohar to a most exalted position, where it was surrounded by an aura of antiquity and a wondrous light" (1994:I. 25). Aspects of its subject mattter were "suited to the spiritual condition of a shattered generation"; and in such a world the Zohar "was able to achieve the highest possible status," gaining "a place in the national consciousness as a canonical text, third only to the Bible and the Talmud" (*ibid.*).

It is to this complex of historical transitions that Mark-Alain Ouaknin appeals in the process of explaining what his *The Burnt Book* is *not* about. Notwithstanding, his impatient summary of sequence and consequence identifies measures "aimed at petrifying Jewish tradition" by way of "the usual methods of repression." They include the fact that the Talmud, after a court case lasting two years, was confiscated and, on 6 June 1242, twenty four cartloads of Talmudic manuscripts were burnt in Paris at the place de la Greve; that all copies of the Talmud were confiscated by Inquisitorial decree and burnt in Rome on 9 September 1553; and that on 21 March 1564 Pope Pius V went back on the various interdicts of his predecessor, adding that the Talmud could be used if the word *Talmud* was not written in full on any copies (1995:xi-xii; also, Lachower and Tishby I 1994:97). Elsewhere, Ouaknin identifies clusterings of Judaism in the "Afro-Spanish" or Muslim world of North Africa and Spain; so, too, in the reach of an "Eretz Israel-Greece-Italy-France-Germany." Rather more consequential here is the fact that one period in the history of Talmudic literature (the *Rishonim*) ends with the expulsion of the Jews from Spain in 1492: "The Jews, fleeing from Spain, spread throughout the world; the great Jewish centers were then established in Holland, in Germany, and particularly in Poland" (46-47).

As I have already suggested, *lo judío* resonates thereafter in the New World in ways that are generic and particular. No less relevant is the strain of anti-semitism to which Aizenberg calls attention by way of the popularity of Julian Martel's *La bolsa* (1890)—a novel in which Martel warned against the descendants of "'Judas' allegedly out to conquer America with an army of Jewish bankers and usurers" (Aizenberg 1984:24-25). In brief: New World judaica is as much the experience of Jewish dis/affiliation and "tropical diaspora" that Levine discusses in Cuba (1993) as it is Nelson Vieira's focus on the "prophetic discourse of alterity" that Jewish voices have contributed to Brazilian literature. "As (Jewish) ethos impacts upon a New World culture," Vieira explains, "it changes, confronting other myths, archetypes, rituals, and ideologies"; it impinges, too, "upon the issue of alterity and national synthesis" (1995:31). Interest in or assumption of *judería* therefore entails cultural transformations that involve "immigrant thematics" as well as philosophical questions about existence (*ibid.*). It does so, too, when Carpentier invokes terrain ("huge Sephardic cemetery at Curaçao") and text (the Zoharic epigraph of *Explosion in a Cathedral*). Judaica of this variety is also at work when, "despite [his] almost complete ignorance of the Hebrew language," Borges preoccupies himself with a "vindication" not so much of the doctrine as of the hermeneutic or cryptographic procedures of Kabbalah. The procedures re-appear in typically Borgesian form in the "congress" and "secret morphology" of "Death and the Compass," for example. Here, a "large octavo volume revealed to [Lonnrot] the teachings of Israel Baal Shem-Tob, founder of the sect of the Pious; another volume, the virtues and terrors of the Tetragrammaton, which is the ineffable name of God; another, the thesis that God has a secret name, in which is epitomized (as in the crystal sphere which

the Persians attribute to Alexander of Macedon) his ninth attribute, eternity—
that is to say, the immediate knowledge of everything that will exist, exists,
and has existed in the universe" (1962:131). Meanwhile, in such places as
"Las luminarias de Hanukah" and "La defensa de Cabala" Borges identifies
with and generates from yet other contexts of *lo hebreo* and *judería*. The same
is true of "Yo Judío," with its "half-serious, half-joking" (Aizenberg) dis/play
of affinities. It was significant, too, that in the 1920s Rafael Cansinos
Assens's "long and flowing sentences" with their "unSpanish and strongly
Hebrew flavor" had stimulated Borges to "far-flung reading." Borges thus
adds to and nuances a convergence of cultures as a consequence of which "his
Argentinians act out Parisian dramas, his Central European Jews are wise in
the ways of the Amazon, his Babylonians are fluent in the paradigms of
Babel" (Kerrigan 1962:9). Aizenberg has elsewhere highlighted the significance of such latitude in her "Aleph Weaver" review of biblical, kabbalistic,
and Judaic elements in Borges's cosmopolitan nativism (1984;1991). She
points to *lo hebreo* that the Jewish presence in Buenos Aires, and elsewhere
in Argentina, provided for the Borges of such narratives as "Emma Zunz," "El
indigno," and "Guayaquil" (1984:26; 1991:1-16). The multiplicity in his
cultural formation is one that Borges himself has best suggested in "La pampa
y el suburbio son dioses" (1926), where he writes about the composite reality
that he finds Buenos Aires to be: "*En este mi Buenos Aires, lo babélico, lo
pintoresco, lo desgajado de las cuatro puntas mundo, es décoro del Centro.
La morería esta en Reconquista y la judería en Talcahuano y Libertad.*"

   Although with a greater bent for subversion, judaica of the esoteric
variety also inflects the complex articulation of terrains and types in *Explosion in a Cathedral*. The text "generates" in signal ways from its Zoharic
epigraph: "*las palabras no caen en el vacío*" (no word falls into an emptiness).
Thereafter, *bruta facta* coincides with epiphenomena that include the conjuration of "witches' Sabbaths and infidels who worshipped one Hiram Abif,
architect of Temple of Solomon." In their "secret ceremonies," the narrative
informs us, "they paid homage to Isis and Osiris and took for themselves the
titles of King of the Tyrians, Builders of the Tower of Babel, Kadosh, and
Grand Master of the Templars" (64;33;184;178). Esoterica of this kind also
involved "the unexpected appearance of Isis and Osiris against the protentous
backcloth of the Temple of Solomon and the Castle of the Templars." In such
a con/fusion of epiphanies men would pray to Lucifer; insult Christ in
Hebrew; and spit on the crucifix and hold abominable feasts on Holy
Thursday (*Explosion* 64). Given *topographia* of this variety, it is no wonder
at all that Carpentier's protagonist could lie as he does in a "water-drunken-
ness" and "with such an expression of joy on his face that he looked like some
fortunate mystic, favoured with an ineffable vision" and "lucid intoxication"
(174-175).

Actually, there are degrees of what I take to be studied and anti-utopian irony in the fact that Carpentier introduces his century of lights by way of a zoharic declaration about the generative power of the word. We learn in *Explosion*'s embedded Allegory of the Discovery, for example, that "Gradually, from talking so much about the Empire of the North, men began to acquire propriety rights over it." In effect, "Words handed on from generation to generation had created so many things that these *things* became a sort of collective patrimony" (242). Elsewhere in Carpentier, there is the esoteric display which the Consul of *Reasons of State* makes of "root-sculptures, sculpture-roots, root-forms, root-objects—baroque roots or roots that are austere in their smoothness": "It was enough to mention the name of a port to the collector for him to pass from the root found there to the invocation, evocation, present-name, or the proliferative activity of the letters—so he said—a process such as was foreshadowed in the Hebrew Cabbala" (258). Parenthetically, this "activity" takes place in a chapter that begins with Descartes's "It sometimes happens that after listening to a speech whose meaning we have perfectly understood, we cannot say in what language it was uttered" (252) and ends with "And that afternoon I wept. I wept because a dictionary—*Je sème à tout vent*—was unaware of my existence" (265). At any rate, although the activity of the word is not quite as calculatedly referenced as it is in Borges's preoccupation with the letters of "the Name" in "Death and the Compass," Carpentier's emphasis on profiles that are "multiplied infinitely in opposing mirrors" (Borges) suggests the zoharic affinities that matter here. After all, in its "all-embracing" response to "emanation, creating, formation, and making" "The Book of Splendors" does invite us to "Come and see. The world was engraved with forty-three letters, all of them a crown of the holy name. . . . The Holy One, blessed be He, made large letters above and small letters below. Hence, we have *bet*, *bet*: *bereshit bara*; *alef*, *alef*: *elohim el*—the letters above, and the letters below, and they were all as one from the upper world and from the lower world" (Lachower and Tishby II 1994:561; 567).

There is studied sub/version, all the same, when Carpentier "epigraphs" the Enlightenment with the *Zohar*'s invocation of sign and surplus. The dis/affiliation highlights certain measures of *Explosion*'s own embrace of the contraindicative. It is worth recalling here that it was in the century of lights that—echoing the discomfort of Rabbi Modena's *Sefer Ari Nohem* (1639)—certain scholars "regarded the kabbalah as a black stain on the fabric of pure Judaism." This judgment was especially evident in "the utmost clarity and precision" with which Heinrich Graetz representatively articulated his own "strong antipathy" to kabbalah and to the *Zohar*, which he portrayed as "a compendium of falsehood, perverse imaginings, and puerile beliefs." He also saw in its putative author, Rabbi Moses de Leon, little more than "a wretched prattler, a forger, and a conscienceless deceiver" (Lachower and Tishby I 1994:44; Scholem 1976:12-13).

Nelson Vieira's account of Jewish voices in Brazilian is also preoccupied with the making of the Americas and with its implications for ethnicity and "authoritarian closure" of identity (1995:19-50). His approach to "metacognition and pluralism" allows us language with which to summarize here. *Jewish Voices in Brazilian Literature* calls attention to the gravitational pull of diasporism on the one hand and, on the other, the national ideology and realities of Brazil's social relations (x). In addition, Vieira's judaica is used to account for a certain "labyrinthine process of questioning existence or identity using Jewish metaphors." *Jewish Voices* examines the politics of its convergent histories in useful ways. This is especially so, since, by promoting "the myth or ideology of national unity/homogeneity; the myth of racial democracy; and the myth of Brazil as a nonviolent nation" (*ibid.* 40), Brazil has labored to impose closure of a peculiar kind on allegiance and identity. Vieira elaborates on difference within the tensions of so hegemonic a grid, emphasizing the point that "the reality that identity is constituted along multiple axes (race, gender, nationality, sexual preference, etc.) makes any univocal or representative solution unacceptable" (*ibid.* 47). *Jewish Voices in Brazilian Literature* summarizes the question of identity and cultural formation in ways that merit being quoted in full at this juncture:

> Interestingly, Borges borrows the first letter of the Hebrew alphabet for his famous story "The Aleph," in which normal human beings cannot grasp the concept or the unlimited multiplicity of the universe. In his story, Borges affirms the impossibility of total sameness or oneness and reveals the possibility of the differing and deferring shadow of language. In *Aqua viva* (*The stream of life*), Lispector's female narrator speaks metaphorically of nontotality, diversity, and difference in a colloquial but penetrating manner: "Não me posso resumir porque não se pode somar uma cadeira e duas maçãs. Eu sou uma cadeira e duas maçãs. E não me somo" (75). ["I can't sum myself up because it's impossible to add up a chair and two apples. I'm a chair and two apples. And I don't add up." (60)]. In another telling passage, the same narrator, reacting to the notion that her language may be interpreted as promiscuous, attempts to convey her sense of diversity and difference: "mas sou caleidoscópica: fascinam-me as minhas mutações faiscantes que aqui caleidoscopicamente registro" (34) ["But I am kaleidoscopic: my sparkling mutations, which here I kaleidoscopically register, fascinate me" (25)].

Mutações faiscantes—in other words, sea-change and the embrace of something rich and strange, be it Ariel's or Clarence's—confirm the New World in its in/continence. It does so in ways that will be familiar, below, when "great chimerical nation" surfaces out of the promiscuous speech that the Wise Man of Nueva Córdoba delivers at the Olympic Stadium of Carpentier's *Reasons of State.* There will be kindred reproductions elsewhere, in the prodigious display of racial consciousness and sexual appetite of Luis Rafael Sánchez's *Macho Camacho's Beat,* for example.

Mutações faiscantes is very much an organizing principle in the Benítez-Rojo of *The Repeating Island,* dealing as he does in identities and experiences that are "heteroclitic, fractual, baroque, fugitive by nature." Characteristically, he roots cultural heterogeneity in fragmentation and in a topography that is everywhere grounded in productive instability. Very much preoccupied with "lack of historiography and historical continuity," he also improvises and engenders in categories that are so apparently provisitional that they result in the exceptionalist index that we get in:

> "certain way, a": of being, of people of Antilles, 12; of connecting (Antilles), 4; of (dis)organizing text, 155; of expressing oneself, 21; meaning of, 4-5; of performing, 16; of reading, 5; of reading text, 23; of two old women, 10, 11; of walking, 18-19, 22, 79. (295)

In effect, and succinctly in Barbara Einzig, "Benítez-Rojo hears the Caribbean story—as well as its ways of being told—not only in the story of the people but also in that of the waters, the plants, the sky, even the insects. He frees the Caribbean from the pathetic situation of needing to be put on the map by destroying the map" (1992:31).

Meanwhile, the now ab/original, now mimetic terrains and types of the still-vex'd Bermoothes move as they do in Carpentier's *The Lost Steps:* like "some modern analogue to [creatures] from another century [that had] strayed into unknown latitudes from perhaps four or five hundred years ago" (174). They do so only to experience, if they are the Africans in Robert Hayden's "Middle Passage," landfall on "New World littorals" that are "mirage and myth and actual shore." There is a similar base of design in the promiscuous embrace of form and deformation that we come upon in the autumn of Márquez's patriarch. For there is a telling knot of dis/affiliations in the pretext with which *El otoño del patriarca* (1975) celebrates its annunication of "the living creature of a mortal sin . . . in our obscene bellies [who] would be named Emmanuel which is the name by which other gods know God." Márquez's contraindicative new testament makes a *missa damnata* out of its New World gospel. What follows is an incarnation in which, its hour come round at last, "the terrible creature rolled over completely in his equinox of thick waters, corrected his compass and found the direction of the light." In effect, Márquez presents us with sub/versions of the Virgin's *Magnificat* and of the Incarnation. He counters the genre of great-compass representations in which, as variously above, The Discovery is "consecrated moment" and "all-embracing sacramental drama," "consummation" and "the greatest event since the creation of the world, excluding the incarnation and the death of Him who created it" (Gómora). And all this on "virgin lands, especially, where a man can start from scratch." Parenthetically, Carpentier limns other measures of the same in *Explosion* when he has Sofia risk an unproductive virginity, one in which the years would pass, "leaving no mark, arousing no emotion, between an Epiphany without Kings, and a Christmas without meaning for those who could not lay the Great Architect to bed in a manger" (312).

The haunt of prophecy is rather more straightforwardly mock-apocalyptic elsewhere in *Explosion*. This much is clear in the New World of Cayenne when a dog barks at a drunkard who went along the street scratching his sores as he shouted "terrible prophecies about the scattering of the just, the punishment of regicides, and the appearance of all before the Throne of the Lord that was to take place—why?—in a valley in Nova Scotia" (312). At any rate, this condition of being rooted in dis/affiliation and sub/version is substantively *the* moment of birth by the time we get to *The Autumn of the Patriarch*. In Márquez's *auto sacramental* of the latter days, the incarnation takes place on a marriage-altar that is nothing if not, representatively, *the* floor of Heaven and roof of Pandemonium. It is here that

> [Leticia Mercedes María Nazareño] doubled over sobbing oh my father and my lord have pity on this your humble servant who has taken pleasure in breaking your holy laws and accepts with resignation this terrible punishment, but biting her lace wristlet at the same time so the sound of the disjointed bones of her waist would not reveal the dishonor held in by the linen petticoat, she squatted down, she fell to pieces in the steaming puddle of her own waters and withdrew from among the muslin folds the seven-month runt who had the same forlorn unboiled-animal look of a calf fetus [and who] was to bear without honor the name Emmanuel. (168)

Meanwhile, and like a beacon off the Island of Pearls and far-off Trinidad, the New World is also the Land-in-Waiting at the "tip of whose nipple grew the Tree of Life." At the same time, no less of a reality attached to the "beef ships" which plied the Caribbean waters between Havana and Barcelona, leaving behind them their "powerful smell of smoked meat" (302). The same is true of that failed version of the future ("Ah! the Indies! the Indies!") in which "men were dragging out the most wretched existence that could be found anywhere on this earth, among Indian servants stinking of rancid oil and negroes smelling like skunks" ("The Road to Santiago" 40). For here, and fully emblematic, "clothes rotted away, weapons rusted, mushrooms sprouted from documents, and when a carcass was thrown into the middle of the street, black-headed vultures [unwound] its tripe like the ribbons on a maypole" (*ibid.* 41-42). It is no surprise, then, that, representatively utopian and bent, Carpentier's New World protagonists

> went up on to the roof, wrapped in their dressing-gowns, and carrying blankets and pillows on which at last they fell asleep, after talking, with their faces turned upwards to the sky, about habitable—and surely inhabited—planets, where life would perhaps be better than it was on this earth, everlastingly subjected to the processes of death. (*Explosion* 23)

James Turner's *The Politics of Landscape* makes for an especially deft summary here, when he observes that "*topographia* cannot be written as a simple increase in actuality." Although Turner produces the argument in relation to contexts that are considerably less complicated, the conclusion to which it brings him, by way of Raymond Williams, is an important one. "There is no longer any excuse," he insists, "for taking topoi at face value [since] we can sometimes discover a 'precise set of social relationships' behind the mystifications of ideal landscapes." Besides which, the making (up) of such terrain "demand[s] sufficient realism to be convincing, and sufficient idealization to be dissociated from immediate reality; different political and economic conditions demand different ways of resolving the contradictions that follow" (1979:xii-xiii).

Aksident store—all part availebul

Everything is fantastical: tales of El Dorados and Potosis, fabulous cities, talking sponges, sheep with red fleece, Amazons with
only one breast, big-eared Incas who eat Jesuits.

Alejo Carpentier, *Concierto barroco*

Here is one example: More's *Utopia* is neither England nor
America, neither the Old nor the New World; it is the in-between
of the contradiction at the beginning of the sixteenth century of
the Old and New Worlds.

Louis Marin, *Utopics: Spatial Play*

In the pages that follow, I propose to further map the spatial and conceptual
play of such *aksident-store* terrains and typologies of the ideal. Their New
World contexts will range accordingly: from Ras Tafarite geoeschatology to
the *hebreo* of "PaRDes; from the tropological conceit according to which
Jerusalem is the rock at the center of the world to the expulsion-from-paradise
motif that Earl Lovelace's *Wine of Astonishment* re-situates when it raises the
question: "But what sin we commit? What deed our father or we do that so vex
God he rain tribulation on us?" (1983:1), and which, in his *A Brief Conversion,* delimits the Land-in-Waiting that looms just beyond the San Juan,
Puerto Rico, airport of "Joebell and America." For this last is the context in
which we learn that "Joebell find he seeing too much hell in Trinidad so he
make up his mind to leave and go away. The place he should go is America,
where everybody have a motor car and you could ski on snow and where it
have seventy-five channels of colour television and never sign off" (1988:111).
Meanwhile, the origins of the terrain of the ideal in the Brazil of Jorge
Amado's *Os Pasôres Da Noite* (1964) lie in a syncretist con/fusion that owes
quite a lot to at least one of "The Lords Back There" (Carpentier, *The Kingdom
of This World*). The Brazilian incarnation is as (predictably) sensual as it is
religious. For in the Bahia of Amado's *Shepherds of the Night* "Who but Exu
could fill the slope of Pelourinho and the blue eyes of Wing-Foot with the
beautiful and lascivious mulattas?" (1966:10). Pelourinho thus lay ahead of
Wing-Foot, "a sea of breasts and thighs, swaying haunches, perfumed napes."
They had "disembarked by the dozen from the clouds of heaven" to become
a "sea of mulattas, and on this heaving sea, Wing-Foot set sail." Here, "a
breast grew till it touched the sky." The path was full, too, of "rumps, large
and small, all well-fleshed; you had only to choose." It was, after all,

the first hour of Exu, the hour of twilight shadow when Exu sets
out on his travels. The women would have completed their round

of visits to all the places of worship, carried out their indispendable
ceremony in honor of Exu, or had one perhaps forgotten her
obligation? Who but Exu could fill the slope of Pelourinho and
the blue eyes of Wing-Foot with the beautiful and lascivious
mulattas? (*ibid.*)

Of course, the "thalasso-graphic" confusion of signs (*eu-topos* and its sub/
version *ou-topos*) which Louis Marin underscores in *Utopics: Spatial Play* is
of some consequence in all this; so, too, other considerations of "determinate
negation" (Hegel) and the dis/equilibrium that it causes in the language of
paradise. For which reason, "Utopia is not only a distant country on the edge
of the world," Marin explains; "it is the Other World, the world as 'other,' and
the 'other' as world. Utopia is the reverse image of this world, its photo-
graphic negative." It is, therefore, "the product of a process by which a
specific system complete with spatial and temporal coordinates is changed
into another system with its own coordinates, structures, and grammatical
rules. This limit is thus an index and zero-space; it is also the bridge to the
'other'" (1984:243). The fact that in Thomas More information about the
precise location of the island is interrupted by "noise" is telling: "More does
not want to give away the place because it is nothing but a name." Marin
underscores the premise when he writes: "*Utopia is not a topography but a
topic*" (115). For his part, the Paz of *Alternating Current* proposes that
"Paradise would appear to be ruled by two warring sisters, [and from within]
a nexus of contrary meanings [that ocscillates] between water and light" (91-
92). Elsewhere, and this time in the baroque erotics of *Conjunctions and
Disjunctions,* the Mexican's rather singular suggestion is that "Our sex organs
and all their images—from the most complex down to jokes in a barroom—
remind us that there was a time when our face was down close to the ground
and to our genitals. . . . Our sex organs tell us that there was a golden age; for
the face, this age is not the solar ray of light of the Cyclops but excrement"
(20).

In this regard, Peter New's study of fiction and purpose in utopia,
whether in More's Renaissance or in the latter days of Samuel Johnson's *The
History of Rasselas, Prince of Abissinia*, provides an instructive configuration of and point of departure into such terrains. And New is nowhere more
helpful here than in the map that he provides of the contraindicative signals
with which *Rasselas*'s Happy Valley, for all that it gives the "appearance of
security and delight," is both "artifice of pleasure" and "new competitor for
imprisonment" (1985:94-95). New identifies and then breaches the boundaries of the ideal in a patient summary of particulars. In the process of doing
so he calls attention to the intrusive nature of "darker hints" that progressively
embed utopian happiness in its negation. He notes that the pleasing security

of the Valley involves coercion in which "everyone was *required* to propose whatever might contribute to make seclusion pleasant." He adds that "temporarily the tone hovers"; that after "the alarming final phrases of [a sentence about 'vacancies of attention' and 'tediousness of time'] there comes a short, emphatic, apparent reassurance: 'Every desire was immediately granted.' But from 'seclusion', the emphasis shifts steadily via 'blissful captivity' to the blunt, unqualified final word of the paragraph, 'imprisonment'" (95).

> Alarm signals are built into the first two sentences which describe the Valley: '. . . Rasselas was confined . . . till the order of succession should call him to the throne'—that is for the fourth son, probably for life. 'The place, which the wisdom or policy of antiquity had destined for the residence of the Abissinian princes'—when policy is [thus] distinguished from wisdom it is potentially ugly. But the dominant impression at first is of a secure haven, indeed a womb-like refuge. . . . Mountains overhang it, but it is 'spacious', so they do not yet seem oppressive. The 'dreadful noise' of falling water is safely outside the Valley. But as the suggestions of resemblance to paradise accumulate, so do further alarm signals. The first half of the sentence seems harmless ('The sides of the mountains were covered with trees, the banks of the brooks were diversified with flowers'); the second becomes cloying and decadent ('every blast shook spices from the rocks, and every month dropped fruits upon the ground'). The summarising sentence is seen to contain a quiet irony, as one looks back over the preceeding two. 'All the diversities of the world were brought together, the blessings of nature were collected together, and its evils extracted and excluded.' 'Nature' is referring here only to the world outside man, for whereas the beasts of prey are excluded, 'the beasts of chase' are there for man to continue to kill. (*ibid.* 93-94)

Whether conceptualized through Soyinka's *aksident store*, in Carpentier's tales of the "fantastical," or in the play of Marin's utopic spaces, it is along such a trajectory of great expectations that the *insulae fortunatae* also lie in Fitzgerald's *The Great Gatsby* when "the white wings of [a] boat [move] against the blue cool limit of the sky" in the assurance that "ahead lay the scalloped ocean and the abounding blessed isles" (1991:118). Negation and disequilibrium follow, of course. How else are we to account for the truncated syntax and ellipses that consign us to an "orgastic [*sic*] future that year by year recedes?" Or to an awkward reach for the ideal in which "blocks of sidewalk formed a ladder [that] mounted to a secret place above the trees." No less consequential, then, is the accompanying challenge of incompletion, with its

"And one fine morning—"; so, too, the utopian bent with which, "boat against the current," we are borne ceaselessly back into memories of the future (126). In effect, the oscillations of what interests me here are reflected in a narrative that moves "like the leg of transit" on water that is marked by a thin blood-red circle; for it is one, Fitzgerald writes, upon which "a small gust of wind that scarcely corrugated the surface was enough to disturb" what is, in the end, an "accidental burden" whose "accidental course" moved it "irregularly"—indeed, "urged" it—toward the drain at the opposite end of any great expectation.

"As every season seems best to us in its turn," Thoreau once observed, "so the coming in of spring is like the creation of Cosmos out of Chaos and the realization of the Golden Age" (1960 [Walden]: 214). All the same, Thoreau makes a point of observing elsewhere that "a ticket to Heaven must include tickets to Limbo, Purgatory and Hell" (Paul 1960:x). Wallace Stevens, for his part, contains the flow of the "honey of heaven" in a no less instructive counter-flow, in "Le Monocle de Mon Oncle." "The honey of heaven may or may not come," he also wrote in 1944, "but that of earth both comes and goes at once. But would the honey of heaven be so uncertain if the mules that angels ride brought a damsel heightened by eternal bloom, that is to say, brought a specifically divine revelation, not merely angelic transformations of ourselves. The trouble with the idea of heaven is that it is merely an idea of the earth. To imagine a heaven that is what heaven ineffectually strives to be" (1966:464). In what follows, Stevens's response to the "Sunday Morning" question, "where, then, is paradise?" will be an illuminating and wide-angled one, for all that the issue is raised amid the "complacencies of the peignoir and late / Coffee and oranges in a sunny chair, / And the green freedom of a cockatoo." Stevens's bent away from and yet toward the paradisiac is (en)gendered from his character's preference for "April's green," her "remembrance of awakened birds," and out of her "desire for June and evening, tipped / By the consummation of the swallow's wings." In the process of thus containing *eu-topos* in a tidier sensuousness, Stevens also dislodges entire categories of figures and forms that have played a role in representations of the lands of America as utopia.

But more about this later, both here and in the sections, "Chimerical Nations" and "The Unreturnable Heaven's Town." For now, I approach cities of the blest and enclaves of the damned in light of the complex of referents with which they converge in the (re)construction of the City Utopian that we get in, say, Elizabeth Langgässer's *Märkische Argonautenfahrt* (1950). For it is in this exploration and pursuit of the ideal that we get "Tower of David, Ivory Tower, and Golden House"; so, too, "Beloved of Heaven, beloved of earth, mysterious rose" (1953:55-56). Simultaneously Judaeo-Christian iconography and Graeco-Roman paganism, the *Argonautenfahrt* is not unrelated to the "prophetic significance" of Seneca's *Medea* that Columbus invokes in *The Harp and the Shadow*. Langgässer's *The Quest* also builds its Heavenly City within the language of "*Adams tyme.*" Its appeal is to an "incarnation of pure compassion and kindness" in which the divine would hold "a hunchback, a hydrocephalic, and a dwarf" in the "baroque beauty" of a transfiguring "embrace" (166). It is out of this elaborate reprise of paradisiac pre-texts that the City Utopian rises; that

> from the depths rise words and sentences that resembled quadratic blocks, pillars, and architraves. They built Vineta, built Troy, built Jerusalem. They were the city that stood there from time immemorial and her measures, according to which all other cities had been secretly patterned. She was beyond the reach of destruction, this utterly indestructible city. She did not age, she was without blemish. She was beloved of the creator, who spoke thus: "Thou art my fair one, my dove, my cedar and palm . . . ." She played before Him. . . . She had been created, but not in time, though neither had she existed from eternity. . . . Beloved of Heaven, beloved of the earth, mysterious rose of the cathedral windows of Europe above the high altar. Tower of David, Ivory Tower, and Golden House. (55-56)

In Carpentier's *Explosion in a Cathedral* and its centuries of Discovery and Lights, taking the utopian measure of the Indies had once been conceived of as a "great all-embracing, sacramental drama" that promised to make an "immense stained glass window" out of the Caribbean and its sea of islands (245; *Concierto barroco* 46). And where the lands of America did not quite allow for high altars that would lie beyond the reach of blemish and destruction, there had been, all the same, the

> century and half (1606-1767) [during which] Paraguay—with its *ceibo* trees and orange groves along its large rivers, altars and church roofs made of American mahogany—would be a land of utopian fancy. Here war and economic discord were abolished, and here—as in Lucian's dream, which Vasco de Quiroga recalled now and then—the golden age had returned, those allegedly happier, more tranquil days of the world. (Picón-Salas 1971:62)

Elsewhere in the lands that the likes of Pedro de Alvarado and Diego de Landa, or Pizarro and Cortés, had "pacified," Mariano Picón-Salas (1944) records that *The Book of Chilam Balam* bewailed and explained the disaster of its encounter with Europe by turning, in the "deep crevasse of sorry defeat," to a "golden age" when "all men lived in health"; when there was "no illness, no aching bones, no smallpox, no fever in the chest, no pain in the stomach, no wasting away" (1971:62;16-17).

For their part, Carpentier's ironic *Te Deums,* Stevens's preference for apostasy, Thoreau's extra "ticket"—and *The Tempest's* anticipation of "nettleseed" and ruination—all counter the notion that "Adam's time in paradise" could ever have been as Arthur Golding's 1567 translation of Ovid's *Metamorphoses* represents it:

> Moreover by the *golden [age]* what other thing is ment,
> Than *Adams tyme in Paradyse,* who being innocent
> Did lead a blist and happy life until thurrough sin
> He fell from God? From which time foorth all sorrow...

The circumstances of any such ideal planting had, in any case, been suggestively uncertain even in the apparent orthodoxy of Thomas Browne's "The Garden of Cyrus." If as "wiser Divinity concludeth," Paradise "were indeed planted the third day of the Creation," Browne had remarked, then "the Nativity thereof" was certainly "too early for Horoscopie; Gardens were therefore before Gardiners, and but some hours after the earth" (129). In effect, beyond—or rather, outside—the "blist" of "thurrough" certainties lies the succinctness with which Emily Dickinson, for one, grounds her "Forbidden Fruit" in the proposition that "Heaven is the interdicted Land—behind the Hill—the House behind." In short, in "what I cannot reach! / there Paradise—is found!" (Shattuck 1996:56). We learn from another of Dickinson's "banquet[s] of abstemiousness" that "Paradise" or "Eden will be so lonesome" on "Bright Wednesday afternoons." Furthermore, if "unto the Dead / There is no Geography," the question arises whether "Heaven [can be] a Place—a sky—a Tree" (Johnson 1993:373;481). As might be expected, Borges's several labyrinths add to this topography of the ideal not so much by moral division as by a rich equivocation on Dante. When Borges revisits "*Paradiso* XXXI, 108" he does so in recognizably idiosyncratic ways. His is a reprise that manages to combine the reach for utopia with what Anthony Kerrigan has identified as a "nostalgia of non-belief" (1967:vii). "Mankind has lost a face, an irretrievable face," Borges writes, "and everyone would like to be that pilgrim (dreamed of in the empyrean, under the Rose) who sees Veronica's handkerchief in Rome and murmurs with faith: *Jesus Christ, My Lord, True God, this, then, was Your Face?*" (1967:176). Kerrigan summarizes the peculiar bent of this quest by observing that the Argentinian "is most poignantly and hauntingly interested in what men have believed in their doubt"; that in his "equivocation regarding heresies and dogmas [Borges] renews them all, though he may be the unique evocative source of his own nostalgic non-belief in Belief or prescient belief in non-belief" (*ibid*.vii). As Borges himself puts it at the end of his excursus into Dante, "Who knows whether we may not see [the face] tonight in the labyrinths of dreams and remember nothing tomorrow" (*ibid*. 176).

Given the constellation of issues here, there is, once again, heuristic "material" in the map of limitations that Milton draws in the *Areopagitica* with the observation that "To sequester out of the world into Atlantick and Eutopian polities, which can never be drawn into use, will not mend our condition" (Hunt 1987:127). By somewhat the same token, his single-gated Eden idealizes and interdicts to relevant effect in Book IV of *Paradise Lost*. Here, Eden does indeed "crown with her enclosure green" the summit "of a steep wilderness, whose hairie sides / With thicket overgrown, grottesque and wild, / Access deni'd" (133-137). Satan will nonetheless slip inside with an ease that is, so to speak, Soyinka-esque. He does so precisely because he has explored and taken the measure of the "steep savage Hill" with its "brake" and "undergrowth / Of shrubs and tangling bushes," and its "One Gate . . . that look'd East." But then, principle of determinate negation and sleeping chrysalis *in* the word that he is, it is in quite the appropriate way that "th'arch-fellon" cancels "due entrance" and "access deni'd," when with

> one slight bound high [he] overleap'd all bound
> Of Hill or highest Wall, and sheer within
> Lights on his feet. (IV 172-184)

For my purposes here, any and all such sub/versions of the "utopic figure" (Marin 1984:262) are conjointly relevant in the "still-vex'd Bermoothes." The lands of America have, after all, involved dis/affiliations of terrain and type that have extended as they will: from Age of Kabbalah to Age of Anxiety in *Explosion in a Cathedral*; and from the Afro-Biblical eschatologies of Ras Tafarite drama in *The Kingdom of This World* and *O Babylon!* (Walcott) to the myth-sanctioning premise in Columbus's *Book of Prophecies* that the rock at the center of the world was nothing if not Jerusalem. Columbus was marvelously possessed by the notion, Stephen Greenblatt writes, "that his voyage on the round rim of the world would lead back to the rocks at its sacred center." For "one moment at least, a moment at once of perfect wonder and of possessive madness," Greenblatt adds, the man could at last see himself "become king of the Promised Land" (1991:85). Columbus finds dominion, that is, in a space of faith for which that Judaic and Christian archetype, Jerusalem, is "the earthly city where pilgrims travel, but [which], allegorically, indicates the church in the world. Tropologically, Jerusalem is the soul of every believer, and anagogically the word means the heavenly city, the celestial fatherland and kingdom" (West and Kling 1991:17). The terms of the archetype are no less translatable, of course, into the esoterica and revolutionary politics that Carpentier's *Explosion in a Cathedral* associates with "Cabbala and Platonism," and which it relates to a certain treatise on "The Coming of the Messiah" by one Juan Josaphat Ben Ezra, "an author whose name concealed, under its Arabic appearance, the identity of an active American revolutionary" (79;100).

There are revelant constellations of the utopian bent in the judaica that variously contextualizes Borges's interest in secret morphologies. It is in one such, "Death and the Compass," that his protagonist duly seeks his bearings by trying to take the measure of "the virtues and terrors of the Tetragrammaton, which is the ineffable name of God"; by his preoccupation with "the thesis that God has a secret name, in which is epitomized (as in the crystal sphere which the Persians attribute to Alexander of Macedon) his ninth attribute, eternity—that is to say, the immediate knowledge of everything that will exist, exists, and has existed in the universe" (1962:131). "PaRDes," in this respect, presents us with a relevant index of the heteroclitic nature of the nostalgia for paradise. It goes with resonances that echo in the *hebreo* or *judío* that I have variously identified above—in an "Indies," that is, in which the convergence of meridians involves invocation of the *Sefer al-Zohar* as well as other forms of the "prophetic discourse of alterity" which, Nelson Vieira writes, Jewish voices contribute to Brazilian literature (1995). We are in a tropical diaspora (Levine), moreover, in which, as *Explosion in a Cathedral* puts it, one could readily come upon "a Masonic Street as well as a Synagogue Street" (305).

That being the case, it is within *lo hebreo* and its corollary sub/versions of the ideal that the Isaac Bashevis Singer of "The Slaughterer" provides us with an instructive because conflicted re-constitution of PaRDEs and its circumstances. Singer's narrative rather more sharply delineates the great divide between ideal(ized) and contingent realities, and it does so with the starkness that the title promises. Not surprisingly, contagion of history and "*Adams tymes*" play themselves out in "The Slaughterer" into a madness-inducing and ultimately suicidal obsession. Singer grounds the utopian bent of the paradisiac when his protagonist, Yoineh Meir, confronts the difference that marks off "Paradise [where] the mysteries of the Torah were revealed to souls [and where] every holy zaddik inherited three hundred and ten worlds and wove crowns for the Divine Presence." This constellation of the ideal, where "Angels were flying, and Seraphim and Holy Wheels and Holy Beasts," lies unbridgeably beyond the Elul and the World of Deeds which could only bring with it, given Yoineh Meir and his troubled election to butcher in contingent time, "holidays of slaughter" and "millions of fowl and cattle now alive [but] doomed to be killed" (1996:209-211). His role as slaughterer delimits his perspective on transcendence in rather stark categories. As a consequence, he is quite unable to function within that zoharic recognition of "activity of the 'other side'" in which "a flow of blessing descends from time to time from the world of emanation into the realm of 'the other side'" (Lachower and Tishby II 1994:509). But then, it is not Singer's kosher butcher *malgré lui* but *The Wisdom of the Zohar* which further explains that this convergence "is part of the anti-dualistic tendency that sees the power of evil as a servant of God, which is allowed to exist simply in order to carry out His orders." In addition, "another way in which 'the other side' is supported is through the portion assigned to it in the performance of specific religious duties" (*ibid.*).

The horror-stricken insight with which the ex-rabbi, and now slaughterer of animals, seeks to escape the specific duty that his obligations impose on him counters the blending of perspectives with which, in Idel's *Kabbalah*, "The Lord planted a garden east of Eden," and in which kabbalah is "conceived as the real force maintaining the Garden as ongoing activity rather than a return to, or attainment of, a primordial state." The "theosophical Paradise," Idel explains, "is not a sublime psychological experience"; nor is it "nostalgia for Paradise" (1988:181-188). Yoineh Meir's suicidal preference for division in "The Slaughterer" also closes off the accommodating measures of the "theurgy" that Marc-Alain Ouaknin summarizes in *The Burnt Book*. PaRDes, "where *Remez* is included in *Drash,"and* may thus be accounted for at three levels; and these levels, Ouaknin writes, provide exegetical proof that, "insofar as they are discourses on . . ., The Zohar itself," and all the texts of the Cabbala and of Hasidism, "are at a *Pshat* level of *Sod*, but not yet *Sod* (let us remember that the *Zohar* is also known as *Midrash Ha-Zohar)*" (235). Meanwhile, the passage in which Idel's *Kabbalah* accounts for "Pardes" merits full quotation at this juncture. For it offers a specific as well as generic summary of the paths into and around the paradisiac that I have been mapping thus far:

> [T]he ancient description of Jewish esotericism employs the term *Pardes*—a garden—as a designation for esoteric speculations, and "the cutting of the branches" as a designation of heresy. Accordingly, the preceeding Kabbalistic theosophy can be conceived as an elaborate interpretation of the esoteric significance of the Paradise account and the mystical role of human activity. The perfect activity is the maintenance of the sefirotic pleroma in its state oriented toward the world, as in the talmudic-midrashic views. . . . This activity maintains the *Ma'aseh Bereshit*—a symbol of the Sefirot—in its exteriorized state, not allowing it to

be reabsorbed into the innermost part of Divinity. Kabbalah is thus conceived as the real force maintaining the divine Garden, as Adam was commanded to do by God. This cultivation of the Garden is an ongoing activity rather than a return to, or attainment of, a primordial state. The theosophical Paradise is not a sublime psychological experience, as the ecstatic Kabbalah would assume, but a dynamic attempt to maintain this world in the best status quo—not a 'nostalgia for Paradise,' oneself always and without effort in the center of the world at the heart the core of the theosophical Paradise, but the effort to construct it continuously and actively. (183)

In effect, and as New does in the contexts of his study of the utopian bent, Singer's "The Slaughterer" records yet another collapse in the attempt to imagine a heaven that heaven ineffectually strives to be (Stevens).

There is a sense, of course, in which the "nostalgia for paradise" cannot escape its own radical negation. In *Politics, Writing, Mutilation*, Allan Stoekl's introductory remarks to his study of Bataille and Kristeva, among others, comes under the heading "Utopias of Conflict, Urtexts of Deconstruction." Stoekl begins his work with a review of preoccupations with "disruptions of language that [are presumably] the product of a predenotative 'semiological flux'—that is, of a state of language outside the repressive strictures of logic and signification" (1985:xii). Thereafter, he calls attention to "not only the utopian denial or denegation of various political problems, but their *return* as well." The thrust is toward instances of "inner violence" that mirror "the self-directed violence of language (in silence, in wordplay, in *writing*)." The utopian effort, here, is "to imagine, somehow implemented in society, the radical negativity and unrecoverable (but crucial) violence that occurs between sacrificer and victim, [or ultimately,] between two opposing ideological forces that collide head on. But the question always returns: what will be the political manifestation of the squandered energy or sacrifice in society?" (*ibid*. xii-xiii). Stoekl thus frames "the trouble with the idea of heaven" (Stevens).

The New World context of Paz's *Conjunctions and Disjunctions* relates the utopian expense of spirit and the extravagance of its politics to a "proud and excremental squandering"; for historically, it was one in which Spain extracts gold from the Indies in "rites of perdition and waste," and of "sacrifice and defecation." The extraction was "at first from the altars of the devil [from pre-Columbian temples, that is] and later from the bowels of the earth. In both cases, it is a product of the lower world, the dominion of barbarians, Cyclopes, and the body." In the end, "gold [is] more twilight than dawn because of the advancing shadow." Far from engendering a golden age, this g(u)ilt-edged pursuit of the ideal leads to "a sort of fabulous privy, except that now the operation does not consist in the retention of gold but in its dispersion. The dominant tone is not moral but mythical" when the "solar metal" spreads over "the fields of Europe in the form of senseless wars and mad undertakings, [of] a proud excremental squandering of gold, blood, and passion: a monstrous, methodical orgy that is mindful of the ritual destruction of the American Indians" (24). Elsewhere, the negations in the paradisiac produce, severally, the Golden Age of silver and piss that *Concierto barroco* limns; the "poetry of corruption" that Little Aberlon becomes in Lamming's *Natives of My Person*; and the *dépense*, the economy of excess, into which Carpentier's *Explosion in a Cathedral* translates the Indies of Pointe-à-Pitre, where "gold glittered in the sun, in a reckless stream of *louis*, quadruples, British Guineas, and Portuguese '*moedas*,' stamped with the effigies of John V, Queen Mary and Pedro III." In effect, the Golden House (Langgässer) that "discoverie" and "plantation" built in the Indies explains the early-modern City Utopian that Lamming's narrative presents to us in a Kingdom of Lime Stone that had "grown fabulous with the rewards of adventure."

> Half the fortunes of the trading vessels were concentrated [in Little Aberlon]. . . . The taverns multiplied overnight. Men deserted their homes and congregated all day under the marquees. . . . They drank amidst a loud and repetitive licentiousness. Fortunes flooded their throats. . . . Affairs of state were conducted from the beds of concubines. Negotiations or the fitting of ships were sealed by the passing of a rumour. One slip of paper had the power of winds to sail men to conquest of lands they had never seen. (*Natives of My Person* 259)

Point-à-Pitre refracts the surplus back to an Indies, and in a century of lights, no less, that was fabulous enough to make it hard to believe that even the Mexico of *Concierto barroco* could be comparable, notwithstanding its goldsmiths and silversmiths. It is in this Point-à-Pitre that "gold glittered in the sun, in a reckless stream of *louis*, quadruples, British guineas, and Portuguese '*moedas*'." In addition, what with erstwhile small shopkeepers turned outfitters to privateers or otherwise associated into companies and partnerships,

> The old India Companies, with their coffers and jewel cases, were being revived here in this remote extremity of the Caribbean Sea, where the Revolution [French] was making many people happy in a very real sense. The folios of the register of captures had been swelled by the inscription of the five hundred and eighty ships, of all types and ports of embarkations, which had been boarded,

sacked and towed back by the squadrons. *(Explosion in a Cathedral* 197)

Soyinka's *The Road* and its subversion of the City Utopian undergird my line of thinking here, precisely because we are quite some distance removed from that City of the *Argonautenfahrt* and its celebration of a quest that "built Vineta, built Troy, built Jerusalem." With him we leave the city that has stood from "time immemorial" and according to whose measures "all other cities had been secretly patterned." For she it was who "did not age [and] was without blemish," and who, "beloved of the creator, had been called "my fair one, my dove, my cedar and palm." Absent any such embrace, Soyinka grounds the premise and its icons in the convergence that *The Road* makes of topography (shack that has been cobbled out of the back of a *bolekaja*— mammy wagon—, lop-sided and minus its wheels), revelation (cross-surmounted steeple tapering out of sight), and language (*AKSIDENT STORE— ALL PART AVAILEBUL*). The ramshackle configuration of wreckage and asylum confirms even as it subverts the utopian assurance that chaos can be translated into cosmos. For all that language promises a "golden nugget on the tongue," Soyinka's Professor is obsessed by evidence that "there are dangers in the Quest"; that "the Word may be found companion not to life, but Death" (1974a:156,186). The drama insists on the impossibility of governing the commonwealth at all, much less its being governed "with such perfection / T'excel the golden age." Implosion thus accounts for the "thin air" and "baseless fabric" into which any and all such visions of covenant and contract melt; and as a result of which "cloud-capp'd towers, the gorgeous palaces, / The solemn temples, the great globe itself" dissolve, as they must, into "insubstantial pageant" (*The Tempest* IV.i.150-156). "My old brain is troubled," Prospero says, when *he* dissolves his pageant into nothing, leaving "not a rack behind." Of course, he does so in the certainty of restoration: of "calm seas, auspicious gales"—and of "sail so expeditious" into History and ideal governance (V.i.315-317). Because Soyinka's Old Man in *Madmen and Specialists* is disinclined to transcendence—witness that "cyst" in "system" and the "dog in dogma"—he dissolves thesis and antithesis in the climactic negation of his "HOLE IN THE ZERO of NOTHING." As the vernacular measures of the play will have it: "*bi o ti wa / ni yio se wa / bi o ti wa / ni yio se wa, / bi o ti wa l'atete ko se*"; in effect, "As Is Was Now / As Ever Shall Be" (1974b:244).

In quite other words, then, Soyinka plays out to the extreme the collapse of a dynamic according to which propositions pass over into and are fulfilled by their opposites. Working through Hegel, Peter Singer sounds a relevant, though redemptive, note when he explains that a "determinate negation" is "itself something"; since a "something that is the result of the discovery that a form of consciousness is inadequate, is itself a new form of consciousness" (1983:51-53). The transforming note is especially evident when "Hegel in the 1790s [talked] about man (i.e. *homo religiosus*) in terms of an eschatology that required active human participation (in a politico-teleological sense) to move it forward" (Dickey 1989:131). According to the Hegel in Alexandre Kojeve, "Man exists humanly only to the extent that he really transforms the natural and social World by his negating action and he himself changes because of this transformation; or, what is the same thing, to the extent that he transforms the World as a result of an active auto-negation of his animal or social 'innate nature'." For to "negate the given without ending in nothingness is to produce something that did not yet exist; this is precisely what is called 'creating'." In this presentation of a "real" that is so "omnipres-ent and dense," there is "nothing" but that "Nothingness" out of which "newness can penetrate into Being and exist only by taking the place of given-Being—that is, by negating it" (Kojeve 1947:222-223). Meanwhile, for the Heidegger that Paz seeks to modify in *Conjunctions and Disjunctions*, "the method of 'total nihilism' involves not so much the change of values or their devaluation as the reversal of the value of values. Denying that the suprasensible—the Idea, God, the Categorical Imperative, Progress—is the supreme value does not necessarily imply the total destruction of values but rather the appearance of a new principle as the source and basis of all values. This principle is life. And life in its most direct and aggressive form: the will to power. The essence of life is will, and will expresses itself as power" (Paz 1974:119). *Madmen and Specialists* moves along a somewhat parallel path; but then, it veers off into a counterpoint in which satirical panache and a greater cynicism do not allow for any translation of "*something*, another thing," into Terrestrial Paradise. Only the likes of Columbus could believe that such a place could exist, even if it had to do so "outside the known world, beyond Asia, in the unknown ocean surrounding all land masses" (West and Kling 1991:18).

All the same, and to make summary use of the Foucault in Gloria House's study of place and power: "A whole 'history of spaces' could be written, that would at the same time be a 'history of the forms of power,' from the major strategies of geopolitics to the tactics of housing, [and] institutional archtecture." For which reason, we must "cease to think that space merely predetermines a particular history which in turn reorganizes it through its own sedimentation" (1991:4-5). Marin plays out his "utopics" in relevant fashion when he points out that "To live in utopia means constructing the represen-tation which will speak its impossibility and simultaneously indicate it as that which it excludes." Now, he explains, "we can understand the despair that accompanies all utopic representations: the instant of prediction, the moment of good news and time outside of the time of pure difference is broadcast in the time of mourning" (*ibid.* xxvi). The times-to-come of a "public universal happiness" had been less ambiguously accommodated, of course, as is clear from the summation that we get in Keith Thomas's review of such matters: "Works like *Christianopolis* or *New Atlantis* were, in this view, "witty ficions" and "mere chimeras," "airy castles and "romantic whimsies": "Perfection was impossible in this world, went the chorus. Human nature could never be reformed and if one evil was eliminated another would spring up in its place. 'Dream not of other worlds', said Milton's Angel to Adam" (1987:43).

Stephen Baehr makes the generic point elsewhere that the terrain of the ideal has included "the land of the Hyperboreans (etymologically 'beyond the North')" (1991:10). It has also been a place enclosed or rendered difficult of access, even in the pre-lapsarian Eden of *Paradise Lost*. Needless to say, Augustine's City of God had been no easier to get into, and More's Renaissance Island was reachable only after crossing the waters that surround it. In other measures, paradise is hemmed in by high mountains, like the ones that surround the Eldorado of Voltaire's *Candide*. "Frequently, womb symbols and other symbols of birth, rebirth, or beginning, were used," Baehr writes in a discussion of disequilibrium in the language of paradise. At any rate, after depicting this return to beginnings, "many works portrayed (either implicitly or explicitly) a complete absence of time, for without time chaos and evil (i.e. change for the worse) could not be." Baehr's survey of the theological import of such enclaves is equally suggestive when it calls attention to a corollary idealization of boundary and containment. He notes that the taxonomy usually calls for a mode of differentiation in which "the words 'mine' and 'yours' were frequently associated with the undesirable and the word 'ours' with the good, just as 'we' usually predominated over 'I'." As a consequence, the individual was marked as 'good' only to the extent that he or she fulfilled the norms and needs of the community." There is a symptomatic con/fusion of attributes, too, in the paradisial "return of androgynous beings (unifying both sexes in themselves as Adam supposedly had before the creation of Eve)"; and of an alchemy that would "restore base metals to gold (through a process called *coniunctio* or the unification of male and female opposites)" (9-10). Still, Baehr rightly makes much of the fact that the utopian "ideal" is in principle always separated from the world of contingent reality "by some physical or symbolic boundary that provides an ethical demarcation." The primary "lexical and syntactic patterns" of the motif have been variously strengthened by "ancillary themes, motifs, and images," as much by way of

Montaigne's New World cannibals as by "the ascendancy of an architecture over the horticulture of Paradise—given the essential vulnerability of the unenclosed garden" (Hunt 1987:135). Other ancillary themes have ranged from postulations of a "prelapsarian language to the assumption of an *axis mundi* in the form of a tree, mountain, or cosmic pillar connecting, and hence unifying, heaven and earth" (Baehr 1991:9). By the same token, witness New's reading of the Happy Valley in *Rasselas*, Baehr notes that "many anti-utopias have created irony by having a narrator recite surface panegyrics to a 'paradisal' state that context subsequently shows to be a totalitarian hell" that is, indeed, very much enclosed in its architecture of the ideal (*ibid.*).

In the end, it is virtually the entirety of this "reservoir of paradisal motifs" about good times and ideal enclaves, interchangeable by the eighteenth century, that the Wallace Stevens of *The Palm at the End of the Mind* (1972) empties out in his "Sunday Morning." He does so in a reprise that is directly aimed at both the primary and ancillary images that Baehr identifies when he points out that by the eighteenth century utopian spaces no longer signified differently whether the labels identified paradise or peaceable kingdom; Elysium or Fortunate Islands; or whether by the golden age was meant Eden, Arcadia, or Hesperides (2). It is this ensemble of idealizations that Stevens's secessionist lines bring under erasure, representing it as "Seraphic proclamations of the pure / Delivered with a deluging onwardness," in "The Comedian as the Letter C." As a result, by "Sunday Morning" the paradisiac no longer lies in "silent Palestine, / Dominion of the blood and sepulchre"; nor does it do so

> in any haunt of prophecy,
> Nor any old chimera of the grave
> Neither the golden underground, nor isle
> Melodious, where spirits gat them home. (1972:6)

When the imperfect is our paradise utopian transcendence can hardly be as discoverable as it once was in some "visionary south, [or] cloudy palm / Remote on heaven's hill." Given, as above, the Gulf of Paria and the apparent re-entry into Eden that it once allowed Columbus's *Book of Prophecies*, this certainty that paradise is certifiably lost, or unregainable, was not always the case, of course. After all, man's progress had been landmarked by a route that led from the Garden of Eden at one end of time to the City of God at the other. Thus, pedigrees of subversion and goodness-of-fit make it appropriate to once again recall that it was in his third-voyage reports to king (1498) and pope (1502) that Columbus had famously engendered that image of a female-bodied hemisphere which "has the shape of a pear, which is everywhere very round, except where the stalk is, for there it is very prominent [and] placed something like a woman's nipple." This part, he had declared, "where the protuberance is found, is the highest and nearest to the sky. I call that 'the end of the East' where end all the land and islands" (Colon 1987:30; O'Gorman 1961:96-99; West and Kling 1991:67-68). Succinctly put, the utopian bent and its reach for paradise required that "There was, there had to be, it was essential that at any given moment there should be, a Better World. The Caribs had conceived of this Better World in their own terms, just as in his turn Ferdinand and Isabella's High Admiral had imagined it, here by the seething Dragon's Mouths" (*Explosion* 247).

Compared to what obtains in *Explosion*, the New World seduction of paradise is a decorous affair in Fitzgerald when his protagonist "gulp[s] down the incomparable milk of wonder"; when, at the end of *The Great Gatsby* to which I have already referred, "the inessential houses began to melt away" into that assurance of access to the *insulae fortunatae*. This is the context in which as the moon rose higher and higher, Nick Carraway, at once sybarite and puritan, at once anti-utopian and utopian, gradually became aware of "the old island here that flowered once for Dutch sailors' eyes—a fresh, green breast of the new world." Carraway thereupon speculates in the usual and contradictory registers: "For a transitory enchanted moment man must have held his breath in the presence of this continent, compelled into an aesthetic contemplation he neither understood nor desired"—even as, *pace* Stevens, paradise "pandered in whispers to the last and greatest of all human dreams" (140). In Carpentier, meanwhile, Columbus does come upon his "shining thought" rather more extravagantly, and it is one that finally erases his doubts. "I cannot find, nor have I found," the Admiral had once written, "any Latin or Greek author who states categorically where the Earthly Paradise is situated in this world, nor have I seen it marked on any map" (246). But of course this was all before the Gulf of Paria, and *Explosion*'s re-telling of its import. "Here then at the Dragon's Mouths, where the water turned transparent in the rising sun, the Admiral could shout his exultation aloud, having understood the meaning of the age-old struggle between the fresh water and the salt water." Carpentier is elaborate and baroque, and full, too, of enlightenment apostasy, when he moves to dis/confirm the issue in the template of its own prophecy: "Let the King and Queen, the Princes and all their Dominions, give thanks to our Saviour Jesus Christ who has granted us this victory," his Admiral exults. "Let there be processions; let solemn celebrations be held; let the churches be filled with palms and flowers; let Christ rejoice on Earth, as there is rejoicing in Heaven, to think that salvation is at hand for so many people hitherto consigned to damnation." For this voyage to "the Gulf of Pearls in the Land of Grace" had led to this discovery of a shape "at the tip of whose nipple grew the Tree of Life." In sum, "the prophecies of the Prophets had been fulfilled, the divinations of the ancients and the inspired intimations of the theologians confirmed," after "an agonising wait of so many centuries" (*ibid.*).

Meanwhile, Stevens's retreat from so overwrought a "visionary south" and "cloudy palm / Remote on heaven's hill" had come to a circum-Caribbean climax in "Farewell to Florida." There, in a somewhat ambivalent act of exorcism he had headed away from a "sepulchral south" where "the palms were hot / as if I lived in ashen ground."

> How content I shall be in the North to which I sail
> And to feel sure and to forget the bleaching sand.
>   . . . carry me
> To the cold, go on, high ship, go on, plunge on. (1972:126)

In thus heading towards an ultimate "palm at the end of the mind," itself a revisionist version of Hyperborean ("beyond the North") narratives of migration to an Empire of the North (*Explosion*), Stevens bids adieu to a world of "convolvulvus and coral / buzzards and live-moss" which, "lasciviously as the wind," had been "tormenting" and "insatiable" in "O Florida, Venereal Soil." This suffocating sensuousness had not been much diminished in "Fabliau of Florida" in which, so it seemed, there would "never be an end" to the "droning of the surf"; to a landscape of "night blues" and "sultry moon-monsters"; of "black hull" and "white moonlight" (46-47). With its "big-finned palm / and green vine angering for life," the torments of "Nomad Exquisite" were no less radiant with "immense dew"; with all that "flinging" about so of "forms, flames, and flakes of forms" (44). Stevens also grounds this pursuit of the paradisiac, and a relevant clustering of circum-Caribbean themes, in the mock-epic through which "The Comedian as the Letter C" rediscovers the New World and the "idea of a colony." Here, and in that discounting of "Seraphic proclamations of the pure / Delivered with a deluging onwardness," the language of and desire for paradise are ultimately reduced to continent measures of "jollified" things" (74). In effect, "odd discoverer" that Crispin is, he surrenders the emblematic and the baroque to the skepticism of Voltaire's Candide, "yeoman and grub, but with a fig in sight" (71). "So may the relation of each man be clipped" is the conclusion to which "The Comedian as the Letter C" then comes (75), having "concocted doctrine from [the] rout" of yet another pursuit of the best of all possible worlds. This is the context in which Stevens brings the voyage of his discoverer to an end. Crispin abandons "mere blusteriness that gewgaws jollified, [and] abates in taste [from] a fancy gorged / By apparition." Having begun "with green brag / [but] concluding fadedly," he surrenders to the "illumination of plain and common things."

> The world, a turnip once so readily plucked
> Sacked up and carried overseas, daubed out
> Of its ancient purple, pruned to the fertile main,
> [Was] sown again by the stiffest realist.

Before it settles on this move into a calmer north, "The Comedian" had variously invoked "Maya sonneteers," "Caribbean amphitheatre," and radiant "Atlantic coign." There had thus been suggestions of that Yucatan where Fray Diego de Landa and his *autos da fe* had demonstrated to "the Indians through their own wincing flesh [the redemptive value of] 'a willingness to become good Christians'"—while their "priests and lords twisted and moaned, as surrendered idols burned" (Clendinnen 1995a:118). In the baroque phase of Crispin's experience of discovery, his consciousness of place, like Columbus's in *The Harp and the Shadow*, had been made "vivid with the sea," and by a "polyphony" that was "beyond [the] baton's thrust," even if it all risked being dissolved, being "washed away by [a] magnitude" that spanned "a rumbling, west of Mexico." The concommitantly subversive, or, if you wish, *Te deum*, experience in "The Comedian as the Letter C" allowed for "dissertation of delight" and "green barbarism [turned] paradigm"; so, too, for a *concierto barroco* of sorts in which the "wind" came "bluntly thundering, more terrible / Than the revenge of music on bassoons." And all this engendered,

> In beak and bud and fruity goblet-skins,
> [An] earth [that] was like a jostling festival
> Of seeds grown fat, too juicily opulent,
> Expanding in the gold's maternal warmth. (58-63)

Anthony Pagden has observed with some saliency that "imagined states" will always, where the only option is a realism without a reality, be in danger of becoming 'a world that is in some sense fantastic, that can be made to justify the past and authorize the future'" (158). Such a premise helps to acount as much for that "mountain on a mountain," the Citadel La Ferriere in *The Kingdom of This World,* as it does for the Creek of Deception where Lamming inverts the architecture of the City Utopian and subverts the assurance of ideal governance. It is on *Natives of My Person*'s Demon Coast that Master Cecil— whose "cause," so he believed, "the future would purify"—leaned over to limn the contours of yet another utopia. He was "begging the stones and the grass to tunnel his message underground," where the Tribes had sought refuge from the terror of his discovery of them: "They had no reason to resist. With a little luck he would put the gifts of the Kingdom at their service; correct their tongues, which knew no language; introduce them to some style of living"

(71). In short, "Lunacy, he was warning the sulphur peaks of the cliff, it was lunacy to desecrate such gifts with an open insult, to resist. The Kingdom would ask no more than a painless subjection to a contract that would leave them free. . . . Nothing would change except increase of crops, which the natural vegetation now conceals." Unless, of course, rejecting the brave new world, the tribes continued their "insult underground" (71).

Meanwhile, it is from Henri Christophe's Haitian Citadel, with its "lush growth of red fungi mounting the flanks of the main tower" (Carpentier 1970:20), that Carpentier (1949), the Martinican Césaire (1963), the Colombian Enrique Buenaventura (1963), and the St. Lucian Walcott (1970) derive utopian sign and surplus in, respectively, *El reino de este mundo*, *La tragédie du roi Christophe*, *La tragédia del Rey Christophe*, and "What the Twilight Said" (1970). This is all as it should be, of course: after all, during its construction "several bulls had [had] their throats cut" every day in the middle of the square; "so that their blood could be added to the mortar to make the fortress impregnable" (*Kingdom* 120). In figure and in sum, the Citadel was both historical and concrete and *eu-topos* and *ou-topos*. In the "bowels" of the "vast edifice" that it was being set to become "hundreds of men worked, [always] under the vigilance of whip and gun, accomplishing feats seen only in the imagined architecture" of Giambattista Piranesi's *Carceri d'invenzione* (*Imaginary Prisons*).

> Hoisted by ropes up the face of the mountain, the first cannons were arriving and being mounted on cedar gun-carriages in shadowy vaulted rooms whose loopholes overlooked all the passes and approaches of the country. There stood the *Scipio*, the *Hannibal*, the *Hamilcar*, satin smooth, of a bronze that was almost gold in hue, [and] several of a larger bore and more ornate barrel, stamped with seal of the Sun King insolently proclaiming his *Ultima Ratio Regum*. (*ibid.* 121)

But then, Carpentier explains, "I was standing on soil where thousands of men, desiring freedom, believed in the lycanthropical powers of Macandal, and to such a degree that that faith produced a miracle on the day of his execution."

> I had breathed in the atmosphere created by Henri Christophe, a monarch of incredible endeavors, much more surprising than all the cruel kings that the surrealists invented, very susceptible as they were to imaginary tyrannies, though not actually suffered. I discovered "marvelous realism" [*lo real maravilloso*] at every step of the way.

Meanwhile, and as counterpoint to that ancillary image of the City Utopian as "fair one, my dove, my cedar and palm" (*The Quest*), there is a telling otherness to the figures around which the terrains and types of the century of lights unbecome themselves in *Explosion in a Cathedral*. For here, Langgässer's "Beloved of Heaven, beloved of the earth, mysterious rose" assumes darkly sensual shades with *mulatas*, for example, who could play out fresh articulations of an ancient promiscuity in the gesture and language of knotted headdresses whose "three-pointed madras" proclaimed, "I've still got room for you." The cluster of effects is nowhere more exposed than in the constellation that Carpentier's *Explosion* makes of Pointe-à-Pitre's mosquitoes and Mademoiselle Athalie Bajazet, *mulata* and *coiffeuse pour dames* (160-61); so, too, of the French Revolution and a Caribbean Place de la Victoire from which the guillotine had been removed—"The boards were brushed and scrubbed to remove all traces of blood"—so that its platform could be converted into a theatre. At the end of the performance of Jean-Jacques's *The Village Soothsayer*, into which some couplets had been improvised in the spirit of the Revolution, there were shouts of enthusiasm. In response, Carpentier writes, the Finale had to be repeated five times (203). It was to this New World performance of revolutionary visions about utopia from the Old World that "a sparkling, transformed Mademoiselle Athalie Bajazet [had come], flashing spangles, and stark naked under a Greek tunic in the very latest fashion." But then, determinate negation, it had proceeded to rain hard, and with far too contraindicative a *tropicalismo*:

> [As a result,] Mademoiselle Athalie Bajazet, after taking off her classical-style sandals, pulled her Greek tunic up to her thighs in order to wade through the puddles left by the previous day's rain. Finally, increasingly alarmed at the risk of being splashed with mud, she pulled the dress right over her head, and left it rolled up on her shoulders. "It's hot tonight," she said, by way of an excuse, swatting the mosquitoes which were attacking her buttocks. (*ibid.* 204)

Carpentier's displays of the female body as Land-in-Waiting are on the whole quite supple, as will become evident in the next section. "We need women. Don't you agree?": this question of Victor Hugues's in *Explosion* arouses the narrative to an appropriate remembrance of bodies past. The century-of-lights context of the response that we get also carries with it suggestions of that catalogue of effects with which the Marquis de Sade had contributed his share, too, to the Enlightenment. For the men of *Explosion* had known "Rosamund, of course, the German girl of the Palais Royal; or Zaïre, of the

Voltairean name; or Dorinna, with her pink muslin dresses; or that entresol where, for a payment of two *louis*, one was offered in succession the variegated skills of Angélique, Zephire, Zoé, Esther and Zilia, who each embodied a different feminine type." These women "comported themselves—in strict observance of dramatic ritual which accorded magnificently with the character of their beauty—as frightened virgins, dissolute bourgeoises, fallen ballet-dancers, a Mauritian Venus (this was Esther) or a drunken Bacchante (that was Zilia)." After having been the object of the "expert attentions of these feminine archetypes, the visitor was thrown into the firm lap of Aglaé, she of the "high pointed breasts and chin of a queen of antiquity whose person always quenched, in peerless manner, the ascending scale of one's desires" (121-122). When not the *mulatas* of Amado's *Shepherds of the Night*—with its *nouveau monde amoureux* "proverb": "A man cannot sleep with all the women in the world, but he should try"—other objects of desire are black women "whose buttocks [jut] out like choirstalls," in "The Road to Santiago," and who, when they appear in *Explosion*, only do so to be "ringed" by "aggressive concupiscence."

Still, there is the sedate virgin, Beloved of God, that the Caribbean and its sea of islands had once seemed ready to become in *Explosion* when, "with a leap of some thousands of years," the New World's "Mediterranean Sea had become the heir of the other Mediterranean, and received the Christian Laying of Hands" (244-245). It was then that those "islands, islands, islands" of *The Harp and the Shadow* had engendered the image which Carpentier re-maps in *Explosion* as a constellation of the "whitened . . . coralliferous labyrinth of the Eleven Thousand Virgins—as impossible to count as the *Campus Stellae*." But then, in his "pourtraicte" of "Madame Ste Ursule" and her "unze mille vierges," Stevens had in fact fleshed out the virgin and "the good lord in his garden" to special effect. He had done so in a world whose new testament could not be "writ / In any book," not surprisingly; for it was in a spot "where none can see" that Ste Ursule had made "Him" an offering "in the grass / Of radishes and flowers" (1972:3). She weeps, though, for fear that the Lord would not accept, preferring instead the "marguerite and coquelicot, / And roses / Frail as April snow" which she had left, "My dear / Upon your altars." The making of the paradisial in "Cy Est Pourtraicte, Madame Ste Ursule, et les Unze Mille Vierges" is thereafter engendered on other than orthodox grounds when

> The good Lord in His garden sought
> New leaf and shadowy tinct,
> And they were all his thought.

But then, "He heard her low accord, / Half prayer and half ditty, / And He felt a subtle quiver." When the Lord enters this virgin Land-in-Waiting, "What he felt was not heavenly love, / Or pity," and therefore, says Stevens, is not Writ (*ibid:*3-4).

Whether the quest is in Langgässer's City Utopian, in Carpentier's "choirstalls," or else in Columbus's "there had been only one woman for me in the world" (*The Harp and the Shadow*), it is not especially surprising, of course, that discovery, access, and dominion are so instrusively played out on the body of the woman. There is a certain conceptual logic, for example, in the language in which C. L. R. James and Herman Melville coincide to celebrate amplitude and engendering in the New World; in their shared view that "We are not a narrow tribe of men," since "our blood is as the flood of the Amazon, made up of a thousand noble currents all pouring into one. We are not a nation, so much as a world." Citing the thought from the Melville of *Redburn,* which he makes the epigraph in his *Mariners, Renegades, and Castaways* (1953), James thus celebrates a writer of the "Americas" who had lodged himself in a vast increase where he sought nothing less than to span "the universe [and grope] down into the bottom of the sea where he [would have] his hands 'among the unspeakable foundations, ribs, and very pelvis of the world'" (103).

Meanwhile, about the genre of governance that More's *Utopia* represents, Marijke Rudnik-Smalbraak's "reflections about and explorations of women and utopia" make the necessary observation that "women and their concerns play" a primarily "subordinate role in Utopia's strictly patriarchal organisation. For although every utopian, irrespective of sex, works at farming and is taught special trade, and both sexes are given military training, authority within the household plainly resides with the man." That being the case, "equality" can go only so far; thus, before Utopia's religious feasts, for example, "wives kneel down at home before their husbands. . . . to confess their sins . . . and ask to be forgiven"—with the husbands "needing no such domestic cleansing" on their part (1987:175). For his part, Bernal Díaz's *The Conquest of New Spain* had been casual but full of consequence with regard to La Malinche. Before proceeding any further, and before even giving an account of Montezuma himself, Díaz wrote, "I should like to say that in every town we passed through and in others that had only heard of us, they called Cortés Malinche, and I shall call him by this name henceforth in recording any conversations he had with Indians, both in this province [Tlascala] and in the city of Mexico, and I shall only call him Cortés in such places as it may be proper. The reason why he received this name was that Doña Marina was always with him, especially when he was visited by ambassadors or *Caciques,* and she always spoke to them in the Mexican language. So they gave Cortés the name of 'Marina's Captain,' which was shortened to Malinche" (172).

This woman from Paynala, about twenty four miles from Coatzacoaloc, knew the language of Coatzacoaloc, which is that of Mexico; and the Tabascan language, too, which is common to Tabasco and Yucatan. She was "a good interpreter in all the wars of New Spain, Tlascala, and New Mexico," and was thus positioned at "the great beginning of our conquests"; for which reason, "praise be to God, all things prospered with us." Díaz makes a point of foregrounding her role because, he explains, "without Doña Marina we could not have understood the language of New Spain and Mexico" (66). Inga Clendinnen's *Aztecs* recognizes this grounding of the "disquieting Doña Marina" in the business of men when she discusses the role of the Aztec *tlatoani* ("He Who Speaks"). "The conquest," Clendinnen writes, "was a male affair, at least in the male telling of it. Women had no right to speak on [Aztec] high public occasions, and this in a polity in which the highest office was that of *tlatoani* ('He Who Speaks'). (Hence the perturbation at the physical prominence and verbal dominance of Doña Marina, Cortés's native interpreter, during Spanish negotiations with native lords)" (156; 157).

Eviatar Zerubavel has quite sensibly pointed out that "America was not discovered on a single day by Columbus (or anyone else, for that matter)," so apparent are the tropological superimpositions that everywhere merged to translate the Land-in-Waiting from *terra incognita* into *terra cognita*—into the "mirage, myth and actual shore" of the "barracoons" of the Florida in Robert Hayden's "Middle Passage" as well that "virgin of boorish birth" and "womb" of the "dreadful sundry of the world," in Wallace Stevens. Terrains and types are signally embodied, then, in the voice of that "she" whose singing makes the world articulate through the "ghostlier demarcations, keener sounds" of Stevens's Key West. From that circum-Caribbean lands-end Stevens had once recognized the "rage" for "order" and "origins" within and yet beyond "theatrical distances, bronze shadows heaped / on high horizon, mountainous atmospheres / of sky and sea" (1972:98). For his part, when Zerubavel points to origins and evolution he foregrounds "glaring epistemo-logical" voids in the discourse about the European discovery of America, underscoring the point that "very little actually happened in 1492" itself (1992:x). In effect, *Terra Cognita* rightly proposes that the making of America was a "long, slow process which lasted almost three hundred years" (5), and that "October 12, 1492, marked the beginning of a long mental voyage that was *fully completed* only in the late eighteenth century" (*ibid*. 5; my emphasis). The premise reads better, of course, from being nuanced by the turbulent commerce in gold, god, and prophecy that Carpentier limns in *The Harp and the Shadow*; so, too, from contemplating the idea of "discovery" that Edmundo O'Gorman famously elaborated in *The Invention of America* (1961), and for which he crafted his allegory of the Caretaker and the Professor:

Let us suppose that the caretaker of an archive comes across an ancient papyrus in a cellar. The next day he brings it to the attention of a professor of classical literature, who after careful study realizes it is a hitherto unknown text by Aristotle. Who is the discoverer of this document, the caretaker who found it or the professor who identified it? It is evident that if we consider in Kingston's re-vision of such encounters with fabulous alterity it as a physical object, a mere piece of papyrus, the caretaker is the discoverer. . . . It is equally evident, however, that if we are considering the document as an original text by Aristotle, the discoverer would be the professor, since it was he who was aware of the nature of its contents. (15)

The title of the historicized allegory that opens Maxine Hong Kingston's *China Men* is "On Discovery." The formality of the title is an ironic echo of a recognizable genre of texts. It also opens a prologue in which Kingston re-contextualizes the male telling and (en)gendering of the Land-in-Waiting. "Once upon a time," we learn in her opening move, "a man named Tang Ao, looking for the Gold Mountain, crossed an ocean, and came upon the Land of Women. . . . In the Women's Land there are no taxes and no wars. Some scholars say that that country was discovered during the reign of Empress Wu (A.D. 694-705), and some say earlier than that, A.D. 441, and that it was in North America" (3-4). Soon enough, Kingston's women make a fully heuristic point of preparing the discoverer to meet their queen. In the process, "On Discovery" resonates with pre-texts and dis/affiliations that relate as much to European "discoverie" and tales of Amazons as they do to the "Old Gold Mountain" narratives that K. Scott Wong identifies in, say, "The *Shan Hai Jing* (Classic of Mountains and Oceans)," an anonymous, illustrated compilation that appeared sometime during the Zhou or Han periods (sixth century B.C. to first century A.D.). This "oldest traveller's guide in the world"—with its "images of the Chinese as paragons of the true human social being"—is one that purports to describe lands and peoples well beyond the borders of China (1996:205-207). Gender-inflected as it is, Kingston's Land of Women re-configures and re-presents Tang Ao's discovery of fabulous alterity to quite telling effect:

They locked him in a canopied apartment equipped with pots of makeup, mirrors, and a woman's clothes. "Let us help you off with your armor and boots," said the women. They slipped his coat off his shoulders, pulled it down his arms, and shackled his wrists behind him. The women who had kneeled to take off his shoes chained his ankles together. . . . The women who sat on him

turned their attention to his feet. They bent his toes so far
backward that his arched foot cracked. The old ladies squeezed
each foot and broke many tiny bones along the sides. They
gathered his toes over and under one another like a knot of ginger
root. Tang Ao wept with pain. As they wound the bandages tight
and tighter around his feet, the women sang footbinding songs to
distract him: "Use aloe for binding feet and not for scholars." (3)

It is in *The Star-Apple Kingdom* that Walcott is summarily dramatic about the
male affairs in and the male telling of such matters; so, too, about related
issues in the discussion that follows next. Walcott's imagery conjoins female
body and Land-in-Waiting in an especially "negative imprint of domination"
(Pfaelzer); for it is one in which, succinctly, the woman's "sex was the slit
throat / of an Indian" (1988:51). Meanwhile, Gayl Jones's "sort of" hermit-
woman makes a no less consequential point—with its "I am an explorer too,
/ but I stay in one place, / and strangers come to me, / like bears to wild honey"
(*Hermit-Woman* 1983).

Placed Something Like a Woman's Nipple

[The men] all displayed a restlessness which was not wholly due to the
satisfaction of having reached the end of a prosperous voyage; waiting on the
shore at the foot of that mountain, whose outline was growing clearer now
against the high cordillera, was Woman—unknown, almost abstract Woman,
still without a face, but prefigured already by the proximity of port. [All the
while] a fabulous smell, of the humidity of a continent not yet properly awake,
came still from [the] waters, where the seed from the sea was about to be
washed up by a vast last thrust from the waves.
        Alejo Carpentier, *Explosion in a Cathedral*

        I cross my hands over breasts
        that are no longer there...

        I lay on my back,
        put my hands over my breasts.
        "I thought my breasts were gone.
        The soldier [cut them off]."
                Gayl Jones, *Song for Anninho*

Women, Fire, and Dangerous Things is the productive title under which George Lakoff makes the observation that "Metonymy is one of the basic characteristics of cognition. It is extremely common for people to take one well-understood or easy-to-perceive aspect of something and use it to stand either for the thing as a whole or for some other aspect or part of it" (1987:77). For my purposes here, there are entire archives—and catalogues enough—of what Carpentier's *The Lost Steps* will elsewhere refer to as "the female principle, genesial, womb, to be found in the secret prologue to all theogonies." There have been New World measures of the same, too, in Columbus's "woman's nipple" view of the Terrestrial Paradise, in Nick Carraway's "fresh, green breast of the New World" in *The Great Gastby*, and in the "woman's tit" version of the same in Carpentier's reprise of the Columbus story in *The Harp and the Shadow*. Other (en)genderings of terrain and type in what follows will be played out in the cultural politics of the Mesoamerican Virgen de Guadalupe in Norma Alarcón's "Traduttora, Traditora" as well as in the "meta-archipelagic" Virgen del Cobre of Benítez-Rojo's *The Repeating Island*. There will be New World and syncretist virgins, too, in the Mariolatry of that Okotbatam liturgy which Alfonso Villa records among the Maya of east central Quintana Roo. Its introit invokes "*Kanleox, señora hermosa*" (beautiful lady, Kanleox), "*hermosa señora Magdalena*," and "*hermosa señora Guadalupe*" as intercessory figures with *Señor Díos*. Thereafter, the Roman Catholic and the Mayan merge in an offering of flesh and fruit:

> I deliver to your right hands these virgin thirteen breads
> and the virgin nine-breads, and the virgin eight-breads
> and the virgin seven-breads, and the thirteen bowls
> and the virgin large breads, and the virgin first offering.
> (1947:160)

There is, too, the *chingada* that the Amerindian woman has become, ever since Cortés, for the "sons of La Malinche" in the Paz of *El laberinto de la solitude*. For its part, "The Indies! Ah! The Indies" of Carpentier's "The Road to Santiago" *(The War of Time)* will have the likes of Doña Yolufa, "whose buttocks," so we learn, "jutted out like choirstalls." As laid out in *Chronicle of a Death Foretold*, meanwhile, Gabriel García Márquez's circum-Caribbean is as much Arab-Caribbean as it is the "main harbor mouth at Cartagena de Indias." Here, we map bodies private and politic that are numinous things—a "trickle of light from the Saint Elmo's fire in the cemetery, the sad swamps, and the phosphorescent line of the Caribbean on the horizon"—and hard commerce: Santiago Nasar "pointed to an intermitent light at sea and told us that it was the soul in torment of a slave ship that had sunk with a cargo of blacks from Senegal" (1982:77). When daylight breaks in *The Autumn of the Patriarch*, with that "rare visible splendor which precedes the imminent rising of the sun in the Caribbean," Márquez's latitudes converge on a certain "slave platform" and "nightmare beauty." Although still very much touched by the erotic, the Antillean *negra* shades off here into darkly moral oscillations, exposing the "terrible temptation of the black flesh" (Lamming), especially the female. For in the Patriarch's *Autumn*, the splendor rises only to fall on a "former slave platform still in use where on another Wednesday of another time in the nation before him they had sold at public auction a captive Senegalese woman who brought more than her own weight in gold because of her nightmare beauty" (180).

The epigraph from Gayl Jones's *Song for Anninho* (1981) re-embodies a history of New World dis-membering, and does so with considerable intensity. But then, significance of a complex sort does attach to Almeyda's breasts being cut off and thrown away, accomplished as the mutilation was during the destruction of the maroon stronghold of Palmares (1612-1694), the circumstances under which *Song* articulates its constellation of woman, fire, and dangerous things. The times are therefore the last days of that *quilombo* African state in Brazil during which it was finally conquered, a process that was completed when Zambi was taken alive, decapitated on November 20, 1695, and his head publicly displayed to dispel the legend that he was immortal. From *Hermit-Woman*, Jones provides other details of a time of "the sword / within the rage and outrage." It is here that her "Machete Woman" tells us that "In 1637 [she] took sanctuary / in a nun's convent"; that she contemplated "horror / because it is there"; because

> It is a crime for an African
> to cut down a tree,
> or to ride a horse,
> or to own a print shop.
> It is a crime to work with gold or silk.
> It is a crime to pick fruit,
> or to wear a cape, or to sell wine.
> It is a crime to sew lace,
> to make candles.
> 50 lashes, 100 lashes, 200 lashes,
> genitals gone, mutilation, death. (1983:68)

The destruction proper of Palmares was accomplished between February 5th and 6th, 1694. It came after a twenty-day siege by Domingo Jorge Velho, field-master of the regiment of the Paulistas, and resulted in the capture and

Brazilian re-enslavement of most of the inhabitants who, at one point, numbered over twenty thousand (Nuñez 1980:370-710; Price 1979). In the *real maravilloso* narrative that Carpentier's *Explosion in a Cathedral* makes of the facts, "The Palisade of the Palm Trees established in the heart of the Brazilian jungle by the high chief Ganga-Zumba [was in this way destroyed after lasting] sixty-five years" (231). Before those February days of 1694 the "pliant fortification of wood and fibre [had dashed to pieces] more than twenty military expeditions, both Dutch and Portuguese, their artillery useless against a strategy which resurrected old tricks from the Numidian wars, and sometimes used animals to strike panic into the white men's hearts. Field Marshall Zumbi, the nephew of King Zumba, was invulnerable to bullets, and his men could travel across the roof of the jungle, dropping on to the enemy columns like ripe fruit" (*ibid.*). This is the torrid zone into which Jones's *Song* drops the female body, and in proof of which Almeyda has her breasts cut off and tossed into a river: "The battle of Palmares / ended, we escaped; Portuguese soldiers / caught us at the river." The inability, or the refusal, of her memory to "go beyond that" is supplemented by Zibatra who found

> "Only the globes of your breasts
> floating in the river.
> I wrapped them decently and hid them." (11)

By way of summary, then: Derek Walcott's *The Star-Apple Kingdom* makes a heuristic composite of the women, fire, and other dangerous things that interest me here. For with him, we come upon "black umbrella blown inside out"; on "La Madre Dolorosa / a black rose of sorrow, a black mine of silence / raped wife, empty mother, Aztec virgin." This figure is also a "she" who is "transfixed by arrows from a thousand guitars," and whose "sex" is, *tout court*, "the slit throat of an Indian." She is a "stone full of silence" which, "if it gave tongue to the tortures done in the name of the Father," as Phyllis Trible's *Texts of Terror* reading of certain biblical models does below, "would curdle the blood of the marauding wolf" (Walcott 1979:51-52).

My contexts are such, then, that, in addition to Lakoff's highly suggestive title, I find considerable value in the epigraph that Marina Warner makes of Artemidorus's thought that "In dreams a writing tablet signifies a woman, since it receives the imprint of all kinds of letters," this in her study of allegories of the female form, *Monuments and Maidens* (1985). The same is true of the degree of interest that Warner shows in the exceptionalist premise with which Caelius Sedulius once accounted for the Virgin Mary. It is an interest that produces an epigraph in and the title of *Alone of All Her Sex*,

Warner's study of the myth and cult of the Virgin Mary (1976). Sedulius had thus celebrated the exceptionalism of a *Mater Dei* who "had no peer / Either in our first mother or in all women / Who were to come. But alone of all her sex / She pleased the Lord." As Alarcón does when she explores the contraindicative politics of La Virgen de Guadalupe and La Malinche, Warner makes a point of underscoring the economy of representation that is involved here. "Together the Virgin and the Magdalene form a diptych of Christian patriarchy's idea of woman." There is, she adds, "no place in the conceptual architecture of Christian society for a single woman who is neither a virgin nor a whore." Christian culture is thus inclined to venerate "two ideals of the feminine—consecrated chastity in the Virgin Mary and regenerate sexuality in the Magdalene" (1976:235). In the latter days of Walcott's "Adam's Song," in *Sea Grapes*, "The adulteress stoned to death" is "still killed." For there is a sense here in which "Nothing has changed," since "men still sing the song that Adam sang / against the world he lost to vipers" (1976:13). Change registers in Juan José Arreola's Mexican *Bestiario* (1959) only because it conflates narratives of genesis into the "dense currents of maternity" with which he accounts for the "obscene rite" and "primitive alliance" that unite Adam and Eve in a new-ancient paradise lost. Adam once lived inside Eve "in an intimate paradise—imprisoned like a seed in the sweet flesh of a fruit, effective as an internal secretion, asleep like the chrysalis in a cocoon of silk, the wings of his spirit deeply folded." But then, Arreola notes, "like all fortunate ones, Adam hated his glory and sought everywhere for an exit." He therefore set out to swim "against the dense currents of maternity" and, through an "awkward tunnel," to cut "the cord of his primitive alliance." Of course, "the inhabitant and the inhabited could not quite live apart," a development that has since engendered, in Areola's words, "a ceremony full of prenatal nostalgia" that is now relived as "an intimate and obscene rite" (Fremantle 1977).

Meanwhile, Ned Ward's 1698 and quite unnostalgic appproach to the New World results in the discovery, on the island of Jamaica, of terrain and type upon which to be "*Wicked* without *Shame*," and "*Whore* without *Punishment*." Here then, Ward declared, was nothing less than *the* place where "Pandora filled her box" (Abrahams and Szwed 1983:12). With this embodiment of the shape of dangerous things, we return to a genre that Joseph's Kestner's *Mythology and Misogyny* describes as being rich in "Sirens, mermaids, nymphs, nixies, and Harpies, all images of predatory, hypersexual, terrifying females" (1989:10). We return, too, to the latter days of palimpsest and primal matter that Machado de Assis calls upon his Pandora to articulate in *The Posthumous Memoirs of Braz Cubas* (1881). In a sequence of hallucinatory experiences that range from Eden to Delirium, Braz is at first a Chinese barber shaving a Mandarin, then a deluxe, illustrated edition of St. Thomas Aquinas's *Summa Theologica*. When he finally returns to his own person, he is carried off on the back of a talking hippopotamus that travels swiftly backward through the ages—past Eden to the beginning of time, a region of eternal ice and snow. Here, "a great female creature who called herself Pandora hulked at him. She defined herself as Imperishable Nature with all things in her box, death as well as life, and her law as egoism" (Caldwell 1970:73; 88). Pandora is consequentially identified in Warner's *Monuments and Maidens* as the "prototype passive recipient of divine or male energy" at the same time that she is "an agent of calamity, a danger to men" (xxii). Her appearance in the Hesiod of *Theogony* and *Works and Days* is surrounded with dangerous significations. They include the fact that Epimetheus accepts the woman as his bride against his brother Prometheus's advice; and that her "box" releases terror on the world. Marylin Arthur's view is that in Hesiod "we come up against the earliest and most extensive formulation of the misogynistic attitude that was to become a veritable *topos* in Greek life and literature of later periods" (1973:22). In this view power in the female body is beneficial—if at all—only "when it was regulated by the male principle of order" (49). And even if we reject the symbolic association of Pandora's box with the vagina, Warner adds, "Hesiod's message [is] that sexual desire for a woman lies at the root of man's undoing" (217). Pandora thus embodies a "lethal amalgam" (Horst), being the vengeful creation of a Zeus angered by Prometheus's theft of fire. Robert ter Horst works through Calderón's several explorations of Pandora—as in *La estatua de Promoteo*—to produce a reading according to which the woman's "emanations express the cooperative duality of divinity that has come to reside among men." But then, although at first "unalloyed," the bestowals of the gift of fire and Pandora "have on closer examination a lethal amalgam already apparent to the senses in the freezing component of the rays from Pandora's touch.... Such a gift involves donor, recipent, and other interested parties in a complicated, dangerous complicity that creates a partly criminal social contract" (1982:26).

With the men of the epigraph from Carpentier's *Explosion*, we are, granted, complexly bound to a geography in which the bent for utopia requires that there be "immense esplanades, virgins' baths, and unimaginable buildings" (242). For on that "one morning" of their sea voyage in *el siglo de las luces*, in the "century of lights," the men had indeed been New World bound when, "against the indistinct green haze of the horizon," the shape of Saddle of Caracas loomed as it did for them. Just south of Trinidad, the shape had surfaced within sight of the place where a couple of centuries before Columbus had made that discovery of his of a Terrestrial Paradise that was "shaped something like a woman's nipple." It was with such latitude and import, then, that the "fabulous smell of Woman" became at once the substance and simulacra of "ruddy ones, copper-colored ones, pale ones and dark ones; women who wore high-heeled shoes under the lace of their petticoats, women who smelt of frangipani, lemon water, veviter, and—best of all—of women" (133). Be it in Eve, Pandora, and Virgin—or else in *Explosion*'s Madame Athalie Bajazet, mulatta *coiffeuse pour dames*, and "stark naked under a Greek tunic"—such figures embody, or else threaten to produce, world-(un)making material of a certain kind. They have aroused variously consequential ideas, among them that Lusotropical and utopian "metarace and brown skins" that Gilberto Freyre conceives of in his Brazilian New World. They account, too, for the facts and fictions of the "unholy concubinage" that so preoccupies Pierre, Carpenter of Lime Stone in Lamming's *Natives of My Person.*

In what had once looked to be a continent resolution of the issue, Carpentier's Columbus had declared with unadorned succinctness: "If I could contain myself, they could do the same! We didn't come here to fuck but to find gold, the gold that was beginning to appear, that was showing up on every island." (85). This, he calculated, was to be the case. Matters could be contained in such a way, notwithstanding the pull toward women who went about naked as the day they were born, "except for little cotton patches that barely covered their sex"; and notwithstanding, too, the likes of Michel di Cuneo to whom, during the second voyage, the "Lord Admiral" had himself given a "very beautiful Carib woman" whom he (Cuneo) had captured—"she being naked according to their custom." Cuneo had wanted, he explained, to put a certain "desire" of his into action; she, however, "did not want it," and instead " treated [him] with her finger nails in such a manner that [he] wished [he] had never begun." But then,

> (to tell you the end of it all), I took a rope and thrashed her well, for which she raised such unheard of screams that you would not have believed your ears. Finally we came to an agreement in such a manner that I can tell you that she seemed to have been brought up in a school of harlots. (Sale 1990:140; Todorov 1984:48-49; Colon 1987:209-208)

As for Columbus himself, in spite of the "swollen flies" of his Spaniards, and his own eyes that "strayed at times," he had been far more enchanted by an overriding experience of his own: "I said: GOLD. Seeing this marvel, I felt a sort of internal shock. A lust the likes of which I had never known rumbled in my gut" (84). Productive and "inconsistent in his hermeneutics" as Columbus was (West and Kling 1991), he certainly allows Carpentier a con/fusion of registers with which to account for his objects of desire. As *Christophoros* and Last Messiah of Christ, the Admiral of the Ocean Sea's "guiding light" and "surpassing moment" had led him to *the* discovery in his "great compass," to that mountain in "the shape of a woman's tit, or more precisely, of a nipple on a pear." It was a place which "no man had ever seen," and his encountering of it "establish[ed] that the Garden of Genesis is *there* [south of Trinidad], and nowhere else" (119). It bears some contemplating that the place lies as it does, and in language that is so proximate to the image of some native woman who "went naked—or nearly so—as the day [she] was born," and "whose exposed breasts," Columbus reports in Carpentier, "were studied by my men, who wanted to touch them, with a lust that [so] raised my fury that I was forced to cry out in an inappropriate manner, unable to maintain the solemn demeanor appropriate to one bearing the standard of Their Highnesses" (83).

The "making of more Americans" in Maxine Hong Kingston's *China Men* confronts us with world-(un)making material of a relevant sort. It is according to the plain facts and apparent fictions of this dispensation that Grandfather Ah Goong shouts his "Look at me!" against the vertiginous heights of the Sierra Nevada Mountains. It is there that, railroad builder and man-in-a-basket, he "pulled open his pants, and pissed overboard, the wind scatterring the drops. 'I'm a waterfall,' he said," then.

> One beautiful day, dangling in the sun above a new valley, not the desire to urinate but sexual desire clutched him so hard he bent over the basket. He curled up, overcome by beauty and fear, which shot to his penis. He tried to rub himself calm. Suddenly he stood up tall and squirted out into space. 'I am fucking the world,' he said. The world's vagina was big, big as the sky, big as a valley. He grew a habit: whenever he lowered in a basket, his rushed to his penis, and he fucked the world. (1980:132-133)

But then, we are also caught in an (en)gendering of things in which Land-in-Waiting does not always translate into "colony of joys" (Lamming)—notwithstanding Surgeon's assurance in *Natives of My Person* that "virgin lands [make] for the most blessed territory, [where] a man can start from scratch" (119). In *China Men* Kingston sets up a sexual topography that is at once *ou-topos* and *eu-topos* against a rock face along which "men were blown up. One knocked out or killed by the explosion fell silently, the other screaming, his arms and legs struggling" (131-132). Here, when "Ah Goong struck with his pickax [he] jarred his bones, chattered his teeth"; here, too, "he swung his sledgehammer" only to feel "the impact [ring] in the dome of his skull." Aboriginal beyond dreams of conquest, gold, and god, "the mountain [was here] millions of years old [and] locked against [the men] and was not to be broken into. The men teased him, 'Let's see you fuck the world now.'

'Let's see you fuck the Gold Mountain now'" (134). We are genres and sub/
versions removed, it is clear, from that Renaissance conflation of issues with
which Ralegh, for one, celebrated his 1595 "discoverie" of a Guiana whose
"madenheade"—rich, large, and beautiful—was ready to be "broken [into]
with sledges."

 In a parenthetical thought about Marvell's "To His Coy Mistress "—
and therefore about what is certainly an impolitic convocation of invading
worms, long-held virginity, and shattering gates—Francis Barker's *Tremulous Private Body* (1984) makes the observation that the poem reflects an
affect of power in one of its more "spectacular" forms: the "delight to be had
from dismembering a woman's body" (86-89). He points out that beyond the
"interpretative chatter" engendered by themes of love, sex, and virtue, "the
literal body is in fragments"; that what is at work involves

> [a] discursive aggression which dissects the body it has made
> word; and doubly so because, like Rembrandt's *Anatomy Lesson*,
> the dynamics of the body are, historically speaking, complex
> . . . . The body is still recalcitrantly and defiantly on display, even
> if in radically analysed form. It is still there to be seen, and is
> acknowledged openly as the object and site of desire. But in tune
> with an entire developing perception of the dangerous passion-
> ateness of the pre-disciplinary flesh, the text rounds on this first
> condition of the body of the woman, and having first torn it to
> pieces, not satisfied even by this act of violation, seeks to quell the
> restless anger of its own desire by consigning it to the darkness
> and silence of the "marble Vault." (89-90)

That being the case, for all that intercourse may have been a matter of
"radishes and flowers" and "subtle quiver" in the Lord's "garden" in Stevens's
"Cy Est Pourtraicte, Madame Ste Ursule, et les Unze Mille Vierges," there is
a quite other arrangement of things in "The Worms at Heaven's Gate," when
the worms re-produce the body parts that were once Bradroulbadour from the
tomb. Stevens's procession heads into the Promised Land in a text that is
baroquely in tune with what *The Tremulous Private Body* represents as the
object of desire. And it is thus that the worms deliver the "bundle of the body
and the feet"; so, too,

> . . . an eye. And here are, one by one,
> The lashes of that eye and its white lid.
> Here is the cheek on which that lid declined,
> And, finger after finger, here, the hand. (18)

Stevens's relationship to my New World terrain and type had been even more clearly mapped out, of course, when his Crispin negotiated the "Andean breath" and "thunderstorms of Yucatan" in "The Comedian as the Letter C"; so, too, in those circum-Caribbean contexts in which Florida is "virgin of boorish births" and a "venereal soil" that is "womb enough for the dreadful sundry of the world"—from "Polodowsky" to some "negro undertaker / Killing time between corpses" (1972:78-79).

For now, I summarize figures from the previous chapter to make the "still-vex'd Bermoothes" point that we are back on terrain upon which Ralegh and Donne, and Montaigne and Cortés, had all (en)gendered versions of the same "material." It is therefore worth recalling the geography of body parts with which Shakespeare's *The Comedy of Errors* maps Dromio of Syracuse's Land-in-Waiting, that "kitchen wench, and all grease." About this "beastly" yet "wondrous fat marriage" and "reverend body," we learn with Antipholus that "America, the Indies" lie "upon her nose," where they are all "o'er embellished with rubies, carbuncles, sapphires"; that the woman surrenders "their rich aspect to the hot breath of Spain, who [has sent] whole armadas of carracks to be ballast" there (III.ii.137-141). The reach for consummation with the Indies is a rather more jolly affair in *The Merry Wives of Windsor* when, echoing Ralegh (or mocking him, some have suggested), Falstaff identifies but fails to plant any colony of joys in Mistress Page and Mistress Ford. He is aroused in true generic form, all the same; for he does believe that he has been actually urged on by the torrid zones themselves, by "the appetite of [eyes] that scorched [him] up like a burning-glass." There are reasons enough, he tells Robin, to "sail like [a] pinnace" to those "golden shores," to a "region in Guiana" that is "all gold and bounty" where he will be "cheaters" to the two Mistresses: "They shall be exchequers to me; they shall be my East and West Indies, and I will trade to them both" (I.iii.57-70). Before Falstaff so burned to traffic and trade in the New World, Ralegh had celebrated the erotic economy of a country that "hath yet her Madenheade." His Guiana was virgin territory that had never been "sackt, turned, nor wrought, nor the vertue and salt of the soyle spent by manurance." Here, "the graues haue not beene opened for gold, the mines not broken" (96).

In others of its heuristic display as Columbian exchange during the early modern period, the female body had clustered in gynecological maps of "First Discoveries." Consider, here, a set of redactions that relate the nineteenth century of Dr. Marion Sims to the early modern period of Renaldus Columbus; and the fact that the conceit of choice is couched in the language of First Observation and of the rights of governance. Designated "Architect of the Vagina" by one twentieth-century historian, Sims had adapted "a spoon handle for the holding open of the vaginal opening, calling it a 'speculum'."

Sims recalled "introducing the bent handle of the spoon" into the vagina, whereupon he "saw everything no man had ever seen before. . . . I felt like an explorer in medicine who views a new and important territory." In effect, Sims "could see himself as [Christopher] Columbus, his new world the vagina" (Barker-Benfield 1976:95). Meanwhile, and with due resonance, Thomas Laqueur (*Making Sex*) summarizes "the somewhat silly but complicated debate around who discovered the clitoris" at a time when, amid "echoes of antiquity, a new and self-consciously revisionist science was aggressively exploring the human body":

> In 1559, for example, Columbus—not Christopher but Renaldus—claims to have discovered the clitoris. He tells his "most gentle reader" that this is "preeminently the seat of woman's delight." Like a penis, "if you touch it, you will find it rendered a little harder and oblong to such a degree that it shows itself as a sort of male member." Conquistador in an unknown land, Columbus stakes his claim: "Since no one has discerned these projections and their workings, if it be permissible to give names to things discovered by me, it should be called the love or sweetness of Venus." Like Adam, he felt himself entitled to name what he found in nature: a female penis. (1990: 64).

The seduction of the fabulous notwithstanding, Laqueur notes that "a militant empiricism pervades the rhetoric of Renaissance anatomists." Columbus's colleagues mapped and laid claims to the sweetness of Venus with equal vigor. Gabriel Fallopius insisted on his own priority: his having seen the clitoris first made everyone else a plagiarist. However, Kaspar Bartholin, from the seventeenth century and out of Copenhagen, "argued in turn that both Fallopius and Columbus were being vainglorious in claiming the 'invention of first Observation of this Part,' since the clitoris had been known by everyone since the second century" (65).

It is clearly the case, then, that with his 1699 "Mistress Going To Bed" (Elegy XIX), John Donne had sought intercourse with his "new-found-land" in familiar enough ways: "Licence my roaving hands / and let them go, / Before, behind, between, above, below, / O, my America!".../ How blest am I in this discovering thee!" It is in the language of commerce and of imperial expansion, and in sexual plainsong, too, that Donne then reached into his "Myne of precious stones" and "Emperie," into a "Kingdome" that is "safeliest when with one man mann'd." But then, witness Walcott's sex-as-slit-throat representation of the issue, "sledges" and "roaving hands" also make for consummation that is neither "safeliest" nor "merry"; and this is a point that no less a character than Richard III was quick to recognize when he sought to arouse his fighting men. He knew well enough to attempt to fend off invasion with: "Shall these enjoy our lands? Lie with our wives? / Ravish our daughters?" (*Richard III* V.iii.334-36). In Paz's Mesoamerica, meanwhile, the "Sons of La Malinche" have since found themselves transfixed by the conquistadorial (in)difference with which Cortés had in fact turned the Amerindian woman into just such a native of his person, by way of an ab/use in which, infamously, the "*chingón* rips open the *chingada*, who is pure passivity, defenceless against the exterior" (1961:77).

There is, too, the threat posed by the "tropicalization" of those who seek to conquer the tropics. The revelation here is that to inhabit the tropics is to seriously risk being in turn sexually inhabited by the torrid zone, and thus to change from being "gentle and generous" to a man who will "have a heart like stone"—witness Jean Rhys on the making of Cosway's bastard in *Wide Sargasso Sea* and Lamming's Pierre on "unholy concubinage" in *Natives*. One needs to add to all this the dissonance of having "been reared in the European belief system in which life was envisaged as a trip, a pilgrimage, yet where one's reflexes and one's common sense said stay at home." The likes of William Holland's "Johnny Newcome in Love in the West Indies" had once reduced the material of such encounters to that line drawing and comic print of his in which the protagonist had been "infected with all the germs of savage life," (Abrahams and Szwed 1983:12). Sexual passion had led him, in addition, "to consort with black sorcerers, leading further to polygamy and the breeding of a bastard race" that was marked by the "half-African, half-European" names given to the offspring of a (de)generation that also carried "the contagion of revolution." There is an obsessiveness to such preoccupations, Abrahams and Szwed suggest, that make it reasonable to conclude that it is all suffused with European "fears of a reversion [to] their own savage past" (12-14). Be that as it may, "unholy concubinage" underscores the degree to which sexual intercourse in the tropics could not possibly make for "peace beyond the line," especially when the line straddles "the ambivalence existing toward the exotic dark-skinned savage" (*ibid.*). Crucial for this line of descent into "dreadful sundry" is access to the body of a certain kind of woman. *Wide Sargasso Sea*'s Daniel-Esau, half-breed and bastard son in the Indies, explains about his *chingón* of a father that: the "man have a heart like stone." For all that "his white marble tablet [hang] in the English church at Spanish Town for all to see, [sometimes] when he sick of a woman which is quickly, he free her like he free my mother, even he give her a hut and a bit of land for herself (garden some call that), but it is no mercy, it's wicked pride he do it. . . . He walk like he own the earth" (Rhys 1982:122).

Whether because of Pandora's box, because of the fabulous smell of Woman, or else on account of some apocalypse-inducing racial nakedness, the facts of the Indies have always been prone to being fiction in a certain genre. Such had been the case when, famously in *Jane Eyre* (1847), Charlotte Bronte's Rochester made his appearance to certify that the Caribbean had been inbred to degeneracy, and right from the start. "I now inform you," Rochester explained, then, "that [the mysterious lunatic kept under watch and ward] is my wife, whom I married fifteen years ago,—Bertha Mason by name." The accompanying certification, so we learn,

> [will] affirm and can prove that on 20th October, A.D., —— (a date fifteen years back) Edward Fairfax Rochester, of Thornfield Hall, in the country of ——, and of Ferndean Manor, in —shire, England, was married to . . . Bertha Antoinetta Mason, daughter of Jonas Mason, merchant, and of Antoinetta, his wife, a Creole —— at —— church, Spanish Town, Jamaica. (1959:275)

The signal value of this certification lay in the dramatic revelation that "Bertha Mason is mad; [that] she came of a mad family;—idiots and maniacs through *three* generations! Her mother, the Creole, was both a mad woman and a drunkard!—as I found out after I had wed the daughter; for they were silent on family secrets before" (277; my emphasis).

Contamination from the past and failure of the future are thus writ large in and through the body of woman. The point is made, with a perhaps too heavy hand, when Naipaul concentrates certain sex-and-conquest obsessions in the black Eden of *The Mimic Men.* Of his relationship with this character Naipaul's protagonist recalls: "Its poison remained with me. It was with me at school. Eden said he wished to join the Japanese army: the reports of their rapes were so exciting. He elaborated the idea crudely and often; it ceased to be a joke" (1977a:151). The starkness of the violence that George Hicks reports in *The Comfort Women* underscores the enormity of the assault that Naipaul launches against his no doubt eponymous Eden. Hicks's focus is on the brutal regime of enforced prostitution that Japanese soldiery inflicted on Korean women. *The Comfort Women* also provides theoretical and historical frames of reference when it points to "superstitions [that] are universal in armed forces," among them "the belief that sex before going into battle worked as a charm against injury, [and that] amulets could be made with the pubic hair of comfort women." Hicks condenses this sexualization of violence into the story of a woman who "refused to bathe—presumably to discourage men from going near her." She was, Hicks writes, "suspended upside down from a tree, battered by rifles, had her nipples cut off, and was finally shot through the vagina" (1995:234). In Naipaul's *Guerrillas* (1975), meanwhile, the degradation of the female body is rather more explicit than it is in *The Mimic Men's* Eden. It is in the graphic clarity of *Guerrillas* that "He covered her mouth with his; her lips widened and she made a strangled sound; and then he spat in her mouth. She swallowed and he let her face go. She opened her eyes and said, 'That was lovely'." Terrain and type come in even more explicit formations in *A Bend in the River*. For here, "Her body had a softness, a pliability, and a great warmth. Only once or twice before I had known her like that. I held her legs apart. She raised them slightly—smooth concavities of flesh on either side of the inner ridge—and then I spat on her between the legs until I had no more spit. All of her softness vanished in outrage" (1979:228).

Even if idiosyncratically associated with "the long slow agony of death by ants" (Rhys), there is familiar business in the *Jane Eyre* story that Rhys reconstitutes into a creolized story of tropical madness and seduction in *Wide Sargasso Sea*. And so, for all that the Rochester of *Wide Sargasso Sea* is apparently unprepared for the sadness that he came to feel, he could indeed look at his "shabby white house"— as "more than ever it strained away from the black snake-like forest"—and *hear* it call out "louder and more desperately: Save me from destruction, ruin and desolation. Save me from the long slow agony of death by ants. But what are you doing here you folly?... Don't you know that this is a dangerous place.... If you don't, you soon will, and I can do nothing to help you" (1982:167). It is in Rhys that Grace Poole finally explains tropical turmoil and white discomfiture in the following way: *"I knew him as a boy. I knew him as a young man. He was gentle, generous, brave. His stay in the West Indies has changed him out of all knowledge"* (178). This is no surprise, of course, as Pierre knows in *Natives of My Person*, where it had already been "said by wiser heads than [his] that unless a man be powerful in the discipline of spirit, his nature will change with every radical change of the sky, becoming loose and base if it be the will of stars to captivate his lust" (Lamming 1971a:125). On this score, Lime Stone's [England's] "chief rival" in the tropics did leave a "most terrible record of debauchery and unjust licence... [For] it was told on authority how they [Antarctica/Spain] would defile their blood by unholy concubinage with the women of this black coast, and wherever their ensigns fly you witness, as indeed on the river we saw, how they spawn a numerous population of half-castes which do confuse the issues of government and rule" (125). And such, too, is the "dismal record" of Antarctica on the Isles of the Black Rock. For there, and

> *Against the will of God and the sacred need of their own blood*
> *they do enter into the most uncritical acts of fornication with*
> *these heathen women, blaspheming against their own body and in*
> *a manner not fit even for the pleasure of beasts; for such is known*

> *of their custom that they would forsake all normal practice in the*
> *arts of love to enhance their pleasure by entering into the most*
> *bestial experiments of lust, like fitting their organs through the*
> *mouth and up the fundaments of the woman's hindmost parts.*
> (125-126)

It is not utopian governance but biology and compulsion—the breaking of
"virgin knot" and the rank sowing of seed—that best account for such brave
new worlds and all who dwell in them. Heuristic focus on this quite different
contexture helps to explain why revenge and hegemonic control, not desire
or honor, define the thrust of Caliban's interest in Miranda's alien(atable)
womb. As he makes clear to Prospero, intercourse with his daughter would
have have been a consummation devoutly to be wished, and very much
political:

> O ho, O ho! would't had been done!
> Thou didst prevent me; I had peopled else
> This isle with Calibans. (I.i.349-351)

The embrace of something rich and strange is best accounted for not by the
language of religous consummation with which Stevens teases us about what
has been wholly Writ; nor yet by the nature of the reach for utopian
governance which Shakespeare's Gonzalo borrows from Montaigne's idealization of the cannibal and his new world. The Montaigne that certainly counts
here is, instead, the *homme* of the "oscillatory dynamic" that Robert Cottrell
emphasizes in *Sexuality/Textuality* when he focuses on *accouplage* and
contexture. As Montaigne uses the word, Cottrell explains, "*accouplage* is a
'conjunction,' a 'pairing,' a 'coupling' that signals the linking together of
opposites, of male and female." The dynamic entails attraction and repulsion;
and within its compass Montaigne develops a vision in which, "timeless and
limitless," the "principle of sexuality" emerges triumphant (1981:xii;5). The
insistence here is on a natural teleology of the body, one that is aimed at
nothing less than a "climactic fertilization of the womb." This much is clear
from Montaigne's own extended general statement of the centrality of sex in
the scheme of things:

> The gods, says Plato, have furnished us with a disobedient and
> tyrannical member, which, like a furious animal, undertakes by
> the violence of its appetite to subject everything to itself. To
> women likewise they have given a gluttonous and voracious
> animal which, if denied its food in due season, goes mad,
> impatient of delay, and, breathing its rage into their bodies, stops
> up the passages, arrests the breathing, causing a thousand ills,

until it has sucked in the fruit of the common thirst and therewith
plentifully irrigated and fertilized the depth of the womb. (Cottrell
1981:5-6; Freccero1994:78)

In an essay, the title of which is "She: The Inappropriate/d Other," Trinh T.
Minh-ha explores what she describes as a "horizontal vertigo" in which
identity is a "multiple layer whose process never leads to the True Self, or to
Woman, but only to other layers, other selves" (1986:3). Her references
coalesce in yet another New World embrace of the dreadful and the sundry by
way, this time, of Argentina's Alicia Dujovne Ortiz and the "Uncertainty of
the personal me, the national me, the sexual me" that Ortiz makes of the
"tragic mixture of blood" that runs in her veins. "Jews, Genovese, Castillians,
Irish, Indians, maybe Blacks, find in me," Ortiz explains, "a bizarre and
motley meeting place. I am a crowd, I am a one-woman march, procession,
parade, masquerade" (1984:3-4).

    Whether *sotto voce* ("maybe") or fully on parade, Ortiz reproduces
even as she skirts a genealogy of con/fusions that will be rather more
provocative, and spectacularly so, in Luis Rafael Sánchez's "slippery and
peppery, purgative and instructive, prophylactic and didactic, scatological"
Macho Camacho's Beat with its Puerto Rican *guaracha* of "black masses
from Timbuktu and Fernando Po [that] wiggle asses, that cock it, that open
their legs to white classes from Extremadura and Galicia." Of course, as does
Pierre in *Natives of My Person*, one could very well argue that the New World
had been well-positioned to be just such a bizarre and motley "meeting place"
when, in that 1506 *Mundus Novus* of his, Amerigo Vespucci fashioned its
inhabitants into natives of *his* person:

> They marry as many wives as they please; and son cohabits with
> mother, brother with sister, male cousin with female, and any
> man with the first woman he meets. . . .The women as I have said
> go about naked and are very libidinous; yet they have bodies
> which are tolerably beautiful and cleanly. . . . When they had the
> opportunity of copulating with Christians, urged by excessive
> lust, they defiled and prostituted themselves. (Sale 1990:141)

The descent into this line of consummation is no doubt recognizable even
where it has been translated into the capacity for wonder that explains Samuel
Eliot Morison's 1942 "life" of Columbus and its thought that "Never again
may mortal man hope to recapture the amazement, the wonder, the delight of
those October days in 1492 when the New World gracefully yielded her
virginity to the conquering Castilians" (1983:236). In the reprise of the same
that we get in Ramón Díaz Sánchez's 1936 novel of petroleum and exploita-

tion in Venezuela, *Mene*, it was some four hundred years before that the Land-in-Waiting had first aroused and experienced the "rending" and "digging manoeuvre[s]" of such a "*gesto de dominio y de enamoramiento*" (gesture of domination and passionate embrace). With "black prows tearing into her blissful virginity," and with "the grey lymph torn asunder," Sánchez wrote, "the hymen [was] broken from America in her hymenal latitude." Still, *Mene* temporizes: "it was less frenetic then; more parsimonious," Sánchez's proposes. For the "ancient prows [had] advanced with smiles which masked their deeds of domination and love-making," raising their "lofty forecastles as if to let the latin voice reach lyrically to the ears of the Indian mermaid" [*al oído de la sirena indiana*] (Sánchez n.d.:31).

Once again, Carpentier's reach for ampleness in such matters is a telling one. For example, contra the "hallelujahs of dazzling geographies" in *The Harp and the Shadow*, the Indies in *The War of Time* are very much a place of the latter days where "clothes rotted away" and "mushrooms sprouted from documents" (1970:41). Under such circumstances a man could indeed develop "a taste for such novelties as tomatoes, sweet potatoes and prickly pears." He could fill "his nostrils with tobacco, and on days when food was short—as it was more often than not—[dip] his manioc bread in cane syrup, afterwards burying his face in his bowl and licking it clean." It was in such a world that a man could dance, "when the ships' crews came ashore, with the enfranchised negresses who kept a wooden enclosure with bug-ridden mattresses, close to the careening-dock—they were ugly as sin, but women were scarce" (*ibid.* 41). It is here that Juan of Antwerp pairs off with the "two negresses" who waited on him and served "to gratify his lust whenever the urge seized him." This "tropicalization of the white man" (Oviedo) is duly embodied in Doña Mandinga, the "tall one, with ample breasts and her hair divided by eight partings"; so, too, in that smaller one of the two, the Dõna Yolofa whose "buttocks jutted out like choirstalls " and who "had only a few hairs in that place where good Christians have a thick tuft" (47). As though in response, Gayl Jones's "Ensinança" would record being "*weary of this / new-ancient world*" from which she "would disappear," but for a "malady that keeps [her] visible" as a "conspicuous hairy nevus" with " the top of me all black / the bottom all white," and a "protuding navel" that divides into day and night *(Hermit-Woman*,12)

When she is aboriginal or native, or otherwise tropical and dark, the figure that the New World Land-in-Waiting turns into is variously but typically represented as primal and atavistic. Its *womanshenegro* (Faulkner) attributes lead to climaxes of a somewhat generic variety, be they encounters that are Brazilian (as in Freyre's "Plantation Boy" and Olinto's *The Water House*) or circum-Caribbean (as in *Macho Camacho's Beat*). The same is true of the metaphysics of the fecund in Carpentier, but most dramatically so, I believe, in the sensual archaeology that *The Lost Steps* makes of a "certain clay figure" whose new-ancient world material harks back to an archetypal imperative to fertilize the womb. "Baked in the sun," the figure was "a kind of jar without handles, with two holes opposite each other in the upper part, and a navel outlined in the convex surface by the pressure of finger when the clay was still soft." With this encounter, Carpentier's protagonist looked upon and into no less an embodiment than "the Mother of the Infant Gods, of the totems given to men so that they would acquire the habit of dealing with the divinity, preparing the way of the Greater Gods. The Mother, 'lonely, beyond space, and even time,' whose name, *Mother*, Faust twice uttered with terror" (1956:183). Here, *tout court*, "was God." In fact,

> More than God, it was the Mother of God. It was the Mother, primordial in all religions. The female principle, genesial, womb, to be found in the secret prologue to all theogonies. The Mother, with swollen belly, which was at one and the same time breasts, womb, and sex, the first figure molded by man, when under his hands the possibility of the object came into being. (*ibid.*)

Paz limns other measures of the same when he writes about "Diana and her bow, Coatlicue and her skulls, goddesses covered with blood, [embodying] life itself, the perpetual rebirth and death of the seasons, time unfolding and turning back on itself" (1973). And the Mesoamerican Ilhuica Cihuapipiltin, the Celestial Princesses, or Cihuateto, the Goddesses, haunt the crossroads in Clendinnen's *Aztecs* to relevant effect. "Malevolence incarnate," they descend to their place of convergence on five special days of ill-fortune. In what is attributed to them, Clendinnen explains, we glimpse "the classic lineaments of the witch, the inverted image of social woman, implacably malevolent, inexhaustibly envious, inimical to life, who destroys rather than nurtures children."

> It was they who as Tzizime, the "Devil Women," were the monsters destined to destroy [the] Fifth World, when the Sun would at last fail to rise and the earth powers would burst forth to devour people. At the New Fire Ceremony every fifty-two years, when the world was poised on the rim of destruction and the Fire Priest whirled his Fire Drill to mark the Sun in his rising, children were nudged and pinched to be kept awake; should they sleep they could turn into mice. Pregnant women were masked with the thick leaves of the maguey cactus and shut away in the granaries to subdue their dangerous, involuntary power. (1991a:180)

In this light, latitudes converge to signal but not surprising effect in the gravitational pull that "Africa proper" exercises on the sixteenth- and seventeenth-century Runaway Blacks of the New World in *Explosion in a Cathedral*. They regress, as regress they must, "to forgotten tongues, to rites of circumcision, the worship of earlier gods, who had preceeded the recent gods of Christianity." In this way, the coming "undergrowth" in the Americas "close[s] behind men who were retracing the course of history, to regain an age when Creation had been ruled by the Fertile Venus, with her huge breasts and her ample belly" (Carpentier 1979:211).

The voyage-sanctioning and Euro-Christian figure that we get in a 1502 painting by Alejo Fernández depicts, for its part, the Virgin of Navigators offering her protection to Columbus and to the natives of the New World. This figure is a consequential one in narratives of the "still-vex'd Bermoothes," as Carpentier demonstrates when he revisits and inflects the Virgins of *Explosion* and *Concierto barroco*. "All lost! To prayers, to prayers! All lost!" Shakespeare's characters had responded when *they* were caught in the thunder and lightning of *The Tempest* (I.i.53-54). There is a similarly focused even if passing "tempest of weather" in Lamming's *Natives of My Person*; however, it is in Carpentier's *Explosion* that *L'Ami du peuple* runs into "the frenzied ebulliency of a sea stirred up of its own free-will." Here, "one could feel one's viscera moving from side to side the moment one's body was stretched out." The ship's deck is thereafter very much haunted by the genealogy of its storms. Its "sailors [joined] in a great chorus, . . . shouting a canticle at the tops of their voices to the Virgin of Perpetual Help, the seaman's intercessor with Divine Wrath" in the hope that "the Mother of the Redeemer" would "placate the waves and still the wind" (193-194). *Concierto barroco* repeats but nuances the Virgin of Navigators and the approach to the Land-in-Waiting. Filomeno prays, but he does so "in a low voice to a black Virgin, the patron saint of fishermen and travelers"; it is she that he asks "to protect their voyage and [to] bring them safely to port in Rome which, being an important city, must, as he imagined, be situated at the ocean's edge with a good bank of reefs to protect it from [the] hurricanes" that were so much a fixture of the "still-vex'd" world of the Caribbean (64). Carpentier captures his *negro* in an act of syncretism and sub/version. It is one that his fellow Cuban, Benítez-Rojo, contextualizes when he takes his turn at recording the "flow of marine foam that connects two civilizations [from] within the turbulence of chaos." *The Repeating Island* proposes, then, that

> (the) cult of the Virgen de la Caridad del Cobre can be read as a
> Cuban cult, but it can also be reread—one reading does not negate
> the other—as a meta-archipelagic text, a meeting of or confluence

of marine flowings that connect the Niger with the Mississippi,
the China Sea with the Orinoco, the Parthenon with a fried food
stand in an alley in Paramaribo. (16)

Elsewhere, sardonic excess and grotesque violence account for other women-
and-dangerous-things maps of the lands of America. One such appears in a
nineteenth-century reference that Peter Mason's *Deconstructing America*
represents as being, perhaps, the "most baroque" of them all. In it, America
"is a female form, long, thin, watery, and at the forty-eighth parallel ice-cold.
The degrees of latitude are years—woman is old at forty-eight" (1990:27).
But then, there is Benítez-Rojo; and his way in *The Repeating Island* is to
spread-eagle the body of the circum-Caribbean against a global economy of
sexual violence. His "accusatory and militant rhetoric" effectively reinforces
"the delight to be had from dismembering a woman's body"—that affect of
power in Barker's *Tremulous Private Body*—and the "profit on't," too.
Benítez-Rojo reproduces the premise in a form that is nothing if not *the*
conceit for the state of being a "madenheade" that has been fully broken into
by "sledges"—as Ralegh and his contemporaries had hoped to do, and had
variously done, by the end of the seventeenth century.

   The Repeating Island also develops this past tense of the genre against
the backdrop of, say, the "desiring-machine" urges that Benítez-Rojo deploys
from the Gilles Deleuze and Felix Guattari of *Anti-Oedipus, Capitalism and
Schizophrenia*. We travel quite some distance, then, beyond the early modern
period in *Natives of My Person* where, "a colony of joys given over to his
care," Lamming's Lady of the House could feel "his flesh rising again,
making it press against her arms," and "the wave of heat [that] was coming
up from his loins" as he went hard with longing. Her experience of him was
as "though his appetite had opened like an ocean, soothing and merciless in
its greed." The climax brought her to "a noise like a wounded bird" (65). In
the *The Repeating Island*'s dispensation of this terrain and type, "the Atlantic
is the Atlantic, because it was once engendered by the copulation of Europe—
that insatiable solar bull—with the Caribbean archipelago." For which
reason, and "let's be realistic," if the Atlantic is now the space of capitalism,
it is

> because Europe . . . conceived of the project of inseminating the
> Caribbean womb with the seed of Africa, and even of Asia; the
> Atlantic [is also NATO, European Economic Community, and so
> on] because it was the painfully delivered child of the Caribbean,
> whose vagina was stretched between continental clamps, be-
> tween the encomienda of Indians and the slaveholding planta-
> tions, between the servitude of the coolie and the discrimination

toward the criollo, between commercial monopoly and piracy, between fortress and surrender; all Europe pulling on the forceps to help at the birth of the Atlantic: Columbus, Cabral, Cortez, de Soto, Hawkins, Drake, Hein, Rodney, Surcouf. . . . After the blood and saltwater spurts, quickly sew up torn flesh and apply the antiseptic tinctures, the gauze and surgical plaster; then the febrile wait through the forming of a scar: suppurating, always suppurating. (1995:5)

Carpentier's *Explosion in a Cathedral* does attempt, through Ogé, to return the Edenic to the experience of the sexual. Given the atavism that so animates narratives of *mulata* and *negra* sexuality in the New World, and given the "psychopathological and philosophical explanation of the *state of being* a negro" that Frantz Fanon so strenuously underscores in *Black Skin, White Masks*, there is some irony here that it is the San Dominican who *voices* the view that

original sin was not perpetuated by the sexual act, but washed away by it each time. Making use of discrete euphemisms, he averred that the couple were realising a return to primal innocence, when out of the total and paradisiacal nakedness of their embrace there swam an appeasement of the senses, a jubilant and gentle calm, which was an eternally repeated intimation of the purity of Man and Woman before the Fall. (Carpentier 1979:79)

This thought is only fleshed out, so to speak, when, Victor Hugues's attempt to rape her thwarted, the sexual act finally occurs between himself and Sofia. It is here that Sofia is "exalted by surrender"; that "her whole body" acquires "a new awareness" in the "supreme munificence" that comes with the "gift of one's whole body." In addition, the "language of the lovers went back to the roots of language itself," and "the word was born from their contact, as elemental and pure as the act which generated it. The rhythm of their bodies was so closely adjusted to the rhythms of Creation that a sudden rainstorm, the flowering of plants in the night or a change of the direction of the wind was enough for their desire to well up at dawn or at twilight" (313-314). Consummated between "the ascent of orgasm and the relapse into half-sleep—the delectable calm of a state of grace—[their sexual embrace] seemed to have lasted the whole night" (314).

As I have said, there is some irony here, given Ogé. For all that he comes as physician, his reception in the novel's Cuban household had been a defining one. In Sofia's eyes, "the relatively light colour of his complexion made him look as though this were an artificial skin covering a real negro's face, one with those wide nostrils and wooly hair." She had made a slight bow in the newcomer's direction, without offering him her hand (*Explosion* 43). "But he's a Negro!" she had whispered into Victor's ear. She does so "with a gasp" (43) the origins of which lie in some significant measure in the New World's preoccupations with purity of blood, and thus with vexations that once accounted for the "Royal Decree" of 27 May 1805, in which the concern was with "marriages between persons of known nobility with members of the castes"; so, too, for the one which, on 15 October 1805, clarified matters when it decreed that "those persons of known nobility and known purity of blood who, having attained their majority, intended to marry a member of the said castes [negroes, mulattos and others] must resort to the Viceroy, Presidents and Audiencias of the Dominions who will grant or deny the corresponding licence" (Martínez-Alier 1974:12-13). But then, the Americas could not *not* make for a certain conmingling of natives and persons. In effect: as with Juan of Antwerp in the Indies, so with Monsieur Lenormand de Mezy on the sugar plantations of *The Kingdom of This World*. There is, too, that circum-Caribbean ring of "aggressive concupiscence" which *Explosion in a Cathedral* will represent as prodigal and *mulata*, when it is not *negra* and naturally incontinent. "Since I was born in the Antilles, my observations and my conclusions are valid only for the Antilles, at least concerning the black *at home*," Fanon would explain when he points out in *Black Skin, White Masks* "what is important to us here": to show that "with the Negro the cycle of the *biological* begins," especially so to the degree that *the* cognate for the Negro is sex: "No anti-Semite, for example, would ever conceive of the idea of castrating the Jew. He is killed or sterilized. But the Negro is castrated. The penis, the symbol of manhood, is annihilated, which is to say denied. . . . It is in his corporeality that the Negro is attacked" (Fanon 1967:161-163).

All in all, what with its choirstall buttocks, nightmare beauty, and "three-knotted" head scarf, the *mulata*'s and *negra*'s flesh has on the whole required that the woman's body be laid out in certain predictable ways. In one commingled instance in Carpentier's *Explosion*, the context is the "iridescent colony" of Paramaribo, where magnificent balls took place on board foreign ships at the foot of Fort Zeelandia and where Dutch girls "were prodigal with their favors." There, "one could sample every wine and liqueur in the world." Banquets were served by "negresses decked in bracelets and necklaces and wearing skirts of Indian silk, with delicate, almost transparent blouses stretched tight over their hard, quivering breasts." This experience of the erotic was subject to "opportune dignity," of course. A French poet, *Explosion* notes, had once alluded to Persian slave-girls who wore a similar costume in the palace at Sardanapolis (32). There is a note of studied topicality in the picture that we get here; for, to my mind, it echoes nothing so much as the genre of libidinous exotica in which Gustave Flaubert had once experienced his passage through Egypt, among the women at Esna. Flaubert had come upon "negresses [there] in dresses of sky-blue; others in yellow, in white, in red—loose garments fluttering in the hot wind. Odors of spices. On their bare breasts long necklaces of gold piastres, so when they move they rattle like carts. They call after you in drawling voices: Cawadja, cawadja, their white teeth gleaming between their red or black lips, their metallic eyes rolling like wheels" (1996:128). In the span of "one day," the Frenchman declared, "I came five times and sucked three. I say it straight out and without circumlocution, and let me add that I enjoyed it" (128). Elsewhere, in the brothels at Kena, that is, "my dear sir, in a land where women go naked. . . . I have lain with Nubian girls whose necklaces of gold piastres hung down to their thighs and whose black stomachs were encircled by colored beads—they feel cold when you rub your own stomach against them. And their dancing! *Sacré nom de Dieu!!!*" (126).

There is certainly no "opportune dignity" and, at best, only a pseudo-pastoral version of the language of lovers that went back to the roots of language itself when the sailors of *L'Ami du peuple* descend upon a certain "deserted, wooded coast" of the New World in *Explosion*. There is no coming either upon some *mulata* stark naked under a Greek tunic. We are even further removed from any awareness of the "supreme munificence" that could only be represented in a whole and white body like Sofia's. Instead, sexual intercourse is more nearly of the stretched-vagina variety that we get in *The Repeating Island*, though rather more steeped in the atavistic, because darker. The embrace of something rich and strange is, *tout court*, unceremonious copulation, given the terrible temptation of the black flesh ("There are some with buttocks like this"; "some of them are stark naked . . . there's one in particular. . . ."). Soon enough the black women arrive, "to be ringed by an aggressive concupiscence; tearful, supplicant, *perhaps* genuinely frightened, they nevertheless submitted to the men, who hauled them off towards the nearby thickets" (187; my emphasis). The narrative moves to soften this class-and-race hauling away, by shifting into a semi-pastoral mode. Esteban comes upon and takes one of the slave girls to a "sort of cradle, carpeted with dry lichen." She was, Carpentier writes, "very young," and "submitted docilely, preferring this to other, and worse brutalities, and unwound the torn stuff she was wearing." But then, because the woman is in fact *womanshenegro*, she carries the pastoral to a climax that is quite the predictable one—whether it comes, as follows below, in the *jitanjáforas* of Luís Pales Matos, the *guaracha* of Luís Rafael Sánchez, or else in Rosario Ferré's Isabel La Negra, "black like the grounds at the bottom of the coffee pot, like the mud at the bottom of the gutter." In effect, *Explosion*'s young black girl performs in true biology-and-blood fashion when "she *offered* the young man the tense smoothness of her adolescent breasts, the nipples liberally smeared with ochre, and her firm fleshy thighs, which were *ready* to clasp, to arch, or bend till her knees touched her chest" (187-88; my emphasis). There is no "subtle quiver" at all here when the "good Lord in His garden" seeks "New leaf and shadowy tinct," as had been the case once before, with Madame Ste Ursule, virgin, Christian, and white.

As now conceived, the lie of the land does not encourage utopian transcendence; the descent is, instead, into a compelling biology. For all that Esteban attempts to recreate the pastoral's bower of bliss, it is obvious that wherever the woman's "tits" are liberally smeared with ochre, they point to neither the "fundamental geoeschatological significance" of the Terrestrial Paradise, one that could launch "a crusade to Jerusalem" (West and Kling 1991:68), nor to "fresh green breast of a New World," young though they may be. The circumstances are certainly "all foison, all abundance," but not quite to feed "innocent people," as Gonzalo would have it appear in *The Tempest*. "If I had not been devoted to the ideal that I pursued," Columbus well understands in *The Harp and the Shadow*, "I would have lain with Indians— many of whom were quite desirable in their Edenic nakedness... But that they can never accuse me of, however much they rummage through old papers, examine old archives, or lend their ears [to] slanders" (153). The language of what they can never accuse him of is elsewhere, in the Carpentier of *The Lost Steps*, the stuff of the "inexhaustible mimetism of virgin nature" and of that "female principle, genesial, womb [and] secret prologue to all theogonies." It is the stuff, too, of that "Fertile Venus, with her huge breasts and her ample belly" to which *Explosion* returns those Blacks on the run in the New World.

"It was an Eve being tempted by the Serpent." With this summary view of a painting in *Concierto barroco* Capentier returns us to a version of the new world that lies ready to be unmade. Already, there is contagion in the fact that, as Filomeno notes, Eve is "too heavily shrouded in tresses in times still incognizant of carnal wickedness." She stands, as fascinated and she is hesitant, before a green-striped Serpent whose "enormous eyes [are] brimming with evil." Although in hindsight, the victim that she is set to become has reasons enough to hesitate—"when one considers what her acquiescence cost us," and the fact that "the fruit [would] cause her to give birth with the pain of her entrails" (81). Moreover, as Henry Krause explains elsewhere, it is "not without meaning that the sculptured presentation of the Vice of Unchastity which one finds on so many church facades of the twelfth century should invariably be a woman, suffering eternally in Hell. She is usually shown in a revolting posture, her naked body entwined by serpents which feed on her breasts and sexual organs. Sometimes, too, she is accompanied by the Devil, who assumes an intimate relationship to her" (1982:81). Be that as it

may, Eve being tempted by the Serpent to unmake the world is what drives
Filomeno to that *cantar para matar una culebra* which Carpentier orches-
trates and brings to a climax in *Concierto barroco*. It is here that Filomeno
slowly approaches the canvas. As if bent on "a strange ritual ceremony," he
beats "on a tray that gave out a hoarse sound" as he sings his Afro-Cuban "*The
snake is dead, / Ca-la-ba-son, / Son-son*," while swiping "at the air with a huge
carving knife as though killing the snake in the picture." This reach for the
"peaceable kingdom" (Walcott) is the genesis for that orchestration of the
baroque in which,

> "*Kabala-sum-sum-sum*," chorused Antonio Vivaldi, out of eccle-
> siastical custom giving the refrain an unexpected inflection of
> Latin litany. "*Kabala-sum-sum-sum*," chorused Domenico
> Scarlatti. "*Kabala-sum-sum-sum*," chorused George Frideric
> Handel. "*Kabala-sum-sum-sum*," repeated the sixty-six female
> voices of the Ospedale. (82-83)

Filomeno's attempt at exorcism fails, of course, and the loss of Eden is
recognizably the consequence, even when, as happens in the latter days of
Walcott's *Sea Grapes*, Adam's song "ascends to God" who, wiping his eyes,
then declares: "Heart, you are in my heart as the bird rises" (*ibid.*). Eden fails,
too, in "The Brother" and the sly consummation of its climax: "And when
your love is spent, / in Eden," the poem asks, "who sleeps happiest? / The
serpent." For then there is a "fire" which, lit "in the brain," cannot "let you
rest" (Walcott 1976:16). Besides which, there is, that larger concession that
Walcott grants in "New World," in its recognition that when "Adam was
exiled to our New World, in the ark's gut" it was "willed" that the "coined
snake [would coil] there for good / fellowship also" (12). Even more
consequential had been the fact that the snake on his "forked tree admired
labor"and that Adam himself "had an idea": he and the snake would "share
/ the loss of Eden for a profit." They did: "So both made the New World. And
it looked good" (12). Thereafter, "good fellowship" and "labor" conjoined to
account for the "awe" of the "first bead of sweat"; the sowing of "all flesh"
with "salt," and, significantly, the beginnings of a "joy" which, for all that it
was "difficult," was "at least [Adam's] own" (12).

    Hesiod and his Pandora, not Adam and his Eve, provide the once again
gendered ground upon which the New World was little more than "shrill
lampoonery" when Ward chose to sow all flesh with salt on the island of
Jamaica in 1698. Not that the inspiration behind "Adam's song" is absent.
Multiple languages of genesis and a great deal of recalcitrant material
converge in Ward's recreation of a "shapeless Pile of Rubbish confusd'ly
jumbled into an Emblem of Chaos, neglected by Omnipotence when he

form'd the World into its admirable Order." The same is true of the site where "*Vulcan* Forg'd *Joves* Thunderbolts," and where "Phaeton, by his rash misguidance of the Sun, scorched into Cinder." Very much disinclined to be romantic about such a place, it is to irredeemably dystopian effect that Ward's "True Character of the People and the Island" re-populates the new-ancient world of Jamaica in a crescendo of images of rubbish: "They are stigmatized with *Nick-Names,* which they bear, not with *Patience* only, but with *Pride*, as *Unconscionable Nan, Salt-Beef Peg, Buttock-de-Clink Jenny*, &c." Far from being garden and "admirable order," nature here is "Subject to Turnadoes, Hurricanes and Earthquakes, as if the island, likke the People, were troubled with the *Dry Belly-Ach*" (*ibid.*). Here at last, in this conflation of woman, fire, and other dangerous things, was *the* place where "Pandora fill'd her box" (Abrahams and Szwed 1983:12).

In the latter days, Naipaul will reinforce this Caribbean fall from grace when he blends into *The Mimic Men* the "famous" story of the visit of that "pathologically gloomy man" and "imperialist pamphleteer" James Anthony Froude to Isabella/Trinidad. During an expedition to Devil's Cauldron, Naipaul writes, "the sight of every Negro forest hut drove Froude to rage at Negro idleness, and to pessimistic conclusions about the future of that race." Still, Naipaul does make a point of remembering that, according to Froude, the only hope for Isabella "lay in the Asiatics, who 'to the not inconsiderable merits of picturesqueness and civilization add virtues of thrift and industry'." At any rate, the climax—and a rather emblematic one at that—comes at the Cauldron itself when "a solitary Negro was discovered, totally naked, washing some clothes" (77). With Froude himself—in *The English in the West Indies* (1888)—we find ourselves on board a ship plying Caribbean waters. We are in the company, too, of "perhaps two or three hundred coloured people going from one island to another, singing, dancing, and chattering all night long, as radiant and happy like chickens as soon as they are able to peck." Froude was very much persuaded that "It is [all] a very peculiar state of things, not to be understood, as priest and missionary agree, without long acquaintance. There is evil, but they sin only as animals, without shame, because there is no sense of doing wrong." For which reason, "these poor children of darkness have escaped the consequences of the Fall, and must come of another stock after all" (*ibid.* 50). Black bodies thus shadow the reach for Eden here.

"Their naked privies were probed to make sure that they still possessed the hymen unruptured; after this humiliation they were sent away from the land that had been their home." The voice is Mark Twain's, and the context is the *Letters from the Earth* in which he maps on to the Americas the Biblical tradition of exodus to and inheritance of the Promised Land, a tradition that has so delimited the archives of Eden in the New World. Terrains and types of the Scripture had been at work, of course, in the unstable hermeneutics of *The Harp and the Shadow*'s Columbus, even if at cross purposes, so to speak:

> In spite of the Franciscan habit in which I now enveloped myself, my flesh was like that of the Pseudo-Cyprian, the Cartagenian heretic who pledged his soul to regain his lost youth and shamefully take advantage of the innocence of a maiden—a virgin pure and innocent of the Evil of Gold as were the lands that I had opened to the greed and lust of men from here: *Kyrie eleison*. (*The Harp and the Shadow*, 117)

The Bible resonates as well in the Christianography and election that Mather's *Magnalia Christi Americana* celebrated with the thought that "the Church of our Lord Jesus Christ, well compared unto a ship, is now victoriously sailing round the globe after Sir Francis Drake's renowned ship, called *The Victory*, which could boast, *Prima ego velivolis ambivi cursibus orbem* [I first, with canvas to the gale unfurld, / Made the wide circuit of the mighty world]" (17).

Of course, there are the darker registers of the tradition, too; and these explain a great deal in Trible and in Twain. "Detail for detail," and "out of history of yesterday's date"—involving an 1862 massacre in Minnesota—"the red Indian of America [would duplicate] God's work, and [do so] in the very spirit of God." Twain makes much of the fact, here, that the "official report" of the campaigns of the Elect in the Promised Land against the Canaanites does not furnish incidents, episodes, and minor details. Instead, it deals with "information in masses: all the virgins, all the men, all the babies, all 'creatures that breathe,' all houses, all cities; it gives you just one vast picture [and] storm-swept desolation" (Twain 1974:Letter XI, 52-54). Mieke Bal's reading of *Judges* in *Death and Dissymmetry* has a nicely summative view to offer. The coherence of its politics and the politics of its coherence, Bal explains, are heavily invested in what she refers to as "scattered virginity." For "The Book [is] full of virgins. Collective virginity is at stake in the bride-stealing scenes at the end of the book, as in the formulaic transitional . . . mini-narratives of the 'sons' taking and giving 'daughters,' exchanging virgins with other, pagan tribes" (69). Twain works within and against this scriptural template with literalist ferocity, pointing to an investment in scattered virginities that yielded a total harvest of 32,000 virgins, and graphically verified, as above, to be indeed virginal. How else?

Phyllis Trible devotes the third chapter of her *Texts of Terror*, "An Unnamed Woman, The Extravagance of Violence," to a feminist-literary reading of the gang-rape, death, and dismemberment of a woman "out of

Bethlehem-judah" who had been concubine to a Levite "sojourning on the side of mount Ephraim." After the rape, and as narrated in the *Book of Judges* (chapters 19-21), the Levite "took a knife, and laid hold on his concubine, and divided her, together with her bones, into twelve pieces, and sent her into all the coasts of Israel." Thus dispersed, the woman is re-constituted into a cause for re-membering and revenge in the Promised Land. It is a re-membering which, when it had "utterly destroyed every male, and every woman that hath laid by man," yielded its own harvest of hundreds of "young virgins that had known no man by lying with any male." This edge-of-the-sword undertaking in Jabesh-Gilead, and the merrier version among the daughters of Shiloh, compelled a new politics of restoration. Because the Lord had "made a breach in the tribes of Israel," there needed to be a return to inheriting the Promised Land according to a certain pious arithmetic. The harvesting of female bodies assures lines of succession and "the right of conferring the heritage" (Stern). The yields are important since, as Moshe Weinfeld claims in his "privilege versus obligation" discussion of the inheritance of the Land, "No other people in the history of mankind was as preoccupied as the people of Israel with the land in which they lived. The whole biblical historiography revolves around the Land. The pivot of the patriarchal stories is the promise of the land for the Patriarchs and their descendants" (Weinfeld 1993:183). The colonization of the Promised Land was thus configured within the haunt of prophecy. And it is one that has since stabilized the conquest of Canaan into a functional genre that would otherwise be "made extraordinarily complex by contradictions in the biblical sources" (99). Trible's reading, for its part, is a determined re-cognition of patriarchal election and female erasure. "The betrayal, rape, torture, murder, and dismemberment of [the] unnamed woman is a story we want to forget but are commanded to speak. It depicts the horrors of male power, brutality, and triumphalism; of female helplessness, abuse, and annihilation. To hear [the] story is to inhabit a world of unrelenting terror" (1984:65).

The pull of contraindicative values is recognizable in Philip Stern's *The Biblical Herem, A Window on Israel's Religious Experience* (1991), preoc-cupied as his study is with repeatedly huge acts of violence in a politics of extermination, fecundity, and inheritance. Stern's ground is the scatterring, slaughtering, and gathering-in that are associated with *herem*, that is, with a "theology of war" that is grounded in the logic of "extirpation[s] consecrated to god." Here, world-making prophecy and expropriation conjoin as they must in an exceptionalist covenant, since, as Mircea Eliade has suggested, for any people to settle into a new territory is a cosmogonic event in which the sacred and profane are implicated (1959). Stern discusses this taking of territory within the constraints of *herem*. His explanation is duly indexed to an "Omnasticon" and to exegeses of a war-faring that has "long been considered as a singular 'consecration-to-destruction' of a designated enemy," or as a "consecration-through-destruction" (16-17; 1). In *The Promise of the Land*, meanwhile, Weinfeld also broaches questions that relate to the inheritance of the land of Canaan by the Israelites and the undertaking's concommitant acts of "expulsion, dispossession and extermination." *The Promise of the Land* is in part framed by the explanatory context of "the book of Deuteronomy [which] conceived of the *herem* as a commandment applying automatically to all inhabitants of the land, whether or not they fought. This *herem* is not conditional on any vow or dedication but is an *a priori* decree, which belongs more to utopian theory than to practice. Indeed, in practice, the inhabitants of Canaanite cities were not to be destroyed but rather placed under corvee labor, as we learn from I Kings 9:20-21" (89-90).

The Biblical Herem explains its organizing principle in conceptual clusters that are broadly relevant. For example, it is Stern's understanding that the collapse of Jericho is a "myth of creation" that was only possible through destruction of the walled city. The event's "seventh day" therefore involved "war, Holy War *par excellence*. A special heightening of activity (sevenfold!)" was thus necessary to effect "the collapse of the forces resisting the new world order" (141). Quite so; considering the constellation of rites and rights that converge at this signal moment, including as it does the "covenant of blood" that re-circumcision again confirms. "Make thee sharp knives, and circumcise again the children of Israel the second time," Joshua is instructed by Jehovah. And he does make him sharp knives, and circumcise the children of Israel at "the hill of the foreskins" (Joshua 5, 2-3). Manna and visitation from the "captain of the host of the Lord" follow the climactic arrival at the plains of Jericho. They confirm that "the Lord sware unto [the fathers of the children of Israel] that he would give us a land that floweth with milk and honey" (*ibid.* 6-15). Thereafter, ark, trumpet, and sword coincide in the taking of Jericho. Then they took the city: "And every man straight before him, . . . they took the city. And they utterly destroyed all that was in the city, both man and woman, young and old, and ox, and sheep, and ass, with the edge of the sword" (Joshua 6, 20-21).

But then, insofar as *herem* is writ large upon and in Woman, such "gigantic violence" merits second thoughts, writes Trible. "To replenish itself, in one such instance, the Benjamites must have women for the tribe's six hundred male survivors," she continues. In consequence, they attack "the derelict town of Jabesh-gilead, murdering all the inhabitants except four hundred young virgins." But the arithmetic of violence and sex falls short: "the Benjamites are unsatisfied because four hundred women cannot meet the demands of six hundred soldiers. This time the daughters of Shiloh must pay the price. To gratify the lust of males," *Texts of Terror* reports, "the men of Israel sanction the abduction of two hundred young women as they come out to dance in the yearly festival of Yaweh" (1984:83). In *Sexism and God-Talk,* Rosemary Radford Ruether effectively summarizes the implications of so reductive a teleology of the body:

> Women are symbolized as "closer to nature" than men and thus fall in an intermediate position between culture as the male sphere and uncontrolled nature. This is due both to woman's physiological investment in the biological processes that reproduce the species rather than in processes that enhance her as an individual and to the ability of male collective power to extend women's physiological role into social roles confined to child nurture and domestic labor. Female physiological processes are viewed as dangerous and polluting to higher (male) culture. Her social roles are regarded as inferior to those of males, falling lower on the nature-culture hierarchy. (Ruether 1983:72)

Trible's reading of the politics and affect of wasted female bodies and scattered virginity is rather less accommodating than is Daniel Boyarin's in *Carnal Israel, Reading Sex in Talmudic Culture* (1993). The disjuncture is especially clear in the "Concluding Forward" where Boyarin finally explains what is central in his agenda. His purpose, he indicates there, is to effect a reconciliation with feminism, and by way, not so parenthetically, of Mieke Bal (Boyarin 1995:228). Because his goals are "redemptive and cultural-critical" (230), Boyarin works a complex weave of issues, past an unapologetic re-cognition of the Augustinian imputation of carnality to Jews (1), into a "dialectics of desire." In "Different Eves" (77-106), he also explores engendering and its import in light of exegeses that are derived from traditions which are now Babylonia, now Palestine. His approach is further nuanced by differentiated readings, rabbinical as against patristic, of Eve and Pandora (100). In the end, Boyarin makes the point that "finding only misogyny in the past produces misogyny; finding only lack of female power, autonomy, and creativity refies female passivity and victimhood" (227). In consequence, he had found it necessary "to facilitate a feminist critique of the rabbinic formation, but also to exculpate that same formation from charges of a founding misogyny that would render it irredeemable" (230).

Beyond Boyarin and Trible, it bears recalling that Woman has been fabulous *for* the Land-in-Waiting in roles that have been other than passive, or *chingada.* In pursuit of primogeniture and right inheritance, Sarah straight-forwardly has Hagar and Ishmael disinherited; Miriam foregrounds her disapproval of the Ethiopian wife of her brother Moses. Signally, Deborah and Barak will celebrate in song the fact that Jael, Heber's wife, took "a nail of the tent, and took a hammer in her hand, and went softly unto [Sisera], and smote the nail into his temples, and fastened it into the ground: for he was fast asleep and weary" (Judges 4; *Concierto barroco* 116):

> She put her hand to the nail, and her right hand to the workmen's hammer; and with the hammer she smote Sisera, she smote off his head, when she had pierced and stricken through his temples. At her feet he bowed, he fell, he lay down: at her feet he bowed, he fell: where he bowed, there he fell down dead. (Judges 5:26-27).

Of course, Deborah and Barak had celebrated while the "mother of Sisera looked out at a window, and cried through the lattice, Why is his chariot so long in coming? Why tarry the wheels of his chariots?" Henry Kraus's "Eve and Mary: Conflicting Images of Medieval Women" looks elsewhere in this tradition to account for an apocryphal Judith who "is shown [in a capital relief at Vezelay] returning from her self-imposed task [the beheading of Holofernes]. She stands, magnificently conscious of her accomplishment, brandishing Holofernes' head before the astonished eyes of the men cowering on the city's walls" (1982:88). Parenthetically, as with Sisera's mother there is a certain native-woman symmetry in the frisson of a *malinchista* role that the biblical narrative assigns to the woman of Jericho, Rehab the harlot. For she takes in and hides Joshua's spies—to the great good fortune of herself, "her father, her mother, and her brethren, and all that she had" when Jericho fell (Joshua 7:23). All the same, the Trible of *Texts of Terror* is persuaded, and persuasive, I might add, in her view that material such as "the betrayal, rape, torture, murder, and dismemberment" of her unnamed woman makes for a story that "we are commanded to speak" about—insofar as it depicts the "horrors [of] female helplessness, abuse, and annihilation" in the taking of virgin territory.

"Wild arithmetic of murder" and "colony of joys" coalesce in Lamming's narrative of the making of the New World in *Natives of My Person*, in which context, so we have learned, "virgin lands" are "the most blessed territory," because "a man can start from scratch, turn any misfortune into a fact of triumph. You can only manage it in virgin lands where you can start from scratch." There is a certain coherence to all this investment in virginity, and it highlights some ironic juxtapositions in sex-and-conquest tales of the New World. Consider, here, the circumstances under which patriarchs and virgins converged on a certain day in September 1519, in the Tlascala of Bernal Díaz's *The Conquest of New Spain*. Díaz's record is that Caciques of the land showed up with an offering of note for the Castilians. For what they brought "with them [were] five beautiful Indian maidens, all virgins. They were very handsome, for Indian women, and very richly adorned, and each one being the daughter of a chief brought a maid to serve her. Then Xicotengo said to Cortés: 'This is my daughter. She is unmarried and a virgin. Take her for yourself'— he put the girl's hand in his—'and give the others to your captains'" (1963:176). The Inca offering that Guaman Poma records in the Andes of *Nueva crónica del buen gobierno* (c 1615) is a familiar one, though nuanced in one detail. We learn here that the presents that Atahaulpa sent to Pizarro and Almagro and the factor Illan consisted of "male servants and sacred virgins"; that some of the virgins were also offered to the Spaniards' horses because, seeing them eating maize, the Peruvians took them for a kind of human being. Until that time, horses were unknown to our people and it seemed advisable to treat them with respect" (1973:107). This is protocol and gift-giving— commerce and unequal exchange, too—that Carpentier's *Explosion in a Cathedral* also embeds in the allegorical history that he makes of the Carib's pursuit of an "Empire of the North" where there had to be the seduction of those imaginable "virgins' baths." In it, and with the Caribs hell-bent for a utopia of "unimaginable buildings," "all the males of other races were ruthlessly exterminated, and the women kept for the propagation of the conquering race. Thus there came to be two languages; that of the women, the language of the kitchen and of childbirth, and that of the men, the language of warriors, to know which was held to be a supreme privilege" (1979:243).

This traffic and trade in women is apparently countered when, in *The Divine Narcisus*, Sor Juana Inés de la Cruz depicts America as "a noble Indian woman" in ceremonial regalia. The same effect would appear to hold in that picture of Doña Marina in "sandals and Yucatean huipil" that we get from Carpentier's *Concierto barroco* (1988:35). The cast of characters in the *auto sacramental* consists of The Occident, America, Zeal, Religion, and Musicians and Soldiers. At the end, "All" will make their exit dancing and singing: "Blessed the day / I came to know the great God of the Seeds!" This female-embodied America and her great God of Seeds had by then been re-cognized in the Christian nun's drama of contact and conversion. "God of Seeds," Margaret Peden explains, "might refer to several Aztec gods, but here he is most obviously Huitzilopochtl, the most powerful of the gods of Tenochtitlan" (135). "*Díos tutelar*," Huitzilopochtl had been singularly important in the celebrated, and to non-Aztecs sinister, emergence of Aztec hegemony around the year 1323, when the god "*dío a conocer su designio*" (Leon-Portilla 1962: 41). At any rate, the surrender to Euro-Christian triumphalism is absolute in the *auto sacramental*, for all that Sor Juana has America responding to Zeal of Religion in full regalia, with "the mantas and huiptiles worn when singing tocotin" (1985:91). *The Divine Narcissus* redeems the Amerindian from the designs of her erstwhile *díos tutelar*, and does so in absolute terms, notwithstanding the nativist emphases to which Peden calls attention. These include the apparent defiance with which the *auto*'s female America declares, "though my person come to harm, / and though I weep for liberty, / my liberty of will, will grow, / and I shall still adore my Gods!" The same is true of the moral ecology of such lines as "what value precious ores untold / if their excrescences befoul / and sterilize a fertile earth."

Still, the greater persuasion lay in Christian conversion, and in the fiercer logic of European penetration and domination. It is worth keeping in mind that Sor Juana's *auto* had been responsibly dedicated to "Madrid, the Royal Town / the Center of Our Holy Faith, / the Jewel in the Royal Crown, / the Seat of Catholic Kings and Queens" by whose authority the "Indies have been sent the blessing of Evangel Light" (123). Destined for performance in Madrid, it had been composed under the colonial patronage of the Most Excellent Countess of Parades, Marquesa of Laguna, Vicuregal Lady of New Spain. Besides which, and quite above and beyond this level of principalities and powers, there was Christian Scripture; and Religion had reinforced her appeal to America with due authority—in the prophetic voice of a St. Paul according to whom, all unknowing, the Indians had been worshipping the Christian God: "THE UNKNOWN GOD [who] is not unknown, but One you laud," only ignorantly (111-12). In the end, Pauline pre-text and redemptive subservience converge to fashion a new world in which "all" could agree that

> there is but One
> True God of Seeds!
>   [and] with tender tears
> by joy distilled,
> raise[d] voices high
> with gladness filled. (127)

The dis- and re-membering of the *mujer presa* in New Spain is a rather more ambiguous matter when we move from the *auto sacramental* to the Sor Juana of the *Respuesta a Sor Filotea*. This is the document—Peden persuasively identifies it as an "intellectual autobiography"—in which Sor Juana responded to a letter from the Bishop of Puebla. Dated November 25, 1690, and signed "Filotea" (lover of God), the Bishop's letter had sought to put constraints on the nun's extra-religious intellectual interests. It is arguably the case, here, that Sor Juana responds with and through a cluster of experiences that re-present the Christian apologist and *auto* sacramentalist as Juana de Asbaje of Napantla and Mexico City, that is, as a colonized woman of the Americas who had been contraindicatively educated to be Sor Juana Inés de la Cruz. In the New Spain of Mesoamerica, Paz has observed, "Religion was the pivot of society and the true spiritual food of its component parts. But religion was on the defensive, seated firmly on its dogmas, for the apogee of Catholicism in America coincided with its decadence in Europe" (1973b:26). Meanwhile, and from the Andean context of the Inca world, Irene Silverblatt makes the case that the life history of Francesca Guacaquillay, a "pagan" virgin priestess,"was emblematic of the terrible years of extirpation campaigns." Silverblatt uses her terrain and its type to make the point that the likes of Guacaquillay were representatively conflated into virgin and witch, and therefore illustrate the "common pattern of Andean colonial purity with its mixing of female chastity and prohibitions against contamination by Church rites and doctrine" (1994:269). Contentious Andean circumstances ("colonial cauldrons") made such women "devil-inspired underminers of colonial disorder"; elsewhere, they stood for "'pure,' uncontaminated ministers of 'idolatory'" (*ibid.* 271).

At any rate, the letter from Don Manuel Fernández de Santa Cruz y Sahagún, Bishop of Puebla, had not too subtly suggested that Sor Juana might do better to dedicate herself to "more suitable pursuits" than had been evidently the case when, for example, she subjected the Portuguese priest Antonio de Vieyra's 1650 "Sermon on the Mandate" (on the exemplary singularity of Christ's washing of feet on Maunday Thursday) to a searching critique (Peden 1982:2). For all that the sum of the Bishop's response was benign, he had nonetheless invoked Saint Paul to make the point that women should be content to study for the love of learning, and not in order to teach. "I do not intend, by this advice," he wrote, "that you alter your natural inclinations by renouncing books, but, rather, that you better them by reading occasionally in the book of Jesus Christ" (3). Sylvia Molloy contextualizes: "More than excluding women, [such] language assigns women to a subordinate place and, from that position of authority, deauthorizes woman's word. That is, it includes that word but in a position of weakness. This happens on more than one level, from the practice of language—the Bishop of Puebla belittling Sor Juana, [Ruben] Dario belittling Delimira Augustini—to editorial policies" (1991:143).

The supple cleverness with which the *Respuesta* challenged Pauline authority and the episcopal right to dis-member provides indices of a Euro-Mesoamerican conversion that was perhaps more nuanced than the gladness of the *auto sacramental* allows. There is the added fact that, for all that it was written from the margins of the imperial world, the *Respuesta* resonates, too, with the *querelle de femmes* (woman question) to which the likes of Helisenne de Crenne, for one, had contributed in 1539. This woman's *Les Epistres invectives* should be read, Mustacchi and Archambault suggest, "as a dialogue between two voices, one the voice of abstract antifeminism, sustained by many centuries of misogynic commentary, and the gentler voice of experience and good sense, which can draw equal sustenance from that same tradition. If *Les Epistres familières* are an account of the victory of life over abstract reasoning, *Les Epistres invectives* are a response—reasoned, dignified, hurt, ironic, and playful by turns—to a long tradition of classical and Judaeo-Christian antifeminism (1986:13). Considered in this light, Sor Juana was indeed the *sorpresa* that she was, and thus the prodigy that she remains in Peden's *A Woman of Genius* (1982). It is also significant that the *Respuesta* manages to both clash with and cloister a *sor* who was nothing if not a *sor presa*, a captive nun (Peden 1982:9), and perhaps *the* "image of a society on the verge of schism" (Paz 1973b:29).

It is this *Sor/presa* whose versions of things resonate so when the "Response to Filotea" gives due recognition to Pauline truth by accepting a "philosophy of the kitchen," in a concession that speaks about "natural secrets" that may be discovered only while cooking. She takes their measure, and their chemistry, in egg and sugar, butter and oil. To this recipe she adds, "I often say, when observing these trivial details: had Aristotle prepared victuals, he would have written more" (Peden 1982:62). There is, meanwhile, the latitude and the challenging import of the set of rhetorical questions that the *Respuesta* asks:

> How without Logic, could I be apprised of the general and specific way in which the Holy Scripture is written?" Moreover, how without Rhetoric and Physics, and without Arithmetic and History, could there be fullness of perception and of meaning? "How should I know whether Saul's being refreshed by the sound of David's harp was due to the virtue and natural power of Music, or to a transcendent power God wished to place in David? . . . Without Geometry could one measure the Holy Arc of the Covenant and the Holy City of Jerusalem, whose mysterious measures are foursquare in their dimensions? (34).

The "Response to Sor Filotea" was, Peden declares, the "passionate yet icily rational outburst" that "an intellectual woman in a world of male dominance and, especially, ecclesiastical dominance" was led "inexorably to produce." It was, in this respect, "the first document in our hemisphere to defend a woman's right to teach, to study, and to write." It was also followed by "four years of total silence. [Sor Juana] acceded to the insistent demands of the Church hierarchy; she surrendered her books, and her collections of musical and mathematical instruments; she ended her communication with the world of the Viceregal court" (*ibid.* 1).

In the latter, and darker, days of the circum-Caribbean, the *mujer presa* would be otherwise incarnate, of course. She becomes, for example, that *womanshenegro* in Luís Pales Matos who causes the "West Indies" to burn in its "Nañigo blood" and "wanton calendas"; and in the "rumba, macumba, candombe, bámbula" rhythms with which some "honey-colored amber," say,Tembandumba of Quimbamba, walks through "the inflamed Antillean street" to where Haiti "offers its calabashes," Jamaica its "fiery rums," and "Cuba tells you: 'Get it mulatta!'" (Johnson 1977:123-126). In Ferré's "Cuando las mujeres quieren a los hombres" ("When Women Love Men"), this doubly possessed woman is acidly etched out in the bitterness with which the narrative's middle-class and white Isabel Luberza counterpoints Isabel la Negra, a character that Ferré based on a "legendary Isabel la Negra who was originally from the Barrio San Anton in Ponce, Puerto Rico" (Meyer and Olmos 1983:82). Ferré's version of the character provokes the eruption of the repressed with which Isabel Luberza re-articulates herself against the figure of her husband's mistress, and therefore against the certain kind of woman that only *la negra* could be: because "someone must show them the first time and that's why they go to Isabel la Negra, black like the grounds at the bottom of the coffee pot";

> because it isn't proper for a nice girl to dislocate her pelvis, because nice girls have vaginas of polished silver and bodies of carved alabaster, because it isn't right for a nice girl to get on top and gallop for her own pleasure and no one else's, because they wouldn't have been able to learn any of this with a nice girl because that wouldn't have been proper, they would not feel like machos, because the macho must always take the initiative but some must show them the first time and that's why they go to Isabel la Negra, black like the grounds at the bottom of the coffee pot, like the mud at the bottom of the gutter . . . .(Olmos 1983:85)

To my knowledge, nowhere else has the New World sum of this certain kind of woman been as far-reachingly conceived of as in Sánchez's *Macho Camacho's Beat*, with its remembering of Las Casas's "African solution," its "all the dark skin is from there," and the proofs that it is ready to offer that "life is a phenomenal thing," and therefore a "slippery and peppery, purgative and instructive, prophylactic and didactic, scatological" affair. The fabulous smell of Woman is now a hugely orgasmic matter, and incarnate in the "strong, dazzling, shiny darkness" of "Bartolomé de Las Casas's recruitments." The phenomenal scatology is represented as the fulsome product of a white Puerto Rican Senator caught in a hallucination-inducing traffic jam—while on his way to an assignation with his black mistress. Here, then, is *the* place in a genre in which "COLORED FEMALES HEAT me up," made up as they are of "black masses from Timbuktu and Fernando Po, black masses

that wiggle asses, that cock it, that open their legs to white classes from
Extremadura and Galicia, white classes that wiggle asses, that cock it, that
open their legs to Taino lasses from Manatuabon and Otoao, Taino lasses
from Manatuabon and Otoao that wiggle their asses, that cock it, that open
their legs to black masses from Timbuktu and Fernando Po: fuck about, suck
about, and anybody without a Dinga has got a swineherd from Trujillo and a
squaw: all milks the milk: the dark skin is from here." And with it, we move
into a "decocking" of the lands of Americas when "a goodly time" was had
by all.

> A LONG TIME: the reality round about abolished by closed
> eyes, the reality round about invented by closed eyes: strong
> winds that blow and carry off big women, great big women like
> the Amazons of California: dark, darkies, very dark, vanilla-
> colored, black as telephones, black as coal; big women, great big
> women like the Amazons of California, their natural condition of
> big women, great big women like the Amazons of California
> adulterated by the furious multiplication of their hairy, cavernous
> sexes distributed on every body, bursting forth like mushrooms,
> bursting forth like thistles: indiscriminately; big women, great
> big women like the Amazons of California who jumble around
> him, around the hooved satyr, his normal condition of hooved
> satyr adulterated by the furious multiplication of his hairy,
> lengthened sex: twenty hairy, lengthened sexes distributed about
> his body, bursting forth like weeds, bursting forth like diplomas:
> indiscriminately. The big women, great big women like the
> Amazons of California begin the seduction of the hooved satyr,
> like hissing squids, they force the entry of his twenty hairy,
> lengthened sexes into their hundreds of hairy cavernous sexes.
> The numerical disproportion fatigues the hooved satyr, the hooved
> satyr prepares his flight, to the courtyard of the Corona Brewery.
> The big women, great big women like Amazons of California,
> dark, darkies, very dark, vanilla-colored, black as telephones,
> black as coal, receive the message sent them by the monitor of
> their women's intuition and surround him and proceed to decock
> him: a goodly time at the decocking, a lot of time and a lot of
> shouting: the reality round about reconquered by a horde of
> horns. (Sánchez 1982:20-21)

Carpentier's heteroclitic imagination had of course orchestrated a similar
ensemble of effects in *Concerto barroco*. But the horns of that consummation
had been of a considerably less heated variety, for all that its profiles and
accents had been brought to a climax in that explosive finale into which Louis

Armstrong's trumpet had led the whole in "a glorious jamming of 'I Can't Give You Anything But Love, Baby' with dazzling variations" (1988:131). But then, Carpentier had chosen to re-score materials which, for all that they were led by the *negro* Filomeno, only involved "cornetto" finding and mating with "viola, flautino with chitarrone, while the violini piccoli alla francese joined in quadrille with the trombones" (84).

As in *Macho Camacho's Beat*, the sexual and cross-racial making of brave new worlds and all who dwell in them has produced narratives that purport to trace the genealogy of psychosexual consciousness and the longing for national form in the Americas. Gilberto Freyre, the Paz of "The Sons of La Malinche," and Frantz Fanon are among others who have sought, like Sánchez, to tease out such matters and to exalt them into design. They have done so in predictable fashion, because unable to avoid the "mythic subtext," "discursive debris," and "risible simulacra" within which Doris Sommer, for one, believes that Latin America has been inclined to fashion its "irresistible romance," "foundational fictions," and "plagiarized authenticity" (1990:130-55). Consider, in this light, the nature of the argument—or, if you wish, the "misperceiving modern Portuguese" framework and "Lusotropical myth" of "plasticity" (Miller 1985:128)—that have been *the* point in Freyre since *Casa grande e senzala* (1933). There is good reason to think, Freyre proposes, that not all slaves were victims of cruel treatment; that the typical slave in agrarian, patriarchal Brazil was happier in lots of ways than the working men in the first period of the industrial society in Brazil; that the Portuguese followed the Arab rather than the European concept of slavery, treating slaves as "part of the family." Arab custom thus contributed polygamy to sixteenth-century Brazil, a polygamy which benefitted the idea of the patriarchal family. Freyre's *O menino de engenho*, his plantation boy, had reasons enough, then, for the view that, "no doubt," he "lived a happier life." Innocent of and yet privileged by race, when "the cane was ripe / there was always a farm hand / who'd cut him a fine juicy point to suck." Even better, "one day a naked black slave girl" would come "to launch the plantation boy / on his first adventure in love." For in bodies such as theirs was material with which to "*conhecer negras nuas*" and "*viver seus primeiros romances de amor*" (1974:193-194). In this respect, the dark-skinned woman's ways had been marked and common enough— witness the ease of entry with which Antonio Olinto's *A Casa da Agua* (*The Water House*) accomplishes its ends when the priest "asked [Epifania] to lie down":

> She got into the bed and lay down without embarrassment, lay motionless, a cricket was singing in the window, the first daylight was coming through a crack in the door, when Father José opened

her legs, played a little with the hairs on her sex and entered her calmly. She had never felt it like this. A serene enjoyment, the priest's penis went in and came out, the morning light grew stronger, and she felt herself utterly suffused by it as the church bell began to sound. (1970:24)

"I wonder what happens to his kind in the tropics," Conrad's Marlow had speculated, darkly, about a European in *Heart of Darkness*. In his time, Oviedo had been preoccupied with this tropicalization of the libido in the sixteenth century of his *Sumario* and *Historia*. The same is true of the latter-day "*determinismo biológico*" and "*barroco científico*"—couched in a "*linguagem*" that was "*virtuosística e acumulativa*"—with which, among others, the Euclydes da Cunha of *Os Sertões* and the Henrique Coehlo Netto of *Rei Negro* all engaged the issue. In *Rei Negro*, for example, Julinho "grew up robust and free in that dissolute atmosphere, surrounded by shameless little mulattas, precociously licencious, and lazy urchins with whom he went to their hangouts or danced wildly in the narrow road and, the longer all this went on, growing stronger, the more there rose up in his blood a swinish sensuality which led him to sniff out the mulattas, rubbing up against them with a rolling motion, grabbing at them, feeling them over wherever he met them, in a frenzy of burning lust" (Johnson 1984:234).

Giorgio Marotti's *Il negro nel romanzo brasiliano* (1982) sums up a genre in which one comes across "lustful and voluptuous Black and mulatto sirens" in book after book. The list that makes up this *romance bárbaro* genre of man-eating mulattas and uncontrollable Black sensuality goes "on and on monotonously," with Manoel Macedo's *Pai Rayol, o feitiçero*, in Aluiso Azevedo's *O cortiço*, in Graça Aranha's *A viagem maravilhosa* (Marotti 1987:393). In full ideological bloom, Freyre would fashion the genre into a "lusotropicological" utopia in which consummation is emphatically, even if *sotto voce*, between Euro-patrician males and dark/native women. They engender the "metarace and brown skins" that he could still celebrate in a Lisbon speech, on May 29, 1970:

Under the sun of Copacabana and other Brazilian beaches, morenidade is definitely on the upswing. To Brazilians it means a denial of race and an affirmation of metarace. As a metaracial human type, the Brazilian is a living retort to any exclusivist mystique of racial purity such as the Aryan ideal, or Negritude, or the mystique of "yellow power" embraced by certain imperialist groups in the Far East. Apropos of "yellow power," though, it should be pointed out that the sallow hue of the so-called Brazilian amarelo is not always the result of malaria or some other pathological condition but it is as often as not an ecological, and therefore healthy, yellow. (1974:84)

In *Reasons of State* Carpentier mocks his novel's Head of State into a self-justifying and *reductio ad absurdum* articulation of so "round" a bed upon which "being a Latin did not mean having 'pure blood' or 'clean blood'—as the out-of-date phraseology of the Inquisition used to put it. All the races of the ancient world had been mixed together in the great Mediterranean basin, mother of our culture. In that tremendous round bed Romans had lain with Egyptian women, Trojans with Cartaginians, the famous Helen with people of dull complexion." Thus, to say "Latinity was to say mixed blood." Besides which, and should it come to that, "there's always Walker lotion, or something of the sort, to smooth our hair, hidden away in the family closet" (1976:114).

Of course, Carpentier's way with the M. Lenormand de Mezy of *The Kingdom of This World* had been considerably less involuted. This man suffered, quite simply, "from a perpetual erotomania that kept him panting after adolescent slave girls, the smell of whose skin drove him out of his mind" (1970:60). De Mezy had quickly recognized that "return to France" was not for him—this, after a few months of a "growing longing for the sun, for space, for abundance, for command, for Negresses tumbled alongside a canefield" (59). Meanwhile, in the *romance-bárbaro* version of this erotomania in *Explosion*, "dusky mistresses put many white men" under strange compulsions——after their "first scruples" had been overcome. The women did so with the "warmth of [their] black flesh"; or else with "infusions, drugs, and mysterious liquids, surreptitiously administered to a pale-skinned lover in order to 'bind' him, to hold him, and to alienate his will to such an extent that he ended up by becoming indifferent to women of his own race" (240). In Marotti's judgment, "the palm" for this type of narrative "goes to José Lins do Rego, whose artistic ability to create lost worlds is equaled only by his morbid capacity to cry over his fate." It is in his *Menino de engenho* and *Doidinho*, as well as in *Meus verdes anos*, that we find "Black and mulatto women who with their aggressive sexuality rob [youth] of innocence and contrive to turn *menino de engenho* (plantation boy) into *menino perdido* [lost boy]." They do so with consequences enough: for initiated by such women into erotic activity, the *menino* of Freyre's idyll would thereafter run wild, "deflowering she-goats and mother hens," not to speak of engaging in "homosexual relations" (Marotti 1987:394).

Whether they are of the metaracial variety, as in Freyre, or else outright *romance bárbaro*, these clusterings of issues about women, fire, and other dangerous things have since provoked the plain-speaking that we get from Afro-Brazilian Abdias do Nascimento. He is quite clear, for example, about all this when he refers to "*processo de um racismo mascarado*" and to "*o genocidio do negro brasileiro*. In English, *Mixture or Massacre*? (1978) is the succinct title under which Nascimento spells out the details, in a work that he dedicates to "the hundreds of millions of Africans and their descendants assassinated by the slavers, oppressors, ravagers, racists, rapists and white supremacists." In his "three sad races" view of Brazil, meanwhile, David Haberly negotiates the gaps between the utopian sexuality in Freyre, the dystopian libido of the *romance bárbaro*, and Nascimento. Haberly notes that "White Brazilians, after 1850, were especially preoccupied with female slaves"; and that there were "relatively few women slaves in the senzalas." Their "low fertility rate was [in effect] a major obstacle to the continuance of slavery. The [literary model] of the Pitiful Slave . . . was almost always a woman, and her usual fate—suicide after immense suffering—could be interpreted by Abolitionists as a great moral tragedy; pro-slavery Brazilians, on the other hand, must have been moved by the immoral waste of good breeding stock" (1972:38-39).

Metaracial exceptionalism is a matter of harder discrimination in Esteva Fabregat, and one that demands rather less service from native women, especially the darker ones. There is a eugenic thrust to the argument in his *El mestizaje en Iberoamérica* that is not unlike the preoccupation with "offscourings" and hybridity in the father of Carpentier's protagonist in *The Lost Steps*. "The so-called New World had become a hemisphere," the father worried, "without history, alien to the great Mediterranean traditions, a land of Indians and Negroes peopled by offscourings of the great nations of Europe, not to mention the boatloads of prostitutes shipped out to New Orleans by tricorned gendarmes to the sound of fifes" (Carpentier 1956:87-88). In Fabregat's *El mestizaje*, superior and aggressive attributes—not offscouring propensities—had to have been necessary to effect the conquest and colonization of the Americas. In the case of Spain this required that the *encuentro* and conquista involve "*individuos enérgicos, vigorosos, asimismo seleccionados para el esfuerzo físico y para la ejecución inteligente de las estrategias de dominio social.*" Granted, this coming to the Americas produced mixed-blood descendants. However, there was a preferential, indeed survival-of-the-fittest gradation that involved white paternity on Indian women and, less desirably, on black ones: "*los productos de mezcla . . . vivieron un mundo inestable que contribuía a desarrollarles tendencias agresivas, y al mismo tiempo, y dada la energía selectiva de sus progenitores poseían el vigor híbrido inherente a productos de mezcla resultantes de individuous enérgicos en su misma movilidad y confrontación ambiental permanente*" (Fabregat 1988:305).

In the Paz of *The Labyrinth of Solitude* (1961) Cortés and La Malinche make for the *confrontación ambiental permanente* that so vexes bodies private and politic in his Mesoamerica. It is, for example, this "memory of an infamy" (Candelaria) that arouses Carpentier's criollo in *Concerto barroco* to frustration and indignation against Vivaldi's opera ("The public doesn't like traitors. No singer of ours would have accepted such a part. To be a great figure deserving of music and applause, that Indian woman would have had to do as Judith did to Holophernes") (1988:116). It is also the occasion for the outrageously casual conceit that Thomas and Carol Christensen introduce in the preface to their translation, *The Harp and the Shadow*, of Carpentier's *El arpa y la sombra*. Here, the Christensens write, quoting Tzvetan Todorov, "'We are all the direct descendants of Columbus'"; they then go on to make the remarkably egregious statement: "Likewise, all American translators—that abject lot!—are descendants of our mother La Malinche, Cortés's informer, the famous whore and traitor" (1990:xii). The "memory" is similarly at work in the anxiety-ridden genealogical terrain that chicano Nash Candelaria explores in *Memories of the Alhambra* (1977:173). He does so by way of a flight into descent ("A kind of grudging accord one gives a rapist [Cortés] whose victim gave you birth") as well as a flight from one ("Certainly no Malinche. . . . So not Malinche, a quiet voice continued. Perhaps Pocahontas. Or Desert Blossom. Mestizo. Child of the Old World and the New"). In Paz, *machismo* and alien(ating) consummation are rather more consequential, as I have indicated. His sons of La Malinche do not end up being the metaracial ideal of Freyre's world; they do not quite harden, either, into Fabregat's gene-ripened *mestizajes*. Instead, Paz emphasizes a Mexican exceptionalism that is all the same over-determined by a common enough sex-and-conquest genealogy, as with Benítez-Rojo's over-worked Caribbean vagina and womb. Paz's *The Labyrinth of Solitude* is circumscribed as a result by those two "bad words (*chingón/chingada*), the only living language in a world of anemic vocables." "Corrosive" and irredeemably "shaming" words, "the idea of violence rules darkly over all the meanings, [for in them] the dialectic of the 'closed' and the 'open' fulfills itself with almost ferocious precision. The *chingón* is the macho, the male, he rips open the chingada, the female, who is pure passivity, defenceless against the exterior world" (1961:77). In sum, a critical consequence of this engendering of culture and identity is that the female body is called back into service as the vessel in which the body politic is (man)-made and (woman)-unmade.

There are reasons enough, then, to call attention to Otilia Meza's *Malinalli Tenepal, La gran calumniada*, a biography of La Malinche, and its claim to being a "*verídica historia*" (true history). Urgent and polemical, Meza insists on producing a counter-narrative to the tradition that inscribed degeneration and dystopia with and in the body of the Amerindian female: "*Según se ha asegurado siempre, la Malinche fue una nefasta figura para México, pues contribuyó con su inteligencia a la destrucción de Tenochtitlan.*

Quienes ese aseguran estan en un error" (1988:5). [We are invariably told that La Malinche was an ominous presence in Mexico's history; that she abused her intelligence to contribute to the destruction of Mexico. Those who persist in making this assertion are mistaken (*ibid.* my translation)]. "The woman [has been] interchangeably called by three names: Malintzin, Malinche, Marina," writes Norma Alarcón (1983:182-90), in the elaborate mission of recuperation that she embarks upon in "Chicana's Feminist Literature: A Re-Vision Through Malintzin or Malinche: Putting Flesh Back on the Object." Her essay appears, appropriately enough, in an edited volume entitled *This Bridge Called My Back*. It is there that Alarcón makes the point that the woman's "historicity, her experience, her true flesh and blood were discarded"; and that a "Kantian, dualistic male consciousness stole her and placed her on the throne of evil, like Dante's upside down frozen Judas, doomed to moan and bemoan" (182-90). The issue is one to which Alarcón returns, extensively examining narratives in which La Malinche is (nationalistically) worked up into—or else out of—the "monstrous double" of La Virgen de Guadalupe, in "Traduttora, Traditora: A Paradigmatic Figure of Chicana Feminism." Here, in what is at heart a subversion of investments like Paz's in La Virgen de Guadalupe, Alarcón explores invention, disempowerment, and recuperation in what is ultimately an extended hermeneutic of suspicion about constructions of gender and modes of social divison. It is the case, Alarcón argues, that "as historical subject Malintzin remains shrouded in preternatural silence, and as object she continues to be on trial for speaking and bearing the enemy's children and continues to be a constant source of revision and appropriation—indeed, for articulating our modern and postmodern condition" (*ibid.* 85).

The Loss of Eden for a Profit

> *There be creatures here as no man can in his ordinary language describe, monsters that do try to resemble men as though the power of Satan was marvellous enough to rival the Almighty. I saw creatures that would swim one moment and take to the air the next, huge giants with the face and shoulders of horses, but turning to human shape at the waist and standing upright on occasion like any man would do to show the full measure of his height.*
> Extract from "Voyages of Pierre, A Carpenter of Lime Stone" (George Lamming, *Natives of My Person*)

"What I want to know," Rolena Adorno indicates in *Guaman Poma, Writing and Resistance in Colonial Peru*, "is how the literary subject took up the challenge of cross-cultural communication in the frst hundred years after the Spanish invasion and conquest in the New World" (1986:3). Meanwhile, Sabine MacCormack's "Atahualpa and the Book" pursues the issue from the tangent that she derives from the alternative context in which New World native and Old World book are embedded in, principally, Garcilaso de la Vega's *Comentarios reales de los incas*. MacCormack does so to make the following point about "Atahualpa's incomprehension of the book he held in his hands"; and why, in Andean eyes, "the book either remained silent or disappeared." She proposes that "the different portrayals of that moment of violence and confusion" at Cajamarca on Saturday, November 16, 1532 "demonstrate that a historical event in itself and the means whereby or reasons for which it can be rendered intelligible are not necessarily the same thing" (1989:165). For example, a century later Guaman Poma invoked the Renaissance "literary conceit" of the "speaking book" to depict runners, both an Indian *chaski* and a colonial, "transporting letters held by a short stick." He does so, MacCormack explains, in an attempt at a re-constitution of things in which

> He also recalled his compatriots's first impressions of Spaniards; Andeans had noted, he observed, that Spaniards, apart from eating silver and gold, "talked with their papers day and night" and never slept. Atahualpa's speaking book is of a piece with the speaking books of literary conceit and especially of ethnographic experience. It could thus provide a concrete and intelligible explanation for the Inca's perceived behavior, and with that, a justification of sorts for Pizarro's attack. However, this explanation satisfied Guaman Poma only partially and Garcilaso not at all. (MacCormack 1989:159)

Meanwhile, in his "mediating among many worlds," Adorno's Guaman Poma had made use of extended visual and verbal allegory to confront what he recognized as the impossibility of the situation that he and his compatriots faced, caught as they were between hope that the colonial order could be reformed and the belief that reform in Peru was impossible, that "*todo es aca mentira.*" In Adorno, then, the first of the two "rhetorical problems" that Poma therefore needed to address was "how to attack and condemn the colonists, who are the vassals and subjects of the Spanish King"; the second was how "to situate himself vis-a-vis the ancient Incas whom the king, as champion of Counter-Reformational and missionary efforts, would view as pagan idolaters" (Adorno 1986:122).

Of course, there had been that Spanish man of the sword (Pizarro) and Spanish man of the book (Fray Valverde) and their framing of the issues at the Plaza de Armas, about which more later. For now, the significant point of departure is the premise that power—the stick at the end of the book, if you will—is the capacity to produce intended results, as Bertrand Russell once observed. Put even more discriminatingly, and as Omotunde Johnson has pointed out by way of Dennis Wrong, power is also "the capacity of some persons to produce intended and foreseen effects on others" (1994:403). "Whatever interpretation can be provided to better understand the complexities of Guaman Poma's world map," Mignolo writes in his summary vision of the dark side of the Renaissance, what really remains telling in any and all such versions of the *encuentro* is not so much a transcending of decolonization as it is measures of the "coexistence of conflictive territorial conceptions" and "fractured perception[s] of the world" (1995:252-253). Thus, and as in José María Arguedas's *Los ríos profundos* (1958) with its "transmutating [of] everything into that Cuzco music that opened the doors of memory," it is apparently the case that the Conquest's "chiseling" of the Inca stones—when the Spaniards "reworked them"— "must have broken their enchantment." But then, "even in the twilight one could see the edge; [for] the lime that joined the cut stones made them stand out" *(Deep Rivers*, 11-12). Of course, Spanish power had earlier clarified matters. It had made for a disaffiliation of the Native and the Book in which, after a summary trial, the Inca Atahualpa had been sentenced to death by the Spaniard, and executed in the city of Cajamarca—for all that, as required by Pizarro, he had effectively had himself translated into "booty that came to a value of 1,326,000 pieces of gold" (110). Small wonder, that the cathedral which later rose up on the Plaza of the Incas, and which had been built with Inca stones, would appear as it does in *Deep Rivers*: rather too large, "as the gates of glory must seem to those who have suffered up until the hour of their death" (10). But then, it was not as if the challenge of the smaller Jesuit church could be any less wounding. After all, "what other stones would the Spanish have used" in its construction? In addition, both churches stood on the Plaza de Armas: on "the plaza where the Incas used to hold their ceremonies"—and which "Inca Pachakutek, Renewer of Earth, made" (11).

Meanwhile, when, "without twisting the facts in any way," Bernal Díaz produced his recollections of the conquest of "New Spain" in the Indies, he put on record a *historia* that is as full of brutality as it is of signs and wonders. The men engaged in the enterprise were all "true conquerors," Díaz wrote; and they had "served His Majesty" accordingly, "in the discovery, conquest, pacification, and settlement of the provinces of New Spain; one of the finest regions of the New World yet discovered, this expedition being undertaken by our own efforts, and without His Majesty's knowledge" (1963:15). Díaz was himself no less full of import and latitude, being "Citizen and governor of the most loyal city of Santiago de Guatemala, one of the first discoverers of New Spain and its Provinces, and the Cape of Honduras and Higueras, native of the most noble and famous city of Medina del Campo, and son of its former governor Francision Díaz del Castillo, known as the Courteous—and his legal wife María Diez Rejón—may their souls rest in glory!" His narration of just the facts seems all the more *maravilloso* for being so casual. In one such encounter, so we are told,

> [the Indians] left about seventeen dead, not counting many wounded. This skirmish was fought on level ground where there were many houses and plantations of maize and *maguey*—the plant from which they make their wine. We slept near a stream, and we dressed our wounds with the fat from a stout Indian whom we had killed and cut open, for we had no oil. We supped on small dogs, which the Indians breed for food. For the houses were deserted and the provisions had been carried away. They had even taken their dogs with them, but these returned home at night, and we captured them. They proved good enough for food. (143-144)

In the Aztec accounts of such clashes, "broken spears lie in the roads"; "the houses are roofless" and their walls "red with blood." We learn, too, that "worms are swarming in the streets and plazas" (Leon-Portilla 1966:137). Such, then, was the world that the Fourth Sun had surrendered to the Fifth World. It is one in which "the Sun [itself] would at last fail to rise and the earth would burst forth to devour the people" (Clendinnen 1995a:179). The apocalypse of *Quinto Sol* was truly elaborate, for "*La Luna aún esta aterida . . . ya va el díos llagado y se arroja al fuego*" (Garibay 1985:15-16). As happened with the terror-struck moon and wounded god, the jaguar and the eagle also descended into the night of the Fifth Sun. In the end, extinction was all-embracing, and even took in Teotihuacan itself: "*todos los dioses mueren allí en Teotihuacan*" (*ibid.* 17). Historicized and measured in human terms, the imprisonment of Cuauhtemoc and the fate of the besieged Aztecs and Tlatelolcas were the occasion, too, for a truly disruptive re-cognition of the self:

> The walls are black,
> the air is black with smoke,
> the guns flash in the darkness.
> ...
> Who is that at the side of the Captain-General?
> Ah, it is Doña Isabel, my little niece!
> Ah, it is true: the kings are prisoners now!" (*ibid.* 148-149).

Notwithstanding such wreckage, evidence remains in the Amerindia that makes up Gordon Brotherston's *Book of the Fourth World* (1992) of what Leslie Silko's *Ceremony*, for one, traces to "an old sensitivity" from before "the fifth world [became] entangled with European names"; from before the divided reality in which "the names of rivers, the hills, the names of animals and plants—all creation—suddenly had two names, an Indian name and a white name" (1978:70). In the facts and fictions of times past about which Silko writes "the people shared a single clan name and they told each other who they were"; "they recounted the actions and words each of their clan had taken, and would take"; and they "had known with the simple certainty of the world they saw, how everything should be." Although the thought is more thinly articulated, one still recognizes in *Ceremony* the "script" of the Native Americas that resonates both against and within the gravitational pull of the *encuentro* that Borges so dramatically illustrates in the Magician of Qaholom; so, too, when Paz's *Conjunctions and Disjunctions* proposes that "The Aztec or the Tarahumara had only to pronounce the name, and immediately the presence would descend." We have "lost the names," Paz goes on to say, in what amounts to a *Quinto Sol* of "triviliaties" and "miserable miracle," in a world of "causes and effects, antecedents and consequences" (1974:81).

For his part, Angel Garibay records a native memory of things past in *La literatura de los Aztecas* that is as much trauma and nostalgia as it is utopian and bent. Here, the founding myth and con/fusion of experiences provoke the return to an "*Edad Dorada*" (golden age) that had been in Tula. There, once upon a time, "*todo era riqueza: fino y rico lo que so comía*"; it could be recorded, then, that "*las calabazas eran inmensamente gruesas.*" But then, not only squash was of extraordinary size; the same was true of corn. Cotton grew by itself in multicolored beauty, from red through blue to yellow and purple, all undyed: "*se producía variada forma de algodón: rojo, amarillo, rosado, morado, verde claro, azul, verde oscura, anaranjado, negrizo, puprino, rojizo, bayo. Todo ese algodón nacía asi teñido, nadie lo metía en tinta*" (Garibay 1985:26-27). In another map of ideal time and disaster—that of the Guaranis, this time—the people had journeyed through a "condemned land"; they had gone "from the sea coasts to the center of America" where they "sought paradise. They have skirted jungles and mountains and rivers in pursuit of the new land, the one that will be founded without old age or sickness. . . . The chants announce that corn will grow on its own. . . . [And] neither punishment nor pardon will be necessary" (Abreu y Gomez 1982). In the Yucatan, and for all that its narrating was in fact syncretist, the Maya *Book of Chilam Balam* reached back, too, to a time "when all lived in health, when there was no illness, no aching bones, no smallpox, no fever in the chest, no pain in the stomach, no wasting away." All "men walked erect and straight," then (Picón-Salas 1971:16-17; Clendinnen 1995a:154; Rendón 1984). Needless to say, this was all before the *dzules* (the invaders) taught fear to the Yucatan, and before "they hurt the plant and sucked the honey of the flowers of others so that their own blossoms might bloom" (Picón-Salas *ibid.*). They brought with them new beginnings to the world, as the *Book of Chilam Balam* puts it. However,

> with the true God, the true Díos, came the beginning of our misery. It was the beginning of tribute, the beginning of church dues, the beginning of strife with purse snatching, the beginning of strife with blow-guns, the beginning of strife by trampling on people. . . . [A] beginning of vexation. This was the origin of service to the Spaniards and priests, of service to local chiefs. (Clendinnen 1995a:139).

Succinctly: "The foreigners made it otherwise when they arrived here" (Clendinnen *ibid.*). Paz's *Conjunctions and Disjunctions* is of some considerable help here when it summarizes the dynamic of such oscillations. For its discussion of "Paradises" introduces us to a constellation that is "a dawning age, a world of paradiasiac meanings in which we can hardly fail to be reminded of the images of Genesis, or Arab tales, of the myths of the South Pacific or Central Asia, of the Teotihuacan paradise of Tlaloc." But then, there is a corollary vision, one that is "of another sort." It traps us in "deserts, rocks, thirst, panting, the dagger-eye of the sun"; it contains us in what, in certain conventions, is "the landscape of damnation, the 'wasteland' of the Grail legend," with their "[t]ransparent infernos, a geometry of crystals; circular hells; hells of garish, clashing colors." The sum of it all is a "pullulation of forms and monsters, temptations of Saint Anthony, Goya's Sabbaths, Hindu copulations." In short, Paz conjoins and disjoins to give us representations of Hell as "*petrification*" and of "the image of heaven" as *levitation, dissolution of the self*" (1974:90).

In Kamau Brathwaite's *Middle Passages*, Columbus's "charted mind's desire" sets out once again on uncharted waters into the New World and its conditions of possibility. He sails now along, now athwart an aboriginality in which his eyes climb "towards the highest ridges / where our farms were hidden." What he hears from his height on Brathwaite's after-deck are "soft voices mocking in the leaves." As yet resistant to the cross and the sword, the voices are again undecipherable, and provoke questions about the nature of the Land-in-Waiting:

What did this journey mean. this

new world mean. dis
covery? or return to terrors
he had sailed from. known before?

Then he was splashing silence
  Crabs snapped their claws
and scattered as he walked towards our shore. (1993:11)

The *dzules* and their "scatteration" (Smart 1984) in the New World subsequently involved more than silence and encompassed more than crab.
Thenceforth, as Brathwaite puts its, all flesh, especially aboriginal, would be
sown with salt, and brought in to feel the edge of fear and of awkward harvest
(*ibid.*). Las Casas would then declare, balancing Amerindia on the razor's
edge of coercion and conversion, that "War against unbelievers for the
purpose of subjecting them to Christian control, and to compel them by this
means to accept the Christian faith and religion, or to remove obstacles to this
end that may exist, is reckless, unjust, perverse and tyrannical." All the same,
the "sole and definitive reason of the Papacy for granting the supreme rule and
imperial sovereignty of the Indies to the monarchs of Castile and Leone was
to preach the gospel, spread the faith, and convert the inhabitants; it was not
to make these monarchs richer princes or greater lords than they already were"
(Picón-Salas 1971:48).
          Configured in this way, the lands of the Americas delimit a space within
which God, a European Christian, had before hand left hints, clues, and
encoded suggestions. Once decoded, Carpentier would declare in the mocking exaltation with which *Explosion in a Cathedral* returns to the fifteenth
century of this persuasion, signs and wonders would transform the "disputed
Archipelago" of the circum-Caribbean into a "Theological Archipelago."
After all, the Caribbean and its sea of islands were in the process of being
"integrated into [a] great, all-embracing sacramental drama," and of being
fashioned into that "immense stained glass window." There is a great deal of
irony, of course, in the fact that it is the "exploding" of just such an emblematic
representation of things that preoccupies *El siglo de las luces*, witness the
emphasis with which the narrative displays the painting "Explosion in a
Cathedral" and its representation of "a great colonnade shattering into
fragments in mid-air, and pausing a moment as its lines broke, floating so as
to fall better—before it dashed its tons of stone upon the terrified people
beneath." Lodged in a Cuban household of the eighteenth century, but
refracted throughout the superimposed centuries of the narrative, the painting
"confounded all the laws of plastic art by representing the apocalyptic

immobilisation of a catastrophe" (1979:18). Earlier, Esteban had made the painting the subject of a conflicted exegesis on consciousness. Thereafter, he had launched a decidedly heretical attack at its "huge fragments of column, sent into the air by the deflagration," and which "remained suspended, as if in a nightmare." He says, then, "Even the stones I'm going to break now were present in this picture. And seizing a stool he threw it against the painting, tearing a hole in the canvas" (296). In the end, apostate ambiguity seems to best explain the blend that Carpentier makes of the (by then torn) painting and the "bituminous darkness" into which it falls, still leaving a trace of itself (349). Emblematically, Carpentier's *Explosion* ruptures the pious economy that had once justified St. Ireneus in his belief that the church is planted as a paradise in this world, and in which light, as Stephen Baehr notes, "the idea is repeated that the church is a terrestrial paradise." The view is as much a certainty in Origen's third-century "equation of baptism with the entry into paradise" as it is in "Eusebius fourth-century *Ecclesiastical History* (where the church is referred to as the earthly likeness of heaven)"; so, too, in St. Ephraem's fourth-century *Hymns on Paradise,* where the church is said to be "similar to paradise," and in St. Germanus's eighth-century writings, in which context "the church is called 'the heaven on earth, where God, who is higher than the heavens, lives')" (Baehr 1991:15). In effect, Carpentier's New World explosion discounts the central proposition that Baehr reviews: succinctly, the proposition that *ex ecclesia non est vita.*

Given such pre-texts of the Columbian exchange between the Old World and the New one, the word "columbarium" is a fortuitous one with which to trace certain patterns of continuity and containment. Borrowing from Nietzsche, Stoekl's *Politics, Writing, Mutilation* identifies the word as meaning "edifice of concepts." More to the point, the columbarium is a "structure that houses dead metaphors, metaphors removed from their original and stunningly unique but not necessarily [logical] significations" (80). About one such clustering of sexually-charged images, this time, Pierre Ragon writes, *"Il est ici question d'images, de fantasmes, de phobies nés au contact des realités américaines et de leur circulation dans le monde des conquistadores espagnols."* He goes on to make the point that *"Des la fin du xve siècle, la decoverte du Nouveau Monde, son exploration, sa conquête et sa colonisation ont engendré dans les imaginaires européens un foisonnement d'images et d'interpretations. Ces figures ne furent ni spontanées ni gratuites. Elles étaient le produit d'expériences anterieures, vecues ou imaginaire"* (1992:7). In sum, Ragon's columbarium—*foisonnement d'images et d'interpretations*—puts on exhibit a harvest of images that was neither spontaneous nor arbitrary. Juan Gil recognizes a relevant premise in the epistemology of the discovery that he traces in *Mitos y utopías del descubrimiento* (1992). Briefly: there is a sense in which Columbus discovered nothing. Instead, what he did was to re-member according to a template of great expectations and common assumptions. Gil writes: "*no descubre nada; antes bien, rememora vivencias ya sentidas por otros y que por ello todo el mundo puede comprender y hacer suyas, vibrando con el al unísono*" (190). Wherever Columbus discovered "new worlds" or otherwise shaped them, Gil declares, he did so within the unanimity of certain conceptual and psychological constraints, among them imperfectly mediated strains of medieval Christianity and Graeco-Roman antiquity.

> Cuando descubre nuevas estrellas, islas paradisíacas, oro a espuertas, Colón se mueve, en consecuencia, dentro de las coordenadas mentales de los nautas portugueses, y en este sentido es un epígono de la tradicion que se esponja a mediados del siglo XIV, si bien hunde sus raíces en tiempos mucho mas remotos, en la Antigüedad greco-latina, tamizada despues por el Cristianismo. (191)

For which reason, O'Gorman's *The Invention of America* insists, the "history" in all this "will no longer be that which *has happened to* America, but that which *it has been, is, and is in the act of being*" (1961:46). Thus, "instead of starting from a preconceived idea of America" in order to explain how Columbus and his times received revlation about the Indies, we should start with what they did in order to explain how such a being was conceived (*ibid.*).

Sacramentally, for example, the Americas and the Indies were circumscribed in the haunt of that "UKNOWN GOD" the pre-text for which, witness Sor Juana's *The Divine Narcissus*, Saint Paul had already articulated. It is all of one *auto-sacramental* piece, then, that in the *Log* entry for Tuesday, 27 November 1492, Columbus made a point of urging their Castilian Highnesses not to "allow any foreigner to set foot or trade [in the New World], except Catholic Christians, since it was the beginning and the end of this enterprise that it should be for the increase and the glory of the Christian religion. No one should come to these regions who is not a good Christian" (Fuson 1987:120). Furthermore, and as Campanella speculated, if not in confirmation of prophecy, why should the discoverer of the Indies have been named "Christopher, the *Christus ferens*?" There was proof enough that "the discovery of America had fulfilled the prophecies of Psalm 2 (Ask of me and I shall make the nations / your heritage / and the ends of the earth your possessions)" (Pagden 1990:54). Mather's *Magnalia Christi Americana* treads familiar ground when it sounds that millenerian note according to which "the Church of God must no longer be wrapped up in Strabo's cloak" since, succinctly, "geography must now find work for a Christianography in regions far enough beyond [where] the ancients once derided them that looked for any inhabitants" (1970:16). In this, the *Magnalia*'s expansionist language echoes the *Religio Medici* in which Sir Thomas Browne had passed judgment on "the vulgarity" of those who would "wrap the Church of God in *Strabo's* cloake and restraine it unto Europe"; the deluding nature of such "bad Geographers" was as great as that of "*Alexander*, who thought hee had conqur'd all the world when he had not subdued the halfe of any part thereof" (1898:52).

Elsewhere, the Scriptures, political hegemony, and a barely disguised threat of excommunication are unmistakably etched into the document, "*Contra los que menosprecian o contradicen la bulla del Papa Alexandro Sexto*": that Scripture-laden condemnation of "those who deprecate or contradict the Bull and the Decree of Pope Alexander VI in which he grants the right to their Catholic Majesties and to their successors, and exhorts that they conquer the Indies, subjugating those savages and afterwards converting them to the Christian religion, and submitting them to their rule and jurisdiction" (Jara and Spadaccini 1989:417). After all, papal families and "dynastic manipulations" of such families were no less involved in the marshalling of forces that contributed to the invention of America. Manipulation had worked to produce "two Borgia, two Piccolomini, two della Rovere, and two Medici popes" (Marino 1994:342). To the degree that popes and conclaves openly worked to delimit the who and the where of global navigation and territorial claims, the somewhat "extreme ambitions of Alexander VI and his son Cesare Borgia appear less aberrant" (*ibid.*). For one thing, between Pope Sixtus IV (and his 1481 *Aeteri Regis*) and Alexander VI (with his *Inter Caetera II* of 1493) no less than six Papal Bulls pronounced on the rights of discovery and the privilege of sovereignty—in addition of course to Lateran Council and Great Debate in Valladolid between 1512 and 1550. The weight of commercial charters and agreements had been no less telling, and one such complex of agreements managed to represent Columbus as a corporate Adam of sorts. For it made "designate" to the said Don Christopher Columbus "during his lifetime, and after his death, his heirs and successors in perpetuity, with all those privileges and prerogatives" appertaining, all the lands of the Americas "discovered or obtained" by "his efforts and industry." A necessary prologue to the enterprise of the Indies, this juridico-economic election was "transacted and dispatched" through "Articles of Agreement," with the replies of their Highnesses at the end of each Article, in the village of Santa Fe of the region of Granada, the seventeenth of April in the year of 1492 after the birth of Our Saviour Jesus Christ. And it was thus confirmed by "I, the King. I, the Queen. By order of The King and The Queen. Juan de Coloma" (Jara and Spadaccini 1989:383-385). The kind of Book that the Ledger is was equally consequential. It duly accounted for itself as "purser's voucher" and "assigned pay allotment," and docmented the contractual arrangement according to which the "aforementioned Admiral be provided with the best caravels, pilots and sailors for the fleet." Here, transport meant and required of "Juan Garcia [de Soria that he] keep a record book in which the stores and supplies and provisions that shall be carried will be recorded" (*ibid.* 388-89).

In effect, from before even Pope Julius II and his Fifth Lateran Council distribution of terrains and types, as above, there was much in the Scripture's mapping of things that made for a certain unanimity of thought in the invention of America; so, too, for a columbarium of pre-texts that were filled with crises no less than with articles of faith and commerce. Conflicts in the record that we get from Oviedo suggest something of the cultural and racial dissonance that Biblical authority, commercial rights, and territorial claims never quite resolved. Like Bartolomé de las Casas, though the two men were much divided in the final orientation of their loyalties, Oviedo's would report that the New World was the victim of "conquistadors, who would more accurately be called depopulators or squanderers of the new lands"; it was no less that of "private soldiers, who like veritable hangmen or headsmen or executioners or ministers of Satan, [caused] various and innumerable cruel deaths . . . as uncountable as the stars." Oviedo passed judgment thus, even as he himself was declaring, *auto da fe* fashion, that "gunpowder used against Indians ('dirty, lying cowards who commit suicide out of sheer boredom, just to ruin the Spaniards by dying') should be considered incense to God" (Sale 1990:158). There was, all the same, the crucial matter of dis/affiliation; and it is clear enough in the wholly rhetorical question that las Casas posed in his *Apologetica*: how could "Divine Providence have been negligent in the creation of such innumerable peoples" as the Indies had? (Rabasa 1989:270).

Generating answers was not much helped, needless to say, by the apparent "discovery" of sodomites in the paradise of the New World. The cover of Ragon's *Les amours indiens, ou l'imaginaire du conquistador* (*Indian Loves, or the Conquistador's "Imaginary"*) (1992) is graced by two terra cotta Mesoamerican figures. They are both naked, and have their faces turned toward the reader/spectator. The bodies are angled forward; and the nether region of one is pushed back in obvious readiness for penetration. The whole resonates with the ambiguous discomfort of reports in such places as in the Dominican Palatino de Curzola's declaration that "he saw with his [own] eyes the Indians committing these crimes of sodomy and other crimes against nature." In other testimonies pederasty was variously imputed to circum-Caribbean aboriginality. Michele di Cuneo, for one, had opined that the Caribbean Arawaks had "caught" sodomy from the "wilder" Caribs coming from Terra Firma of South America: "They had perhaps seen the later raping the former, and taken to it themselves." Oviedo had been persuaded along similar lines when he mapped out the thrust in sodomitic behavior throughout Hispaniola and Terra Firma (Trexler 1995:147; 173). Still, it is worth recalling here the sex-and-conquest and therefore geo-political context in which Girolamo Benzoni wrote that the Spaniards once "seized two local boats and put fifty Indians in them with their bows and spears. And they sent them out to the [French] ship, giving them to understand that the people in it were sodomites, and if they did not kill them, they would land and seize many of them and use them as they would women" (*ibid*. 64). The Europeans that were "our sources for American institutions," Trexler observes, "did not want for long views on homosexual practices" (142). Quite so; there was, for example, the disrelish and fascinated horror ("Are you here, Ser Brunetto?") with which in *Inferno*'s Canto XV Dante Alighieri had exposed his teacher among sodomites; that is, had put him among the condemned who "when they had raced up to us" elsewhere in *Inferno* (Canto XVI) "linked their bodies in a wheel" (Pinsky 1994:151; 161).

Granting the closeness of Amerindia to *inferno*, it was crucial indeed that the acts of no freshly mapped peoples delay unduly the coming of the kingdom of gold, much less that of God, as had nearly happened when the "Fall" threatened the Scriptures on that Inca plaza at Cajamarca in 1532. On that spot, to repeat, Fray Valverde had sought to explain to Atahualpa how the Christian God had created the world; how he had sent his only Son to earth to save mankind; and how the pope had granted the emperor of Spain the right to subdue the natives of the New World. In the course of the "interchange" Valverde presented the Incan emperor with a book containing either the Scriptures or some Christian prayers, which Atahualpa rejected, causing it to fall to the ground (Martin 1974:31; MacCormack 1989:141). When the book was first handed to him, Atahualpa "began to eye it carefully and listen to it page by page. At last he asked: 'Why doesn't the book say anything to me?'" as Guaman Poma's *Crónica* would later record (Dilke 1978:103). At any rate, it was in the avenging of this Fall of Scripture upon Amerindia that artillery men fired their weapons, that the cavalry rushed into the square, and that foot soldiers led by Pizarro charged the mass of Indians. For according to Cristobal de Mena's eye-witness report, the priest had turned round, and he had shouted: "Come forth, come forth Christians, and attack these dogs our enemies, who do not want the things of God. Because this cacique has thrown the book of our holy law on the ground" (MacCormack 1989:143). Meanwhile, as depicted by Guaman Poma, the Inca's downfall was completed at Cajamarca; for it was there that, "enthroned on an *usnu,*" and thus on a throne, an observation point for astronomical data, and an opening to the inner parts of the earth, all in one, he had confronted Pizarro and Valverde. Like the reworked Inca stones of Arguedas's *Deep Rivers*, the captured Inca/*Usnu* thereupon lost its religious and political significance, and Andeans "entered into a period of sterility, 'a world upside down' as Guaman Poma expressed it, which unlike the sterile months of the year, did not come to an end at a fixed point" (MacCormack 1989:163). One recalls here other measures with which the beginnings of *quinto sol* had been recognized elsewhere, as in Fray Bernadino de Sahagún's native informants: *"Injc chicunavi capitulo: vnca mjotoa in quenjn chocac Motecucomatzin, yoan in chocaque mexica, in jquac oqujmatque, ca cenca chicaoque in Espanoles."* That is, in the Mesoamerican details of the contact and declension that we get in the ninth chapter of the twelfth book of *The General History of New Spain* where "it is told how Moctezuma wept; and the Mexicans wept when they learned that the Spaniards were very powerful" (Anderson and Dibble 1955:25). In that *relación* flight had been Moctezuma's desire; and departure his wish." In addition, "much did he consult" with those to whom "he confided his heart." And they in turn had said: "There are [some] who know the road to Mictlan and Tonatuh ichan, and to Tlalocan, and to Cincalco, that one may rest." But, of course, "Moctezuma could only await [the Spaniards]; only steel his heart and tax himself. He quieted and stilled his heart, and resigned himself to whatsoever he might behold and marvel at" (*ibid.* 26). It is in the later but concommitant days of the New Wor(l)d that there then to came to be *"creatures here as no man in his ordinary language can describe"* (Lamming). For what with Inca, Book, and Fall consubstantiated and imbricated (Carpentier) in the alienating power of the god's script (Borges), we are left with the conjunctions and disjunctions (Paz) in which Arguedas grounds his *Deep Rivers*:

> Every year the Franciscan priests go to the haciendas to preach. You should see them . . .! They speak in Quechua, bringing consolation to the Indians and making them sing mournful hymns. The *colono*s crawl around the hacienda on their knees; moaning and groaning, they touch their faces to the ground and weep, day and night. And when the priests leave, you should see them! The Indians follow them. They ride off rapidly and the Indians run after them, calling to them, leaping over the fences, bushes, and ditches, taking short cuts; shouting, they fall down, only to stumble to their feet again and climb the hills. They come back at night, and go sobbing in the chapel doorways. (*Deep Rivers* 145-146)

Great Chimerical Nations

> [Then] one night [Ts'ai Yen] heard music tremble and rise like
> desert wind. She walked out of her tent and saw hundreds of
> barbarians sitting upon the sand, the sand gold under the moon.
> Their elbows were raised and they were blowing on flutes. They
> reached again and again for a high note, yearning toward a high
> note, which they found at last and held—an icicle in the desert.
> . . . It translated well.
>
> Maxine Hong Kingston, *The Woman Warrior*

Face to face with "the constant incipiency of chaos" or "the contaminations
of contingency," the utopian bent is the consequence of an all too insistent
"wager against the unpredictable" (Paz 1974:189-201). To my knowledge,
nowhere else in the literature has wagering against but *within* the gravitational
pull of *ou-topos* and *eu-topos* generated quite the language of the body politic
into which Carpentier translates the exercise in *Reasons of State* (1974). The
occasion involves the Man who had been "hailed as restorer and custodian of
Liberty"; who had made "a triumphal entry riding on a black horse—but
without boots and in the white drill suit he had always worn at the university."
It is this man, awaited "with unction and eager impatience," who delivers the
speech in question before an immense crowd at the Olympic Stadium. In it,
the "Wise Man of Nueva Córdoba" unleashes "a torrential onslaught—
without pause to take breath—as if a dictionary were unbound, let loose, with
pages in confusion, words in revolt, a tumult of concepts and ideas, accelerated impact of figures, images and abstractions in a vertiginous flood of words
launched to the Republic, from the Logos to foot-and-mouth disease, from
General Motors to Ramakrishna." From beginning to end the speech, which
will in fact leave behind "a total mental emptiness—blank brains and an
agnostic trance," is a veritable encyclopaedia of figures, schemes, and
fantasies, all of them utopian and bent. Appropriately, the de- and transvaluation of all values does not prevent the Wise Man and Austere Doctor
from coming to the synthetic conclusion that "from the Mystic Marriage
between the Eagle and the Condor, and as a result of the fertilization of our
inexhaustible soil by foreign investment, our America would be transformed
by the vigorous Technology that would come to us from the North, [for we
are] on the threshold of a century which would be the Century of Technology
for our Young Continent." And out of this version of the extraordinary
concretion that is the Americas,

a synthesis would be born between the *Vedanta*, the *Popul-Vuh*, and the parables of Christ-the-first-socialist, the only true social-ist, nothing to do with Moscow Gold or the Red Peril, or an exhausted dying Europe, without sap or talent—and it would be as well for us to break finally with its useless teaching. . . . The start of this new Era, in which the thesis-antithesis of North-South was complemented by the telluric and the scientific, would be manifested in the creation of a New Humanity, the Alpha-Omega, the party of Hope, expressing the sturm-und-drang, the political pulse of new generations, marking the end of Dictator-ships in this Continent, and establishing a true and authentic Democracy, where there would be freedom of syndical action, provided that it did not break the harmony between Capital and Labour; . . . and, finally, the Communist Party would be legalized, since it in fact existed in our country, provided that it did not obstruct the functioning of institutions nor stimulate class war. (Carpentier 1976:289-290)

The peroration, which also left his audience with "the impression that time had stood still, independently of the ticking of clocks," is highly suggestive of that "great, empty mouth of chaos with its fatal seduction for man and the universe" which, it is worth recalling, is how Paz had once proposed that we understand the central image of the Aztec Sun Stone (1974:26). The pedigree adds relevant dimensions to what, using Marin, I have been referring to as a thalasso-graphic confusion of utopic signs. In any case, there is wor(l)d-making material here that Paz has succinctly represented in another context as "copulation of syllables [and] fornication of meanings." The formulation, in *Alternative Current* (1973:81), highlights the narratives of the chimerical bodies politic that matter here. The convergence of terrains and types thus relates *Reasons of State*'s "veritable encyclopaedia of figures" to that "*some-thing*, another thing" which Columbus's "quill" makes of the "optical illusion" of the Indies in *The Harp and the Shadow*. The same is true of that *orbis tertius* of Perfect Order which Augusto Rao Bastos's *Yo El Supremo* associates with "a cylindrical pen of the sort manufactured by prisoners serving life sentences in order to pay for their food." We learn from this narrative that its wor(l)d-making pen is evidently "not a product of the unaided imagination of the prisoner, but was made according to precise instructions":

It is of white ivory, a material not available to prisoners. The upper end is shaped like a small spatula: it bears an inscription blurred by traces of years of nibbling. "What is the use of one tooth biting on another?" was one of *El Supremo*'s favorite expressions. "To blur inscriptions by the superimposition of other more visible, though more secret, ones," *He* himself would have answered himself. [Meanwhile,] mounted in the hollow of the cylindrical tube, scarcely larger than a very bright point, is the memory-lens that turns it into a most unusual instrument with two different yet coordinated functions: writing while at the same time visualizing the forms of another language composed exclusively of images, of *optical metaphors*, so to speak. (1987:197)

There is much in the "superimposition" that helps to affiliate Supremo's dispensation with structures that Paz grounds in Coatlicue and the Aztec Pyramid. It resonates, too, in that phenomenal promiscuity with which, as above, Luis Rafael Sánchez's *guaracha* couples, copulates, and engenders bodies private and politic in *Macho Camacho's Beat*. In the end, what we get is a promiscuous pluralism in which heterogeneity is driven off-scale in the pursuit of utopian wholeness. In the pre-texts and text of Bastos's *Yo El Supremo* language and reality coincide in an "infinity of repeaters" and "pitiless inhuman slandererers"; in the "perfidy" fermented by "successive incurable scoundrels" who "cook up potfuls of infamies," and in "rats," too, which the Perpetual and Absolute Dictator's prisoners "continually train to carry clandestine communications." No less consequential is "the memory of an archive-cockroach [that is] three hundered million years older than homo sapiens." To follow the trail of so palmpsestic a "handwriting through the labryinths" of what has not been "torn" from the Perfect Order of the Supremo is to come upon "the filigreed fleuron in the vergered-perjured paper, the flagellated letters [that] now mark the unreality of the inexistent." For which reason, *El Supremo* recognizes, "I too must guard against against being deluded by the delirium of similarities. . . I am not always **I**. The only one who doesn't change is **HE**. . . . If I close my eyes, I still see him, infinitely repeated in the rings of the concave mirror" (45).

The purpose of all this conmingling of "ruminant's memory. Indigestive-disgestive Repetitive. Disfigurative. Sulliative" has both a utopian bent and a dictatorial politics to it, of course; they are not unlike the terrains and types that animate, or otherwise justify, the purpose of the speech in *Reasons of State*. In Bastos, the utopians duly prophesy that they would turn their country into a new Athens, "The Areopagus of the sciences, the letters, the arts of this Continent." But then, given the counterpoint that defines El Supremo's major preoccupation—any fall from "Absolute Power to Absolute Impotence" (409)—what "they" were really after with "their chimeras was to hand Paraguay over the highest bidder" (6-7). Bastos's "Supreme Dictator for Life" thus enters into his apparently first-person narrative as "the very image" of a "chimera," according to which "Forms disappear, words remain, to signify the impossible" (11). He looms large in a pre-text—found "nailed to the door of the cathedral, Excellency"—that is as much a signature of his presence as it is a sign of subversion and erasure:

I the Supreme Dictator of the Republic

Order that on the occasion of my death my corpse

be decapitated; my head placed on a pike for

three days in the Plaza de la Republica, to

which the people are to be summoned by the

sounding of a full peal of bells.

All my civil and military servants are to be

hanged. Their corpses are to be buried in

pastures outside the walls with neither

cross nor mark to commemorate their names.

At the end of the aforementioned period, I

order that my remains be burned and my

ashes thrown into the river. . .(3)

There is, meanwhile, that "icicle in the desert" of my epigraph from Kingston's "memoir of a girlhood among ghosts." The conclusion to which this recuperative exercise in the making of more Americas comes is that "It translated well." For out of Ts'ai Yen's tent of exile among barbarians had come a voice and a singing "so high and clear, it matched the flutes. Her words seemed to be Chinese, but the barbarians understood their sadness and anger. Sometimes they thought they could catch barbarian phrases about forever wandering." That this convergence of latitude and import translated well is, as I have said, the affiliative note on which the narrative rounds out one of the three songs from the "savage lands," with its "Eighteen Stanzas for a Barbarian Reed Pipe,"which, so we learn, "has been passed down to us" (1977:243).

By contrast, "colonial doubt and malice"; "disorder" and "greater disorder"; and "from play acting to disorder": this is "the pattern" in the chimera that Naipaul makes of his terrain and type. His *The Mimic Men* is deeply lodged in the persuasion that "to be born on an island like Isabella, an obscure New World transplantation, second-hand and barbarous, was to be born to disorder"; to be "inbred to degeneracy" even (121; 118; 184; 147). It is in a much-vexed Caribbean that Naipaul writes about his "mimic men" pretending "to be real, to be learning, to be preparing for life" in "one unknown corner" of the New World, with all its "reminders of the corruption that came so quick to the new." This thorough advocacy of determinate negation is more aggressive than is the Caribbean norm, of course; for Naipaul is quicker to confirm the terminal nature of the "symptoms of disease and fantastic growths" which every territory produces, and examples of which may be found on Isabella on any Sunday with its "twenty bizarre processions" of belief and worship. Here, too, the likes of "Cecil visited degraded Negro whores. [For] pleasure for him appeared to lie in an increase in self-violation," as though he were a man "testing his toleration of the unpleasant" (*Mimic Men* 158). In the *mapa mundi* that we get in *Guerrillas* the descent into hell is as graphic as it chimerical:

> And then he was on the highway, locked in the afternoon traffic and he was being taken past all the stations of that familiar drive. The sun, already yellowing, picked out all the ridges and dips of the scorched hill, that smoked. . . The junked cars beside the road. . . the burning rubbish dump, lorries and people amid the smoke and the miniature hills of confetti-like refuse, the big-breasted black corbeaux squatting on the fence posts or hopping about on the ground. . . the bauxite pall, the hot squalling afternoon city, melting tar, honking buses and taxies, enraged, sweating cyclists. (McWatt 1985:35-36)

In effect, "the general shipwreck" that the Caribbean cannot *not* be generates real dystopia out of utopian mirage, creating "disorder where previously everyone had deluded himself there was order. Disorder was drama, and drama was discovered to be a necessary human nutriment" (*Mimic Men* 127). Elsewhere, and this time about Argentina's contribution to the constellation of chimerical bodies, Naipaul would write of a place in which *Díos arregla de noche la macana que los Argentinos hacen de dia:* about God putting right at night the mess the Argentines make by day. This is not at all surprising, of course, for once again, sheer inauthenticity defines the boundaries of what Naipaul sees. For which reason, *The Return of Eva Peron* insists, to be an "Argentine is to be inhabit a magical, debilitating world," one in which "wealth and Europeanness concealed the colonial realities of an agricultural society which had needed little talent and had produced little, which had needed no great men and had produced none" (1980:116). This is the context in which, so Naipaul reports,

> "Nothing *happened* here," Norman di Giovanni said with irrita-
> tion one day. And everyone one, from Borges down, says,
> "Buenos Aires is a small town." Eight million people: a mon-
> strous plebean sprawl, mean, repetitive and meaningless: but
> only a small town, eaten up by colonial doubt and malice. When
> the real world is felt to be outside, everyone at home is inadequate
> and fraudulent. (*ibid.* 116-117)

Within a few years, Naipaul concludes in a typical flourish, Eva Peron "shatterred the myth of Argentine as an aristocratic colonial land. And no other myth, no other idea of the land, has been found to takes its place" (117). Its circumstances are not much helped, in this respect, by Borges's "inflated and bogus" Anglo-American reputation as a "blind, elderly Argentine, the writer of a very few short and very mysterious stories," a reputation that has possibly cost him the Nobel prize. Naipaul notes this about a man who, he writes, was given to a "curiously colonial performance," especially when he "talks about Chesterton, Stevenson and Kipling, and about Old English and his English ancestors, "with all the enthusiasm of a man who has picked up an academic subject by himself" (122).

Elsewhere, Naipaul reconfigures the Asia of his Indies into a disorder-liness which has never translated well, of course. Gordon Rohlehr addresses the import of "character and rebellion" in *A House for Mr. Biswas* (1961) to relevant effect; and here he points out that "on the surface," at least, the Tulsis appear to have "effected an admirable reconstruction of the clan in a strange and sometimes hostile environment." Naipaul's re-figuration of India in the Indies has "its leaders, its scheme of prescribed duties and responsibilities, its own law and order, its religious ritual, and it tries to provide the indivudual with the sort of job for which his talents equip him." Looked at this way, Biswas's "rebellion is inexplicable when one considers his prospects in colonial Trinidad. Because he has no alternative to life in Hanuman House, his rebellion suffers from a lack of direction, and he has to return to the protective warmth of Tulsidom, time and time again" (Rohlehr1977:87). But the fact is, of course, that Naipaul grounds his Asian Americans in the disordered circularity of a vision that mocks their recent "yet already remote voyages" from the East to the Indies. Naipaul's terrains and types breed confusion—his preferred word is "disorder"—that is fully on exhibit in the arcade of the House of Hanuman, a place that was "grey and insubstantial in the dark" with its "evening assembly of old men." These were men who could speak no English; who "were not interested in the land where they lived." At once *eu-topos* and *ou-topos*, the arcade is the reality and simulacrum of a place to which Naipaul's Caribbean Hindus "had come for a short time and stayed longer than they expected." Here, the West Indians "continually talked of going back to India." However, "when the opportunity came, many refused, afraid of the unknown, afraid to leave the familiar temporariness. And every evening they came to the arcade of the solid, friendly house, smoked, told stories, and continued to talk of India" (174).

The New World Indian muddledom is most elaborately and all the same rather benignly limned in "that blatant product of cultural cross-breeding" Mr. W. C. Tuttle, of *A House for Mr. Biswas*. This Tuttle is a strict Hindu who is no less interested in material than he is in spiritual life; "and while he is a modern man, his manner of blowing his nose is definitely uncivil in terms of modern society" (Warner-Lewis 1977). His Shorthills estate is an acquired relic from the old days of plantation slavery and creole plantocracy. Now his neighbours are French-patois-speaking Negroes. Not surprisingly, when Tuttle reaches for pedigree, telling "changes occur in architecture—the toilet becomes a sewing-room, the electric plant provides W.C. Tuttle, the physical culture enthusiast, with dumbells, a cowshed is raised on the cricket pitch, a temple is created" (*ibid.*). Out of the embrace of the contraindicative emerges the following portrait of cultural and psychological confusion:

W.C. Tuttle began with a series of photographs, in large wooden frames of himself. In one photograph W.C. Tuttle, naked except for dhoti, sacred thread and caste marks, head shorn except for the top knot, sat crosslegged, fingers bunched delicately on his upturned soles, and meditated with closed eyes. Next to this W.C. Tuttle stood in jacket, trousers, collar, tie, hat, one well-shod foot on the running-board of a motorcar, laughing, his gold tooth brilliantly revealed. There were photographs of his father, his mother, their house; his brothers, in a group and singly; his sisters, in a group and singly. There were photographs of W.C. Tuttle in various transitory phases: W.C. Tuttle with beard, whiskers and moustache, W.C. Tuttle with beard alone, moustache alone; W.C. Tuttle as weightlifter (in bathing trunks, glaring at the camera, holding aloft the weights he had made from the lead of the dismantled electricity plant at Shorthills); W.C. Tuttle, in Indian court dress; W. C. Tuttle in full pundit's regalia, turban, dhoti, white jacket, beads, standing with a brass jar in one hand, laughing again (a number of blurred, awestruck faces in the background). In between there were pictures of the English countryside in spring, a view of the Matterhorn, a photograph of Mahatma Ghandi, and a picture entitled "When Did You Last See Your Father?" It was W.C. Tuttle's way of blending East and West. (*House for Mr. Biswas* 460-461)

The body politic in Bastos's *I The Supreme* is grounded in a recognizably fabulous disarray that is not unlike, though rather less sensual than, what we get behind the "Cyclopean walls" of Christophe's Citadel in Carpentier (*The Kingdom of This World*) and Césaire (*The Tragedy of King Christophe*); so, too, in the circum-Caribbean of Márquez's *The Autumn of the Patriarch* and the Macondo of his *One Hundred Years of Solitude*. The making of the chimerical nation in Bastos is likewise subject to an engendering that is not really "childbirth." Instead, it is the "wildbirth" of terrain and type that we get when the dictator's civil and military functionaries foist off the task of counting heads onto clerks who then proceeded to do so "by counting on their fingers, lying stretched out in their hammocks after having chased after peasant girls, mulattas and Indians all over the backlands, in all the brakes and brambles, round the remotest farmhouse. One sniff at the papers and you can smell the stink of their breeches. . . . I find here, [*El Supremo* observes], one Erena Cheve, a woman those clerks have had the balls to give 567 sons to, all with the oddest names and ages, the youngest still unborn and the oldest older than his mother." The body politic that surfaces then is a habitation of "phantoms come from the heights of the imagination [of] profligate figure-flingers who have made their trousers flies their principal pieces of military equipment" (Bastos 1987:402-403). But then, the utopian bent of *Yo El Supremo*'s reformist seekers of the Land-without-Evil are no less constrained in a theater of universal voracity, one in which like was eaten by like, and then consubstantiated and imbricated (Carpentier). For which reason, there is instruction to be had in the fact—"Absolutely true, Sire!"—that once upon a time the "First-Grandfather of the Indians of the forest, according to a dream told and sung in their traditions, made his way out of the bowels of the earth by raking it with his fingernails." Ant-bears, too, had also emerged. But then, for an earth which necessarily "devours men in search of the Land-without-Evil," "red hair, bones, teeth, couldn't matter less. Mere baubles." It is thus that the waiting earth bears us on its back in Bastos, "some for a fair time, others less." But be that as it may, it soon enough "gets tired, rolls us off, and eats us." Afterwards, "other men, double-men, come out of its insides." But, she "always ends up eating [all] those who come into and those who come out of her inside. She's down there waiting" (259). Given the added thought that "these vapors [also] issue forth from me," El Supremo wonders, what is one to do, when one is oneself "the pit that exhales mortal emanation, the oven that spews forth burning clouds of smoke, the mine that vomits out a suffocating damp?" All the more so where the left hand continues to engender, even when the right one has already "fallen dead: "It writes, it drags itself across the Book, it writes, it copies. I dictate the inter-dict beneath the rule of another hand" (414).

In Márquez's *Autumn*, meanwhile, the Patriarch's way is to "unbutton the nine buttons of his fly" and to vast increase "show his huge tool" in erotic surges that then spawn short-order (that is, seven-month) "runts" (1987:19). There is the mosaic, too, of this narrative's "Babelic labyrinth of [a] commercial district, [with] its lethal music, the labara of lottery tickets, the pushcarts with cane juice, the strings of iguana eggs, the Turks and their sunlight-faded bargains, the fearsome tapestry of the woman who had been changed into a scorpion for having disobeyed her parents, the alley of misery of women without men who would emerge naked at dusk to buy blue corbinas and red snappers . . . the everyday light of the pelicans around the corner, the disorder of the colors of the Negro shacks on the promontories of the bay" (14). Here, the utopian bent of Márquez's terrains and types oscillate against, or else collapse into, a "vast mournful realm" that may then surface as "orchid sprigs, birds of paradise, and jaguars sleeping on native barren uplands" (15).

The world-making *dépense*, or surplus, of this material is related, Carpentier has famously argued in the preface to *The Kingdom of This World*, to the newness of the "formations" that have made the "history of all of America" nothing if not "a chronicle of marvelous realism." C. L. R. James has elsewhere appreciated the import of such bodies by way of Wilson Harris's rather more involuted genealogies, according to which "*We are the potential parents that can contain the ancestral house*" (James 1967:417). Meanwhile, when Fitzgerald's *The Great Gatsby*'s commits itself to the "following of [such] a grail" his narrative ends up mapping an "unfamiliar sky" which, as seen through "frightening leaves," caused one to shiver with the "discovery of what a grotesque thing a rose" can be, and with the recognition of how "raw the sunlight [can be] upon scarcely created grass." Given *The Great Gatsby*'s transitions—from "fresh, green breast" through "ladder leading up to a secret place above the trees" to "valley of ashes"—we end up in and as the chimera of a "new world, material without being real, where poor ghosts, breathing dreams like air, drifted fortuituously about" (162). It is reasonable enough to argue that there are topographic conceits in all this that help to account for settings in Márquez's *Autumn* that are now "the prophetic waters of soothsayers' basins," now a presidential palace which looked more like a marketplace." In such a place,

> a person had to make his way through barefoot orderlies unload-
> ing vegetables and chicken cages from donkeys in the corridors,
> stepping over beggar women with famished godchildren who
> were sleeping in a huddle on the stairs awaiting the miracle of
> official charity, it was necessary to elude the flow of dirty water
> from foul-mouthed concubines who were putting fresh flowers in
> the vases in the place of nocturnal flowers and swabbing the floor
> and singing songs of illusory loves to the rhythm of dry branches.
> (1976:12)

Meanwhile, there is a great deal of *recien formación* (Carpentier) in the
Macondo of *One Hundred Years of Solitude*. For one thing, this world of
Márquez's is tellingly situated on "the bank of a river of clear water that ran
along polished stones, which were white and enormous like prehistoric eggs.
[On this site] the world was so recent that many things lacked names, and in
order to indicate them it was necessary to point" (11). Macondo's emergence
thus contributes its share to the dis/play of becoming-signs in the New World,
among them the "growing economy of [a] Creation" that had been "barely
named as yet by the torpid, hesitant tongue of the Man-Child" in *Explosion
in a Cathedral* (176); so, too, that appeal in Walcott (*Another Life*) and
Carpentier (*The Lost Steps*) to that responsibility that man was proving
unequal to the New World: "Adam's task of giving things their names"
(Walcott 1976). No less consequential is the "natural history" through which
Walcott's "Names" evolves its "I" from a "race [that] began as the sea began
/ With no nouns, and with no horizons / with pebbles under [the] tongue" (*Sea
Grapes*). There is a fine recapitulation of the import of such topographical
features in Regina Janes's "revolution in wonderland" summary of being and
becoming in Márquez's Macondo:

> Our first glimpse of Macondo is pre-Adamic and Arcadian,
> things lack names in a primitive, egalitarian idyll before "original
> sin." Mixing Cain and Moses, the founders come to a land no one
> had promised them because one of them has killed a man, and the
> murderer stops in Macondo because he has dreamed of a great
> city. (Cain is the founder of cities.) Thereafter, we descend in the
> violent complications of nineteenth- and twentieth-century poli-
> tics, with events prophesied before they occur, plagues, a deluge,
> and a final "apocalyptic wind," a "biblical hurricane" that ends
> the novel by destroying the town and the last Buendia, who is
> really a Babilonia and thus related to the scarlet whore with her
> cup of abominations, who is a great city, fallen. (50-51)

When we again come upon the circum-Caribbean in *Autumn of the Patriarch*,
this narrative's prolific "father of the nation" is virtually disseminated

throughout the wonder-working paradoxes of his brave new and "great, chimerical, shoreless nation." It is an intriguing matter here that the Colombian novelist has his "odd discoverer" (Stevens) orienting himself toward the Caribbean archipelago from a vantage point that is very much like Columbus's at The Dragon's Mouths site of the Terrestrial Paradise. Márquez's Patriarch-Politician, a "false dead man" with the "open eyes of a sleepwalker in the shadows" (82), is accordingly positioned to "contemplate [a] line of islands as lunatic as sleeping crocodiles in the cistern of the sea" (152). It is from that "alchemical plateau" (Walcott) that the Patriarch, now "somewhere between 107 and 232 years old," conjures up the alternative future and its utopian bent. He does so in imagery that once again makes "the whole universe of the Antilles from Barbados to Veracruz" a "*something*, another thing" (Carpentier) that is couched in the language of paradise. Márquez's Patriarch dreams, then, of a certain "one island" that "doesn't even have a sea to get there by [of that] saddest and most beautiful [of] islands in the world that we go on dreaming about until the first light of dawn." He does so in the face of the "blandishments of death" and of the ambiguous temptation of other islands that are as extravagant and myth-inducing "in the showcase of the sea" as they are mundane and myth-mocking in the "breeding ground of islands which is the Caribbean." Therefrom,

> the perfumed volcano of Martinique . . . the tuberculous hospital, the gigantic black man with a lace blouse selling bouquets of gardenias to the governors' wives on the church steps . . . the infernal market of Paramaribo. . . . the crabs that came out of the sea and up through the toilets, climbing up onto the tables of ice cream parlors, the diamonds embedded in the teeth of black grandmothers who sold heads of Indians and ginger roots sitting on their safe buttocks under the drenching rain . . . the solid gold cows on Tanaguera beach . . . the blind visionary of La Guayra who charged two reals to scare off the blandishments of death. . . . Trinidad's burning August, automobiles going the wrong way, the green Hindus who shat on the middle of the street . . . [the Patriarch also sees] the rebirth of Dutch tulips in the gasoline drums of Curacao . . .the stone enclosure of Cartagena de Indias. (39-40)

Meanwhile, utopian sign and dystopian surplus explain the emphasis of the "last major turning" point in Pablo Neruda's *The Heights of Macchu Picchu* where—like Carpentier contemplating the building of that mountain on a mountain, the Citadel La Ferriere—"Neruda begins to wonder [about] the men who built up stone on stone, in long-past time"; to consider "whether the geometrical precision of the citadel might not in fact have been erected on a

base of human suffering [with] 'Stone above stone on a groundwork of rags'."
If, for example, that Andean aspiration to the sun required the work of slaves,
"in what conditions did these live? Was Ancient America—that not only
'bore the rose in mind' but could translate it 'into the radiant weave of
matter'—based on starvation, hoarding 'the eagle hunger' in its depths?"
(Pring-Mill 1966:xviii). In this respect, the constellation that Neruda makes
of "las alturas de Macchu Picchu" is familiar in the simultaneity of what it
encloses: in its reach for genesis ("High reef of the human dawn") and
recognition of eschatology ("Spade buried in primordial sand"). *Las alturas*
explores this chimera of an Inca presence and absence—"tall city of stepped
stone, / home at long last of whatever earth / had never hidden in her sleeping
clothes"—through and past "the barbed jungle's thickets" and "the ladder of
the earth." Yet another evidence of the numinous and the concrete, here,
finally, "was the habitation, this was the site" where Neruda confronts his
Americas with a moral imperative about governance and the ideal: "And
man, where was he?" His answer is a New World one, embedded as it is in
the contraindicative embrace of

> . . . two lineages that had run parallel [and who]
> met where the cradle both of man and light
> rocked in a wind of thorns. (Neruda 1966:27)

The "hymn," "theology," and "discourse in stone" of the Aztec Pyramid and
of Coatlicue are the Mesoamerican structures within which the Paz of
Alternating Current grounds his answers to such questions. They constitute
forms of "the broken mirror where the world sees itself destroyed"; and it is
in them, Paz writes, that Coatlicue strikes us "as a cluster of meanings"; that
its "symbolic richness dazzles us, and [that] its sheer geometrical proportions,
which have a certain grandeur all their own, may awe us or horrify us"
(1973a:26). Close encounter with the weave of matter that the figure represents yields import of a telling sort: "If we really study it, rather than simply
thinking about it," we come to recognize that "It is not a creation; it is a
construction. Its various elements never fuse into a form. The mass is the
result of a process of superposition. . . . A dense jumble of forms, Coatlicue
is the work of semicivilized barbarians: it attempts to say everything, and it
is not aware that the best way to express certain things is to say nothing about
them. It scorns the expressive value of silence: the smile of archaic Greek art,
the empty spaces of Teotihuacan. As rigid as a concept, it is totally unaware
of ambiguity, allusion, indirect expression. Coatlicue is a work of blood-
thirsty theologians: pedantry and cruelty" (*ibid.*). For Paul Westheim, the
figure is "montrosity monumentalized to the sublime. The history of the
world knows of only one similar case, only one visionary creation where

monstrosity has been shaped with identical vigor: Dante's Inferno" (Keen 1990:520). The darkly panegyric image that Diego Rivera once made of the Aztec use of or response to the "Great Material"—he saw in it "the joy and moral clarity of the Sacrifice, mystic culmination, from which anaesthesia eliminated pain, for pain would destroy the magical efficacy of the act" (525)—moves us along into the farther reaches of the utopian bent toward which Paz (1972) heads when he conjures up a vision of "deserts, rocks, thrists, panting." It all makes for a context in which context the "dagger-eye of the sun" looks down upon and fires into existence a certain kind of response:

> The Aztec version of Mesoamerican civilization was grandiose and somber. The military and religious groups, and also the common people, were possessed by a heroic and inordinate belief: that they were the instruments of a sacred task that consisted in serving, maintaining, and extending the solar cult and thus helping to preserve the order of the cosmos. The cult demanded that the gods be fed human blood in order to keep the universe operating. A sublime and frightening idea: blood as the animating substance of the motion of the worlds, a motion analogous to that of the dance and to that of war. The war dance of the stars and planets, a dance of creative destruction. (1972:90)

In Leon-Portilla (1959), the great main temple in Tenochtitlan, dedicated to that god of seed and sun Huitzilopochtli, had become "the scene of innumerable sacrifices of captives" from nearby places as well as from "such distant regions as Oaxaca, Chiapas and Guatemala" (1966:xxi). To understand this convergence of dark descent and angle of ascent, with its "superficially elevating and reassuring identification," Clendinnen's *Aztecs* explains, "it is necessary to grasp something of how the Mexica understood time"; for they, like Mesoamerica generally, knew that Four 'Suns', or world-creations, had preceded the one in which we and the Mexica live, which is the Fifth and last Sun" (1995a:35). The motions of history thus helped to fashion "the great tangle of ideas" in which the Mexica embedded "apprehension and comprehension of the world" (209), as much in the figure of Coatlicue as in the war dance of the stars. "After Talacaelel [nephew to Itzcoal and royal counselor] inculcated the idea that [the Sun] had to be fed with ['that most precious food of all, human blood'], war became a cultural institution of primary importance in Aztec life, since was a means of obtaining victims to appease the god's insatiable hunger" (Leon-Portilla 1966:xxv). Thus, "the Aztec warriors never forgot that their first duty was to take captives to be sacrificed" (*ibid*). It is in the anethesticized constellation that Rivera makes of this pre-text that we read: "After a purifying preparation with beautifiul living for two years, after having left in the bellies of two virgins, two new lives in exchange for his own, the victim converted himself into a sacred book of the revealing entrails of the Macrocosm, and his heart, like a splendid bleeding flower was offered to the Father Sun, irradiating center of all possibility of life. Or [else] to the magnificent and beautiful Huitzilopochtli" (Keen 1990). It is easy enough to recall here that Magician of Qaholom, in Borges's "The God's Script," transfixed by the language of the jaguars that he can no longer celebrate as he once did when "With the deep obsidian knife I have cut open the breasts of victims." Devastated as he now is by Pedro de Alvarado, can only "imagine the first morning of time"; filled with pity, he imagines, too, his "god confiding his message to the living skin of the jaguars, who would love and reproduce without end, in caverns, in cane fields, on islands, in order that the last men might receive it." But then, Tzinacan also acknowledges a "net of tigers, [a] teeming labyrinth of tigers, inflicting horror upon pastures and flocks in order to perpetuate a design" (Borges 1964:171).

"What stuns and paralyzes the mind," Paz writes about the embrace of the contraindicative, is "the use of realistic means in the service of a metaphysic both rigorously rational and delirious, the insensate offering up of lives to a petrified concept" (1972:94). A signal feature of what Paz refers to above as "the dance of creative destruction" is the concommitant fact that its misalliances of politics and metaphysics are of the sort that invariably prove to be "so intimate, so exacerbated, and so deadly" (*ibid.*). And it is in precisely one such misalliance that Aimé Césaire grounds the history, body politic, and that chimera of an architecture of the Haitian Revolution, La Ferriere, that he accounts for in his 1963 *La tragédie du roi Christophe* (*The Tragedy of King Christophe*). The same is true in the version which Carpentier had produced earlier, in 1949, as *El reino de este mundo* (*The Kingdom of This World*)—with its "Lords Back There" of Guinea and its Macandal and his remembrance of things past, especially when, "with terrible gestures, he recalled his trip, years earlier, as prisoner before he was sold to the slave-traders of Sierra Leone"; so, too, its M. Lenormand de Mezy, who was an "assiduous visitor to the Cap theater, where actresses from Paris sang Jean-Jacques Rousseau's arias or loftily declaimed tragic alexandrines, pausing between hemistichs to wipe the sweat from their brows" (1970:59). No less consequential, there were the mastiffs sent from Santiago de Cuba, on a ship of dogs "to eat [the] niggers" of the slave uprising (89). In 1943, Carpentier had thus discovered "marvellous realism"at "every step of the way" when he learned of the fantastic story of Bouckman, the Jamaican initiate of the uprising; he had ventured into La Ferriere, that work of unparalleled architecture, where he breathed in the atmosphere created by Henri Christophe, a monarch of incredible endeavors, much more surprising than all the cruel kings invented by the surrealists, very susceptible as they were to imaginary tyrannies, though not actually suffered. Carpentier had thereupon expanded the import of it all into that *real maravilloso* vision of the Americas. The formulation served as the preface to *The Kingdom of This World*, the narrative that he made of his experience of finding himself standing on soil where thousands of men, desiring freedom, had put their faith in the lycanthropical powers of Macandal who, "with wings one day, spurs another, galloping and crawling, had made himself master of the courses of the underground stream, and caverns of the seacoast, and the treetops." Not surprisingly, dogs did not bark at such a man; "he changed his shadow at will." Because of him "a Negress gave birth to a child with a wild boar's face"; and it was he that would give the "sign for the great uprising [when] the blood of whites would run into the brooks."

> The wait lasted four years, and the alert ears never despaired of hearing, at any moment, the voice of the great conch shell which would bellow through the hills to annnounce to all that Macandal had completed the cycle of his metamorphoses, and stood poised once more, sinewy and hard, with testicles like rocks, on his own human legs. (Carpentier 1970b:41-43)

In Césaire's case, meanwhile, a corollary transvaluation of values adds a tragi-comic edge to the historical parable that he, too, makes of the two Haitian states that came to co-exist, none too peacefully, after the revolution—after "the Lords Back There, headed by Damballah, the Master of the Roads, and Ogoun, Master of Swords, [indeed brought] the thunder and lightning and [unleashed] the cyclone that [had rounded] out the work of men's hands" (Carpentier 1970:42). In the south that followed there was a mulatto republic, with Petion as president. In the north was a kingdom [where], "Yes, Christophe was King," a "King like Louis XIII, Louis XIV and a few other. And like every king, every true king, every white king I mean, he created a court and surrounded himself with a nobility" (Césaire 1970:9-10). Césaire has Vastey exult in the appropriate register in *The Tragedy of King Christophe*: "A black king! It's like a fairy tale, isn't it? This black kingdom, this court, a perfect replica in black of the finest courts the Old World has to offer" (21). Besides which, Christophe had crowned himself at his coronation, having kissed the Gospels and responded "*Profiteor*" to the latin of Corneille Brelle (the Archbishop officiating): "*Profiterisne carissime in Christo Fili et promittis coram Deo et angelis eius deinceps legem justitiam et pacem, Eccclesiaeque Dei populoque tibi subjecto facere ac servare . . . ac invigulare ut pontificibus Ecclesiae Dei condignus et canonicus honos exhibeatur?*" Thereupon, announced the Master-at-Arms, "His great and most serene Highness Henry King of Haiti [was] crowned and enthroned" (27-28). He had then embarked upon that "patrimony of pride": the construction of that "enigmatic prow, spewing the blood and foam, plowing through the sea of shame" (44-45).

"Against fate, against history, against nature" (44), Christophe had had his City of Stone built on the summit of a chain of rugged mountains at an altitude of almost one thousand meters over the vast spaces of the Plaine du Nord. The justifications for La Ferriere went equally against the grain of conventional territorial defense. Howard W. French, limning the relevant conflation of contexts in his "Milot Journal" report (1991) on the restoration work of contemporary Haitian architect Albert Manganes and the Haitian Institute for the Preservation of the National Patrimony, notes that "for all the Citadelle's architectural splendor, Christophe's choice of a site for his fort, far too distant from the water to guard Haiti's shores, was seen as stubborn folly." Over time, however, "a more generous view of his strategy has taken hold. Without a navy to ward off Napoleon's avenging forces, whose defeat had won independence in 1804 for a nation of slaves, Haiti's early rulers conceived a large network of internal defenses to repel invaders overconfident for having easily taken lightly defended shores." French relevantly cites Roger Kennedy's observation that although "it is conventional to dismiss all this as an expression of madness, [the fact of the matter is that] it is not that at all." Witness, for example, the "elaborate water collection and drainage system . . . that would enable a 5,000-man garrison to withstand siege for a year" (1991:A4).

It is equally significant that French recalls the Haitians' profound need to exalt tribe and self beyond abuse, injury, and erasure. Legend has it that Christophe "dedicated the fortress with the words, 'To a people they would have on their knees, I offer this upright monument.'" La Ferriere is similarly transfigured in Césaire's *Tragedy*, and becomes for the "spellbound" Christophe that "enigmatic prow" which would cancel "out the slave ship"; as a result, those who had been "flung ashore by the surf" would be suffused with "the tide smell of the future" (1970:45). The exceptionalist conclusion to which Manganes comes is, quite simply, "There is nothing like this in the whole hemisphere" (French 1991:A4). In the end, though, it was the singular, and darker, coalescing of ironies in this metamorphosis of man and stone that Carpentier would capture when he wrote, "Henri Christophe would never know the corruption of his flesh, flesh fused in its architecture, integrated with the flying buttresses. Le Bonnet de L'Evêque, the whole mountain [would eventually] become the mausoleum of the first King of Haiti" (Carpentier 1970:156).

What Césaire's play described as a "phantom vessel, riding the swell of a magic ocean suddenly stilled in the middle of the storm" (44) may appear to be a remarkable instance of what Robert Hughes meant when he posited architecture as "the carapace of political fantasy" in a discussion of "trouble in utopia" (1980:164), and when, as above, Carpentier relates the structure to Giambattista Piranesi's *Carceri d'invenzione*. Still, La Ferriere was quite plausibly grounded, so to speak, in a historical reality that took cognizance, as it had to, of Napoleon and his General Leclerc and Chief of Staff General Boyer. So, too, of the Slave Trade and Versailles, and of slave-hunting dogs from Cuba and Jamaica that were set upon Haiti. Just as foundational for La Ferriere were the self- and other-consuming excesses of the French Revolution and its reverberations in the Antilles. So, too, were the events of that night of August 22, 1791 when, "with torch in one hand and knife in the other, the slave of Saint-Domingue [began the destruction of] a society which had oppressed him for nearly one hundred years" (Ott 1987:ix). The spectacle that followed, wrote J. Dennis Harris in his 1860 "A Summer on the Borders of the Caribbean Sea," presented "earth and heaven such spectacles of horror as to cause even Europe, accustomed as it is to blood and fire, to stand aghast, and which will serve Americans as a finger-board of terror so long as slavery there exists." In effect,

> The torch of conflagration and the sword of destruction have marched in fearful union through the land, and covered the hills and plains with desolation. Tyranny, scorn, and retaliating vengeance have displayed their utmost rage, and in the end have given birth to an empire which has not only hurled its thunderbolts on its assailants, but at this moment bids defiance to the world. (Bell 1970:149)

The Kingdom of This World had limned certain of its configurations "straight from horror." For "on holidays Rochambeau began to throw Negroes to his dogs, and when the beasts hesitated to sink their teeth into a human body before the brilliant, finely clad spectators, the victim was pricked with a sword to make the tempting blood flow. On the assumption that this would keep the Negroes in their place, the Governor had sent to Cuba for hundreds of mastiffs: 'They'll be puking niggers'" (104). "On such a soil as San Domingo slavery," C. L. R. James would conclude, "only a vicious society could flourish. Nor were the incidental circumstances such as to mitigate the demoralisation inherent in [the] method of production" that slavery was (1963:27). In addition to which, the French Revolution collapses to quite relevant effect in *Explosion in a Cathedral* when, "like a long and fearful roll of thunder in summer, heralding cyclones that will blacken the sky and tear down cities, the cruel news rang around the Caribbean, amid shouts and the lighting of torches: the Law of the 30th Floreal of the Year Ten had been promulgated—slavery was reinstituted in the French colonies in America." And so, in this return to the old ways of the New World

There was great rejoicing amongst the landowners, ranchers and planters. . . . .In Guadeloupe, Dominica and Marie Galante, the news was greeted with salvoes and illuminations, and thousands of "former free citizens" were led back to their old hutments once more, beneath a rain of sticks and ropes' ends. The Big Whites of the old days set out into the countryside, with packs of dogs at their heels, to look for their former servants, who were brought back to their compounds with chains around their necks. (Carpentier 1979:319)

In Césaire's equally tendentious *real maravilloso* re-construction of the La Ferriere, Christophe's architecture of the (im)plausible does become a "very unusual platform, turned toward the north magnetic pole," with walls that were "one hundred and thirty feet high and thirty feet thick, lime and bagasse, lime and bull's blood" (44). Indeed, defiant transfiguration and subversive consubstantiation extend to Christophe himself. Ex-slave and ex-cook at the Sign of the Crown, he quite (un)becomes himself as "Henri, by the Grace of God and the Constitutional Law of the State, King of Haiti, Ruler of the Islands of La Tortue and Gonave, and others adjacent, Destroyer of Tyranny, Regenerator and Benefactor of the Haitian Nation, Creator of its Moral, Political, and Military Institutions, First Crowned Monarch of the New World" (Carpentier 1970b:147; Césaire 1970:27).

"Not for nothing," Carpentier observes, "had those towers risen, on the mighty bellowing of bulls, their testicles toward the sun." For in the event of any attempt by France to retake the island, "He, Henri Christophe, God, my cause and my sword, could hold out here," outside, or rather, beyond history: "above the clouds for as long as necessary, with his whole court, his army, his chaplains, his musicians, his African pages, his jesters." Hell-bent on being utopian, Christophe was persuaded that fifteen thousand men could live within its "Cyclopean walls and lack for nothing." It is in *The Kingdom of This World* that we then read:

Once the drawbridge of the Single Gate had been pulled up, the Citadel La Ferriere would be the country, with its independence, its monarch, its treasury, and all its pomp. Because down below, the sufferings involved in its building forgotten, the Negroes of the Plaine would raise their eyes to the fortress, replete with corn, with gunpowder, iron, and gold, thinking that there higher than the birds there, where life below was a remote sound of bells and the crowing of roosters, a king of their own race was waiting, close to heaven, which is the same everywhere, for the thud of the bronze hoofs of Ogoun's ten thousand horses. (124-125)

"Majesty," Engineer Martial Besse had pointed out in Césaire's dramatic version, "these are terrifying slopes to build on" (44). Or, as Madame Christophe puts it in the politics-of-intimacy translation that she makes of affairs and reasons of state: "Take care, Christophe!/ If you try to put the roof of one hut on another/ it will be too little or too big!" (41). But then, as yet another Caribbean would one day propose, the slave-kings of Haiti, Dessalines and Christophe, were "men who had structured their despair" into, among other forms, the "only noble ruin in the archipelago: Christophe's massive citadel." It was, Derek Walcott continues in ambivalent celebration, "a monument to egomania, more than a strategic castle" (1970:12). For all of its concrete and contingent reality, La Ferriere was what such constructions are—at once *ou-topos* [no-place] and *eu-topos* [place of happiness]. With its "head in the clouds" and "its feet [digging] into the valleys," the Citadel was, so Christophe announces, "a city, a fortress, a battleship of stone, [and] impregnable." It is "solid cornerstone and firm foundation" as well as "assault on heaven or the sun's resting place" (Césaire 1970:44). It is not surprising, then, that Christophe's "*Ultimo Ratio Regum*," that "stronghold, unique in the world [but] too vast for one man" (Carpentier 1979:148), provokes ambivalence that in part recalls Neruda at the heights of Machu Picchu. "In the days of imperial Rome," J. Dennis Harris would comment further, "it was the custom of Cicero and his haughty contemporaries to sneer at the wretchedness and barbarity of the Britons, just as Americans speak of Haytiens today; yet when we reflect how analogous the history of the seven-hilled city and that of the United States promises to be, that Hayti may yet become the counterpart of England, head-quarters of a colored American nationality, and supreme mistress of the Caribbean Sea" (Bell 1970:149).

> In both prophetic and utopic discourses, [Marin remarks], there exist a background and a base of "reality" that is simultaneously kept and rejected, conserved and suppressed, in the same gesture and at the same time. The "symbols" of negation that these proper names carry with them indicate the rejection of this real positivity in the very act by which this positivity is designated, in the very way it is gathered and acepted in speech. But in this act of possession surrounded by nothingness reality itself undergoes a profound change, worked on as it is by these symbols. Reality springs back, not to be perceived truly or felt in its fullness, but to haunt subliminally the words and phrases that utter it. In the margins of discourse and in the intervals that are sculpted in the proper names themselves—"Not-My-People," "No-Place," "Non-sense," etc.—reality returns to be the other side of what it is: thickness, obstacle, and presence. (1984:95-96).

In "What the Twilight Says," an early artistic manifesto, this is how Walcott
finally confronted Christophe's monumental effort to arrest a history of racial
degradation by bringing history itself to an end in one last stone gesture. "The
only noble ruin" in the archipelago was "an effort to reach God's height,"
Walcott concluded. Even if "the slave had surrendered one Egyptian darkness
for another, that darkness was his will, that structure was the image of the
inaccessible achieved. To put it plainly, it was something we could look up
to. It was all we had" (1970:12;14)—even if, as Márquez (1976) writes about
such patriarchs, it was ultimately a case of "our never knowing who he was,
or what he was like, or even if he was only a figment of the imagination, a
comic tyrant who never knew where the reverse side was and the right of this
life which we loved with an insatiable passion." Besides which, for all that the
incarnation was "arduous and ephemeral" there "wasn't any other" kind
(268). Ambivalence of this kind is, it may be argued, an act of historical and
moral generosity, of aesthetic gratitude even, so caught (up) was Walcott, for
one, in the blinding clarity of a trance/fixing illumination: "Now, one may see
such heroes as squalid fascists who chained their own people, but they had
size, mania, the fire of heretics." He was, said Walcott of himself, "in awe of
their blasphemy" (1970:13). But, Georges Bataille and Octavio Paz would
appear to be of some cautionary use here—especially so in the focus that
Michelle H. Richman gives to Bataille's view of "reactionary exaltations,"
as merely "Icarian illumination." Richman provides us with a relevant—and
synoptic—reading when she examines Bataille's position on the *dépense* (the
extravagance) of "aspirations to the sun" within which "idealistic utopiani-
sm" offers itself up as *the* "redeeming light, rising above the world, above
classes, [as] the epitome of the spirit" (1982:50-51). Hell-bent on resisting the
contaminations of contingency, such utopian visionaries do steal fire. But
they do so within a closed economy, and so only manage to annihilate
themselves. In other wor(l)ds, it is the fate of what Cabrera Infante (1973) has
called the "misfired Midas" to produce a Golden Age that is very much iron-
bound. And such, indeed, is the case when "anti-utopian" Cabrera Infante
engages in an "avatar of Attila" (Che Guevara) and a "West Indian version of
Jehovah" (Castro) representation of *fidelismo*.

The re-presentation of the failure of political vision in Márquez's
Autumn of the Patriarch and in Brathwaite's *Black + Blues* (1977) is similarly
one of extravagant dis/enchantment. "Sons, dreamers, lovers (we could have
had them)" in the "Springblade" of *Black + Blues*. That we did not do so was
the consequence of a post-independence of "figment, scheme, and fantasy"
that was shot through with the "psychedelic flashes of madmen" (44). In the
aksident-store body politic that followed—that is, after "all should have been
soaked in real blood" and been "anchored in the real bone"—

> . . . we set them up here
> some to build crazy
> palaces, imperial shops, super-
> markets that have become cages
> that have become prison . . . (*ibid.* 40)

Meanwhile, in the radiant corruption and the "dog-days sun of high noon" of Márquez's *Autumn*, the likes of the patriarch-politician, "whose real existence was the simplest of enigmas" (1976:194), was himself not beyond appreciating the myth-inducing dispensation within which he is lodged behind "the three bars of his sleeping dungeon," with its "three bolts" and its "three locks." But then, he is nothing if not the "indecipherable satrap" in a romance of fabulous disarray. Here, the utopian bent manifests itself in various ways, doing so as much in the enchantment and "marketplace disaster" of a palace in which "tenured civil servants found hens laying eggs in desk drawers, and the traffic of whores and soldiers in the toilets, and the tumult of birds, and the fighting of street dogs in the midst of audiences" (12) as in the architecture of the ideal that we get in the "largest baseball stadium in the Caribbean [where] he imparted in our team the motto of victory or death, and [where he] ordered a free school established in each province to teach sweeping where the pupils fanaticized by the presidential stimulus went on to sweep the streets after having swept their houses and then highways and roads so that piles of trash were carried back and forth from one province to another without anyone knowing what to do" (37). In the end, Utopia unbecomes itself as circus and prison. Márquez thus records cycles of descent from and into the extravagance of *ou-topos*. For once upon a time, what with his "ten pips of general of the universe," this visionary had been proclaimed by "dauntless adulators and lettered politicians" to be "corrector of earthquakes, eclipses, leap years, and other errors of God"; he had been besieged too by other seekers of the good life, "mobs of lepers, blind people and cripples who begged for the salt of health from his hand" (28; 5). But then, in the determinate negation (*bi yio ti wa*) that followed, when one asked about a sign that soldiers were busy erasing, "they answered eternal glory to the maker of the new nation although he knew it was lie, of course, if not they wouldn't be erasing it, God damn it" (226).

Fully disenchanted, the terminus of arrested motion in the body politic soon enough becomes that "Jail Me Quickly" in Martin Carter where "Men murder men as men must murder men to build their shining Governments of the damned" (Dabydeen and Wilson-Tagoe 1988:58). Whether in Carpentier or Césaire, or in Márquez and Carter, the vision of things is, in the end, one that Bastos's extravagant patriarch of the nation, "I The Supreme Perpetual Dictator," is well-positioned to generate and to sustain when he "summons" us to his body politic:

Do you think that the reality of this nation to which I gave birth and which gave birth to me accommodates itself to your phantas-magorias and hallucinations? Conform to the law, you layabouts and loafers, you airy-fairy merry-andrews! The world is as it ought to be. The law: the first pole. Its counterpole: anarchy, ruin, the desert which is the non-house, non-history. Choose if you can. There is not a third world beyond. There is not a third pole. There are no promised-lands. Less still, much less are there such for you, you virtuosos of rumor, you artful farters, you buzzing ball-less bees! I'll have you know that once and for all, you worthless know-nothing turds, you sepals of shit in bloom! (Bastos 1987:168)

Notwithstanding this assurance from the Perpetual Dictator that there are no promised lands, we remain infected with the "insatiable illness" of the utopian bent that *The Autumn of the Patriarch* cycles again and again in its narrative; for it is one in which "frantic crowds [would take] to the streets singing hymns of joy"; in which "the music of liberation and the rockets of jubilation and the bells of glory would announce to the world that the uncountable time of eternity had come to an end" (Márquez 1976:269). *Autumn* does so notwith-standing, or else because of, apocalyptic visions in which mud from the swamps would "go back upriver to its source"; in which "it would rain blood, hens would lay pentagonal eggs, [and] silence and darkness would cover the universe once more" (80; 125).

There is, meanwhile, yet another dimension to the convergence of Old World import and New World latitude in *The Tragedy of King Christophe* and *The Kingdom of This World*. It is one that helps us re-locate Christophe's attempt to "shake off the first sleep of chaos" in a Yoruba-based cautionary tale about the "Lords Back There." In this regard, there was nothing casual in the fact that Caliban, as above in the last chapter, had invoked the "Lord's Back There" when Césaire transformed Shakespeare's play into *A Tempest*: "Forget to give [Shango] room if you dare! /...Refuse to have him under your roof at your own risk!. . . He'll tear off your roof and wear it as a hat!" (1992:20). Césaire had turned, too, to the consequential because slip-sliding nature of Eshu who, Caliban recognizes—and Miranda intuits—"can throw a stone yesterday / And kill a bird today"; who "with his dick /...can whip you, whip you..." (49). In effect, "Shango strikes, and money expires"; mean-while, "Give Eshu [he of the "many tricks"] twenty dogs, / [and] you will see" (48). This dispensation of things from the "Old Shore" informs the imagery of the utopian bent in Césaire's *Tragedy*—with its "Look at the swelling chest of the earth, the earth stretching and tensing its loins as it shakes off sleep, the first sleep of chaos"—and in Carpentier's representation of his *Kingdom*['s] "new castle somewhere near Pierrot's Ridge. And what a castle! Something out of the Thousand and One Nights" (44;73). Christophe's New World and its tragedy thus build on the Yoruba foundation that interests me here—whether at the Citadel's dizzying height or on the grounds of Sans Souci whose destruction provides Carpentier with the epigraph that he makes of Karl Ritter's eye-witness account of the place: "Everywhere one came upon royal crowns of gold, some of them so heavy that it was an effort to pick them up." Such had been the shape of things in that "marvelous world" which, when Ti Noel first came upon it, was "the favorite residence of King Henri Christophe, former cook of the rue des Espagnols, master of the Auberge de la Couronne, who now struck off money bearing his initials above the proud motto *God, my cause and my sword*" (1970:114-115). It is no casual matter at all, then, that *The Tragedy of King Christophe* invokes the myth and history of Shango—that "storm on the edge of a knife" (Thompson 1984:85). The salute that Shango receives from Césaire's African Page is an encompassing one, for as is his due, Shango is "Power of night, tide of the day / [who rides] / through the halls of heaven / mounted on the flaming ram of the tempest" (95). By the same token, Carpentier is hardly being casual either when he invokes that millenial "waiting for the thud of the bronze hoofs of Ogoun's ten thousand horses" at La Ferriere. *The Kingdom of This World* is also historically and emblematically engaged with "The Lords Back There" when its Macandal announced that great uprising in which the work of men's hands would be rounded out by the Master of the Swords and the Master of the Roads; so, too, by "gods who ruled the vegetable kingdom and [who] appeared, wet and gleaming, among the canebrakes" (20). There is an instructive aboriginality, clearly, in the "great rejoicing" with which *The Kingdom of This World* had earlier indexed the prophetic signs and wonders of its "strangest news": "a green lizard had warmed its back on the roof of the tobacco barn; someone had seen a night moth flying at noon; a big dog, with bristling hair, had dashed through the house, carrying off a haunch of venison; a gannet—so far from the sea!—had shaken the lice from its wings over the arbor of the back patio" (41). Equally significant was that roll-call of vernacular forces with which the Jamaican Bouckman had initiated the revolution, under the aegis of Ogoun, and in which context a bony, long-limbed Negress had brandished the ritual machete.

> *Fai Ogoun, Fail Ogoun, Fai Ogoun, O!*
> *Damballah m'ap tiré canon,*
> *Fai Ogoun, Fail Ogoun, Fai Ogoun, O!*
> *Damballah map tiré canon!*

Ogoun of the Irons, Ogoun the Warrior, Ogoun of the Forges, Ogoun Marshal, Ogoun of the lnaces, Ogoun-Chango, Ogoun-Kankanikan, Ogoun-Batala,

Ogoun-Panama, Ogoun-Bakoule were thus invoked by the priestess of the Rada:

> *Ogoun Badagri*
> *General Sanglant,*
> *Saizi z'orage*
> *Ou scell'orage*
> *Ou fait Kataoun z'eclai!* (67-68)

Revolution and ecstasy in the New World therefore reach back to Yoruba Ogun in special ways; for it is he who lives on the cutting edge of iron; in the flames of the blacksmith's forge; and on the battlefield. It was Ogun who cleared the primordial forests with his iron and who, according to his *oriki*, is the "terrible guardian of the sacred oath"; the "owner of high fringes of palm fronds" to whom is due "the salute of iron on stone" (Thompson 1984:52-53). "To dare transition," Wole Soyinka explains in *Myth, Literature, and the African World*, "is the ultimate test of the human spirit, and Ogun is the first protagonist of the abyss" (1976:157-58). Césaire and Carpentier variously emphasize this aboriginal and consuming significance of the "Lords Back There." When the import is not Ogun's, it is Shango's—he who "dances savagely in the courtyard of the impertinent"; who "carries fire as a burden on his head" (Thompson 1984:86). Besides which, Shango was "the tempestuous mythic king" whose wife is the whirlwind; it was he who recklessly experimented with a leaf that had power to bring down lightning from the skies. Inadvertently, he caused the roof of the palace of Oyo to be set afire by lightning. In the blaze his wife and children were killed. Half-crazed with grief and guilt, Shango goes to a spot outside his royal capital, and there hangs himself. "He thus suffers the consequences of playing arrogantly with God's fire, and became lightning itself." In sum, "in the lightning bolt Shango met himself" (88). There is considerable irony, of course, in the fact that when Christophe dies his suicide's death at the Citadel he is immured, upright, in one of its walls. He thereupon becomes, in Césaire's drama, "a king erect holding [his] own memorial tablet over the abyss" (1970:95). But then, again, only Ogun could have "experienced the process of being literally torn asunder in cosmic winds, and of then rescuing himself from the precarious edge of total dissolution by harnessing the untouched part of himself, the will" (Soyinka, *ibid*). His aspiration to the sun notwithstanding, Christophe of Haiti is grounded in the *bruta facta* of history. Only the double-gestured Ogun could be at once successful as "cosmic gesture in space" and "warrior on earth" (Tidjani-Serpos 1996:12).

		Such, then, are the chimeras the pursuit of which leads Césaire's Engineer Martial Besse to point out to Christophe: "Majesty, these are terrifying slopes to build on"; or upon which to await, as in Carpentier's *Kingdom*, an apocalypse that will be announced by the bronze hoofs of Ogoun's ten thousand horses. Elsewhere, utopian bent and dis/affiliation in so double-gestured a world help to account for the body politic over which Carpentier's Head of State presides in *Reasons of State*, and for its "scenes of revelry, or appeals for rain or calls for revolution." The contours of the great chimerical nation are especially emblematized when this narrative's "El Supremo" or "Patriarch" reaches symbolic conclusion in what he had been looking for; it is significant that he does so after having gone from "bone sewing needles to the ritual masks of the New Hebrides, from negro amulets to gold breastplates, from Chaman rattles to stone axes." Thereafter, latitude and import coincide to instructive effect "in the middle of the room" and in front of a rectangular glass case mounted on a wooden base. Inside it was a mummy, "eternally sitting," which had been found in a cave during a thunderstorm. At once *memento mori* and memories of the future, it is no surprise that this "piece of human architecture" is made up

> of bones wrapped in shreds of material, its skin dry, full of holes, worm-eaten, supporting a skull bound with an embroidered fillet, a skull whose hollow eyes were endowed with a terrifying expression; whose hollow nose looked angry in spite of its absence, and with an enormous mouth battlemented with yellow teeth, as if immobilized forever in a silent howl at the pain in the crossed shin-bones, to which there still adhered rope-soled shoes a thousand years old, yet seeming new because of the permanence of their red, black and yellow threads. (1976:302)

Small wonder, then, that in the template of the body politic that the Guatemalan Miguel Angel Asturias had made of his *El Señor Presidente* (1942), the "rain dance" of the Maya-Guatemala divinity Tohil could only be of a certain kind. It had been nothing if not a *quinto sol* confirmation of "darkness, chaos, confusion and the astronomical melancholy of a eunuch" (200). In the end, its terms of reference had been duly grounded in "instructions received"— and nowhere more so than when the Chief of the Secret Police finally puts his signature ("This is all I have to impart to the President" [283]) on a narrative that had begun with a clamor of dis/affiliation, "In the Cathedral Porch" with its

> "Boom, bloom, alum-bright, Lucifer of alunite!" The sound of the church bells summing people to prayer lingered on, like a humming in the ears, an uneasy transition from brightness to gloom, from gloom to brightness. "Boom, bloom, alum-bright,

Lucifer of alunite, over the sombre tomb! Bloom, alum-bright,
over the tomb, Lucifer of al unite! Boom, boom alum-bright
. . .bloom....alum-bright...bloom, alum-bright..bloom, boom."
(1983:7)

As with Christophe's double-gestured reach for an *ultimo ratio regum*, and as
in the latter days of the Patriarch's autumn, we return here to material that is
as much *floor* of heaven as it is *roof* of pandemonium (Rajan). The utopian
bent of the genre and its way with annunciation and incarnaton are recognizable enough when *El Señor Presidente*'s Camila—"thin and wrinkled as an
old cat with nothing left of her face but eyes," but "barely twenty years old"
all the same—gave birth to a little boy. For, then, a day came at last which
"shed light on the dark night of her grief, as she wandered like a shadow
between the pines, the orchard fruit trees, and the tall trees in the field." It
would be on a "Whit Sunday," moreover, when her son would "be anointed
with salt, oil, water and the priest's saliva, and given the name Miguel"—
while mocking-birds caressed each other; sheep were busy licking each other;
foals raced after moist-eyed mares; and calves mooed with delight, their jaws
slavering, as they nuzzled swollen udders (277).

The Unreturnable-Heaven's Town

> If I was bound for hell let it be hell. No more false heavens.
> Jean Rhys, *Wide Sargasso Sea*

> Things are working out
> towards their dazzling conclusions. . .
> So it is neither here nor there,
> what ticky-tackies we have
> saddled and surrounded ourselves with,
> blocked our views,
> cluttered our brains.
> Ama Ata Aidoo, *Our Sister Killjoy*

Beverley Ormerod observes that the corollary concept of paradise lost has
become a "most plangent and enduring" motif. By way of a choice of
Caribbean writers, Ormerod develops the thesis with appropriate metaphoric
force: "Time guards the gates of Eden . . . as sternly as any angel with drawn
sword." That being the case, there can be no returning to eras of "simplicity
and optimism, with [their] divine illusion of permanence" (1985:1). Mali's

Yambo Ouologuem is characteriscally disinclined to deny legitimate genealogy to the utopian bent. As a consequence, his conviction that we are always
already (duty-) bound to violence and violation makes *le devoir de violence*
the ground upon which he concludes that "Often, it is true, the soul desires to
dream the echo of happiness, an echo that has no past" (1971:181). For
purposes that relate to my conclusions here, there is an equally instructive
con/fusion of signs in that coinage of Amos Tutuola's, the "Unreturnable-
Heaven's Town," whose predictably "very clean road" in *The Palm-Wine
Drinkard* leads into an enclosure within whose "thick and tall wall [we] saw
that if [the inhabitants] wanted to climb a tree, [they] would climb the ladder
first before leaning it against [a] tree" (1953:56).

From Aztec dance of creative destruction to Yoruba bush of ghosts, and
from Mesoamerica to Ethiopia and the sevententh-century Jesuit paradise of
Paraguay, there is a certain assault-on-paradise dispensation to all this. Its
embrace of the contraindicative reinforces Marin's "utopics: spatial play"
observation that "Living at the origin—and at the founding moment—is
impossible. [For] after space comes the rude reality of time" (1984:276). It is
true, of course, that less implosive assessments of the utopian bent are
possible, as happens to be the case when Frank and Fritzie Manuel emphasize
condition of being, rather than teleology. The Manuels view "the truly great
utopian" as "a Janus-like creature, time-bound and free of time, place-bound
and free of place," with a duality that "should be respected and appreciated"
(1979:13). They also call attention to the fact that "particularly rich utopian
moments have been attached to political revolutions and the dictatorships that
follow in their wake." These are periods, after all, in which all things seem
possible, and the utopian appears no madder than other men" (24)—for all
that Àjàlá Alàmò the Yoruba Potter of Heaven has warned that it is not
possible to tell which footsteps on a road belong to a mad man: *a ki i da ese
asiwèrè mò l'ójú òna*. Roger Garaudy's *Alternative Future* rather more
circumspectly makes the point that "a utopia is not born just anytime; only at
a turning point of history" (1974:107). Teresa da Silva covers a relevant
topography in "A repressão da utopia" (1991) when she emphasizes the
utopian work of negotiating the lacunae between *bruta facta* and the imaginary. Briefly put: because it is the place *natus sine flores* (Ovid), utopia is of
necessity the space where Art completes the work of History.

> O espaço da utopia é o espaco da ficção. E é a ficção que permite
> o salto final do poeta leitor da História. Resgantando os vazios,
> as brechas, as lacunas que a História reconhece em suas fontes,
> em seus documentos, é com o imaginário que o artista cumprirá
> a missão do historiador, e que seria, segundo Lucien Febvre, a de
> saber "fabricar o seu mel, mesmo onde não haja flores" (Reis
> 1991:123).

Mariano Picón-Salas (1944) has, for his part, identified one such Ovidian metamorphosis in "the sunlit land of Michoacan." He does so through the agency of Vasco de Quiroga, judge of the Audiencia and later elevated to the rank of Bishop of Michoacan. Quiroga is, in Picón-Salas, a Sir Thomas More-influenced person of "high caliber" who "started the first great utopia in the New World to create a human order bordering on divine harmony." Picon-Salas also underscores the "Platonic dream—now impregnated with Christian fervor"—which marked the "hearts of the missionary humanists." He makes the point through the 1547 *Christian Rule* of Bishop Zumárraga—a friend and confidant of Quiroga's (and no less influenced by More's *Utopia*)—and its proposition that one of "the signs to determine whether something is truly of God and created by His divine hand, the Apostle Saint Paul teaches, is its order and law, for everything that God creates has order and law to which it adheres by nature" (1971:60-61)

There was always the attraction of such alternative futures, of course; and with it the pull toward the "another life" which the likes of Walcott and Carpentier have variously limned in their works. The invocations of "lost steps" and "memories of the future" converge in a familiar remembrance of things past when, as above, we were blest "with a virginal, unpainted world / with Adam's task of giving things their names" (Walcott 1976:45). This reach for "intransitive beginnings" (Said) is a defining one—nothwithstanding the counter-narrative that we get in Peter Abrahams's *This Island, Now*; or else in Martin Carter's arrangement of things in "Jail Me Quickly" where men must murder men to build their "shining Governments of the damned" (Dabydeen and Wilson-Tagoe 1988:58). There is, too, that politics-writing-mutilation dispensation in *The Autumn of the Patriarch* where Márquez's "ephemeral image," "stud," and "illusory monarch" shows himself quite prepared to exile the poet from the republic. All other political dissidents would be granted amnesty and allowed to return to his "homeland of misery," except for "men of letters, of course, them never, he said, they've got a fever in their quills like thoroughbred roosters when they're moulting so they're no good for anything except when they're good for something" (105). Abrahams, for his part, employs a perhaps too emblematic hand in *This Island, Now* to foreground a post-independence politics of betrayal. With it had come the collapse of a liberation theology as a consequence of which President Moses Joshua "could no longer be called names like 'The Liberator,' 'The Dark Crusader,' 'The Guardian of the People'." Its aspirations subverted by such a chimera of utopian politics, "This island, now," has become nothing if not "an unjust society"; one that is "harsh and cruel to the majority of its people." Its political history is one in which "forces have been manipulated first to run the slave state, then to run the colonial state, then to run the independent state which was handed over not to the mass of the people but to the descendants of the slave-owners and the heirs of the colonial state" (1967:259). In effect, and as Brathwaite put it when he assessed the political culture of such a "homecoming" and its "trade winds" in his *Islands* (1969), "the wheel turns / and the future returns / wreathed in disguises" (Dabydeen and Wilson-Tagoe *ibid.*:59). This much is evident in Carpentier's *Reasons of State* where, "contemplating the panorama of swindling and gangsterism every morning," the Head of State could all the same rejoice in the absence of "stealth" with which he had become "Master of Bread and Fish, of Corn and Herds, of Ice and Springs, of Fluid and the Wheel, beneath a multiplicity of identities, syndicates, trade names and always anonymous societies immune from failure or setbacks" (1976:166).

Given the congeneric nature of latitude and import in the Americas, it is no surprise that its narratives of dis/affiliation have so much ground to cover. Or that in one such instance "the star-apple kingdom" suffers a dystopian reduction that makes it little more than a "whole fucking island" for the Shabine of Walcott's "The Schooner, 'Flight'." But then, from Monos to Nassau" the kingdoms of this world are just as apt to reach back to a time "when these slums of empire was paradise," as the same Shabine would have it elsewhere in the poetry of *The Star-Apple Kingdom* (1979). Walcott adopts a prophetic stance to present us with cycles of the same in *Omeros* where the dystopian certainty is that "One day the Mafia / will spin these islands round like a roulette . . . and ministers cash in on casinos with their old excuses / of more jobs." That being the case, "Where? / Where could [the] world renew the Mediteranean's / innocence?"—if not "on [this] other side of the world [with] its sunlit islands" (1990:28-29). Equally haunted as the brave new world of Carpentier's *Reasons of State* is by such a cultural and moral economy, it comes as no surprise that its Head of State felt as he did:

> that there was *something*, something that his men had been unable to grasp, nor torture, nor a state of siege could put a stop to; something that was moving in the subsoil, underground, that arose from urban catacombs not previously known to exist; something new in the country with unpredictable manifestations, mysterious mechanisms. . . . It was as if the atmosphere had been charged by the addition of some impalpable pollen or hidden ferment, an elusive slippery, occult but manifest force, silent although throbbingly alive [with] circulation. (Carpentier 1976:166)

The persistent circulation of this world-(un)making material is manifest as such in the memories of the future that haunt Márquez's Patriarch. This is clearly the case in the emblematic "three caravels" that he imagines he sees "anchored in the shadowy sea"; so, too, in that "mirror of premonitory waters [where he could see] himself lying dead [and] face down on the floor as he had slept every night of his life since birth, with the denim uniform without insignia, the boots, the gold spur, his right arm folded under his head to serve as a pillow, and at an indefinite age somewhere between 107 and 232 years" (1976:84). The ferment in *Reasons of State* helps to account, too, for *The Autumn of the Patriarch*'s "trail of yellow leaves of our uncountable years of misfortune" as well as for the narrative's reach for an *eu-topos* in which "frantic crowds [would take] to the streets singing hymns of joy at the jubilant news of [the Patriarch's] death and alien forevermore to the music of liberation and the rockets of jubilation and the bells of glory that announced to the world the good news that the uncountable time of eternity had come to an end" (269). But then, it very much matters that "that was how they found him on the even of his autumn, when the corpse was really that of Patricio Aragones, and that was how we found him again many years later during a moment of such uncertainty that no one could give in to the evidence that the senile body there gouged by vultures and infested with parasites from the depths of the sea was his" (85).

There is a "throbbing" here that reverberates as much in Henri Christophe, Emperor, by the grace of God, as in "the congeries of volatile and fissiparous Jamaican movements known collectively as the Ras Tafarites" (Wilson 1973:63). And never mind, either, that with the Rastafari the utopian bent derives from a particular space-of-faith, one in which the defining genea-theo-logical conceit is deeply yet subversively lodged in the haunt of a certain pre-text and prophecy, the signal point of which is that

> De spirit of the Lawd went over into Ethiopia when Israel was parted among the nations. De twelve tribes were scattered an' lost. But de spirit of de Lawd passed over into Ethiopia, after the Queen of Sheba came to Solomon and learned all his wisdom, an' passed over back to her own land. So it was black men out of Africa who became God's chosen people, for they had learnt de Way. (74)

As a result, and in the lyrical re-statement that we get from Walcott's Sufferer in *O Babylon!* (1978), "You shall believe / that the Emperor Selassie, Jah Rastafari, / Lion of Judah and King of Kings, is one God." Here, too, lies the supreme conviction that "all which is not Zion is Babylon" (168); that in the Ethiopian Lion of Judah

> is beauty. In him is wisdom.
> For when Sheba travel to Ethiopia,

> her jangling procession on the horizon
> a moving oasis in the desert rise up to look. (167-168)

Sheba "couple with Solomon" in this context, and "from the their seed sprang / Ras Makonnen, the vine and the fig tree of fragrant Zion" (168).

Babylonian captivity and cultural dissonance are equally catalytic here; so, too, the politics of misgovernance that has produced "Men, women and children stark naked, lunatics of wants" and "Executives in horseless chariots [who] sometimes pass through [and] hold their noses" (Barrett 1977:12). Writing in the Caribbean context of the late sixties, Walter Rodney was able to record that "the Rastafarians have represented the leading force of the expression of black consciousness. They have rejected . . . philistine white West Indian society. They have sought their cultural and spiritual roots in Ethiopia *and* Africa" (61, my emphasis). Selwyn Cudjoe concurs in his parenthetical discussion of the Ras Tafari in Caribbean literature. Cudjoe's favorable characterization —"a positive and progressive force, concerned with the welfare of the dispossessed masses" (1980:165-169)—relied primarily on Roger Mais's *Brother Man* and its sympathetic depiction of the movement's beginnings in the late forties and early fifties. Mais had written of the period as one in which anti-Rasta sentiment ("a secret cult and a menace to society") was "carefully fanned to a nice conflagration by political opportunists and a partisan press." As a consequence, "many members of the Ras Tafarite persuasion were forced to shave their beards in secret, or suffer public humiliation of another kind" (1974:175). All the same, in surveying those who have been "liberated from the obscurity of themselves," Cudjoe notes that Rex Nettleford underscores the Rastafarians, their "unashamed commitment to Africa and a yearning for knowledge of the African past . . . the unfaltering expressions of wrath against an oppressive and what the Rastafarians regarded as a 'continuing colonial society' . . . the expressed hatred for the humiliating 'white bias' in the society though not necessarily for white people [and] the deprecation of the agonizing logic of a history of black slavery and white domination" (169). For his part, Horace Campbell is convinced that the (now widely diffused) drama of Rastafarian symbols— flag, lion, drum, chalice, [dread]locks, and distinctive language [*I an I Gwine Beat Down Babylon; Let The Power Fall On I*] are indices of a bent that is "neither crazy nor millenarian" (1987:89). Seen in this light, even when Rasta Time seems eschatological, as in Brathwaite's "Conqueror," its machine gun beat clocks an apocalypse of the here and the now: "like a rat/like a rat/like a rat-a-tap tapping . . ."

> an we burnin babylone
> haile selassie hallelu/jah

> haile selassie hallelu/jah
> haile selassie hallelu/jah (1977:10-11)

For his part, Walcott frames the Rastafari of *O Babylon!*, "squatters on a beach that faces the harbor of Kingston, Jamaica," in the complex nexus of their dis/affiliations: "Their doctrine is non-violent; their faith is Peace and Love." He makes the point that "there are few true Rastafari"; so too that "they have invented a grammar and a syntax which immure them from the seductions of Babylon, an oral poetry which requires translation into the language of the oppressor" (1978:155-156).

In the treatment of Rastafarian Ethiopianism that we get in the 1964 novel, *The Children of Sisyphus*, Orlando Patterson reorients matters in decidedly dystopian ways. He does capture, it is true, the requisite "by the rivers of Babylon" anguish and radical insight into "Ethiopia, the land of our Fathers, / The land where all Gods love to be," which so distinguishes the Chosen of Ethiopia among the "red-seamed agents of Babylon."

> Our redeemer is calling us home
> We see there is no truth in Rome
> Our heaven is in Ethiopia
> With King Rasta and Queen Ethiopia (1982:97)

But by emphasizing the Rasta investment in the return of an unreturnable fiction, Patterson also portrays them as pathos-filled and self-consuming. In the process, he attaches to their utopian idealism the tragi-comic bent of the quixotic. The Rastafarian assault on the ideal is accordingly arrested "across the dark-brown, silty shore" where the inadequate provisions of experience and the recalcitrance of the known have left "so many silhouetted majesties swallowed over with all the harvest of their expectancy." Stranded "upon the undulating, stale, delicious filth," they had "ravished and exhausted their living hell. So now there was only the dead nothingness of joy" (173).

Resignation and retreat are inconceivable, however. Thus, there can be no acceptance of, for example, those "new combinations" identity that Harris's Guiana Quartet associates with "branches and sensations we've missed" because "*we're the first potential parents who can contain the ancestral house.*" Consummation of the right sort would not come, either, in the "cross-over" that the calypsonian Sparrow plays out in *Marajhin Sister*; so, too, in the knowing ironies of *Marajhin*, with its "You are the genesis of my happiness / [when] I see you in your sari or your *ohrni*"; and its "Shower me with your kiss, gih me eternal bliss." There is, too, that "I'll learn to grind *massala* and / *chookay dhal* / and jump out a tune to sweet pan for Carnival"— as well as the fact that if it weren't "for your *nani* and *bowgi* / I would marry you and take you in the country" (*Sparrow, the Legend*). It is equally the case that not much Ras Tafarite comfort can be derived from the "divided to the vein" identity which, because of his tolerable "far cry from Africa," Walcott has come to exercise as his being and his due. Nor, yet again, can there be much Rasta consolation when, in "Back to Africa?," Jamaican Louise Bennett descends to that vernacular skepticism of hers in which, true, "Granma was African." But then, "great great great / Granpa was Englishman." In addition to which, what if

> yuh great granmodder fader
> By yuh fader side was Jew?
> An you grampa by yuh modder side
> Was Frenchie parlez-vous? (1982:104)

The point is that even in versions of dis/affiliation that appear to be more negotiable than Bennett's—such as Nicolás Guillén's Cuban "Balada de los dos abuelos" ("Ballad of the Two Grandfathers") or Earl Lovelace's *The Wine of Astonishment*—West Indian identities and allegiances appear to invite crises in (un)becoming. And this disturbance holds, for all that one grants that Guillén resolves his New World *ansia blanca, ansia negra* in an embrace in which he unites the two "in shouts, dreams, tears, songs / in dreams, cries, songs / in tears, songs / singing" (Johnson 1971:149). There is ironic insufficiency, too, in the syncretist stoicism with which Lovelace's Trinidad Spiritual Baptist community responds in *The Wine of Astonishment* to its experience of the passing of the *Prohibition Ordinance* (1917-1951). It is as a consequence of that colonialist version of the *ansia blaca / ansia negra* that England's Government could "say we sing too loud. We disturbing the peace." And Government send the police, too, "with a paper to make us move." But then, "God don't give you more than you can bear"; besides which, "for hundreds of years we bearing what He send like the earth bears the hot sun and the rains and the dew and the cold, and the earth is still the earth, still here for man to build house on and fall down on, still sending up shoots and flowers and growing things" (1983:1). Majorie Thorpe does well, of course, to identify the land-of-look-behind genealogy that the community also represents. The transport of its worship is syncretist, born out of Africa's encounter with Europe in the New World. The Spiritual Baptists, she argues, made of their "'Africanization of Christianity' a living example of the creative and regenerative impulses inherent in the black creole tradition" (1983:viii).

"The black flesh is a terrible temptation": Priest acknowledges this in what he contributes to Lamming's chronicling of the early modern period of colonial domination in *Natives of My Person* (1971:112). Priest had "given his blessing to the traffic in black flesh, but he had also maintained in "those glorious days when faith was a weapon in his hands and men waged war with

words to justify some divinity of right over these black cargoes," that the black
flesh "contained a soul." In the end he had won "both ways," after wrestling
with the illumination that the "black flesh was a challenge which nature had
flung back in the face of God" (116-17); and after confirming the counter-sign
to that Lockean premise that (European) persons can be owners of themselves
which accounts, one suspects, for Lamming's title, *Natives of My Person.*
Meanwhile, in the amazing grace of that conceit of John Newton's in
Thoughts Upon the African Slave Trade, the black flesh would "lie in two
rows, one above the other, like books upon a shelf." He had known them to
lie "so close," Newton recalled, "that the shelf could not, easily, contain one
more" (1788:33-34). There was pre-text enough, all the same, for that mid-
nineteenth century testimony of Captain Theodore Canot's in which his
Adventures of an African Slaver (1854) had called upon the rich and strange
poetry of Coleridge's "Rime of the Ancient Mariner" when his transport
found itself be-calmed on its way to the Americas:

> There we hung—
> 　　　A painted ship upon a painted ocean!
> I cannot describe the fretful anxiety which vexes a mind under
> such circumstances. Slaves below; a blazing sun above; the
> boiling sea beneath; a withering air around; decks piled with
> materials of death; escape unlikely; a phantom in chase behind;
> the ocean like an unreachable eternity before; uncertainty every-
> where; and, within your skull, a feverish mind, harassed by doubt
> and responsibility, yet almost craving for any act of desperation
> that will remove the spell. It is a living nightmare, from which the
> soul pants to be free. (Johnson 1980:67-68)

But then again, the "still nigher approach" that we get to all this in Herman
Melville's *Benito Cereno* makes the commerce with the African connection
"plain." For when this narrative unveils its "shadows present, foreshadowing
deeper shadows to come," painted ship upon a painted ocean proved to be a
Spanish merchantman of the "first class" that was carrying "Negro slaves,
among other valuable freight, from one colonial port to another" (1983:141-
143). It carried the violence, too, with which, led by a "small negro from
Senegal [whose] negro name was Babo," the slaves had acted out their
yearning for a Land-in-Waiting that was not the New World of the Indies but
the Old one of Senegal (240). The inversion was an illegitimate one, of
course, and its attempted execution a criminal offense. This much is clear
enough in the redemptive naivete of the North American Captain Delano. It
is categorically so when the whole affair underwent investigation in the
colonial and viceregal court of the post-Inca "City of Kings" that Lima, Peru,
had by then become. Melville takes the measure of its laws in the "declara-

tion" and "deposition" of Don José de Abos and Padilla, "His Majesty's Notary for the Royal Revenue, and Register [and] Notary Public of the Holy Crusade of the Bishopric" (207-220).

All in all, "the black flesh is a terrible temptation" here in ways that are freighted with traffic and trade, with the fictions and facts of marvelous possession. Witness the convergence of issues that it produces in *Natives of My Person*, from the economy of Priest's theology to the mothers of the Demon Coast that so haunt the Lady of the House. There is, too, the genre of "travells" and "discoverie" to which Lamming resorts by way of those "excerpts" from the voyages of Pierre, carpenter of Lime Stone:

> *Creeks navigable for seven days.   Delicacy be fish and safe for provisioning. Canoes abound, being only known means of jour-ney safe to inhabitants.   Slaves given as token of respect or in exchange for mere trifles. Infidels show great love of knives and bells. Marvellous bay for traffic in the flesh.* (1971a:100)

Shorn of Melville's involuted ironies, meanwhile, Césaire's 1939 *Return to My Native Land* takes stock of this exchange in mere trifles in the plainest of terms, seeing it as a "prying of vermin among weary bodies" that were bound for

> islands that are scars upon the water
> islands that are evidence of wounds
> crumbled islands
> formless islands
>
> islands that are waste paper torn up and steewn upon the water
> islands that are broken blades driven into the flaming sword of the sun.
> (1969a:82)

Return to My Native Land grounds this consubstantiation of waste, water, and black body in the simple enough fact that "for centuries" it was "repeated that we are brute beasts" and that "the human heart stops at the gates of the black world." Small wonder that "We, the vomit of the slave-ship / We, the hunted meat of Calabar" were brought down, and that "we slept in our shit." Ours was a commodification that was so complete, Césaire declares, that "we were sold in public squares and a yard of English cloth and salted Irish meat were [all that could be any] cheaper than we came to be" (67).

Conceived of this way, the slave platform upon which Africa came to rest in the Americas resists the pre-texts of the Yankee captain in Melville and the poetry of the Ancient Mariner in Canot's Coleridge. Still, it is all hedged about with ambiguous horror, of the variety that we encounter when Márquez's

Autumn of the Patriarch recalls the splendor with which the Caribbean sun
had once fallen on Babo's compatriot, that nightmare beauty of Senegal who
had brought in more than her own weight in gold. An equally numinous and
yet consequential view of history as nightmare haunts "the groves of blue
bananas trees in the moonlight, the sad swamps, and the phosphorescent line
of the Caribbean" in *The Chronicle of a Death Foretold*. For it is here that
Márquez's Arab-Caribbean character Santiago Nasar makes a beacon of a
certain "intermittent light at sea" which, so we are informed, "was the soul of
torment of a slaveship that had sunk with a cargo of blacks from Senegal
across the main harbor mouth at Cartagena de Indias" (1982:77). In the end,
Melville's *Benito Cereno* had also set up its Senegalese black body for
emblematic display in the colonial world of Peru: Babo had been "dragged
at the tail of a mule [to meet] his voiceless end" (258), and then, like the Zumbi
of post-Palmares Brazil, he had been decapitated. His head—"that hive of
subtlety" which had plotted so violent a return to the Other Shore of the Lords
Back There—was then mounted on a pole in the plaza. It was from that height
in the New World that the body in question "met unabashed, the gaze of
whites" (258).

     Robert Hayden's "Middle Passage" echoes such pre-texts in the temp-
tation of the black flesh. It charts lines of succession which duly record the
fact that the "Deponent further sayeth" that "The *Bella* / [had] left the Guinea
Coast / with a cargo of five hundred blacks and odd / for the barracoons of
Florida" (1975:119). Thereafter, the ships of "Middle Passage" move with a
dark lyricism; and there is a studied elegance, too, in the way in which *bruta
facta* and the marvelous lie in the "effluvium of living death" and in "charnal
stench." Imbricated and consubstantiated, "the living and the dead, the
horribly dying / lie interlocked, lie with blood and excrement." It is thus that
the transport weaves its way, in a "voyage through death / to life upon these
shores." The "angle of ascent" is one in which the ships leave in their wake
a familiar conscripting of the names for god and gold:

> *Jesus, Estrella, Esperanza, Mercy—*
>
> Shuttles in the rocking loom of history
> the dark ships move, the dark ships move
> their bright ironical names
> like jests of kindness on a murderer's mouth
>
> *Desire, Adventure, Tartar, Ann.* (1975:118)

With jest, Jesus, and murder—and a dead reckoning of "the profit on't" all—
the transport heads into "New World littorals" that are "mirage and myth and
actual shore" (*ibid.*). This is land which, in Stevens's "O Florida, Venereal

Soil," is also a virgin of boorish births, ready to be fecund with "the dreadful sundry of this world":

> The Cuban, Polodowsky,
> The Mexican women,
> The negro undertaker
> Killing time between corpses
> Fishing for crayfish... (1972:78)

"I am going to take off for Africa," declares Bastos's El Supremo. "Why Africa, Loco-Solo? Because I want strong impressions, not that shitty little war with Bolis. Balls on that!" (1987:99). He limns a familiar enough terrain; so, too, the human type to go with it. Caught between being crayfish and corpse, *lo negro* in the Americas has again and again manifested itself in myth-making and myth-mocking forms. Its "strong impressions" have ranged accordingly, from the "soiled gods" that the Aztecs assumed the blacks in Cortés's party to be to that "pubic" bush where Cabrera Infante locates its essential identity in *Infante's Inferno*. In the several centuries that Carpentier collapses into *Explosion in a Cathedral*, "the black flesh" would be re-constituted, too, in the now pragmatic and revolutionary, now utopian body politics of maroon societies. These included the "Valley of the Negroes in Mexico and along the coast of Veracruz" where the Viceroy Martin Enriques ordered that all fugitive slaves be castrated, "without further inves-tigation of their crimes of excess" (1979:23); so, too, the Caribbean of *The Kingdom of This World*, and the Palmares of *Song for Anninho*. It was in the Venezuela of 1552-1555, and to the accompaniment of drums, that the Negro Miguel, for one, had led that rebellion of miners at Buria; that he had emerged transfigured into mirage and myth. He had done so with "the negress Guiomar" at his side—she who had been consecrated when a Congo or Yoruba Archibishop, unknown at Rome yet possessing both crozier and mitre," placed a "royal garland about her brow." It was thus that the man and the woman had founded that kingdom of theirs in a landscape of such dazzling whiteness that it looked like "ground glass" (*Explosion* 231; Nuñez 1980:315-316; Rout 1976:111).

There were occasions, of course, in which the Other Shore conjured up itself in the ordinary and the apparent: in "the work," that is, of Blood, Feathers, and Parrots' Beaks; in Dogs' Teeth and Alligators' Teeth; so, too, in Broken Bottles, Grave Dirt, and in Rum and Eggshells (Barrett 1979:74). With them the *loas* could be re-embodied as the "Lords Back There," especially the historical import of their readiness to "round out the work of men's hands" in the New World. Needless to say, the "Lords Back There" were themselves caught up in the haunt of other theologies and ceremonies of conquest. As a result, there were restraining orders of various sorts. Anathemas were pronounced, and interdictions enforced, according to which— (and "anything in this Act or any other Act or any other Law to the Contrary notwithstanding")— beyond "the first Day of January which will be in the year of our Lord One thousand Seven hundred and Sixty one, Any Negro or other Slave who shall pretend to any Supernatural Power and be detected in making use of [any] materials related to the practice of Obeah or Witchcraft in Order to delude and impose on the Minds of others shall upon Conviction thereof before two magistrates and three Freeholders suffer Death" or, peculiar irony, suffer "Transportation" (Barrett *ibid.*).

Be that as it may, reasons of state no less than the demands of prophecy required that the *loas* be severely policed should they ever descend upon the New World. C. L. R. James's *The Black Jacobins* duly records the fact that following the example of the Spaniards in Cuba and the English in Jamaica, the French brought 1500 dogs into San Domingo to hunt down blacks (1963:275; Carpentier 1979:232). A day thus arrived in the Haiti of *The Kingdom of This World* when, "with rapid clicks of the beads of the abacus," a French official counted hundreds of mastiffs from a "ship of dogs" as they disembarked "to eat niggers!" (1970:89). The Governor's calculation was that this display of appetite would keep the Negroes in their place. But then, the extravagance of violence notwithstanding, Napoleon also aimed at nothing less than *eu-topos* on the island. He sent out an expeditionary force that did not only involve dogs, his brother-in-law General Leclerc, and an "infinite number of soldiers with great talent, good strategies, great tacticians, officers of engineers and artillery, well-educated and very resourceful." James adds that Leclerc's wife, Pauline Bonaparte, and their son went along too. She brought with her musicians, artists, and all the paraphernalia of a court in the expectation that "slavery would be re-established, civilisation restarted, and a good time would be had by all" (*ibid.*). In the course of events, ceremonies of some consequence did take place in an amphitheater constructed on the grounds of a former Jesuit convent. The presiding official was General Rochambeau who, having concluded that he was no longer engaged in a war but in "a fight of tigers," had embarked on an extermination of the island's mulattoes, and elsewhere drowned "so many people in the Bay of Le Cap that many a long day the people of the district would not eat fish" (359). At any rate, Rochambeau had arrived at the amphitheater surrounded by his staff, and to the sound of martial music.

> But when the dogs were let loose they did not attack the victim [a young black man]. Boyer, chief of staff . . . jumped into the arena and with a stroke of his sword cut open the belly of the black. At the sight and scent of the blood the dogs threw

themselves on the black and devoured him in a twinkling. . . . To encourage them in a liking for blood blacks were daily delivered to them, until the dogs, though useless in battle, would throw themselves on blacks at sight. (*ibid.* 359-360)

All in all, Césaire's *The Tragedy of King Christophe* is worth re-situating here. With La Ferriere's "delirious clouds overhead," and "at our feet the sea vomited out by two worlds," we are back in that "extraordinary concretion" of Vastey's, and thus "situated at the focal point of every ebb and flow. And what a view it offers on all sides!" (1969:73). In Fernando Ortiz's version of the same the influx is of "Jews, French, Anglo-Saxons, Chinese" who join an earlier and "steady stream of African Negroes" from the continent's coastal regions, having been transported from Senegal, Guinea, the Congo, and Angola and as far away as Mozambique on the opposite side (1947:98). As *The Pleasures of Exile* rather more elaborately summarizes this converging of latitudes,

> A fantastic human migration [had moved] to the New World of the Caribbean; deported crooks and criminals, defeated soldiers and Royalist gentlemen fleeing from Europe, slaves from the West Coast of Africa, East Indians, Chinese, Corsicans, and Portuguese. The list is always incomplete, but they all move and meet on an unfamiliar soil, in a violent rhythm of race and religion. (Lamming 1992:17)

One consequence of the Caribbean being the site of so much variousness is that it forever promises to be—or risks being—itself only within the inventory of dis/affiliations that we get in *The Repeating Island*'s dizzying (but still inadequate) account of "the black who studied in Paris; of the white who believes in the Yoruba orichas or in the voodoo *loas*." So, too, in the story "of the mulatto who wants to be white; of the white man who does not want his daughter to marry a black man; of the white man who loves a mulatto woman; of the black woman who loves a white man; of the black man who despises the mulatto; of the rich black and the poor white; of the white who claims that race does not exist" (Benítez-Rojo 1995:105). There remains, too, the sexually charged ethnic division that so disturbs the "Indian party" in Sparrow's composition, *Marajhin Sister*, with its "Seem like you have a weakness for Indian / Well, get it from somebody else not me." For his part, the suitor is nothing if not dedicated:

> Though bigotry is threatening our love
> *Pakray pakray parkay ham say*
> Where there is a will there is a way.

All the same, "honourable intention" or not, the warning that "If you touch me *lah-tee-mangay*, cutlass go pass" is one that does resonate, and on so tight an island too (*Sparrow, the Legend*).

Ras Tafarite accommodation to such registers of conmingling is especially problematic. It is no less so with the mediation that Lamming's Pa suggests in *In the Castle of My Skin* when he makes his peace with "the silver of exchange [that] sail across the sea" and with a scatteration, "like clouds in the sky when the waters come" that led to Jamaica, Antigua, Grenada, or to Barbados and the island of oil and the mountain tops (1975:233-34). Still to be resolved, then, is the story that Benítez-Rojo identifies as that "of the black who wants to return to Africa after so many centuries. In the case of the Ras Tafari in Orlando Patterson's *The Children of Sisyphus*, the Great Return insisted on Ethiopia *unbound and unadulterated*—in spite, or precisely because, of other impatient Caribbean voices, with their "if you hear some young fool fretting about going back to Africa, keep far from the invalid and don't force a passage to where you won't yet belong" (Lamming 1975:234). As represented in Patterson, Ras Tafarite insistence on disaffiliation results in a conflation of desire with an anxiety that is obsessive, hysterical, even, in its conviction that "the ship would come. They talked. They laughed. The ship of the great Emperor would show itself in the morning with the glory of the sun" (173).

> [On] the morrow would not the holy ship be coming for them? Could not the spirit of the Holy Emperor bring [them] back to life? Babylon was wicked. He had never realized it could be so wicked. But no matter what they did, there was nothing which the Holy Emperor could not repair. He made all things; he destroyed all things; and he could remake all things.
>
> And so he kissed her gently on her lips. He said a short prayer for her. "Tomorrow," he whispered with all the deep fervour of his faith. "Tomorrow we shall meet in Paradise." (190)

Conceived of in this way, the messianic-millenarianism of *The Children of Sisyphus* is necessarily limited to avoidance and rebuke, to awaiting the demise of the offending society. "And when the end comes, the disinherited will survey the ruins and gather themselves to await the call to come home . . . in the case of the Rastafarians, to Africa. To Ethiopia. To be with Ras Tafari, Negus Negast, the Conquering Lion of Judah" (Wilson 1973:67). In *O Babylon!* Walcott's Rastafarian "Four Horsemen" mime something of this vision, to the accompaniment of music and of Aaron's words:

> I stood on the sand, I saw
> black horsemen galloping
> They were all white like the waves
> and turbanned, too, like the breakers,
> their flags thinning away into spume;
> white, white were their snorting horses.
> I saw them. It was no dream.
> They rode through me,
> they came from my home,
> as fresh as the waves and older than the sea. (1978:166)

But then, notwithstanding so other-worldly a pre-text, there is historical record of a counter-text; so, too, of paradise regained. Walcott's drama of exile and exploitation, and of the utopian bent in "Babylon," was in fact occasioned by the signs-and-wonders visit of "His Imperial Majesty Haile Selassie," the Conquering Lion of Judah, to Jamaica on April 21, 1966. For some, it could have been nothing short of the kerygmatic return of an unreturnable fiction, of an End-Time "when every cultist on the island began to prepare for what the Greek New Testament called a *parousia*." All the same, it was a thing of the kingdom of *this* world, too. Rastafarian chronicles would record that "The King of Kings and Lord of Lords did not think too highly to leave his High Throne in Ethiopia to sit on a chair in the King's House among the servants of the earth." And this his coming, it would be noted, "lifted us from the dust and caused us to sit with princes of this country" (Barrett 1977). Indeed, it did. For so massive was "the outpouring of support for [the] African monarch that the State had to call upon Rastafarian leaders, such as Mortimer Planno, to participate in the official functions" (Campbell 1987:127; Lewis 1994:16-17).

A favorite *sranan tongo* aphorism of Suriname's J.G.A. Koenders effectively captures the divided-to-the-vein appeal—and the threat—that are involved in all this: "*Yu kan kibri granmama, ma yu no kan tapu kosokoso*— you may hide your grandmother, but you cannot prevent her from coughing" (1975:137). That being the case, the oscillations of root and renovation in the New World may indeed be Rasta eschatology, or the racial-cleansing in the Thomas Jefferson that Michelle Cliff cites in *Abeng*: "While we are . . . Scouring our planet, by clearing America of Woods, and so making this Side of our Globe reflect a brighter Light to the Eyes of Inhabitants in Mars and Venus, why should we in the Sight of Superior Beings, darken its People?" (1984:38). There is, too, the apocalypse into which "The Lords Back There" lead *The Kingdom of This World*. Carpentier duly records the fact that "Henri Christophe, the reformer, had attempted to ignore Voodoo, molding with whiplash a caste of Catholic gentlemen." However, when he is faced with a native insurrection of subjugated knowledges on the last night of his life,

Christophe comes to recognize that "the real traitors to his cause" had been St. Peter with his keys, the Capuchins of St. Francis, the blackamoor St. Benedict along with the dark-faced Virgin in her blue cloak; so, too, the Evangelists whose books he had ordered kissed each time the oath of loyalty was sworn. In addition to which, there were all those "martyrs to whom he had ordered the lighting of candles containing thirteen gold coins." The consequences are clear enough in the alternative future to which Christophe turns in his suicide: "Africa, help me to go home, carry me like an aged child in your arms. Undress me and wash me. Strip me of my nobles, my nobility, my scepter, my crown. And wash me, oh, wash me clean of their grease paint, their kisses, wash me clean of my kingdom" (Césaire 1970:90). The night of the Great Return and insurrection had been "dense with drums. Calling to one another, answering from mountain to mountain, rising from the beaches, issuing from the caves, running beneath the trees, descending ravines and riverbeds, the drums of Bouckman, the drums of the Grand Alliances." In effect, the "Lords Back There" of the Other Shore were closing in, and doing so in a "vast encompassing percussion" and with a "horizon of thunder" (148).

In both Césaire and Carpentier, such crises of allegiance and identity have as much import for Emperor as they do for Commoner. This is clearly the case in *The Kingdom of This World* when the narrative foregrounds the telling nature of Soliman's exile in Rome and the vernacular move that he makes toward the Other Shore of the Land-in-Waiting, this time by way of *Eshu* [childless wanderer, alone, moving as a spirit] *Elegbara* [owner-of-the-power]. His prayer is appropriately for "Papa Legba" to "lift up the barrier; open up the gate, and let [him] pass."

> In vain did [Christophe's widow] Queen-Marie Louise attempt to calm him with an infusion of bitter herbs which she had received from the Cap, via London, as a special token from President Boyer. Soliman was cold. An unseasonable fog was chilling the marbles of Rome. The summer was veiled by a mist that thickened by the hour. The Princesses sent for Dr. Antommarchi, who had been Napoleon's doctor on St. Helena, and who was credited by some with exceptional professional gifts, as a homeopath. But his prescribed pills never left the box. Turning his back on all, moaning to the wall papered with yellow flowers on a green background, Soliman was seeking a god who had his abode in far-off Dahomey, at some dark crossroad, his red phallus on a crutch he carried for that purpose.

> *Papa Legba, l'ouvri barrie-a pou moin, ago yé,*
> *Papa Legba, ouvri barrie-a pou moin, pou moin passé.* (1970:168)

Given the generic habit of trapping *mulata* and *negro* in the eroteleptic, this instance of the Great Return to the "crossroad" may benefit from the greater historical and cultural sensitivity that Galeano's *Open Veins of Latin America* brings to bear on the genre. He points out that in Cuba "some slaves committed mass suicide, mocking their masters, as Fernando Ortiz has put it, 'with their eternal strikes, their unending flight to the other world'." They thought, explains Galeano, that they would thus be brought back to life, body and soul, in Africa. However, "by mutilating the corpses so they would return to life castrated, maimed, or decapitated, the masters dissuaded many from killing themselves." There is a narrative from the *back-there* of Chinua Achebe's *Things Fall Apart* which provides us with a measure of the genealogy that the slave owners in Cuba understood well enough to disrupt. For it is in the telling ritual of dealing with the *ogbanje* that a "medicine man" of the Other Shore had "ordered that there should be no more mourning for the dead child. He brought out a sharp razor from his goatskin bag slung from his left shoulder and began to mutilate the child. Then he took it away to bury it in Evil Forest, holding it by the ankle and dragging it on the ground behind him. After such treatment it would think twice before coming again, unless it was one of the stubborn ones who returned, carrying the stamp of their mutilation—a missing finger or perhaps a dark line where the medicine man's razor had cut them." By 1870, Galeano reports, "Afro-Cubans were, on the whole, no longer committing suicide; instead, "a magic chain gave them power and they 'flew through the sky and returned to their own land'" (1973:98). Esteban Montejo's flight into descent in the Cuba of the *Autobiography of a Runaway Slave* limns a now distant metaphysics:

> The strongest gods are African. I tell you it's certain they could fly. . . . I don't know how they permitted slavery. The truth is . . . I can't make head or tail of it. To my mind it all started with the scarlet handkerchiefs, the day they crossed the wall. There was an old wall in Africa, right round the coast, made of palm-bark and magic insects which stung like the devil. (1973:16)

It has ever been the case, then, that "The People Who Could Fly" to the Other Shore always sought to do exactly that (Hamilton 1985). Cliff's *Abeng* explains the facts in the fiction: "Africans could fly. They were the only people on this earth to whom God had given this power. Those who refused to be slaves and did not eat salt flew back to Africa, [but] those who were slaves and ate salt to replenish their sweat, had lost the power, because the salt made them heavy, weighted down" (63-64); and Toni Morrison counter-points its exuberant epiphany ("He could flyyyy!") with moral gravity ("You can't just fly off and leave a body") in *Song of Solomon* (1980:332). Galeano makes a reprise of the whole through Carpentier's master-poisoner, Macandal. The year is 1758, and the place Cape Français: François Macandal, he who had announced "the hour of those who came from Africa," is in the process of being burnt alive at the stake when, all of a sudden, a shriek splits the ground, a fierce cry of pain and exultation. Macandal breaks free and is lost in the air to the accompanying and knowing cry of "Macandal *sauvé!*" [Macandal is saved, and gone!] (Galeano 1987:26). In *The Kingdom of This World*, "the slaves [had] returned to their plantations laughing all the way. Macandal had kept his word, remaining in the Kingdom of This World. Once more the whites had been outwitted by the mighty Powers of the Other Shore" (52). For their Land-in-Waiting was a "Back There [where] there were princes hard as anvils, and princes who were leopards, and princes who knew the language of the forest, and princes who ruled the four points of the compass, lords of the clouds, of the seed, of bronze, of fire" (15).

As things turn out, this future-past fails; and it fails in the kingdoms of this world where, as Carpentier notes, "the word of Henri Christophe had become stone and no longer dwelt among us." For in the end, "all of his fabulous person that remained was in Rome, a finger floating in a rock-crystal bottle filled with brandy" (1970:177). Carpentier also links the failure to gene-soaked anxieties—to black skin/white masks obsessions—in "the king-dom of this world." Meanwhile, in Césaire's *Tragedy*, Christophe's sover-eign state, that "tide smell of the future" (45), would become a race-(de)graded dystopia, having by then forgotten its ancient properties. Simply put: "a spurious aristocracy [made up of a] caste of quadroons" that "not even Henri Christophe would have suspected that the land of Santo Domingo would bring forth [had taken over] the old plantations, with their privileges and rank" (Carpentier 1970b:177).

In the final analysis, then, and as has been very much the case in the various sections of this chapter, Carpentier's *Explosion in a Cathedral* is richly various in its stories of utopian excursions and dystopian arrivals. The narrative's several voyages to abounding blessed isles make a palimpsest of Mesoamerica and its Caribbean Sea; and it plays out in extravagant form the ironies that ensue when Arawak and Carib; Carib and Maya; Africa and Europe; Euro-Conquistador and Carib; and Caribbean and Yankee pursue ideal enclaves and imagined communities that have been conjured into and out "immense esplanades, virgins' baths, and unimaginable buildings" (1979:242). This is the context in which, a self- and other-consuming artifice, the Empire of the North forever remains the Land-in-Waiting that makes and unmakes, even as it is itself made up. This had been true, once upon a time, when the Other Shore had seemed almost to appear before the eyes of the Caribs. In pursuit of that Land-in-Waiting they had embarked upon their canoe-driven and Arawak-destroying assault on paradise. Moreover, from "talking so much about the Empire of the North, men began to acquire proprietary rights over it. . . . Three more islands, two more, perhaps only one." Then, "they would reach the Land-in-Waiting" (243-4). It was at precisely the same time that, irony of ironies, the Caribs encountered other "unsuspectable invaders, from no one knew where"; for there began "to loom on the horizon strange, unrecognized shapes, with hollows in their sides, and trees growing on top of them, beating the canvas which billowed and fluttered, and displayed unknown symbols." As a consequence, that Carib/bean "Great Migration would no longer have an objective, the Empire of the North would fall into the hands of these unexpected rivals" (244). Meanwhile, for the unsuspected others, gold-driven and cross-sanctioned, "the prophecies of the Prophets had been fulfilled, the divinations of theologians confirmed. The everlasting Battle of the Waters, in such a spot as this, proclaimed that they had finally reached the Promised Land, after an agonizing wait of many centuries" (247). In short order, Carpentier writes, the disputed Archipelago would suddenly become a "Theological Archipelago" when the first island "discovered" received the name of Christ, San Salvador. "The Antilles were being transformed into an immense stained-glass window": Santo Domingo, Santiago, Our Lady of Guadeloupe, all set up in the showcase of a sea now "whitened by the coralliferous labyrinth of the Eleven Thousand Virgins— as imposssible to count as the *Campus Stellae*" (245). But then, all that would soon remain, myth-making and myth-mocking, of the earlier Amerindian reach for the utopian Land-in-Waiting would be "the reality of Carib petroglyphs . . . with their human figures, inlaid in the rock, a proud solar symbolism" (245). Aspiration to the sun had been "dealt a death blow" and turned into *aksident* and determinate negation just as it was about to climax in yet another "age-old design" on the best of all possible worlds. In effect, as Soyinka's vernacular measure will have it in *Madmen and Specialists*: "*bi o ti wa / ni yio se wa / bi o ti wa / ni yio se wa, / bi o ti wa l'atete ko se*": "As Is Was Now / As Ever Shall Be" (244).

Tutuola's Yoruba landscapes lead us deeper into the nexus of such contraindications. The terms of reference in *The Palm-Wine Drinkard and His Dead Palm-Wine Tapster in Dead's Town* are as inimitably as they are representatively caught in the con/fusion of the signs that mark the boundaries of *eu-topos* and *ou-topos*. For here again we are led by a "very clean road" to an "UNRETURNABLE-HEAVEN'S TOWN" that "was surrounded with a thick and tall wall."

> There we saw that if one of them wanted to climb a tree, he would climb the ladder first before leaning it against that tree; and there was a flat land near their town but they built their houses on the side of a steep hill, so all the houses bent downwards as if they

were going to fall, and their children were always rolling down
from these houses, but their parents did not care about that; the
whole of them did not wash their bodies at all, but washed their
domestic animals; they wrapped themselves with a kind of leaves
as their clothes, but had costly clothes for their domestic animals,
and cut their domestic animals' finger nails, but kept their own
uncut for one hundred years. (1953:56-58)

In 1958, workmen uncovered "a coffin of heavy metal, a coffin of huge
proportions," while digging near the churchyard of a High Anglican Church
founded in Kingston, Jamaica in 1692. So writes Michelle Cliff in her
complexly Caribbean-Mesoamerican narrative, *Abeng*. Sacrament and cargo
cult, war and death by water, the womb contained and despoiled, superimpositions of epochs, all of them alive—all these are clustered in the details of the
unearthing. The find was, after all, not really in the shape of a coffin at all.
Instead, it was more like "a monstrous packing case, made of lead and welded
shut" (1984:7). As Paz does through the archaeology of Coatlicue, it is richly
appropriate that in explaining this Caribbean exhumation, Cliff invokes, only
to subvert, the play of tropes that has dominated narratives of the utopian bent:
exodus to a promised land and sea voyages to blessed isles; migration
(ideological or physical) to an Empire of the North and the haunt of pre-text
and prophecy. In the process, she refigures the cluster of ideas that Carpentier
makes the nuclear fable in *Explosion*, and in which context,

> the children of the Castilian plain would dream . . . of the Valley
> of Jauja after a supper of crust of bread with olive oil and garlic.
> The Encyclopaedists . . . a Better World in the society of the
> Ancient Incas, [and in which] the United States had seemed a
> Better World, when they sent ambassadors to Europe without
> wigs, who wore buckled shoes, spoke clearly and simply, and
> bestowed blessings in the name of Freedom. (247)

A brass plate affixed to the monstrous packing case in *Abeng* informed the
vicar of the High Anglican Church that within were the remains of a hundred
plague victims, part of a shipload of slaves from the Gold Coast, who had
contracted the plague from the rats on the vessel which brought them across
the Atlantic from Africa to Jamaica. On no account, the inscription insisted,
was the coffin to be opened as the plague might still be viable—and no doubt
"still-vex'd." Thereupon, and given the latter days of the utopian bent in the
still-vex'd Bermoothes, Cliff's vicar concludes the matter appropriately: he
commissions "an American navy warship in port to take the coffin twenty
miles out and sink it in the sea" (8).

Meanwhile, in the "bituminous darkness" that followed when the last door had been closed on Carpentier's century of lights, "the picture of the 'Explosion in a Cathedral', which had been left behind—perhaps deliberately left behind—ceased to have any subject." In the growing darkness the painting merged with "the dark crimson brocade" which covered the main wall of the drawing room of a house upon whose roof it had once upon a time been possible to talk, with one's face "turned upwards to the sky, about habitable—and surely inhabited—planets, where life would perhaps be better than it was on this earth, everlastingly subjected to the processes of death" (23). This is the context in which, finally, the cathedral's "scattered and falling columns became invisible against the background which, even now that the lights had gone, retained the colour of blood" (349). Thus, for all that its "charms are all o'erthrown" (*The Tempest*) this "*Something*, another thing" would remain imbricated in the dis/play of darkness and light in the Indies.

"Africa, ma'am, as Nature meant her to be, the home of the black man and the quiet elephant."

Aloysius Smith or *Trader Horn* or Ethelreda Smith or Metro-Goldwyn-Mayer Pictures.

Chapter 3

Postscript:
How To Breathe Dead Hippo Meat, and Live

The earth for us is a place to live in, where we must put up with
sights, with sounds, with smells, too, by Jove!—breathe dead hippo,
so to speak, and not be contaminated.
> Jozef Teodor Konrad Korzeniowski (aka Joseph Conrad),
> *Heart of Darkness*

After that I hinted to them about the "SECRET-SOCIETY OF
GHOST" which is celebrated once in every century. I told them that
as it is near to be celebrated I like to be present there so that I may
bring some of its news to them and other people.
> Amos Tutuola, *My Life in the Bush of Ghosts*

H enrietta Street, London, England, makes for a starting point that is
as implausible as it may be said to be unavoidable, given the oddly
syncopated rhythms of our "high life." In *The Mysterious Mr. Eliot,*
a biographical documentary about the St. Louis-born writer turned
High Anglican and High Modernist English poet, one of the persons inter-
viewed recalls a visit to T.S. Eliot's desk when he was employed at Lloyd's
Bank: "There he was, poor man, *the* poet of our time, adding up figures in a
bank." And all day the heels of passersby went *clok clok, clok clok* six inches
overhead, on the pavement of Henrietta Street. Such bits of information, at
once useful and exotically pointless—very much like dead hippo meat,
perhaps, or like news from a bush of ghosts—do have a way of developing into
critical noises in one's head. At any rate, my being thus crossed up at and into
Henrietta Street may not have been altogether that odd, or unproductive. For
I happened upon Henrietta Street at about the same time, in the 1970s, that I
embarked upon the three-volume poetry sequence that would culminate in
Carnival of the Old Coast. To explain further the coincidence of dislocation
and inspiration that the Sierra Leone trilogy has since worked to contain, I
borrow from George Lamming's *The Pleasures of Exile* what amounts to a
manifesto and poetics of exile: "The pleasure and the paradox of . . . exile is

that I belong wherever I am. My role, it seems, has rather to do with time and change than with the geography of circumstances; and yet there is an acre of ground in the New World which keeps growing echoes in my head. I can only hope that these echoes do not die before my work comes to an end" (50).

After a rather extended stay away from Sierra Leone, my concern in the poetry trilogy was to return in a way that would recover the years from the 1500s to the 1960s; and to do so by way of a strategic deployment of contexts in my Sierra Leone Krio heritage. I decided then that I would focus on the remarkably elastic features of this culture's peculiar history of scatterration and re-grouping. In brief, *Highlife for Caliban* (1940s-1960s), *Hand on the Navel* (1914-1945), and *Carnival of the Old Coast* (1500s-1950s) would ride out and into the various affiliations and languages of Sierra Leone's creolization. The volumes thus negotiate a complex cultural genealogy; they also traffic and trade with "yron works of sundry sorts / manillos and jingling bracelets anon" in a "highlife for traders." After all, it was in the "stout talk" of "charlatan lions" that we once learned that

> it was for this darkskinned
> *this-one* that a stout *this-one*
> came to know 2 bags
> of lead and the weight of 10
> yards in a king's cloth
> of scarlet; and for this *that-one,*
> two bajude pants of cloth,
> 2 patna do & 2 blue
> and one half of cotton:
> weight enough, fit so
> to make a nakedness of us. (62)

For all of this the length and the weight of genealogy were as much Yoruba as Afro-Brazilian; as much Liverpool and Hull as Nova Scotia and Jamaican Maroon. The product, too, of the Carolinas and the Gullah Islands, terrain and type in the trilogy would answer as much to Afro-Christian *shout* as it would to the call of the Afro-Islamic Aku Krio concentration at Fourah Bay, in the East-end of Freetown. Small wonder that on December 20, 1902 an item in *The Sierra Leone Weekly News* had rather elaborately understood the arrangement of lines and succesion to mean that "Being a Creole or Sierra Leonean [could] not be a nationality; it is an act of grace."

Carnival of the Old Coast, Hand on the Navel, and *Highlife for Caliban* have collectively sought to thicken "grace" with historical edge and sensuous detail—as happens in "Giddy Appetites," among the "scholars," as we were called, of the Sierra Leone Grammar School Choir (1956-1958):

The song cycles are done.
they have gone quiet, the quinqueremes
of Ninevah, row their way
home, and become nothing to us.

I slip down a morning peculiar
to this coast; freighted with gold bits,
salt, really, paraguay tea; these
nine books for buenos ayres; a like
a parcel of guinea grain and negro
sails with us, weighs with us into port.

oigame, y que díos nos bendiga
and for those stately spanish galleons
too, remember, that made
brightness and bone structure a puzzle
in apes and peacocks for us.

still, that children never know
the measure and the full
beat of things, or learn too
well the native shift of difference
in the unquiet privilege of song
—all this means nothing;
we were, after all, smaller
then than the disfiguring joke.
we were giddy so with appetite.
we could hold so to notes played
out beyond even the tenor of our days. (*Carnival* 5)

In the unquiet privilege of other maps, the volumes also sought out the
implications of disfiguring joke and appetite in Krenakore Brazil and in the
Africa of "queen Victoria days"; with Aborigine Australia and along the
sidewalk cafes of the Cours Mirabeau, in Aix-en-Provence. So, too, riding the
trains from Paris to Venice, by way of Florence. And here, as I recall, when
"the train clattered out of Milan / the men, inside our compartment, /
[scratched] so at their groins." I recall, too, that *i signiori veneziani* flogged
their forefingers so inside the palm of the hand, "wondering how well you
(blonde of hair) and I 'did' it." But then,

there are fishbones in Venice,
too, and the screams of urgent cats
and small streets they call Pavarotti.
water sucks at the rotting stones of our hotel.

we do not give birth with ease
here. . . (*Highlife* 68)

No less relevant than Nineveh could have been, there were memories, too, of mosques and long-jointed minarets to attend to—whether along the Niger and Benue Rivers in Nigeria or else under the shade of an "*Arabia felix*" of black eunuchs ("radiant cut, blessed / in the dividing blade / that is Allah's eye"). In places, that is, with "names jingling so like oases / and jewels on a golddark belly" (*Carnival* 18-20). But then, here where "there are no new ways left us / truly to know evil. . . / or the evidence for god,"

> . . . why, after all,
> should fine silk be friend to wool?

Besides which, when, by the hill of Arafa, "Abraham, peace be upon him, / stoned the devil," it was "in his own anger, not in ours."

> our economy is continence itself,
> and austere; tart so with bitter
> trouble . . .
>
> we who can contain no such
> history of hell; why, after all,
> should fine silk become the friend of wool? (*Carnival* 19)

"You can't breathe dead hippo meat waking, sleeping, and eating, and at the same time keep your precarious grip on existence," Korzeniowski-Conrad's Marlow had once said, caught in the act of being very nearly at impossible odds with himself, and in the heart of a certain kind of darkness, no less. True enough, I should think. Of course, it is no easy thing to "take twelve stiches in mouth" either; for which reason—and to keep "brittle bones polite"— *Highlife for Caliban* had moved in various ways to account for its calculus of allegiances by re-siting Henrietta Street. It did so in "Letter to My Tailor," in which context, "Lately," so the confession goes, "I have taken to trousers / with buttons on a long fly; being / lately, in no hurry to ease myself." In addition to which,

> lately, I have taken to walking,
> here, with my elbows close to my body.
>
> if you like, you may say,
> I do not like the climate, or, again

you may say, if you like, you may say
"this one has taken twelve stitches inside
the corners of his mouth; his elbows,
now, keep the rebellion in his brittle bones polite." (62)

In one of its meanings, *highlife* is a West African dance. All the same, the
elbow-room movements to which this Caliban devotes his attention have
much in common with all those back-to-the-native-land steps that Martinique's
Aimé Césaire had so decisively played out in *Cahier d'un retour au pays
natal*, in 1939. As things turn out, the poems of *Highlife* recalculate the
temptation and the weight of ideas accordingly—whether they appear on sale,
or merely hung up for display, on the Henrietta Streets of our various exiles
among Tarzans or Hegels. Subsequent shifts in the valuing of high life, or low,
coalesce in the elbow-room anxieties of the class of "we" that gets to speak
in "Exorcism":

narrow
as a calvinist's ark
this, too,
is the place
built for us
by strangers...

why else
would old photographs
turn yellow
against the walls?

why else
would glass
refuse
our reflection
turning
to the wall? (*Highlife* 48)

Meanwhile, neither "ariel-spirit" nor "daughter-flesh," Caliban reflects in the
ora pro nobis of his calypso on the fact that "is so I set down so to substance
/ and to sum, but, seduced, think / to be elf with printless foot / is admiration
and nice" (*Highlife* 39).

One of the perquisites of Power, no doubt, is the capacity to determine
when and if one's Truth can have Universal weight. Naturally, I oppose the
heft and muscle of such capital-letter formations to the parochial density of
folk who can be ever so easily pushed outside History. The capacity to stand,

bulwarked, against the subversive penetration of strangers certainly has its advantages. So, too, are there disadvantages to being forever available for assimilation. This is especially the case with participant-outsiders, with *gastarbeiter* folk, if you wish. It is peculiarly so, I would think, for the alien(ated) who see themselves as permanently exiled from clusterings that confer citizenship and the comfort and power of belonging. The cluster of effects is succinctly captured when Ralph Ellison's *Invisible Man* calls attention to the existential weightlessness of it all: "Outside the Brotherhood, we were outside history; but inside it they didn't see us. It was a hell of a state of affairs."

The roles that exile-participants assume under these circumstances invite comparisons; and one such is that of model Alien/Visitor/Guest Worker. One might think here of Othello in Venice, *before* he misunderstands the degree to which Desdemona can be available. Still, close encounters of the model kind may be sustained with decorum and apparent good grace. Therefrom might emerge a kind of Naipaulian Exile-as-Honorary-Gentleman. On the other hand, the honorary status could become charged, modulating into the exile as Noble and Necessary Mercenary; especially if, as in the case of Othello when we first meet him, truly illegal aliens in the likes of infidel/circumcized Turk/moslem *Ausländer* are already within shooting distance of Venice, and shooting. Fully inverted, the role of Othello-the-model falls back upon itself when the exile becomes hired gun. In effect, The Moor turns, or is turned, into a self- and ethno-traducing spear carrier who withers, dangerously, in assimilationist illusions of distinterested merit and esteem. "Are we turned Turk?" Othello then asks.

In part, it is this conflict in perspectives about the exile as hired, or noble, gun that accounts for character and voice in the second volume of the Sierra Leone trilogy, *Hand on the Navel*. The preoccupation also explains why the volume's circumstances pivot as they do, around the years 1914-1918 and 1939-1945. After all, did not *The Sierra Leone Weekly News* (1884 to 1951), for one, take note on April 29, 1939 that Herr Hitler had pointedly remarked that "From time to time it is brought to notice that a Negro has become a lawyer, teacher, tenor or the like. This is a sin against all reason; it is criminal madness to train a born Semi-Ape to become a lawyer. It is a sin against the Eternal Creator to train Hottentots and Kaffirs to intellectual professions."

But then, at the 1914 Feast of the Greater Biram—celebrated at Bonthe Island, Shebro, Sierra Leone—special prayers had been "recited in solemn tones by Alpha Moukhtahr" and two other Imams, Alimamy Duramany and Alpha Davendo. We recall, too, that on the occasion of that Biram, after the recital of the ceremonial prayers, "a special form of prayers prepared for the present troubles of the war affecting Europe, the Empire and the civilised world were repeated." The people there gathered had affirmed each prayerful request with "*Amina*" as they offered themselves up "on behalf of King George V, leader of his people, in the Kingdom and amongst the people whose capital is London. May God be merciful and hear our prayers, and the people say, *Amina*!" The Imam had led them further: "Grant that our armies be aided by angels and that they may have success and will speedily conquer their foe! *Amina*! The Kaiser is desirous to be dominant ruler over all, may he be unstable and fail in his purpose of tyranny. May God the merciful help the armies of the King and all who are concerned in the war on his side. *Amina*!" Appropriately, along with that November 14, 1914 Biram report, the *Sierra Leone Weekly News* had also carried the prediction of a certain Mme de Thebes, the celebrated French Prophetess, that "the Allies [would] win a crushing and total victory, and that the Kaiser [would] die a mental and physical wreck."

Granted, it was true that we were latitudes away from so "Yankee-boy" a thing that happened on August 31st, 1943. Since it was then that a white private would tell a negro officer who had reprimanded him for not observing the usual military courtesies: "If you would take your clothes off and lay them on the ground I would salute them but I wouldn't salute anything that looks like you." But then, that was in another country; and as yet to be recorded in the collection of letters from World War II "nigger-man" soldiers that Phillip McGuire would call *Taps for a Jim Crow Army* (1991). Such "taps" could hardly have been a live, and lived, thing with us; and it was not.

Small wonder, that, "ancient and loyal," the *Sierra Leone Weekly News* could reach out so as it did to record, on November 7, 1914, the anxious agony of our exclusion: "'Oh, if the Government will only come to our aid and give us our desire. Talk of the coolness of the Turcos and the Senegalese as being cool under fire? Below the biggest zero will stand our coolness when we know we are on the path to meet the atrocious Kaiser and his infernal and barbarous host.' That's strong, isn't it? The sentiment, I am sure, will find an echo in every Creole boy's heart." For "the Creole boy loves the soldier life. He loves the smart uniform and the swaggery gait of the *so'jer* man. But he wants a chance to join the colours. Give him the hope of an epaulet, a star and a sword and, by Jingo! you'll see what stuff he is made of. How grand it would be, eh, if we could get a response called 'The King's Own Creole Boys'." Furthermore, and in an October 7, 1939 appeal for "deeds not words," the SLWN would recall that in that other war against the atrocious Kaiser there could never have been any doubting the loyalty ("most gladly shown") of Sierra Leone. It was in due recognition, then, that on September 3, 1939 His Excellency the colonial Governor-General signed two orders "relating to the use of lights in Freetown." The orders affected buildings with windows that faced the sea since, "for the present time," it was "not thought to be necessary to order that windows which do not face the sea should be covered." However,

> As from today no light shall be shown and householders are advised to take immediate steps to see that windows which face the sea are fixed in such a way so that no light, however dim, can penetrate. This is best done by fixing cardboard or several thickness of paper over the window.

Of course, this was all under circumstances in which it was not a matter to be taken lightly that His Majesty's Broadcast to the Empire had taken place on September 3, 1939. Moreover, on September 1, after it had been learned that Germany had invaded Poland, His Majesty had driven to No. 10 Downing Street for a talk with the Prime Minister Mr. Chamberlain. In 1941, he would again visit No. 10 to see, this time, Mr. Churchill who had succeeded Mr. Chamberlain in May 1940. In any case, within a few years one of the largest sequestrations ever of the Empire's fleet of ships would take place in Freetown's well-positioned harbor. "I want to tell you a story," the Right Honourable Harold MacMillan, M.P., and then Parliamentary Under-Secretary for the Colonies, said in a broadcast on 28 July 1942. "It is about an African. I have never seen him or, I'm afraid, the country he lives in. . . . He is of the Nandi tribe and calls himself the Son of Kibet. He was born in a village in an outlying district of Kenya, far from civilisation, far from the railway. . . . Then one day when the threat of war came," there was "in fact no need for conscription." For this Son of Kibet "counted himself lucky" to join one of the local regiments, "the King's African Rifles."

Such events could hardly ever be forgotten, needless to say; and they would not be—neither in *Hand on the Navel* nor in *Highlife for Caliban*'s "The King of a Distant Country (1940-45)." For, pressed as "a memory in 78 rpm," they all came through in the wild and counterfeit passion of "baroque radios we did not invent":

> for there once was a close and dry
> knocking of stone against stone
>   (and this we heard too)
> for *there'll always be an England!*
> *and England shall be free!*
> *if only England means as much*
> *to you as me.* so, do nothing . . .
> Oh, do nothing till you hear from me,
> marching, in the beauty of all my person
>   (*Hand on the Navel* 26)

All in all, as that chronicle of record, *The Sierra Leone Weekly News*, put it in October of 1939, "It was deeply felt that we were part and parcel of the British Empire and that in England we lived and in England we died." And this politics of passion and assimilation was certainly consistent with what an SLWN "Jottings" item had declared on November 21, 1914, at a time when "undoubtedly we [were also] concerned." It never was "an over-estimation of ourselves" to know that we were British subjects"; that we were "part and parcel of that conglomerate whole forming the population of the British Empire." And no statement to the contrary, "however trenchant, could eradicate from us the idea that the weal or woe of the British Throne or nation, has a more or less reactionary (sic) influence on us." The "Jottings" columnist had been moved to respond thus because of a contrary opinion about the meaning of our place in the imperial scheme of things. It was the columnist's conviction that so counter an opinion could not but be "merely a twaddle worked up to sincerity by prejudice (race prejudice) which generally reduces to temporary distortion the intellect of man." Besides which, another "Jottings" item noted, a donation to the British Red Cross war effort was "a positive indication that despite his ebony appearance, the Negro is in no way devoid of the spirit of humanity"; and in this, "Jottings" was quoting a certain Dr. Awunor-Renner. By the same token, and from a Gazette dated 30th September 1942, there was the announcement from just up the coast from us that the sum of £4,170 had been subscribed to the Gambia Spitfire Fund. The Ministry of Aircraft Production was therefore able to state that a Spitfire firefighter would be named "Gambia" as soon as the contribution reached a total of £50,000.

Meanwhile, in the light of such pamphlets as *Uganda for Victory* and *Nigeria for Victory*, and in such places as in *The History of the Battalion of the Royal West African Frontier Force*, compiled by the likes of Lt. R.P.M. Davies from "the Official Records and Documents and from the Letters and Papers of Old Frontier Officers," it would be chronicled that, in the hundreds of thousands, Frontier Boys had indeed "been called upon to take part in a great struggle, the rights and wrongs of which they can scarcely have been expected dimly to perceive. They have been through the, to them, novel experience of facing an enemy with modern weapons, and led by highly trained officers. Their rations have been scanty, their bare-footed marches long and trying, and their fighting at times extremely arduous, yet they have not been found wanting either in discipline, devotion to their officers, or in personal courage." As for some of those who came back "no longer at ease," well—and this is how Chinua Achebe recalls them—they "spoke of Abyssinia, Egypt, Palestine, Burma, and so on. Some of them had been village ne'er-do-wells, but now they were heroes. They had bags and bags of money, and the villagers sat at their feet to listen to their stories. One of them went regularly to market in the neighbouring village and helped himself to whatever he liked. He went in full uniform, breaking the earth with his boots."

In effect, what *Hand on the Navel* explores within and against the template of such service is the model of Othello at war with himself and against his own, for Venice and Desdemona. Affiliation and quarrel were all resonant with, yet again, Europe and Ottoman when Euro-America and Japan's quarrels turned into global catastrophes. For us, then, it had a resonance that could not *not* "take the biscuit"—and that it certainly did when the *Sierra Leone Weekly News* chose to declare on November 14, 1914: "In the name of all that is sensible, what has possessed the 'sick man in Europe' to become entangled in the European imbroglio! . . . For consummate ingratitude Turkey, as John Bull would put it, 'takes the biscuit.'"

The figures and the shade of such matters account for the dedication of *Hand on the Navel* to a knowable, and known, soldier of the Royal West African Frontier Force (RWAFF), Sierra Leone Regiment. So, too, for the fact that there was one summer during which,

> in the antics of odd corners, he kept the eye
> of a ravaged penis tight
> in his left hand (10)

> there are no rabbits in Malaya,
> sir.
> there was one who knew that, saying
> so (despite the nets, the
> mosquitoes insistent); and quinine is
> bitter as death is not sweet (11)

Whether on the encrusted portuguese stone steps of the harbor in Freetown or knee-deep in jungle-rot in Burma, the particulars of quinine, gun, and left hand converge to become the record of the half lives that *Hand on the Navel* reproduces as "The Book of Corporal Bundu, RWAFF—who came back insane"—and of

> those others who apprenticed our youth to an enchantment of
> sorcery and madness; and teased magic out of the fire of strange
> women singing of blue birds over the white cliffs of Dover. This
> then is a recording of memories and half memories, of songs and
> half-songs—and of half lives. (1)

For sooner or later, the evidence is that Othello will pretty much stab himself—or be stabbed—into a suicidal recognition of *how* he means in

Venice. For Corporal Bundu and the RWAFF, the reality had been a matter for plain chant; it was also a matter of dying to no good effect so far from "*the banks of old Moa River / where the moon shines so bright*"; and where, "private no more, in brass / octaves and 'huptwos!',

> *I leave my mother*
> *I leave my father*
> *I leave them farrr-rah-wayyy...*
>
> at Arnheim...
> in December
> we went
> slate-grey with cold
> and we left the corpses
> under a shred a moon
> and the dry wind cropped
> them into a white stone.
> the ground was a hard thing, sir... (25)

Others of The Frontier Boys died prodigiously; and they did so in figures that have since come to speak of 700,000 Ethiopians, nearly one in every family. In battles against General Rommel's troops in Libya about 50 percent of the 10,000 Gabonese troops were killed; and, the figures continue, between 30,000 and 40,000 African lives were lost in the campaign to liberate Italy. The remains of tens of thousands of Nigerians, Ghanaians, Kenyans, and Sierra Leoneans—Frontier Boys all—are buried in Burma and Malaysia. It was in the understanding that followed that the question then became: "to what end aim a dry root / at italian carrara, thinking / of villas and fine pissoirs?" Besides which,

> Mussolini died upside down.
> [and] Rosa posed, but not for us,
> with a dulcimer. in Venice. You remember
> the picture. in Florence.
> what can a dry root do among them?
> in Venice the stones suck so at a green misery
> and sink so far now down from Ethiopia;
> and to what end? to have come
> this far with irregular steps, marching.
> to what doxologies does one pander
> now? Nijinsky danced and went mad.
> did you know? at the end. (39)

"So I would like to say to you," Under-Secretary Harold MacMillan had meanwhile said in his broadcast, "if you see a man in uniform in the street, with a dark skin and a smiling face, think of the Son of Kibet—don't pass him by. Stop him and ask him what Colonial territory he comes from. Give him a welcome."

"The mind of man is capable of anything," so Korzeniowski-Conrad's Marlow tells us. The observation is true, perhaps. Still, the confrontation with Difference, or to put the matter somewhat more gently, the exile from Sameness, that the man proposes with so much flair is no easy matter. Indeed, Marlow makes the observation shortly after the following disorienting convergence of Self and Other:

> It was unearthly, and the men were—No, they were not inhuman. Well, you know, that was the worst of it—this suspicion of their not being inhuman. It would come slowly to one. They howled and leaped, and spun, and made horrid faces; but what thrilled you was the thought of their humanity—like yours—and the thought of your remote kinship with this wild and passionate uproar.

Here the "passionate uproar" underscores rather starkly, even melodramatically, the ambivalence that being foreign and being made to feel foreign can generate. It is noteworthy, of course, that in Conrad the feeling originates and is resolved in a somewhat stereotypical production of *nigger* strangeness. As a result, the experience of being exiled from the normal is compensated for by a prior advantage in which the mind of *man* is already gifted with a familiar pre-text: pre-existing condition of superiority.

Consider, in this light, the refinement and regression in which Verdi, Placido Domingo, and Othello meet in a vignette from the 1994 New York Metropolitan Opera season. The passion and the uproar come, here, when Verdi's Otello is deprived of vision. The social crisis and psychological scatteration that follow are ones that the Moor's "*Dio! me potevi scagliar tutti mali*" (Act 3, Scene 2) tries—and hardly surprising this—fails to contain.

> God! You could have rained upon me
> all evil; all the misery, the affliction,
> shame, have made my trophies
> and bold triumphs a ruin—a lie...
> and I would have borne the cruelty of that cross
> of anguish and shame; would have
> resigned myself to the will of heaven;
> calm, I would bear it all.

> But, the grief, the suffering!
> they have deprived me of the vision
> in which I found joy, kept peace in the soul.
> The sun has gone dark, that smile
> and the radiance with which it quickened me....
> Clemency, you immortal power, once
> a red-rose smile; now, cover up your
> holy face in the horror of a hell-hot rage.
> (Verdi/Boito; my translation)

Significantly, when Placido Domingo gives voice to a pedigree for this anguish, the tenor of what he makes up is predictable, and lodged at the edge of a black and incomprehensible frenzy, as Conrad well knew. "At one point," writes *The New York Times* critic Edward Rothstein in "Mr. Domingo Explains How He Does What He Does" (4/6/94), "Mr. Domingo changed the timbre of his voice, making it seem pale, stripped of resonance or physicality. He does it again now, slowly gasping out the scarcely audible monotone Verdi wrote for the Moor. '*Dio—me potevi—scagliar*'; it has the quality of a recitative,' he says, taking long breaths between phrases. 'I try to think of the almost guttural sound that this black man in a moment of desperation will have. He is a noble character,' Mr. Domingo continues, stepping back from the role, 'and he has been very much refined by the new culture, by the new religion, by the new people. What I like sometimes is when he feels deceit from everybody. He goes back to his roots, into his own world'."

In the heart of his darkness, Marlow had retreated into the comfort of his own voice when he found himself unable to tell whether a certain prehistoric man was "cursing us, praying to us, welcoming us—who could tell?" As Conrad reported the matter, it was certainly true that Kurtz had dropped low enough—stepped back—to take a "high seat amongst the devils of the land—I mean literally" (1963:50). But, Marlow insists, "By Jove!" the key of note lies in a readiness "to breathe dead hippo meat, so to speak, and not be contaminated." For which reason, he steps back into his own world: "I have a voice too, and for good or evil mine is the speech that cannot be silenced."

The exemplary meeting of human voice and hippo meat that Monsieur Theodore Monod records in *L'Hippopotame et le philosophe* (1941) is quite the appropriate one. Its goodness-of-fit is nowhere more evident than when Monsieur Monod leads us to a moment of epiphany in the life of Dr. Albert Schweizter—missionary doctor to equatorial Africa; German-born in 1875 at Kaysenberg, Upper Alsace (now in France); groomed in philosophy and theology at Strasbourg (also in France, now). Schweitzer's enlightenment is rooted in the heart of darkness; on the forested banks of the Ogowe river, no less. The errand into the wilderness generates well; for light does dis/play against and scatters the dark: "*tout à coup, dans ces ténèbres va briller la lumière.*" And indeed it was so, even if Schweitzer's management of insight and elbow-room was "somewhat patriarchal"—as the *Encyclopaedia Britannica*, fifteenth edition, gently notes.

There was light, all the same. "*Ecoutez le philosophe lui-même,*" Monod exhorts, when Schweitzer recalls the signal moment of his translation from blindness to insight, and on the third day, no less. "*Au soir du troisième jour, précisément lorsque nous traversions un troupeau d'hippopotame, il me fut donné, tout soudainement, d'entrevoir la solution: respect de la vie. La porte de fer avait cédé. Je commençais à voir clair.*" In effect, where Newtonian physics had been, so to speak, "eureka'd" by the gravity of an apple's fall, for Schweitzerian insight into the decline and reconstruction of moral culture, into the import of Christianity and the religions of the world, for such insights to come there was hippo meat. Monod is succinct: "*C'est la pomme de Newton*" (337).

Such conditions of exile and insight resonate in various ways in *Carnival of the Old Coast*. These include the volume's concerns with women, from Penelope and how "Ithaca sits with her / where she sits / to knit out the noise / of men sailing off to Troy" (*Carnival* 13) to the nine-poem sequence, "Hagar, or, The Insufficiency of Metaphor." In its treatment of exile and the temptation of allegiance, this sequence draws from Judaic and Christian narratives, and from the Islamic texture that Al-Bukhari, Jalal-Ud-Din Rumi, and the *Qur'an* contribute to making "Hagar, paradise beyond paradise." But the poetry does so to consider the fact that

> how a slavewoman misunderstand
> contract for fact of grace
> jahweh too and miss sarah
> —no less— is instructive;

> —so too
> how a business can get
> full so of wilderness and stone talk;
> why it waits, still, to laugh
> back, and rearrange.

The poems of *Carnival* also place the mind of man and the speech that cannot be silenced in various ports of call." They range from the Dardanelles, "south of Istanbul," to the Manhattan of "The new year exiles" and the Argentina of "Witness" to the "Caribbean sugar" of Matilda's Corner (Kingston). "Banzo" brings with it a certain "temptation of Brazil," in world "world without / ever an end to it / either." For here "the head swivels in fever and carnival," and seduction lies in the "bright dangle, the dainty peace / of a mulatta nipple." Here, *banzo* (an inconsolable sadness that invariably drove slaves to commit suicide) also leads to re-cognition of a certain kind:

> *senhor, o senhor do bomfin*
> lord of ends that are good . . .
> there is so much and more
>
> to blood that is in blood
> in this world without
> an ever-loving end to it. (70)

Meanwhile, in the Peru of the sixteenth century, Pizzaro pits himself against Atahualpa. Up to a man's height in ransom gold, the Spaniard nonetheless leaves the Inca dead, to "grope in darkness":

> a showerdust
> in gold fell here, where the tribe,
> a light held to its heart,
> looked to see if Self remained, or would
> mirror some such thing in the dead reckoning of joy.

So, too, in the Mexico of 1519 does Cortés set himself up against Montezuma. As I interpret their meeting, what the European offers the Aztec is the "consolation" of resurrection into a new identity. His promise—his guarantee, even—to Tenochtitlan is that "the most miraculous roses will grow / once again; take their root / in the choked residue of grief." After all, in the light and "bracing romp / that quickens [all] into worth," History, he explains, can have "no embarrassment / that endures higher than its rehearsal." For which reason,

> Whether this language
> I speak hears only itself
> out, and then is stranded
> —*ad maiorem gloria dei*—
>
> what you have yet to hear is true
> ... the most miraculous roses will grow
> once again; take their root
> in the choked residue of grief. (51)

Finally, and in the "Pedigree, with Weight" section of *Carnival of the Old Coast*, "Corpse Cooking at Night" also engages a history that appears to have no embarrassment. There being, after all, no such thing as an anthropology of (native) shame,

> note, I am told,
> the long firehardened wooden spear.
> —and I do— Wooreddy holds it. others too.
> their names cluster in consonants,
> the vowels exuberant, drunk, weaving so:
> "Maori Warrior Rings Bell at Whakariwarena"
> "A Dinka in His Dancing Dress . . . "
>
> with magnifying glass I go over
> and over again the jawlines I see
> nothing that I look at falls right
> where the sunlight falls,
> "Bantu Female, high arse, with deep face"
> in the camera's shallow eye.

However, my own feeling is that it does do us some good to record refusals to surrender to the erasure of good sense and resilient sensibility, for all that we are sorely tempted to see nothing but "like to like, organizing chaos." After all, "the gods stand up for bastards" in a "defiance of figures in wood." For which reason, "ambitious as salt water itself," we could "kneel, too, on the sea, / and not sink" (63):

> call us Ishmael (if you please) or Barabbas;
> Habibatu or Zenobia. Cain, too.
> we take a count in figure and in sum,
> no matter how hissed as injury into the ear.
> we barter coinage for coin, and do not sink. (*ibid.*)

Works Cited

Abbot, Wilbur Cortez. *The Expansion of Europe: The Foundations of the Modern World*. 1. London: H. Holt, 1918.

Abrahams, Peter. *Mine Boy*. 1946. New York: MacMillan, 1970.

_____ *This Island, Now*. New York: Alfred K. Knopf, 1967.

Abrahams, Roger D. and John F. Szwed. *After Africa, Excerpts from British Travel Accounts and Journals of the Seventeenth, Eighteenth, and Nineteenth Centuries Concerning the Slaves, their Manners, and Customs in the British West Indies*. New Haven: Yale University Press, 1983.

Abreu y Gomez, Ermilio. *Canek. Historia y leyenda de un heröe maya*. Mexico City: Oasis, 1982.

Achebe, Chinua. *Things Fall Apart*. 1959. New York: Fawcett, 1989.

Adams, Percy G. *Travel Literature and the Evolution of the Novel*. Lexington: University of Kentucky Press, 1983.

Adorno, Rolena. *Guaman Poma, Writing and Resistance in Colonial Peru*. Austin: University of Texas Press, 1986.

Aers, Lesley and Wheale, Nigel, eds. *Shakespeare in the Changing Curriculum*. London: Routledge, 1991.

Afonso, María Joao da Rocha. "Simão de Melo Brandao and the First Portuguese Version of *Othello*." *European Shakespeares, Translating Shakespeare in the Romantic Age*. Eds. Dirk Delabastita and Lieven D'hulst. Amsterdam: John Benjamins, 1992:129-146.

Agbaw, Ekema S. "Africanizing Macbeth: 'Down-fall'n birthdom." *Research in African Literatures* 27 (Spring 1996):102-109.

Aguirre Beltrán, Gonzalo. *La población negra de México 1519-1810*. Mexico D.F.: Ediciones Fuente Cultural, 1946.

Aidoo, Ama Ata. *Our Sister Killjoy, or, Reflections of a Black-Eyed Squint*. London: Longman, 1977.

Aizenberg, Edna. *The Aleph Weaver: Biblical, Kabbalistic, and Judaic Elements in Borges*. Potomac, Maryland: Scripta Humanitas, 1984.

_____ Ed. *Borges and His Successors: The Borgesian Impact on Literature and the Arts*. Columbia: University of Missouri, 1991.

Alarcón, Norma. "Chicana's Feminist Literature: A Re-vision Through Malintzin/or Malintzin: Putting Flesh Back on the Object." *This Bridge Called My Back, Writings By Radical Women of Color*. Eds. Cherrie Moraga and Gloria Anzaldua. New York: Kitchen Table/Women of Color Press, 1983:182-190.

_____ "Traddutora, Traditora: A Paradigmatic Figure of Chicana Feminism." *Cultural Critique* (Fall 1989):57-87.

Alberti, Leon Battista. *On Painting*. 1435. Trans. John R. Spencer. New Haven: Yale University Press, 1956.

Amado, Jorge. *Shepherds of the Night*. Trans. Harriet de Onis. New York: Avon, 1978.

Ammannati, Franceso, "Toscanelli e Colombo: gli errori della ragione e i dubbi della fede." *La Carta perduta: Paolo dal Toscanelli e la cartografia delle grande scoperte*. Ed. Francesco Ammannati. Firenze: Alinari, 1992:61-86.

Amphlett, H. *Who Was Shakespeare?* London: Heinemann, 1955.

Anand, Mulk Raj. *Caliban and Gandhi, Letters to 'Bapu' from Bombay*. New Delhi: Arnold Publishers, 1991.

Andrew, Edward. *Shylock's Rights: A Grammar of Lockian Claims*. Toronto: University of Toronto Press, 1988.

Angelou, Maya. *I Know Why the Caged Bird Sings*. New York: Random, 1993.

Appadurai, Arjun. "Global Ethnoscapes: Notes and Queries for a Transnational Anthropology." *Recapturing Anthropology: Working in the Present*. Ed. Richard G. Fox. Santa Fe, New Mexico: School of American Research Press, 1991:191-210.

Arac, Jonathan and Harriet Ritvo, eds. *Macropolitics of Nineteenth-Century Literature: Nationalism, Exoticism, Imperialism*. Durham: Duke University Press, 1995.

Arguedas, José María. *Los ríos profundos*. 1958. Trans. as *Deep Rivers* by Frances Horning Barraclough. Austin: University of Texas Press, 1989.

___ *Yawar Fiesta*. 1941. Trans. Frances Horning Barraclough. Austin: University of Texas Press, 1985.

___ "The Novel and the Problem of Literary Expression in Peru." *Yawar Fiesta*. Trans. Frances Horning Barraclough. Austin: University of Texas Press, 1985:xiii-xxi.

Arnold, Matthew. *Civilization in the United States*. Boston: DeWolfe, Fisk, 1900.

Arthur, Marylin. "Early Greece: The Origins of the Western Attitude Toward Women." *Arethusa* 6 (1973):7-58.

Asad, Talal. "From the History of Colonial Anthropology to the Anthropology of Western Hegemony." *Colonial Situations: Essays on the Contextualization of Ethnographic Knowledge*. Ed. George W. Stocking, Jr. Madison: University of Wisconsin Press, 1991:314-324.

Assis, Machado de. *The Posthumous Memoirs of Braz Cubas*. 1881. Trans. William Grossman. New York:Noonday Press, 1952.

Asturias, Miguel Angel. *El Señor Presidente*. 1946. Trans. Frances Partridge. New York: Atheneum, 1983.

Atkins, Douglas. G. "Dehellenizing Literary Criticism." *College English* 41 (1980):769-779.

Atkinson, William C. Introduction. Camoens's *The Lusiads*. Trans. William C. Atkinson. New York: Viking, 1987.

Bachrach, A.G.H. "*Luna Mendax*: Some Reflections on the Moon-Voyages in Early Seventeenth-Century England." *Beyond Dream and Nature: Essays on Utopia and Dystopia*. Eds. Dominic Baker-Smith and C. C. Barfoot. Amsterdam: Rodopi, 1987:70-90.

Bacon, Francis. "Of Empire" and "Of the True Greatness of Kingdoms and Estates." *The Works of Francis Bacon*. Vol. II. London: C. and J. Rivington, 1826.

Baehr, Stephen Lessing. *The Paradise Myth in Eighteenth-Century Russia*. Stanford: Stanford University Press, 1991.

Bajan, R. *Paradise Lost and the Seventeenth Century Reader*. 1947. Ann Arbor: University of Michigan Press, 1967.

Bakan, David. *Maimonides on Prophecy*. Northvale, N.J.: J Aronson, 1991.

Baker, Houston. "Caliban's Triple Play." *"Race," Writing, and Difference*. Ed. Henry Louis Gates, Jr. Chicago: University of Chicago Press, 1986:381-395.

Baker-Smith, Dominic and C.C. Barfoot. Eds. *Between Dream and Nature, Essays on Utopia and Dystopia*. Amsterdam: Rodopi, 1987.

Bal, Mieke. *Death and Dissymmetry: The Politics of Coherence in Judges*. Chicago: University of Chicago Press, 1988.

Bald, R.C. Introduction. William Shakespeare's *Measure for Measure*. New York: Penguin, 1987.

Baldwin, James. *Another Country*. 1962. New York: Random House, 1993.

Barfoot, C.C. "'A Paradise Unlost': Edward Young Among the Stars." *Beyond Dream and Nature*. Eds. Dominic Baker-Smith and C.C.Barfoot. Amsterdam: Rodopi, 1987:139-171.

Barker, Francis. *The Tremulous Private Body, Essays on Subjection*. London: Methuen, 1984.

Barker, Francis, and Peter Hulme. "Nymphs and Reapers Heavily Vanish: The Discursive Con-texts of *The Tempest*." *Alternative Shakespeares*. Ed. John Drakakis. London: Methuen, 1985:191-205.

Barker-Benfield, G.J. *The Horrors of the Half-Known Life: Male Attitudes Toward Women in Nineteenth-Century America*. New York: Harper and Row, 1976.

Barnes, Leonard. *Caliban in Africa*. London: Victor Gollancz, 1930.

Barrett, Leonard. *The Sun and the Drum: African Roots in Jamaican Folk Tradition*. Kingston, Jamaica: Heinemann, 1979.

_____ *The Rastafarians: Sounds of Cultural Dissonance*. Boston: Beacon, 1977.

Barthelemy, Anthony Gerard. *Black Face, Maligned Race: The Representation of Blacks in English Drama from Shakespeare to Southerne*. Baton Rouge: Louisiana State University Press, 1987.

Bary, Leslie. "Civilization, Barbarism, 'Cannibalism': The Question of National Culture in Oswald de Andrade." *Toward Socio-Criticism: "Luso-Brazilian Literatures."* Ed. Roberto Reis. Tempe: Center for Latin American Studies, 1991:95-100.

Bastos, Augusto, Roa. *I The Supreme*. Trans. Helen Lane. New York: Aventura, 1987.

Bate, W. Jackson. *The Burden of the Past and the English Poet*. New York: Norton, 1970.

Battacharya, Hiranmoy. *Raj and Literature: Banned Bengali Books*. Calcutta: Firma KLM Private, 1989.

Beck, Brandon H. *From the Rising of the Sun*. New York: Peter Lang, 1987.

Bedford, Simi. *Yoruba Girl Dancing*. 1992. London: Penguin, 1994.

Behague, Gerard H. *Music and Black Ethnicity: The Caribbean and South America*. Boulder: Lynne Reinner, 1994.

Behn, Aphra. *Oroonoko or, The Royal Slave*. 1688. New York: W. W. Norton, 1973.

Bell, Howard H. Ed. *Black Separatism and the Caribbean*. 1860. Ann Arbor, Michigan: University of Michigan Press, 1970.

Benítez-Rojo, Antonio. *The Repeating Island*. Trans. James E. Maraniss. Durham: Duke University Press, 1995.

Benjamin, Walter. *Illuminations*. Trans. Harry Zohn. New York: Schocken, 1969.

Bennett, Louise. *Selected Poems.* Kingston, Jamaica: Sangster, 1982.

Bhabha, Homi. "Of Man and Mimicry: The Ambivalence of Colonial Discourse." *October* 28 (1984):15-33.

Blakely, Allison. *Blacks in the Dutch World.* Bloomington: Indiana University Press, 1993.

Biobaku, S.O. *Sources of Yoruba History.* London: Oxford University Press, 1973.

Bishop, John Peale. "Speaking of Poetry." *Collected Poems of John Peale Bishop.* Ed. Allen Tate. London: Chatto and Windus, 1960.

Böckler, Carlos Guzman. Prólogo. *Pop Wuj, Libro del tiempo. Poema mito-histórico.* Buenos Aires: Ediciónes del sol, 1987.

Bohannan, Laura. "Shakespeare in the Bush." *Conformity and Conflict, Readings in Cultural Anthropology.* Eds. James P. Spradley and David W. McCurdy. Boston: Little, Brown & Co., 1977:13-23.

Boito, Arrigo. Libretto for Verdi's *Otello.* EMI Digital CDS 7 47450 8. 1986.

Bonfil, Robert. "Jews and Antijudaism." *Handbook of European History 1400-1600, Late Middle Ages, Renaissance and Reformation.* Eds. Thomas A. Brady, Jr, Heiko A. Oberman, and James D. Tracy. Leiden: E.J. Brill, 1995:263-302.

Borges, Jorge Luis. *Prosa Completa,* vol. 2. Bruguera: Spain: Editorial Bruguera, 1980.

_____ *A Personal Anthology.* Ed. Anthony Kerrigan. New York: Grove Press, 1967.

_____ *Labyrinths, Selected Stories and Other Writings.* Eds. Donald A. Yates and James E. Irby. New York: New Directions, 1964.

_____ *Ficciones.* New York: Grove Press, 1962.

_____ *El Hacedor.* Buenos Aires: Emece Editores, 1960.

Bourget, Paul. *Outre-mer: Impressions of America.* New York: Scribner's, 1895.

Boyarin, Daniel. *Carnal Israel, Reading Sex in Talmudic Culture.* 1993. Berkeley: University of California Press, 1995.

Bracken, Henry M. "Philosophy and Racism," *Philosophia* 8, 2-3. (1978).

Bradley, A.C. "Shakespeare's *Antony and Cleopatra.*" 1901. *The Tragedy of Antony and Cleopatra.* Ed. Barbara Everett. New York: Signet, 1988.

Brantley, Ben. "*Tempest* Deepens as It Goes Indoors." *New York Times.* 11/2/95. B1.

Brathwaite, Edward. "Caribbean Critics." *New World Quarterly* 5, 1-2 (1969):5-12.

Brathwaite, Edward Kamau. *Black + Blues.* Benin City, Nigeria: Ethiop, 1977.

Brathwaite, Kamau. *Middle Passages.* New York: New Directions, 1993.

Brenton, Marcela. Ed. *Rhythm and Revolt, Tales of the Antilles.* New York: Penguin, 1995.

Bronte, Charlotte. *Jane Eyre.* 1847. Cambridge, Mass.: Riverside Press, 1959.

Brooke, Tucker, John William Cunliffe, and Henry Noble MacCracken. Eds. *Shakespeare's Principal Plays.* New York: Appleton-Century, 1935.

Brotherston, Gordon. *Book of the Fourth World, Reading the Native Americas through their Literature.* New York: Cambridge University Press, 1992.

Browne, Thomas. *Religio Medici and Other Essays.* Ed. D. Lloyd Roberts. London: Smith, Elder, 1898.

Bruner, Charlotte. "The Meaning of Caliban in Black Literature Today." *Comparative Literature Studies* xiii. 30 (1976):240-253.

Brushwood, John S. *The Spanish American Novel.* Austin: University of Texas Press, 1975.

Budden, Julien. "Verdi, Milano and *Othello*." EMI Digital CDS 7 47450 8. 1986.

Buhle, Peter. "Mr. Jones, He Dead." *The Village Voice Literary Supplement.* July 1966. (18-19)

Burt, Richard. *Licenced by Authority, Ben Jonson and the Discourse of Censorship.* Ithaca: Cornell University Press, 1996.

Busia, Abena. "Silencing Sycorax: On African Colonial Discourse and the Unvoiced Female." *Cultural Critique* 14 (1989):81-104.

Cabrera Infante, Guillermo. Interview, in *Seven Voices, Seven Latin American Writers Talk.* Ed. Rita Guibert. Trans. Frances Partridge. New York: Knopf, 1973.

_____ *Infante's Inferno.* Trans. Suzanne Jill Levine. New York: Harper and Row, 1984.

_____ *Three Trapped Tigers.* 1965. Trans. Donald Gardner and Suzanne Jill Levine. New York: Harper, 1978.

Calderón, Pedro de la Barca. *The Schism in England.* Trans. Kenneth Muir and Ann L. Mackenzie. Warminster, England: Aris and Phillips Ltd., 1990.

Caldwell, Helen. *Machado de Assis: The Brazilian Master and His Novels.* Berkeley: University of California Press, 1970.

Callaghan, Dympna. "Re-Reading Elizabeth Cary's *The Tragedie of Mariam, Faire Queene of Jewry.*" In: *Women, "Race," and Writing in the Early Modern Period.* Eds. Margo Hendricks and Patricia Parker. New York: Routledge, 1994:163-177.

Campbell, Horace. *Rasta and Resistance, From Marcus Garvey to Walter Rodney.* Trenton: Africa World Press, 1987.

Cameons, Luis Vas de. *The Lusiads.* Trans. William C. Atkinson. New York: Viking, 1987.

Campion, Thomas. *The Works.* Ed. Walter R. Davis. London: Faber and Faber, 1969.

Candelaria, Nash. *Memories of the Alhambra.* Ypsilanti, Michigan: Bilingual Press, 1977.

Canot, Theodore. *Adventures of an African Slaver.* 1854. New York: Dover, 1969.

Carlin, Murray. *Not Now, Sweet Desdemona.* Nairobi: Oxford University Press, 1969.

Carlyle, Thomas. *English and Other Critical Essays.* 1915. London: J.M.Dent, 1940.

Carpentier, Alejo. *The Harp and the Shadow.* Trans. Thomas and Carol Christensen. 1979. San Francisco: Mercury House, 1990.

_____ *Concierto barroco.* Trans. Aza Zatz. Tulsa: Council Oak Books, 1988.

_____ *Explosion in a Cathedral.* 1962. Trans. Harriet de Onis. 1962. New York: Harper and Row, 1979.

_____ *Reasons of State.* Trans. Francis Partridge. 1974. New York: Alfred A. Knopf, 1976.

_____ Interview, with Miguel Roa, "Recourse to Descartes," in *Granma* (La Habana) June 2, 1974.

_____ *The War of Time.* Trans. Frances Partridge. London: Victor Gollanz, 1970a.

_____ *The Kingdom of This World.* 1949. Trans. Harriet de Onis. New York: Collier. 1970b.

_____ *The Lost Steps.* 1953. Trans. New York: Alfred A. Knopf. 1956.

Cartelli, Thomas, "Prospero in Africa: *The Tempest* as Colonialist Text and Pretext." *Shakespeare Reproduced: The Text in History and Ideology.* Ed. Jean E. Howard and Marion F. O'Connor. London: Methuen, 1987:99-115.

Casas, Bartolomé de las. *In Defense of the Indians.* Trans. Stafford Poole. Dekalb: Northern Illinois University Press, 1992.

Cavanagh, Sheila T. *Wanton Eyes and Chaste Desires.* Bloomington: University of Indiana Press, 1990.

Césaire, Aimé. *A Tempest.* 1969. Trans. Richard Miller. New York: Ubu Repertory Theater Publications, 1992.

_____*Return to My Native Land.* 1939. Trans. John Berger and Anne Bostock. Middlesex, England: Penguin, 1969a.

_____ *Une Tempête: d'après la tempête de Shakespeare: Adaptation pour une théâtre nègre.* Paris: Seuil, 1969b.

_____*The Tragedy of King Christophe.* Trans. Ralph Manheim. New York: Grove, 1970.

Chamoiseau, Patrick. *Texaco.* Trans. Rose-Myriam Rejouis and Val Vinokurov. New York: Pantheon Books, 1997.

Chatterjee, Sudipto. *"Mis-en-(Colonial-) Scene*: The Theatre of Bengal Renaissance." *Imperialism and Theatre, Essays on World Theatre, Drama and Performance.* Ed. J. Ellen Gainor. New York: Routledge, 1995:19-37.

Chávez, Adrian I. *Pop Wuj, Libro del tiempo: Poema mito-histórico ki-che traducido del texto original*: Buenos Aires: Ediciones del Sol, 1987.

Chen, Jack. *The Chinese in America.* New York: Harper and Row, 1980.

Cheyette, Bryan. "Neither Black Nor White: The Figure of 'the Jew' in Imperial British Literature." *The Jew in the Text: Modernity and the Construction of Identity.* Eds. Linda Nochlin and Tamar Garb. London: Thames and Hudson, 1995: 31-41.

Cheyfitz, Eric. *The Poetics of Imperialism: Translation and Colonization from* The Tempest *to* Tarzan. New York: Oxford University Press, 1991.

Christensen, Thomas and Carol. Introduction. Carpentier's *The Harp and the Shadow.* San Francisco: Mercury House, 1990.

Ciplijauskaite, Birute. *La novela feminina contemporanea (1970-1985).* Barcelona: Editorial Anthropos, 1988.

Clarke, Austin. *Growing Up Stupid Under the Union Jack.* Toronto: McClelland and Stewart, 1980.

Cliff, Michelle. *Abeng.* Trumansburg, New York: The Crossing Press, 1984.

_____ *No Telephone to Heaven.* New York: Vintage, 1985.

Clifford, James and George E. Marcus. Eds. *Writing Culture: The Poetics and Politics of Ethnography.* Berkeley: University of California Press, 1986.

Clendinnen, Inga. *Aztecs.* 1991. New York: Cambridge University Press, 1995a.

_____ *Ambivalent Conquests.* 1987. New York: Cambridge University Press, 1995b.

Coetzee, J.M. *Waiting for the Barbarians.* London: Secker and Warburg, 1980.

Coghill, Nevill. "The Basis of Shakespearian Comedy." *Shakespeare Criticism 1935-1960.* Ed. Anne Ridler. London: Oxford University Press, 1963.

Colón, Cristóbal. *The Log of Christopher Columbus*. Trans. Robert H. Fuson. Southampton: Ashford, 1987.

Columbus, Christopher. *Libro de las profecías*. Trans. Delno C. West and August Kling. Gainesville: University of Florida, 1991.

_____*The Four Voyages, A History in Eight Documents, Including Five by Christopher Columbus*. 1498. Trans. and Ed. Cecil Jane. New York: Dover Publications, 1988.

Conley, Tom. "Montaigne and the Indies: Cartographies of the New World in the *Essaies*." *1492-1992: Re/Discovering Colonial Writing*. Ed. Réné Jara and Nicholas Spadaccini. Minneapolis: University of Minnesota Press, 1989:225-262.

Conner, W. Robert. "Milton as Misogynist, Shakespeare as Elitist, Homer as Pornographer." *Chronicle of Higher Education*. December 5, 1990. A48.

Conrad, Joseph. *Heart of Darkness*. 1899. Ed. Robert Kimbrough. New York: Norton, 1963.

Cortés, Hernán. *Cartas de relación de la conquista de México*. Mexico, D.F.: Espasa-Calpe Mexicana, 1986.

Cottrell, Robert D. *Sexuality/Textuality, A Study of the Fabric of Mointaigne's Essais*. Columbus: The Ohio State University Press, 1981.

Craik. T. W. Introduction. *The Jew Of Malta*. New York: Norton, 1983.

Crewe, Jonathan. "Out of the Matrix: Shakespeare and Race-Writing." *The Yale Journal of Criticism* 8, 2 (1995):13-29.

Crosby, Alfred W. *The Columbian Exchange: Biological and Cultural Consequences of 1492*. Westport, Connecticut: Greenwood, 1973.

Cudjoe, Selwyn R. *Resistance and Caribbean Literature*. Athens: Ohio University Press, 1980.

Cunliffe, John William. Introduction to *The Tempest*. *Shakespeare's Principal Plays*. Ed. Tucker Brooke, John William Cunliffe, and Henry Noble MacCracken. New York: D. Appleton-Century, 1935:899-902.

Curtiss, Thomas Quinn. "Peter Brooks' Inventive *Tempest*." *International Herald Tribune*. 10/17/90.

Dabydeen, David and Nana Wilson Tagoe. *A Reader's Guide to West Indian and Black British Literature*. London: Hansib/Rutherford Press, 1988.

Dante, Alighieri. *Inferno*. Trans. Robert Pinsky. New York: Farrar, Straus and Giroux, 1995.

Davidhazi, Peter. "Providing Texts for a Literary Cult: Early Translations of Shakespeare in Hungary." *European Shakespeares, Translating Shakespeare in the Romantic Age*. Eds. Dirk Delabastita and Lieven D'hulst. Amsterdam: John Benjamins, 1993:147-162.

Davies, Neville H. "*Pericles* and the Sherley Brothers." *Shakespeare and His Contemporaries*. Ed. E.J.A. Honigmann. Manchester: University of Manchester Press, 1986.

Davis, Carole Boyce and Elaine Fido. Ed. *Out of the Kumbla, Caribbean Women and Literature*. Trenton: Africa World Press, 1990.

Davis, Walter R. *Thomas Campion*. Boston: Twayne Publishers, 1987.

Decker, Thomas. *Juliohs Siza*. Ed. Neville Shrimpton and Njie Sulayman. Umea, Sweden: Umea University, 1988.

_____ *Udat di Kiap Fit*. Umea, Sweden: Umea University, 1972.

De Certeau, Michel. "Montaigne's 'Of Cannibals': The Savage 'I.'" *Michel de Montaigne's Essays*. Ed. Harold Bloom. New York: Chelsea House. 1987:120-132.

Defoe, Daniel. *The Reformation of Manners*. 1702. London ms.

Delabastita, Dirk. "*Hamlet* in the Netherlands in the Late Eighteenth and Early Nineteenth Centuries: The Complexities of the History of Shakespeare's Reception." *European Shakespeares, Translating Shakespeare in the Romantic Age*. Eds. Dirk Delabastita and Lieven D'hulst. Amsterdam: Rodofo, 1992:219-234.

Deleuze, Giles and Felix Guattari. *Anti-Oedipus, Capitalism and Schizophrenia*. Trans. Robert Hurley and Helen R. Lane. New York: Viking, 1972.

Derrida, Jacques. *Specters of Marx, The State of Debt, the Work of Mourning, and the New International*. Trans. Peggy Kamuf. New York: Routledge, 1994.

Devisse, Jean and Michel Mollay, eds. *The Image of the Black in Western Art*. II. Trans. William Granger Ryan. Cambridge: Harvard University Press, 1979.

Díaz del Castillo, Bernal. *The Discovery and Conquest of New Spain*. Trans. J.M. Cohen. New York: Penguin, 1963.

Dickey, Laurence. *Hegel: Religion, Economics, and the Politics of Spirit, 1770-1807*. New York: Cambridge University Press, 1989.

Dickinson, Emily. *Further Poems*. New York: Little, Brown, and Company, 1929.

Dilke, Christopher. Ed. Huaman Poma, *Letter to a King*. New York: E.P. Dutton, 1978.

Doane, Mary Ann. *Femmes Fatales: Feminism, Film Theory, Psychoanalysis*. New York: Routledge, 1991.

Dobell, Bertram. *The Poetical Works of William Strode*. London: The Editor, 1907.

Donne, John. *The Poems of John Donne*. Ed. Herbert J.C. Grierson. London: Oxford University Press, 1912.

Drakakis, John. *Alternative Shakespeares*. London: Methuen, 1985.

Dryden, John. *Annus Mirabilis: The Year of Wonders, 1666. An Historical Poem Counting the Progress and Various Successes of Our Naval War with Holland*. London: Henry Herringman, 1607.

_____ *The Indian Emperour, or, The Conquest of Mexico by the Spanairds, being a sequel to the Indian Queen*. London: H. Herringman, 1668.

_____ "The Grounds of Criticism in Tragedy." 1695. *The Works of John Dryden*. Ed. Edward Niles Hooker, H.T. Swedenberg *et al*. Berkeley: University of California Press, 1984:239-240.

duBois, Page. *Torture and Truth*. New York: Routledge, 1991.

Du Bois, W.E.B. *The Oxford W.E.B. Du Bois Reader*. Ed. Eric Sundquist. New York: Oxford University Press, 1996.

Dusinberre, Juliet. *Shakespeare and the Nature of Women*. 1975. New York: St. Martin's Press, 1996.

The Economist. "Queen Margaret, or, Shakespeare Goes to the Falklands." 25 December-3 January, 1982-83:13-20.

_____ "The Dawn of Modern Navigation." 26 December 1992-8 January 1993:121.

Eilberg-Schwartz, Howard. *The Savage in Judaism: An Anthropology of Israelite and Ancient Judaism*. Bloomington: Indiana, 1990.

Einzig, Barbara. "Water Music, Sailing Away with Antonio Benítez-Rojo." *The Village Voice Literary Supplement*. December 1992:31.

Eliade. Mircea. *The Sacred and the Profane*. Trans. Willard Trask. New York:1959.

Eliot, Valerie. Ed. *The Letters of T.S. Eliot*. Vol. 1, 1898-1922. New York: Harcourt Brace Jovanovich, 1988.

Emecheta, Buchi. *The Joys of Motherhood*. New York: George Braziller, 1979.

Erickson, Peter. "Rewriting the Renaissance, Rewriting Ourselves." *Shakespeare Quarterly* 38 (1987):327-37.

Evans, Blakemore G., Harry Levin, Herschel Baker, Anne Barton, Frank Kermode, Hallet Smith, and Marc Edel. *The Riverside Shakespeare*. Boston: Houghton Mifflin, 1974.

Everett, Barbara, Ed. *The Tragedy of Antony and Cleopatra*. New York: Signet, 1988.

Fabian, Johannes. *Time and the Other: How Anthropology Makes its Object*. New York: Columbia University Press, 1983.

_____ "Anthropology Against Time." *Transition* 53 (1991):55-61.

Fabregat, Esteva. *El mestizaje en iberoamérica*. Madrid: Alhambra, 1988.

Fanon, Frantz. *Black Skin, White Masks*. 1952. New York: Grove, 1967.

Farley-Hills, David. *Shakespeare and the Rival Playwrights 1600-1606*. New York: Routledge, 1990.

Farriss, Nancy M. *Maya Society Under Colonial Rule: The Collective Enterprise of Survival*. Princeton: Princeton University Press, 1984.

Faulkner, William. *Light in August*. 1932. New York: Vintage, 1990.

Fell, Barry. *America B.C., Ancient Settlers in the New World*. New York: Demeter, 1977.

Fenton, James. "Goodbye to All That." *New York Review of Books* XLIII (8) 1996:59-64,

Ferré, Rosario. *Fábulas de la garza desangrada*. Mexico City: Joaquin Mortiz, 1984.

Fergusson, Margaret W., Maureen Quilligan, and Nancy Vickers. Eds. *Rewriting the Renaissance: The Discourse of Sexual Difference in Early Modern Europe*. Chicago: University of Chicago Press, 1986.

Fiedler, Leslie. *The Stranger in Shakespeare*. New York: Stein and Day, 1973.

Fiscal, María Rosa. "Siete mujeres y el mito." *Proceso* 28 (28 Mayo, 1990):54-55.

Fitzgerald, F. Scott. *The Great Gatsby*. 1925. New York: Cambridge University Press, 1991.

Flaubert, Gustave. *Flaubert in Egypt*. Trans. Frances Steegmuller. New York: Penguin, 1996.

Foakes, R.A. "The Descent of Iago: Satire, Ben Jonson, and Shakespeare's *Othello*." *Shakespeare and His Contemporaries*. Ed. E.A.J. Honigman. Manchester: University of Manchester Press, 1986:16-30.

Forbes, Jack D. *Africans and Native Americans, The Language of Race and the Evolution of Red-Black Peoples*. Urbana: University of Illinois, 1993.

Forster, Ricardo. "Dialogue Along the Margins." *American Visions/Visiones de las Americas: Artistic and Cultural Identity in the Western Hemisphere*. Eds. Mary Jane Jacob, Noreen Tomassi, and Ivo Mesquita. New York: American Council for the Arts Books/Allworth Press, 1994:35-40.

Foss, Michael. *Undreamed Shores: England's Wasted Empire in America*. London: George C. Harrap, 1974.

Fothergill-Payne, Peter. "A Prince of Our Disorder: 'Good Kingship' in Camoes, Couto, and Manuel de Melo." *Empire in Transition: The Portuguese World in the Time of Camoes*. Ed. Alfred Hower and Richard A. Preto-Rodas. Gainesville: University of Florida, 1985:12-21.

Foxe, John. *The Book of Martyrs, or, The Actes and Monuments of the Christian Church*. Philadelphia: J.& J.L. Gihon, 1813.

Franco, Jean. "The Nation As Imagined Community." *The New Historicism*. Ed. H. Aram Veeser. 1989:204-212.

Fraser, Russell. *Shakespeare, The Later Years*. New York: Columbia University Press, 1992.

_____ *Essential Shakespeare, Nine Plays and the Sonnets*. New York: Macmillan, 1972.

Freccero, Carla. "Cannibalism, Homophobia, Women: Montaignes 'Des Cannibales' and 'De l'amitie'." *Women, "Race," and Writing in the Early Modern Period*. Eds. Margo Hendricks and Patricia Parker. New York: Routledge, 1994:73-83.

Freemantle, Anne. Ed. *Latin-American Literature Today*. New York: New American Library, 1977.

French, Howard M. "Milot Journal: Haitian Fortress Saved From Nature's On-slaught." *New York Times*. September 25, 1991.

Freyre, Gilberto. *The Gilberto Freyre Reader: Varied Writings*. Trans. Barbara Shelby. New York: Alfred Knopf, 1974.

_____ *The Masters and the Slaves, A Study in the Development of Brazilian Civilization*. 1946. New York: Knopf, 1956.

Frost, William. *John Dryden, Dramatist, Satirist, Translator*. New York: AMS Press, 1988.

Froude, James Anthony. *The English in the West Indies, or, The Bow of Ulysses*. London: Longmans, Greene & Co., 1888.

Fukuyama, Francis. *The End of History and the Last Man*. New York: Free Press, 1992.

Fuson, Robert H. *The Log of Christopher Columbus*. Southampton: Ashford, 1987.

Fyfe, Christopher. *Sierra Leone Inheritance*. London: Oxford University Press, 1964.

Galeano, Eduardo. *Memory of Fire*. Vol 2, *Faces & Masks*. New York: Pantheon, 1987.

_____ *Open Veins of Latin America*. New York: Monthly Review Press, 1973.

Gamba, Margaly Martinez. *Restos y cenizas*. Mexico City: UNAM, 1988.

Garbini, Giovanni. *History and Ideology in Ancient Israel*. 1986. Trans. John Bowden. New York: Crossroad Press, 1988.

García Pinto, Magdalena. *Women Writers of Latin America: Intimate Histories*. Austin: University of Texas Press, 1991.

Garaudy, Roger. *The Alternative Future*. New York: Simon and Schuster, 1974.

Gates, Henry Louis. Ed. *"Race," Writing, and Difference.* Chicago: University of Chigaco Press, 1986.

Garibay, Angel M. *La literatura de los Aztecas.* Mexico, D.F.: Editorial Joaquin Mortiz, 1985.

Geertz, Clifford. *After the Fact, Two Countries, Four Decades, One Anthropologist.* Cambridge: Harvard University Press, 1995.

Gide, André. *Travels in the Congo.* Trans. Dorothy Bussy. Berkeley: University of California Press, 1962.

Gil, Juan. *Mitos y utopías del descubrimiento. I. Colón y su tiempo.* Madrid: Alianza, 1992.

Gilchrist, Alexander. *The Life of William Blake.* London: John Lane, 1906.

Giraldus, Cambrensis. *History and Topography of Ireland.* New York: Penguin, 1982.

_____ *The English Conquest of Ireland, A.D. 1166-1185.* Ed. Frederick Furnivall. New York: Greenwood Press, 1969.

Gilman, Sander L. "Salome, Syphillis, Sarah Bernhardt, and the Modern Jewess." *The Jew in the Text.* Eds. Linda Nochlin and Tamar Garb. London: Thames and Hudson, 1996: 97-120.

Gilmour, David. *Curzon.* London: John Murray, 1994.

Gilroy, Paul. *There Ain't No Black in the Union Jack: The Cultural Politics of Race and Nation.* London: Hutchinson, 1987.

Glantz, Margo. Interview. *Women Writers of Latin America.* Ed. Magdalena García-Pinto. Austin: University of Texas, 1991:105-122.

Glissant, Edouard. *Monsieur Toussaint, A Play.* 1961. Trans. Juris Silenieks. Washington, D.C.: Three Continents Press, 1981.

Gómez-Mariana, Antonio. "Narration and Argumentation in the Chronicles of the New World." *1492-1992: Re/Discovering Colonial Writing.* Ed. Réné Jara and Nicholas Spadaccini. Minneapolis: University of Minnesota Press, 1989:97-120.

Gonzalez, Eduardo. "American Theriomorphia: The Presence of *Mulatez* in Cirilo Villaverde and Beyond." *Do the Americas Have a Common Literature?* Ed. Gustavo Perez Firmat. Durham: Duke University Press, 1990:177-197.

Gorra, Michael. "The Autobiographical Turn." *Transition* 68 (Winter 1995):143-153.

_____ "Tact and Tarzan." *Transition* 52 (1991): 80-91.

Greenblatt, Stephen. *Marvelous Possessions, The Wonder of the New World.* Chicago: University of Chicago Press, 1991.

_____ *Learning to Curse, Essays in Early Modern Culture.* New York: Routledge, 1990.

_____ *Shakespearean Negotiations, The Circulation of Social Energy in Renaissance England.* Berkeley: University of California Press, 1988.

_____ *Renaissance Self-Fashioning, From More to Shakespeare.* Chicago: University of Chicago Press, 1984.

Greenfield, Jeannette. *The Return of Cultural Treasures.* New York: Cambridge University Press, 1989.

Gregg, Veronica. *A Certain Kind of Woman.* (Unpublished manuscript).

Gross, John J. *Shylock: A Legend and Its Legacy.* New York: Simon and Schuster, 1992.

Guillén, Nicolás. *Man-making Words: Selected Poems*. Trans. Robert Marquez and David Arthur McMurray. La Habana: Editorial de Arte y Literatura, 1973.

———— *Patria o Muerte! The Great Zoo and Other Poems*. Trans. and ed. Robert Marquez New York: Monthly Review Press, 1972.

Guillermo Wilson, Carlos (Cubena). *Short Stories by Cubena*. Trans. Ian Isidore Smart. Washington, D.C.: Afro-Hispanic Institute, 1987.

———— *Chombo*. Miami: Ediciones Universal, 1981.

Guitierrez, Ramon A. *When Jesus Came, The Corn Mothers Went Away: Marriage, Sexuality, and Power in New Mexico, 1500-1846*. Stanford: Stanford University Press, 1991.

Haberly, David T. "Abolitionism in Brazil: Anti-Slavery and Anti-Slave." *Lusophone Brazilian Review* 9, 2 (1972):38-39.

Hadfield, Andrew and John McVeagh. Eds. *Strangers to that Land*. Gerrards Cross: Colin Smythe, 1994.

Hall, Edith. *Inventing the Barbarian: Greek Self-Definition through Tragedy*. Oxford: Clarendon Press, 1991.

Hamana, Emi. "Let Women's Voices Be Heard: A Feminist Re-Vision of Ophelia." *Japan Shakespeare Studies* 26 (1988):21-40.

Hamilton, Virginia. *The People Who Could Fly*. New York: Knopf, 1985.

Hampson, Norman. *A Cultural History of the Enlightenment*. New York: Pantheon, 1968.

Hanke, Lewis. *Selected Writings on the History of Latin America*. Tempe: University of New Mexico Press, 1971.

Hardin, Richard F. *Michael Drayton and the Passing of Elizabethan England*. Lawrence: University of Press of Kansas, 1973.

Harris, Hendon M. *The Asiatic Fathers of America*. Taitung, Taiwan: Harris, 1973.

Harris, Wilson. *The Palace of the Peacock*. 1960. New York: Faber, 1981.

Harris, Dennis J. "A Summer on the Borders of the Caribbean Sea." *Black Separatism and the Caribbean, 1860*. Ed. Howard H. Bell. Ann Arbor, Michigan: University of Michigan Press, 1970.

Hartman, Geoffrey H. *Criticism in the Wilderness*. New Haven: Yale Univesity Press, 1980.

Harvey, L. P. *Islamic Spain: 1250 to 1500*. Chicago: University of Chicago Press, 1990.

Hawkins, Harriet. *The Classics and Trash: Traditions and Taboos in High Literature and Popular Modern Genres*. Toronto: University of Toronto, 1990.

Hayden, Robert. *Angle of Ascent: New and Selected Poems*. New York: Liveright, 1975.

Hegel, Georg Wilhelm Friedrich. *Lectures on the Philosophy of World History*. Ed. Johannes Hoffmeister. Trans. H.B. Nisbet. London: Cambridge University Press, 1980.

Henderson, William. *Who Wrote Shakespeare?* London: D. Stott, 1887.

Hendricks, Margo and Patricia Parker. Eds. *Women, "Race," and Writing in the Early Modern Period*. London: Routledge, 1994.

Herren, Ricard. *Doña Marina, La Malinche*. Mexico, D.F.: Editorial Planeta, 1993.

Herrmann, Claudine. *The Tongue Snatchers*. Trans. Nancy Kline. Lincoln: University of Nebraska Press, 1989.

Herzog, Don. *Happy Slaves, A Critique of Consent Theory*. Chicago: University of Chicago Press, 1989.

Hicks, George, *The Comfort Women*. St. Leonards, NSW: Allen & Unwin, 1995.

Hill, Wayne F. and Cynthia J. Ottchen. *Shakespeare's Insults*. Cambridge: Mainsail, 1994.

Hollinger, David A. *Postethnic America*. New York: Basic Books, 1995.

Honigman, E.A.J. Ed. *Shakespeare and His Contemporaries*. London: Manchester University Press, 1986.

Hood, John. *Aquinas and the Jews*. Philadelphia: University of Pennsylvania Press, 1995.

Hourani, Albert. *A History of the Arab Peoples*. Cambridge: Belknap, 1991.

House, Gloria. *Power and Dungeon: A Study of Place and Power in American Culture*. Detroit: Casa de Unidad Press, 1991,

Hughes, Robert. *The Shock of the New*. New York: Knopf, 1980.

_____ *The Fatal Shore*. New York: Knopf, 1986.

Hughes-Hallet, Lucy. *Cleopatra, Histories, Dreams and Distortions*. New York: Harper & Row, 1990.

Hull, Suzanne W. *Chaste, Silent & Obedient: English Books for Women, 1475-1640*. San Marino: Huntington Library, 1982.

Hulme, Peter. *Colonial Encounters, European and Native Caribbean 1492-1797*. London: Methuen, 1986.

Hunt, John Dixon. "Gardens in Utopia: Utopia in the Garden." *Between Dream and Nature: Essays on Utopia and Dystopia*. Eds. Dominic Baker-Smith & C.C. Barfoot. Amsterdam: Rodopi, 1987:114-138.

Hurston, Zora Neale. *Their Eyes Were Watching God*. 1937. Urbana: University of Illinois, 1978.

Huttington Theatre Company. News Release. May 13, 1996. Boston.

Idel, Moshe. *Kabbalah, New Perspectives*. New Haven: Yale Unversity Press, 1988.

Ioppolo, Grace. *Revising Shakespeare*. Cambridge: Harvard University Press, 1991.

Irby, James E. "Borges and the Idea of Utopia." *The Cardinal Points of Borges*. Eds. Lowell Dunham and Ivar Ivask. Norman: University of Oklahoma Press, 1973:35-46.

Irele, Abiola F. "Editor's Comments: Shakespeare and Company." *Research in African Literatures* 27 1 (1996):1-2.

James I, King of England. *Counterblast to Tobacco*. London: John Hancock, 1672.

James, C.L.R. *The Black Jacobins, Toussaint L'Ouverture and the San Domingo Revolution*. 1938. New York: Vintage, *1963*.

_____ *Mariners, Renegades, and Castaways*. New York: C.L.R. James, 1953.

James, Henry. *The Critical Muse: Selected Literary Criticism*. Ed. Rogerd Gard. New York:Penguin, 1987.

Janes, Regina. *Gabriel García Márquez, Revolution in Wonderland*. Columbia: University of Missouri Press, 1981.

Jara, Réné and Nicholas Spadaccini. Eds. *1492-1992: Re/Discovering Colonial Writing*. Minneapolis: University of Minnesota Press, 1989.

Jefferson, Thomas. *Notes on the State of Virginia*. 1787. New York: Norton, 1972.

Jelloun, Tahar Ben. *The Sacred Night*. Trans. Alan Sheridan. New York: Ballantine, 1987.

Jeyifo, Biodun. "The Nature of Things: Arrested Decolonization and Critical Theory." *Research in African Literatures* 21, 1 (1990):33-48.

Johnson, Lemuel. *Carnival of the Old Coast*. Trenton, N.J.: Africa World Press, 1995.

_____ *Highlife for Caliban*. Trenton, N.J.: Africa World Press, 1995.

_____ *Hand on the Navel*. Trenton, N.J.: Africa World Press, 1995.

_____ "The *Romance Bárbaro* as an Agent of Disappearance: Henrique Coelho Netto's *Rei Negro* and its Conventions." *Voices from Under: Black Narrative in Latin America and the Caribbean*. Ed. William Luis. Westport: Greenwood Press, 1984: 223-248.

_____ "The Middle Passage in African Literature: Wole Soyinka, Yambo Ouologuem, Ayi Kwei Armah." *African Literature Today* 11. Ed. Eldred Durosimi Jones. London: Heinemann, 1980:63-84.

_____ "*El Tema Negro*: The Nature of Primitivism in the Poetry of Luis Pales Matos." *Blacks in Hispanic Literature*. Ed. Miriam DeCosta. Port Washington: Kennikat Press, 1977.

_____*The Devil, the Gargoyle, and the Buffoon*. Port Washington: Kennikat, 1971.

_____ Trans. "Night and War in the Prado Museum." *Modern Spanish Theatre*. Eds. Michael Benedickt and George Wellwarth. New York: E. P. Dutton, 1969.

Johnson, Omotunde. "Managing Adjustment Costs, Political Authority, and the Implementation of Adjustment Programs, with Special Reference to African Countries." *World Development* 22, 3 (1994):399-411.

Johnson, Randal. "*O futuro nos pertenece. E agora que fazer?*: The *Estado Novo* and the Social Relations of Brazilian Literature." *Toward Socio-Criticism: "Luso-Brazilian Literatures"*. Ed. Roberto Reis. Tempe: Center of Latin American Studies, 1991:101-114.

Jones, Adam. Ed. *West Africa in the Mid-Seventeenth Century, An Anonymous Dutch Manuscript*. African Studies Association Press, 1995.

Jones, Eldred. *Othello's Countrymen, The African in English Renaissance Drama*. London: Oxford University Press, 1965.

Jones, Gayl. *The Hermit-Woman*. Detroit: Lotus Press, 1983.

_____ *Song for Anninho*. Detroit: Lotus Press, 1981.

Jorgens, Jack J. *Shakespeare on Film*. New York: University Press of America, 1991.

Jorgensen, Paul A. *Redeeming Shakespeare's Words*. Berkeley: University of California Press, 1962.

Juana Inés de la Cruz, Sister. *Poems*. Trans. Margaret Sayers Peden. Binghamton, New York: Bilingual Press, 1985.

_____ *Woman of Genius: The Intellectual Autobiography of Sor Juana Inés de la Cruz*. Trans. Margaret Sayers Peden. Salisbury, Conn.: Lime Rock Press, 1982.

Kafadar, Cemal. *Between Two Worlds: The Construction of the Ottoman State*. Berkeley: University of California Press, 1995.

_____ "The Ottomans and Europe." *Handbook of European History, 1400-1600*. Eds. Thomas Brady, Heiko A. Oberman, and James D. Tracy. Leiden: E. J. Brill, 1994:589-636.

Kakutani, Michiko. "Books of The Times." *New York Times*. 5 June, 1990: B2.

Kamen, Henry. "The Hapsburg Lands, Iberia." *Handbook of European History*. Ed. Thomas Brady, Heiko A. Oberman, and James D. Tracy. Leiden: E. J. Brill, 1994:467-98.

Kaplan, Caren. "The Poetics of Displacement in *Buenos Aires*." *Discourse* 8 (1986-87):84-100.

Kar, Sisir. *Banned Bengal*. Howrath, India: Shiva & Co., 1992.

Keen, Benjamin. *The Aztec Image in Western Thought*. 1971. New Brunswick: Rutgers University Press, 1990.

Keegan, William F. "Columbus's 1492 Voyage and the Search for His Landfall." *First Encounters*. Ed. Jerald T. Milanich and Susan Milbrath. Gainesville: University of Florida Press, 1989.

Kermode, Frank. Introduction. *The Tempest*. London: Methuen, 1986.

Kerrigan, Anthony. Ed. and Trans. *Jorge Luis Borges: A Personal Anthology*. New York: Grove Press, 1967.

_____Introduction. Borges's *Ficciones*. New York: Grove Press, 1962.

Kestner, Joseph A. *Mythology and Misogyny*. Madison: University of Wisconsin Press, 1989.

King, Preston. "Historical Contextualism: The New Historicism?" *History of European Ideas*. Eds. Ezra Talmor and Sasha Talmor. 21 2 (1995):212-33.

Kingston, Maxine Hong. *China Men*. New York: Knopf, 1980.

_____ *Woman Warrior*. New York: Vintage, 1977.

Knight, Wilson G. *The Crown of Life: Essays in Interpretation of Shakespeare's Final Plays*. 1947. New York: Barnes and Noble, 1987.

_____ *The Imperial Theme*. London: Methuen, 1951.

Koenders, J.G.A. "Wi Tongo" ("Our Language"). 1943. *Creole Drum, An Anthology of Creole Literature in Surinam*. Eds. Jan Voorhoeve and Ursy M. Lichtveld. Trans. Vernie A. February. New Haven: Yale University Press, 1975.

Kojeve, Alexandre. *Introduction to a Reading of Hegel*. Trans. James H. Nichols. New York: Basic Books, 1947.

Kott, Jan. *Shakespeare, Our Contemporary*. Trans. Boleslaw Taborski. Garden City, N.Y.: Doubleday, 1964.

Kristeller, Paul Oskar. *Renaissance Concepts of Man and Other Essays*. New York: Harper & Row, 1972.

Lachower, Fischel and Isaiah Tishby. Eds. *The Wisdom of the Zohar*, I & II. Trans. David Goldstein. London: The Littman Library, 1994.

La Guma, Alex. *Time of the Butcherbird*. 1979. London: Heinemann, 1986.

_____ *A Walk in the Night, Seven Stories of Cape Town*. 1962. London: Heinemann,

Lakoff, George. *Women, Fire, and Dangerous Things, What Categories Reveal about the Mind*. Chicago: University of Chicago Press, 1987.

Lamb, Mary Ellen. *Gender and Authorship in the Sidney Circle*. Madison: University of Wisconsin Press, 1990.

Lamming, George. *The Pleasures of Exile*. 1960. Ann Arbor: University of Michigan Press, 1992.

_____ *In the Castle of My Skin*. 1953. New York: Collier, 1975.

_____ *Natives of My Person*. New York: Holt, 1971a.

_____ *Water With Berries*. London: Longman, 1971b.

Landa, Fray Diego de. *Landa's Relación de las cosas de Yucatan*. Trans. Alfred M. Tozzer. Cambridge, Mass.: Harvard University Press, 1941.

Langgässer, Elizabeth. *The Quest*. Trans. Jane Bannard Greene. New York: Knopf, 1953.

Laqueur, Thomas. *Making Sex: Body and Gender from the Greeks to Freud*. Cambridge: Harvard University Press, 1990.

Lawrence, D.H. "The Man Who Died." 1925. *The Man Who Died* and *Saint Mawr*. New York: Vintage, 1953.

Lawal, Babatunde. "*Ori*: The Significance of the Head in Yoruba Sculpture." *Journal of Anthropological Research* 41 (1):1988.

Lenz, C.R.S., G. Greene and C.T. Neely. Eds. *The Woman's Part: Feminist Criticism of Shakespeare*. Urbana: University of Illinois Press, 1980.

Leon-Portilla, Miguel. Ed. *The Broken Spears, The Aztec Account of the Conquest of Mexico*. Boston: Beacon, 1966.

Leschemelle, Pierre. *Montaigne, or The Anguished Soul*. Trans. William J. Beck. New York: Peter Lang, 1994.

Levine, Robert M. *Tropical Diaspora: The Jewish Experience in Cuba*. Gainesville: University of Florida, 1993.

Lewis, Rupert. "Walter Rodney: 1968 Revisited." *Social and Economic Studies* 43:3(1994):7-56.

Limon, Jerzy and Joy L. Halio. *Shakespeare and His Contemporaries: Eastern and Central European Studies*. Newark: University of Delaware Press, 1993.

Loomba, Ania. "The Color of Patriarchy: Critical Difference, Cultural Difference, and Renaissance Drama." *Women, "Race," and Writing in the Early Modern Period*. London: Routledge, 1994:17-34

Lorde, Audre. "An Open Letter to Mary Daley." *This Bridge Called My Back, Writings by Radical Women of Color*. Ed. Cherrie Moraga and Gloria Anzaldua. Watertown, Mass.: Persephone, 1981.

Lovelace, Earl. "Jobell and America." In *A Brief Conversion and Other Stories*. Oxford: Heinemann, 1988.

_____ *The Wine of Astonishment*. London: Heinemann, 1983.

Lowry, Malcolm. *Under the Volcano*. Intro. Stephen Spender. New York: Plume, 1971.

Macaulay, James. *Table-Talk and Anecdotes of Martin Luther*. New York: J.B. Allen, 1885.

MacCormack, Sabine. "Atahualpa and the Book." *Dispositio* 36-38 (1989):141-168.

MacCracken, Henry Noble. Introduction to *The Winter's Tale*. *Shakespeare's Principal Plays*. Eds. Tucker Brooke, John William Cunliffe, and Henry Noble MacCracken. New York: D. Appleton-Century, 1935:855-856.

_____ Introduction to *Much Ado About Nothing*. *Shakespeare's Principal Plays*. Eds. Tucker Brooke, John William Cunliffe, and Henry Noble MacCracken. New York: D. Appleton-Century, 1935:373-374.

Mack, Maynard. *Everybody's Shakespeare*. Lincoln: University of Nebraska, 1993.

Mackenzie, Ann L. Introduction. Calderon's *The Schism in England.* Trans. Kenneth Muir and Ann L. MacKenzie. Warminster, England: Aris and Phillips Ltd., 1990:1-46.

Mais, Roger. *Brother Man.* 1954. London: Heinemann, 1974.

Maja-Pearce, Oluwale. *Who's Afraid of Wole Soyinka?* Portsmouth, New Hampshire:Heinemann, 1991.

Malti-Douglas, Fedwa. *Woman's Body, Woman's Word: Gender and Discourse in Arabo-Islamic Writing.* Princeton, N.J.: Princeton University Press, 1991.

Maltin Leonard. *Leonard Maltin's TV Movies and Video Guide.* New York: Plume, 1990.

Mannoni, Octave. *Prospero and Caliban, The Psychology of Colonialism.* 1950. London: Methuen 1956.

Manuel, Frank and Fritzie. *Utopian Thought in the Western World.* Cambridge, Mass.: Belknap Press, 1979.

Marcus, George E. "Afterword: Ethnographic Writing and Anthropological Careers." *Writing Culture.* Eds. James Clifford and George Marcus. Berkeley: University of California Press, 1986.

Marcus, Leah S. *Puzzling Shakespeare: Local Readings and Its Discontents.* Berkeley: University of California Press, 1988.

Marin, Louis. *Utopics, Spatial Play.* 1984. Trans. Robert A. Vollrath. Atlantic Highlands: Humanities Press, 1984.

Marino, John A. "The Italian States in the 'Long Sixteenth Century'." *Handbook of European History.* Eds: Thomas Brady, Heiko A. Oberman, and James D. Tracy. Leiden: E. J. Brill, 1994:331-368.

Marlowe, Christopher. *The Jew of Malta.* New York: Norton, 1935.

Marotti, Girogo. *Black Characters in the Brazilian Novel.* 1982. Trans. Maria O. Marotti and Harry Lawton. Los Angeles: Center for Afro-American Studies, 1987.

Marques, A. H. de Oliveira. "A View of Portugal in the Time of Camões." *Empire in Transition, The Portuguese World in the Time of Camões.* Eds. Alfred Hower and Richard A. Preto-Rodas. Gainesville: University Presses of Florida, 1985:3-11

Márquez, Gabriel García. *The General in His Labyrinth.* Trans. Edith Grossman. New York: Knopf, 1990.

———— *Chronicle of a Death Foretold.* Trans. Gregory Rabassa. New York: Ballantine Books, 1982.

———— *The Autumn of the Patriarch.* Trans. Gregory Rabassa. New York: Harper and Row, 1976.

———— *One Hundred Years of Solitude.* Trans. Gregory Rabassa. New York: Harper and Row, 1970.

Marshall, Paule. "Brazil." 1961. *Soul Clap Hands and Sing.* Washington, D.C.: Howard University Press, 1988.

Martin, Luis. *The Kingdom of the Sun, A Short History of Peru.* New York: Scribner, 1974.

Martin, Milward W. *Was Shakespeare Shakespeare?* New York: Cooper Square Publishers, 1965.

Martinez-Alier, Verena. *Marriage, Class and Colour in Nineteenth-Century Cuba.* London:Cambridge University Press, 1974.

Mason, Peter. *Deconstructing America.* London: Routledge, 1990.

Mather, Cotton. *Magnalia Christi America, or the Ecclesiastical History of New England.* New York: Frederick Ungar, 1970.

Matus, Jill L. *Unstable Bodies: Victorian Representations of Sexuality and Maternity.* Manchester: University of Manchester Press, 1995.

Matus, Irvin, Leigh. *Shakespeare, in Fact.* New York: Continuum, 1994.

Mazrui, Alamin M. "Shakespeare in Africa: Between English and Swahili Literature." *Research in African Literatures* 27 1 (1996):64-79.

McEachern, Claire. "Fathering Herself: A Source Study of Shakespeare's Feminism." *Shakespeare Quarterly* 39 (1989): 269-290.

McGovern, James R. "Columbus, a Renaissance Man." *The World of Columbus.* Ed. James R. McGovern. Macon: Mercer University Press, 1992.

McLuskie, Kathleen. "The Patriarchal Bard: Feminist Criticism and Shakepeare: *King Lear* and *Measure for Measure.*" *Political Shakespeare: New Essays in Cultural Materialism.* Eds. Jonathan Dollimore and Alan Sinfield. Manchester: Manchester University Press, 1985.

McWatt, Mark. "The Two Faces of El Dorado: Contrasting Attitudes Towards History and Identity in West Indian Literature. *West Indian Literature and Its Social Context.* Cave Hill, Barbados: Department of English, 1985:33-47.

Melville, Herman. "Benito Cereno." *Billy Budd, Sailor and Other Stories.* New York: Penguin, 1983.

_____ *Moby Dick or The Whale.* New York: Holt, Rinehart and Winston, 1964.

Menocal, Maria Rosa. *The Arabic Role in Medieval Literary History.* Philadelphia: University of Pennsylvania Press, 1987.

Merrim, Stephanie. "The Apprehension of the New in Nature and Culture" Fernández de Oviedo's *Sumario.*" *1492-1992: Re/Discovering Colonial Writing.* Eds. Réné Jara and Nicholas Spadaccini. Minneapolis: University of Minneapolis Press, 1989:165-200.

Messenger, Phyllis Mauch. Ed. *The Ethics of Collecting Cultural Property.* Albuquerque: University of New Mexico Press, 1989.

Meyer, Doris and Margarite Fernandez Olmos. *Contemporary Women Authors of Latin America.* Brooklyn: Brooklyn College Press, 1983.

Meza, Otilia. *Malinalli Tenepal, La gran calumniada.* Mexico City: Edamex, 1988.

Michaud, Christopher. "Sir Ian McKellen Wins Raves for his *Richard III.*" Reuters. *International Herald Tribune* 9/17/92.

Michael, Robert. "Antisemitism and the Church Fathers." *Jewish-Christian Encounters over the Centuries: Symbiosis, Prejudice, Holocaust, Dialogue.* Ed. Marvin Perry and Frederick M. Schweitzer. New York: Peter Lang, 1994:101-130.

Michell, John. *Who Wrote Shakespeare?* London: Thomas and Hudson, 1986.

Midgley, Mary. "On Not Being Afraid of Natural Sex Differences." *Feminist Perspectives in Philosophy*, eds. Morwenna Griffiths and Mary Whitford. Bloomington: Indiana University Press, 1988:29-41.

Mignolo, Walter. *The Darker Side of the Renaissance.* Ann Arbor: University of Michigan Press, 1995.

Milanich, Jerald T. and Susan Milbrath. Eds. *First Encounters, Spanish Explorations in the Caribbean and the United States, 1492-1570.* Gainesville: University of Florida Press, 1989.

Miller, Arthur. *Death of a Salesman*. 1949. New York: Penguin, 1976.

Miller, Joseph C. "Angola in the Sixteenth Century: Um mundo que o Portugues encontrou." *Empire in Transition: The Portuguese World in the Time of Camoes*. Ed. Alfred Hower and Richard A. Preto-Rodas. Gainesville: University of Florida Presses, 1985:118-134.

Miller, Perry. *Errand into the Wilderness*. Cambridge: Belknap Press, 1956.

Milton. John. *The Complete English Poetry*. Ed. John T. Shawcross. New York: New York University Press, 1963.

_____ *The Complete Poetry and Selected Prose*. New York: Modern Librarn, 1950.

Minh-ha, Trinh T. "Difference: 'Special Third World Women Issue'." *Discourse* 8 (1986-87):11-37.

_____ *Woman, Native, Other, Writing Postcoloniality and Feminism*. Bloomington: University of Indiana Press, 1989.

Mitter, Partha. *Much Maligned Monsters: A History of European Reactions to Indian Art*. Chicago: University of Chicago Press, 1992.

Molière [Jean-Baptiste Poquelin]. *Le bourgeois gentilhomme*. Version by Nick Dear. Bath, England: Absolute Classics, 1992.

Molloy, Sylvia. Interview. *Women Writers of Latin America*. Ed. Magdalena García Pinto. Austin: University of Texas Press, 1991:125-143.

Monegal, Emir Rodriguez. "In the Labyrinth." *The Cardinal Points of Borges*. Eds. Lowell Dunham and Ivar Ivask. Norman: University of Oklahoma Press, 1973:17-24.

Monod, Theodore. *L'Hippotame et le philosophe*. Paris: Julliard, 1941.

Montaigne, Michele de. *The Essays*. Vol. 1. Trans. E. J. Trechmann. London: Oxford University of Press, 1927.

Montejo, Esteban. *The Autobiography of a Runaway Slave*. Trans. Miguel Barnet. New York: Vintage, 1973.

Montesquieu, Charles Secondat. *Persian Letters*. Trans. C.J. Betts. New York: Penguin, 1993.

_____ *The Spirit of the Laws*. Trans. Thomas Nugent. New York: Hafner, 1949.

Moraga, Cherrie and Gloria Anzaldua. Eds. *The Bridge Called My Back*: *Writings by Radical Women of Color*. New York: Kitchen Table Press, 1983.

Morejón, Nancy. *Where the Island Sleeps Like a Wing*. Trans. Richard Weaver. San Franciso: Black Scholar Press, 1985.

Morison, Samuel Eliot. *Admiral of the Ocean Sea*. 1942. Boston: Northeastern University Press, 1983.

Morrison, Toni. *Song of Solomon*. New York: Knopf, 1980.

Motohashi, Edward Tetsuya. "'The Suburbs of Your Pleasure': Theatre and Liberties in *Julius Caesar*." *Shakespeare Studies* 26 (1988):41-75.

Mudimbe, V.Y. *Between Tides*. 1973. Trans. Stephen Becker. New York: Simon & Schuster, 1991a.

_____ *Parables and Fables: Essays, Textuality, and Politics in Central Africa*. Madison:University of Wisconsin Press, 1991b.

_____ *The Invention of Africa, Gnosis, Philosophy, and the Order of Knowledge*. Bloomington: Indiana University Press, 1988.

_____ *L'Odeur du père*. Paris: Presence Africaine, 1982.

_____ *L'Autre face du royaume*. Paris: L'Age d'homme, 1973.

Mullan, John. "Look on't again I dare not." *Times Literary Supplement*. October 6, 1995.

Mullaney, Steven. *The Place of the Stage: License, Play, and Power in Renaissance England*. Chicago: University of Chicago Press, 1988.

Mullin, Michael and David McQuire. "A 'Purge on Prettiness': Motley's Costumes for *A Midsummer Night's Dream*, Shakespeare Memorial Theatre, Stratford-upon-Avon, 1954." *Shakespeare Studies* 27 (1989):65-78.

Munro, John H. "Patterns of Trade, Money, and Credit." *Handbook of European History*. Eds. Thomas A. Brady, Jr., Heiko A Oberman, and James D. Tracy. Leiden: E.J. Brill, 1995: 147-196.

Mustacchi, Marianna M. and Paul J. Archambault. Trans. and Eds. *A Renaissance Woman*. Syracuse: University of Syracuse Press, 1986.

Myrick, Kenneth. Ed. *The Merchant of Venice*. New York: Signet Classic, 1987.

Naipaul, V.S. *The Return of Eva Peron, with The Killings in Trinidad*. New York: Knopf, 1980.

_____ *A Bend in the River*. New York: Knopf, 1979.

_____ *The Mimic Men*. 1967. New York: Penguin, 1977a.

_____ "Conrad's Darkness." *Critical Perspectives on V. S. Naipaul*. Ed. Robert D. Hamner. Washington, D.C.: Three Continents Press, 1977b. 54-65.

_____ *The Loss of Eldorado, A History*. London: Deutsch, 1969.

_____ *Guerrillas*. New York: Knopf, 1975

_____ *A House for Mr. Biswas*. London: Heinemann, 1961.

Neill, Michael. "Unproper Beds: Race, Adultery, and the Hideous in *Othello.*" *Shakespeare Quarterly* 40. (1989):383-412.

Neruda, Pablo. *Song of Protest*. New York: William Morrow, 1976.

_____ *The Heights of Macchu Picchu*. Trans. Nathaniel Tarn. New York: Farrar, Straus, Giroux, 1966.

Nesim, Aziz. *Istanbul Boy*. Trans. from the Turkish by Joseph S. Jacobson. Austin, Texas: Center for Middle Eastern Studies, 1977.

New, Peter. *Fiction and Purpose in Utopia*. New York: St. Martin's Press, 1985.

Newton, John. *Thoughts upon the African Slave Trade*. 1788. London: Epworth Press, 1962.

Ngate, Jonathan. *Francophone African Fiction, Reading a Literary Tradition*. Trenton: Africa World Press, 1988.

Nicholl, Charles. *The Creature in the Map: A Journey to El Dorado*. London, Jonathan Cape, 1995.

Nixon, Bob. "Caribbean and African Appropriations of *The Tempest*." *Critical Inquiry* 13 (1987): 557-578.

Nkosi, Lewis. *Home and Exile*. London: Longman, 1965.

Nochlin, Linda and Tamar Garb, eds. *The Jew in the Text*. London: Thames & Hudson, 1996.

Nuñez, Benjamin. *Dictionary of Afro-Latin American Civilization*. Westport, Connecticut: Greenwood Press, 1980.

Obeyesekere, Gananath. *The Work of Culture, Symbolic Transformation in Psychoanalysis and Anthropology*. Chicago: University of Chicago Press, 1990.

Ockman, Carol. "When Is a Jewish Star Just a Star? Interpreting Images of Sarah Bernhardt." *The Jew in the Text: Modernity and the Construction of Identity.* Eds. Linda Nochlin and Tamar Garb. New York: Thames and Hudson Ltd. 1996:121-139.

O'Callaghan, Evelyn. "Selected Creole Sociolinguistics in the West Indian Novel." *Critical Issues in West Indian Literature.* Ed. Erika Sollish Smilowitz and Roberta Quarles Knowles. St. Croix: Caribbean Books, 1984:125-136.

_____ Oestreich, James. "Rare Verdi Sketches Up for Sale." *New York Times.* 11/8/95.

Ogburn, Charlton. *The Mysterious William Shakespeare, The Myth and the Reality.* New York: Dodd, Mead, 1984.

Ogburn, Charlton and Dorothy, *The Renaissance Man of England.* New York: Coward-McCann, 1955.

O'Gorman, Edmundo. *The Invention of America.* Bloomington: Indiana University Press, 1961.

Ojo-Ade, Femi. "Of Culture, Commitment, and Construction: Reflections on African Literature." *Transition* 53 (1991):4-24.

Okri, Ben. "Meditations on Othello." *West Africa* 23 March (1987):562-64; 30 March 1987:618-619.

Olinto, Antonio. *The Water House.* Trans. Dorothy Heapy. London: Rex Collings, 1970.

Olmos, Margarite Fernández. "From a Woman's Perspective: The Short Stories of Rosario Ferré and Ana Lydia Vega." *Contemporary Women Authors of Latin America.* Ed. Doris Meyer and Margarite Fernandez Olmos. Brooklyn: Brooklyn College Press, 1983:78-90.

Orgel, Stephen. "The Authentic Shakespeare." *Representations* 21 (1988):1-25.

_____ Ed. *The Tempest.* London: Clarendon, 1987.

_____ "Prospero's Wife." *Representations* 8 (1984):1-13.

Ormerod, Beverley. *An Introduction to the French Caribbean Novel.* London: Heinemann, 1985.

Ortiz, Alicia Dujovne. *Buenos Aires.* Sesseyl, France: Editions du Champ Vallon, 1984.

Ortiz, Fernando. *Cuban Counterpoint: Tobacco and Sugar.* New York: Knopf, 1947.

Ota, Kazuaki. "Shakespeare's Romances and the Court." *Shakespeare Studies* (The Shakespeare Society of Japan) 27 (1989):1-21.

Ott, Thomas O. *The Haitian Revolution, 1789-1804.* Knoxville: University of Tennessee Press, 1987.

Ouakin, Marc-Alain. *The Burnt Book: Reading the Talmud.* 1986. Trans. Llewellyn Brown. Princeton: Princeton University Press, 1995.

Ouologuem, Yambo. *Bound to Violence.* 1968. Trans. Ralph Manheim. London: Heinemann, 1971.

Overton, Bill. *The Merchant of Venice, Text and Performance.* Atlantic Highlands, N.J.: Humanities, 1987.

Pagden, Anthony. *Spanish Imperialism and the Political Imagination.* New Haven: Yale University Press, 1990.

Palmer, Colin A. *Human Cargoes: The British Slave Trade to Spanish America, 1700-1739*. Urbana: University of Illinois, 1981.

Pamuk, Orhan. *The White Castle*. Trans from the Turkish by Victoria Holbrook. New York: Braziller, 1991.

Parker, Patricia. "Fantasies of 'Race' and 'Gender': Africa, *Othello*, and Bringing to Light." *Women, "Race", and Writing*. 84-100.

Partridge, Eric. *Shakespeare's Bawdy*. London: Routledge, 1947.

Patterson, Orlando. *The Children of Sisyphus*. 1964. Essex, England: Longman, 1982.

Paul, Sherman. Ed. *Walden* and *Civil Disobedience*. Boston: Houghton Mifflin Company, 1960.

Paz, Octavio. "The Power of Art in Ancient Mexico." *The New York Review of Books*. December 1990. 18-21.

_____ *Conjunctions and Disjunctions*. New York: Viking Press, 1974.

_____ *Alternating Current*. Trans. Helen R. Lane. New York: Viking, 1973a.

_____ Ed. *An Anthology of Mexican Poetry*. Trans. Samuel Beckett. Bloomington: Indiana University Press, 1973b.

_____ *The Other Mexico: Critique of the Pyramid*. Trans. Lysander Kemp New York: Grove, 1972.

_____ *The Labyrinth of Solitude*. 1950. Trans. Lysander Kemp. New York: Grove, 1961.

Pechter, Edward. "The New Historicism and Its Discontents: Politicizing Renaissance Drama." *PMLA* 102 (1987):292-303.

Pecora, Vincent P. "The Limits of Local Knowledge." *The New Historicism*. Ed. H. Aram Veeser. New York: Routledge, 1989.

Peden, Margaret Sayers. *A Woman of Genius, The Intellectual Autobiography of Sor Juana Inés de la Cruz*. Salisbury, Connecticut: Lime Rock Press, 1982.

Peyrefitte, Alain. *The Immobile Empire*. Trans. Jon Rothschild. New York: Knopf, 1992.

Pfaelzer, Jean. *The Utopian Novel in America 1886-1896: The Politics of Form*. Pittsburgh: University of Pittsburgh Press, 1988.

Philip, Marlene Nourbese. "The Absence of Writing, or, How I Almost Became a Spy." *Out of the Kumbla, Women In Caribbean Literature*. Ed. Carol Boyce Davies and Elaine Savory Fido. Trenton: Africa World Press, 1990:271-278.

Phillips, Caryl. *The European Tribe*. London: Faber, 1987.

Picón-Salas, Mariano. *A Cultural History of Spanish America, From Conquest to Independence*. 1944. Berkeley: University of California Press, 1971.

Pinsky, Robert. Trans. *The Inferno of Dante*. New York: Farrar, Straus, Giroux, 1994.

Pittarello, Elide. "*Arauco Domado* de Pedro de Ona o la via erotica de la conquista." *Dispositio* xiv, 36-38 (1989):247-270.

Placoly, Vincent. *Frères volcans*. Montreuil: Editions La Breche, 1983.

Pollard, Dennis Darrell. *Rhetoric, Politics and the King's Justice in Pineda y Bascunan's* Cautivero Feliz. Unpublished dissertation. University of Michigan 1986.

Poma, Huaman. *Letter to a King: A Peruvian Chief's Account of Life Under the Incas and Under Spanish Rule*. Trans. Christopher Dilke. New York: E.P. Dutton, 1973.

Pound, Ezra. *Selected Poems*. New York: New Directions, 1957.

Pratt, Mary Louise. *Imperial Eyes, Travel Writing and Transculturation*. New York: Routledge, 1992.

Price, Richard. Ed. *Maroon Societies, Rebel Slave Communities in the Americas*. Baltimore: Johns Hopkins, 1979.

Pring-Mill, Robert. Preface. Neruda, *The Heights of Macchu Picchu*. Trans. Nathaniel Tarn. New York: Farrar, Straus, Giroux, 1966.

Provost, Foster. *The Columbus Dictionary*. Detroit, Michigan: Omnigraphics, Inc., 1991.

Rabasa, José. "Columbus and the New Scriptural Economy of the Renaissance." *Dispositio* XIV, 36-38 (1989):271-302.

Rabelais, François. *Gargantua and Pantagruel*. London: Penguin, 1955.

Rachewiltz, Boris de. *Black Eros*. Trans. From the Italian *Eros Nero* (1963) by Peter Whigham. New York: Lyle Stuart, 1964.

Ragon, Pierre. *Les Amours Indiennes, ou l'imaginaire du conquistador*. Paris: Armand Colin, 1992.

Ralegh, Walter. *The Discoverie of the Large, Rich and Bewtiful Empyre of Guiana. 1596.* Amsterdam: Theatrum Orbis Terrarum, 1968.

Ramchand, Kenneth. "Partial Truths: A Critical Account of V. S. Naipaul's Later Fiction." *Critical Issues in West Indian Literature*. Ed. Erika Sollish Smilowitz and Roberta Quarles Knowles. St. Croix: Caribbean Books, 1984:65-89.

Reinard, Wolfgang. "The Seaborne Empires." *Handbook of European History*. 637-64.

Reis, Roberto. Ed. *Toward Socio-Criticism: "Luso-Brazilian Literatures"*. Tempe: Arizona State University. 1991.

Remnick, David. "*Hamlet* in Hollywood." *The New Yorker*. (11/20/95):66-71.

Rendón, Alfred Barrera Vasquez y Sylvia. *El libro de los libros de Chilam Balam*. 1948. México, D.F.: Fondo de Cultura Economica, 1984.

Retamar, Roberto Fernández. *Caliban and Other Essays*. Trans. Edward Baker. Minneapolis: University of Minnesota Press, 1989.

Rhys, Jean. *Wide Sargasso Sea*. New York: Norton, 1982.

Rich, Frank. In: Christopher Michaud, "Sir Ian McKellen Wins Raves for His *Richard III*." Reuters. *International Herald Tribune*. 9/17/90.

Richman, Michele H. *Reading Bataille: Beyond the Gift*. Baltimore: Johns Hopkins, 1982.

Rifkin, Adrian. "Parvenu or Palimpsest: Some Tracings of the Jew in Modern France." *The Jew in the Text*. Ed. Linda Nochlin and Tamar Garb. London: Thames and Hudson, 1996:276-291.

Robinson, Jeffers. "V.S. Naipaul and the Sexuality of Power." *West Indian Literature and its Social Context*. Ed. Mark A, McWatt. Cave Hill, Barbados: Department of English, 1985:69-77.

Rodó, José Enrique. *Ariel*. 1900. Trans. Margaret Sayers Peden. Austin: University of Texas Press, 1988.

Rodrígues, José Honori. "The Victory of the Portuguese Language in Colonial Brazil." *Empire in Transition: The Portuguese World in the Time of Camoes*. Eds. Alfred Hower and Richard A. Preto-Rodas. Gainesville: University Presses of Florida, 1985.

Rohlehr, Gordon. "Character and Rebellion in *A House for Mr. Biswas.*" *Critical Perspectives on V. S. Naipaul.* Ed. Robert D. Hamner. Washington, D.C.: Three Continents Press, 1977:84-93.

Rojas, Alfonso Villa. *The Maya of East Central Quintana Roo.* Washington, D.C.: Carnegie Institution, 1945.

Rosador, K. Tetzeli von. "'Supernatural Soliciting': Temptation and Imagination in *Doctor Faustus* and *Macbeth.*" *Shakespeare and His Contemporaries.* Ed. E. A. J. Honigmann. Manchester: Manchester University Press, 1986.

Root, Deborah. *Cannibal Culture: Art, Appropriation, and the Commodification of Difference.* Boulder: Westview Press, 1996.

Rosenberg, Marvin. *The Masks of Othello.* Newark, New Jersey: University of Delaware Press, 1961.

Rouillard, Clarence Dana. *The Turk in French History, Thought, and Literature (1520-1660).* Paris: Boivin et Cie, 1938.

Rout, Leslie. *The African Experience in Spanish America from 1502 to the Present Day.* New York: Cambridge University Press, 1976.

Rubinstein, Frankie. *A Dictionary of Shakespeare's Sexual Puns and their Significance.* New York: St. Martin's Press, 1995.

Rudnik-Smalbraak, Marijke. "Women and Utopia: Some Reflections and Explorations." *Between Dream and Nature, Essays on Utopia and Dystopia.* Eds. Dominic Baker-Smith and C. Barfoot. Amsterdam: Rodopi, 1987.

Ruether, Rosemary Radford. *Sexism and God-Talk: Toward a Feminist Theology.* Boston: Beacon Press, 1983.

Ruppersburg, Hugh. *Reading Faulkner:* Light in August, *Glossary and Commentary.* Oxford: University of Mississippi Press, 1994.

Rushdie, Salman. *East, West.* New York: Vintage, 1994.

Saadawi, Nawal el. *She Has No Place in Paradise.* Trans. Shirley Eber. London: Minerva, 1989.

Sade, Marquis de. *Justine, Philosophy in the Bedroom, and Other Writings.* Ed. and Trans. Richard Seaver and Austryn Wainhouse. New York: Grove Weidenfeld, 1990.

Sagahún, Fray Bernadino de. *General History of the Things of New Spain.* Trans. Arthur J.O. Anderson and Charles E. Dibble. Santa Fe, New Mexico: The School of American Research and The University of Utah Press, 1955.

Said, Edward W. *Culture and Imperialism.* New York: Knopf, 1993.

____ *Orientalism.* New York: Pantheon, 1978.

_____ *Beginnings: Intention and Method.* New York: Basic Books, 1975.

Saldívar, José David. *The Dialectics of Our America.* Durham: Duke University Press, 1991.

Sale, Kirkpatrick. *The Conquest of Paradise.* New York: Knopf, 1990.

Salih, al-Tayyib (Tayeb Salih). *Mawsim al-Hijrah ila al Shawal.* (*Season of Migration to the North*). Trans. Denys Johnson-Davies. Portsmouth, N.H.: Heinemann, 1970.

Sánchez, Luis Rafael. *Macho Camacho's Beat.* Trans. Gregory Rabassa. New York:1982.

Sánchez, Ramon Diaz. *Mene.* Trans. Jesse Noel St. Augustine, Trinidad: Multimedia Production Centre, n.d.

Sanders, Ronald. *Lost Tribes and Promised Lands, The Origins of American Racism.*
1978. New York: Harper, 1992.

Sarmiento, Domingo Faustino. *Conflict and Harmony Among the Races in America.*
Buenos Aires: S. Ostwald, 1883.

Saunders, A.C. de C.M. *A Social History of Black Slaves and Freedmen in Portugal,
1441-1555.* New York: Cambridge University Press, 1982.

Schama, Simon. *The Embarrassment of Riches, An Interpretation of Dutch Culture in
the Golden Age.* Berkeley: University of California Press, 1988.

Schaub, J. Diana. *Erotic Liberalism, Women and Revolution in Montesquieu's
Persian Letters.* London: Roman and Littlefield, 1995.

Schedel, Hartmann. *Liber Chronicarum.* Nuremberg: Anton Koberger, 1493.

Scheper-Hughes, Nancy. Review of Clifford Geertz, *After the Fact. New York Times
Book Review* 100 (May 7, 1995):22-23.

Schoenbaum, Samuel. *Shakespeare's Lives.* Oxford: Clarendon, 1993.

_____*Shakespeare and Others.* Washington, D.C.: Folger, 1985.

Scholem, Gershom. Ed. *Zohar, The Book of Splendor.* New York: Schocken, 1976.

Schultz, Brigitte. "Shakespeare's Way into the West Slavic Literatures and Cultures."
European Shakespeares, Translating Shakespeare in the Romantic Age. Eds. Dirk
Delabastita and Lieven D'hulst. Amsterdam: John Benjamins, 1993:147-162. 55-
74.

Schweitzer, Frederick M. "Perception of Jews and Judaism." *Jewish-Christian
Encounters over the Centuries: Symbiosis, Prejudice, Holocaust, Dialogue.* Ed.
Marvin Perry and Frederick M. Schweitzer. New York: Peter Lang. 1994:131-168.

Scribner, Robert W. "Elements of Popular Belief." *Handbook of European History.*
231-262.

Seneca. *The Tragedies.* Trans. Frank Justus Miller. 1917. Cambridge: Harvard
University Press, 1979.

Sensabaugh, George F. *Milton in Early America.* Princeton: Princeton University
Press, 1964.

Seth, Vikram. *A Suitable Boy.* New York: Harper, 1994.

Shakespeare, William. *The Complete Works.* Ed. Stanley Wells, Gary Taylor, John
Jowett, and William Montgomery. Oxford: Clarendon Press, 1988.

Shattuck, Roger. "Emily Dickinson's Banquet of Abstemiousness." *New York Review
of Books* XLIII 8 (1996):55-59.

Shatzmiller, Joseph. *Shylock Reconsidered, Jews, Moneylending and Medieval
Society.* Berkeley: University of California Press, 1990.

Sherbo, Arthur. *Shakespeare's Midwives: Some Neglected Shakespeareans.* Newark:
University of Delaware Press, 1992.

Sibony, Daniel. *El otro incastrable.* Trans. Italo Manzi. Barcelona: Ediciones Petrel,
1981.

Sicherman, Carol. "Ngugi's Colonial Education: 'The Subversion. . . of the African
Mind." *African Studies Review* 38, 3 (1996):11-41.

Silko, Leslie. *Ceremony.* New York: Signet, 1978.

Silva, Teresa Cristina Cerdeira da. "O memorial do convento e a repressao da utopia."
Toward Socio-Criticism: "Luso-Brazilian Literatures". Ed. Roberto Reis. Tempe:
Center for Latim American Studies, 1991:115-124

Silverblatt, Irene. "Andean Witches and Virgins: Seventeenth Century Nativism and Subversive Gender Ideologies." *Women, "Race," and Writing in the Early Modern Period.* Eds. Margo Hendricks and Patricia Parker. London: Routledge, 1994:259-271.

Singer, Isaac Bashevis. *The Collected Stories.* 1982. New York: Noonday, 1996.

Singer, Peter. *Hegel.* New York: Oxford University Press, 1983.

Singh, Jyotsna. "Othello's Identity, Postcolonial Theory, and Contemporary African Rewritings of *Othello*". *Women, "Race," and Writing in the Early Modern Period.* Eds. Margo Hendricks and Patricia Parker. London: Routledge, 1994:287-299.

Sisson, C.H. Trans. *The Song of Roland.* Manchester: Carcanet, 1983.

Sisson, C.J. *Shakespeare in India.* London: Oxford University Press, 1926.

Slotkin, Richard. *The Fatal Environment: The Myth of the Frontier in the Age of Industrialization, 1800-1890.* Middletown, Connecticut: Wesleyan University Press, 1986.

Smart, Ian. "Nancy Morejón as Guillén's *Mujer Nueva.*" *Afro-Hispanic Review* 15 1 (1996):50-55.

_____ *Central American Writers of West Indian Origin: A New Hispanic Literature.* Washington, D.C.: Three Continents, 1984.

Smith, Bruce R. "The Presidential Message 1994-95." *Bulletin.* The Shakespeare Association of America, 1995.

_____ *Homosexual Desire in Shakespeare's England.* Chicago: University of Chicago Press, 1991.

Sodi, Demetrio M. *De la literatura de los Mayas.* Mexico, D.F.: Joaquin Moritz, 1983.

Sommer, Doris. "Plagiarized Authencity: Sarmiento's Cooper and Others." *Do the Americas Have a Common Literature?* 1990:130-155.

Soren, David, Aicha Ben Abed Ben Khader, and Hedi Slim. *Carthage.* New York: Touchstone, 1990.

Sorrentino, Fernando. *Seven Conversations with Jorge Luis Borges.* Trans. Clark M. Zlotchew. Troy, New York: The Whitson Publishing Company, 1982.

Soyinka, Wole. "Shakespeare and the Living Dramatist." *Art, Dialogue, and Outrage.* Ibadan: New Horn Press, 1988.

_____ *Myth, Literature and the African World.* London: Cambridge University Press, 1976.

_____ *The Road.* In *Collected Plays 1.* New York: Oxford University Press, 1974a.

_____ *Madmen and Specialists.* In *Collected Plays 2.* New York: Oxford University Press, 1974b.

Sparrow [Slinger Francisco]. *Sparrow, the Legend.* Port of Spain: Inprint Caribbean, n.d.

Spenser, Edmund. "A View of the Present State of Ireland." *Ireland Under Elizabeth and James the First, described by Edmund Spencer, Sir John Davies, and by Fynes Moryson.* Ed. Henry Morley. London: Routledge, 1890.

Sperati-Pinero, Emma Susana. *Pasos hallados en El reino del mundo.* Mexico: El Colegio de Mexico, 1981.

Steinberg, Leo. *The Sexuality of Christ in Renaissance Art and in Modern Oblivion.* New York: Pantheon, 1983.

Steiner, George. *No Passion Spent, Essays 1978-1995*. New Haven: Yale University Press, 1996.

_____"Master and Man." *The New Yorker*. July 12, 1982:102-103.

Stern, Philip. *The Biblical Herem, A Window on Israel's Religious Experience*. Atlanta, Georgia: Scholars Press, 1991.

Stevens, Wallace. *The Palm at the End of the Mind*. New York: Vintage, 1972.

_____*Letters*. Ed. Holly Stevens. New York: Knopf, 1966.

_____*The Necessary Angel*. New York: Vintage, 1951.

Stoekl, Allan. *Politics,Writing, Mutilation, The Cases of Bataille, Blanchot, Roussel, Leiris, and Ponge*. Minneapolis: University of Minnesota Press, 1985.

Stoll, Elmer Edgar. "Shylock." *The Merchant of Venice*. Ed. Kenneth Myrick. New York: Signet Classic, 1987:157-172.

Strauss, Gerald. "Ideas of *Reformatio* and *Renovatio* from the Middle Ages to the Reformation." *Handbook of European History, 1400-1600*. 2. 1995:1-30.

Strode, William. *The Poetical Works*. Ed. Bertram Dobell. London: Bertram Dobell, 1907.

Sturm, Fred Gillette. "'Estes tem alma como nos?': Manuel da Nobrega's View of the Brazilian Indians." *Empire in Transition: The Portuguese World in the Time of Camoes*. Ed. Alfred Hower and Richard A. Preto-Rodas. Gainesville: University of Florida Press, 1985:72-82.

Summers, Montagu. *Shakespeare Adaptations*. London: Jonathan Cape, 1922.

Talmor, Ezra and Sascha Talmor. Eds. *History of European Ideas* 21, 2 (1995).

Taylor, Gary. *Reinventing Shakespeare, A Cultural History from the Restoration to the Present*. New York: Oxford University Press, 1989.

Taylor, Gary and John Jowett. *Shakespeare Re-Shaped*. Oxford: Clarendon Press, 1993.

Tedlock, Dennis. Trans. *Popul Vuh: The Definitive Edition of the Mayan Book of the Dawn of Life and the Glories of Gods and Kings*. New York: Simon and Schuster, 1985.

Tedlock, Dennis and Bruce Mannheim. Eds. *The Dialogic Emergence of Culture*. Urbana: University of Illinois, 1995.

ter Horst, Robert. *Calderon, The Secular Plays*. Lexington: University of Kentucky, 1982.

Thomas, Keith. "The Utopian Impulse in Seventeenth-Century England." *Between Dream and Nature*. 20-46.

Thompson, Robert Farris. *Flash of Spirit, African and Afro-American Art and Philosophy*. New York: Vintage, 1984.

Thorpe, Marjorie. Introduction. Earl Lovelace, *The Wine of Astonishment*. London: Heinemann, 1983.

Thoreau, Henry David. *Walden* and *Civil Disobedience*. Ed. Sherman Paul. Boston: Houghton Mifflin, 1960.

Tidjani-Serpos, Noureini. "The Postcolonial Condition: The Archeology of African Knowledge: From the Feast of Ogun and Sango to the Postcolonial Creativity of Obatala." *Research in African Literatures* 27 1 (1996):3-18.

Tillyard, E. M. W. *The Elizabethan World Picture*. London: Chatto and Windus, 1943.

Tishby, Isaiah. Ed. *The Wisdom of the Zohar*, vol III. Trans. David Goldstein. London: The Littman Library, 1994.

Todorov, Tzvetan. *The Conquest of America*. Trans. Richard Howard. New York: Harper and Row, 1984.

Tokson, Elliot H. *The Popular Image of the Black Man in English Drama 1550-1688*. Boston: G. K. Hall, 1982.

Tonkin, Humphrey. *The Faerie Queen*. London: Unwin Hyman, 1989.

Tooley, R.V. *Maps and Mapmakers*. New York:Dorset Press, 1990.

Torres-Rioseco, Arturo. *The Epic of Latin American Literature*. 1942. Berkeley: University of California Press, 1970.

Trexler, Richard C. *Sex and Conquest*. Ithaca: Cornell University Press, 1995.

Trible, Phyllis. *Texts of Terror: Literary-Feminist Readings of Biblical Narratives*. Philadelphia: Fortress, 1984.

Turner, James. *The Politics of Landscape*. Oxford: Blackwell, 1979.

Tutuola, Amos. *My Life in the Bush of Ghosts*. New York: Grove, 1970.

_____*The Palm-Wine Drinkard, and His Dead Palm-Wine Tapster in the Dead's Town*. New York: Grove, 1953.

Twain, Mark. *Letters From the Earth*. 1942. Ed. Bernard DeVoto. New York: Harper and Row, 1974.

Updike, John. "Fool's Gold." *Critical Perspectives on V. S. Naipaul*. Ed. Robert D. Hamner. Washington, D.C.: Three Continents Press, 1977.

Vaughan, Alden and Virginia Vaughan. *Shakespeare's Caliban: A Cultural History*. New York: Cambridge University Press, 1991.

Vaughan, Virginia Mason. *Othello, A Contextual History*. London: Cambridge University Press, 1994.

Vega, Lope de. *El nuevo mundo descubierto por Cristobal Colon*. Madrid: Instituto de Cultura, 1598.

Veeser, H. Aram. *The New Historicism*. New York: Routledge, 1989.

Vieira, Nelson H. *Jewish Voices in Brazilian Literature: A Prophetic Discourse in Alterity*. Gainesville: University of Florida, 1995.

Vignaud, Henry. *Toscanelli and Columbus: The Letter and Chart of Toscanelli*. New York: E.P. Dutton, 1902.

Villa, Alfonso R. *The Maya of East Central Quintana Roo*. Washington, D.C.: Carnegie Institution, 1945.

wa Githiora, Cege. "The Afro-Mexicans: An Ignored and Forgotten People." *CAAS Newsletter* 6, 1, 1990.

Walcott, Derek. *Omeros*. New York: Farrar, Straus & Giroux, 1990.

_____*Another Life*. Washington, D.C.: Three Continents Press, 1982.

_____ *The Star-Apple Kingdom*. New York: Farrar, Straus & Giroux, 1979.

_____ *The Joker of Seville and O Babylon!: Two Plays*. New York: Farrar, Straus, Giroux, 1978.

_____ *Sea Grapes*. New York: Farrar, Straus & Giroux, 1976.

_____ "What the Twilight Says," in *Dream on Monkey Mountain and Other Plays*. New York: Farrar, Straus & Giroux, 1970.

_____*In a Green Night: Poems 1946-1960*. New York: Farrar. Straus & Giroux, 1962.

Wald, Priscilla. *Constituting Americans: Cultural Anxiety and Narrative Form.* Durham: Duke University Press, 1995.

Warner, Marina. *Monuments and Maidens, The Allegory of the Female Form.* New York: Atheneum, 1985.

_____*Alone of All Her Sex: The Myth and the Cult of the Virgin Mary.* London: Picador, 1985.

Warner-Lewis, Maureen. "Cultural Confrontation in *A House for Mr. Biswas.*" *Critical Perspectives on Naipaul.* Ed. Robert D. Hamner. Washington, D.C.: Three Continents Press, 1977.

Webster, Margaret. *Shakespeare Without Tears.* New York: Capricorn Books, 1975.

Weinfeld, Moshe. *The Promise of the Land: The Inheritance of the Land of Canaan by the Israelites.* Berkeley: University of California Press, 1993.

Wells, Stanley, Gary Taylor, John Jowett, and William Montgomery. *William Shakespeare, The Complete Works.* Oxford: Clarendon Press, 1988.

West, Delno C. and August Kling. Trans. *The Libro de las profecías of Christopher Columbus.* Gainesville: University Presses of Florida, 1991.

Westheim, Paul. *Arte antiguo de Mexico.* Trans. Mariana Frenk. México: Fondo de Cultura Economica, 1950.

Whitman, Walt. *Leaves of Grass.* New York: Modern Library, 1950.

Williams, Eric. *Capitalism and Slavery.* New York: Perigee Books, 1980.

Wilson, Bryan R. *Magic and the Millenium: A Sociological Study of Religious Movements of Protest Among Tribal and Third-World Peoples.* New York: Harper, 1973.

Winkler, John. *The Constraints of Desire: The Anthropology of Sex and Gender in Ancient Greece.* New York: Routledge, 1990.

Wisse, Ruth. R. Introduction. Isaac Bashevis Singer's *Satan in Goray.* (1935). New York: Noonday Press, 1996.

Womersley, David. "The Clubman's Editor." *The Times Literary Supplement.* August 4, 1995.

Wong, K. Scott. "The Transformation of Culture: Three Chinese Views of America." *American Quarterly* 48 (2) 1996:201-232.

Wright, Handel Kashope. "What Is Shakespeare Doing in My Hut?" *Canadian International Education* 22 (1) 1993:66-86.

Wynter, Sylvia. "Beyond Miranda's Meanings: Un/silencing the 'Demonic Ground' of Caliban's 'Woman'." *Out of the Kumbla: Caribbean Women and Literature.* Ed. Carole Boyce Davies and Elaine Savory Fido. Trenton, N.J.: Africa World Press, 1990:355-372.

_____ "The Poetics and the Politics of a High Life for Caliban." Afterword. Lemuel Johnson, *Highlife for Caliban.* Trenton, N.J.: Africa World Press, 1995.

_____*The Hills of Hebron.* Essex, England: Longman, 1984

Yamashita, Karen Tei. *Brazil-Maru.* Minneapolis: Coffee House Press, 1992.

Yates, Frances A. *Majesty and Magic in Shakespeare's Last Plays: A New Approach to "Cymberline," "Henry VIII," and "The Tempest."* Boulder: Shambhala, 1978.

Zarrilli, Phillip B. *Critical Theory and Performance.* Eds. Janelle G. Reinelt and Joseph R. Roach. Ann Arbor, Michigan: University of Michigan Press, 1992:16-40.

Zerubavel, Eviatar. *Terra Cognita, The Mental Discovery of America.* New Brunswick: Rutgers University Press, 1992.

Zimra, Clarisse. "In the Name of the Father: Chronotopia, Utopia and Dystopia in *Ti Jean l'horizon.*" *L'Esprit Createur* 23, 2 (1993):59-72.

_____ "Righting the Calabash: Writing History in the Female Francophone Narrative." *Out of the Kumbla.* Eds. Davies and Fido. Trenton, N.J.: Africa World Press, 1990:143-159.

Zorilla, Juan de San Martin. *Las Américas.* Montevideo: Editorial Cribo, 1945.

Index